*The
Conservative
Intellectual Movement
in America*

THE
CONSERVATIVE
INTELLECTUAL MOVEMENT
IN AMERICA

SINCE 1945

GEORGE H. NASH

INTERCOLLEGIATE STUDIES INSTITUTE
WILMINGTON, DELAWARE
1996

Library of Congress Catalog Card Number:
96-075872

ISBN: 1-882926-12-9

Published in the United States by:

Intercollegiate Studies Institute
3901 Centerville Road
P.O. Box 4431
Wilmington, DE 19807-0431

Manufactured in the United States of America

To my mother, father, and sister

Contents

PREFACE TO THE 1996 EDITION

Two decades have now elapsed since the book before you was published in its original form—and nearly a decade since it was last in print. In the lives of men and women, as well as the cycles of book publishing, such a period of time can constitute an epoch.

So it has been for the subject of the pages that follow. When *The Conservative Intellectual Movement in America Since 1945* was first published, Ronald Reagan was a former governor of California with no apparent political future, and Newt Gingrich a professor at a small college in Georgia. While intelligent conservatism was clearly on the upswing in the 1970s, it was still a minority phenomenon, especially in the academic community. Abroad, Lech Walesa was an unknown Polish electrician, Vaclav Havel a persecuted Czech playwright, and Margaret Thatcher the new leader of a British Conservative Party that was out of power. The pontificate of Pope John Paul II had not yet begun, and the Berlin Wall stood firm. The Cold War was very much a reality.

And yet, as I reread these pages, mostly written in graduate school, I am struck by how contemporary their subject still seems. Despite the corrosive passage of time and the ephemerality of so much public discourse, the conservative intellectual movement chronicled in this book has not faded into quaint irrelevance. It has not become history. To the contrary, in the years since 1976 it has *made* history and is still making history—to the point that, for adherents and detractors alike, it is more relevant to our nation's life than ever before.

For this reason alone, it seems fitting to make my book readily accessible once more, with an Epilogue devoted to the swirling intellectual and political currents of recent years. There is another reason as well: in the 1990s the conservative movement has entered a period of introspection not seen, in such acute form, since the early 1960s. So close to political triumph, yet so far from assurance of it, many on the Right are seeking to refine, and even redefine, the conservative mission. In such confusing circumstances, it is usually helpful to "remember who we are" or have come to be. As thoughtful conservatives (and some of their critics) go "back to basics," perhaps this study of modern American conservatism's intellectual history will provide some edifying perspective.

"The only thing that's new in the world is the history you don't know," Winston Churchill once remarked. It is my hope that students of all persuasions, especially students who call themselves conservatives, will find in this book some history that they "don't know" but will want to know, if they would truly understand the national debates raging around them.

Many people have influenced and facilitated the preparation of this volume. In my Acknowledgments pages I cite those individuals who contributed to the process of study and reflection that culminated in the first edition. In this Preface it is a pleasure to acknowledge those who made a second edition possible. I particularly thank Jeffrey O. Nelson of the Intercollegiate Studies Institute for initiating this reprint project and for encouraging me to write an Epilogue. To Mr. Nelson and Brooke Daley at ISI, I offer additional thanks for skillfully shepherding the book to publication. For able and conscientious proofreading assistance, I am grateful to Andrea Gralenski, Catherine Lulves, Michael Hancock, Mary Slayton, Jean Nash, and G. Harlan Nash.

ACKNOWLEDGMENTS

Probably every historian who engages in scholarly research soon becomes aware of the dual nature of his craft. On the one hand, his work is usually solitary; on the other, it is supported by, and even dependent upon, the contributions of those who make him aware of the larger community to which his work is eventually addressed. As this project now passes from the scholar's study into public view, it is with deep satisfaction that I contemplate the many people who at one stage or another contributed, directly or indirectly, to my undertaking. With particular pleasure I thank Donald Fleming of Harvard University for his unfailing encouragement, scholarly example, and wise counsel. To Frank Freidel of Harvard I express my appreciation for his helpful advice and continuing interest as my work developed. I am pleased to thank Bernard Bailyn, Oscar Handlin, and my other professors at Harvard for their roles in the process of professional training which has culminated in this volume.

I am indebted as well to the many conservative intellectuals and others (listed in the Appendix) whom I corresponded with and, in many cases, interviewed. Their cooperation was invaluable, and their assistance to my research has been one of the most enjoyable aspects of my entire project. Although it would be impossible to cite here every instance of their courtesy and helpfulness, I must record my special thanks to William F. Buckley, Jr. for granting me complete and unrestricted access to his collection of papers at Yale University—a generous and thoughtful act for which I am grateful. I am happy to acknowledge the permission of Mrs. T. S. Eliot to quote from three of her husband's unpublished letters to Russell Kirk; the permission of Mrs. Maxwell Anderson and Brandt & Brandt to quote from Maxwell Anderson's poem

"Churchill," copyright © 1965 by Gilda Oakleaf Anderson; and the permission of Holt, Rinehart and Winston to use a passage from Robert Frost's poem "Reluctance." In addition, I express my thanks and appreciation to the persons and institutions that graciously permitted me to quote from correspondence, interviews, and other sources essential to this study.

An additional list of friends, associates, and acquaintances helped to make my own research experience a fundamentally agreeable one and, in ways great and small, affected the preparation of my book: Paul Neuthaler and Keri Christenfeld at Basic Books, Geoffrey Horn, professors, fellow graduate students, colleagues at the Charles Warren Center and in the Senior Common Room at Lowell House, my students and other inquiring Harvard undergraduates, a bevy of typists, and the archivists of the libraries listed in the Bibliographical Essay. Rather than attempt to compose a long list which would risk omitting some who belong on it, I simply offer here my gratitude—no less sincerely felt, I hope, for being extended to so many. If any of them read this book, I trust they will recognize that it is to them that I render my thanks for making this project so rewarding to me and, I hope, worth the effort.

And, of course, my family—indefatigable cheerleaders, ever thoughtful critics, proofreaders extraordinary: qualities that cannot begin to exhaust my reasons for dedicating this book to them.

INTRODUCTION

This book is about conservative intellectuals—those engaged in study, reflection, and speculation; purveyors of ideas; scholars and journalists. It is not a chronicle of political campaigns or an examination of the careers of such right-wing politicians of recent times as Robert Taft, Barry Goldwater, and Ronald Reagan, men primarily involved in the hurly-burly of everyday politics. Nor is it concerned with the much-publicized "Radical Right" organizations which received extraordinary attention in the 1960s. While extremists of the Right were often energetic in the period covered by this study, their contribution to conservatism as an intellectual force was negligible.

The focus of this book is on a "movement"—a movement of ideas, but one with visibly nonacademic and political aspirations. Conservatism in America after World War II was no closet philosophy or esoteric sect, at least not for long. It was a decidedly activist force whose thrust was outward toward the often uncongenial America of the mid-twentieth century. An intellectual movement in a narrow sense it certainly was, yet one whose objective was not simply to understand the world but to change it, restore it, preserve it.

Because this is an examination of what I have labeled "conservatism" in the postwar period, readers may perhaps expect a definition: what is conservatism? For those who have examined the subject, this is a perennial question; many are the writers who have searched for the elusive answer. Such an a priori effort, I have concluded, is misdirected. I doubt that there is any single, satisfactory, all-encompassing definition of the complex phenomenon called conservatism, the content of which varies enormously with time and place. It may even be true that conservatism is inherently resistant to precise definition. Many right-wingers, in fact, have argued that conservatism by its very nature is not an elaborate ideology at all.

There are, to be sure, a number of definitions which are inadequate and tendentious. Thus, on occasion conservatism is equated with mindless defense of the status quo, *any* status quo; under such a usage even Stalinist Russia, Maoist China, or any other revolutionary state could be called "conservative" once the revolutionaries had managed to entrench themselves. Sometimes conservatism has been blandly defined as an attitude toward "change"; under such a usage even Fabian Socialists who believed in "the inevitability of gradualness" might be labeled conservatives. Such definitions seem superficial and undiscriminating. On the other hand, some are unduly restrictive. Thus, intellectual conservatism has sometimes been confused with the Radical Right. Frequently, it has been associated with European experiences, such as feudalism, aristocracy, and the Middle Ages—a device often used to explain away conservatism (Mr. X is not conservative, he is "really" something else; America has no conservatives; we are "really" all liberals). Attempts to define conservatism abstractly and universally or in terms of one peculiar set of historical circumstances have led many writers into a terminological thicket.

How shall we extricate ourselves? Great as is the temptation to construct a pattern of my own, I have deliberately refrained from what I believe to be a dubious enterprise. The subject of this book is conservatism as an intellectual movement *in America, in a particular period*. Not all conservatism; not conservatism as an illustration of an archetype derived, perhaps, from a study of feudalism or the Middle Ages. Rather, conservatism as it existed, in a certain time and in a certain place. Conservatism identifiable as resistance to certain forces perceived to be leftist, revolutionary, and profoundly subversive of what conservatives at the time deemed worth cherishing, defending, and perhaps dying for.

At some point, however, an insistent reader may still object to my use of the word "conservative." How, it may be asked, can you label someone a conservative when he was "actually" a nineteenth-century liberal? How can you include an émigré royalist from Europe in a study of the American Right? How can you discuss individuals who deny that they are conservatives or even intellectuals? To these questions one answer, I hope, will suffice: I have designated various people as conservatives either because they called themselves conservatives or because others (who did call themselves conservatives) regarded them as part of their conservative intellectual movement. I have counted diverse people within the conservative fold because study shows that, existentially, they belonged to the American conservative ranks in the postwar period. Whatever our sense (or their sense) of the propriety of these alignments may be, that was the way it was. The reality was that all sorts of people have comprised the conservative intellectual movement in the United States in the years since 1945. This is the reality I have attempted to portray.

So I offer here no compact definition of conservatism. In fact, American conservatives themselves have had no such agreed-upon definition. Instead, the very quest for self-definition has been one of the most notable motifs of their thought since World War II. All the more reason, then, to examine this movement in its intriguing complexity, on its own terms, and to illuminate the various streams of conservative consciousness. All the more reason to dispense with defining "true" conservatism and to get on with the task of explaining what conscious conservatism in the United States has been since World War II.

In 1945 no articulate, coordinated, self-consciously conservative intellectual force existed in the United States. There were, at most, scattered voices of protest, profoundly pessimistic about the future of their country. Gradually during the first postwar decade these voices multiplied, acquired an audience, and began to generate an intellectual movement. In the beginning one finds not one right-wing renascence but three, the subjects of the first several chapters of this book. First, there were "classical liberals" or "libertarians," resisting the threat of the ever expanding State to liberty, private enterprise, and individualism. Convinced that America was rapidly drifting toward statism (socialism), these intellectuals offered an alternative that achieved some scholarly and popular influence by the mid-1950s. Concurrently and independently, a second school of thought was emerging: the "new conservatism" or "traditionalism" of such men as Richard Weaver, Peter Viereck, Russell Kirk, and Robert Nisbet. Shocked by totalitarianism, total war, and the development of secular, rootless, mass society during the 1930s and 1940s, the "new conservatives" urged a return to traditional religious and ethical absolutes and a rejection of the "relativism" which had allegedly corroded Western values and produced an intolerable vacuum that was filled by demonic ideologies. Third, there appeared a militant, evangelistic anti-Communism, shaped decisively by a number of influential ex-radicals of the 1930s, including Whittaker Chambers, James Burnham, Frank Meyer, and many more. These former men of the Left brought to the postwar Right a profound conviction that the West was engaged in a titanic struggle with an implacable adversary—Communism—which sought nothing less than conquest of the world.

While no impassable gulf separated these three components of the intellectual Right, and while each shared a deep antipathy to twentieth-century liberalism, the need for consolidation of the conservative camp was urgent by the mid-1950s. Through the medium of various journals and organizations this task was gradually accomplished. Still, the forging of a movement out of such extremely diverse materials created certain intellectual problems for the Right by the early 1960s. What—besides a common foe—bound them together? Behind what principles and aspirations could they coalesce? What intellectual legitimacy did the conservative movement have? In addition, conservatives confronted a second crucial intellectual challenge: the search for an authentically American conservative heritage. What was conservatism in America? How should the Right refute the recurrent criticism that conservatism was "un-American" because the United States was really a "liberal" country? To these fundamental questions conservatives gave a variety of answers. Their responses—and their continuing efforts to achieve coherence and self-understanding—are the subject of Chapters Five through Eight.

But conservatives were by no means constantly preoccupied with internal, theoretical issues and controversies. For in the 1960s a momentous transformation of the Right began to occur: a transition from minority to potentially majority status in American politics and culture. These were years of preparation for American conservatives. Right-wing critiques of liberal foreign and domestic policies were expounded with increasing sophistication and effectiveness, while conservatives strove to develop intellectually serious and practical alternatives. Although the polarization of the 1960s produced tensions within the conservative community, it also generated new alignments that facilitated the emergence of conservatism as a powerful intellectual and political force. Through a proliferating network of journals, books, organizations, and political alliances, the intellectual Right steadily approached maturity and recognition—until, in the late 1960s and early 1970s, it achieved its long-sought breakthrough. Twenty-five years earlier it had been almost an underground phenomenon. By 1972 conservatives had gained a national audience and had won a chance to exercise national leadership.

During the period under review, conservative intellectuals produced a large—and, toward the end, enormous—literature. It has not been possible to analyze here every book and essay written by every conservative intellectual, major and minor, since 1945. Nor has it been possible to examine the thought of every person who might be labeled a "conservative" in every field from politics to literature, and from science to art. It has been necessary to be selective, to concentrate on the writings of those individuals who, in my judgment, contributed most to the post-war conservative resurgence as an organized intellectual (and ultimately political) force. In 1945 "conservatism" was not a popular word in America, and its spokesmen were without much influence in their native land. A generation later these once isolated voices had become a chorus, a significant intellectual and political movement which had an opportunity to shape the nation's destiny. This transformation and its architects are the subject of the pages that follow.

ONE

The Revolt of the Libertarians

To many Americans who believed in the existence and value of Western civilization, 1945 was a year of victory and foreboding. Europe was liberated but prostrate; the price of Hitler's extirpation had been the rending of what men once called Christendom. In far-off Asia, the Rising Sun had set—but not before seeing the future in the atomic bomb. And after all the sacrifices of war, there stood across eastern and central Europe, ominously, enigmatically, the Colossus of the East. Like the Abbé Sieyès, who had lived through the French Revolution, historically minded Americans might simply have said to one another: We survived.

For those Americans who believed in the creed of old-fashioned, classical, nineteenth-century, liberal individualism, 1945 was especially lonely, unpromising, and bleak. Free markets, private property, limited government, self-reliance, laissez-faire—it had been a long time since principles like these had guided governments and persuaded peoples. The 1930s—what had they been? Uncongenial years of workers' utopias, New Orders, and marching feet abroad; Blue Eagles, the WPA, and increasing regulation of the economy at home. The war—the Popular Front war, the crusade for freedom—had been little comfort to many thoughtful adherents of the old liberal faith. President Roosevelt may have announced the demise of "Dr. New Deal" in favor of "Dr. Win-the-War," but to many of his foes the end of domestic reform could hardly be welcomed.

For what had war and victory brought? A domestic superstate, a partially controlled economy, millions of conscripts under arms, and widespread fears of reversion to depression once demobilization set in. Further success for a philosophy of "tax and tax, spend and spend, elect and

elect."[1] If, seeking solace or perspective, these apprehensive "individualists" turned to ravaged Europe for a portent of the future, they could
only be further disheartened. In the summer of 1945, Americans were
stunned to learn that Britain had voted Socialist. Britain—home of so
much of the classical liberal tradition, of John Locke and Adam Smith,
Herbert Spencer and John Stuart Mill. Britain—home of the dauntless
Tory, Churchill, who had warned the voters about the dangers of socialism, only to be turned out into the cold. "We are the masters now," boasted
a Labour Party M.P. In Parliament, August 1, 1945, exultant socialists
sang the "Red Flag" for the first time since the Spanish Civil War.[2]

Was the whole Western world going Left? Many old-time American
liberals feared that it was. Their dejection was sharply reflected in an
article written by the historian Mortimer Smith and published three days
after the Yalta conference in the year of victory. The "central fact" of the
last seventy-five years, he declared, had been the march of men to collectivism; this trend was certain to gain "terrific momentum" from the
war.

> Through the cacophonous chorus of the postwar planners runs
> one harmonious theme: the individual must surrender more
> and more of his rights to the state which will in return guar-
> antee him what is euphemistically called security.

No matter what their ideology, said Smith, the leaders of the Grand Alliance agreed on one goal: "enhanced state power" after the war. The
fact was inescapable that "old-fashioned liberalism...is all but dead in
our present world."[3]

And yet. And yet. The situation, gloomy though it appeared to many
whom we may designate libertarian conservatives, was not hopeless. History, in fact, is rarely without hope, for history is possibility. There is no
such thing as a lost cause, said T.S. Eliot, for there is no such thing as a
gained cause. In 1945 classical liberalism was neither dead nor dying.
Even then, as Mortimer Smith acknowledged in his article, there were
"faint twitchings and stirrings"[4] in the land. In a world of overweening
statism, entrenched bureaucracy, and seemingly triumphant philosophies
of the Left, the old indigenous American tradition of "individualism"
was about to enjoy an unexpected revival. It was to become one branch
of the postwar conservative intellectual movement.

However old and indigenous this stream of thought may have been,
much of the initial impetus for its renascence came not from America
but from Europe. Indeed, it is doubtful that this resurgent libertarian-

ism would ever have achieved the respectability and impact that it eventually did attain without the contributions of two émigré scholars from the nightmare world of the Thousand Year Reich. The roots of postwar American conservatism must first be sought in Europe, in the revulsion from dictatorship and war.

In the spring of 1944 a little book called *The Road to Serfdom* appeared in Britain and soon caused a great storm. Interestingly enough, it was not written by a native Englishman but by an Austrian economist named Friedrich A. Hayek, then teaching at the London School of Economics. Born in Vienna in 1899 and educated at its university, an economist and lecturer in Austria during the 1920s, Hayek had gone to the London School of Economics as a professor of economics in 1931. Watching from afar the deepening crisis in central Europe in the 1930s, Hayek became a British subject in 1938. As World War II enveloped Europe, he grew increasingly alarmed about the tendency toward governmental planning of the economy and the consequences of this trend for individual liberty. He decided to write a learned polemic, which he dedicated "to the Socialists of all parties."[5]

The thesis of Hayek's work was simple: "Planning leads to dictatorship"; "the direction of economic activity" inevitably necessitates the "suppression of freedom."[6] By "planning" Hayek did not mean any kind of preparation by individuals or governments for the future; he meant only "central direction of all economic activity according to a single plan," or "planning against competition."[7] Such comprehensive controls, he argued, would necessarily be arbitrary, capricious, and ultimately destructive of liberty.

> Economic control is not merely control of a sector of human life which can be separated from the rest; it is the control of the means for all our ends. And whoever has sole control of the means must also determine which ends are to be served, which values are to be rated higher and which lower—in short, what men should believe and strive for.[8]

Collectivism, in short—all collectivism—was inherently totalitarian; "democratic socialism" was illusory and "unachievable."[9] Pointing to Nazi Germany as the incarnation of his fears, Hayek argued that "the rise of fascism and nazism was not a reaction against the socialist trends of the preceding period but a necessary outcome of those tendencies."[10] His book, in short, was no academic matter. The path to socialism which

Britain was taking was the very path Germany had already chosen: the road to serfdom.

Against this specter Hayek opposed "the abandoned road" of individualism and classical liberalism. The "fundamental principle" of this creed was "that in the ordering of our affairs we should make as much use as possible of the spontaneous forces of society, and resort as little as possible to coercion...."[11] This did not mean, Hayek insisted, that government should be inactive;[12] he strenuously denied that his brand of liberalism was identical with laissez-faire.[13] Instead, he proposed the concept of the Rule of Law: "government in all its actions is [to be] bound by rules fixed and announced beforehand...."[14] Such a principle would often require vigorous government action designed to facilitate competition and the continued functioning of a free society. Under such a system, in fact, limitations of working hours, sanitary regulations, and even minimum wage laws and social insurance would be permitted.[15] But always the design of such interventions must be the *preservation* of competition, private initiative, and private property, and the rules of the game would have to be applied equally. There was, he contended, a world of difference between his version of the liberal state and the centralized, capricious, privilege-granting, collectivist state—aggrandizing power and "planning against competition."[16]

The response to Hayek's work in Great Britain was immediate. Intended "as a warning to the socialist intelligentsia of England," *The Road to Serfdom* incited many readers to vigorous reply.[17] So important a challenge did it offer that two book-length refutations appeared—one by a prominent Labour Party M.P.[18] At one point in 1945, Hayek even briefly became an election issue when Clement Atlee accused the Conservative Party of adopting the Austrian economist's allegedly reactionary principles.[19]

The British reception of Hayek's book was mild and restrained, however, compared to its fate in the United States following publication on September 18, 1944. The book had not been expected to make much of an impact; in fact three publishing houses—at least one of them apparently motivated by political opposition to Hayek—rejected it.[20] When the University of Chicago Press finally published the book, it printed only 2,000 copies.[21] Clearly, as Hayek later recalled, this book was "not intended for popular consumption."[22]

Hayek's expectation was wrong. Instantly his book was recognized, not just as a scholarly polemic but as a fervent tract for the times. Within a week a second printing of 5,000 copies was undertaken;[23] a few months later the *Reader's Digest* eagerly condensed the book for its readers and arranged for the Book-of-the-Month Club to distribute more than a million reprints. Soon Hayek—who had thought of himself as something of a voice in the wilderness—was lecturing all over the United States. "Seldom," said one observer, "have an economist and a nonfiction book reached such popularity in so short a time." [24]

Many book reviewers contributed to the growing controversy with excited and sometimes extravagant remarks. In a front-page article in the *New York Times Book Review*, the veteran journalist Henry Hazlitt proclaimed *The Road to Serfdom* "one of the most important books of our generation," comparable in "power and rigor of reasoning" to John Stuart Mill's *On Liberty*.[25] In *Fortune*, John Davenport judged the book "one of the great liberal statements of our times," an effective restatement of the faith in individualism, "the faith after all in Western Christian civilization."[26] Mortimer Smith predicted that Hayek's work might become a "milestone in a critical age," like Thomas Paine's *The Rights of Man*.[27] Meanwhile, the hostile *New Republic* editorialized that Hayek's work was having little scholarly impact and was simply being used by reactionary business interests.[28] Stuart Chase asserted that the volume was fulfilling a "deep spiritual need in American men of affairs" for "the fundamentalist doctrine that those of us beyond fifty were brought up on."[29] Writing early in 1946, Professor Charles Merriam, a wartime vice-chairman of the National Resources Planning Board, vehemently dismissed Hayek's book as "over-rated," "dismal," "cynical," and "one of the strange survivals of obscurantism in modern times."[30] Even in academic circles the debate became tempestuous, so much so that the editor of *American Economic Review* took the unusual step of publishing two reviews of the book. Needless to say, they disagreed.[31]

No one was more startled—and admittedly embarrassed—by this uproar than the scholarly Professor Hayek himself.[32] As he later observed, the emotions the book engendered amazed him.[33] Why should a work aimed at experts and written by an Austrian émigré living in London stir the passions of Americans? Perhaps it was true, as the *New Republic* charged, that chambers of commerce, advertising interests, and other businesses were boosting demand for the book by bulk orders, thereby concealing its actual public appeal.[34] But why should they have bothered? And if, as one critic alleged, Hayek had merely presented "an old nostrum attractively packaged,"[35] why should many liberals (new style) have become so angry and even dismayed? Why should one self-proclaimed "left-of-center" reviewer confess that the book had "shaken" him and proved to be "one of the most unsettling books to come along in many years"?[36]

The reason for the Left's malaise was partially supplied by Hayek in his retrospective essay of 1956. In contrast with Britain, where the question of freedom versus planning had become a familiar issue by 1945, the United States remained at the stage of enthusiasm. For many American intellectuals, the ideal of a "new kind of rationally constructed society" still seemed novel, vibrant, and "largely unsoiled by practical experience." To criticize such heady beliefs was to attack something nearly sacred—even if it was, in Hayek's view, an illusion.[37]

The Austrian economist's analysis suggests another reason for the Left's reaction to his book. It had not, after all, been such a long time since modern liberalism (statism to its detractors) had attained power in America. It had not been so terribly long—twelve years, in fact, in 1945—since professors, lawyers, and many others had turned to Washington, D.C. and to President Roosevelt for leadership and the New Deal. For many of these people, one suspects, the pleasures and gains of those days were not quite consolidated in 1945. Theirs was still an uncertain triumph, not yet ratified by time and consensus. Consequently, when a bold challenge like Hayek's appeared—and few denied his competence and polemical power—it could not be airily dismissed. It was a threat, and it had to be vigorously repulsed. In 1948 and 1949 some American liberals would react in a similar but even more intense way to another formative controversy of the postwar era, the Hiss-Chambers trial. In 1945 their uneasiness about the future was already evident.

Yet if, at war's end, many self-designated progressives, for all their power and prominence, may still have felt insecure, the Right did not know it. There a far different sentiment prevailed. Outnumbered and beleaguered, it could only rejoice when a compelling restatement of its case appeared. Stuart Chase might ridicule it as "the true faith we have lost";[38] John Davenport might hail it for the very same reason. But both sides agreed that an old tradition had acquired an articulate voice again. No doubt, as many critics eagerly observed, Hayek's defenders did not always realize just how critical of laissez-faire and business he was. Still, their impulse was correct; Hayek *was* on their side. And that was precisely part of his significance: he enabled those who felt routed to draw the lines and confidently take sides once more. At last they had a champion who made the enemy squirm. It is a measure of their rout and of the paucity of libertarian thought in America in this period that they were obliged to rely on an Austrian professor for leadership.

Hayek was not the only European intellectual who provided intellectual sustenance to the American Right in the mid-1940s. Less dramatic but equally noteworthy was the widening influence of another Austrian: Hayek's mentor, the indefatigable Ludwig von Mises. Born in Austria-Hungary in 1881, Mises studied law and economics at the University of Vienna, where he obtained his doctorate in 1906. To be a young economist at Vienna in those days was to live in an environment dominated by the great *Methodenstreit* (clash over methods) of the late nineteenth century. Carl Menger, an eminent "classical liberal" Austrian economist, had opened the "war" in 1883 with an attack on Gustav Schmoller and the German Historical School of economists. To Menger and his allies—soon known as the Austrian School—the Historical School's relativistic rejection of universal economic laws in the name of history was a dangerous repudiation of science and a justification for government intervention and socialism. After all, if there were no immutable economic laws, why shouldn't the government direct affairs as it wished? This dispute did not quickly subside. Instead, as Mises later observed, each camp produced its disciples. In the direct line of the Austrian succession, from Menger to Eugen von Böhm-Bawerk (another Austrian economist) and beyond, was Ludwig von Mises. By the 1920s he had become internationally known as an economic theorist and author of a trenchant critique of socialism.[39] He was also, like Hayek, an unremitting opponent of Nazism (or National Socialism, as its classical liberal critics carefully noted). In 1934 he left the University of Vienna to become a refugee at the Graduate Institute of International Studies in Geneva. In 1940 the "patriarch of the modern Austrian school"[40] emigrated to the United States.[41]

He was not the only one of his circle to depart. During his years in Europe such men as Gottfried Haberler and Fritz Machlup, as well as Hayek, had studied with or been deeply influenced by Mises. As Europe careened toward catastrophe, these three disciples and others took up residence abroad; several came to America.[42] If, as is now recognized, the "Great Migration" of intellectuals from central Europe in the 1930s was a crucial event in the intellectual history of our time, the diaspora of the Austrian School to England and America was likewise one of the significant chapters in the history of modern American conservatism.

In 1944 Mises published two books that increased the debt of American "classical liberals" or "libertarians" to the European refugees. The subject of *Omnipotent Government* and *Bureaucracy*[43] was the same: governmental intervention in all its forms. With analytical skill and erudition that even his opponents respected, and with a supreme logical rigor that even his friends sometimes considered excessive,[44] Mises fought on. He was uncompromising; one reviewer called him "Cato-like."[45] More totally devoted to pure laissez-faire than his pupil Hayek, Mises insisted that the choice was stark: capitalism or statism, capitalism or "chaos."[46]

> The essential teaching of liberalism is that social coop-
> eration and the division of labor can be achieved only in a
> system of private ownership of the means of production, i.e.,
> within a market society, or capitalism. All the other principles
> of liberalism—democracy, personal freedom of the individual,
> freedom of speech and of the press, religious tolerance, peace
> among the nations—are consequences of this basic postulate.
> They can be realized only within a society based on private
> property.[47]

Indeed, Mises was convinced that "private property is inextricably linked with civilization" and that lasting peace could arise only "under perfect capitalism, hitherto never and nowhere completely tried or achieved."[48] According to one reviewer, statism was for Mises "the great pervasive evil of the modern world."[49] Another reviewer asked, "Could it be that the city of Manchester is actually located in Austria?"[50]

Like Hayek, Mises was writing in the somber days of war, and like his pupil, he was convinced that the abandonment of nineteenth-century liberalism had led to twentieth-century catastrophe. Dismissing arguments that Nazism was somehow a product of capitalism, Mises traced totalitarianism to the ideology of etatism, of which Nazism was one variant. Etatism—"the trend toward government control of business"[51]—led to economic nationalism and war. Nazism, he strenuously contended, was *anti*-capitalistic, socialistic, and thus necessarily undemocratic.[52] The true lesson of our era was not any failure of the free market but the ominous ascendancy of its foes. It was no coincidence that the rise of the socialist panacea was accompanied by the rise of Nazi and Soviet totalitarianism and the outbreak of total wars. To Mises, Hayek, and their disciples, these phenomena were profoundly related. Again and again, Mises, like Hayek, stressed the utter incompatibility of centralized planning and the preservation of liberty. "The main issue," he said, "...is whether or not man should give away freedom, private initiative, and individual responsibility and surrender to the guardianship of a gigantic apparatus of compulsion and coercion, the socialist state."[53] That was what socialism inescapably meant.

They call themselves democrats, but they yearn for dictatorship. They call themselves revolutionaries, but they want to make the government omnipotent. They promise the blessings of the Garden of Eden, but they plan to transform the world into a gigantic post office. Every man but one a subordinate clerk in a bureau, what an alluring utopia! What a noble cause to fight for![54]

Although Mises's writings did not create the sensation produced by Hayek's book, his services to the cause did not go unnoticed. Pointing out that *Bureaucracy* had been published just one day after *The Road to Serfdom*, Henry Hazlitt remarked how "ironic" it was that "the most eminent...defenders of English liberty, and of the system of free enterprise which reached its highest development in America, should now be two Austrian exiles."[55] Far from New York, an obscure sergeant in the Chemical Warfare Service named Russell Kirk had also discovered and enjoyed both *The Road to Serfdom* and *Bureaucracy*. He wrote to a friend that the Vienna of Freud "also had its great school of economists of a very different and much sounder mind."[56] In 1945 Mises's grateful and admiring American friends arranged for him to become a visiting professor of economics at New York University's Graduate School of Business Administration, a position he would hold for more than twenty years.[57]

The culmination of Mises's early contributions to the classical liberal revival came in 1949, when Yale University Press published his massive tome *Human Action*.[58] Nearly 1,000 pages long, this prodigious effort was the synthesis of Mises's system of "praxeology." Many critics considered the work to be dogmatic and "hectoring"; one complained that a reader encountering the work "continually has the sense of being argued out of existence."[59] Everyone, however, agreed that the 68-year-old economist had written a "Capitalist Manifesto,"[60] "a truly unvarnished and unconditional defense of laissez-faire."[61] Once more Henry Hazlitt suggested the book's importance for the intellectual history of the American Right:

> *Human Action* is, in short, at once the most uncompromising and the most rigorously reasoned statement of the case for capitalism that has yet appeared. If any single book can turn the ideological tide that has been running in recent years so heavily toward statism, socialism, and totalitarianism, *Human Action* is that book.[62]

Single books usually do not instantly turn ideological tides. Still, it would be difficult to exaggerate the contributions of Friedrich Hayek and Ludwig von Mises to the intellectual rehabilitation of individualism in America at the close of World War II. One right-wing journalist, William Henry Chamberlin, called the redoubtable Mises (whom he knew personally) "a true St. George fighting the dragon of collectivism."[63] To those Americans who remained shell-shocked by the New Deal and the wartime growth of government, it was a pleasure to find scholarly "saints" to lead them.

If Hayek, still living in London, had taken the time to examine the American situation in 1944 or 1945, his gloom and discouragement would not have abated very much. As the furor caused by his book indicated, libertarianism was still alive in the United States, but it gave no promise of becoming the wave of the future. Here and there, of course, one could find dissenters from the prevailing orthodoxy. There were journalists: Henry Hazlitt; John Chamberlain, who wrote the introduction to the American edition of *The Road to Serfdom*; Isabel Paterson, whose *The God of the Machine* (1943) had assailed collectivism and argued the need for individual freedom in a technological society; Garet Garrett, author of *The Revolution Was* (1944), a fierce denunciation of the New Deal; and John Flynn, whose *As We Go Marching* (1945) contended that America under welfarism was following the very road that Italy and Germany had already traversed to disaster. There were Felix Morley, William Henry Chamberlin, and Frank Hanighen, the founders of *Human Events* in early 1944. In time this journal would become an important organ of libertarian journalism, but in 1945 it was still a small-circulation weekly news sheet concentrating on foreign policy. Among the various academic classical liberals, probably the most notable were Professors Henry C. Simons and Frank H. Knight of the University of Chicago— the nucleus of the nascent Chicago School in economics.

Yet all these voices of protest hardly comprised a movement in 1945. Looking back on those early days, Frank Meyer, later a conservative leader, correctly assayed the libertarians' plight: "scattered remnants of opposition...remained after Roosevelt's revolution of 1932."[64] Henry Regnery, the conservative Chicago book publisher, concurred:

> Liberalism [new style] reigned supreme and without question; the Liberal could believe, in fact, that no other position

was conceivable. The war, which represented the triumph of good over evil, had been won. Fascism, militarism and colonialism had been banished from the earth; the Peace-Loving Nations, joined together in San Francisco in a perpetual bond, would preserve peace, protect the weak, and guarantee the rule of democracy—the future seemed assured. It was a beautiful picture and questions about its conformity to the facts of life were not welcome.[65]

One must agree with Robert Crunden: "The war period, 1939-45, marked the nadir of individualistic, Jeffersonian thought in the United States."[66]

One indication of the almost forlorn minority status of libertarianism in these years was the quiet discovery by many future conservative intellectuals of the writings of Albert Jay Nock. Probably best remembered today as the founder of *The Freeman* in the 1920s and as the author of *Memoirs of a Superfluous Man*, the highly cultivated, eccentric Nock came to exert a significant influence on the postwar Right. Increasingly pessimistic and elitist in his later years, Nock verged on anarchism in his denunciations of the inherently aggrandizing State.[67] *Our Enemy, the State* he entitled one of his tracts.[68] Deeply affected by Ralph Adams Cram, Nock abandoned his early Jeffersonian idealism in revulsion from the hopeless, uneducable masses. Nock the classicist, the man of culture, became convinced that the masses could never be saved. But—and here he appealed to many later conservatives—the Remnant could. For in every age there existed a small Remnant of truly intelligent people; it was the task of each would-be Isaiah, alarmed at decay and impending doom, simply to preach. The members of the Remnant would eventually find him; they would come.[69]

In 1945 Nock died; already, however, a kind of Remnant had made its way to him. Out in the South Pacific during the war, a young serviceman named Robert Nisbet read and "practically memorized" Nock's *Memoirs of a Superfluous Man*.[70] Stationed in the desolate wastes of the Great Salt Lake Desert, Russell Kirk read Nock's work and corresponded with him.[71] In Massachusetts, a Unitarian minister named Edmund Opitz discovered Nock's writings just before World War II and read *Our Enemy, the State*.[72] Opitz later recalled Nock's impact:

> Nock has a way of becoming an event in a man's life.... after World War II I picked up a secondhand copy of the *Memoirs*...and sat up reading it during a long train trip across the country. By the time I reached the East Coast I had chosen sides. But I was not Nock's man; I was more than ever my

own man, I felt, as a result of AJN's gentle prodding.[73]

Still others acknowledged their debt; the journalist John Chamberlain, for example, revealed that *Our Enemy, the State* had "hit me between the eyes when I read it in the thirties."[74] In one important case—that of William F. Buckley, Jr.—Nock's impact was direct. Since Nock knew Buckley's family and lunched often at their home in Connecticut, it was no surprise that the young Buckley was personally affected by Nock in the 1940s. It was Nockian libertarianism in fact, which exercised the first conservative influence on the future editor of *National Review*.[75]

Why did Albert Jay Nock appeal so compellingly to so many who were to lead the postwar conservative renascence? One reason, of course, was that he articulated their thoughts so fully and so well. His passionate antistatism, his stern educational traditionalism (with its disdain for "progressive" education), his scorn for the masses, and his prewar isolationism were likely to attract people whose hopes for the future differed from those of Franklin Roosevelt, John Dewey, or Henry Wallace. A second reason may have been equally important, particularly in the mid-1940s: Nock's distinctive stance and style. In the century of the "common man" and the era of the welfare state, Nock did not pretend to hold out political hope. Instead, adopting a stoic, aristocratic pose, he presented himself as a sublimely *superfluous* man. This very concept of superfluity was, one suspects, part of Nock's charm (certainly his aristocratic aloofness from vulgarity may well have influenced Buckley). To be a philosophical individualist in 1945 was to feel alone and probably superfluous—or so, at least, Nock and other right-wing intellectuals appeared to think. But then, there were other goods in this life than pleasing the crowd—a useful and consoling lesson for a minority, and a lesson that Nock taught. Perhaps history and the masses had passed us by. So much the worse for history and the masses.

If Albert Jay Nock had lived on, he might have become the "grand old man" of postwar American libertarianism. With his death, however, the mantle passed to his principal disciple. The task of promulgating his thought to a larger audience was accomplished by a remarkable, individualistic son of a poor Russian Jewish immigrant peddler in New York: Frank Chodorov. Born on the lower East Side of New York City in 1887, Chodorov graduated from Columbia and started work as a teacher. Discontented with petty bureaucratic conformity, he soon resigned and spent several years as an advertising man and manager of a clothing factory. An early exposure to *Progress and Poverty* convinced Chodorov that Henry George was a prophet; in due time he became director of the Henry

George School of Social Science. When, in 1936, he met Albert Jay Nock, Chodorov had already imbibed deeply of the American libertarian tradition: men like Thoreau, Sumner, Mencken, and (he believed) George. A close friendship with Nock for nearly a decade thereafter intensified his convictions.[76]

In the late 1930s Chodorov revived *The Freeman* under the auspices of the Henry George School. It was not long before his pungent writing got him into trouble. Unabashedly antiwar and isolationist, Chodorov embarrassed his cautious and politically sensitive trustees. One day he was fired; the militant individualist was now fully on his own.[77]

At this point the career of Frank Chodorov began to shape directly the intellectual development of the postwar Right. Anxious to proselytize and undaunted by adversity, he established in November 1944 a four-page monthly broadsheet called *analysis*.[78] It is a vivid illustration both of the virtually underground character of much of the "classical liberal" movement in this period and of the perseverance of its devotees that this little journal appeared at all. Frank Chodorov was a practicing individualist; he produced his own magazine in a few rooms in an unpretentious building in Manhattan.[79]

In a promotional letter to readers of *analysis*, Chodorov described his "venture in personal journalism."[80] It was, he said, "an individualistic publication—the only one of its kind in America"; the tradition it espoused was that of Herbert Spencer, Adam Smith, Thoreau, George, and Nock. "I have tried...to interpret events and trends in the light of Nock's philosophy," he added.[81] In another such letter Chodorov was more explicit:

> ...*analysis*...stands for free trade, free land and the unrestricted employment of capital and labor. Its economics stem from Adam Smith and Henry George.
>
> ...*analysis* goes along with Albert Jay Nock in asserting that the State is our enemy, that its administrators and beneficiaries are a "professional criminal class," and interprets events accordingly. It is radical, not reformist.
>
> In short, *analysis* looks at the current scene through the eyeglass of historic liberalism, unashamedly accepting the doctrine of natural rights, proclaims the dignity of the individual and denounces all forms of Statism as human slavery.[82]

The reverse side of this letter contained an endorsement of Chodorov's effort by Nock himself, who declared that *analysis* was "by far the best contribution to our minor literature of public affairs." [83]

That Chodorov's intent was not mildly reformist was soon evident to his few thousand readers. Hayek's *Road to Serfdom*, he complained, had given him a "let-down." After demonstrating "that this road [to serfdom] is paved with planning he offers 'planning for competition' as a way out. How silly!"[84] Like so many other "individualists" in this era, Chodorov stated his case in a sweeping and zealous manner. And like them also, he was endowed with energy and will. Early in 1947, for instance, an *analysis* bookstore was set up in New York. Among the titles offered were books by Henry George and Nock, Vernon Louis Parrington's *Main Currents in American Thought*, Charles Beard's *Economic Interpretation of the Constitution*, Thoreau's *Walden*, and Ayn Rand's novel *Anthem*.[85]

By October 1946 *analysis* had attracted only 2,786 subscribers;[86] up to the time of its merger with *Human Events* in 1951, circulation reached a peak of only 4,000.[87] These were not easy years financially for the crusading libertarian.[88] Still, it was not money or a mass audience that he wanted; it was a Remnant. And, sure enough, by one route or another, it found him. About a year after *analysis* was founded, William F. Buckley, Jr. discovered it; this and other writings by Chodorov impressed him greatly.[89] Through his essayist-friend Henry Beston, Edmund Opitz learned of the magazine and enthusiastically urged it on his friends.[90] A future revisionist historian, James J. Martin, first learned about World War II revisionist works by such men as Harry Elmer Barnes and John T. Flynn in *analysis*; it was for Martin the "voice" of "the intellectual libertarian underground."[91] In 1946 Murray Rothbard, a graduate student at Columbia who would one day be a leading libertarian, discovered *analysis* and "eagerly imbibed" the writings of Chodorov, Nock, Mencken, and others; Chodorov's essay "Taxation Is Robbery"[92] had a "big impact" on him.[93]

During these years in which Chodorov was helping the libertarian Remnant to attain self-consciousness and intellectual coherence, a trenchant and sophisticated classical liberal literature was gradually beginning to develop. In 1946, Henry Hazlitt published his conspicuously pro-capitalist *Economics in One Lesson*, which eventually achieved a substantial circulation. Among those whom he praised in his introduction was Ludwig von Mises, who had read the manuscript. [94] In 1947 Frank Knight of the Chicago School published his *Freedom and Reform*, a collection of essays which argued forcefully a more or less Hayekian liberal position.[95] A year later another influential set of essays restated the Chicago case. Entitled *Economic Policy for a Free Society*, this volume represented most of the significant output of Knight's colleague, the late

Henry C. Simons. Only 46 at his death in 1946, Simons had already come to hold "a unique position in American economics.... [H]e was slowly establishing himself as the head of a 'school.' Just as Lord Keynes provided a respectable foundation for the adherents of collectivism, so Simons was providing a respectable foundation for the older faith of freedom and equality." [96] Author of the famous 1934 essay "A Positive Program for Laissez-Faire," Simons, along with his friend Knight, would come to achieve immense influence on the American Right through their brilliant disciple, Milton Friedman.[97]

In 1948, also, the University of Chicago published a collection of essays by Friedrich Hayek entitled *Individualism and Economic Order*, a work reflecting his profound distrust of "rationalist" attempts deliberately to design an improved society.[98] Hayek attacked the notion, which he traced to Descartes and other continental thinkers, that human society could be totally comprehended and manipulated by conscious human reason. Opposed to this "rationalistic pseudo-individualism" which "leads to practical collectivism"[99] was a primarily English tradition of "true individualism" expounded by Adam Smith, Adam Ferguson, Burke, Tocqueville, and Acton. This tradition, said Hayek, was antirationalistic, deeply convinced of the limits of reason and of the fallibility of any one individual. Men simply could not *know* enough to presume to direct consciously an entire society. "The fundamental attitude of true individualism is one of humility toward the processes by which mankind has achieved things which have not been designed or understood by any individual and are indeed greater than individual minds."[100] Hayek remained confident that the spontaneous actions of men and women were fundamentally beneficent: "if left free, men will often achieve more than individual reason could design or foresee."[101] As if to consolidate his forces with the congenial Chicago School of Knight, Simons, and Jacob Viner, Hayek became a professor at the University of Chicago in 1950s. It was one more sign of the times that, like Ludwig von Mises, Hayek was forced to rely on private sources to subsidize his entry into American academic circles.[102]

Other signs of rejuvenation were slowly surfacing. In 1949, for instance, came Felix Morley's *The Power in the People* and John T. Flynn's *The Road Ahead*—both responses to what the authors perceived as a socialist or statist threat to libertarian, individualistic America.[103] In 1947, Henry Regnery founded the publishing house bearing his name, intending, as he later put it, to publish "books which didn't necessarily fit the liberal ideology which so dominated publishing as to constitute a particularly effective form of censorship."[104] Two other publishers were also adding to the right-wing output: Devin-Adair of New York and the Caxton Printers of Caldwell, Idaho.[105]

Yet books alone do not create a coherent intellectual movement. They may alter the life of individual minds and, ultimately, the *weltanschauung* of a generation. But the construction of networks of influence with political impact—this, print alone cannot accomplish. Members of the Remnant needed to find one another and come together if their ideas were to have immediate and discernible consequences. If William F. Buckley, Jr. had become a businessman; if Frank Chodorov had remained in advertising; if Edmund Opitz had remained a minister in Hingham, Massachusetts; if Henry Regnery had not founded a publishing house; if countless other libertarians, individualists, and classical liberals had chosen to remain a scattered, hidden Remnant—they might still have had some personal influence. But it is unlikely that these individuals would have achieved broader intellectual significance were it not for their impulse in the 1940s to proselytize and organize. The example of the lofty, passive Albert J. Nock, exuding indifference toward the twilight struggles about him, was no doubt an inspiration, especially in moments of loneliness and despair. It was not, however, a formula for turning the tide here and now.

And that was what most individualists really wanted to do. As Hayek, Mises, and many others realized, the hour was late in 1945. What was to be done? It is imperative to recognize that the postwar libertarian intellectual movement was a movement of ideas *in action*. It was not solely a phenomenon of academic journals, lectures, and seminars, although many of its most distinguished and influential leaders lived in academe. Instead, it was the intellectual flank of what became a political movement, or, to put it differently, an intellectual movement with political implications. Its goal was not conventional power and prestige but the implementation of ideas. Parallels on the Left included the Fabian Socialists and the Americans for Democratic Action.

Yet just as in the case of the Fabian Socialists and the ADA, so, too, with the individualists of the Right: the Remnant had to be mobilized in order to be effective. It was not enough for individuals to protest the *zeitgeist* here and there; it was not enough for a few books to be written. An intellectual movement, like a political movement, requires form as well as spirit. In the years following 1945, several groups arose to fill this need.

"An institution is but the lengthened shadow of a man." In an article in *The Freeman* in 1952, John Chamberlain used this aphorism of Emerson's to describe a little organization called the Foundation for Economic Education and its energetic founder-president, Leonard Read.[106] The application of Emerson's wisdom to this case could not have been more apt; once more the quiet, almost obscure, and highly individualistic origins of postwar libertarian conservatism become apparent.

Born in 1898, Leonard Read by 1945 had already enjoyed a long career as an evangelist for classical liberalism. He had not always been a libertarian; in 1932, as manager of the western division of the Chamber of Commerce of the United States, he merely echoed the ideas of its national leader, Henry Harriman, a proponent of interventionist ideas which became the basis of the NRA a year later. One day in 1932, Read recalls, he paid a visit to an ideological opponent, W.C. Mullendore, then executive vice-president of Southern California Edison Company and later a supporter of many right-wing causes. Within an hour, Read's mind was completely changed; Mullendore had converted him to a free-market, limited-government philosophy. It was the turning point in his life.[107]

As Read, newly won to a libertarian perspective, surveyed the political scene in California, pernicious radical nostrums and panaceas seemed to be everywhere; EPIC, Ham-and-Eggs, Production for Use, and Townsendism were some of the most alluring. He soon became convinced that only a profound educational reorientation would suffice to quell the forever bubbling cauldron of erroneous doctrine; in 1935 he wrote a book embodying that thesis. Gradually Read became known as a dedicated believer in educational methods; in 1938 he left the national organization to become manager of the Los Angeles Chamber of Commerce, the largest of any city in the world. His task was explicit: to combat radicalism in California by a campaign of education.[108]

During World War II, Read worked energetically to spread his gospel. As one activity, he organized a little group called Pamphleteers, Inc., with a mailing list of 3,000. In 1935 Professor Thomas Nixon Carver of Harvard had introduced Read to the works of Frederic Bastiat (1801-1850), a French economist, politician, and polemicist for classical liberalism. Delighted by Bastiat's brilliant essay *The Law*, Read mailed it to his readers in 1943. Another nineteenth-century figure he enthusiastically introduced to his clientele was William Graham Sumner.[109]

Despite all this activity, Read by 1945 was dissatisfied with his accomplishments. Negative critiques of statism were not enough; a positive philosophy, a "freedom philosophy," was needed.

> ...I made several interesting discoveries.... Number one, it
> wasn't issuing from any place on the face of the earth. Num-
> ber two, there wasn't a magazine in the country that would
> take one of our articles. Three, there wasn't a book publisher
> that would take one of our books. Number four, just twenty-
> six years ago [1945] there did not exist a consistent literature
> of this philosophy written in modern American idiom. That's
> how far down the drain this philosophy was.

Resigning from the Los Angeles Chamber of Commerce, Read came to
New York to organize a challenge to the prevailing orthodoxy. He was
convinced that socialism, statism, Communism, the planned economy,
the welfare state—"it's all the same thing"—were successful principally
because "there [are] so few persons on earth who understand and can
explain socialism's opposite, which is this free-market, private ownership, limited government philosophy."[110]

In March 1946, with a number of distinguished associates,[111] Read
established the Foundation for Economic Education in Irvington-on-
Hudson, New York. Gradually he collected a staff, including three economists from Cornell University (W.M. Curtiss, F.A. Harper, and Paul
Poirot)[112] and Ludwig von Mises, whom Read put on the payroll at an
early date.[113] Among FEE's early friends was Friedrich Hayek, who occasionally lectured for it and supported its activities.[114]

As a nonpolitical foundation, FEE did not seek publicity in its early
days; so thorough was its belief in voluntarism that it invariably relied on
voluntary donations[115] and sent its literature to anyone free for the ask-
ing. At first Read believed that "economic illiteracy" was the chief ill to
be cured; soon he realized that the problem was deeper than that: it was
moral.[116] Consequently, much of FEE's literature became homiletic in
character. Intellectually, another staff member has recalled, a key question for FEE was: What are the proper functions of government?[117] Government strictly limited to the prevention of "aggressive force" was FEE's
answer.

From its inception, Read's foundation was clearly influenced by
Nock's concept of the Remnant; one sympathetic observer even likened
FEE to a kind of secular monastery.[118] But FEE's importance was greater
than its austere avoidance of controversy might suggest. By the summer
of 1952 it had developed a mailing list of 28,712 people,[119] to whom it
offered a growing array of literature of the "freedom philosophy." Bastiat's
The Law was reissued in a new translation in 1950; it became the
foundation's all-time best-seller. (By 1971 more than 500,000 copies had

been sold.) Henry Hazlitt's *Economics in One Lesson* was also distributed by FEE; it, too, had passed the 500,000 mark by 1971.[120] In 1952 the foundation collected its best releases in a volume entitled *Essays on Liberty*; among the contributors were Chodorov, Hazlitt, Mises, William Graham Sumner, and Bertrand de Jouvenel of France.[121]

The principal function which the Foundation for Economic Education served in these early years, in short, was to facilitate the recovery of a tradition and the dissemination of ideas. Classics of the "freedom philosophy" were being dusted off and published again; forgotten writers were now providing sustenance for a libertarian renascence. Many living individualist writers—well or little known—were finding an outlet for their efforts. Moreover, FEE's staff was assiduously compiling an expanding list of "clichés of socialism" and writing brief rebuttals for mass distribution. These "twitchings and stirrings" were not the kind to generate headlines or affect events at once. No one peering into FEE's stately old mansion on the Hudson would have thought he perceived the wave of the future—not yet. Nevertheless, the import of these activities should not be underestimated. Perhaps Read himself assessed the phenomenon most judiciously in 1951:

> The substance for a thorough-going twentieth century revolution is in the making.... That this spirit [of individualism] at present is evident among only a minority need not necessarily deject the devotee of liberty. Everything begins with a minority of one, extends to a few, and then to many.[122]

The Foundation for Economic Education in these years was extending its version of classical liberalism from the few to the many, one by one.

As FEE quietly went about its work, another organization founded in 1947 thousands of miles away was also contributing substantially to the growing self-consciousness and interrelatedness of what some were soon calling the neo-liberal movement in the United States and Western Europe. The earliest stimulus for this aspect of the revival emanated from the United States in 1937, when Walter Lippmann published *The Good Society*. Among those quick to perceive its importance was Friedrich Hayek, who considered it a "brilliant restatement of the fundamental ideals of classic liberalism."[123] At the University of Paris, Professor Louis Rougier was similarly elated and called for an international colloquium of liberal-minded scholars to discuss Lippmann's "maître-livre, un livre-clé,...la meilleure explication des maux de notre temps."[124] Among those who attended in August 1938 were Lippmann himself and a number of prominent European scholars, including Hayek, Mises, Raymond Aron, Étienne Mantoux, Michael Polanyi, Wilhelm Röpke, and Jacques Rueff. After several days of earnest discussions, the conference established the Centre International d'Études pour la Rénovation du Liberalisme.

Before this organization could take form, conflict descended upon Europe, and the "renewal" of liberalism yielded to the demands of war. Soon after the war ended, however, the effort was revived, this time by Hayek. He had become convinced of the need for scholars then "working in isolation" and scattered by war, men united by a common faith in traditional liberalism, to unite, exchange views, and consolidate their forces. Among the people to whom he confided his hopes were Sir John Clapham, the eminent British economic historian, and Professor Henry Simons at Chicago. Finally, on April 1, 1947, nearly forty prominent European and American scholars gathered at Mont Pélerin, Switzerland for a ten-day conference. Almost half of those in attendance were Americans, or Europeans living in America.[125]

The mood of this conference was somber; the participants, high in the Swiss Alps, were only too conscious that they were outnumbered and without apparent influence on policymakers in the Western world. All across Europe, planning and socialism seemed ascendant. The conference's concluding declaration revealed its trepidation:

> The central values of civilization are in danger. Over large stretches of the earth's surface the essential conditions of human dignity and freedom have already disappeared. In others they are under constant menace from the development of current tendencies of policy. The position of the individual and the voluntary group are progressively undermined by the spread of creeds which, claiming the privilege of tolerance when in the position of a minority, seek only to establish a position of power in which they can suppress and obliterate all views but their own.
>
> The group holds that these developments have been fostered by the growth of a view of history which denies all absolute moral standards and by the growth of theories which question the desirability of the rule of law. It holds further that they have been fostered by a decline of belief in private property and the competitive market; for without the diffused power and initiative associated with these institutions it is difficult to imagine a society in which freedom may be effectively preserved.[126]

Eschewing all partisan alignments and merely propagandistic motives, the group called for study of several issues pertinent to its central goal, "the preservation and improvement of the free society."[127] After some discussion, the conference decided to call itself the Mont Pélerin Society.[128]

The immediate impact of the society was perhaps best stated by one of its members, Milton Friedman: "The importance of that meeting was that it showed us that we were not alone."[129] This in itself was no small gain in those uncongenial years. As Friedman later put it, the conference served as a "rallying point" for outnumbered troops.[130] But the advantages of cooperation soon transcended the reassurance of comradeship in adversity. Reassembling in 1949 and almost every year thereafter, the Mont Pélerin Society gradually became a kind of international "who's who" of the classical liberal and neo-liberal intellectuals.[131] At its conferences papers were presented which were often eventually published;[132] ideas were exchanged and friendships formed. For the American Right, already indebted to Europeans for help in its resuscitation during the 1940s, this exposure to wider currents was, one suspects, particularly important; it stretched the web of influence and tended to make American conservative thought more cosmopolitan. Whatever the "grass-roots" of American conservatism may have been in this period, its intellectual leadership was not xenophobic. For this increasing cosmopolitanism, for this consciousness of compatriots in Europe, the Mont Pélerin Society—and the network it created—must be given partial credit. In 1952 its founder, Friedrich Hayek, was justifiably proud to report:

> Gone are the days when the few outmoded liberals walked their paths lonely, ridiculed and without response from the young....
> ...at least personal contact among the proponents of neo-liberalism has been established....
> Thus the period of drought...seems to have come to an end.[133]

That the drought was indeed ending was evident in the appearance of *The Freeman* on October 2, 1950. Combining with Isaac Don Levine's anti-Communist journal *Plain Talk*, the new journal unabashedly declared its dedication to "traditional liberalism and individual freedom" and pledged to uphold such principles as these:

> ...economic freedom, as embodied in the free market, is the basic institution of a liberal society....

> The free market economy not only provides the maxi-
> mum of economic liberty but insures maximum production....
> ...True liberalism rests on the common law, on clear and
> definite statute law, and on a government of limited powers....
> And true liberalism means local autonomy and the decen-
> tralization of political power.[134]

Edited by two experienced classical liberal journalists, John Chamberlain and Henry Hazlitt, with the assistance of Suzanne La Follette (formerly on the staff of Albert Jay Nock's *Freeman* in the 1920s), the magazine welcomed as contributors to its first issue such veterans of the struggle
for old-style liberalism as Raymond Moley, George Sokolsky, and John T.
Flynn.[135]

By the end of its first year of publication, *The Freeman* had attained
a modest circulation of about 12,000.[136] This rather low figure does not,
however, adequately reflect either its influence or its significance in the
early 1950s. Here at last was a respectable journal ("a fortnightly for
individualists")[137] which was providing a regular forum for hitherto dispersed writers. Here at last was a periodical applying libertarian theories
to daily realities. Not only professional journalists but also scholars like
Hayek, Mises, and Germany's neo-liberal economist Wilhelm Röpke appeared in its pages. Men as diverse as Senators Harry Byrd and John
Bricker, John Dos Passos, Roscoe Pound, and General Albert Wedemeyer
acclaimed its value.[138] It is difficult to convey a sense of the crucial role of
The Freeman at the height of its prestige, between 1950 and 1954. The
American Left, in these years, had many well-known and reputable journals from which to choose; the American Right had almost none. It fell
to *The Freeman*, almost alone among popular journals, to focus dissent,
to marshal its forces, to articulate practical alternatives to the chimeras
and schemes of its foes. It did so with recognized skill and success.

Still, the way was uphill. Financially the journal was a disaster; by
mid-1954 it had lost $400,000. In July 1954 the Irvington Press (whose
capital was owned by the Foundation for Economic Education) purchased
the magazine, which now became a monthly. Leonard Read hired Frank
Chodorov as editor, and under his guidance the magazine increasingly
emphasized economics. When after eighteen months Read had lost
$90,000 in the venture, he was forced to alter the scope and format of
the journal.[139]

The Foundation for Economic Education, the Mont Pélerin Society, and *The Freeman* were not the only groups and organizations that
were providing leadership and an institutional framework for the devel-

oping libertarian wing of the conservative movement in the late 1940s and early 1950s. Others of varying intellectual and political respectability were also at work. One was the *American Mercury*, which served as a useful outlet for some conservative intellectuals in the 1950s. [140] Another was *Faith and Freedom*, established in 1950 as the organ of Spiritual Mobilization, a group founded in 1935 "to arouse ministers of all denominations in America to check the trends toward pagan stateism [sic]."[141] Among the contributors to this monthly were Hazlitt, Mises, Morley, and Read. It also featured in April and May 1953 a notable exchange on government and economics between Edmund Opitz and his former teacher, Dr. John C. Bennett of Union Theological Seminary.[142] Opitz had discovered the magazine through his friend Frank Chodorov; not long thereafter he became the conference director for Spiritual Mobilization, where he stayed until 1955.[143] While neither of these two periodicals had as central a role in the rebuilding of the intellectual Right as did *The Freeman*, their contributions to the cause were not negligible in its formative years.[144]

Meanwhile, yet another organization was getting under way in the early 1950s; it was, from the beginning, the "lengthened shadow" of the tireless Frank Chodorov. Slowly the editor of *analysis* was becoming known; his friend Devin Garrity published Chodorov's *One Is a Crowd* in 1952 and *The Income Tax: Root of All Evil* in 1954.[145] "Absolutely unyielding" in his libertarianism,[146] he liked to boast that no one stood to his right; perhaps for this reason he was beginning to acquire a following on college campuses.[147]

As Chodorov surveyed trends in academe, he was increasingly disturbed by what he saw. In an article in *analysis* in 1950, he asserted that the most significant development in the first half of the twentieth century had been "the transmutation of the American character from individualist to collectivist." Why had this revolution come about? Partly because "the collectivist seed was implanted in the soft and fertile student mind forty-odd years ago." Chodorov traced the long, slow process by which socialistic ideas had allegedly permeated campuses, captured many of the best young minds, and laid the foundations for the New Deal. Yet this trend had *not* been inevitable. It had been the product of conscious effort, manifest injustices of the status quo, the intellectual sloth of the defenders of natural rights and capitalism, and the vigor of the socialist idea. With a similar effort on the campuses, the cause of individualism could itself, he believed, eventually prevail.

> We are not born with ideas, we learn them. If socialism
> has come to America because it was implanted in the minds
> of past generations, there is no reason for assuming that the
> contrary idea cannot be taught to a new generation. What the
> socialists have done can be undone, if there is a will for it.

There would be no instant reversal, though; it might take fifty years for the cause to triumph.[148]

Chodorov was not the only libertarian dismayed by "collectivism on the campus" in the 1950s. In 1951 a young Yale graduate, William F. Buckley, Jr. published a book that produced a sensation, dwarfing even the reception of *The Road to Serfdom* a few years before. Widely, often angrily reviewed, *God and Man at Yale* has probably been the most controversial book in the history of conservatism since 1945, and its importance for this movement is manifold. Of immediate interest here is only one aspect: Buckley's contention that individualism—the philosophy of free enterprise, private property, and limited government—was "dying at Yale, and without a fight."[149] By analyzing allegedly lopsided courses and textbooks in economics, Buckley tried to prove "the net influence of Yale economics to be thoroughly collectivistic."[150] In his introduction to the book, John Chamberlain echoed Buckley's complaint. It might be permissible, he said, to expose students to left-wing economic viewpoints as part of a truly balanced fare. "But where [at Yale] are the countervailing quotations from Röpke, von Mises, Hayek, Frank Knight, the Walter Lippmann of *The Good Society* and other believers in the economics of free customer choice?"[151]

One result of this ferment was Chodorov's founding, in 1953, of the Intercollegiate Society of Individualists (ISI)—with William F. Buckley, Jr. as president.[152] Intended as an antidote to the Intercollegiate Society of Socialists of an earlier generation, ISI reflected Chodorov's personality and interests. There was virtually no organization, no salesmanship, and no fanfare. All materials were free on request; all members were self-elected. It was indeed, in Chodorov's own words, "an organization of ideas"—and a reflection of his expectation that the Remnant would find him.[153] By 1956 a total of 10,000 people had done so and had received more than 500,000 pieces of the burgeoning literature of libertarianism.[154]

In later years ISI became extremely influential as a clearinghouse of conservative publications and as a coordinator of the conservative intellectual movement.[155] But by the mid-1950s its significance was already noticeable. First, ISI was doing for intelligent conservative youths what other groups were doing for adults: it was giving them an intellectual home and a focus for disparate energies. This, Chodorov acknowledged, was one of its purposes: "to inform nonconformists that they have company." [156] Certainly the need was obvious. As one college graduate wrote, "The youthful libertarian is faced with an environment utterly hostile.... To be a libertarian is a lonely, sometimes heartrending job."[157]

ISI was notable for a second reason: its success revealed that the classical liberal revival was increasingly self-conscious and articulate. ISI could not have flourished had there not already emerged an array of respectable books bearing its message. Among the works which it distributed to its eager youthful Remnant were Chodorov's own *One Is a Crowd*, Hazlitt's *Economics in One Lesson*, Bastiat's *The Law*, Buckley's *God and Man at Yale*, Hayek's *The Road to Serfdom*, and William Graham Sumner's *What Social Classes Owe to Each Other*.[158] ISI's work in the 1950s was thus a testimony to the intellectual spadework that had begun in the 1940s. Indeed, one might even say that William F. Buckley's *God and Man at Yale* could not have been written without the revival of the classical liberal tradition. For how could he have criticized Yale's monolithic "collectivism" had not a scholarly alternative to Keynes and Marx already been developing?

In this task of creating and sustaining an intellectual movement, then, ISI joined FEE, the Mont Pélerin Society, and *The Freeman* as the principal architects of the libertarian reconstruction.[159] To these four groups belongs most of the credit for giving "classical liberalism" some initial coherence as a movement. Each strengthened the network of influence and personal contacts so indispensable to widely dispersed dissenters.

"Everything begins with a minority of one, extends to a few, and then to many."

By 1955—the year *National Review* was founded—the libertarian revival in America had reached a new plateau. If classical liberals and individualists had not escaped from what they regarded as an intellectual ghetto, at least they had emerged from the storm cellars.[160] Many of their intellectual leaders were becoming happily aware of their changing status. As early as 1952, Friedrich Hayek had celebrated a "rebirth" of liberalism on both sides of the Atlantic.[161] A year later, examining European intellectual currents, the conservative Austrian author and scholar Erik von Kuehnelt-Leddihn acclaimed a "resurgence" of liberalism.[162] In 1954, Hayek edited a provocative book, *Capitalism and the Historians*. Drawing heavily on recent trends in British economic historiography, it was a hard-hitting, deliberate counterattack on "the legend of the deterioration of the position of the working classes in consequence of the rise of 'capitalism'...."[163] The early Industrial Revolution was *not* an era of exploitation and suffering caused by "capitalism," the contributors insisted. Significantly, Hayek's book was also a direct product of the deliberations of the Mont Pélerin Society. Even Frank Chodorov, not one to expect quick results, detected cheerful portents by 1954:

> There wasn't much you could do with the merchandise of freedom, ten years ago.... Therefore, the very volume, if not the quality, of literature that arose from the arid desert of 1944 is something to be thankful for. Things *are* looking up. The Socialists...in the intellectual field...are meeting more and more opposition.[164]

Old-style liberals could have no illusions, however, that their troubles were over; the response in many left-of-center quarters to *Capitalism and the Historians* was a case in point. One hostile reviewer accused Hayek of "whitewashing the Industrial Revolution."[165] Another disliked the book's appeal for "unqualified affirmations of its viewpoint."[166] Most critical of all was Professor Arthur Schlesinger, Jr. Accusing Hayek of "fiery dogmatism," Schlesinger denounced the book as "a summons to a witch-hunt," adding: "Americans, one would think, have enough trouble with home-grown McCarthys without importing Viennese professors to add academic luster to the process."[167] If "classical liberalism" had established itself as a viable and significant intellectual force by 1955, obviously it had not routed its opposition. It was still very much a minority among educated Americans.

Moreover, it was to some extent a divided movement. Despite their common opposition to socialism, Keynesian economics, and the welfare state, libertarian intellectuals disagreed about the extent to which government activity was compatible with individual freedom and the market system. Clearly there was a considerable gap between the passionate antistatism of Chodorov and Mises and the more moderate views of Hayek, who dissociated himself from pure "laissez-faire" and argued the need for vigorous government action to establish the "rule of law" and to maintain the "design" of a free market. The scope of government acceptable to the Foundation for Economic Education seemed much more narrow than that proposed by the Chicago School's Henry Simons, whose "Positive Program for Laissez-Faire" in 1934 actually called for nationalization of enterprises deemed incapable of operating within a framework of competition.[168] How much government was needed simply to make capitalism function? Should we adhere to a rigid gold standard or adopt flexible exchange rates?[169] To these questions libertarians gave divergent answers. Furthermore, while some were relatively indifferent to larger social and philosophical problems, others—led particularly by the increasingly influential German economist Wilhelm Röpke—insisted that "the ethics of freedom can only be derived from the religious values embodied in the Judaeo-Christian tradition."[170] One observer, analyzing European developments, distinguished Röpke's "Neo-Liberal" group from nineteenth-century "Paleo-Liberalism."[171] Similar tensions existed among the Americans, as disputes in the years ahead would reveal.

Nevertheless, for all the skepticism from the Left and for all its own internal differences, the movement of classical liberals, libertarians, and individualists was having a certain impact by the mid-1950s. The question becomes: Why was it having any impact at all? Why had not this alleged "survival," this "obscurantism" (to borrow Charles Merriam's words) simply disappeared in the postwar decade? Two factors seem most responsible. First, many circumstances in these years combined to give the creed continued relevance and respectability. At home, the New Deal era was "only yesterday," and as the election returns suggested, a sizable bloc of Americans had not reconciled themselves to its permanence. The issues of government and the economy, of balanced budgets versus Keynesianism, continued to define political battle lines. In 1951, Senator Robert Taft could identify the choice for the nation as liberty or socialism;[172] Hayek, Chodorov, or Buckley could not have said it more succinctly. The very success of such books as *The Road to Serfdom* and *God and Man at Yale* attested to the national uncertainty—and to the existence of an audience for right-wing publications.

Abroad, too, certain political developments were giving resonance to libertarian arguments. By the early 1950s, it was evident to nearly everyone that Stalinist Russia was a "god that failed." In the tense cold war against this totalitarian state, it was not surprising that many Americans felt the need to reassert national ideals. In such an environment, old American traditions—including individualism—no longer seemed obsolete.[173] Also instructive, right-wingers believed, was the example of socialist Britain. There the Labour Party victory of 1945 had turned, they contended, into a dreary failure by the time of Churchill's return to power in 1951. To Friedrich Hayek, writing in 1956, the British "experiment" had only "strengthened my concern" about totalitarian pressures inherent in socialism.[174] Other libertarians echoed him. Had not rationalistic, coercive statism failed? Was not the "invisible hand" preferable to the all too visible hand of the bureaucrat and the secret police? In both Europe and America, the early 1950s were, for many intellectuals, years of what Max Eastman called "reflections on the failure of socialism."[175] Compared to tarnished utopias abroad, "capitalist" America did not look so bad or so backward anymore.

In glittering contrast to the Soviet Union and Britain, American libertarians triumphantly cited the astonishing economic recovery of West Germany. The German "miracle" was especially welcome to them, for they regarded it as directly attributable to the theories of one of their European mentors, Wilhelm Röpke. As one of the first German professors to be dismissed by the Nazis in 1933, Röpke had endured years of exile in Turkey and Switzerland. Upon his return to his homeland after World War II, Röpke quickly became one of the founders of the neoliberal school of economists, a prominent member of the Mont Pélerin Society, and an influential adviser to the West German government.[176] So immense, in fact, was his impact on Ludwig Erhard's economic policies that Röpke was acclaimed by the American Right as the intellectual father of the German recovery. Erhard himself agreed: "My own services toward the attainment of a free society are scarcely enough to express my gratitude to him who, to such a high degree, influenced my position and conduct."[177] Not surprisingly, Röpke's influence on the American Right increased during the early 1950s; by 1954 he had contributed several articles to *The Freeman*.[178] Libertarians claimed to find proof in Germany of the superiority of the free market and the validity of their views. Gleefully they pointed out that the Germans were again prosperous precisely because they had ignored the advice of Keynesians from the United States and had instead adopted Röpke's "neo-liberal" recommendations.

Yet external events and trends alone cannot fully explain the resurgence of classical liberalism as an intellectual force in America in the first decade after 1945. What seems, in retrospect, most remarkable about the leaders of this movement in these early years was their tenacity in the face of an often hostile environment. The Olympian Nock, Hayek in war-torn London, Chodorov living on a meal a day, Read in a "monastery" outside New York City, Buckley seemingly alone at Yale—these and the others seem especially noteworthy for their refusal to abandon what frequently appeared to be a doomed position. In their contempt for the cult of easy security, passive conformity, and acceptance by the "lonely crowd," they exhibited an "inner-directedness" that many of their contemporaries believed was dying. If Disraeli was correct—that "men are not the creatures of circumstances; circumstances are the creatures of men"— his aphorism should be applied to these libertarian conservatives during their years in intellectual exile.

In 1954, Professor H. Stuart Hughes of Harvard reflected on their altered circumstances:

> The publication ten years ago of F.A. Hayek's *The Road to Serfdom* was a major event in the intellectual history of the United States.... [I]t marked the beginning of that slow reorientation of sentiment—both in academic circles and among the general public—toward a more positive evaluation of the capitalist system which has marked the past decade.[179]

Years later Milton Friedman, casting a backward glance, agreed. *The Road to Serfdom*, he remarked, was "an extraordinarily insightful and prescient" book which had decisively affected many, many people. Above all, it had demolished the "stereotype" that defenders of the free market were necessarily "tools of the interests" and that all decent men had to be socialists.[180] Libertarianism and capitalism had become intellectually defensible again.

"That slow reorientation of sentiment"—how obscure and unpretentious were most of its origins, how incomplete its victories. Still, by 1955, classical liberals—one branch of American conservatism—had considerable reason to think that T.S. Eliot was right. There was indeed no such thing as a lost cause.

TWO

The Revolt Against the Masses[1]

A t the end of World War II, classical liberals or libertarians, peering at the "monuments" of global conflict, apprehensively discerned in the State a landmark on the road to serfdom. They were not alone in their attempts to extract meaning from the nightmare of destruction in which America and scores of other nations had just participated. Other men—scattered, like the libertarians, and unknown as yet to one another—were beginning to analyze the crisis the war had precipitated and to reconstruct the civilization it had threatened. Out of these efforts emerged the "new conservative" or traditionalist wing of the postwar conservative intellectual movement in the United States.

Let us examine a representative figure. One morning in the autumn of 1945, an obscure professor of English at the University of Chicago sat in his office contemplating the devastation of a world so recently at war. The experience of the past few years had been a "progressive disillusionment" to Richard M. Weaver. As the war had continued it had become more "total" than ever; old restraints had failed to control man's propensity to evil. When Finland, in Weaver's opinion, was "thrown to the wolves," and when the "political insanity" of Yalta was perpetrated, his faith in the "honesty of our case" diminished even further.[2]

He began to ponder "whether it would not be possible to deduce, from fundamental causes, the fallacies of modern life and thinking that had produced this holocaust and would insure others." Curiously, he later admitted, it was "the bygone ideal of chivalry" that decisively influenced his thinking. Chivalry, he thought, "offered a plan whereby civilization might contain a war and go on existing as civilization." War could not be eradicated, but it might be controlled. Chivalry at least incorporated "the conception of something spiritual which stood above war itself and included the two sides in any conflict."[3]

This interest in a medieval code of ethics and "something spiritual which stood above war itself" was no mere vagary; Weaver had come to his position by an illuminating intellectual odyssey. Born in 1910 in North Carolina, he entered the University of Kentucky in 1927; there he became convinced that "the future was with science, liberalism, and equalitarianism...."[4] Upon graduation in 1932, the young North Carolinian joined Norman Thomas's Socialist Party of America and served as secretary of a local for about two years. Weaver's affinities for the Left were soon exposed to a disconcerting challenge. As a graduate student in literature at Vanderbilt University from 1933 to 1936, he became acquainted with several leading Southern Agrarians, whose company he preferred to that of the "dry, insistent" socialists "of shallow objectives."[5] As a student of John Crowe Ransom, Weaver was particularly attracted to his teacher's concept of the "unorthodox defense of orthodoxy," developed in *God without Thunder*. "I began to perceive," he later wrote, "that many traditional positions in our world had suffered not so much because of inherent defects as because of the stupidity, ineptness, and intellectual sloth of those who for one reason or another were presumed to have their defense in charge."[6]

When Weaver left Vanderbilt in 1936, he was still "poised" between socialism and Agrarianism.[7] The direction of his thinking, however, was soon evident. As a teacher at Texas A&M in the late 1930s, he was appalled by "rampant philistinism, abetted by technology, large-scale organization, and a complacent acceptance of success as the goal of life." To this experience he later attributed his "poetic and ethical vision of life."[8] The final conversion occurred late in 1939, when Weaver realized that the "clichés of liberalism" had become "meaningless" to him. In 1940, he gave up his job and "went off to start my education over." He was 30 years old.[9]

For the next three years, as war encircled the globe, Richard Weaver studied the American Civil War. It was a quest not just for knowledge but for self-knowledge and escape from the "stultifying" Whig theory of history. He began to be impressed by the sheer givenness and incomprehensibility of the world, and he veered more than ever from "egotistical and presumptuous" attempts to reform it. The study of Southern history was for Weaver a road to the Right.

One product of his immersion in the story of the "losing side" was a doctoral dissertation completed at Louisiana State University in 1943, dedicated to John Crowe Ransom and influenced by Ortega y Gasset's *The Revolt of the Masses*.[10] According to Weaver, the antebellum South was different; it was tenacious, and it was in many ways superior as a civilization to that which triumphed with the Civil War. The Southern tradition had four distinct features: a feudal theory and organization of society, a code of chivalry, the concept of the gentleman, and a peculiar, unintellectual, "older" religiousness. This civilization, more akin to Europe than to any other American region, was defeated by the unleashed might of the "modern" North in the 1860s. Yet—and this was his principal theme—the Old South had not been spiritually obliterated. Instead, for decades after 1865, it had persisted in defending its antebellum mores and wartime behavior. Politicians, soldiers, diarists, novelists—nearly all had united to assert the rightness of the past in the face of defeat by an alien culture.

Weaver's dissertation was not simply a historical investigation; it was an apologia. The South, he argued, has "an ethical claim which can be described only in terms of the mandate of civilization."[11] For instance, "the South, alone among the sections, has persisted in regarding science as a false messiah."[12] Southern feudalism, he noted, "possessed stability, an indispensable condition for positive values.... It was a rooted culture which viewed with dismay the anonymity and the social indifference of urban man."[13] Although Weaver on occasion criticized his native region, his loyalty to it was supreme. He contended that it had been "right without realizing the grounds of its rightness."[14] The Old South had been *"the last non-materialist civilization in the Western world."*[15] By 1943 Richard Weaver was a devoted Agrarian.[16]

Like so many of his Agrarian mentors, Weaver soon joined in the diaspora from the South; by 1945 he was at the University of Chicago, reflecting soberly on the cataclysm of modernity. Perhaps, as he sat in his office on that fall day, he recalled the statement by Ortega y Gasset which he had cited in his dissertation. "The simple process of preserving our present civilization," said Ortega, "is supremely complex, and demands incalculably subtle powers."[17] Richard Weaver wished to make the attempt; by late 1947 he had completed a book which he wanted to call *The Fearful Descent*.[18] His publisher, however, selected another title and, early in 1948, *Ideas Have Consequences* at last appeared. It was to become, in the opinion of many, "the *fons et origo* [source and origin] of the contemporary American conservative movement."[19]

The subject of Weaver's book was nothing less than "the dissolution of the West."[20] Its deterioration as a culture was traceable to an intellec-

tual failure in the late fourteenth century, when, Weaver argued, Western man had made an "evil decision": enticed by the philosophy of nominalism expounded by William of Occam (d. *c.* 1349), he had abandoned
his belief in transcendental values or "universals" and thus the position
that "there is a source of truth higher than, and independent of, man...."[21]
In short, "the defeat of logical realism [by nominalism] in the great medieval debate was the crucial event in the history of Western culture...."[22]

The "consequences" of this revolution in ideas, Weaver believed,
were stark and disastrous. "The denial of everything transcending experience," he declared, "means inevitably...the denial of truth. With the
denial of objective truth there is no escape from the relativism of 'man is
the measure of all things.'"[23] This was only the beginning. Nature ceased
to be seen as an "imperfect reality" and was instead perceived as a self-
contained entity. The doctrine of original sin was abandoned; the "goodness of man" replaced it. Since only the physical world of the senses was
held to be real, religion declined, rationalism arose, and materialist science increasingly became the most prestigious way to study man. With
knowledge limited to sensory experience, man was eventually lost in "endless induction" and "multiplicities." Man, in sum, had been in retreat for
centuries, from first principles, from definition, from true knowledge—
that is, the knowledge of universals.[24]

After establishing his historical perspective on the decadent modern world, Weaver concentrated on the maladies of the contemporary
West. Again and again, he insisted that civilization must be based on
vision, principle, hierarchy, structure, distance, and restraint. The modern world could hardly have been more remote from his ideals. Culture,
in Weaver's definition, was "sentiment refined and measured by intellect."[25] It confronted in 1948 an assault on privacy, a tidal wave of raw
experience, "the desire of immediacy."[26] Civilization, said Weaver, depends on "distinction and hierarchy"; it faced in 1948 rampant equalitarianism and the cult of the mass. As Weaver remarked, "society and
mass are contradictory terms."[27] Everywhere his ethic of self-discipline,
orderliness in thought and life, and reflective humility was under siege:
in the "fragmentation and obsession" that empiricism and specialization
were producing; in such "egotistic" movements as jazz music and im-
pressionist art; in the immersion in disorderly experience produced by
the "Great Stereopticon" (Weaver's phrase for the mass media); and in
the "spoiled-child psychology" of modern man, who had "not been made
to see the relationship between effort and reward."[28] Repeatedly Weaver
traced this orgy of mindlessness to the failure of modern man to achieve

an integrated world picture, a "metaphysical dream." And he warned that "the closer man stands to ruin, the duller grows his realization; the annihilation of spiritual being precedes the destruction of temple walls."[29]

It was not Weaver's intention merely to write a jeremiad, however; in the final three chapters he offered proposals for reform.

> The first positive step must be a driving afresh of the wedge between the material and the transcendental.... That there is a world of ought, that the apparent does not exhaust the real—these are so essential to the very conception of im- provement that it should be superfluous to mention them.... To bring dualism back into the world and to ebuke the moral impotence fathered by empiricism is then the broad charac- ter of our objective. [30]

But how? First we must defend the right of private property—"the last metaphysical right remaining to us."[31] By this Weaver did not mean im- personal, corporate property but "the distributive ownership of small properties."[32] Here an individual could maintain perspective and pri- vacy; here he could find a refuge from the encroaching state; here he could defend "the logos against modern barbarism."[33]

Next Weaver proposed that language be purified and rescued from "the impulse to dissolve everything into sensation,"[34] represented cur- rently by the nominalistic semantics movement. Language, far from be- ing a trap, was "a great storehouse of universal memory,"[35] a "metaphysi- cal community,"[36] an inherently value-giving power. Accordingly, he ad- vocated discipline in language, through poetry, dialectic, and foreign lan- guages. Possibly reflecting the thought of his Agrarian mentors, Weaver asserted that "poetry offers the fairest hope of restoring our lost unity of mind."[37] We must, he concluded with a distinctive phrase, restore "a respect for words as things."[38]

Finally, Weaver pleaded for an attitude of piety toward nature, other human beings, and the past. This, he believed, would be a partial anti- dote for modern man's egotism, "hysterical optimism," and aggressive "war against substance."[39]

The response to Weaver's audacious book was varied and sometimes venomous. "People seem to be for or against it violently," he wrote to Donald Davidson.[40] Paul Tillich, Reinhold Niebuhr, and John Crowe Ransom praised it highly.[41] The antinaturalist philosopher Eliseo Vivas called Weaver "an inspired moralist,"[42] while Willmoore Kendall, a con- servative Yale political scientist, nominated him for "the captaincy of the anti-Liberal team."[43] Others were far less laudatory. Charles Frankel, who would eventually write *The Case for Modern Man*, criticized Weaver's "absolutist" defense of the humanist tradition.[44] Howard Mumford Jones accused him of irresponsibility;[45] another reviewer labeled him "a propagandist for a return to the medieval papacy."[46] In perhaps the most intemperate review, one critic denounced the book as a "pompous fraud," "essentially evil," "notorious," and part of a University of Chicago Press "chain of reaction" that included books by Hans Morgenthau and Friedrich Hayek.[47] No wonder Weaver observed that his little opus "carries a whip lash."[48]

Why? The extreme response to *Ideas Have Consequences* invites comparison with the furor that greeted *The Road to Serfdom* a few years earlier. Both authors were austere intellectuals, little interested in popular acclaim; neither anticipated the success and notoriety he gained.[49] Indeed, so quietly had Weaver prepared his book that neither his family nor his colleagues knew that he was writing it.[50] Moreover, both Hayek and Weaver, in their separate domains, perceived the same phenomenon: the decline of the West as a result of the triumph of pernicious ideas. Each man was shocked by the experience of World War II;[51] each book was in part a jeremiad; each book touched the raw nerve of an uncertain nation.

Weaver's tour de force was not, however, just one more addition to the literature of lamentation about the decline of the West. The frequently outraged response to it suggests its true significance: probably more than any other book in the early postwar years, *Ideas Have Consequences* starkly revealed the chasm dividing the intellectual Right and Left. In a review in 1949, Herbert J. Muller focused repeatedly on this gulf. The trouble with Weaver, he wrote, was that he believed in "absolute, immutable, eternal" truths. But not only did Weaver fail to demonstrate the existence of such truths; he also sought to implement a "quixotic," neo-feudal program based on "positive illiberality." The "political equivalent of Mr. Weaver's metaphysical certitudes," Muller asserted, was authoritarianism. Not tolerant, "relativistic" liberalism but the "illusion of certainty" was really "at the root of our troubles."[52]

The profound differences between Muller and Weaver reflected with unusual clarity the developing intellectual cleavage between liberalism and what came to be called the "new conservatism" in the postwar era. At issue, in part, was the true significance of totalitarianism. Hitler's gas ovens, Stalin's enormous purges, Orwell's vision of 1984—how had this new barbarism happened? What were the sources of totalitarianism and the best defense against it? How could we prevent history from repeating itself? Which road led to tyranny, to serfdom—corrosive, skeptical relativism, or militant reaffirmation of tradition "absolutes"?[53] On what basis could we erect a "moral foundation for democracy"?[54] By secular, pragmatic, scientific intelligence (personified by John Dewey), or by religious faith and the "Great Tradition" of Western philosophy? The very appearance of the notion that democracy required a "moral basis" was a sign of the times. These were some of the questions raised by Weaver's book in 1948, and the divergent answers of his reviewers clarified the lines of intellectual force for years to come.

Although Weaver effectively expressed many postwar conservative concerns, he was by no means the only dissenter from liberal orthodoxy in these years. Here and there other voices of protest were contributing to what Muller called "the revival of the absolute." One such individual was the chief editorial writer for the *New York Herald Tribune*, August Heckscher, whose book *A Pattern of Politics* appeared in 1947.[55] The assumption of his work, he averred, was "the need of restoring to our social life some moral content, some valid meaning and purpose."[56] Like Weaver, Heckscher had been pondering the impact of the war, and like Weaver, he turned to ideas as the source of our discontents. Heckscher was especially disconcerted by what had seemed to him to be the moral indifference of college students just before World War II. A generation of students had been taught, he contended, to be cynical about truths and ideals.

> ...a generation came to live in a pallid world, from which all the qualities that affirm manhood and declare character had been drained. Because loyalty and will and hope seemed to have played no part in the studies to which they had gone for light upon the nature of man and the communities which he builds, they doubted that these things existed. They lived with phantoms. They fed upon the dry husks of truth.... Freedom had been a few privileges exacted from the crown at Runnymede by a grasping aristocracy, and afterwards elaborated by fifty-five rich men at Philadelphia. Truth had been the propaganda that made the loudest noise; justice, the settlement achieved by the side that happened to be the strongest.[57]

Who was responsible for this relativism and reductionism? The teachers of politics, Heckscher charged. Separating politics from ethics, divorcing their scientific hypotheses from value judgments, political scientists had misled their students. They had made it easy for students hungry for truth to mistake the cautious, dispassionate methods of the scientist for palpitating truths about the everyday world. The students had sought ethical judgments; they had been given tentative and abstract generalizations. Heckscher's solution was to reaffirm the Great Tradition that had originated in Plato and to *teach* that tradition with conviction.

Some of Heckscher's complaints were echoed a few years later in an influential book, *The Republic and the Person*, written by President Gordon Keith Chalmers of Kenyon College.[58] The history of the United States in the 1920s and 1930s, wrote Chalmers, was substantially the history of a "disintegrated" and sentimental liberalism. True liberalism had been characterized by granitic belief in such values as individual dignity, moral responsibility, and justice under law. Liberalism before the war, however, had too often been suffused with silly Rousseauistic notions of the rationality and goodness of man and the easy eradicability of "social" ills, coupled with a willingness to excuse dictatorships, particularly Russia's. Moreover, too many intellectuals had succumbed to the prewar fad of semantics. Like Weaver in *Ideas Have Consequences*, Chalmers criticized this new science which Alfred Korzybski and S.I. Hayakawa had developed. The "new semantics was nominalism," he declared;[59] its corrosive popularity had helped to confuse Americans about which side we should support just before the war. Chalmers forcefully noted the contrast: semantics was skeptical about words like "honor," "courage," "democracy," and "freedom," yet it was just these words for which Americans had supposedly fought in World War II.

Another evil was relativism; here a recent statement by Chief Justice Fred A. Vinson particularly dismayed Chalmers. In *Dennis et al.* vs. *U.S.* (1951), while upholding the conviction of eleven leaders of the Communist Party, Vinson observed:

> Nothing is more certain in modern society than the principle that there are no absolutes, that a name, a phrase, a standard, has meaning only when associated with the considerations which gave birth to nomenclature.... all concepts are relative.[60]

To Chalmers, such views, traceable to the academy in the era of John Dewey and Justice Holmes, were not only false but dangerous. For "what has really made possible the liberty of the individual has been not only its root in truth but the constancy of human agreement about the relation of men to God, right and wrong, good and evil. Stress in letters, philosophy, and law upon the inconstancy and, indeed, uncertainty of the essentials of this relation has contributed to the disintegration of liberalism."[61]

Relativism, semantics, amoralism—to this growing list of the solvents of traditional values the political scientist John Hallowell of Duke University added another: positivism. As the world war ground on in 1944, Hallowell wrote a controversial attack on the influence of the natural sciences in his profession.[62] "Are we right," he demanded to know, "in believing that the study of politics can or should be approached with a 'scientific' detachment divorced from all ethical considerations? Have we been traveling the right road in seeking to 'emancipate' ourselves from history, philosophy, law, and ethics?"[63] While Hallowell's answer was obviously negative, he felt that the trend was against him. For in the late nineteenth century an "empirical, positivistic" outlook, serving the gods of science and technology, had arisen and conquered. Metaphysics and qualitative description soon became suspect. "Value judgments were considered to be expressions of subjective preference rather than objective truth. At best judgments of right and wrong, good and bad, justice and injustice, were thought to be based upon utility or expediency."[64] After demonstrating various fallacies in positivist theory, Hallowell discussed its social and intellectual implications. Positivism, with its studied indifference to values, produced "nihilism in thought and anarchy in practice."[65]

> If, as the positivist insists, no rational justification is ever genuine, sincere, or real, then differences of political opinion can, in the last analysis, be decided only in the arena of force, and politics must be conceived as a species of warfare....
> ...Implicit in positivism is a nihilism closely akin to, if not identical with, the gospel of cynicism and despair that produced the mentality of fascism.[66]

In a subsequent article Hallowell elaborated on the link between positivism, liberalism, and twentieth-century totalitarianism. Under assault by positivism, liberals had increasingly abandoned concepts like justice as outmoded, unverifiable, and "metaphysical." But the result of this "scientific" impulse was helplessness in the face of Fascism and Nazism. "How can you condemn a tyrant as unjust when you have purged the word *justice* from your vocabulary? How, indeed, can you recognize tyranny?"[67] The liberals, said Hallowell, had paved the way for Lidice and Dachau by repudiating the idea of the inalienable rights of man. Hallowell thus joined Heckscher and Chalmers in finding pre-war liberalism intellectually and morally bankrupt:

> Vitiated by fear and by a lack of conviction in the truth of his
> own doctrine, the modern liberal has neither the courage born
> of conviction nor the words to condemn despotism. That was
> true in 1933 and it is true in 1947. Modern liberalism is an
> invitation to suicide.[68]

Ideas have consequences, then: this was the message of the proliferating critiques of liberalism in the early postwar years. Liberalism, with
its cult of the suspended judgment, was flabby and confused; it had too
long allowed itself to be seduced, even raped, by totalitarian ideologies.
In its relativistic, bend-over-backward, secular, scientistic, pragmatic way,
it was—said a rising chorus of critics—undermining a civilization in which
it no longer believed. But should we not beware of absolutism, liberals
asked? Hallowell replied: "Despair disguised as humility and indifference parading as tolerance are manifestations of the sickness of the modern spirit." [69]

As conservative intellectuals examined the fruits of liberal ideas, they
frequently noted with special distaste the spectacular rise of a mass society and the cult of the common man. They did not fail to notice that a
liberal, Henry Wallace, had proclaimed the twentieth century to be the
century of the common man. This was true, Bernard Iddings Bell acknowledged, but it did not follow that we should celebrate the fact.[70] To
Bell, an Episcopal clergyman, former warden of St. Stephen's (later Bard)
College, and close friend of Albert Jay Nock, the United States of the
early 1950s was a "crowd culture." In a little book of that title dedicated
to the "Common Man," Bell unsparingly castigated the so-called civilization around him.[71] "The chief threat to America comes from within
America"[72]—from the complacent, vulgar, mindless, homogenized, com-
fort-seeking, nouveau riche culture of the common man. Was this perspective undemocratic? Of course it was, Bell cheerfully conceded. One
of the most dangerous assumptions of our time is that the common man
"can be entrusted...without skilled critical leadership, safely to run himself and society."[73] Instead, the masses require "an elite, a democratic
elite," that will exemplify excellence and "a more urbane and humane
way of living."[74]

It was easy enough to criticize liberal dogmas and mass culture in
the 1940s and 1950s. But what was the connection between the two? In
the early 1950s a young conservative poet and journalist essayed an answer. Born in 1925 in New York City, Anthony Harrigan graduated from
Bard College, where Bernard Iddings Bell had once been warden and
Albert Jay Nock a professor. Harrigan had then gone to Charleston, South

Carolina, to become an assistant to the crusty, ultraconservative William Watts Ball, the elderly editor of the *News and Courier*. Imbibing deeply at these founts of aristocratic disdain for the mass man, Harrigan lashed out at the liberal-positivistic-collectivistic erosion of the moral and ethical fiber of Western man. According to Harrigan, this process of decay had been fostered by a "fierce and subtle" modernist orthodoxy which was developing a code of "immorality." "Modernists are determined," he claimed,

> to force the acceptance of pornography as medical science, filth as artistic realism, and abnormality as a mere difference of opinion.... Though the life of the country is basically decent, Americans are in the hands of a cultural ruling class which, having led to destruction the humane elements in our civilization, is conducting us to ruin.[75]

One organ of this diseased liberal culture was the *New Yorker*, a "smug, self-satisfied court gazette" that was "contemptuous of values."[76] And to what end? The rise of "the liberal-bred barbarian," "motivated by a destructive impulse" and unchecked by "traditional values and restraints."[77]

The decline of old ways and values in the 1940s and 1950s could not, of course, be attributed solely to journals like the *New Yorker*. The relation between liberal ideologies and the emergent mass man was more complex than that. How had liberal errors become so pervasive? For many "new conservative" intellectuals in the postwar decade, one solution to the puzzle lay in the widespread penetration of the American school system by the doctrine of progressive education espoused by John Dewey.

One of the earliest examples of what became a minor genre of social criticism in the 1950s was Bell's *Crisis in Education*. Published in 1949, this book contained the same themes that would recur in his later writings: disdain for the common man (who could, however, be assisted by *proper* education), disapproval of our "childish" and vulgar culture, and concern for the education of all children, including a "gifted few," in the moral and religious tradition of our civilization. "Make moral philosophy once more the central consideration in education," he exhorted.[78] Although Bell mentioned John Dewey only rarely in his book, his antipathy to Dewey's ideas was obvious. Again and again, for example, he insisted on the necessity for religion and for religious education in the schools: "If there is no God...free love is entirely defensible, and politics based on force is inevitable."[79] Bell was also vehemently critical of the secular "intelligentsia" who gaped admiringly at science, scoffed at religion, and thought that "mere freedom from standards and restraints" would facilitate the seeking of truth.[80] In his antipathy to egalitarianism, secular education, and government control, and in his emphasis on discipline and a traditional curriculum, Bell was far removed from the "progressive education" ethos of his day. No "progressive" would have praised, as Bell did, Ortega y Gasset's *The Revolt of the Masses* and Albert Jay Nock's *Our Enemy, the State*. As if to drive the point home, Bell dedicated his book to Nock's son.

In the years after 1949, other critics of Dewey began to be heard—notably Arthur Bestor, Mortimer Smith, and Gordon Keith Chalmers.[81] By the mid-1950s a vigorous reaction against Dewey and what Russell Kirk called "the patronage network of Teachers College, Columbia" was obviously under way. Among the most trenchant opponents of Dewey was a philosopher then at Ohio State University, Eliseo Vivas. Once a leading younger light of the naturalist philosophical movement, Vivas, profoundly affected by the evils of World War II,[82] had increasingly moved away from naive, optimistic naturalism with its acceptance of "the secularistic direction of the *Zeitgeist*."[83] By 1950 he had become an "axiological realist," convinced that "values are real and antecedent to our discovery of them...." Values, that is, had "ontic status," a reality independent of the human beings who perceive it.[84]

In 1950 Vivas published a searing indictment of naturalist philosophies, including Dewey's. Among his manifold criticism of instrumentalism was that it adhered to a totally secularistic world view. Far from opposing the fearsome trends of the day, Dewey encouraged conformity to them:

> Dewey thinks of himself as a critic of his world and its values; but he is doing nothing more than throwing his weight behind some of the most sinister forces that are...leading us toward Orwell's and Huxley's nightmares, since the effect of his philosophy is to thin and trivialize the dignity of men....
>
> ...He has, unwittingly, undertaken to soften us up for the Red push. He is the biggest of the bigtime promoters of the "brave new world." What he has never seen is that, in his haste to get rid of all the values that the historical process has weakened, he has advocated the destruction of all the values that are basically constitutive of our humanity....
>
> No Deweyian can give one good, radically theoretical reason, one that goes beyond expedience, why he prefers democracy to totalitarianism....[85]

There was the key, in many ways, to the conservative complaint. The era of the 1930s and 1940s was, for them, a time of liberal retreat and abdication before the apocalypse of fascism, Communism, and total war. The "beast-men" controlled almost all modern life, Bernard Iddings Bell lamented.[86] Not only had liberalism failed to contain the "brutality...passions and lusts" that Vivas said existed in everyone. [87] Liberalism, according to its right-wing critics, had encouraged and in part caused the moral decline of western civilization. Was this the century of the common man? To conservatives such as Eliseo Vivas, "one of the essential marks of decency today is to be ashamed of being a man of the twentieth century."[88]

It was not enough, however, merely to locate and denounce the contemporary manifestations of the West's malaise. Repeatedly there arose a series of questions particularly compelling for those who wished to salvage old traditions: How had we arrived at our present misfortunes? How had the past been subverted? Why the decline of the West? Why, above all, the twentieth century, with its monstrous record of totalitarianism, genocide, and total war?

It was no accident, then, that one of the characteristics of the emerging conservative intellectual movement was a fascination with intellectual genealogy, with tracing declension through the history of ideas. Richard Weaver had made that attempt in grand style, delineating "the fearful descent" from Occam in the fourteenth century. In the late 1940s and early 1950s others undertook similar efforts.

Weaver was not the only conservative intellectual to discover the source of Western decadence in the Middle Ages. Another was a Central European refugee from Nazism, Eric Voegelin. Born in Germany in 1901 and educated at the University of Vienna, Voegelin was dismissed from his professorship by the Nazis in 1938. With the assistance of Professor William Y. Elliott of Harvard, Voegelin escaped to the United States, where he eventually settled for many years at Louisiana State University.[89] In 1952 this learned political scientist published what became one of the most important books by postwar intellectuals of the Right, *The New Science of Politics*. In it he propounded the thesis that "the essence of modernity is the growth of gnosticism."[90]

What was gnosticism? In one sense, of course, it was an ancient heresy that had threatened Christianity in its early centuries.[91] But as Voegelin used the term, gnosticism ceased to be anything quite so esoteric or remote. Instead, it was a deep-seated, persistent tendency in Western thought to "immanentize the Christian eschaton," to transfer Christian hopes and symbols from an otherworldly orientation to an "intramundane range of action." Christianity in the Roman Empire had achieved the "de-divinization of the temporal sphere of power." Gnosticism, however, sought the "re-divinization of society" and "eschatological fulfillment" within this world alone. "The Gnostic revolution," he contended, "has for its purpose a change in the nature of man and the establishment of a transfigured society."[92]

Voegelin believed that the revival of Gnostic speculation occurred in the works of Scotus Eriugena in the ninth century. More important was the upsurge of Gnostic thinking in the "expansive" twelfth and thirteenth centuries. Until then, "the desire for a re-divinization of society" had lacked "a definite symbolism" and "comprehensive expression."[93] This deficiency was remedied by the speculations of Joachim of Flora, who proclaimed a periodization of history based on the Trinity. The Age of the Father had occurred; the Age of the Son was ending; the Age of the Spirit was about to begin. According to Voegelin, Joachim's "speculation was an attempt to endow the immanent course of history with a meaning" which the Christian philosophy of history of St. Augustine had not supplied. Moreover, Joachim's theory had "decisively" influenced the "structure of modern politics"; he had "created the aggregate of symbols which govern the self-interpretation of modern political society to this day."[94]

It was still a long way, however, from Joachim to the truly modern world. The Gnostic impulse remained "marginal," Voegelin contended, until a "revolutionary eruption" in the sixteenth century: the Reformation. Indeed, the Reformation could be defined as "the successful invasion of Western institutions by Gnostic movements."[95] Using the English Puritans as a case study of revolutionary gnosticism, and analyzing Hobbes's attempt in the *Leviathan* to define the nature of order in an increasingly Gnostic-ridden society, Voegelin examined the fallacies of this "counterexistential dream world."[96] Does all this analysis perhaps seem remote from the United States at midcentury? Voegelin took care to make its relevance plain. Communism, liberalism, Nazism, the French Revolution, positivism, scientism—all these modern movements were identified as variants of the heretical effort to merge heaven and earth. He could, at times, become very specific: "...the Gnostic politicians have put the Soviet army on the Elbe, surrendered China to the Communists, at the same time demilitarized Germany and Japan, and in addition demobilized our own army."[97] From Joachim to Harry Truman was not so great a distance after all. Where might it all end? "Totalitarianism, defined as the existential rule of Gnostic activists, is the end form of progressive civilization."[98]

For Leo Strauss, another émigré from Nazi Europe in the 1930s, the upheaval of the sixteenth and seventeenth centuries also appeared to be critical in the decline of Western man. Born to an Orthodox Jewish family in Germany in 1899, a soldier in the German army in World War I, Strauss received his doctorate at Hamburg University in 1921. From 1925 to 1932 he worked at the Academy of Jewish Research in Berlin. Like several other Europeans who markedly affected postwar American conservatism, Strauss had witnessed as a young man the steady erosion of the Weimar Republic and the frightening ascent of Adolf Hitler. In 1938 he, too, came to the United States, where he began a decade of teaching at the New School for Social Research. In 1949 he became a professor of political philosophy at the University of Chicago—a position he retained for nearly twenty years.[99]

Although Strauss would eventually identify Machiavelli as the principal villain of his intellectual genealogy, in the early 1950s it was Thomas Hobbes who seemed to him to be the father of modern political philosophy. It was Hobbes who initiated a revolutionary break with ancient or classical teachings. It was Hobbes who repudiated the natural law tradition for natural "rights":

> For Hobbes obviously starts, not, as the great tradition did, from natural "law," i.e. from an objective order, but from natural "right," i.e. from an absolutely justified subjective claim which, far from being dependent on any previous law, order, or obligation, is itself the origin of all law, order, or obligation.[100]

Strauss emphasized repeatedly the gap between Hobbes and the more healthy ancient tradition: "the absolute priority of the individual to the State, the conceptions of the individual as asocial, of the relation between the state of nature and the State as an absolute antithesis, and finally of the State itself as Leviathan."[101] In all these theories Hobbes broke with the past. Strauss also took note of Hobbes's rejection of reason in his philosophizing:

> ...because reason is impotent [in Hobbes's view], the rational "law of nature" also loses its dignity. In its place we have the "right of nature" which is, indeed, according to reason but

dictated not by reason but by the fear of death. The break
with rationalism is thus the decisive presupposition for...the
supplanting of the primacy of obligation by the primacy of
claim. This break with rationalism is, therefore, the fundamental presupposition of modern political philosophy in general. The acutest expression of this break which can be found
in Hobbes's writings is that he conceives sovereign power not
as reason but as will.... The explicit break with rationalism is
thus the reason for the antithesis of modern political thought
to classical....[102]

In *Natural Right and History* (1953), Strauss traced the development of modern natural rights theories from Hobbes through Locke to
Rousseau and Burke; none of them, in Strauss's opinion, equaled the
wisdom of the ancients. Moreover, the nineteenth century had witnessed
the birth of two new challenges—positivism and historicism—and Strauss
felt obliged to mount powerful attacks on each. Like Voegelin and Weaver,
Strauss believed that his subject was no academic matter: "The contemporary rejection of natural right [i.e. natural law] tends to nihilism—nay,
it is identical with nihilism."[103] And like Hallowell and others, he was
earnest in his warning of the consequences of relativism, skepticism, and
liberal doubt:

> Once we realize that the principles of our actions have
> no other support than our blind choice, we really do not be-
> lieve in them any more. We cannot wholeheartedly act upon
> them any more. We cannot live any more as responsible be-
> ings. In order to live, we have to silence the easily silenced
> voice of reason, which tells us that our principles are in them-
> selves as good or as bad as any other principles. The more we
> cultivate reason, the more we cultivate nihilism: the less we
> are able to be loyal members of society. The inescapable prac-
> tical consequence of nihilism is fanatical obscurantism.[104]

To this abyss Hobbes and his followers had brought us.

Strauss's strictures against Hobbes found support in yet another intellectual genealogy, one supplied by the sociologist Robert Nisbet in
The Quest for Community.[105] Nisbet's thesis (reminiscent of Tocqueville,
whom he admired) was that the emergence of the "centralized territorial
State" was "the single most decisive influence upon Western social organization."[106] The history of the West since the end of the Middle Ages
was the story of the decline of intermediate associations between the
individual and the state. The weakening and dissolution of such ties as

family, church, guild, and neighborhood had not, as many had hoped, liberated men. Instead, it had produced alienation, isolation, spiritual desolation, and the growth of mass man. But man cannot live in Hobbesian isolation, and so, to satisfy his longings, he seeks out ersatz community—eventually finding it in the totalitarian state.

One aspect of this disintegration and "reintegration" of Western man was the development of the theory of the total state. From Bodin to Hobbes to Rousseau, Nisbet traced an increasing theoretical antipathy to intermediate power structures between an omnipotent government and the naked individual. Indeed, said Nisbet, "the whole tendency of social thought" from Bodin to Burke was "to deprecate, even dissolve, all forms of association that could not be rationalized by natural law or by the will of the State."[107] The culmination of this evil trend came in the totalitarian thinking of Rousseau, for whom society ought to be "an aggregate of atoms held rigidly together" by the State.[108] The pluralist Nisbet noted that Rousseau's ideal, "the redemptive power of the sovereign State,"[109] did not die with him. Rather, it was expounded with clarity by men like Bentham and Marx. The nineteenth century may have been the great era of freedom and progress, but it was also the era of the rise of the masses, without whom there could have been no totalitarianism. In short, Nisbet was propounding the "vacuum" theory of totalitarianism[110] popular among many conservatives: atomistic liberal individualism had been unable to fill the needs of men and to contain the tramping feet of the 1930s. It had overlooked the fundamental fact that its own ideals were unattainable except in a *community*, and it was community which individualism had disparaged. Liberals, said Nisbet, had failed to recognize the dependence of their thought on "the subtle, infinitely complex lines of habit, tradition, and social relationship...."[111]

At this point Nisbet's analysis merged remarkably with that of John Hallowell. Like Strauss, Voegelin, and Nisbet, Hallowell saw in the Renaissance and Reformation the period of crisis from which the "acids of modernity" began to flow. This was preeminently the era of a new creed: liberalism. The novelty of this new system was striking; in its emphasis on the "autonomy of reason" and the "essential goodness of man," it departed substantially from the classical tradition.[112] But if all men were so reasonable, good, and autonomous, why or how should they obey any authority? According to Hallowell, the "keystone" of liberalism was conscience: "Only conscience bids the individual to follow the dictates of reason rather than those of interest, and upon the consciences of individuals alone rests the choice between order and anarchy."[113] Only conscience restrained the willful individual. Part of the trouble with this ideal, Hallowell argued, was that it did not survive the test of history. As the centuries passed, liberalism—*formed in a Christian matrix*—had come to take for granted or even to despise the inherited cultural capital on which it depended. "Conscience" had lost the guidance that tradition had given it. Positivism, for instance, had corroded its very foundations.[114] Here Hallowell adumbrated one of the recurrent conservative arguments of the postwar era: liberalism was a parasitic philosophy, increasingly estranged and adrift from its cultural heritage. Vitiated by self-doubt, reduced to genteel negations, it was, conservatives would say, "the ideology of Western suicide."[115]

Not everyone located the genesis of modernist "errors" in the sixteenth and seventeenth centuries. Several authors popular among traditionalist conservatives felt they had only to look to the cataclysmic French Revolution and its aftermath. To the Jewish scholar J.L. Talmon, for instance, not all democratic forms were pernicious; "empirical and liberal democracy," with its pragmatic, nondoctrinaire approach to politics, was acceptable. However, a radically new "totalitarian Messianic democracy," originating in the thoughts and deeds of such French revolutionaries as Robespierre and Babeuf, was not. Coercive, plebiscitary, totalist, perfectionist, it sought through an omnipotent government to create utter equality. "Nothing was [to be] left to stand between man and the State."[116] (Echoes of Tocqueville again.) Lord Percy of Newcastle concurred with Talmon; in *The Heresy of Democracy* he too argued that a new form of democracy—in fact, a new religion—was born with the French Revolution, and it led from Rousseau to Marx to Lenin.[117] Albert Salomon, yet another Central European émigré, added a genealogy of his own: Saint-Simon, Comte, and other early sociologists paved the way for totalitarianism. Hegel and Comte "introduced into Western philosophy the idea of the total immanence of society";[118] society, in their utopia, was to be "omnipotent, all-knowing," and "the collective substitute for the divine meaning."[119] In addition, they made another error: they extolled the methods of the natural sciences as a means to radical reformation of society. Was all this reminiscent of Weaver or Voegelin? Indeed it was, and it suggests the degree to which right-wing intellectual critiques of the Left were converging in the 1950s.[120]

What some of these conservatives considered to be effects, others took to be causes of subsequent evils. Nineteenth-century nationalism, socialism, and racism, for instance, were to someone like Nisbet attempts to fill the vacuum left by atomistic liberalism; to someone like Voegelin they were forms of gnosticism. To one young historian, Peter Viereck, they were the essential ingredients of "the worst single catastrophe in human history"—World War I.[121] The nineteenth century, said Viereck, saw the rise of the values of "blood and iron"; this was the "'ethical revolution' of modern Europe."[122] A concatenation of "blood and iron nationalism," "blood and iron socialism," and statism had rebelled against Europe's tradition of ethical universalism and respect for individuality. The turmoil of the Great War had enabled them to triumph; the legatees of this world conflict were Lenin and Hitler.[123]

As one surveys these ventures in conservative historiography in the postwar years, several features stand out. First, despite different terminology, emphasis, and initial points of reference, the genealogies seem consistent with one another. All these conservative analysts implicitly repudiated optimistic theories of history. All seemed to agree that totalitarianism was either an offspring of liberalism or the result of liberal failure; it was not the sole product of the Right and was certainly not to be confused with the new conservatism. All tended to emphasize two crucial turning points: the Renaissance-Reformation period and the French Revolution. All agreed that in the nineteenth century—the so-called liberal century—lay germs of twentieth-century madness. Ah, that sunny, placid century with its pretty illusions of progress, its confidence that truth would always prevail in the marketplace. If that were so, why had the Nazis won in highly literate Germany? Why? The insistency, the driving urgency of that question was evident in these writings time and time again.

Above all, the most noteworthy feature of this body of thought is the simple fact that it was overwhelmingly *intellectual* history. In nearly all these accounts of the decline of the West, relatively little attention was paid to "material" or "social" forces. Instead, ideas were alleged to have been decisive; *ideas* had had consequences. Evil thoughts had generated evil deeds. At the root of modernity was *intellectual error*.

Why was this mode of interpretation so pronounced? Why did these writers come to believe that ideas were so crucial in modern history? Presumably they would say: because the evidence compelled such belief. But another factor may also have influenced their outlook. Despite all their disdain for the vulgar, rootless masses against whom they rebelled, the "new conservatives" did not really regard the masses as the primary cause of the present crisis. The disease had originated elsewhere—with Hobbes, Rousseau, or Saint-Simon, for example—and had *created* the modern phenomenon of the masses. In a sense, an explanation which made ideas the principal engines of history was an explanation which offered hope. Perhaps it is harder to battle the direction of events if one thinks that the whole impersonal weight of industrialism or secularism or urbanization is bearing down on the present. Perhaps it is easier to resist one's age if "only" ideas and not "forces" seem to be the foe. For presumably ideas can be altered. If bad ideas have consequences, so can good ideas. One thinks here of Frank Chodorov's "Fifty-Year Project" to reverse the dominance of socialist ideology, and of Leonard Read's patient efforts to spread the libertarian gospel by voluntary means. One thinks of Friedrich Hayek's attack on the bloody consequences of "rationalism" and Ludwig von Mises's blasts at "etatism." One thinks of congressional investigations of Communism in the 1940s and 1950s: what a person *believed* was held to make a difference. This belief in the potency of ideas pervaded all segments of the postwar American Right.[124]

It was clearly not sufficient, however, simply to chronicle the mistakes of modernity. What were we fighting *for*? In the face of "disintegrated liberalism," the new conservatives sought to recover what some of them called the Great Tradition. Although Weaver wrote of universals, Strauss of natural right, and Hallowell of natural law, a common impulse was evident: the yearning for some sort of bridge over the gaping chasm. The approaches and terminologies were diverse, but a unifying thread was present: the search for a bulwark of ideas, tradition, and truth against "a wash of lies / That eats like acid at the feet of men." *

*From "Churchill," by Maxwell Anderson, Copyright 1965 by Gilda Oakleaf Anderson. Reprinted in the *New York Times*, January 31, 1965, p. 35.

THREE

The Recovery of Tradition and Values

B efore one can defend or refine a tradition, one must find one. This was the task facing traditionalist conservatives in America after 1945.

On the surface, at least, the traditionalists were not in so weak a position as the classical liberals at the close of the war. Abroad, the traditional conservatives could find men of stature like T.S. Eliot, C.S. Lewis, and Ortega y Gasset—indeed, a whole array of celebrated nonliberal thinkers whom one critic dubbed the "Counter-Enlightenment."[1] At home, the New Humanism movement of the early 1930s, led by Irving Babbitt and Paul Elmer More, was not so long gone as to be forgotten. Nor were the Southern Agrarians, who remained active although scattered. In fact, not long after the war, one liberal intellectual professed to see in the flourishing New Criticism movement (itself an outgrowth, in part, of Agrarianism) a major intellectual force and powerful vehicle for the ideas of a nineteenth-century French counterrevolutionary, Joseph de Maistre:

> Over the last two decades, in the journals of the New Criticism, *authority, hierarchy, catholicism, aristocracy, tradition, absolutes, dogma, truths* became related terms of honor, and *liberalism, naturalism, scientism, individualism, equalitarianism, progress, protestantism, pragmatism,* and *personality* became related terms of rejection and contempt. As programmatic social movements, the New Humanism and Agrarianism seemed short-lived.... But during the forties, with the intense reaction against Stalinism, the socio-historical patterns of acceptance and rejection established by the humanist-agrar-

ian movement quietly triumphed on the higher literary levels....[2]

There is no doubt, then, that in the mid-1940s the resources for a nonliberal intellectual revival were present. Yet it would be wrong to claim that in 1945 a coherent, explicitly conservative movement was flourishing in America. So barren did the Right side of the intellectual landscape seem to many in those years that one observer actually contended in 1950 that "the American conservative has yet to discover conservatism."[3] And in 1950, in a famous comment, Lionel Trilling complained of the absence of conservative ballast in American intellectual life:

> In the United States at this time liberalism is not only the dominant but even the sole intellectual tradition. For it is the plain fact that nowadays there are no conservative or reactionary ideas in general circulation. This does not mean, of course, that there is no impulse to conservatism or to reaction. Such impulses are certainly very strong, perhaps even stronger than most of us know. But the conservative impulse and the reactionary impulse do not, with some isolated and some ecclesiastical exceptions, express themselves in ideas but only in action or in irritable mental gestures which seem to resemble ideas.[4]

Trilling, of course, was too harsh; moreover, even as he wrote, conservative thought was beginning to appear. It could not expect, though, to rely indefinitely on an older generation of pioneers—on Eliot and Ortega, Babbitt and More, Chesterton and Belloc, Ransom and Davidson. A "new" or revived conservative movement, although indebted to these men, must develop on its own.

Of the many aspects of the recovery of tradition in the decade after Hiroshima, one of the most pervasive was the renewal of interest and belief in Christian orthodoxy. On a popular level, signs of this "return to religion" were everywhere.[5] Some might doubt its sincerity or profundity; some might jibe at "foxhole religion"; none could doubt that religiosity, at least, had come back into favor. In 1940 fewer than 50 percent of the American people were church members; by 1955, 60 percent had joined. These years also witnessed the spectacular rise of Billy Graham, the addition of "under God" to the "Pledge of Allegiance," and the printing of "In God We Trust" on certain postage stamps. President Eisenhower unexpectedly opened his inaugural address with a prayer, joined the National Presbyterian Church (and attended it often), gave a nationally broadcast speech on the need for religious faith, and supported the American Legion's "Back to God" campaign.[6] Many observers were astounded when a Roman Catholic bishop named Fulton J. Sheen surpassed entertainer Milton Berle in the television ratings. The best-selling book in the United States in 1953 and 1954 was *The Power of Positive Thinking*, by the Reverend Norman Vincent Peale. The new impulse extended to intellectuals, too, as theologians like Kierkegaard, Paul Tillich, and Reinhold Niebuhr came into vogue. Nor did trends abroad go unnoticed. The brilliant Christian apologetics of C.S. Lewis were becoming popular in America. And when, in 1948, C.E.M. Joad, a British philosopher and hitherto staunch agnostic, wrote a defense of Christianity, *Time* was quick to take note. The horrible evils of World War II, Joad explained, had "hit me in the face.... Human progress is possible but so unlikely." *Time* also quoted Joad as saying: "I see now that evil is endemic in man, and that the Christian doctrine of original sin expresses a deep and essential insight into human nature."[7]

Sympathy toward neo-orthodoxy in religion did not necessarily mean faith; the secular-liberal Arthur Schlesinger, Jr. was one of the greatest admirers of Reinhold Niebuhr in these years.[8] Others also believed that religion could serve a useful function. Writing in *Partisan Review* in 1950, Ernest van den Haag, an émigré sociologist from Mussolini's Italy then teaching at the New School for Social Research, conceded that religious faith could not be "logically justified." Still,

> Religious sanction is required—just as the police force is—for any society which wishes to be stable without being totalitarian....
>
> Religion is useful, even a necessary opiate—a sedative protecting us from excessive anxiety and agitation and from those who, like Marx, thrive on agitation and therefore hate the sedative and would replace it by the murderer's hashish.[9]

Some adopted a similar attitude toward the Catholic Church. The anti-Communist journalist James Rorty, for instance, acclaimed the "faith of Catholics" as one of the "strongest forces that today confronts the evil combination of faith and force that is Communism." Rorty quoted approvingly the statement by Douglas Hyde, an English ex-Communist and convert to Catholic Christianity: "The sanest things on earth are those for which the allegedly reactionary, unscientific, obscurantist Church stands and for which she is doing battle."[10]

While a few conservatives no doubt welcomed the revival of Christianity because it was useful, many more were convinced that it was *true*. It was the truths of Christianity that needed to be reasserted. "I myself believe that the duel between Christianity and atheism is the most important in the world," wrote William F. Buckley, Jr. in 1951.[11] "Christianity is the most complete and perfect revelation we know of the nature of God and of God's will for man," wrote John Hallowell in 1950.[12] Hallowell, in fact, was particularly bold in his affirmation of Christianity; it was the unifying thesis of his interpretation of modern political philosophy:

> ...the basic insights of the Christian faith provide the best insights we have into the nature of man and of the crisis in which we find ourselves. That crisis is the culmination of modern man's progressive attempt to deny the existence of a transcendent or spiritual reality and of his progressive failure to find meaning and salvation in some wholly immanent conception of reality.... Only through a return to faith in God, as God revealed Himself to man in Jesus Christ, can modern man and his society find redemption from the tyranny of evil.[13]

The Christianity which Hallowell, Buckley, and others defended was not the Christianity of the Social Gospel or liberal Protestantism. It was a Christianity grounded in what was for many neo-conservatives the deepest lesson of World War II: the lesson of evil, of original sin. "We must restore to our vocabulary a word discarded long ago, namely, *sin*," Hallowell asserted.[14] To Richard Weaver, no concept gave "deeper insight into the enigma that is man" than original sin.[15] Evil was not just a "bad dream," an "accident of history," or "the creation of a few antisocial men." It was a "subtle, pervasive, protean force," and original sin was a "parabolical expression" of this "immemorial tendency of man to do the wrong thing when he knows the right thing."[16] Eliseo Vivas concurred; inside every man, he said, lay "brutality" and a "natural tendency" to "define value in terms of his own interests."[17] Bernard Iddings Bell claimed that "exaggerated optimism about man" was "the chief cause of our decay."[18] The social implications of original sin were obvious to the conservatives. It could be a check on what Gertrude Himmelfarb called "presumptuous mass man";[19] it could be, in Weaver's words, "a severe restraint upon democracy."[20] It could suggest the danger of reckless social innovation and turn men's thoughts toward something greater than themselves.

The new conservatives' brand of Christianity was often of a decidedly Catholic, even medieval cast. In his respect for chivalry and his ascription of fundamental error to William of Occam, Richard Weaver had, in effect, encouraged a more positive view of the Middle Ages. So, too, did Hallowell, although he carefully urged "that we go back to the Middle Ages only in the sense that we go back in spirit to a society that, intellectually and spiritually, was God-centered rather than man-centered."[21] Frederick Wilhelmsen, a young Catholic biographer of Hilaire Belloc and a professor of philosophy at the University of Santa Clara, went even further. To understand contemporary conservatism, he averred, we must turn to medieval Christendom. "Medieval man sacramentalized the whole of being"; the "medieval dream" of the "unity of all things in existence" was the "mythic foundation" of the conservative vision. Alas, Calvinism and Manchesterianism had "shattered for all time" medieval tradition; reality became something not to be conserved but to be manipulated. Conservatives, he gloomily admitted, were too weak to alter and save the modern world. "We conservatives have lost our kings and our chivalry; our craftsmen are gone, and our peasantry is fast disappearing.... We have nothing to offer the world but our vision."[22] The Middle Ages had offered a Christian *culture*; this was lacking in the modern "anti-humanistic" age, which was "incapable of incarnating the Gospel."[23]

This revival of traditional Christianity and what *Time* called "pre-Gnostic views of the world" was clearly having an intellectual impact in the 1950s. Perhaps sensing the shift in the wind, *Time* itself, in 1953, devoted an extraordinary five pages to a fulsome review of Eric Voegelin's *The New Science of Politics*.[24] On a less popular level, the editors of *Partisan Review*, long associated with the Trotskyist Left, were also surprised by the new phenomenon:

> One of the most significant tendencies of our times, especially in this decade, has been the new turn toward religion among intellectuals and the growing disfavor with which secular attitudes and perspectives are now regarded in not a few circles that lay claim to the leadership of culture. There is no doubt that the number of intellectuals professing religious sympathies, beliefs, or doctrines is greater now than it was ten or twenty years ago, and that this number is continually increasing or becoming more articulate. If we seek to relate our period to the recent past, the first decades of this century begin to look like triumphant naturalism; and if the present tendency continues, the mid-century years may go down in history as the years of conversion and return.[25]

With these words *Partisan Review* introduced an extended symposium called "Religion and the Intellectuals." A year later H. Stuart Hughes reached a similar conclusion:

> Ten or fifteen years ago no self-respecting "enlightened" in-
> tellectual would have been caught dead with a religious inter-
> pretation of anything. Only the Catholics thought in these
> terms—plus a scattering of Protestants whom we dismissed
> as harmless eccentrics. We were either "idealistic" Socialist-
> radicals or skeptical, hard-boiled Freudian-Paretans. Any
> other attitude would have been considered a betrayal of the
> avantgarde. Now Mr. Hallowell confirms the suspicions that
> have gradually been drifting up to us from the students we
> confront. The avantgarde has become old-fashioned; religion
> is now the latest thing.[26]

Meanwhile, another aspect of the Great Tradition was being revived:
ancient or classical political philosophy. One of its most erudite and formidable advocates in the postwar period was Leo Strauss. It is impossible to summarize Strauss's thought in a few sentences. But central to
his viewpoint were a number of contrasts which he perceived between
the ancients and the moderns. The best of ancient political philosophy
(particularly Plato, Aristotle, and Cicero) was grounded in rational natural law and emphasized the duties of man; Hobbes and the moderns
increasingly stressed natural rights. The ancients sought to discover the
best regime; the moderns, lowering their sights, did not, and were increasingly immersed in barren methodology. The ancients were deeply
concerned with virtue; the moderns paid too much attention to "individuality." Classical political philosophy strove for truth and did not fear
"value judgments"; modern political philosophy was unsure that universal truth exists and was thoroughly suffused with pernicious doctrines
like positivism and historicism. [27]

In presenting the thought of the ancients with vigor and learning,
Strauss was making a number of contributions to the intellectual life of
the 1950s. For one thing, as Gertrude Himmelfarb noted, he was stimulating a new "Battle of the Books" between ancients and moderns and
was having an enormous "pedagogic" impact through his painstaking
method of textual analysis.[28] Strauss's importance to the emerging "new
conservative" movement was especially noteworthy. Indeed, William F.
Buckley, Jr. has said it was "absolutely critical," for Strauss taught two
indispensable lessons: that there was a relationship between common
sense and the natural law, and that "scientific approaches to epistemol-
ogy" were "terribly misleading."[29] In the years to come, Strauss's influence on many conservative intellectuals would increase.

To many writers of the 1950s classical political philosophy meant, above all, natural law. In *The Moral Foundation of Democracy*, John Hallowell argued its tenets. Describing himself as a "classical realist," Hallowell enunciated three principles: (1) "there exists a meaningful reality," an "orderly universe," independent of the knower; (2) man can, by use of his reason, discern the nature of reality; and (3) "knowledge of what man should do in order to fulfill his human nature is embodied in what has traditionally been called the 'law of nature' or the 'moral law.'"[30] Hallowell urged the recovery of belief in "universally valid principles";[31] without them, democracy cannot exist. For democracy requires a "moral foundation"; it will degenerate unless it is based on self-restraint and directed toward the common good. Man, said Hallowell, "is not an autonomous being but the creature of God";[32] in the recognition of this highest allegiance and the consequent "obligation to obey the moral law" lay a bulwark against totalitarianism.

There were other signs of interest in premodern political philosophy. In the 1930s and early 1940s, Plato had come under mounting attack as the father of totalitarianism, notably by Karl Popper in *The Open Society and Its Enemies*. In the early 1950s, however, defenders of the ancient philosopher returned the fire and caused considerable commotion in scholarly circles. Led by such men as Hallowell and John Wild of Harvard, they argued that Plato was a democrat, not a totalitarian—and a natural law democrat, not a relativist.[33] On another front, Richard Weaver in *The Ethics of Rhetoric* applied the ancient tradition of rhetoric to such targets as intellectually flabby, melioristic "social science."[34] In 1955, Walter Lippmann joined the call for a revival of natural law in *Essays in the Public Philosophy*. The "root of the matter," said Lippmann, was this: "Can men, acting like gods, be appointed to establish heaven on earth?" In order to contain the threat from demonic ideologies like Hitlerism and Leninism, our institutions must be strengthened by a revival of natural law—the "public philosophy," or philosophy of civility, without which Western society would not survive.[35]

The revivals of neo-orthodox Christianity and classical political philosophy were broad and multifaceted, but they did not exhaust the impulse to recover a "conservative" past. More modern and secular heroes were needed to complete the conservative pantheon. One of the first to be invoked was Alexis de Tocqueville.

It is perhaps difficult for a generation exposed in college courses and elsewhere to the insights of the great nineteenth-century French thinker to recognize that in the 1930s and early 1940s he was little read and discussed in the United States. A dramatic illustration of this neglect comes from the historical sociologist Robert Nisbet. As a graduate student at the University of California at Berkeley in the late 1930s, Nisbet had discovered the writings of Edmund Burke and a variety of nineteenth-century antagonists of the French Revolution, including Bonald, de Maistre, and von Haller.[36] Incredibly, however, not once did he hear the name Tocqueville mentioned in all his years at graduate school![37] With the publication in 1945 of a widely reviewed new edition of *Democracy in America*, a resurgence of interest in Tocqueville at last occurred.[38] One small sign was the publication later that year of a symposium on the book by a number of scholars at Fordham University.[39] Another was the increasing frequency with which Tocqueville was cited as a critic of democracy and the mass man by Nisbet, Lippmann, Russell Kirk, Erik von Kuehnelt-Leddihn, and others in the postwar years. As one historian later observed, "...Tocqueville, perhaps for the first time, provided [Americans] with the example of a respectable modern thinker who was critical of democracy...."[40]

Kuehnelt-Leddihn was himself a link between the continental European conservative tradition and the conservative stirrings in America in the postwar decade. An aristocratic Catholic monarchist from Austria, a member of the Knights of Malta, a recipient of a doctorate in political science from the University of Budapest in 1929, Kuehnelt-Leddihn had left his native land in the mid-1930s to teach first in England and then at Georgetown, St. Peter's College, Fordham, and Chestnut Hill College—all Catholic institutions—in the United States. The author of *The Menace of the Herd* (1943), Kuehnelt-Leddihn resettled in Austria after World War II. He continued, however, to maintain extensive American contacts. As a historian, novelist, prolific journalist, world traveler, lecturer, and linguist (he eventually became fluent in eight languages, with a reading knowledge of nineteen more), he was one of the most versatile and cosmopolitan contributors to the post-1945 conservative renascence.[41]

In 1952, James H. Gipson's Caxton Printers brought out Kuehnelt-Leddihn's *Liberty or Equality*, an explicitly antidemocratic book laden with learned references to such continental thinkers as Donoso-Cortés, Burckhardt, Berdyaev, Dostoevsky, Ortega, and Tocqueville, as well as to English and American writers.[42] The Austrian's argument must have been breathtaking to many of his American readers. "Liberty and equality are in essence contradictory," he argued.[43]

...democracy and liberalism are concerned with two entirely

different problems. The former is concerned with the question of *who* should be vested with ruling authority, while the latter deals with the freedom of the individual, regardless of who carries on the government. A democracy *can* be highly illiberal: the Volstead Act, quite democratically voted for, interfered with the dinner menus of millions of citizens.[44]

Kuehnelt-Leddihn went even further: "contemporary totalitarianism," he wrote, "...has its roots in the democratic (plebiscitarian, majoritarian, egalitarian), and not in the liberal-libertarian, principle."[45] In addition to discerning in uniformitarian mass democracy the seeds of tyranny, Kuehnelt-Leddihn endeavored to locate the intellectual roots of Nazism in the Protestant Reformation. German National Socialism was the fulfillment, not the antithesis, of the French Revolution[46] and, before that, of the Hussite Reformation:

> National Socialism...is neither a conservative nor a reactionary movement, but merely the synthesis of practically all ideas dominant in the last 160 years. It is obvious that the *roots* of these ideas antedate the French Revolution.[47]

By stressing intellectual genealogy, by finding the origin of evil in the Reformation era, by delineating totalitarianism as a democratic movement, Kuehnelt-Leddihn clearly revealed his membership in the intellectual Right.[48] His use of relatively unfamiliar continental sources reinforced a tendency already apparent in the impact of Ortega on Weaver and in the influence of de Maistre, via Charles Maurras and T.S. Eliot, on American literary critics.

Undoubtedly the most spectacular and audacious attempt to utilize the continental European tradition was made by Peter Viereck in *Conservatism Revisited: The Revolt against Revolt*.[49] Viereck, a poet and professor of history at Mount Holyoke College, had responded deeply to the tragedy of the 1940s. As the son of George Sylvester Viereck, the controversial German-American author and propagandist for the Kaiser in World War I,[50] young Viereck was early exposed to his father's intense loyalties. As a little boy, Peter had even visited the Kaiser in exile in Holland.[51] But at an early date, father and son went separate ways, and it is possible to see in Peter Viereck's conservatism a rejection of all that his father stood for. Educated at Harvard and Oxford, young Viereck moved to dissociate himself from his father's views. In 1940, while his father publicly defended Hitler's Germany and promoted isolationist causes, Peter, at the age of 23, wrote a magazine article expressing his revulsion against Communism, Fascism, the Popular Front Left, and the Liberty League Right. As a defense against the "communazis," Viereck pleaded for an ethical, reformist conservatism based on the "necessity and supremacy of Law and of absolute standards of conduct."[52] It was the first call for a "new conservatism" in America. Viereck's subsequent experience in World War II poignantly reminded him of the cost of preserving civilization and repulsing extremism. While his father was jailed for pro-Nazi activities, Peter and his brother George fought in the American army; George Viereck was killed at Anzio.[53]

With this background of personal involvement, Viereck "revisited" conservatism in 1949. In his book could be found eloquent statements of the conservative concerns of these years. Here were denunciations of the "internal invasion of today: the barbarian invasion from below."

> We don't need a "century of the common man;" we have it already, and it has only produced the commonest man, the impersonal and irresponsible and uprooted mass-man.

Here were quotations from Burckhardt and Ortega, appeals for respect for law, and criticisms of the Rousseauistic "cult" of the "natural man." Here, too, one could find belief in original sin and implicit rejection of progressive education: "In his natural instincts, every modern baby is still born a cave-man baby. What prevents today's baby from remaining a cave man is the conservative force of law and tradition."[54]

Against this welter of chaos and error Viereck posed his conception of conservatism. It was not laissez-faire capitalism that Viereck wanted; it was a conservatism filled with "a humanist reverence for the dignity of the individual soul" that was "incompatible with fascist or Stalinist collectivism." It was a conservatism suffused with such values as "proportion and measure," "self-expression through self-restraint," "humanism and classical balance," and historical continuity. Above all, conservatism for Viereck should be based on Christianity and "the four ancestries of Western man: the stern moral commandments and social justice of Judaism; the love for beauty and for untrammeled intellectual speculation of the free Hellenic mind; the Roman Empire's universalism and its exaltation of law; and the Aristotelianism, Thomism, and antinominalism included in the Middle Ages." In one of his many epigrams, Viereck further defined conservatism as "the political secularization of the doctrine of original sin."[55]

As an exemplar of his values, Viereck selected none other than the old symbol of reaction, Klemens von Metternich. In part Viereck was simply building on recent revisionist scholarship. But the intent of his book was obviously didactic and polemical as well as historical. Viereck admitted that Metternich had often lapsed from ideal behavior; nevertheless, the Austrian diplomat symbolized much that was pertinent to America in the early years of the cold war. In contrast to the often virulent nationalisms of the nineteenth century (and of Viereck's own father), Metternich stood for a cosmopolitan, racially tolerant internationalism. In contrast to realpolitik, the Austrian adopted as his motto: "Force within Law." Despite all his failings, and despite the intransigence of the emperors whom he served, Metternich strove creditably for moderate reform and the containment of the red and brown extremists of his time. He even called himself, on one occasion, a "conservative socialist"; "Stability is not immobility" was his own slogan. To Viereck, a twentieth-century internationalist, antifascist, and anti-national bolshevist," Metternich was a beacon to a "middle way," eschewing the irrational extremisms of our era.

The importance of *Conservatism Revisited* far transcended the renewed interest in Metternich which the book stimulated.[56] This was the book which, more than any other of the early postwar era, created the new conservatism as a self-conscious intellectual force. It was not that Viereck's thoughts and sentiments were altogether novel; many others were uttering similar views. Indeed, Viereck was not even the most trenchant critic of liberalism in the field. As more than one reviewer noted, his principal target was not the liberals, with all their sins, but the totalitarians,[57] against whom a *coalition* of liberals and conservatives was needed. (Viereck himself acknowledged this as his real goal years later.)[58] Nevertheless, it was this book which boldly used the word "conservatism" in its title—the first such book after 1945. At least as much as any of his contemporaries, Peter Viereck popularized the term "conservative" and gave the nascent movement its label.

If Metternich, Tocqueville, and other nineteenth-century figures suddenly seemed surprisingly relevant to American politics after 1945, no European was more acclaimed as the source of conservative wisdom than the towering opponent of the French Revolution, Edmund Burke. According to Robert Nisbet, Burke was not highly esteemed in American academic circles in the 1930s; he was "well-known but not known well."[59] In the crucible of revolution and world war, however, interest in Burke was rekindled. To some extent this was a scholarly phenomenon, attributable to the general release in 1949 of a huge, formerly private collection of Burke's papers in England.[60] Far more important was the changing political climate after World War II. Among the first straws in the wind was the founding of the Burke Society at Fordham University on April 12, 1945—the very day of Franklin Roosevelt's death.[61] The purpose of this society illuminates well the attraction that Burke had for many conservatives. It was to achieve "a recall to the principles, values, and traditions which are the heritage of the political and international society of Christendom."[62] To these Edmund Burke had devoted his career. In a 1949 anthology of Burke's writings, two Fordham University professors, Ross J.S. Hoffman and Paul Levack, vigorously drove the lesson home:

> Never have his great maxims been more contemptuously ignored than during the catastrophic last half-century. Never have "metaphysical sophistries" been so rampant as in this age.... It has been an age of doctrinaire "planning," or as Burke would have said, of "scheming." Its political leaders have forgotten the natural law.... All the rationalistic errors of the age of Rousseau and Paine came coursing back with the upsurge of socialism, communism, and fascism, and hard upon them came the inevitable mad efforts of irrational will to enforce unreason in the name of reason.... To the astonishment of some superficial observers, we emerged from the Second World War as the champions of a conservative cause: the cause of conserving law and liberty against totalitarian despotism. It is the same cause Burke championed....[63]

Others were discovering Burke's usefulness for the present. Reviewing the Hoffman-Levack volume, Crane Brinton praised Burke as an "admirable antidote" to some of the "poisons" loosed on the world by the eighteenth-century Enlightenment.[64] Peter Viereck referred frequently to Burke in *Conservatism Revisited*. And in 1951 another young scholar, Russell Kirk, published *Randolph of Roanoke*, in which he called John Randolph "the American Burke" and emphasized the profound influence of the British statesman on the Virginian.[65]

The ground for receptivity to Burke, then, was well prepared by 1953 when Kirk's *The Conservative Mind* appeared and dramatically catalyzed the emergence of the conservative intellectual movement. Kirk was no stranger to the thinking of the American Right. Born in 1918, the son of a railroad engineer, Kirk grew up in the little villages of Plymouth and Mecosta, Michigan.[66] A romantic traditionalist by instinct, as it were, Kirk early came to share his father's prejudices against the "assembly-line civilization"[67] already penetrating Michigan under the aegis of Henry

Ford. After graduating from high school in 1936, Kirk entered Michigan State College, whose spirit of "conformity," utilitarianism, and "dim animosity toward liberal education"[68] grated against his sensibility, much as Texas A&M was offending Richard Weaver at the same time. By dint of wide reading on his own (and a Depression-induced frugality which meant peanut butter and crackers for many a meal), Kirk persisted in his studies and graduated in 1940.

For the next year Kirk was a graduate student in history at Duke University; there he wrote a master's thesis later published as *Randolph of Roanoke*. In it he clearly sympathized with the Virginian's aristocratic, strict-constructionist, states' rights agrarianism. During this year the young scholar from rural Michigan began to get acquainted with the South—"a conservative society," he later recalled, "struck a fearful blow eighty years before and still dazed...."[69] He read approvingly the Agrarian manifesto, *I'll Take My Stand*;[70] he read Donald Davidson's *The Attack on Leviathan* ("Southern agrarianism at its almost-best").[71] Like many an antebellum Southerner, Kirk was ecstatic about the fiction of Scott: "Sir Walter is the only novelist I can re-read anymore."[72] Simultaneously, his life as a graduate student was ripening his already deep suspicion of progressive education. "There are simply not enough real brains in this country to fill the graduate schools," he complained. "We need far fewer high schools and colleges, not more."[73] In 1941, in his first published article, he revealed his developing conservatism. We must, he said,

> foster Jeffersonian principles. We must have slow but democratic decision, sound local government, diffusion of property-owning, taxation as direct as possible, preservation of civil liberties, payment of debts by the generation incurring them, prevention of the rise of class antipathies, a stable and extensive agriculture, as little governing by the government as practicable, and, above all, stimulation of self-reliance.[74]

It was, in general, the midwestern "individualist" conservatism of Robert Taft.

In the summer of 1941, the "Jeffersonian" Kirk found himself working at Henry Ford's Greenfield Village. A few months later he was transferred to the mammoth Rouge plant, "a fearful and wonderful sight" which made him "shiver."[75] Even before his experiences at the Ford company, Kirk had developed a distaste for big business, big labor, and big government. Unions, he told a friend, were often "more restrictive and selfish than the soulless corporation."[76] He praised the trustbuster

Thurman Arnold and hoped that he would run for president.[77] Kirk's year or so at Ford did nothing to change his attitudes; his letters during this period expressed his scorn of unions, management, and federal "parasites."[78] Indeed, his dislike of bureaucracy was, if anything, increasing. He denounced the military draft as "slavery."[79] He was furious at the government's removal of Japanese-Americans from their homes on the west coast shortly after Pearl Harbor.[80] At one point he dreamed of becoming a farmer; perhaps that would be a refuge from the Leviathan State.[81] On another occasion he thought about becoming a kind of wandering poet for a few months: "the Vachel Lindsay of Michigan."[82] Looking back years later on this period in his life, Kirk described it as one of "marking time." He had fallen victim to "an apathy which the modern industrial system induces...."[83]

Kirk's drifting ended abruptly in August 1942 when he was drafted into the army. For nearly four years he lived in the desolate wastes of Utah (and, later, at a camp in Florida) as a sergeant in the Chemical Warfare Service. Kirk had not wanted to join the army. Although sympathetic to the Allies (he followed the Italian-Ethiopian sector closely), he had opposed American intervention in World War II and had believed that President Roosevelt was deliberately trying to maneuver America into the war.[84] In 1944 he even voted for the Socialist Party's Norman Thomas for president to reward Thomas's anti-imperialist speeches before Pearl Harbor.[85] Kirk's wartime letters showed the persistence of his libertarian convictions; his correspondence was replete with disgust at conscription, military inefficiency, governmental bureaucracy, "paternalism," and socialist economics. He denounced liberal "globaloney"[86] and feared that America was doomed to live in a collectivistic economy.[87]

As the war came to a close, Kirk, anxious to return to civilian life, grew increasingly worried that the army, unnecessarily alarmed about Russia, would strive to perpetuate conscription.[88] On one occasion he even accused New Dealers of seeking a way to maintain scarcity and enhance prosperity: in order to avoid what it thought would be a postwar depression, the administration would prolong the state of war even after the end of hostilities. In this way it could keep the men under arms from glutting the job market. Then, he predicted, the New Dealers would deliberately create an enemy abroad; it could only be the Soviet Union.[89] Vehemently opposed to the peacetime draft, Sergeant Kirk published a vigorous article on the subject in 1946. "Abstract humanitarianism has come to regard servitude—so long as it be to the state—as a privilege," he charged. Yet "...there is no tyranny more onerous than military life."[90]

In one respect, though, Kirk's wartime experience had been extremely valuable: as a clerk with largely routine duties, he found a large amount of time to read. And read he did—Nock's *Memoirs*, Chesterton's *Orthodoxy*, Irving Babbitt's *Democracy and Leadership*, the novels of George Gissing, the political thought of Bagehot, and countless classics of English and ancient literature. One product of Kirk's extraordinary private exposure to a "humanistic" education was a blistering article he published in the *South Atlantic Quarterly* (something of a conservative outpost) in 1945.

> We have turned from the classics to the lathe because of our fetishes of creature comforts and material aggrandizement....
> ...We talk of education for leadership, but actually we educate for mediocrity.[91]

Unabashedly "classical" and aristocratic in his outlook, Kirk denounced the four "sins" of public education: equalitarianism, technicalism, progressivism, and egotism.[92] Fearlessly attacking everything from progressive education to campus sports-mindedness to utilitarian vocationalism to modern psychology ("that muddle of physiology and metaphysics"), Kirk warned against expecting federal aid to solve the ills of higher education.[93] His blast—coming in 1945—was still another sign of the revolt against the masses. Significantly, one of the delighted readers of his essay was Bernard Iddings Bell, who wrote to Kirk, inaugurating a friendship of more than a decade's duration.[94]

After completing service in the army, Kirk divided his time between teaching the history of civilization at Michigan State College and pursuing his doctorate at St. Andrews University in Scotland. Kirk, who was deeply attached to rural and ancestral ways and whose "Gothic mind" cherished "variety, mystery, tradition, the venerable, the awful,"[95] immediately loved Scotland and England. There he saw "the metaphysical principle of continuity given visible reality."[96] As a college professor Kirk believed fervently that his profession was a conservative one.[97] Moreover, during World War II he had planned to write a book about Americans who had fought against their age—men like Fisher Ames, John Randolph, and Henry Adams.[98] In part, no doubt, for these reasons, Kirk selected as his dissertation topic the Anglo-American or Burkean conservative tradition. Here, indeed, was a body of thought that seemed to be against the age.

Deeply pessimistic about the apparent demise of this school of thought in the modern world, Kirk at first intended to call his work *The*

Conservatives' Rout.[99] But when the book was published early in 1953 as *The Conservative Mind*, the sense of despair was lacking. Instead, readers discovered an eloquent, defiant, impassioned *cri de coeur* for conservatism. The essence of this philosophy lay in six "canons":

(1) Belief that a divine intent rules society as well as conscience.... Political problems, at bottom, are religious and moral problems....

(2) Affection for the proliferating variety and mystery of traditional life, as distinguished from the narrowing uniformity and equalitarianism and utilitarian aims of most radical systems....

(3) Conviction that civilized society requires orders and classes.... Society longs for leadership....

(4) Persuasion that property and freedom are inseparably connected, and that economic leveling is not economic progress....

(5) Faith in prescription and distrust of "sophisters and calculators." Man must put a control upon his will and his appetite.... Tradition and sound prejudice provide checks upon man's anarchic impulse.

(6) Recognition that change and reform are not identical....[100]

Who were the conservatives whom Kirk analyzed with such enthusiasm? Above all, Edmund Burke, the "founder" of "the true school of conservative principle." From the incomparable Burke flowed a still vibrant, if battered, tradition: through such men as Scott, Coleridge, Disraeli, and Newman in Britain, and the Adams family, Calhoun, Hawthorne, Brownson, Babbitt, and More in America. Conservatives have been "routed" since 1789, Kirk admitted, "but they have never surrendered." Indeed, Kirk claimed to discern a number of auspicious trends; conservative ideas were now "struggling toward ascendancy in the United States...."[101]

Kirk's text was not only a huge, 450-page distillation of the thinking of 150 years of the intellectual Right; it was also a relentless assault on every left-wing panacea and error imaginable. The perfectibility of man, contempt for tradition, political and economic leveling—these were, in Kirk's view, the most prominent among post-1789 attacks on social order.[102] Liberalism, collectivism, utilitarianism, positivism, atomistic individualism, leveling humanitarianism, pragmatism, socialism, ideology ("the science of idiocy," said John Adams)—these were some of Kirk's targets.

Moreover, at times he criticized capitalism and industrialism; the automobile, for example, he labeled a "mechanical Jacobin."[103] Kirk, in short, left no stone unturned. Here was a full-scale challenge to modernity.

The response to Kirk's massive volume was, in the words of its publisher, "beyond all expectations."[104] Conservatives were delighted. Robert Nisbet, for example, wrote to Kirk that no book could have been better timed for the edification of American intellectuals. Kirk, said Nisbet, had done the impossible: he had broken "the cake of intellectual opposition to the conservative tradition in the United States."[105] T.S. Eliot reported that he was "very much impressed" by *The Conservative Mind*;[106] soon it was published in Great Britain. Kirk, too, was pleased; fortyseven of the first fifty reviews, he wrote to Eliot, were favorable.[107] Everywhere, it seemed, the book was being discussed; Henry Regnery later recalled that its impact was "hard to imagine."[108]

To some extent Kirk's extraordinary success was attributable to an unusual series of accidents. When his *Randolph of Roanoke* appeared in 1951, a friend had reviewed it favorably in the *New York Compass*—at the time, according to Kirk, a fellow-traveling, far-Left newspaper. Kirk believes that his unexpected support in that quarter predisposed segments of the intellectual Left to respond sympathetically to *The Conservative Mind*. More crucial was Kirk's obtaining a favorable review in the *New York Times*; once again, luck was with him. When Gordon Keith Chalmers's *The Republic and the Person* was published, Kirk had praised it in *The Living Churchman*. When Kirk's book appeared, Chalmers, anxious to return the favor, asked the *Times* to give him that book to review. It did so, and in May 1953, Chalmers joined the ranks of laudatory critics.[109]

With the approval of the highly influential *New York Times* now secured (as Kirk tells the story), the fame of his book spread outward. Among those who contributed significantly to its popular impact were the editors of *Time*, who apparently became interested once the *Times* had "endorsed" his book. When the senior editors discovered that their own book review editor seemed adamantly unwilling to review Kirk's work, they called on a former associate, the ex-Communist Whittaker Chambers, for advice. Chambers was blunt: *The Conservative Mind* was the most important book of the twentieth century. That settled it. *Time* quickly selected Max Ways to be the reviewer and devoted its entire July 6, 1953 book section to Kirk's work.[110]

Fortuitous events alone cannot explain the impact of *The Conservative Mind* in 1953; deeper trends favored its success. First, as Kirk him-

self later noted,[111] these were the early days of the apparently conservative administration of President Eisenhower; perhaps Kirk's book could
yield clues about the aspirations of the resurgent Right. More important
than the book's timing was its substance. Here, in one fat volume, was a
fervent synthesis of many conservative criticisms of the Left in the postwar years. Here was a handbook—the ideas not just of one man but of a
distinguished group of men, covering nearly two centuries. Other traditionalists had constructed genealogies of evil men and pernicious thoughts;
here, at long last, was a genealogy of good men and valuable thoughts.
No longer could it be said, as John Stuart Mill had once jibed, that conservatives were the "stupid party." Thanks to Russell Kirk they could
claim an intellectually formidable and respectable ancestry. Kirk had
demonstrated that conservatism should be taken seriously; he had, as a
friend later put it, "devulgarized" conservatism.[112] Like Friedrich Hayek,
Kirk had made it respectable again to be a man of the Right. He had
done even more. If Peter Viereck's *Conservatism Revisited* had given
the postwar conservative impulse a label, *The Conservative Mind* had
decisively catalyzed a self-conscious, unabashedly conservative *movement*.
In the words of Henry Regnery, Kirk had given an "amorphous, scattered opposition" to liberalism an "identity."[113]

Kirk had contributed to American conservatism in another, less obvious way: half of *The Conservative Mind* was devoted to American thinkers. It is customary—and correct—to point to Kirk as the principal disciple of Edmund Burke in the postwar era; less often noted is his recovery of an American conservative tradition. Kirk, of course, was not the
first or only one to undertake such a quest. In the 1940s, Richard Weaver
had delineated Southern conservative traditions in a few articles,[114] and
Kirk himself had done the same in *Randolph of Roanoke*. In *The Case
for Conservatism*, Francis Wilson, a political scientist at the University
of Illinois, had devoted a chapter to the American conservative tradition,
including the *Federalist* and Paul Elmer More, "the greatest of our intellectual conservatives."[115] Elsewhere in these years, Daniel Boorstin, sometimes considered a neo-conservative, reinterpreted the American tradition in *The Genius of American Politics* and singled out its unique,
nonideological, *inimitable* character as a brake on crusading internationalism.[116] By revealing a usable conservative American past, Kirk's book
strengthened this "Americanizing" impulse.[117] Nevertheless, the dominant thrust of the new conservatism before *The Conservative Mind* (and,
two years later, Clinton Rossiter's *Conservatism in America*) was not toward America but toward Europe. The principal perspective in which to

place Kirk's book was Europe and Burke; it was Kirk's argument, in fact, that the American tradition was fundamentally Burkean.

With the advent of Russell Kirk, the new conservative or traditionalist segment of the renascent American Right reached full bloom. Clearly this was a phenomenon of some status and importance, as the rising number of essays about it attested.[118] What was the nature of this movement? What was its significance?

To some extent, no doubt, the term "new conservatism" was merely a journalistic catchword. To a considerable degree, however, it was the creation of Peter Viereck, who had first coined the phrase in an article in 1940.[119] For Viereck, it represented an attempt to distinguish his "ethical" conservatism of values from the "Old-Guard," "Manchester-liberal," "McKinley-style" Republicanism he detested.[120] The "new" conservatism, he later declared, was supposed to be "non-Republican, non-commercialist, non-conformist."[121] Not everyone accepted the label easily. Kirk in particular was distressed by its implied emphasis on novelty: "The cardinal principle of conservative thought is the conviction that new systems and structures incline dangerously toward presumption...."[122] Still, despite the tendentious and partisan usage to which the phrase was sometimes put, it lingered on as a broad, generic classification as well. One critic, in fact, writing in 1955, predicted that the entire decade would be remembered as "the Era of the New Conservatism."[123]

In several ways this powerful impulse of the late 1940s and early 1950s differed from the concurrent libertarian or classical liberal revival (discussed in Chapter One). First, the new conservative movement was overwhelmingly associated with colleges and universities. Virtually every one of its spokesmen held a position in academe. It was much less an "underground" movement in its origins; while libertarians wrote for journals like *analysis* and *The Freeman*, traditionalists submitted their work to learned quarterlies. Indeed, the libertarian revival was to an important degree a journalistic affair; the new conservatism was not. In part this was attributable to a simple fact: thanks to the "Counter-Enlightenment" of men like Eliot, the Agrarians, and the New Critics, the influence of tradition had never disappeared in the universities in the 1930s and 1940s. Instead, in the words of one observer, it had only been "drowned out by the clatter and confusion attendant upon the building of the 'Brave New World.'"[124] After 1945, when the intellectual and political climate began to change, younger voices could appeal to a tradition that was still alive. Perhaps this accounts for another characteristic of the new conservatives: for all their pessimism about modernity, they never seemed quite so despondent or isolated as many of the libertarians did for a time.

A second noticeable feature of the traditionalist group was its extraordinary orientation toward Europe. We have already noted its relative lack of interest in the specifically American past. One must take care not to exaggerate; nevertheless, the principal early acts of recovery were of European conservatives—Burke and Metternich, for instance—not Americans. The revival of Christian orthodoxy and classical, natural law philosophy also strengthened a noticeable tendency to place America in the perspective of the larger civilization of the West. One of the strong undercurrents in the literature of the new conservatives, in fact, was the theme that the United States was not alone; it had become, willy-nilly, the principal defender of the entire West against the Communist East.

This lack of parochialism was reinforced by two factors. First, as outspoken opponents of contemporary "crowd culture" and its potential for totalitarianism, the American neo-traditionalists believed that they were deeply set apart from the triumphant forces in their native land. As blunt critics of liberalism, democracy, and the common man, they knew that they were denouncing the idols of their day. They knew that they were outside the mainstream of contemporary life. As believers in standards and leadership, they were dismayed by the decadent standards and demagogic leaders they saw around them. Why not, therefore, turn to Europe for inspiration and perspective?

"Alienation," however, would be too strong a term for this sense of distance, which appeared in the writings of such conservatives as Kirk, Weaver, Bell, and Harrigan. Although they realized they were a minority, they were not an embittered minority. The tone of *The Conservative Mind*, to take one case, was one of defiance, not misanthropy. Moreover, there was no conservative counterpart in the 1950s to the literary exiles of the 1920s. Although some—like Kirk and Viereck—had studied abroad, they had not fled to Europe. Instead, they imported European insights and took their stand at home.

A second reason for the "Western" rather than simply American consciousness of the new conservatives lay in the striking number of European refugees who contributed to their cause. Leo Strauss, Eric Voegelin, Erik von Kuehnelt-Leddihn, John Lukacs [125]—these and other émigrés and visitors were naturally accustomed to think in more than American categories. It is doubtful that these men were as indispensable to the traditionalists as Hayek and Mises were to the beleaguered libertarians in these same years. A Kirk, a Viereck, or a Weaver would undoubtedly have persevered with or without the assistance of émigrés. Nevertheless, these refugees had been on the edge of hell, and their experience was unforgettable. As living rebuttals to American isolationism and parochialism, they could only further direct attention toward problems abroad and thus increase the European orientation of conservative intellectuals in America.

The case of one such refugee—Thomas Molnar—was especially dramatic. Born in Hungary in 1921, Molnar had actually been imprisoned as a member of a Catholic resistance group in the Nazi concentration camp at Dachau in World War II. Liberation from one tyranny, however, had only exposed him to another; as the Communists tightened their grip on his native land after the war, Molnar escaped to Belgium. After obtaining a master's degree in philosophy and French literature at the University of Brussels, Molnar emigrated to the United States and obtained his doctorate at Columbia University in 1952. At this time the young scholar still considered himself to be vaguely left-of-center in politics. Gradually, however, he began to move to the Right. As a European, he was startled by the "excesses of American democracy." While he considered democracy to be acceptable in politics, he found the sweeping American application of it to culture, universities, and family relations repugnant; democracy, he believed, could be a destructive force. Already an anti-Communist, Molnar was also moving to the Right as a result of his scholarly study of utopianism and of the dangerous role of intellectuals in promoting it. Such components of healthy societies as decency, hierarchy, and integrative symbols seemed to be weakening around him. Gradually, old books—such as those of Dostoevsky—took on a new meaning for him; new books—notably Kirk's *The Conservative Mind*—also had an impact. In the mid-1950s Molnar became acquainted with Russell Kirk and other conservative leaders. More and more this professor of history and French literature found himself writing for conservative periodicals and for Catholic organs (particularly *Commonweal* and *Catholic World*) then open to conservative authors. By the late 1950s Molnar— victim of two totalitarianisms, critic of utopianism and American "democracy"—was a man of the Right.[126]

The distance between many new conservatives and their milieu was evident in another way. One of the most remarkable features of this movement was that, in a country still substantially Protestant, its leadership was heavily Roman Catholic, Anglo-Catholic, or critical of Protestant Christianity. Erik von Kuehnelt-Leddihn, Thomas Molnar, Francis Wilson, Frederick Wilhelmsen, William F. Buckley, Jr.—all were Catholics. Eric Voegelin called himself a "pre-Reformation Christian";[127] Bernard Iddings Bell was an Episcopal clergyman; John Hallowell and Anthony Harrigan were Episcopalians. Although once an atheist, Russell Kirk, by 1953, was on the road to Roman Catholicism.[128] While remaining Protestant, Peter Viereck wrote to Francis Wilson that he considered himself "in many ways [but not all] a fellow-traveler of the Catholic church."[129] In a famous aphorism Viereck remarked, "Catholic-baiting is the anti-Semitism of the liberals."[130]

In a sense Viereck was correct. The early years of the new conservative movement were ones of marked tension between Catholics and other religious groups in the United States. These were the years when Francis Cardinal Spellman and Eleanor Roosevelt argued vehemently about government aid to parochial schools, when President James B. Conant of Harvard urged the abolition of private schools. This was the era in which Sidney Hook asserted that "there is no academic freedom in Catholic colleges...."[131] It was the period in which President Truman appointed General Mark Clark ambassador to the Vatican—only to withdraw the nomination (at Clark's request) after it had aroused furious protest. This was the era in which Paul Blanshard's muckraking *American Freedom and Catholic Power* became a bestseller. To be a Catholic in these years was to occupy an uncertain position in American intellectual life; to be a conservative Catholic was to bear an even heavier burden. Perhaps, then, it is not so surprising that much of the new conservatism seemed so Catholic in composition. Both Catholics and conservatives were outsiders. One is even tempted to say that the new conservatism was, in part, an intellectual cutting edge of the postwar "coming of age" of America's Catholic minority. Politically, one sign was the ascent of Senator Joseph McCarthy—an outsider, a loner, a hero among many conservatives, and a Catholic who enjoyed much support among Catholics. Another sign was the rise in the early 1950s of a young Catholic politician whose early views—on "who lost China," for instance—were often conservative: John F. Kennedy. In short, the "Catholic" temper of much traditionalist conservatism reinforces one's sense of how fundamental a challenge to "official" secular-liberal America the movement was—and was meant to be.

It is not surprising, either, that a considerable distance also existed between the traditionalist and libertarian conservatives in the postwar decade. It was not that the two groups were unaware of each other; [132] William F. Buckley, Jr., in *God and Man at Yale*, had a foot in both camps, defending orthodox Christianity *and* laissez-faire capitalism. What was noticeable was the lack of contact and mingling. Indeed, nearly all of the leading new conservatives took pains to dissociate themselves from the "nineteenth-century liberalism" that was also enjoying a new vogue on the right. Most vehement was Viereck; *his* conservatism, he said, had nothing to do with rootless, "cash nexus," selfish, laissez-faire individualism.[133] Russell Kirk also emphasized that his kind of traditionalism was not a defense of materialistic businessmen or "the dogmas of Manchesterian economic theory." "Conservatism is something more than mere solicitude for tidy incomes."[134] In a lengthy critique of Ludwig von Mises, dean of the Austrian School, Kirk warned of the dangers of rationalistic, atomistic capitalism and utilitarianism: "...once supernatural and traditional sanctions are dissolved, economic self-interest is ridiculously inadequate to hold an economic system together, and even less adequate to preserve order."[135] On one occasion he even rebuked *The Freeman*:

> ...it...subscribes to a kind of ossified Benthamism, preaches Cobden and Bright as Holy Writ, and is edited by a philosophical anarchist [Chodorov] who declares that government is an unnecessary evil and that radicals are the salt of the earth.[136]

Kirk had worked for a "soulless corporation" and had lived in a dreary industrial city; he had no inclination to idealize free enterprise. Robert Nisbet was also critical of the corrosive, antisocial laissez-faire of the nineteenth century: it had weakened social bonds and "accelerated" the aggrandizement of the "omnicompetent State." Nisbet wanted in its place laissez-faire for "autonomous groups."[137] Similar sentiments could be found in the writings of other traditionalist conservatives.[138]

Nevertheless, certain bonds did link the two independent wings of the conservative revival. Both abhorred the totalitarian state and collectivism; both tended to support private property, decentralization, and (at least in a general way) a free economic system. Both evinced a similar minority consciousness: the new conservatives with their general disdain for "crowd culture," the libertarians with their concept of the Remnant. In one case—Albert Jay Nock—they shared a common ancestor: Nisbet, Kirk, and Bell explicitly indicated their appreciation of that "superfluous man." But it is revealing that the Nock to whom the traditionalists turned was less the libertarian who despised the State than the humanist and elitist who scorned the masses as uneducable and appealed only to a natural aristocracy—the Remnant.

Despite some common ground, in other words, the gap between

the two streams of thought was real indeed. While libertarians tended to emphasize economic arguments against the State, the new conservatives were more concerned with what they saw as the ethical and spiritual causes and consequences of Leviathan. On the whole, the new conservatives were little interested in economics—particularly what they regarded as abstract and doctrinaire economics. Instead, they were fundamentally social and cultural critics, for whom conservatism meant the restoration of values, not the preservation of material gains. Viereck informed a friend that he saw little difference between the "rival materialisms" of Adam Smith and Karl Marx in the realm of spiritual values.[139] In its origins, the new conservatism was primarily a philosophic, religious, literary, and aesthetic—not an economic—phenomenon. While libertarians stressed the freedom of the individual in opposition to the State, traditionalists saw in the "masterless man" a threat. While libertarians asserted the *right* of the individual to be free, the *right* to be oneself, traditionalists were concerned with what an individual *ought* to be. Richard Weaver, perhaps, said it best:

> Sentimental humanitarianism manifestly does not speak the language of duty, but of indulgence. The notion that obligations are tyrannies and that wants, not deserts, should be the measure of what one gets has by now shown its destructive power. We have tended to ignore the inexorable truth that rights must be earned.... Man, then, perfects himself by discipline, and at the heart of discipline lies self-denial.[140]

What Weaver said about humanitarianism he might have applied to libertarianism. When libertarians stressed individual rights and denounced the State, they tended to assume that the individual acting for himself would act in a socially beneficial way. To the traditionalists, the history of the twentieth century could not sustain that assumption.

By the mid-1950s the new conservatives had become a recognized, almost fashionable, cultural force—"the dynamic intellectual movement today," said Louis Filler.[141] Attention, of course, did not mean assent, and not without reason did Raymond English refer to conservatism as the "forbidden faith."[142] (Clinton Rossiter called it the "thankless persuasion.")[143] Furthermore, the traditionalists were not in accord on all issues, as subsequent events would demonstrate, and one critic accused them of resembling "pin-wheels roaring in so many different directions."[144] But whatever their weaknesses, they had, at least for a moment, achieved one result: they had made the conservative resurgence, in Rossiter's words, "one of the most remarkable facts of our age."[145]

FOUR

Nightmare in Red[1]

In 1966 the conservative scholar Jeffrey Hart remarked that in the twentieth century the "style" of warfare had drastically changed. The day of traditional conflicts between nation-states was over; the era of the "internationalized civil war" had come. The first such war, said Hart, began in Spain in 1936 when the forces of General Franco rebelled against the Republic. Here was a struggle which divided not only Spain but Europe and the United States as well. To the battlefields of Iberia came men from Germany, Italy, France, Britain, Russia, America. The Spanish Civil War was, in Hart's opinion, the "prototype" of the transnational ideological war between Left and Right; the same "cleavage of opinion" had recurred ever since: "over Yugoslavia, over Greece, Cuba and Vietnam."[2] Spain, to borrow a phrase from Allen Guttmann, opened a "wound in the heart";[3] Jeffrey Hart believed it had never healed.

This sense of a civilization divided within, of the West racked by an "inner civil war," was not peculiar to Hart in the 1960s. Like ceaselessly beating drums—sometimes muffled and distant, sometimes throbbing and close at hand—an air of crisis and urgency haunted the American conservative intellectual movement in the decade after 1945. The sources of its malaise are varied, but one above all was decisive: the experience of Communism and the cold war. This was one of the formative influences on the American Right following World War II.

The magnitude of the "transformation of the Right"[4] is obvious when one recalls the attitudes of prominent American conservatives toward foreign affairs between Versailles and Yalta. From Senator Lodge in 1919 to Senator Taft in 1940, many conservative spokesmen had long been extremely skeptical of extensive foreign involvements and "liberal" interventionism. In the post-1945 decade, however, this aloofness—at least among most intellectuals of the Right—declined. In an age of internationalized civil wars, "isolationism" was abandoned.

It did not happen all at once. One sign of residual conservative bitterness about President Roosevelt's foreign policy and its consequences was the efflorescence of revisionist historical scholarship after World War II. Led by Charles Beard, Harry Elmer Barnes, Charles Tansill, George Morgenstern, and William Henry Chamberlin,[5] the revisionists argued that, in defiance of public opinion and personal pledges, Roosevelt had deceitfully maneuvered the United States into war and had then conducted it disastrously. Some critics claimed that he had deliberately created—or at least allowed—the Pearl Harbor disaster. Others denounced the "unconditional surrender" policy against Germany, the "appeasement" at Yalta, and the "betrayal" of Poland. To the indefatigable Barnes, writing in the early 1950s, the postwar world was proof of "the dolorous record of global meddling."[6] To Chamberlin, who had hoped that Nazi Germany and Communist Russia would balance or destroy each other, our "Second Crusade" had been the "product of illusions."

> It was an illusion that the United States was at any time in danger of invasion by Nazi Germany. It was an illusion that Hitler was bent on the destruction of the British Empire. It was an illusion that a powerful Soviet Union in a weakened and impoverished Eurasia would be a force for peace, conciliation, stability, and international co-operation. It was an illusion that the evils and dangers associated with totalitarianism could be eliminated by giving unconditional support to one form of totalitarianism against another. It was an illusion that a combination of appeasement and personal charm could melt away designs of conquest and domination which were deeply rooted in Russian history and Communist philosophy.
> The fruit harvested from seeds of illusion is always bitter.[7]

In the middle of the fighting, conscript Russell Kirk reflected the revisionist sentiment. This was, he said, "the usual sort of war, fought by Russia for Russian aggrandizement and by America to satisfy a national passion for meddling."[8] The war had been a liberal, internationalist crusade, and the "peace" a liberal creation, too. In the disappointing years after victory, the revisionists—who had generally opposed American intervention in the first place—felt vindicated.

If revisionism was a continuation of World War II on the level of scholarship, its long-range impact was limited for that very reason. For most revisionism was essentially retrospective—a last intellectual gasp, however valid, of isolationism. This is not to deny its importance. It kept the foreign policy pot boiling; it raised plausible (if controversial) doubts about liberal efforts abroad and thus subverted the prestige of the architects of those policies. Nevertheless, as William Henry Chamberlin acknowledged, our foreign affairs "cannot come to a dead stop. Americans cannot wring their hands in hopeless disillusionment."[9] The controversies of the prewar and war years lived on, but their role in reviving the intellectual American Right was supportive, not decisive.

For in the tense and ominous years after Yalta, the follies of past wars necessarily yielded to apprehension about a future holocaust. "From Stettin on the Baltic to Trieste on the Adriatic," a new colossus, warned Churchill, dominated Europe. This perception of Communism as a global menace came to dominate the American Right. The conservative intellectual movement was molded by its vision of Communism and by the relentless "inner civil war" in which it became engaged.

The intellectual roots of anti-Communist conservatism, like so much else in the intellectual traditions of the American Right since 1945, lie in responses to the 1930s. To the classical liberal wing of this heterogeneous movement, the 1930s were a time of collectivism and Big Government. To traditionalists the era was one of philosophical nihilism, totalitarianism, and the disturbing emergence of the mass man. To a small but extraordinarily significant group of ex-Communists and former fellow travelers, the 1930s was the Red Decade.

The term "Red Decade" was the invention of the journalist Eugene Lyons. A radical in the 1920s, Lyons had written a passionate defense of Sacco and Vanzetti and had then gone to Moscow as a correspondent between 1927 and 1933. There he saw the "future" and lost his illusions. Upon his return to the United States, Lyons became a vehement critic of Stalinist Russia and was outraged as significant numbers of prominent American liberals collaborated with Communists in the antifascist Popular Front. In 1941 he retaliated with *The Red Decade*.[10]

This fierce book was, in Daniel Aaron's words, "a melancholy record of self-delusion and even more reprehensible human failings."[11] After boldly challenging the "hobgoblin of red-baiting,"[12] Lyons proceeded to document his contention that "the complex communist United Front tinctured every department of American life while it lasted...."[13] The Communist magnet was *real*, he argued, and dismaying numbers of liberals had been attracted to it. Lyons relentlessly compiled his list of the liberals' sins: they had too often ignored or even apologized for such monstrous Russian behavior as the contrived famines, the grotesque purge trials, and the subversion of Republican Spain. They were repeatedly duped by clever Communists who manipulated scores of "fronts" for the Kremlin's advantage. Men like John Dewey who criticized the Soviet Union were slandered; anti-Communist books were often deliberately "sabotaged." For the acerbic Lyons the "last loony scene" was the famous Open Letter of August 10, 1939. Four hundred of the most distinguished intellectuals in America signed this statement, which denounced "the fantastic falsehood that the U.S.S.R. and the totalitarian states are basically alike." The perpetrators of such foolishness, the 400 declared, were "fascists and their allies," anxious "to create dissension among the progressive forces." The signers insisted that the Soviet Union was "a bulwark against war and aggression," an unflagging supporter of "a peaceful international order." Its policies were "diametrically opposed" to those of the Fascists. Less than two weeks later Russia and Germany signed a nonaggression pact. It was a sordid climax, Lyons felt, to a sordid decade of liberal hypocrisy and self-deception.[14]

While Lyons may have overestimated the strength of the Popular Front,[15] he presented enough evidence to give plausibility to his central image: the 1930s as the Red Decade. He was not alone in his rebellion against that era; by the end of World War II a significant literature of disillusionment with Communism already existed. Lyons's own *Moscow Carousel* and *Assignment in Utopia*[16] were two early contributions. Others included Freda Utley's *The Dream We Lost*, Max Eastman's *Artists in Uniform* and *Stalin's Russia and the Crisis in Socialism*, and William Henry Chamberlin's *Collectivism: A False Utopia* and *The Confessions of an Individualist*.[17] All had seen the Soviet Union; all could speak authoritatively about "the god that failed." Eastman had been an admirer and biographer of the exiled Leon Trotsky. Utley, a former English Communist, had married a Russian who disappeared forever in the purges of the mid-1930s. Lyons and Chamberlin had served as correspondents in Moscow and had learned of such atrocities as the artificial famines of the early 1930s. The effect was profound. "Under the challenge of Soviet collectivism," Chamberlin observed, "I rediscovered with tenfold conviction my instinctive individualist faith."[18] In the decade after Yalta, Lyons, Eastman, Utley, and Chamberlin would help to create the conservative intellectual movement.

There were other expressions of anti-Communism before 1945.

Books by former Communists like Walter Krivitsky, Benjamin Gitlow, and Jan Valtin appeared.[19] *Partisan Review* (linked with Trotskyists) and the *New Leader* (dominated by former Mensheviks) printed frequent criticisms of Stalin's Russia. And yet, for all the disillusionment with Communism generated in the 1930s, the intellectual impact of this early revolt against the Red Decade remained decidedly marginal in 1945. The *New Leader*, for instance, may have been—as James Burnham believes—the most important anti-Communist magazine in the country, [20] but its influence was still limited. Eugene Lyons was among the first to criticize Yalta,[21] but most Americans at the time apparently felt otherwise. As one historian has observed, the "tone of U.S. politics in 1945 was distinctly favorable toward a policy of détente toward the Soviet Union."[22] For the ex-Communists, as for the libertarians and traditionalists, 1945 was not an auspicious year.

Nevertheless, circumscribed as the intellectual revulsion against Communism was at war's end, the groundwork for the future had been laid. If the "premature" anti-Communists and the ex-Communists could as yet claim no major influence on public opinion or on the American Right, they still possessed the advantages of expertise. After all, they had *seen* the revolution. If, after 1945, events were to veer in "their" direction, if One World were to become two, the authors of the literature of disillusionment might acquire an audience.

And when the Iron Curtain did descend and the cold war did break out, the veterans of the "inner civil war" of the 1930s stepped forward to guide the conservative army.

The effects of Communism and the cold war on conservatism may be divided into two categories: responses to threats from abroad, and responses to threats from within.

The menace abroad seemed all too obvious in the early postwar years. In Europe, as the Right saw it, Poland had been betrayed[23] and the rest of the Iron Curtain countries abandoned. Czechoslovakia had fallen in a coup, and Berlin was continually threatened. France and Italy were weakened by substantial domestic Communist parties, while the head of France's atomic energy program for a period was the Communist Frédéric Joliot-Curie.[24] In Asia, the situation seemed increasingly desperate, as China fell and Korea became convulsed in an indecisive war. The execution of the anti-Communist Chetnik leader Mikhailovich in Yugoslavia, the death of Czech Foreign Minister Jan Masaryk, the flight of Chiang

Kai-shek to Formosa, the sudden invasion of South Korea, the massive intervention of the Chinese in Korea—these were *shocks* to conservatives and virtually all Americans. And so the anguished cry naturally went out: Why? Why were we reeling before Communism on the march? Why had the euphoria of Yalta yielded to the daily fear of global war? Who lost China? Who had so glaringly mishandled our foreign policy?

With increasing indignation and bitterness, right-wing critics charged that the liberals were responsible—the liberals who had been in power in Washington since 1933. At best, the liberals had been ineffectual; at worst, they had been duped or infiltrated by Communists. Three journals in particular spearheaded the assault: *Plain Talk*, founded in 1946 by Isaac Don Levine and Ralph de Toledano and heavily subsidized by its publisher, the "China lobbyist" Alfred Kohlberg;[25] *The Freeman*, with which *Plain Talk* merged in 1950; and the *American Mercury*, especially under William Bradford Huie, who became editor late in 1950. In these journals and in books like Freda Utley's *The China Story* and John T. Flynn's *While You Slept*,[26] the conservative case was articulated. Leading the critics were such former leftist sympathizers as Lyons, Chamberlin, Utley, Eastman, Toledano, and Burnham.

The day-to-day details of conservative critiques of specific policies have been examined elsewhere and need not be discussed here.[27] The broad features of their analysis, however, are noteworthy. First, the conservatives alleged that America's reverses abroad were substantially attributable to the failure of domestic liberal leaders to comprehend the inherently revolutionary, expansionary, implacable nature of Communism. To liberal ignorance of Communism could be attributed Roosevelt's myopic "unconditional surrender" policy, which had created a vacuum that Stalin eagerly filled. Fatuous liberalism was responsible for the appeasement of "Uncle Joe" Stalin and the preposterous attempt to impose a coalition government in China; the sins of the Red Decade had not ceased in 1939. Second, relying heavily on congressional investigations of such matters as the *Amerasia* case and the Institute of Pacific Relations, right-wing critics personalized the controversy by pointing to individuals of (to them) dubious judgment and questionable loyalty who had disastrously affected American foreign policy. Alger Hiss, Owen Lattimore, Harry Dexter White, John Stewart Service, John Carter Vincent, and dozens of other government officials and advisers became targets of criticism from the Right.

Another important aspect of developing conservative anti-Communism was the effect upon it of exile scholars. Like the libertarians and traditionalists, the anti-Communists were heavily indebted to Europe. In the early 1950s men like Gerhart Niemeyer, Stefan Possony, and Robert Strausz-Hupé—all émigrés from Central Europe—were becoming known as hard-line anti-Communist scholars;[28] in time all would become leading cold war strategists for the American Right.[29] The process by which an Eastern European exile could become embittered by the foreign policies of the Roosevelt and Truman administrations was abundantly illustrated by Bogdan Raditsa, formerly chief of the foreign press department of the Yugoslav Ministry of Information under Tito. Writing in 1951, Raditsa asserted that political refugees from the Iron Curtain countries were alarmed by the attitudes of their American colleagues. While the Europeans knew that Communism could not be placated, too many Americans did not. Instead, Americans were victims of cautious, relativistic, philistine "Machiavellian liberalism," expounded particularly by Walter Lippmann, George Kennan, and Barbara Ward. The trouble with this philosophy was its "ambivalent attitude toward despots and despotism." It failed to realize that democracy and totalitarianism were irreconcilable; it was too willing to let Communism alone as long as it did not invade Western Europe. Bemused by balance-of-power diplomacy and the desire to be "objective," it feared anti-Communist "hysteria." Raditsa charged that "Machiavellian liberals" were skeptical about the desirability of popular upheavals in the captive nations and were deliberately excluding both exiles and the most anti-Communist Americans from the anti-Soviet effort. Exiles were supposed to be too "emotional" and "prejudiced" about Communism. Raditsa warned that "you cannot destroy an ideological enemy without being yourself ideologically prepared." He therefore advocated an idealistic international crusade for the "universal establishment of liberty."[30]

It was obviously not sufficient, however, for conservatives to berate liberal foreign policies and their makers. Even if liberals had been tainted with ignorance or pro-Communism, what did their critics propose? The title of Raditsa's article supplied a logical answer: "Beyond Containment to Liberation." In the postwar years, many conservative intellectuals demanded just that. In 1953 William Henry Chamberlin published *Beyond Containment*, a history of the cold war which urged the adoption of programs "starting the Soviet empire, the greatest threat to our Western civilization, on the road to decline and fall."[31] Also in 1953, the new conservative Peter Viereck argued for the "overthrow" of the "Stalin terror." To Viereck it was "heartless" to prefer "containment" to liberation, and he cited Raditsa's article in his defense. "For the millions of slaves behind the Iron Curtain," Viereck exclaimed, "'peaceful' coexistence means not peace but a continuation of torture and murder." "How long today," he wanted to know, "can the Christian-Judaic moral basis of American freedom survive our tolerating by 'containment'—as opposed to liberation—the...horrors of the Soviet slave camps?" [32]

It was one thing simply to propose liberation of Communist territories; it was quite another to devise a rationale and strategy to achieve it. This was the task performed by probably the most influential right-wing critic of liberal foreign policies after 1945: James Burnham. More than any other single person, Burnham supplied the conservative intellectual movement with the theoretical formulation for victory in the cold war.

Born in 1905, educated at Princeton and Oxford, Burnham served on the faculty of New York University as a professor of philosophy from 1929 to 1953. Like so many others who eventually found their home on the Right, Burnham had been a man of the far Left in the 1930s. Working with Communist unions in Detroit, Burnham eventually became associated with A.J. Muste and, in 1934, with the Fourth International of Leon Trotsky. Although Burnham later stated that he never became a full ideological Marxist, he was an active Trotskyist and editor of the *New International* for several years. Gradually, disillusionment set in, as it did for so many others. Burnham discovered that he could no longer accept Trotsky's contention that the Soviet Union, despite Stalin's "aberration," was still essentially a progressive "workers' state," to be defended at all costs. Burnham argued instead that the Soviet regime was profoundly "exploitative and imperialist"—a hypothesis confirmed, he believed, by the Nazi-Soviet pact of 1939 and the Russian war with Finland. In March 1940, Burnham severed all ties with the Trotskyists. [33]

A year later Burnham published his provocative book *The Managerial Revolution*, soon followed by *The Machiavellians*. Meanwhile he contributed frequently to *Partisan Review*. During these years, Burnham later reflected, he was undergoing a process of "re-education":

> Having come to know something of the gigantic ideology of Bolshevism, I knew that I was not going to be able to settle for the pigmy ideologies of Liberalism, social democracy, refurbished laissez-faire or the inverted, cut-rate Bolshevism called "fascism." Through the Machiavellians I began to understand more thoroughly what I had long felt: that only by renouncing all ideology can we begin to see the world and man. [34]

Recoiling from the Left, Burnham developed a tough-minded perspective; he refused to be deceived by silly, moral platitudes or verbal camouflage of hard realities. He was determined to be a dispassionate scientist of power, a *realpolitiker*—in that sense, a "Machiavellian."

In the decade after 1945, Burnham turned increasingly to the problems of global politics. Soon he became a formidable polemicist, writing with brisk, lucid self-assurance on the world conflict with Communism. The first of his influential books, *The Struggle for the World*, appeared in 1947; part of it was based on work done for the OSS.[35] Heavily influenced by Arnold Toynbee's *A Study of History*, which he cited often, and by the geopolitical theories of Sir Halford Mackinder, Burnham argued that the world had reached an intolerable crisis.

> The discovery of atomic weapons has brought about a situation in which Western Civilization, and perhaps human society in general, can continue to exist only if an absolute monopoly in the control of atomic weapons is created. This monopoly can be gained and exercised only through a World Empire.... the present candidates for leadership in the World Empire are only two: the Soviet Union and the United States.[36]

Burnham contended that the Communist drive for world domination had already begun; the "Third World War" was a fact. Relentlessly he asserted that the Communist goal was "irrevocable." The Communists wanted total power, the conquest of the planet—a result which would mean the "destruction" of the most "cherished" values of Western civilization. The danger was imminent, the struggle "irrepressible."[37]

What, then, should be done? Only the United States could prevent a Communist triumph. Conciliation and drift meant defeat: "...you can get along with communism in only one way: by capitulating to it."[38] In terms of defense, Burnham proposed measures to prevent Communist consolidation of the Eurasian World Island (Mackinder's term) and to thwart Communist infiltration. The United States should, for example, abandon the notions that its world objective is peace and that all nations are "equal." It should "discard" the "verbal shell" of "non-intervention in the internal affairs of other nations";[39] in the future, more, not less, intervention might be necessary. It should use massive worldwide propaganda, give all necessary aid to allies, and refuse to collaborate with the Soviet Union. It must immediately outlaw and suppress the domestic Communist movement. Offensively, America must initiate a "non-Communist World Federation":

> The reality is that the only alternative to the communist World
> Empire is an American Empire which will be, if not literally
> world-wide in formal boundaries, capable of exercising deci-
> sive world control....
>
> The United States cannot help building an Empire.[40]

As a first step, Burnham suggested "common citizenship and full political union" with Great Britain and its dominions.[41]

Behind Burnham's energetic prose lurked a deep sense of pessimism. While he did not consider all-out war technically inevitable, he
was convinced that it was "very probable"; perhaps it would even occur
before his book came off the presses.[42] Burnham believed that his own
proposals need not provoke war. Still, he argued, "the danger of this war
will not disappear until the present Soviet regime is overthrown, and
world communism as a whole rendered impotent."[43] This must be the
American goal. The problem was that Burnham could discern no such
American resolve. Instead, despite some new official rhetoric of "tough-
ness," Burnham, writing in 1946, detected in American conduct of foreign policy only a "policy of vacillation." If this continued (as he expected),
"the defeat and annihilation of the United States are probable."[44]

In 1950 Burnham produced another fervent polemic, *The Coming
Defeat of Communism*. In many respects this book was a recapitulation
and "extension" of *The Struggle for the World*.[45] Here again was the
mood of crisis, the dramatic insistence that we were already in a war with
aggressive Communism, that compromise and neutrality were impossible, that the United States must mobilize now. Here again were wither-
ing blasts at weak, confused American diplomacy as contradictory, narrow, defensive, and lacking in objectives. Here again were the exhorta-
tions to a single goal: "the destruction of the power of Soviet-based Communism."[46]

There were also new elements in Burnham's analysis. First, he placed
increased stress on signs of current "vulnerability" in the Communist
camp, including restiveness in the satellites, economic disorder, and rigid
bureaucracies. Burnham even conceded that "in a strictly military sense"
the United States had little to fear from Russia for several years.[47] Nevertheless, the time to act was now. For if the Communists consolidated
their postwar gains without hindrance (again the influence of Mackinder
was obvious), and if the Americans continued passively to pretend that
the Third World War had not yet begun, then total war would be inevitable. The immediate exploitation of Communist weakness, however,
would enable the "free world" to defeat its foe *without* full-scale war.

Burnham insisted that we could win at the level of "political-subversive warfare." Indeed, it was "the only rational alternative to immediate armed attack" on the Soviet Union.[48]

Second, and rather uncharacteristically, Burnham in 1950 allowed himself a little hope, as the very title of his book suggested. Between 1946 and 1949 the Communists had made sweeping gains, he observed, but the "net trend" had turned against them. Despite all the inadequacies of past and current U.S. policies, America had at least awakened somewhat to the danger and had slowed the rate of Communist advance. Burnham believed that the defeat of Communism was "inevitable" because Americans had the *will* to survive. This did not mean, of course, that we could get by with Coué-like slogans about improving every day in every way. Burnham's book bristled with practical suggestions, often involving what he labeled "untraditional methods."[49] Aim propaganda directly at the Communist elite. Break the Communist hold on the world labor movement. Initiate a "united front with the Vatican." Establish an East European Institute. Utilize refugees and the resistance movements behind the Iron Curtain. Establish an agency to guide and conduct "unorthodox" operations. Overthrow Albania. Prevent Moscow from reconquering Yugoslavia—even at the risk of war. These were but a few of Burnham's specific ideas—all of which depended on the will to survive and the development of intelligent leadership. At the end of this book, at least, Burnham considered the United States equal to the challenge.

The optimism in *The Coming Defeat of Communism* was gone from Burnham's next major postwar book, *Containment or Liberation?*, published in 1953. Burnham acknowledged that the U.S. government had at last developed a foreign policy of containment, principally devised by George Kennan. Unfortunately, it was totally inadequate. Burnham argued that "containment" was purely defensive, inapplicable to the gigantic Soviet Union, and fundamentally unable "to comprehend the revolutionary nature of the communist enterprise." [50] Moreover, it was spiritually deficient: "Who will willingly suffer, sacrifice and die for containment?"[51] It was simply "a policy of drift" whose "inner law" was "let history do it."[52] But, Burnham pleaded, we cannot rely on history to bail us out:

> If the communists succeed in consolidating what they have *already* conquered, then their complete world victory is certain....
> ...What this means is that liberation is the only defense against a Soviet world victory.[53]

How could liberation be achieved? Burnham dismissed the "west European strategy" of mere containment as "without hope." For one thing, Western Europe could not survive without Eastern Europe; the West would eventually either have to surrender to Moscow or free Moscow's satellites.[54] Nor would the "Asian-American strategy" proposed by Senator Taft suffice; the immediate threat to America lay in Europe, not the Far East. Obviously still reflecting the geopolitical view of Mackinder, Burnham declared that preoccupation with Asia "leaves the enemy free to go about his principal and decisive business: the consolidation of the Heartland and of the surrounding Empire...."[55] He proposed instead a third alternative: an "East European strategy" designed to take the offensive and carry the conflict to the enemy's base. Only this approach could repel the Communist threat. In the final section of his book he urged such initiatives as the recognition of exile governments and the establishment of military units of exiled soldiers as means for the liberation of the captive nations.[56]

The degree to which the foreign policy debate had been personalized by 1953 was also evident in Burnham's volume. In a chapter entitled "Is Political Warfare Possible?" he expressed doubt that this crucial mode of conducting the cold war would ever be effectively employed by the United States. He attributed this American weakness to the presence of an "ideologized minority" of government officials whose views of the world were shaped "in the context of the economic depression of the '30's and the political struggle against Hitler and Nazism."[57] They were products (although Burnham did not use the term) of the Red Decade. Passionately antifascist, these men, said Burnham, never felt quite the same way about Communism.

> Communism was not like fascism, not wholly evil as fascism was, because—they were taught without knowing they were being taught—communism "has the same ideals that we have, even if we differ on the methods." ...It was only about Nazism that they *felt* strongly.[58]

Such men were not comfortable with "hard anti-communists." Who were these men? Burnham named examples: Dean Acheson, Charles Bohlen, John Paton Davies, Jr., and others who defended such men as Alger Hiss, Owen Lattimore, John Stewart Service, and other State Department officials and advisers suspected of treason or gross neglect of America's national interests in the 1940s.[59]

The influence of Burnham's books on American attitudes toward the cold war seems to have been substantial; certainly he gained a respectful hearing both inside and outside the government. When *The Struggle for the World* appeared in 1947, the *Christian Century* contended that Burnham's book coincided precisely with President Truman's new policy toward Greece and Turkey. It might even be no coincidence, the journal noted, that the Truman Doctrine and Burnham's book were published in the same week.[60] Burnham undeniably established significant government connections in the first cold war years. In the early 1950s he lectured "regularly" at the National War College, the Air War College, the Naval War College, and the School for Advanced International Studies.[61] In *The Coming Defeat of Communism* he advocated the establishment of an East European Institute or University; [62] perhaps it was only happenstance that on July 22, 1951, the founding of the Free Europe University in Exile was announced, with James Burnham as one of the trustees.[63] Early in 1950, the *New York Times* quoted New York University as saying that Burnham was "officially on leave to do research from the nation's capital."[64] His "research" may have included work for the Central Intelligence Agency, for which Burnham had been a consultant.[65] He was also very active in the American Committee for Cultural Freedom, which received financial assistance from the CIA.[66]

Outside of government circles Burnham's writings also received careful attention. Each of his books was widely, often vehemently, reviewed and discussed. Moreover, as an editor of *Partisan Review* and contributor to the *New Leader*, Burnham had access to articulate, left-of-center audiences. More important for his later associations was his growing stature on the Right. In the early 1950s he increasingly contributed to the *American Mercury* and *The Freeman*. Substantial excerpts from all three of his foreign policy books were printed in the *American Mercury* in 1947, 1950, and 1952.[67] When *Containment or Liberation?* appeared, Frank Meyer, a former Communist, praised it in the *American Mercury*, while Eugene Lyons of *Red Decade* fame lauded it in *The Freeman*.[68] Another sign of his prominence in and acceptance by conservative groups was a comment in 1952 by Raymond Moley, a *Newsweek* columnist and former adviser to President Roosevelt. Moley claimed that *The Struggle for the World* "had no little influence in shaping the thinking of Republican critics of the Truman-Acheson diplomacy."[69]

It seems safe to say, then, that James Burnham as much as anyone provided the theoretical formulation for the conservative critique of liberal foreign policies in the early cold war period. He as much as anyone made militant, global anti-Communism a characteristic of the postwar intellectual Right. But Burnham, of course, did not do it alone. Events at home combined with reverses abroad to create and exacerbate the "inner civil war" between Left and Right.

In the late 1940s and early 1950s there appeared on the national stage, often before intent congressional committees, a growing band of men and women who had broken with the Communist Party. Unlike many of the intellectuals already discussed, who had been influenced by Communism but had not become fully committed Stalinists in the 1930s, the new group had usually been deeply involved in the party apparatus. To Eugene Lyons's portrayal of the Red Decade as an era of stupidity and hypocrisy was added the stunning new dimension of treason.

As these former Communists paraded before the public, they increasingly received the attention of the intellectual Right. Names of ex-Communist witnesses like Louis Budenz, Bella Dodd, Elizabeth Bentley, Hede Massing, and Nathaniel Weyl became nationally familiar. If—like Budenz, Massing, and others—they wrote books about their experiences,[70] these were usually noted in the *American Mercury* or *The Freeman*. Their testimony, combined with such powerful expressions of disillusionment as *The God that Failed* and *Verdict of Three Decades*,[71] had an enormous educational impact on the Right.

Sometimes the links between the ex-Communists and the conservative intellectual revival were quite direct; Frank Meyer is a case in point.[72] Born in 1909 in Newark, New Jersey, Meyer attended Princeton University and then Oxford, where he received his B.A. during the Depression. At Oxford in 1931, Meyer joined the Communist Party of Great Britain and became director of its Students' Bureau and a member of its Central Committee. While doing graduate work at the London School of Economics, he was elected president of the Students' Union as an avowed Communist, with the aid of Indian students led by Krishna Menon, later a fiery Indian defense minister under Nehru. From 1934, when Meyer returned to the United States, until 1945, he remained, in his words, a "dedicated Communist." He held many responsible positions in the party.[73]

In 1945, when Earl Browder was deposed as the American Communist leader, Meyer broke with the movement—deeply influenced by Friedrich Hayek's *The Road to Serfdom*, which he had read while still a Communist.[74] The process of extrication from the Left was a slow one. At first he simply called himself a non-Communist. But as the pressures of the cold war intensified [75] and as his personal reeducation continued (he was also profoundly affected by Richard Weaver's *Ideas Have Consequences*),[76] Meyer moved to the Right. According to his friend William Rusher, Meyer was at first a "doctrinaire socialist," then a Truman supporter in 1948, and a Republican by 1952,[77] when he began contributing to the *American Mercury* and *The Freeman*.[78]

With Meyer and other recruits from the ranks of ex-Communists, the postwar American Right suffered from no lack of vivid acquaintance with the god that failed. But it is doubtful that the experience of Communism would have seared the conservative consciousness as irrevocably as it did were it not for a man named Whittaker Chambers and the trial of Alger Hiss.

In August 1948, Whittaker Chambers, a senior editor of *Time*, testified before the House Un-American Activities Committee that he had been an underground Communist in the 1930s and had known as a Communist a young State Department official named Alger Hiss. In the subsequent decade Hiss had become a senior State Department officer, a trusted member of the American delegation to the Yalta conference, and, for many, a symbol of the bright, young, successful New Dealer. When Hiss, who was now president of the Carnegie Endowment for International Peace, denied Chambers's story and sued him for libel, Chambers astounded the nation by producing secret government documents which implicated Hiss and Chambers in the Communist espionage apparatus of the 1930s. In 1950, after more than a year of furious litigation, Hiss was convicted of perjury (and, implicitly, espionage) and sentenced to prison.[79]

The bare facts of this case, however, cannot begin to suggest its enduring effect on the post-1945 conservative intellectual renascence. As much as any other event, the Hiss case forged the anti-Communist element in resurgent conservatism. While many men of the Left, like Arthur Schlesinger, Jr., believed Chambers to be truthful,[80] the whole affair tended to become a Left-Right confrontation. As the saying had it, "a generation was on trial"—the generation of the New Deal. To some, Hiss was a martyr to social justice and Chambers a vicious, pathological liar in league with reactionary Republicans led by Congressman Richard Nixon. To others, Chambers was an extraordinarily sensitive and gifted man who was willingly destroying himself in order to awaken the nation to the Communist peril symbolized by the unrepentant traitor Alger Hiss. The tendency to view the contest in partisan terms was augmented by President Truman's dismissal of the case in 1948 as a "red herring" and by Secretary of State Acheson's remark, just after Hiss was convicted: "I do not intend to turn my back on Alger Hiss." (Acheson had long known Hiss and was a law partner of Hiss's brother Donald.) When many prominent liberals of the day—Acheson, Justices Frankfurter and Reed, Adlai Stevenson, Eleanor Roosevelt, and distinguished professors at famous universities—defended Hiss, at least initially, the lines were drawn tighter. "All right we are two nations"—so wrote John Dos Passos of the Sacco-Vanzetti trial. He might have said the same thing about Hiss and Chambers, for the case was undoubtedly the most ideologically divisive since the execution of the two Italian anarchists in 1927.

The ferocity of the dispute was indeed incredible. Arthur Schlesinger, Jr. observed that the "anti-Chambers whispering campaign was one of the most repellent of modern history."[81] James Burnham was more angry: "At Washington dinners and cocktail parties held or attended by State Department and Intelligence officials, no bitterness or contempt was ever expressed against Alger Hiss. At those same gatherings no vile and shameless slander against Whittaker Chambers was omitted."[82] Chambers himself developed a theme which conservatives adopted wholeheartedly:

> No feature of the Hiss Case is more obvious, or more troubling as history, than the jagged fissure, which it did not so much open as reveal, between the plain men and women of the nation, and those who affected to act, think and speak for them. It was, not invariably, but in general, the "best people" who were for Alger Hiss and who were prepared to go to almost any length to protect and defend him. It was the enlightened and the powerful, the clamorous proponents of the open mind and the common man, who snapped their minds shut in a pro-Hiss psychosis, of a kind which,...in a nation, is a warning of the end.[83]

The effect of the case on many who were or would become conservatives was graphically exemplified by the response of a young journalist named Ralph de Toledano. Born in 1916, raised in a very liberal environment, Toledano had entered Columbia University in the 1930s and had become an activist for left-wing causes. While never a Communist, he lived in "the same red haze" on the "cozy periphery" of the party.[84] Disillusioned by such events as the Moscow purge trials and the Hitler-Stalin pact of 1939, Toledano became in the 1940s a hardened anti-Communist. He worked for the *New Leader* and helped Isaac Don Levine found *Plain Talk* in 1946. (It was Levine, incidentally, who accompanied

Whittaker Chambers in 1939 to the home of A.A. Berle, to inform the then State Department security officer of the network of Communist espionage within the U.S. government.) While at the *New Leader* during the war, Toledano had befriended the émigré Italian anarchist, Carlo Tresca, who believed that he was marked for assassination by the Communists. When Tresca was mysteriously murdered in 1943, Toledano notified the police; his story reached the press. One night, not long afterward, as he was walking home, a car with lights off followed him down a dimly lit street. As he walked faster, the car came toward him. He thought: this was just the way death had come to Tresca. But this time the car veered off. Sitting in the back seat was an Italian Communist, Vittorio Vidali, the same man who had probably engineered the killing of Carlo Tresca:

> ...Tresca's murder was a landmark on the road to anti-Communism. It gave me a first-hand view of the MVD at work....
> ...My war against Communism suddenly acquired a very personal dimension.[85]

With this and other chilling experiences affecting him deeply, Toledano covered the Hiss case for *Newsweek* beginning in 1948. For all his seasoned anti-Communism and rejection of the Popular Front mind, he was still, however tenuously, a man of the Left when the case began. But not for long. Embittered by what he regarded as A.A. Berle's craven, dishonest, and politically motivated account of his conversation with Chambers in 1939, Toledano resigned from the New York state Liberal Party, of which Berle was then chairman.[86] As a result, he believed, of his defection, Toledano suffered insults and discrimination from his erstwhile allies on the Left. He was outraged, too, by many liberals' responses to the controversy:

> Identifying themselves with the criminal, they protested that he was innocent. Identifying themselves with the crime, they shouted that it was no crime at all but a commonplace of the era in which it was committed. And, in a triumph of perverse reasoning, they insisted that the evil was not in the cancer, but in the surgeon who had laid open the flesh to expose it....
> ...It was not what Chambers had done, but what he was, which infuriated and stampeded the "liberals." For Chambers was the first man of real and unconquerable stature to stand up before them....
> ...The "liberals" could not accept Chambers as a religious

man. They could not accept his concept of a religious war because they could not accept religion in the first place. It threatened their universe. They were baffled and outraged by a man who said simply that he believed in God and in freedom.[87]

As the controversy grew increasingly bitter, Toledano was driven to reconsider liberalism as a philosophy. He found it wanting—compounded of conformity, statism, and ethical relativism:

To the liberals, from Samuel Adams to Harry S. Truman, there was never any room for disagreement....

In the context of morals, politics, and economics, liberalism was corrupt. And its corruption stemmed from one corrupting influence: the doctrine that all absolutes are evil with the exception of the absolute State.... in a system which held as relative all restraints on human behavior—the values of truth, justice, honor—where could the liberal find balance[?][88]

One source of balance for Toledano was Whittaker Chambers himself. During the turbulent months of the case, Toledano turned an acquaintance with the ex-Communist into "the most significant friendship of my life."[89] To the *Newsweek* reporter and rebel against the Left, Chambers was "a man of sensibility, graced or afflicted by an abiding sense of history, who realized that time was man's commodity, but eternity God's."[90] Ralph de Toledano thus became one of the first to exalt Chambers as one of the saints of the conservative intellectual revival. In 1950 Toledano contributed to Chambers's status as a hero of the Right by writing with another journalist, Victor Lasky, an account of the Hiss-Chambers case entitled *Seeds of Treason*. The book became a major best-seller and did much to familiarize the American public with this complicated and extraordinary affair.[91]

What personal experience did for Toledano was done for many more conservatives by Chambers's publication in 1952 of *Witness*. Recognized at once as "one of the most significant autobiographies of the twentieth century,"[92] the book immediately became a best-seller. When the *Saturday Evening Post* serialized it prior to publication, the *Post*'s circulation jumped by hundreds of thousands.[93] Chambers's 800-page opus was in reality several books: a poignant story of a decadent home, a revelation of Communist infiltration of the government, an account of his famous confrontation with Alger Hiss. Above all, it was—in Chambers's eyes—a desperate attempt to alert the West to the most total challenge in its history. It was one effort to convey to an unheeding world the redeeming truth for which Chambers believed he had suffered.

Three aspects of the autobiography's message appealed compellingly to the conservative consciousness in the 1950s. First, Chambers articulated eloquently the growing conservative conviction that America faced a transcendent crisis. His book was permeated by a sense of tragedy and by what William F. Buckley, Jr. once called "Spenglerian gloom."[94] He was convinced that in forsaking Communism he was probably leaving the winning side for a confused, vacillating, doomed West. Perhaps, he wondered at one bleak moment in the case, God did not *want* this nation to survive any longer. Perhaps the world was irremediably beyond rescue.[95] Still, he strove to find a reason for fighting on. He later wrote to Buckley:

> I never really hoped to do more in the Hiss Case than give the children of men a slightly better, only slightly better, chance to fight a battle already largely foredoomed....
>   ...How odd that most of the world seems to have missed the point in *Witness*; that it seems to suppose that I said: "Destroy Communism and you can go back to business as usual." Of course, what I really said was: "This struggle is universal and mortal, and only *by means of it*, on condition that you are willing to die that your faith may live, can you conceivably recover the greatness which is in the souls of men."[96]

Second, Chambers developed an interpretation of the enveloping crisis which conservative intellectuals, so many of whom were religious, found congenial. In the "Letter to My Children" which opened *Witness*, Chambers argued that the crisis of the twentieth century, of which Communism was both catalyst and symptom, was a crisis of faith. Communism was fundamentally a religion, "man's second oldest faith," man's "great alternative faith." Its promise was "Ye shall be as gods." Its vision was "the vision of man without God," of "man's mind displacing God as the creative intelligence of the world," of "man's liberated mind, by the sole force of its rational intelligence, redirecting man's destiny...."[97] Communism starkly and insistently proclaimed an inescapable choice: "God or Man, Soul or Mind, Freedom or Communism."[98] To Chambers, the "crisis of the Western world exists to the degree in which it is indifferent to God."[99] No wonder, then, that he despaired of the West, for it seemed to him incapable of perceiving that the titanic struggle of the age was the irrepressible conflict of "two irreconcilable faiths."[100]

The logic of his analysis led to a third point of crucial importance to the resurgent Right. If Communism was an expression of the struggle between religion and atheism, between God and man, another form of the enemy—less violent but also unpalatable—was secular liberalism. One of the fundamental tenets of postwar conservatism, in fact, was this theory of the philosophical continuity of the Left. As Eric Voegelin put it in 1952, "...if liberalism is understood as the immanent salvation of man and society, communism certainly is its most radical expression."[101] This interpretation of the Left was naturally an affront to those, such as Arthur Schlesinger, Jr., who regarded pragmatic, anti-Communist liberalism of the "vital center" as the best defense against the Soviet challenge.[102] It was also a reflection of conservative rage at the way in which so many liberals (as they saw it) rushed to the defense of a traitor.

To this stream of conservative thought *Witness* contributed powerfully. Here was a man who spoke openly of God, was a devout Quaker, and interpreted history in religious terms. Moreover, he shed a disconcerting new light on the Red Decade. To most liberals, the New Deal seemed (at least in retrospect) to be a moderate reform movement which had preserved capitalism. To Chambers in 1952, the New Deal era seemed revolutionary. To be sure, the revolution—defined as the replacement of "the power of business" by "the power of politics"—had been nonviolent. But it had been a revolution nevertheless, and "at the basic point of the revolution" the "two kinds of revolutionists"—liberals and Communists—were in accord.[103] Chambers asserted that this essential continuity of the Left explained the Hiss case:

> For men who could not see that what they firmly believed was liberalism added up to socialism could scarcely be expected to see what added up to Communism.... they reacted, not like liberals, but with the fierceness of revolutionists whenever that power was at issue....
>
> Every move against the Communists was felt by the liberals as a move against themselves....
>
> The simple fact is that when I took up my little sling and aimed at Communism, I also hit something else. What I hit was the forces of that great socialist revolution, which, in the name of liberalism...has been inching its ice cap over the nation for two decades.... It was the forces of that revolution that I struck at the point of its struggle for power....
>
> It was the forces of this revolution that had smothered the Hiss Case (and much else) for a decade, and fought to smother it in 1948.[104]

Like *The Road to Serfdom* and *Ideas Have Consequences*, *Witness* assaulted the American Left at a moment of acute uncertainty.

The impact of *Witness* on various conservatives was profound. Chambers's three essential themes—the sense of titanic struggle, the interpretation of that struggle as God versus Man, and the belief in the fundamental continuity of liberalism and Communism—struck deep chords and became part of the conservative "case" in the 1950s and after. According to William F. Buckley, Jr., the book tended to have emotional rather than intellectual influence, for Chambers's "un-American" pessimism limited his effect.[105] But whatever their degree of receptivity to Chambers's predictions of doom, for many conservatives the book was a crucial intellectual experience. William Rusher, then a New York lawyer and later the publisher of *National Review*, has remarked that *Witness* exerted a "tremendous influence" on him; it was the "Alpha and Omega" of his perception of the nature of the American Communist mind.[106] Another man deeply affected was John Chamberlain, a veteran journalist and anti-Communist of the 1930s. Chamberlain had met Chambers in 1939 when both were working for *Time*; at that time Chambers had inspired the anti-Communists in the *Time* section of the Newspaper Guild to fight the Communists intelligently. Chambers's "prophetic insight" had taught Chamberlain and others many valuable lessons. When *Witness* appeared, Chamberlain commended it enthusiastically to the readers of *The Freeman*.[107]

The revolt against the Red Decade and all its works was strengthened in the early 1950s by the self-styled new conservative, Peter Viereck. In *Shame and Glory of the Intellectuals*, Viereck lambasted with wit and erudition the fellow-traveling intellectuals of 1930-1947 who, he insisted, had exerted "very real power." The Popular Front "illusion," he contended, had supplied the "moral sugar-coating to Russia's aggression" at the end of World War II.[108] While most intellectuals had responded quickly to Hitler's challenge (that was their "glory"), many had been much less perceptive and resolute in fighting Communism (that was their "shame"). Citing cases from the intellectual wars of his time, Viereck relentlessly exposes the failings of the left-wing Babbitts, "Lumpen-intellectuals," and "Stalinoid upper-middlebrows" who exhibited "*Nation*-ite mentalities."[109] Viereck believed that there were two menaces to civil liberties: "the McCarthyite exaggeration of communist infiltrations and the *Nation*-ite apathy or indulgence toward them." By all means we should combat hysteria, he continued. "But let us also resist hysteria about hysteria."[110] Viereck criticized the "compulsive" fellow travelers who sought to "whitewash" Alger Hiss and prophesied that Hiss might become "the mythic national symbol of the whole guilty 1930's."[111]

The guilty 1930s. What Viereck argued in academic and liberal journals,[112] dozens of others zealously asserted in rightist-oriented magazines like *Plain Talk*, *American Mercury*, and *The Freeman*. The themes are evident enough in these few randomly selected titles: "Ten Fallacies of Fellow-travelers," "Lattimore: Master of Omission," "The Book Reviewers Sell Out China," "The Value of the Ex-Communist," "The Treason of 'Liberalism,'" "Bankruptcy on the Left," "How Many Other Harry Whites?" and "Men Who Scuttled China." Often these articles were written by former Communists and fellow travelers.

It is sometimes said that this extraordinary upsurge of antiliberal sentiment was merely an unbalanced, retrospective, partisan assault on the New Deal, or only a tactic by which Republican politicians strove to regain power. Certainly the Roosevelt administration was often a target of the scholars and publicists of the anti-Communist Right. It would be a mistake, however, to attribute their attack on liberalism simply to political malice. What many anti-Communist conservatives abhorred about the Roosevelt administration was less its domestic reforms than its alleged appeasement of Communism at home and abroad. The Communist issue was not, in other words, just a convenient pretext for criticizing the New Deal, or seeking votes. It was, at least for many conservative intellectuals, the yardstick for measuring the New Dealers' and the liberals' performance in the struggle not just for office but for *survival*. Motivating the intellectual conservatives was something far more deep-seated than concern for the next election. It was the suspicion (for some the conviction) that liberalism meant treason. For the Communist issue was not an ordinary issue. As Forrest Davis, an adviser to Senator Taft and a contributor to *The Freeman*, asked, "Is it not the prevailing political 'liberalism' of the midcentury, that potpourri of indiscriminate do-goodism trending into statism and Marxism and blending so indistinguishably with treason, that is the deepest enemy of the traditional America and the West?" [113] And not just liberalism, but liberals, *people*: Hiss, Lattimore, and all the rest, and the politicians who excused them. These, said conservatives, *these* were the enemy. The liberal, exclaimed Davis, "has looked upon the face of evil and found it half good."[114]

"All right we are two nations."

In developing their case against the Communists, the liberals, and the wretched Red Decade, conservatives relied heavily on what became, in effect, a significant genre of right-wing literature in the late 1940s and

1950s: the hearings and reports of congressional committees investigating Communist influence on American life and politics. These proliferating sources were taken very seriously indeed. They reveal once more the conservative conviction that ideas—and their purveyors—affect the course of history. In one case—the exhaustive Senate Internal Security Subcommittee investigation of the Institute of Pacific Relations and U.S. China policy—the link between Congress and the conservatives was direct: James Burnham worked for the committee and wrote a portion of its final report.[115] This was the report which concluded in 1952 that Professor Owen Lattimore of Johns Hopkins University—an Asian specialist and a principal target of Senator Joseph McCarthy—was "from some time beginning in the 1930's, a conscious articulate instrument of the Soviet conspiracy,"[116] and that the Institute of Pacific Relations had disastrously influenced American policy in ways "favorable to Communist objectives in China" before the defeat of the Nationalists in 1949.[117] The influence of such documents was obvious and immediate; conservatives quoted them from one end of the country to the other. Sometimes their influence was felt in more subtle ways. During the Korean war, for example, a young New Yorker named Jeffrey Hart enlisted in the navy and was sent to Naval Intelligence school. There he became "political" and read the entire twenty-odd volumes of the Senate investigation of the Institute of Pacific Relations. To Hart this seemed to be, all things considered, a very respectable effort at investigation, and it affected him significantly. It convinced him that there really had been a massive Communist penetration of the government bureaucracy. It was one of several influences that moved Hart on a road to the Right, culminating in the 1960s with a senior editorship at *National Review*.[118]

In 1954 the indefatigable Burnham published *The Web of Subversion*, a survey of Communist penetration of the government since the 1930s. The book was backed by *Reader's Digest*, then edited in part by Eugene Lyons.[119] Relying on the huge amount of testimony compiled by various congressional inquiries, he drew a frightening portrait of massive Communist influence on American foreign policy. Burnham summarized what so many conservatives of the early 1950s believed fervently:

> I do not think that the Communist victory in China was "inevitable." I believe that it would not have occurred without a breakdown in U.S. policy, and that this breakdown could have been avoided—at least sufficiently—if not for the influence of the web of subversion....
> ...[T]he units of the underground provided the political

cover on the American flank for the Soviet Empire's triumphant swallowing of Eastern Europe; for the unimpeded
Communist conquest of the bulk of the Italian and French
trade union movements; for the liquidation, under slogans
of reprisal against "collaborationists," of tens of thousands of
Europe's anti-Communists; for the forced return eastward
of hundreds of thousands of anti-Communist war prisoners,
refugees and deserters. The underground can take legitimate
pride in its clever manipulation of American "anti-colonial"
attitudes in connection with Indonesia, the Middle East and
North Africa; its contribution to our continuing paralysis in
the face of Guatemala's creeping subjection to Communist
rule; its sly use of our genuine concern for civil liberties as a
protective shield for its own treachery....[120]

The "web" had not always achieved its objectives, Burnham recognized,
but it had gained many. And—said the conservatives—it had used many
liberals in the process.

The Hiss-Chambers case and the subsequent investigations left a
residue of bitterness that has not yet disappeared from American life.
Yet this cause célèbre was only a prelude to the even more incredible
and savage controversy remembered today as "McCarthyism." If the Hiss
case presented American conservatives with (in Ralph de Toledano's
words) "a view of the chasm,"[121] in the ensuing "McCarthy era" many
conservatives plunged in.

On January 25, 1950, Alger Hiss was sentenced to five years in prison
for perjury. On February 9, 1950, Joseph McCarthy, an obscure junior
senator from Wisconsin, informed an audience of Republican women in
Wheeling, West Virginia that he had in his hand a list of Communists or
Communist sympathizers affiliated with the foreign policy apparatus of
the United States. Barely had the nation recovered from the Hiss-Chambers storm when a new political tornado swirled across the land.

To what extent was the developing postwar conservative intellectual
movement shaped by the McCarthy controversy? The answer is: substantially. It would, of course, be a gross error to equate conservatism
with McCarthyism. The intellectual roots of the conservative revival were
extremely diverse, and the ex-Communists and fervid anti-Communists
were only one segment of a broad spectrum. Anti-Communism did not
originate with Senator McCarthy; neither did libertarianism or traditionalism. Nevertheless, in the great polarization of the early 1950s, a large

segment of conservative intellectuals found themselves on McCarthy's side of the ideological barricades, and a considerable number proclaimed themselves his allies. Joseph McCarthy left a visible mark on the American Right.

The deep identification of some conservatives with McCarthy was manifested in many ways. When the Wisconsin lawmaker made a lengthy speech denouncing the foreign policy record of General George C. Marshall, his speech was applauded in *The Freeman* by Suzanne La Follette,[122] a former associate of Albert Jay Nock, a member in the 1930s of the American Committee for the Defense of Leon Trotsky (against Moscow purge charges), and, in 1950, a founder and managing editor of *The Freeman*.[123] When McCarthy published in 1952 his book *McCarthyism: the Fight for America*, it received sympathetic attention from John Chamberlain, another survivor of the ideological wars of the 1930s. Chamberlain reiterated some of the standard conservative complaints about the Red Decade:

> In the late thirties and on up to 1945 and 1946 any author who deliberately provoked the Communists could count on a standard smear treatment....
>   ...By their oblique control of writing in the thirties and the early forties, the Communists managed to poison the intellectual life of a whole nation—and the poison has lingered on.[124]

The time had come, he said, to eliminate the disease and its "end-result," subversion in government. Chamberlain was pleased that McCarthy's book was full of "sober citations" and that the formerly "unsophisticated young politician from the Middle West" was maturing as an anti-Communist leader.[125]

Undoubtedly the most systematic—in fact, the only significant—effort to defend McCarthy was undertaken in 1954 by two young Yale alumni, William F. Buckley, Jr. and L. Brent Bozell. Buckley was already famous for *God and Man at Yale*, while his brother-in-law Bozell, a lawyer, had been converted in college to vigorous, anti-Communist Roman Catholicism. In *McCarthy and His Enemies* they examined the record of the senator and his foes through 1952. The two authors strove to give the appearance, at least, of scrupulous fairness. Their analysis of McCarthy's charges was detailed and buttressed by extensive appendices. Rather frequently they criticized McCarthy outright: an "egregious blunder" here, "gratuitous sensationalism" there, occasionally "outrageous," "censurable," and "reprehensible" conduct. But despite McCarthy's faults and lapses,

Buckley and Bozell concluded that the senator was fundamentally correct. There *had* been extensive Communist subversion of the government. The State Department *had* been incredibly negligent in its loyalty-security program. Buckley and Bozell were especially angered by what they regarded as the high-handed, one-sided, partisan misconduct of the Tydings Committee, established by the Senate in 1950 to investigate McCarthy's initial accusations. McCarthy, in short, had not been refuted. He had not created a "reign of terror." Nor were his methods generally objectionable; at worst, they were no more objectionable than those of other rough-and-tumble politicians of his day—like Harry Truman. Buckley and Bozell emphasized that McCarthy had become a leader in mobilizing America's response to Communism and warned that "if McCarthy's enemies are successful in discrediting him, the mobilization will lose momentum and, perhaps, grind to a dead halt."[126] The two authors contended that "on McCarthyism hang the hopes of America for effective resistance to Communist infiltration."[127] In a sentence that affronted many liberals, they declared: "...as long as McCarthyism fixes its goal with its present precision, it is a movement around which men of good will and stern morality can close ranks."[128]

On the day the Buckley-Bozell book was published, a reception for the young authors was held in New York City; among those who attended were Senator McCarthy and his assistant Roy Cohn.[129] At the reception Buckley stated that he did not expect to receive fair treatment because of the "mass distortion of facts" in the controversy.[130] Certainly liberals were critical.[131] In conservative circles, however, the response, not surprisingly, was more favorable. In *Faith and Freedom*, the journal of Spiritual Mobilization, the antistatist Frank Chodorov praised the book.[132] In *The Freeman*, the ex-Trotsky supporter Max Eastman concurred. McCarthy's weakness, Eastman explained, was "a temperamental failure" to do the necessary job in "a mature and thoughtful way." The sins of the "McCarthy-baiters" were far more dangerous: the policies that lost China and much of Europe, and a "refusal" to recognize the desperate struggle of the West with Communism.[133]

The services of Buckley and Bozell to McCarthy's cause went beyond their book. In 1953, for instance, Buckley wrote a speech for McCarthy criticizing President Eisenhower's nomination of James B. Conant to be high commissioner to Germany. In 1954 McCarthy temporarily designated Buckley a stand-in for a televised rebuttal to Edward R. Murrow's attacks.[134] Bozell also worked extensively for the Wisconsin senator by serving as a speechwriter on many occasions.[135]

The authors of *McCarthy and His Enemies* were not the only people to defend the senator energetically. In 1953, twenty-eight right-wing partisans sent a letter to 700 newspapers accusing the media of treating the anti-Communist leader unfairly. Lambasting the book reviewers for ignoring *McCarthyism: The Fight for America* while lavishly and thought-lessly praising Owen Lattimore's *Ordeal by Slander*, the twenty-eight demanded to know what methods the critics of McCarthy had used to defeat the Communist menace within the U.S. government. How accurate, they asked, is the assertion that McCarthy had "attacked and injured innocent people"? Among the signers were several prominent conservative intellectuals: John Chamberlain, Frank Chodorov, Ralph de Toledano, John T. Flynn, Suzanne La Follette, Eugene Lyons, Felix Morley, Frank Hanighen of *Human Events*, Devin Garrity of the Devin-Adair publishing firm, and Henry Regnery.[136] A year later, as the Senate moved toward censure of McCarthy, a number of conservatives again protested. To them the censure proposal of the Watkins Committee was an attempt "to suppress unpopular people and unpopular ideas." Never in the history of Congress, they claimed, had a senator been censured for "discourtesy toward a witness,"[137] and the seven signers doubted that the code being invoked against McCarthy would ever be used again. To the seven the Watkins Committee report was an "abject surrender" to executive power—a clear sign of totalitarian government. The signers included George Schuyler, a black journalist, Frank Hanighen, Eugene Lyons, Freda Utley, James Burnham, William F. Buckley, Jr., and John T. Flynn.[138] When, in mid-1954, the Joint Committee Against Communism in New York held a dinner in honor of Roy Cohn, many right-wing figures, including Buckley, were there. The *New York Times* reported that the audience of 2,000 was "wildly enthusiastic."[139]

Not all conservative intellectuals, by any means, participated in the McCarthy crusade. Peter Viereck was particularly critical of what he perceived as a neo-populist threat to civil liberties. To Viereck, both Lattimore and McCarthy aided Communism, Lattimore "by the way he defended it," McCarthy "by the way he attacks it."[140] Moreover, he wrote in 1955, McCarthyism was not conservative at all. It was status-resentful "radical anti-conservatism," a vengeful expression of "the same old isolationist, Anglophobe, Germanophile revolt of radical Populist lunatic-fringers against the eastern, educated Anglicized elite."[141] It—the New Right—was "the most anti-conservative uprising in native Americana since the Whiskey Rebellion of 1794."[142] It was easy enough to guess the side with which Viereck—an Oxford-educated internationalist in foreign policy and a professor at an Eastern college—identified. To Viereck, this New Right was a revolt of the masses, "the plebeian insurrection of right-wing direct democracy,"[143] of "Rousseauistic mass democracy,"[144] which true, aristocratic, antidemocratic conservatism was duty-bound to oppose. For him, conservatism and McCarthyism were antithetical.

Viereck's analysis was corroborated in part by the respected Jewish sociologist, Will Herberg. A native of New York City with a doctorate from Columbia University, Herberg had been an active Communist during the late 1920s and early 1930s. Expelled from the party in an ideological feud, Herberg eventually became research analyst and educational director for the International Ladies Garment Workers Union (1935-1948). After several years as a writer and lecturer, he joined the faculty of Drew University in 1955.[145]

Although he still considered himself a liberal in 1950, Herberg was gradually moving toward a Burkean conservative position in the 1950s.[146] One sign of his shift was an essay on McCarthyism for the *New Leader* in 1954. "McCarthyism," he argued, was only the latest form of a menacing national phenomenon, "government by rabble-rousing." According to Herberg, the Founding Fathers in their wisdom had established a carefully balanced government designed to prevent turbulent, "irresponsible *mass-democracy*." Now, however, with the advent of mass communications (especially radio), it was possible for political leaders to bypass deliberative institutions and appeal directly to the masses. The first great breach had been made by President Franklin Roosevelt, who used his "fireside chats" to pressure Congress. Indeed, modern liberals from Roosevelt to Senator Kefauver (with his spectacular televised investigations of crime) must bear much of the responsibility, said Herberg, for making "government by rabble-rousing" so commonplace. There was plenty of blame to go around:

> Here is where "McCarthyism" comes in. "McCarthyism" is the logical outcome of the system of government by rabble-rousing initiated in the first years of the New Deal....
> McCarthy, like Roosevelt, is impatient with the restraints and limitations of what are called proper constitutional channels....
> ...Both ["Liberals" and "nationalists"], though of course they would not admit it, are actually *radicals* whose whole approach is subversive of American constitutional democracy.

The remedy, Herberg stated, was "a good, sound, responsible conservatism" of the kind being offered by Viereck and Reinhold Niebuhr.[147]

Once again the new conservatives' aloofness from the masses and "totalitarian democracy" was evident.

Still another new conservative who kept his distance from McCarthy was the historical sociologist Robert Nisbet. As a graduate student at Berkeley in the late 1930s, Nisbet had fought a strong local Popular Front influence. In the mid-1940s he became a charter member of the Berkeley chapter of Americans for Democratic Action, organized in large part, he thought, to eliminate the taint of Communism from liberal ranks. At about that time, Arthur Schlesinger, Jr.'s *The Vital Center* appealed to Nisbet greatly. Within a few months, however, as the ADA became in Nisbet's eyes just one more segment of the liberal wing of the Democratic Party, Nisbet resigned and followed an independent path. In the turmoil of the 1950s, he tried to steer a middle course. On the one hand, as a firm anti-Communist, he "detested utterly" Henry Wallace's Progressive Party and, a little later, the "professional, twenty-four-hour-a-day McCarthy-haters." But McCarthy himself and his crusade were equally distasteful. McCarthy and his supporters seemed to him, as they did to Viereck, to represent a recrudescence of radical, xenophobic populism. Distrustful of both extremes, Nisbet adopted what he considered the appropriate attitude: "A plague on both your houses."[148]

The wariness of McCarthy which Viereck, Herberg, and Nisbet evinced found an echo in an unexpected quarter: Whittaker Chambers, the very symbol for conservatives of the anti-Communist hero. When *McCarthy and His Enemies* appeared in 1954, Chambers and Buckley began a correspondence which lasted until Chambers's death in 1961. While Chambers was impressed by the Buckley-Bozell book, he was dubious about McCarthy from the beginning. In letter after letter he expressed his concern: "...we live in terror that Senator McCarthy will one day make some irreparable blunder which will play directly into the hands of our common enemy and discredit the whole anti-Communist effort for a long while to come." The trouble, said Chambers, was that McCarthy "can't think. He is a slugger and a rabble-rouser" who "simply knows that somebody threw a tomato and the general direction from which it came." When McCarthy died in 1957, Chambers observed that McCarthy never understood the struggle against Communism. He never had any strategy—only one tactic: "Attack." And that was not sufficient.[149]

Chambers's deep reservations about the senator from Wisconsin were shared by his friend Ralph de Toledano. In his autobiography, published a few years after McCarthy's death, Toledano recounted his uneasy role in the great controversy. He had been, undeniably, a "hostage to the

McCarthy forces," driven into the maelstrom by the "malevolence" of the opposition. But Toledano had not really been happy. McCarthy was a "nihilist" who had damaged the conservative cause by irresponsible charges, such as the suggestion that General Marshall was a traitor. Buffeted by Left and Right, Toledano arrived at a point where he felt he could neither defend nor attack McCarthy, so appalled was he by the passions of both sides.[150]

The attitude of one of the principal figures in the conservative revival—Russell Kirk—is especially interesting, for in a sense Kirk was a man in the middle of this controversy. On the one hand, he was, like Viereck, a new conservative, a disciple of Burke, Tocqueville, Ortega, and Nock—critical of the masses, undiluted democracy, and "the silent tyranny of the majority."[151] "I am," he wrote to Viereck,

> a kind of American W.H. Mallock, devoted to the classical tradition in literature and society, wandering about to decaying country houses, and dedicated to the cause of conservatism in all things.[152]

Intellectually and temperamentally he was worlds apart from Senator McCarthy. On the other hand, Kirk was a Midwesterner, an opponent of American foreign policy in World War II, and a supporter of Senator Taft for president in 1952.[153] If Viereck's sociological profile of provincial, "populist" McCarthyites is correct, there is some reason to expect that Kirk might have supported the Wisconsin senator in his heyday.

Perhaps because of his varied intellectual background, Kirk's position in the McCarthy affair cannot be characterized in a single phrase. Kirk was certainly no admirer of the senator: "I think of Joseph McCarthy substantially what I thought of Claude Pepper," he told Viereck.[154] Both men were demagogues. Nevertheless, Kirk was not prepared to dismiss utterly all the charges which McCarthy and his cohorts made.[155] He denounced the Tydings Committee's "indifference to truth" and indicated that he took seriously *The Web of Subversion* and *McCarthy and His Enemies*.[156] With particular relish he scoffed at the notion—spread by "doctrinaire liberals" like Henry Steele Commager and Harold Taylor— that America was in the grip of a near-fascist hysteria. The "curious pretended terror of Senator McCarthy," he called it, noting that "the dispute over loyalty has resulted in very little actual injustice or repression in America, as yet."[157] Like some other conservatives, Kirk believed that the McCarthy "menace" had been exaggerated.[158]

Kirk's views on the loyalty-security issue were developed at length in an article in *Confluence* in 1954. While calling the Buckley-Bozell effort a "sober and well-written book,"[159] Kirk dissociated himself from McCarthy. McCarthy had "abused" his privileges—and so had other senators:

> But to endeavor to convince the friends of America abroad that Senator McCarthy is a dread menace to American society and to the future of humanity, as certain well-meaning "liberals" are doing, is to create a tempest in a teapot and to distort the truth about American politics. Senator Joe McCarthy, whatever one thinks of him, is not undemocratic, being the gift of the Congress of Industrial Organizations to America (which supported him against La Follette) and immensely popular in his own state. Neither does he have any totalitarian program; he has no program at all; he is, instead, in the old line of destructive critics in the American Congress whose function it is to bedevil the executive arm of government for good or ill.[160]

McCarthy was really a product of a vacuum in the Senate, a vacuum left by the death of Taft. Kirk was severely critical of liberals who, having cheered such demagogic investigations as the Nye Committee's exposé of the "merchants of death" in the 1930s,[161] now professed alarm about investigations of Communism. In fact, he strongly implied, the rise of McCarthy was in part the fault of the sinful liberals. Americans in the 1950s were properly anxious to secure "loyalty toward the prescriptive values of American society."

> This is not a loyalty to be derided.... If already certain ugly and ominous tendencies may be discerned in the American insistence upon "loyalty," I suspect that these are the consequences of the mocking of loyalty among many of the *illuminati*, for some years past, and of a growing realization that many persons endowed by the public with high responsibilities had lost all idea of what is loyalty to a nation's traditions.[162]

Not surprisingly, Kirk's position failed to satisfy Peter Viereck. When Viereck attempted to organize conservative intellectuals to oppose McCarthy, Kirk refused—repelled, he later said, by Viereck's overzealous "reverse McCarthyism."[163] Several years later Viereck would accuse Kirk and his "group" of being "McCarthy-corrupted" and of failing to repudiate the "dangerous" senator from Wisconsin.[164]

Thus a fair number of conservative intellectuals—particularly the new conservatives—remained in varying degrees aloof from McCarthy.

But the pressures of the controversy were intense and virtually impossible to avoid. In many cases they hardened the intellectual Right. The careers of two men, William Rusher and James Burnham, exemplify this effect.

Born in 1923 in Chicago of Republican parents (his mother was from Alf Landon's home town), Rusher moved to New York City at an early age and grew up as a moderate-liberal Republican. A supporter of Landon for president in 1936 and of Wendell Willkie in 1940, Rusher dedicated his senior thesis at Princeton in 1943 to Willkie and supported Dewey in 1948. During the postwar years he was "fascinated and surprised" by the House Un-American Activities Committee's exposure of Communism in government; he was affected by the conviction of Alger Hiss, Truman's dismissal of General MacArthur from the Korean War command, and, especially, by *Witness*. Still, in 1952, Rusher was an Eisenhower Republican; he had never been an isolationist and had been little interested in the laissez-faire economics of *The Freeman*.

The McCarthy controversy helped push Rusher further Right. Although never temperamentally attuned to McCarthy, Rusher was "totally sickened" by the "dishonest" attack that the liberals launched against him. By 1954, Rusher was disillusioned with Eisenhower as well, in part because of the President's role in the McCarthy affair, and was "ripe" for the founding of *National Review*, to which he became a charter subscriber in 1955. Rusher, a lawyer, served as a special counsel to the Senate Internal Security Subcommittee in 1956 and 1957, when he became publisher of *National Review*. The liberal, Eastern-oriented Republican had, thanks in part to McCarthyism, become a dedicated conservative.[165]

The effect of the controversy on Burnham was similarly harsh. Shortly after World War II, Burnham still considered himself a man of the anti-Communist Left—rather like Sidney Hook.[166] He remained on *Partisan Review* even while contributing to right-wing journals and assisting a congressional investigation. By 1953, however, Burnham was no longer comfortable at *Partisan Review*. In a letter severing his last ties with the Left, he noted that many felt his presence there an "anomaly" and that the journal seemed to regard "McCarthyism" as "the dominant issue." But, he insisted, it was *not* the dominant issue; in fact "McCarthyism" was "an invention of the Communist tacticians, who launched it and are exploiting it." Burnham professed to be neither "pro" nor "anti" McCarthy the man; like all politicians' records, McCarthy's was a mixture of good and bad. But Burnham refused to be part of an Eastern intellectual anti-McCarthy crusade abhorrently reminiscent of the Red Decade. He therefore resigned from *Partisan Review*;[167] two years later he became a founding editor of the militantly conservative *National Review*.

Obviously, then, the McCarthy episode had a traumatic importance for the American intellectual Right that far transcended the day-to-day argument about loyalty risks, security clearances, and McCarthy's methods. During these years and long afterward, many conservative intellectuals strove to understand what the larger significance of the uproar was. To William Rusher, the key to the dispute lay in the peculiar circumstances of 1950. The conviction of Hiss, he claimed, was the "nadir" of liberalism: guilt ridden and defensive, the liberals "desperately needed an issue upon which to base a counterattack against their tormentors." McCarthy's speech at Wheeling supplied it—so they thought. But when McCarthy, astonishingly, refused to budge, the liberals were driven to escalate the conflict and obtain "some symbolic act of judgment." When that judgment—censure by the Senate—was finally attained, the furor over McCarthyism disappeared.[168] Others emphasized the cleavage between the intellectuals and the rest of the country as a significant element in the turmoil. This, in part, was Viereck's analysis; it was also, in part, Buckley's. To Buckley the country consisted of two groups: the "'university' crowd" and the "'non-university' crowd"; Joe McCarthy appealed to the latter. In doing so, he could not, Buckley argued, use the "protocol" of the graduate student. To make his point he had to be blunt and audacious.[169] Many others also interpreted the debate in terms of a compromised elite versus the mass of the country.[170]

A few years after the affair subsided, James Burnham assessed its larger significance. Clearly something more than the number of Communists in government was at stake. According to Burnham, during the 1930s and much of the 1940s Communism was "legitimized within most of the structure of our community"; it did not hurt anyone to be known as a Communist. But as the cold war intensified, the United States deliberately engaged in "a non-violent manhunt" designed to extirpate Communism as a legitimate force in American life. The "basic strata of citizens" had come to the conclusion that Communists did not belong here, that "the line must be drawn somewhere." And this decision, said Burnham, was resisted by the liberals. Therein lay the crisis of the 1950s:

> The issue was philosophical, metaphysical: what kind of community are we? And the Liberals, including the rationally anti-Communist Liberals, were correct in labeling McCarthy The Enemy, and in destroying him. From the Liberal standpoint—

secularist, egalitarian, relativist—the line is not drawn, Relativism must be Absolute.[171]

As Burnham's article revealed, McCarthyism furnished the context
for the emergence of one of the principal elements of conservative thought
since 1945: the critique of the liberal theory of the open society. In a
sense, McCarthyism *was* this critique. With typical fearlessness, Buckley
and Bozell led the way. No society, they contended, has ever been or
ever can be totally "open" or totally indifferent to its central values.

> Not only is it *characteristic* of society to create institu-
> tions and to defend them with sanctions. Societies *must* do
> so—or else they cease to exist. The members of a society must
> share certain values if that society is to cohere; and cohere it
> must if it is to survive. In order to assert and perpetuate these
> values, it must do constant battle against competing values....
> A hard and indelible fact of freedom is that a conformity
> of sorts is always dominant.... [Therefore] the freeman's prin-
> cipal concern is that it shall be a conformity that honors the
> values he esteems rather than those he rejects.[172]

Liberals, they continued, were hypocritical in pretending that they opposed all orthodoxy; in reality the liberals merely wanted to impose their
own "conformity—with Liberalism"[173]

The question of orthodoxy, the two authors maintained, was the heart
of the McCarthy issue. Yes, they said, America was indeed "rallying around
an orthodoxy": the exclusion of Communism from respectability and influence in national life. Yes, they cheerfully admitted, McCarthyism was
indeed solidifying "conformity"—*"on the Communist issue."* This was
the meaning of the Smith Act, the McCarran Act, and various "social
sanctions" being imposed against domestic Communists and their sympathizers. The American people, Buckley and Bozell argued, had carefully examined and "emphatically rejected" the claims of Communism.
Now, embroiled in a worldwide war against Communism, they were moving—deliberately, properly, and by means of McCarthyism—to penalize
and curtail an unassimilable philosophy and "those in our land who help
the enemy."[174]

At times Buckley and Bozell seemed uneasy about the possible implications of their argument. After all, Buckley in particular had been
influenced by libertarianism and knew personally both Albert Jay Nock
and Frank Chodorov. How, then, could he propose "conformity"? The
two young authors therefore stressed that McCarthyism was aimed "not

at *new* ideas but at *Communist* ideas" and that it was not likely to go beyond that limitation. Moreover, they noted that McCarthyism was "nine parts social sanction to one part legal sanction," and even the legal restriction of freedom was slight compared to "the total tyranny of compulsory military service." They cautioned the "balanced libertarian" to apply legal curbs only when "the exigencies of the situation" require them. But—and here was the transitional argument—that time was now.[175]

The Buckley-Bozell attack upon the "open society" was unmistakably dependent on the theories of a man who had been their teacher and friend at Yale: the political scientist Willmoore Kendall. Indeed, there is evidence to suggest that Kendall himself may have written part of *McCarthy and His Enemies*.[176] A native of Oklahoma, a Rhodes Scholar in the 1930s, Kendall had been a man of the far Left in the Red Decade. But by the late 1940s he was known as a defender of Whittaker Chambers and a vehement, articulate critic of liberalism.[177]

Never one to be cautious, Kendall argued daringly in his dissertation in 1941 that John Locke, far from being a devotee of inalienable natural rights, had actually been a majority-rule democrat.[178] This was what Kendall called himself in the early cold war years, and what he meant by it he made clear in a letter in 1949. It was "not only the right but the *duty*" of the members of a democracy "to use public policy as an instrument for creating the kind of society their values call for...." As an "old fashioned majority-rule democrat," he rejected as inherently undemocratic any effort to limit majorities by bills of rights. Discussing the Nixon-Mundt bill to control Communism, Kendall suggested deportation as a possible sanction against Communists. (Back in the 1930s, the sanction would have applied to Nazis, too.) Kendall acknowledged that "liquidation of a minority" must be a very careful undertaking. But he insisted on two principles:

> ...a) that a democratic society that has a meaning to preserve, as I think ours still does, must stand prepared to make such decisions, and b) that the surest way for it to lose its meaning is for it to tell itself, and its potential dissidents, that where dissidence is concerned, the sky's the limit.

In another letter several years later Kendall amplified his point. *His* campaign against Communists would not depend, as Buckley's and Bozell's ultimately did, on proving that domestic Communists were a clear and present danger. Indeed, at the moment they were not a *clear* and *present* danger at all. His argument was different: "we do not make sense as a community so long as we tolerate Communists and pro-communists in our midst." Or as he put it on another occasion, "The reason for striking at [domestic] Communists is not so much that they are dangerous as that they are incapable of participating in democratic government."[179] Kendall's breathtaking majoritarianism was diametrically opposed to the natural rights philosophy which undergirded so much of the concurrent libertarian conservative revival. It was also, needless to say, anathema to the civil libertarian Left in the McCarthy era.

A few years after the McCarthy episode faded into history, Kendall attempted to explain the true meaning of McCarthyism. The basic issue had not been McCarthy himself; after all, people were "mad" at one another in the Hiss case, long before McCarthy was heard of. Nor had the issue simply been one of different opinions about the seriousness of the Communist threat; this answer could not explain the intensity of the dispute—indeed, its "civil war dimension." The issue had not been one of the executive versus the legislative branch, either; people do not become *that* angry over abstract "separation of powers." The clue to the proper explanation, rather, lay in the fact that each side was really accusing the other of "heresy." The battle was a debate ("with genuine civil war potential") over the fundamental nature of American society. Were we or were we not an "open society"? Could the United States proscribe and "persecute" an "undesirable" movement like the Communists *even if* there were no immediate peril? Did the United States have a consensus—an orthodoxy—which could be defended by legal and other sanctions? Were all questions "open" questions, or did we hold certain truths to be beyond dispute? In all the confusion and maneuvering of the battle, said Kendall, "McCarthyites" (that is, broadly speaking, the Right) answered these questions one way, and "anti-McCarthyites" (the Left) another. The McCarthy episode was thus an intellectual and spiritual crisis of the gravest dimensions.[180]

Kendall was not the only conservative intellectual to plead for orthodoxy and to attack the purely open society. In the same period Peter Viereck, while solicitous of civil liberties and hostile to "thought-control nationalists," called America a properly "semi-closed" society and criticized the "liberalism of suicide" which would allow "a communazi military conspiracy" to function as "a political 'party.'"[181] Similarly, the conservative émigré sociologist Ernest van den Haag argued that the outlawing of groups with subversive and totalitarian aims was quite compatible with democratic principles.[182] But it was Kendall who articulated most systematically this fundamental challenge to liberal theories. It was one of his principal contributions to postwar American conservative thought.

Clearly, then, the inner civil war of the McCarthy years elicited a variety of interpretations of its meaning for conservatives. But whatever their divergent emphases, on one point, at least, many conservatives would have agreed: the crusade of Joseph McCarthy had drawn many of them together in a bruising, common struggle and had helped to forge part of the conservative movement.

Yet it is probable that many conservatives came to realize that this was not sufficient compensation for the defeat they received. For the extraordinarily bitter McCarthy affair[183] was, in a larger sense, a defeat.[184] Ralph de Toledano sensed this in 1960 when he wrote sadly, "We became partisans, and by the dialectics of the situation, we took over some of the characteristics of our antagonists—thereby losing the sense of moral ascendancy we had until then enjoyed."[185] But more than that was involved. If McCarthyism helped shape the conservative intellectual movement, it also left that movement weakened and defensive; the ghost of McCarthy has remained a burden upon it. In 1971, William F. Buckley, Jr. reflected on this fact. Up to 1954, he observed, most conservatives had supported McCarthy, "however fastidiously." Then they began to turn, particularly after McCarthy attacked President Eisenhower. [186] In the turmoil of the Wisconsin senator's downfall, the "backlash" set the conservative cause back to the pre-McCarthy period. Many liberals, according to Buckley, had "genocidal urges" toward any conservatives who had ever defended McCarthy. Right-wing columnists George Sokolsky and Fulton Lewis, Jr. lost business because of their support of the senator. Nearly two decades later, Buckley himself still received criticism because of his earlier support of the Wisconsin senator. He therefore concluded that the whole controversy had injured conservatism "a good deal."[187]

For better or for worse, the domestic cold war branded the American Right for a generation.

By 1955 the contours of conservatism had in some ways changed considerably from those of fifteen or even ten years earlier. Global anti-Communism had triumphed over "isolationism"; the exigencies of the cold war conflicted, at times, with the tenacious antistatism characteristic of much of the Right. The magnitude of this transition was rendered even more striking by the fact that many conservatives of 1955—includ-

ing some of the most militant anti-Communists—had been "isolationists" (even, in some cases, members of America First) before Pearl Harbor. The list included John Chamberlain, Frank Chodorov, William Henry
Chamberlin, Henry Regnery, Devin Garrity, William F. Buckley, Jr.,
Russell Kirk, and Edmund Opitz. Two questions therefore arise: How
easy was the transition? How did conservatives rationalize it?

The tensions between "Old Right" nationalism and "New Right"
internationalism were repeatedly evident in the postwar decade. In 1947,
for instance, James Burnham opposed the rapid demobilization that had
followed the war;[188] yet only three years earlier, Sergeant Russell Kirk,
then in the army, had vigorously applauded demobilization and had skep-
tically noted the army leadership's distrust of the Communists. In 1944
Kirk predicted that New Dealers would prolong the state of war after
the Axis powers' defeat in order to maintain prosperity. They would justify keeping men in arms (and off the job market) by *creating* an enemy:
Russia.[189] While Burnham, formulating global strategy in 1947, considered conscription a sheer necessity, Kirk and many others regarded it as
"slavery."[190] In 1947 the isolationist-revisionist Harry Elmer Barnes castigated Burnham's *The Struggle for the World* as "the most dangerous
and 'un-American' book of the year." It was, Barnes claimed, "a blueprint for aggressive war" and "confirmation" of his thesis that World War
II would cause "the ultimate triumph of Hitlerian attitudes and policies
in this country."[191] Felix Morley, an editor of *Human Events*, was similarly alarmed. He accused Burnham, "as a former Marxist," of failing to
understand American traditions and principles. While Morley shared
Burnham's anti-Communism and agreed that "we must stop trying to
appease" the Russians, Burnham's book revealed that "the very real threat
of Soviet Russia...will be utilized to advocate the dissolution of the American Republic" and "the establishment of an American empire in its
place."[192]

Later, during the Korean war, Leonard Read at the Foundation for
Economic Education criticized American intervention in that conflict.
In a celebrated pamphlet, *Conscience on the Battlefield*, Read repudiated the justification of Korea on anti-Communist grounds alone. Coercion of men to fight there was wrong; indeed, coercion was "the essential
characteristic of communism." If Americans really believed that Korea
was so vital to their country's security, Read implied, they would go to
Korea on their own free will. But "this war could not have happened
short of involuntary service." Moreover,"...interference in strange areas
may make you the initiator of violence rather than the protector of

rectitude."And initiation of violence was evil. "To fight evil with evil is only to make evil general."[193] Read's article, which he considers the best piece he ever wrote, aroused a considerable stir on the Right.[194] It revealed starkly the simmering divergence of views in the heterogeneous conservative intellectual movement.

Another product of the friction between Old Right and New Right was the resignation of Felix Morley as an editor of *Human Events* in 1950. As a classical liberal, antimilitarist, and anti-imperialist, Morley often found himself at odds with coeditor Frank Hanighen about foreign policy issues in the late 1940s. When Morley unhappily concluded that "the Communist grip on Eastern Europe could not and would not be shaken," he urged *Human Events* to support the strengthening of "the German and Japanese barriers to Communism but avoid any direct affronts to Russia...." Hanighen disagreed and argued (according to Morley) that Morley was "tending to be 'soft on Communism.'" Morley returned from a trip to Europe in 1949 "with doubts about the value of the Cold War" and a desire to secure full editorial control of *Human Events*. When, in 1950, Hanighen and Henry Regnery (the other two stockholders of *Human Events*) rejected Morley's proposal, he resigned. A generation later, Morley stated that the "cleavage" between himself and Hanighen had reflected the developing differences between Old Right and New— "between a generally pacific, even isolated, America and an actively interventionist America."[195]

The foreign policy differences among conservatives were felt with special force by William Henry Chamberlin and William F. Buckley, Jr. In a letter in July 1949, Chamberlin praised Senator Robert Taft for his integrity and domestic record but lamented his opposition to NATO. Taft was "so dreadfully wrongheaded" in foreign affairs; if Taft were to be opposed by a liberal but anti-Communist Democrat for President in 1952, Chamberlin said he would face a "painful dilemma."[196] Buckley was also aware of the tensions. An enthusiastic America Firster in 1941,[197] he was, as the pupil of both Nock and Kendall, almost the personification of the conflicting strands of conservative thought. In an election year essay in 1952, Buckley's ambivalence was acute. While the first half of his article bristled with references to Nock, Herbert Spencer, and the "Leviathan State," the second half declared that "the thus far invincible aggressiveness of the Soviet Union" was a "menace to our freedom" and even to American survival. Rather gloomily he concluded that until Communism ceased to endanger us, we would have to acquiesce in the Big Government required to defeat it.[198] The foreign danger came first.

These tensions and pressures burst forth in 1954 and 1955 in a series of polemics in the conservative press. In *Faith and Freedom*, Murray Rothbard debated William Henry Chamberlin and William Schlamm, a former adviser to Henry Luce. In *The Freeman* Schlamm and Frank Chodorov exchanged fusillades. The arguments of the isolationist libertarians (Rothbard and Chodorov) were essentially twofold. First, they denied that the Soviet Union posed any immediate military threat to the United States. The United States had not been attacked, said Rothbard; both men insisted that Russia's recent territorial conquests were a source of weakness. Secondly, both feared that war would enhance the powers of government and destroy liberty at home. The real enemy, they strenuously declared, was the State, of which Communism was but one variant. In reply, Schlamm (a German ex-Communist) and Chamberlin (a former sympathizer with the "Russian experiment") declared vehemently that the Communist threat was imminent and ominous. Communism was *inherently* expansionary, totalitarian, unappeasable, and "incurably aggressive"; the Soviet goal was world conquest. Later, writing in the *New Leader*, Chamberlin characterized as "appeasement" Rothbard's suggestion that the United States trade with the Communists and abandon all its foreign bases. Chamberlin denied that he was advocating crusading liberal internationalism. Invoking the Taft-conservative language of national interest, he contended simply that "vital interests" of the nation were definitely at stake abroad.[199]

Viewing this developing controversy in 1954, Buckley was pessimistic. The dispute between what he called "liberation or interventionist conservatives" and "containment conservatives" represented "an enormous fissure" in the Right, and he was certain that the movement would be harmed by it.[200] In a sense the young activist was correct; in intellectual terms, the two sides were irreconcilable. But in immediate, practical terms, no cataclysmic fissure occurred. The unmistakable tendency of conservative thought was illuminated early in 1955 by that sensitive barometer, Buckley himself. Commenting on the Schlamm-Chodorov exchange, Buckley conceded that the future might bring "both war and slavery." Still, he would rather take his chances later with a powerful domestic State than adopt a foreign policy that would allow Communism to conquer the world. He therefore counted himself, "dejectedly, among those who favor a carefully planned showdown, and who are prepared to go to war to frustrate communist designs."[201] The anti-Communists had won the mind of Buckley and the great bulk of the Right.

One of the most notable features of the transition, as both Buckley and Rothbard later agreed,[202] was precisely the ease with which it occurred. The debates did not last very long, really; the movement was not substantially ruptured. How was it possible? How could such an apparently massive shift take place so smoothly? Four factors account for this remarkable development. First, as Rothbard has noted, the hard-core "isolationist" Old Right was weakened by attrition in the 1950s. Senator Taft died in 1953; the anti-imperialist journalist Garet Garrett (one of Rothbard's heroes) died a year later; Frank Chodorov suffered a paralyzing stroke in the late 1950s. Leonard Read and his colleagues at FEE, after venturing into the Korean war debate, withdrew, Rothbard said, into their more conventional, nonpolitical activities. Rothbard himself drifted away. After supporting Senator Everett Dirksen of Illinois for president in 1952 (he considered Senator Taft a compromising "Socialist sellout"), Rothbard left the Republican Party when Eisenhower "stole" the nomination from Taft. In the mid-1950s, despite his debates on foreign policy, he exerted no significant influence on the Right. Second, according to Rothbard the social base of the Old Right—the Protestant Midwest—yielded in preeminence to the rising Eastern, urban Roman Catholics for whom people like Buckley allegedly spoke.[203] Certainly there is a measure of truth in this observation. A disproportionate number of conservative intellectuals in the 1950s were Catholics, at a time when the Church, headed by Pope Pius XII, was uncompromisingly anti-Communist. Nor should one overlook the fact that many Catholics by birth or ancestry were from Eastern Europe and were thus doubly cognizant of Communism. All these factors tended, no doubt, to pull conservatism—both intellectually and politically—out of the orbit of the Old Right.

A third important lubricant of the transition was the simple fact that for most conservative intellectuals the world of 1955 looked very different from the world of 1940. Hence, American foreign policy, to some degree, had to be different also. Europe and Asia did not seem so remote any longer. This factor explains in particular William Henry Chamberlin's conversion from isolationism. In 1940, he later wrote, there were two evil nations, Germany and Russia; Chamberlin had hoped to balance them off and let them destroy each other. As a result of World War II and the resultant rise of the Soviet Union, such "maneuvering" was now impossible: "There is no balance of power in the world—except as we supply it ourselves."[204] The United States must fill the vacuum.

Finally, despite the complaints in the 1950s of extreme antistatists like Chodorov and Rothbard, and despite the ambivalence of Buckley, active anti-Communism at home and abroad fitted in very well with other

strands of the multifaceted conservative intellectual revival. Most libertarians, for instance, did *not* feel any burning inconsistency between support for individual liberty (especially economic liberty) at home and tough
anti-Communism either at home or abroad. The former depended on
the latter. Indeed, for libertarians such as Chamberlin, Frank Meyer,
and Max Eastman, the experience of Communism—its deification of the
State, among other things—actually reinforced and motivated their acceptance of a free-market, limited-government philosophy. Eastman's
Reflections on the Failure of Socialism, for example, was replete with
condemnations of socialism and Communism, and encomiums of the
"only" alternative—capitalism.[205]

Even the purest antistatists, Chodorov and Rothbard, shared at times
in the anti-Communist crusade. After all, Chodorov himself was a partial
supporter of McCarthy, who, he said, demonstrated the "ubiquity" of
Communists in the government. McCarthy's only mistake, the arch-individualist continued, was that he did not go far enough: "The only thing to
do, if you want to rid the bureaucracy of Communists, is to abolish the
bureaucracy."[206] Rothbard was similarly inclined; when he read in the
New York Times that McCarthy was destroying the morale of the executive branch, he was delighted.[207] Not all the ex-Communists or anti-Communists adopted libertarian economics; James Burnham was one conspicuous exception,[208] Willmoore Kendall another. But many did—enthusiastically—and felt quite comfortable with their position. After all,
why shouldn't we be anti-Communist? Isn't Communism the negation
of everything we believe in?

The revolt against Communism was also easily integrated with traditionalist, often religious conservatism. Was not Communism a secular,
atheistic, messianic challenge to the Christian West? Was this not the
lesson of *Witness*, the lesson dramatized by the return to religion of such
former Communists as Louis Budenz and Bella Dodd? Were not the
anti-Communist critics of the "open" society saying essentially what many
traditionalists were simultaneously observing about the roots of totalitarianism? That the open, indifferent, permissive society was an empty
society. That without values, without absolutes, without consensus, a civilization would degenerate into moral anarchy and eventual tyranny. Ex-
Communists and traditionalists agreed that liberalism—the ideology of
openness—was, in John Hallowell's words, an "invitation to suicide." Was
not Communism an excellent example of all that the traditionalists feared?

Anti-Communism, in short, was for the most part easily assimilated
into the conservative credo of the 1950s. Both libertarians and tradition-

alists discerned in the "god that failed" a case study for their deepest convictions. Communism was a threat to liberty *and* tradition. If conservatism in 1955 was an amalgam, anti-Communism was a vital part of its cement.

In addition to their global perspective, their knowledge of Communism, and their criticism of the "treason" of the intellectuals,[209] the anti-Communists and ex-Communists brought to early postwar conservatism two noteworthy characteristics. First, in contrast to the elitist concept of the Remnant and the disdain for "crowd culture" that permeated much libertarian and traditionalist thinking in these years, the ex-radicals and anti-Communists began to apotheosize Middle America. Whittaker Chambers noted that common people, humble people, "the plain men and women of the nation," had stood by him in his need. James Burnham, leaving the "ingrown" East and driving across the continent in 1948-1949, was almost lyrical in his description of the country. "The United States," he concluded, "is not, not by centuries, ready to quit." Willmoore Kendall, Oklahoma-born, urged in 1950 that foreign policy be based on "the native good sense of the American people." William Schlamm, introducing the Buckley-Bozell book, observed approvingly that Joseph McCarthy had come out of "the heartland of America."[201] Was this sympathy for the American people an unconscious reflection of the ex-Communists' Marxist past? Was this a right-wing variant of the almost mystical faith in the virtue and good sense of the masses? Perhaps. But it was more. If the passions of the cold war drove some pluralist liberals to criticize "populism" and the mass society, [211] these pressures also generated among some conservatives a hitherto forbidden identification with the people. On the Communist issue some conservatives sensed that *they* were on the popular side. This new and more optimistic mood was not dominant—not yet. But in the raging storms of the McCarthy era one catches the first glimpses of later conservative praise for the "silent majority."

Second, the ex-radicals and their allies brought to the conservative intellectual movement the evangelical vigor of an ideological crusade. They supplied much of the "zeal," the "ginger," the "tone"[212]—and helped the articulate Right to acquire a fervent mass following for the first time in years. In part their almost apocalyptic sense of urgency was probably due to the expectation of war. In 1947, James Burnham wondered whether war would break out before his book reached the public. In 1950, just after the Korean conflict began, Peter Viereck wrote that we had only "thirty days to save the peace" by warning the Soviets that we would fight to prevent any impending move against Yugoslavia, Berlin, or Iran.[213] Willmoore Kendall's letters during the early 1950s often expressed the belief that a world war would break out soon.[214] In part this urgency reflected the bitter suspicion of betrayal. Moreover, what if it *really* was too late? What if Whittaker Chambers was right: that the West really was the losing side?

Chambers himself was at times bleakly pessimistic, Nock-like in his resignation. In 1954 he wrote to Buckley:

> No, I no longer believe that political solutions are possible for us.... The enemy—he is ourselves. That is why it is idle to talk about preventing the wreck of Western civilization. It is already a wreck from within. That is why we can hope to do little more now than snatch a fingernail of a saint from the rack or a handful of ashes from the faggots, and bury them secretly in a flowerpot against the day, ages hence, when a few men begin again to dare to believe that there was once something else, that something else is thinkable, and need some evidence of what it was, and the fortifying knowledge that there were those who, at the great nightfall, took loving thought to preserve the tokens of hope and truth. [215]

Most conservative intellectuals did not share Chambers's despair. But in the background...

"*C'est la lutte finale*"—"'Tis the final struggle."

So goes the "Internationale." Partly via the ex-Communists and their supporters, this crusading spirit came to pervade the Right and to make post-war intellectual conservatism a fighting faith.

FIVE

Consolidation

By the mid-1950s, a vigorous, if heterogeneous, conservative intellectual movement had arisen to challenge what Frank Meyer called "the revolution of the twentieth century."[1] Where, just a few years earlier, only scattered voices of intelligent right-wing protest were audible, by the end of President Eisenhower's first term a chorus of articulate critics of the Left had emerged. Although far from dominating the intellectual landscape, they had established a presence, and many of them were increasingly anxious to consolidate their forces.

The need for further welding of divergent tendencies into a coherent movement was self-evident. For in the early 1950s there was no single right-wing renascence. The Right consisted of three loosely related groups: traditionalists or new conservatives, appalled by the erosion of values and the emergence of a secular, rootless, mass society; libertarians, apprehensive about the threat of the State to private enterprise and individualism; and disillusioned ex-radicals and their allies, alarmed by international Communism. No rigid barriers separated the three groups. Traditionalists and libertarians were usually anti-Communists, while ex-Communists generally endorsed free-market capitalism and Western traditions. Nevertheless, the impulses that comprised the developing conservative movement were clearly diverse.

The necessity for coordinating these strands of conservatism was accentuated by the responses of American liberals in the 1950s. Although it would be an error to attribute too much to liberal criticism, many conservatives were quite aware of the evolving attitudes of the Left. As the Right became more vocal, so did its opponents, who thereby illuminated the condition of American conservatism at the end of the first postwar decade.

If the period from 1945 to 1955 was scarcely a blissful one for conservative intellectuals, it was not the worst of times, either. Whether or not they perceived it, one fact at least should have been encouraging: disillusionment and uncertainty on the Left were widespread.[2] Sated with power since the New Deal, blamed for the unsatisfactory postwar settlement in Europe and the disasters in Asia, accused even of complicity in treason, many liberals were afflicted by doubt and by what one observer called "the travail of redefinition."[3] Writing shortly after the 1946 Republican landslide, John Fischer of *Harper's* noted that liberals no longer seemed sure of their objectives. They needed "a brand new set of directions"; instead they were still living off a generation-old congeries of ideas that was now "pretty well used up." Even before the end of the New Deal, Fischer contended, liberalism had revealed its "intellectual bankruptcy." Moreover, it had left no "legacy" for confronting the post-war world.[4] Another liberal spokesman, Arthur Schlesinger, Jr., concurred; liberalism, he wrote in 1947, lacked an adequate grounding in "actuality." "The 'liberal' analysis today is predominantly wishful, sentimental, rhetorical."[5]

Fischer and Schlesinger were not isolated voices in these years; in many quarters signs of liberal self-examination and "tiredness" multiplied. For several months in 1949, *Partisan Review* featured a spirited debate among such men as Richard Chase, Daniel Aaron, William Barrett, and Lionel Trilling on the strengths and weaknesses of the "liberal mind."[6] The very airing of such a question was revealing. In 1952, as Eisenhower campaigned toward victory, Joseph C. Harsch wondered in the *Reporter* whether liberals were "obsolete."[7] A few months later, with Eisenhower triumphantly in the White House, an article by the liberal historian Eric Goldman asked: "After the Fair Deal, What?"[8] Still another indication of the new mood among liberals was the popularity of the Protestant theologian Reinhold Niebuhr. A member of the New York State Liberal Party and an activist in Americans for Democratic Action, Niebuhr preached to his friends on the Left an understanding of man based on original sin, the limitations of reform, and the folly of naive notions about the goodness and perfectibility of humanity. Niebuhr's tempered liberalism was still liberalism, but it was a tough, no-nonsense, pragmatic philosophy that promised no utopias and fitted in well with the sober and tentative mood gripping many American liberals.[9]

The experience of long political success followed by disconcerting jolts at the polls was not, of course, the sole cause of liberal introspection after World War II. Undoubtedly the most wrenching factor was the onset of the cold war abroad and the emergence of the Communist issue at home. In 1947 hundreds of prominent liberal politicians, intellectuals, and labor leaders founded the Americans for Democratic Action (ADA). Vigorously anti-Communist, convinced that the Soviet Union was a menace and that liberalism must be cleansed of Popular Front illusions lingering on from the Red Decade, the ADA battled the Progressive Citizens of America (later the Progressive Party) and its hero, Henry Wallace, who favored conciliation (to their foes, appeasement) of the Soviet Union. Wallace's debacle at the polls in 1948 confirmed the triumph of the ADA and the "right wing" of the liberal community. This emergence of anti-Communist or cold war liberalism was strenuously applauded by Arthur Schlesinger, Jr. in an influential book, *The Vital Center*, published in 1949. While critical of the American Right, which he defined primarily in economic terms and equated with businessmen, Schlesinger relentlessly concentrated most of his fire on the "doughface progressives" who could not or would not see that Communism was a failure, that Russia *was* a threat, that the Progressive Party of 1948 *had* been Communist dominated, and that liberals must rid their house of totalitarians.[10] Some of Schlesinger's criticisms of the far Left might easily have emanated from the Right. In fact, one later self-styled conservative, Robert Nisbet, identified strongly with *The Vital Center* when it first appeared.[11] In the years to come, similar denunciations of fellow travelers, "dupes," and "anti-anti-Communists" frequently appeared in such journals of the anti-Communist Left as *Commentary*, *Partisan Review*, and the *New Leader*.[12]

As a portion of liberalism, recoiling from the radical Left, veered toward the "vital center," some liberals began to evince an unwonted curiosity about contemporary conservatism. Perhaps, a few began to admit aloud, conservatism might have some relevance after all. Perhaps the conservative impulse had some value in an era of liberal retrenchment. Perhaps a modest conservative revival should even be welcomed as a corrective to jejune liberalism. In 1947, for instance, Schlesinger claimed that liberalism's intellectual flaccidity was actually in part "the reflux of the sentimentality of conservatism." Because conservatism had failed, it had "dragged American liberalism down with it."[13] The logic of this analysis suggested that the responsible Left needed a healthy opposition, and Schlesinger did not miss the implication. In April 1950—shortly after the conviction of Alger Hiss and the initial charges of Senator McCarthy—the apostle of the "vital center" acknowledged the importance of intelligent conservatism. The Harvard historian was careful, however, to specify what he meant. True conservatism, he insisted, must support the "public interest," social welfare, civil rights, and freedom of expression; it must not become the property of the National Association of Manufacturers or those right-wing anti-Communist Republican leaders, Richard Nixon and Karl Mundt. It must, in foreign policy, follow the constructive internationalist bipartisanship of Henry Stimson and Wendell Willkie rather than content itself with denunciations of Communism. It must embody the spirit of national continuity rather than the demands of special interests.[14] In another article at the same time, Schlesinger, long a partisan of Andrew Jackson, extended his spirit of magnanimity to one of Jackson's foes, John C. Calhoun. Perhaps, he observed, renewed interest in this iron-willed Southern conservative was "not inappropriate for an age like our own."

> A time of perplexity creates a need for somber and tragic interpretations of man. Thus we find Burke more satisfying today than Paine, Hamilton or Adams than Jefferson, Calhoun than Webster or Clay.[15]

Once again, Schlesinger was not alone in his attitudes toward conservatism. In 1948, on the eve of what appeared to be the return of the Republicans to power, John Fischer revived Calhoun's theory of the concurrent majority as part of a defense of America against "ideological politics," exemplified at the moment by the Progressive Party and Henry Wallace.[16] In the same campaign, no doubt anticipating a victory by Dewey, the liberal stalwart Chester Bowles pleaded for "liberal-conservative understanding" as essential to "national well-being" in the years ahead.[17] In his celebrated introduction to *The Liberal Imagination* in 1950, Lionel Trilling seemed almost to mourn the weakness of intelligent conservatism in American life.[18] It was not entirely surprising, then, that when avowed conservatives like Peter Viereck and Russell Kirk appeared, they initially received respectful attention in many liberal circles. Both Viereck and Kirk contributed often to journals read by liberals, and appeared frequently before academic (hence usually liberal) audiences. Kirk even debated Schlesinger on occasion.[19] At least for a brief period in the 1940s and early 1950s, some liberals professed some interest in some kind of conservatism.

In part this "opening to the Right" reflected the exigencies of the cold war; toleration of—even limited collaboration with—the Right seemed necessary in the face of the Communist enemy. Such reasoning probably motivated the liberal alliance with conservative intellectuals in the American Committee for Cultural Freedom, established in 1950. Another significant motive was the liberals' increasing recognition that they had achieved much and thus had much to conserve. Hence they now found themselves in an unexpectedly conservative *situation*. This perception was developed most forcefully in 1957 by the political scientist Samuel Huntington of Harvard University. Rejecting definitions of conservatism that associated it either with feudalism and aristocracy or with some set of immutable, universal truths, Huntington argued that conservatism was a *situational* ideology "arising out of a distinct but recurring type of historical situation in which a fundamental challenge is directed at established institutions...."[20] According to Huntington, it was the liberals who "must be the conservatives in America today"; it was the liberals whose mission it was to defend "liberal, popular, and democratic" American institutions.

> Until the challenge of communism and the Soviet Union is eliminated or neutralized, a major aim of American liberals must be to preserve what they have created.... In preserving the achievements of American liberalism, American liberals have no recourse but to turn to conservatism. For them especially conservative ideology has a place in America today.[21]

Situational conservatism had its uses—to preserve liberal gains.

These signs of liberal interest in the Right, however, did not obscure the fact that the liberal response to the conservative intellectual movement was highly selective. Who were the leaders of intelligent conservatism in 1950? According to Schlesinger, they included August Heckscher, Peter Viereck, McGeorge Bundy, Wayne Morse, Henry Cabot Lodge, and Jacob Javits—in other words, the most "liberal" of the new conservatives and the left wing of the Republican Party. This limited acceptance of the Right was not untypical. For while many liberals were willing to pay at least polite attention to some of the academic new conservatives, their tolerance for the libertarian and anti-Communist wings of the movement was much less warm. When *The Freeman* was founded in 1950, the *Nation*, while conceding the need for an intellectual conservative journal, hastened to criticize the "whinings," "portentous platitudes," and "sneers and snarls" it found in the first issue.[22] When Friedrich Hayek's *Capitalism and the Historians* appeared in 1954, Arthur

Schlesinger, Jr. accused the Austrian scholar of "fiery dogmatism" and of adding "luster" to the "homegrown McCarthys."[23] If Schlesinger in 1947 had many words of praise for James Burnham's *The Struggle for the World*, in 1953 he harshly condemned Burnham's *Containment or Liberation?* as "an absurd book written by an absurd man."[24] Nor was the Left enthusiastic about conservative defenders of Senator McCarthy. While liberalism in the postwar era was obviously not monolithic, it is clear that the liberal reception (such as it was) of Kirk and Viereck did not, in general, extend to Buckley, Chamberlain, Mises, Burnham, Meyer, or other spokesmen for libertarian and anti-Communist conservatism. The "vital center" had very definite boundaries.

This selectivity of response did not elude the conservatives, many of whom resented what they regarded as a liberal effort to divide and confuse the conservative movement. A young conservative historian, Stephen Tonsor of the University of Michigan, vigorously rebutted Schlesinger's persistent attempts to link conservatism with the business class:

> The leaders of the new conservatism are not now, nor will they be, identified with the American business community. They are clearly identified with natural law philosophy and revealed religion. The seat of the new conservatism is not an hereditary aristocracy which America lacks, but the Churches and theological faculties which are playing an ever more important role in American life.

Tonsor further argued that "the myopic perspectives of economic determinism" could not adequately comprehend the conservative renascence.[25] Reviewing Russell Kirk's *Program for Conservatives* in 1955, James Burnham also alluded to critics of the Right. He praised Kirk for "rescuing" conservatism from "verbalists who by paying out a few modish conservative phrases are at present trying to hitch a ride on the shifting Zeitgeist."[26] Who were these "verbalists"? Although Burnham did not offer any names, other conservatives did. According to Willmoore Kendall, one culprit was Peter Viereck himself, who could inform people "how to be conservative and yet agree with the Liberals about Everything." Another, said Kendall, was the historian Clinton Rossiter, author of *Conservatism in America* (1955). Kendall thought Rossiter so adept at causing confusion that "he could make you feel ashamed of yourself if you were *not* both conservative and Liberal."[27] Or as Gerhart Niemeyer, a political scientist at the University of Notre Dame, gibed, "It is once again fashionable to call oneself a conservative—provided, of course, one does not stray too far from the liberal fold. Clinton Rossiter does not."[28] Frank

Meyer went even further. Not only did he consider Rossiter's "conservatism" compatible with the views of Arthur Schlesinger, Jr. and Adlai Stevenson; he even denounced Russell Kirk himself for lacking a foundation in *principle* for unremitting resistance to statism and totalitarianism. No wonder, said Meyer, that the liberals tolerated the new conservatism:

> They realize that the New Conservatives, with their emphasis
> on tone and mood, with their lack of clear principle and their
> virulent rejection of individualism and a free economy,
> threaten no danger to the pillars of the temple…. Even bet-
> ter, by the magnanimity with which they receive the New Con-
> servatives into polite society, they justify expelling into outer
> darkness the principled champions of limited government and
> a free economy as "crackpots" and "fringe elements."[29]

Here was one more vivid illustration of the chasm that separated Left and Right in the 1950s. If some liberals were willing, for whatever reason, to grant an audience to a few academic new conservatives, many militant right-wing intellectuals were suspicious even of this much accommodation. The "vital center" seemed rather shaky by 1955.

Indeed, by mid-decade, there were increasing indications that the liberal mood of self-criticism was passing and that the faddish aspects of the "new conservatism" discussion were dying. "I'm Sick of Conservatism," the liberal political scientist John Roche entitled an article in the *New Leader*. If conservatism meant Burkean reverence for history and organic change, then it was obvious that an American conservative should be a liberal, for our tradition was liberal. If, Roche continued, conservatism consisted merely of a set of attitudes or a way of living, it lacked programmatic content and reduced itself to a mere "affirmation of human decency." Either way, it was irrelevant to modern America.[30]

The liberals' critique of the intellectual Right now took two basic forms. First, in response to traditionalist new conservatives who tended to glorify European figures like Burke, liberals declared that the American tradition was quintessentially liberal. Fortified by Louis Hartz's *The Liberal Tradition in America*, which appeared in 1955, commentator after commentator insisted that European-style conservatism had no place in the United States. Many cherished the "paradox" that *"to be an American conservative it is necessary to reassert liberalism."*[31] If this was correct, then it followed that the new conservatism was indeed what Schlesinger labeled it: "the politics of nostalgia." According to Schlesinger, Burkean conservatism was simply "the ethical afterglow of feudalism"—

quite inappropriate to the "non-feudal, nonaristocratic, dynamic, progressive business society of the United States." By trying to fuse this European import with laissez-faire, the new conservatives (Schlesinger meant Kirk) were guilty of "schizophrenia." He therefore dismissed the whole movement as a "hothouse growth."[32]

A second and very different liberal criticism was directed primarily at the libertarians and ex-Communists, who were far too indigenous and numerous to consign to the dustbins of "feudal" irrelevance. To these groups a number of primarily left-of-center social scientists applied psychological and sociological analysis. Beginning with *The Authoritarian Personality*, prepared by T.W. Adorno and his associates,[33] this genre reached a climax in 1955 in *The New American Right*, to which Daniel Bell, David Riesman, Nathan Glazer, Richard Hofstadter, Peter Viereck, Talcott Parsons, and Seymour Martin Lipset contributed.[34] Concentrating on the so-called New American Right or "pseudo-conservative revolt," which they linked to Senator McCarthy and *The Freeman*, the authors analyzed the phenomenon not as a rational and respectable response to Communism, the New Deal, or any of the other objects of conservative wrath but as the response of a frustrated, maladjusted, status-conscious, neo-populist Radical Right, led largely by fierce (and implicitly suspect) ex-radicals, to a complex modern world with which they were unable to cope. Much of the conservative intellectual movement, in other words, was interpreted not as a serious challenge to be refuted but as an aberration to be explained. The atmosphere of *The New American Right*—however correct its arguments—was that of the clinic, not the forum.

This tendency to perceive conservatism as a problem of abnormal psychology rather than rational politics was further exemplified by Herbert McClosky of the University of Minnesota, in a 1958 article detailing his research on "conservatism and personality." According to McClosky's controversial findings, conservative beliefs were most frequently held by "the uninformed, the poorly educated, and...the less intelligent." Conservatives tended to be submissive, alienated, lacking in confidence, "bewildered" by modern society, hostile, suspicious, compulsive, intolerant, mystical, and fearful of change. McClosky contended that "conservative doctrines" were "highly correlated" with certain distinct personality patterns and suggested that their doctrines "may tell us less about the nature of man and society than about the persons who believe these doctrines."[35] Once more, then, the implication of this scholarship—whatever its validity—was clear: conservatism need not be examined on its own merits. Conservatives were unattractive people; presumably (although McClosky did not actually say it) that was enough to invalidate their case.

The conservative reception of these studies was naturally unenthusiastic; many regarded the genre as a patronizing attempt to relegate them to obscurity. William F. Buckley, Jr., for instance, criticized the "cult" of *The Authoritarian Personality*, a book whose thesis (that conservatives had "authoritarian personalities") was both "frivolous" and "preposterous." But it was "marvelously convenient," he added pointedly, for people who were looking for ways to claim that conservative protest had no "rational grounds."[36] Frank Meyer tried to turn the liberal social scientists' tools on themselves: it was the liberals who were actually victims of "mass delusion," of neurosis, of escape from reality. What reality? That after "twenty-five years of the welfare state, of Deweyite education, and of control of the press and radio and television by the 'enlightened,'" millions of Americans *still* did not accept liberalism, *still* resolutely supported Taft, MacArthur, and McCarthy, and *still* stood in "principled opposition" to all that had supposedly been settled for years. So "traumatic" was this discovery, Meyer charged, that liberal social scientists could not stand it:

> Not ideas, not principles, nothing by which a reasonable man could be affected, could possibly be the cause of this intractable resistance to the good, the true, and the beautiful.... Since all political, economic and social propositions that form the accepted corpus of Liberal thought are beyond intellectual doubt or question, the only explanation of dissent must be, in the Liberal fantasy, a psychological defect, approaching, it is often hinted, paranoia.[37]

Both Buckley and Meyer cited scholarly critiques of Adorno's volume to bolster their case.[38]

Other conservatives also entered the battle. In a review of *The New American Right*, Russell Kirk complained that not one of the contributors even tried to determine "how far reaction against Communism actually is justified...." Instead, they were content to devise "ingenious" but "thoroughly unconvincing" means of pigeonholing the so-called Radical Right. Moreover, Bell, Hofstadter, and their fellow contributors virtually ignored the fact that "we are in the midst of a natural reaction against practical communism; and that such a reaction from a social catastrophe, at any period in history, always has displayed intolerance and imprudence, together with healthy and necessary indignation against the authors of that catastrophe and their friends."[39] One should not judge a movement, Kirk was saying in effect, solely by its lunatic fringe. As for the McClosky study, Willmoore Kendall contended in a rejoinder that it did not properly examine conservatism at all. According to Kendall, McClosky's methodology was deeply flawed and his article proved nothing about the relationship of conservatism and personality.[40]

These conservative responses did not alter the historical significance of the developing liberal hostility to the Right in the mid-1950s. If, for a moment, portions of the Left had granted conservatives a hearing, by 1955 their two-pronged counterattack revealed how far conservatives had to go before they attained equality of influence over the intellectual life of the nation. For liberal critics had not so much tried to refute conservative arguments about the free market, or secularism, or relativism, or Communism, as they had denied the very legitimacy of the conservative revival itself. If one segment of the Right was an alien "hothouse growth" and another a mere "pseudo-conservative revolt," surely such a hodge-podge could be dismissed and ignored.

All the more reason, then, for consolidation of the antiliberal forces. There was so much intellectual labor still to be done.

One key reason for the conservatives' wish to achieve coherence as a movement in the mid-1950s was their continuing consciousness of how small an intellectual minority they remained. Although Russell Kirk might proclaim that liberalism as an ideology was expiring,[41] William F. Buckley, Jr. realized that the Left as an intellectual movement was still very much alive and that the Right still lacked sufficient focus. "The few spasmodic victories conservatives are winning," he wrote late in 1954, "are aimless, uncoordinated, and inconclusive. This is so...because many years have gone by since the philosophy of freedom has been expounded systematically, brilliantly, and resourcefully."[42]

Why this weakness? Why was what Arthur Krock called in 1949 "the superior articulation of the Left"[43] still extant half a decade later? To Buckley and many other conservatives, the key to the imbalance lay not in any inherent conservative defects but in the overwhelming liberal domination of the nation's universities and influential media. Undoubtedly the *locus classicus* of this belief was Buckley's controversial *God and Man at Yale*, published in 1951. In it Buckley strove to document the monumental anti-Christian and collectivist bias which, he believed, was corrupting his alma mater. Although the young writer stated in his introduction that he expected his book to arouse "bitter antagonism,"[44] he soon realized that he had been "naive beyond recognition."

> Much of what came was unexpected. I should have known
> better, of course, for I had seen the Apparatus go to work on
> other dissenters from the Liberal orthodoxy, and I respected
> the Apparatus and stood in awe of it....[45]

Go to work it certainly did. Yale was furious; across the country, scandalized liberal reviewers denounced Buckley's attack on what he called "the superstitions of academic freedom" and his call for alumni to establish at Yale the orthodoxy *they* wished to pay for and perpetuate. Among the angriest critics was McGeorge Bundy, who labeled Buckley "a twisted and ignorant young man whose personal views of economics would have seemed reactionary to Mark Hanna." [46] But if liberals fulminated, conservatives cheered. In the *American Mercury*, Max Eastman pronounced the book "brilliant," although, as an atheist, he objected to the chapter on religion and to Buckley's call for "indoctrination." In *The Freeman*, Felix Wittmer, a professor at New Jersey State Teachers College, asserted that Buckley had rendered a service to Yale, America, and Western civilization.[47]

Buckley's bombshell was only the most publicized example of what became a recurrent conservative theme in the postwar years. In 1955, for instance, E. Merrill Root published *Collectivism on the Campus*,[48] a compilation of cases of alleged Communist, fellow traveler, and liberal domination of academe and discrimination against conservative students and professors. A year later Felix Wittmer followed with *Conquest of the American Mind*.[49] Meanwhile *The Freeman*, with articles like "God and Woman at Vassar" (written by the daughter of General Bonner Fellers), maintained the attack.[50] While the authors of *The New American Right* tended to perceive these conservatives' complaints as evidence of frustration, anti-intellectualism, and "status anxiety," conservatives considered liberal hegemony in the universities to be an undeniable fact. So solidly liberal did academe appear, in fact, to the administrators of the small, conservative Volker Fund that they actually hired assistants in the 1950s simply to search for conservative scholars who were unaware of the fund and who might be potential recipients of grants from it.[51]

It is not surprising, therefore, that in the face of the "superior articulation" and "field position" of the intellectual Left in the early 1950s, many conservatives increasingly came to believe that a new journal, even beyond *The Freeman*, *Human Events*, and the *American Mercury*, was needed to combat the liberals, to compensate for conservative weakness in academe, and to focus the energies of the diverse movement. Writing in *Human Events* in 1953, John Chamberlain declared that libertarians needed "not new authors" but "supporting media"—especially a *Saturday Review* or "a New York newspaper with a Sunday review supplement that can reach the bookstores of the hinterlands."[52] In a letter to Buckley in 1953, Kevin Corrigan, then employed by the Henry Regnery Company, reported that he had recently asked James Burnham what he considered to be "the most urgent of all anti-Communist tasks." Instantly Burnham had replied, "A magazine," preferably a weekly which would, like the *New Republic* and the *Nation* in the heyday of the New Deal, reach "opinion-makers all over the country every week."[53]

Burnham's views were echoed by Henry Regnery himself, the publisher of Buckley's *God and Man at Yale*. Deeply concerned by what he deemed "the collectivistic indoctrination of American youth in the universities,"[54] Regnery declared in 1953 that the "means of communication in this country are pretty well controlled by the left." Indeed, Regnery had founded his company precisely because "I felt it was time somebody did something to break the almost complete monopoly of book publishing, which is really the key to the whole thing, by New York intellectuals." Contending that Communism was not a mass movement but a "system of ideas," Regnery lamented the conservatives' failure to realize that "men don't live by bread alone, that it is ideas that shape history...."

> So far the left has won nearly every battle, and the left still controls the important positions.... So long as they control the means of communication, they don't have to worry too much about a slight set-back in Washington. If we want to do anything, we must work on the level of ideas.[55]

One man who was determined to do just that was the conservative scholar Russell Kirk. In a 1955 article, Kirk decried the fact that most American periodicals were suffused with the "oppressive ideology" of "ritualistic liberalism"; there was not even one explicitly conservative quarterly in the entire country. Nor was *The Freeman*, then edited by the arch antistatist Frank Chodorov, truly conservative either.[56] There was not, in other words, an adequate outlet for long and more literary articles of a conservative bent.[57] For some time before Kirk's essay was published, he had been attempting to rectify this imbalance. An initial motive was to replace *Measure*, the scholarly publication of the Committee on Social Thought of the University of Chicago.[58] While not overtly conservative, *Measure*, before its demise in 1951, had published articles by Kirk, Wilhelm Röpke, T.E. Utley, and other American and European right-wing intellectuals. In April 1951, Kirk wrote to the Burke scholar Ross Hoffman that he was working on a proposed fortnightly journal to be called *The American Conservative*. For a time he tentatively renamed it *The Federal Review*; then, *The Conservative Review*.[59]

In a prospectus circulated to his friends in 1954, Kirk described the kind of periodical he had in mind. "No monthly magazine of a reflective, leisurely, imaginative, serious, and good-natured character," he began, "is widely circulated in America today." No solid journal with the influence wielded by the *Quarterly Review* and *Edinburgh Review* in nineteenth-century Britain now existed. Kirk proposed to establish one, with a circulation of 30,000 to 50,000—a review that would be read by "professors, clergymen, leaders of business, men in government, professional persons, and those reflective people in obscure walks of life who preserve the equilibrium of any society...." The purpose of such a periodical should be frankly conservative: "to revive the best elements in American and European thought."

> This journal would abjure the cant of yesterday's "liberal" and "humanitarian" and "progressive" cliques, thought surely it would not be illiberal or inhumane or reactionary.... Its intention would be to conserve the intellectual traditions, the free constitutions, and the old heartiness of our civilized society; it would be forthrightly opposed to political collectivism, social decadence, and effeminacy in thought and literature .... It would not be ashamed of an avowed prejudice in favor of religion, in favor of prescriptive justice, in favor of liberty under law, in favor of the wisdom of our ancestors, in favor of manliness in thought and society. But it would not be afraid to face the problems of our age.

Beyond these general positions, the new journal should, said Kirk, have three specific features. First, it should be "frankly theistic," open to "religious and ethical ideas" without being sectarian. It should counteract the "bigoted nineteenth-century secularism" that dominated contemporary media. Second, the journal should articulate "conservative social principles," examine "the whole vast question of the ties that bind man to man," and oppose the "short-sighted contempt for everything old and established" that afflicted most modern journalism. Finally, Kirk wanted his magazine to serve as a forum for "the culture of the Middle West and the heart of the United States generally," and as a partial remedy for the parochialism of the liberal East. Like Henry Regnery (another Midwesterner), Anthony Harrigan, and several other conservative spokesmen, Kirk was alarmed at the concentration of intellectual leadership and publishing in the Northeast.

> A profound misunderstanding of the temper and character of Middle Western life and opinion exists in the Eastern United States, and abroad, because serious thought in the heart of our country is represented only very fragmentarily, or not at all, in Eastern journals of opinion.... America dare not run the risk, in this hour, of relinquishing control of her media of expression to small circles of cognoscenti in two or three cities—who, no matter how well intentioned, cannot truly claim to speak for the whole nation.[60]

For many liberal critics of the Right in the 1950s, Kirk's prospectus (if they had seen it) would probably have confirmed the popular thesis that postwar conservatism was merely a resentful outcry of "hick" Midwestern "populists" against the Eastern establishment. Certainly this dimension was present in some conservative thought; certainly conservatives did see themselves as outsiders who were attacking a "consensus"— to them an imposed consensus—emanating mostly from Eastern sources. Yet to deal exclusively in sociological or psychological categories like "status revolution" or "inferiority complex" is to risk misunderstanding the contours of American intellectual life in the 1950s. Russell Kirk, for instance, was no half-educated hick, nor was he in any meaningful sense a populist. At the same time, he *was* critical of Eastern liberals. Here again we confront the deep cleavages between Left and Right in this period. To Kirk and his allies, Eastern liberal domination of American culture was a *fact* and a *problem* requiring sober analysis and sober response. If any region was provincial and intellectually ossified, it was the liberal East. Hence, for example, Stephen Tonsor's objections to Arthur Schlesinger's classification of conservatism in economic terms. How typical of an Eastern New Dealer! How dated!

Moreover, Kirk intended the scope of his journal to be not just sectional but national—even international. Kirk's list of proposed contributors revealed how widely he cast his nets. In addition to various Midwestern authors, he cited other possibilities, including Richard Weaver, Allen Tate, Friedrich Hayek, Robert Frost, Bernard Iddings Bell, Reinhold Niebuhr, Robert Nisbet, and Whittaker Chambers. Of special interest was his determination to acquire distinguished European contributors, such as T.S. Eliot, Herbert Butterfield, Roy Campbell, Douglas Jerrold, Harold Nicholson, Bertrand de Jouvenel, and Wilhelm Röpke. [61] Obviously, then, Kirk's venture, while hoping to balance (Eastern) liberal journals, cannot be explained as a xenophobic or Anglophobic assault on the establishment. Whatever the characteristics of the mass base of the Right in this era, the conservative *intellectual* movement was more complicated, more cosmopolitan, more sophisticated than that.

After several years of preparation and with the aid of Henry Regnery,[62] Kirk's journal appeared as a quarterly in 1957. Entitled *Modern Age: a Conservative Review*, it immediately became the principal—indeed, the only—scholarly medium deliberately designed to publish conservative thought in the United States. Kirk's enterprise was primarily oriented toward the traditionalist or new conservative segment of the conservative revival. Among the twenty-seven original "editorial advisers," only two—Wilhelm Röpke and David McCord Wright—were economists, while none was widely known as a convert from Communism.[63] Instead, the board included such traditionalist luminaries as Bernard Iddings Bell, Ross Hoffman, Eliseo Vivas, Richard Weaver, Frederick Wilhelmsen, and Francis Wilson. Several, including Weaver, the Agrarian Donald Davidson, and Anthony Harrigan, were Southerners. Another, James J. Kilpatrick, was an Oklahoma native who had become the dynamic editor of the conservative *Richmond News-Leader*. Many, including Bell, Harrigan, Hoffman, Wilhelmsen, Wilson, Leo R. Ward of Notre Dame, and Röpke were either Roman Catholics, Anglo-Catholics, or "pre-Reformation Christians." Nearly all held appointments in universities; one— the Methodist clergyman Lynn Harold Hough—had been associated with Irving Babbitt and Paul Elmer More in the New Humanism movement of the early 1930s.[64] The contents of *Modern Age* reflected this traditionalist influence. Symposia in the early issues carried such titles as "The Achievement of Ortega y Gasset," "Christianity and Our Present Discontents," "The Restoration of American Learning," "The Achievement of Eric Voegelin," and "Humane Political Economy." In the Summer 1959 issue appeared the first *Burke Newsletter*, which eventually became an independent journal. Despite the handicaps of little money or editorial assistance,[65] by the time Kirk resigned in 1959[66] he had established what he wanted: a dignified forum for reflective, traditionalist conservatism. *Modern Age* had filled a desperate need; even after Kirk's departure it remained the principal quarterly of the intellectual Right.

While Kirk's venture unquestionably helped to consolidate the conservative movement, it was obviously not sufficient by itself. For one thing, *Modern Age* was a quarterly, not a weekly, and it refrained from ephemeral political discussions. Moreover, its clientele was largely academic and traditionalist. It could only partially compensate, therefore, for what Arthur Krock might have called the inferior articulation of the Right. In the early 1950s many conservatives sought anxiously to fill the continuing gap.

The crucial figure in initiating a new conservative weekly, curiously enough, appears to have been a European émigré named William S. Schlamm. Born in Austria in 1904, Schlamm had become a Communist as a teenager, had broken when only 25, and had become in the 1930s a prominent anti-Nazi and anti-Stalinist newspaper editor in Berlin and Prague. In 1937 he published *Dikatur der Luge* [The Dictatorship of the Lie], a vehement critique of Stalinism and the Trotsky trial. In 1938, despondent about the future of democratic Europe, he emigrated to the United States, where he soon became a columnist for the *New Leader*. An acquaintance with John Chamberlain helped to lead Schlamm to the editorial staff of *Fortune* in 1941; two years later he became foreign policy adviser and assistant to Henry Luce, editor-in-chief of *Time*, *Life*, and *Fortune*. During these years Schlamm, who had still considered himself a "non-Marxian socialist" in the 1930s, gradually moved to the Right. It was, he said, "my intellectual Americanization."[67]

During his years with Luce, Schlamm became the editor-designate of *Measure* (not the University of Chicago journal), a new intellectual magazine which Luce was planning to add to his publishing empire. For various financial and other reasons, the periodical never appeared.[68] When Schlamm left Time, Inc. in 1951, however, his interest in journalism did not cease. For most of the next three years he helped to edit *The Freeman*; he hoped "to create a new type of Conservative Journalism...." [69] In 1952 he met William F. Buckley, Jr. and was immensely impressed by the young conservative author and debater. Probably recalling his abortive attempt to found *Measure*, and thoroughly convinced that in Buckley he had found an extraordinary recruit, Schlamm sought to interest his friend in founding "a journal of Conservative opinion"; the idea was "obsessive" with him. At last, in 1953—according to Schlamm's account—he secured Buckley's assent to the undertaking. In the next two years he worked closely with Buckley in this effort.[70]

For all of Schlamm's enthusiasm, it is quite possible that a new conservative magazine would never have appeared had *The Freeman* not undergone a severe internal crisis in 1952 and 1953. Before this crisis arose, there had been few if any right-wing complaints about the journal; in the heat of the 1952 election year, however, the atmosphere changed. At the center of the storm was a new *Freeman* editor, Forrest Davis, a journalist and an adviser to Senator Taft. Davis soon clashed with co-editor Henry Hazlitt and offended some pro-Eisenhower members of the board of directors by his pro-Taft activities. Some of the director-stockholders were also distressed by the alleged stridency of the editors and sought to alter the journal's tone. To several of the editors this effort, if successful, would turn *The Freeman* into an arid, academic publication focused exclusively on economics. In October 1952, Hazlitt, who had many reservations about Senator Joseph McCarthy, resigned, complaining about *The Freeman*'s tendency to make the senator a "sacred character." In Hazlitt's opinion the magazine had become too centered on personalities—particularly McCarthy's. In the next few months the situation worsened, as the directors divided almost evenly into seemingly irreconcilable factions. Finally, in January 1953, with *The Freeman* unable to raise money or pay its bills, the three principal editors—Davis, John Chamberlain, and Suzanne La Follette—resigned and began at once to explore the possibility of founding a new journal. William Schlamm joined their exodus.[71]

A change in the nature of *The Freeman* after 1953 further intensified the desire for a new journal. In 1954 Leonard Read and the Foundation for Economic Education bought *The Freeman*, converted it from a bi-weekly to a monthly, and installed the near-anarchist Frank Chodorov as editor.[72] Once more the Right lacked an intellectual weekly or fortnightly journal of opinion. To William F. Buckley, Jr., this development meant that the old *Freeman* had, to all intents and purposes, "folded." Accordingly, he made the final decision to proceed with plans to establish and edit a new magazine; in the next eighteen months or so he strove to amass the necessary capital. Buckley was aided by his comparative youth. Still less than 30, he could not easily be seen as a competitor of the older, established journalists he gathered around him. With surprising ease a diverse "constellation" of right-wing luminaries came together in his enterprise.[73]

The objective of the new magazine, as Buckley conceived it, would be "to revitalize the conservative position" and to "influence the opinion-makers" of the nation. Incredibly, he noted, while conservatives did not possess one weekly journal of opinion in 1955, the liberals had eight. "They know the power of ideas, and it is largely for this reason that socialist-liberal forces have made such a great headway in the past thirty years."[74] Buckley forcefully rejected what he called "the popular and cliché-ridden appeal to the 'grass-roots' "[75] and strove instead to establish a journal which would reach intellectuals. Not all conservatives agreed with this approach, but the young editor-to-be was firm. It was the intellectuals, after all, "who have midwived and implemented the revolution. We have got to have allies among the intellectuals, and we propose to renovate conservatism and see if we can't win some of them around."[76]

At last, in November 1955, a few days before Buckley's 30th birthday, the new periodical, *National Review*, appeared; it was strikingly similar in format to the pre-1953 *Freeman*. In fact, most of the names which initially graced its masthead had worked for or at least contributed to that magazine. But Buckley's journal was not destined to be a mere replica of *The Freeman*. Its function was not solely to renew the attack against the Left but to consolidate the Right.

Buckley's success in welding a coalition was substantial. New conservatives, libertarians, and anti-Communists were represented on the masthead and readily gained access to the pages of the magazine. Among the traditionalists, Russell Kirk contributed a regular column, while Richard Weaver, Donald Davidson, Erik von Kuehnelt-Leddihn, and many others either assisted the magazine in its birth or came to it eventually. But for his unexpected death, the Spanish philosopher Ortega y Gasset would have contributed an essay entitled "The Revolt Against the Masses" to an early issue.[77] The impact of libertarians was also evident, notably in the presence on the masthead of John Chamberlain, Frank Chodorov, the European economist Wilhelm Röpke, and those vehement ex-radical critics of statism, Max Eastman and Frank Meyer. Especially noticeable was the extraordinary concentration of ex-Communists, ex-Trotskyists, and others with radical pasts among the magazine's early editors and associates. James Burnham, Willmoore Kendall, William Schlamm, Frank Meyer, Freda Utley, Richard Weaver, Max Eastman, John Chamberlain, and Whittaker Chambers—all had once been on the Left and all contributed, sometimes profoundly, to the shaping and management of the new magazine. Even before 1955, the radicals-turned-conservative had affected the consciousness of the American Right; through the medium of *National Review* their influence was extended. Without the efforts of such militant, strong-willed ex-radicals as Burnham, Meyer, and Schlamm, *National Review* would never have succeeded. If *The Freeman* was libertarian and *Modern Age* was traditionalist, one distinctive mark of *National Review* was the prominence of ex-radicals in its coalition government.

The principal themes of the journal reflected the varied constituencies from which it drew support. The editors, in their initial declaration of belief, pronounced themselves "irrevocably" at war with "satanic" Communism; coexistence was "neither desirable, nor possible, nor honorable"; victory must be the American goal.[78] In nearly every issue James Burnham, the magazine's chief global strategist, wrote a column called "The Third World War." The journal was also open to Senator McCarthy. Not only did it have him review a book by his foe Dean Acheson,[79] but it also occasionally published defenses of McCarthyism and replies to its critics.[80] Moreover, the editors affirmed the "competitive price system" as "indispensable to liberty and material progress" and asserted that they were "libertarian" in the battle against the growth of government—a threat to freedom which "must be fought relentlessly." On another front they announced themselves to be "conservative" (that is, traditionalist) in the struggle between "the Social Engineers, who seek to adjust mankind to conform with scientific utopias, and the disciples of Truth, who defend the organic moral order."[81] Several of the early leaders of the *National Review* circle, in fact, were Roman Catholics. Buckley was of course the most prominent, while Bozell and Kendall, to take two more examples, were converts. Not surprisingly, another striking characteristic of the journal in its early years was the amount of space it devoted to criticism of the academy. Two columns—Kirk's "From the Academy" and Buckley's "The Ivory Tower"—were repeatedly devoted to the excesses and follies of the people who administered and taught in the universities. The critique of the intellectual class continued to be a prominent feature of postwar conservative thought.

Above all, *National Review* in its first years was dominated by the conviction that its preeminent intellectual enemy—and they insisted that it *was* an enemy—was liberalism. It was the liberals, said Buckley in the first issue, "who run this country."[82] In his column "The Liberal Line," Willmoore Kendall regularly attempted to discern the strategy and tactics of the foe. Kendall's column was predicated on several assumptions which were shared by the other editors: that there did exist a recognizably liberal credo on contemporary issues, that this liberal viewpoint was held by most of the country's "leading opinion-makers," and that these liberals relentlessly sought to pound their views into the public. In short, a powerful liberal "propaganda machine" was

> engaged in a major, sustained assault upon the sanity, and
> upon the prudence and the morality of the American people—
> its sanity, because the political reality of which they speak is a
> dream world that nowhere exists, its prudence and morality

because their values and goals are in sharpest conflict with
the goals and values appropriate to the American tradition....[83]

This fundamental philosophical antagonism even to the non-Communist Left was far removed from the new conservatism of Peter Viereck or the "vital center" liberalism of Arthur Schlesinger. Viereck in particular had sought a kind of alliance between liberals and conservatives to beat back "Communazi" extremists. To many of the *National Review* conservatives, no such accommodation was ultimately possible, certainly not on the level of principle. For they deeply believed—as Whittaker Chambers, among others, had taught them—that the Left was, in basic philosophy, united. As William Rusher put it when he became publisher in 1957, "the Liberal Establishment...shares Communism's materialist principles."[84] A year later Frank Meyer summarized the conservative case with characteristic pungency. The phenomenon called McCarthyism, he explained, had established a number of undeniable truths:

> 1) that contemporary Liberalism is in agreement with Communism on the most essential point—the necessity and desirability of socialism; 2) that it regards all inherited value—theological, philosophical, political—as without intrinsic virtue or authority; 3) that, therefore, no irreconcilable differences exist between it and Communism—only differences as to method and means; and 4) that, in view of these characteristics of their ideology, the Liberals are unfit for the leadership of a free society, and intrinsically incapable of offering serious opposition to the Communist offensive.[85]

It was obvious that the inner civil war between Left and Right had not ended with the censure of Joseph McCarthy.

Such an uncompromising enunciation of principles reflected, in part, the desperate crisis in which *National Review*'s editors believed the nation to be floundering. While the fact that the magazine had appeared at all was a significant accomplishment, no one could deny the magnitude of the task ahead. *National Review*, Buckley proclaimed in the first issue, "stands athwart history yelling Stop...." It is "out of place" in the world today "because, in its maturity, literate America rejected conservatism in favor of radical social experimentation." To be a conservative was to be part of a group of "non-licensed nonconformists" in a world of enormous, liberal-imposed conformity. No wonder, then, that a journal was needed for "radical conservatives"—those ignored by the "irresponsible," "well-fed Right" and abused by the liberals.[86]

Although *National Review* was welcomed by a large number of con-servative intellectuals, not all of them felt entirely comfortable with its tone and substance; several traditionalists in particular were either aloof or critical. Both Peter Viereck and the Southern Agrarian Allen Tate, for example, were asked to contribute pieces to the journal but declined; Tate refused because *National Review* supported Senator McCarthy.[87] Abroad, T.S. Eliot, virtually a patron saint of the new conservatism, ob-jected to certain aspects of the journal. It was, he wrote to Russell Kirk, "too consciously the vehicle of a defiant minority."

> I fear that a reader of "The National Review" who does not already share 100% Mr. Buckley's opinions, might gradually get the impression that it was a vehicle of prejudice, and that all issues were decided in advance.

Eliot thought it especially "ill-advised" to have Senator McCarthy review a book by Dean Acheson. In another letter he reiterated his "very mixed feelings" about the new journal and said he found *Modern Age* "much more welcome." [88]

While regularly contributing a column to *National Review*, Russell Kirk also had definite reservations about the venture. For one thing, he wrote to Eliot, the magazine evinced "too much Yale undergraduate spirit."[89] For another, Kirk had been incensed by Frank Meyer's searing attack on him in the July 1955 *Freeman*[90] and was uncomfortable not only with Meyer but also with other arch-individualists like Chodorov, whom he had recently criticized.[91] To appear on the same masthead with these foes was unacceptable, particularly when it seemed to Kirk that Meyer and Chodorov were conducting a campaign to reduce his influ-ence among conservatives.[92] Consequently, Kirk directed Buckley to take his name off the masthead.[93] He later explained that he did not want to be considered partially responsible for the collective editorial policy of the magazine.[94] Kirk was willing, in short, to do what he could to make *National Review* a success, but he did not wish to become totally identi-fied with *National Review*'s brand of conservatism.

In retrospect, these disputes[95] seem less important than the fact that the journal was gradually beginning to have an impact in the late 1950s. In 1956 Clinton Rossiter, hardly the magazine's favorite scholar, wrote, "*National Review* continues to interest, amuse and anger me, and what more can I ask of a magazine? I don't get this reaction from any other journal these days."[96] To be sure, the magazine's average circulation re-mained small (less than 20,000 in its first three years, 30,000 by 1960),[97] and it continually faced financial disaster.[98] In 1958 it was forced to become a biweekly. Nevertheless, in a fund-raising appeal in 1958, Buckley proudly contended that

> National Review has entered the mainstream of American thought, and it is now an institutional fact of American life. It is no longer a new and experimental magazine. It is no longer a flash fire by the Neanderthal Right. It is the voice of American conservatism, and more and more, it is recognized as such.[99]

Two years later, at the fifth anniversary dinner, Buckley was equally emphatic. National Review, he said, echoing Admiral Lewis Strauss, was "organically American, rooted in the nation's deepest traditions, and beyond that even, in the deepest traditions of Western civilization...."[100]

Buckley's buoyancy was hardly meant to convey the impression that the battle was won. Indeed, his praise of National Review contrasted dramatically with several liberal fusillades aimed at it in the formative months of its existence. According to John Fischer of Harper's, Buckley's new journal was not conservative at all; it was radical, exhibiting such telltale signs of extremism as humorlessness, utopianism, inconsistency, and a persecution complex. Murray Kempton claimed that the magazine was boring and trivial. Most savage of all was Dwight Macdonald, who castigated the new journal as dull, low-quality fare offered by obscure and eccentric "scrambled eggheads" for "intellectually underprivileged" provincials. National Review, he charged, was "the voice of the lumpen-bourgeoisie."[101]

Conservatives naturally offered rebuttals to these denunciations.[102] Willmoore Kendall, for instance, sarcastically noted that for the "Liberal Propaganda Machine" a "'conservative' publication is not really conservative unless it is Liberal."[103] But conservatives were not, according to William Rusher, preoccupied by the liberal attacks.[104] For although these responses from the Left reinforced conservatives' awareness of the long uphill road ahead, nothing could obscure the fact that National Review was beginning to create networks of association and channels of communication. These were essential to any movement, but especially to one attempting to stand athwart history yelling "Stop." National Review, appearing week after week, drawing on an ever-expanding cast of intellectuals, was beginning—slowly, step by step—to compensate for the superior articulation of the Left. It cannot be overemphasized that National Review was not simply one more periodical conveying a modicum of news and comment to the faithful. It was, instead, a forum for disputation, a means by which scattered intellectuals could learn about one another, a framework within which a heterogeneous group of often highly individualistic men and women could come together to work in what seemed to be a common cause. As the only significant avowedly conservative journal of opinion for a long time after 1955,[105] *National Review* was far more indispensable to the Right than any single liberal journal was to the Left. Not all conservatives wrote for *National Review*; not all approved of it; certainly disagreements among its contributors proved to be profound. Nevertheless, if *National Review* (or something like it) had not been founded, there would probably have been no cohesive intellectual force on the Right in the 1960s and 1970s. To a very substantial degree, the history of reflective conservatism in America after 1955 is the history of the individuals who collaborated in—or were discovered by—the magazine William F. Buckley, Jr. founded.

If in the middle and late 1950s, *National Review* and *Modern Age* finally provided essential foci for renascent conservatism, an even more serious task lay before it: to generate intellectual cohesiveness out of the coalitions and "constellations" that had emerged toward the end of the first postwar decade. It was reassuring to conservatives to know that they stood together. What, though, did they stand *for*? What, if anything, bound these disparate people into one movement? What intellectual legitimacy did their movement really have? What, in fact, *was* conservatism? What was conservatism in America? Reflective conservatives, pondering these issues, realized that true consolidation must go beyond journalism and publicity. What Eric Voegelin called, in a different context, "retheoretization" must continue and intensify. But at least—and at last—they knew they were not alone.

SIX

Fission and Fusion: The Quest for Philosophical Order

In the spring of 1956, *National Review* was only a few months old and *Modern Age* was still struggling to be born. But already a sense of possibility was beginning to affect the conservative revival. It was a time, William F. Buckley, Jr. wrote to Russell Kirk, "when the very nature of conservatism is being reexamined."[1] It was a time when people of the Right were beginning to refine their positions and to locate common ground.

That the need for self-definition was urgent seemed increasingly obvious to perceptive conservatives in the mid-1950s. For theirs was no precisely focused, unified vanguard entrenched in the universities, the media, the foundations, the churches, or other leading centers of influence in the nation's intellectual life. Instead, a fervent but embattled minority—not even one movement, really, but three—was striving to gain intellectual coherence. What emerged in 1955 around *National Review* was not a single "voice of conservatism" but a coalition of often competing intellectuals.

It is not surprising, therefore, that one of the distinctive features of conservative thought in the decade after 1955 was an almost Sisyphean quest for philosophical order. Although right-wing intellectuals frequently denied that conservatism was a neatly packaged ideology, many of them strove nevertheless to clarify the meaning of that elusive term and to find an identity. It was a challenge reinforced by Buckley's opening *National Review* to the many instead of to a sectarian few. With aggressive ex-Communists, antistatists of varying purity, and many kinds of traditionalists all rubbing shoulders in a common endeavor, friction was inevitably generated, and from friction came both heat and light.

To anyone who read *National Review* in its first four or five years, it must have been obvious that the search for unity—or even harmony—was going to be difficult. Time and again, disputes about the nature of responsible conservatism broke out—disputes which at least helped to indicate what was acceptable to the *National Review* circle that was coming to dominate the respectable Right.[2] One of the earliest such efforts at self-definition involved Peter Viereck, whose brand of "new conservatism" seemed increasingly divergent from that espoused by Buckley and his associates. To Viereck, conservatism emphatically did not mean Senator Robert Taft, Senator Joseph McCarthy, "Manchester liberalism," laissez-faire, "thought-control nationalism," or total hostility to the New Deal. Instead, it was a centrist philosophy, rejecting doctrinaire, bitter-end extremism of both Left and Right. Liberalism per se was not an enemy but a potential ally against totalitarianism. The New Deal, while imperfect in many respects, was not a revolution but a reform movement that had prevented a revolution. In 1956 Viereck even declared that the new conservatism was "a non-party philosophy close to that of Adlai Stevenson among Democrats, Clifford Case among Republicans,"[3] and enthusiastically commended Stevenson for distinguished conservative leadership.[4]

All this quite naturally aroused the displeasure of *National Review*, and in an early issue Frank Meyer in the "Books in Review" section pronounced an anathema. Meyer was particularly incensed by a tendency among liberal intellectuals to designate Viereck a right-wing spokesman. Viereck was no such thing, Meyer countered; he was a man of "unexceptionably Liberal sentiments" which he was "passing off" as conservatism.[5] To Meyer and most of the Buckley circle, liberalism itself was the target, the New Deal was a revolution to be fought relentlessly, and Adlai Stevenson was not in the least a model for conservative political action. The enemy was the Left, period—not just its extremist fringe. *National Review* was not about to acquiesce in the post-New Deal *zeitgeist*. The lesson of Meyer's denunciation was plain: Viereck-style, nonpartisan, "vital center" conservatism was not going to become the accepted credo of the intellectual Right. While Viereck continued to articulate his views after 1955, he could no longer be considered representative of the decisive thrust of conservative thought.

The "expulsion" of Viereck from what Buckley called "our movement"[6] was easily accomplished; after all, the two sides had never been close. Far more serious was the controversy which raged in the late 1950s over the status of Ayn Rand. Born in 1905 in St. Petersburg, Rand had emigrated to the United States in the 1920s from the bleak totalitarian world of Communist Russia. Gradually she established herself as an author of strenuously anticollectivist novels, such as *We the Living* and *The Fountainhead*; indefatigably she labored to develop a comprehensive philosophy. One product of her effort—a gargantuan novel called *Atlas Shrugged*[7]—appeared in 1957 and introduced the world to Rand's philosophy of objectivism in its most fully developed form.

Rand's system of values held "that man exists for his own sake, that the pursuit of his own happiness is his highest moral purpose, that he must not sacrifice himself to others, nor sacrifice others to himself."[8] Anything that denigrated man's rationality, total self-reliance, and freedom was deemed evil. Hence religion, collectivism, even altruism, were condemned, while the cross of Christianity was denounced as "the symbol of the sacrifice of the ideal to the nonideal."[9] In place of the cross and its ethic she offered rational self-interest and the dollar sign, the symbol of "free trade and, therefore, of a free mind."[10] To Rand the only economic system compatible with human freedom was unmitigated laissez-faire capitalism. Aggressiveness, egoism, energy, rationality, self-respect, the "virtue of selfishness"—these were some of the values she enthroned. With the aplomb of the self-made woman, Rand calmly declared, "I am challenging the cultural tradition of two-and-a-half-thousand years."[11]

Rand's forceful and Nietzschean novel quickly became enormously popular; within a few years it had sold well over a million copies.[12] For many conservatives, especially the young, it was a powerful treatise. Certainly some of its themes—the wickedness and irrationality of the welfare state, collectivism, and all sorts of government intervention; the virtues of capitalism; the celebration of individual self-assertion—were (in somewhat less extravagant form) themes of the libertarian Right. But not all conservatives were pleased by *Atlas Shrugged*, and in a devastating review late in 1957, Whittaker Chambers declared war on Ayn Rand. To Chambers the book was a literary and philosophical nightmare. Its plot was "preposterous," its characterization "primitive" and caricatured, and much of its effect "sophomoric." It was not, in fact, a novel at all, but a "Message": the antireligious gospel of "philosophic materialism," in which "...Randian Man, like Marxian Man, is made the center of a godless world." Moreover, for all her opposition to the State, Rand, according to Chambers, really wanted a society controlled by a "technocratic elite" similar to the absurd heroes of her novel. Indeed, permeating her novel was a "dictatorial tone":

> Out of a lifetime of reading, I can recall no other book in
> which a tone of overriding arrogance was so implacably sus-
> tained. Its shrillness is without reprieve. Its dogmatism is with-
> out appeal.... It consistently mistakes raw force for strength
> .... It supposes itself to be the bringer of a final revelation.
> Therefore, resistance to the Message cannot be tolerated....
> From almost any page of *Atlas Shrugged*, a voice can be heard,
> from painful necessity, commanding:"To a gas chamber—go!"

Chambers's review was appropriately entitled "Big Sister Is Watching You."[13]

Not all conservative intellectuals agreed with Chambers's verdict. E. Merrill Root, a professor at Earlham College and author of *Collectivism on the Campus*, proclaimed the novel a literary and philosophical tour de force. While Rand did reject God and preach atheism, Root argued that this aberration was only superficial. She was still "an artistic and philosophical Atlas" whose metaphysical roots tended toward religion in spite of her denials.[14] John Chamberlain, a free-market conservative as well as an experienced book reviewer, also found merit in the novel. Although repelled by Rand's "dogmatic ethical hardness" and material-ism, he insisted that the book deserved the attention of conservatives. Rand's grasp of economics was "magnificent," and she demonstrated the "indissoluble" links between capitalism and freedom.[15] Other libertar-ians, including the Misesian economist Murray Rothbard, also rose to defend *Atlas Shrugged*.[16]

Yet Chambers had his defenders, too, among them Russell Kirk, who praised the controversial review.[17] A few years later Kirk again dis-cussed Rand; her objectivism, he held, was a false and detestable "in-verted religion." While Kirk supported free enterprise and agreed with Rand's criticism of collectivism, the amassing of wealth was simply not "the whole aim of existence."[18] Frank Meyer was even more sharp: Ayn Rand was guilty of "calculated cruelties" and the presentation of an "arid subhuman image of man."[19] Perhaps the most telling rebuke to Rand and her defenders came from a young classical scholar, Garry Wills. In a rejoinder to E. Merrill Root, Wills denied that Rand—a "fanatic" with "narrow fixations"—was a conservative at all.

> When...John Galt [the hero of *Atlas Shrugged*] repudiates all
> obligations to other men, he denies history, that link with one's
> ancestors and with all human experience which is the first
> principle of conservatism. When Galt asserts the immediate
> perfectibility of man (an *achieved* perfection in his own case),

he is working from the first principle of historical Liberalism.
...Ayn Rand's superman comes from the same source as the
Liberal's perfect society. Her muscular and Malthusian
heroes...are all expressions of Liberalism—the attempt to attain beatitude with a politico-economic program.

Wills emphasized that conservatism and capitalism were not identical. It
was the worst of errors to allow the doctrinaire, laissez-faire, utopian
Objectivists to reside within the conservative fold.[20]

When the furor over Ayn Rand eventually subsided, it became clear
that Chambers and Wills had won: Objectivism did not take conservatives by storm.[21] As William F. Buckley, Jr. reflected in the early 1960s,
Rand's "desiccated philosophy" was inconsistent with "the conservative's
emphasis on transcendence," while her harsh ideological fervor was profoundly distasteful.[22] Rand herself was similarly aware of the unbridge-
able gap. *National Review*, she declared in 1964, was "the worst and
most dangerous magazine in America"; its mixture of religion and capitalism represented a sullying of the rationally defensible (freedom and
capitalism) with mystical, unconvincing obscurantism.[23]

This problem of the relation of religious faith to conservatism (especially the libertarian variety) arose on another front when Max Eastman,
one of *National Review*'s associates and contributors at its founding, resigned from the journal's masthead. Although Eastman had long since
made the pilgrimage from Lenin and Trotsky to passionate belief in laissez-
faire capitalism, he had never abandoned his atheist's suspicion of "eccle-
siastical authoritarianism" and his pragmatist's faith in scientific experiment. Eastman had broken with Communism in part *because* it was a
religion—because, that is, it had not been scientific enough. He therefore spurned the tendency of many other ex-radicals to accept Christianity; he was determined to avoid all entangling alliances with religion and
all threats to the freedom and rationality of man.[24] Finally, in 1958, dismayed by some of *National Review*'s editorial positions and particularly
by its religious perspective, which he considered irrational and even dangerous in its political implications, Eastman departed.[25] He was the only
person ever to leave *National Review* for this reason.[26]

Although the controversies mentioned thus far illuminated significant obstacles to self-definition, in a sense they remained peripheral to
the conservative movement as a whole. Neither Peter Viereck nor Max
Eastman inaugurated any popular alternative to, or massive defections
from, *National Review*-style conservatism. Ayn Rand, for all her pyro-
technics, remained for most conservatives merely the leader of a sect.

None was a central figure in the developing effort to construct (or locate or articulate) a satisfactory conservative consensus. More crucial than the polemics involving Viereck, Eastman, and Rand, who were beyond the pale, were the intramural disputes within the *National Review* circle itself.

Among the first to initiate the search for a viable conservative philosophy was the former Communist warhorse Frank Meyer. An intense, sometimes fiery, heavy-smoking man who worked by night and slept by day, he had slowly fought his way from Communism to libertarian individualism after World War II. Meyer was becoming known as a man who would tolerate no ideological nonsense. "Principles and Heresies" he called his column in *National Review*, and in it he relentlessly exposed deviationists.

One of Meyer's earliest targets was none other than Russell Kirk, whose *Conservative Mind* had done as much as any book to fortify and legitimize the postwar conservative revival. Even before joining *National Review*, Meyer had criticized Kirk in a 1955 article in *The Freeman*. The trouble with Kirk and the new conservatives generally, said Meyer, was a lack of grounding in "clear and distinct principle." For all the froth and tone of their writing, they failed utterly to provide a crisp analytic framework for opposing the statism threatening to engulf us. Conservatism "carries with it...no built-in defense against the acceptance, grudging though it may be, of institutions which reason and prudence would otherwise reject, if only those institutions are sufficiently firmly established." Kirk simply had no standards, no "principle," for achieving his goals. Conservatism? What should one conserve? Meyer was additionally angered by Kirk's denunciations of "individualism." The ex-radical, who believed that "*all* value resides in the individual," felt that Kirk did not comprehend the principles and institutions of a free society. No wonder, then, that some liberals applauded the new conservatism, Meyer concluded bitterly. This amorphous movement was no threat to them.[27]

In an early issue of *National Review*, Meyer again crossed swords with Kirk; this time the issue was one of Meyer's heroes, John Stuart Mill. According to Kirk, history had "refuted" Mill's faith in progress, enlightenment, and rational discussion:

> It is consummate folly to tolerate every variety of opinion, on every topic, out of devotion to an abstract "liberty"; for opinion soon finds its expression in action, and the fanatics whom we tolerated will not tolerate us when they have power.
>
> ...An incessant zeal for repression is not the answer to the complex problem of liberty, either; but...liberty cannot be main-

tained or extended by an abstract appeal to free discussion,
sweet reasonableness, and solitary simple principle.

The threat today, Kirk added, was not, as Mill thought, conformity to custom. It was the very destruction of custom and tradition by "the lust after
novelty."[28] To Meyer, however, such strictures were misleading and unjustifiable. To be sure, Mill's thought was mired in utilitarianism and did not
acknowledge "the source of man's rights in the realm of value beyond history." Mill had not been "absolute" enough! Nevertheless,

> in vindicating the individual person as the measure of value
> over [and] against the collective instrumentalities of state and
> society, and in demanding that the worth of a society should
> be judged by the degree to which it makes possible the free-
> dom of the individual, he vindicated the first principle of
> morality (for no man can act morally unless he is free to choose
> good from evil).

Mill still had much to teach us, particularly in the battle against the State.
Meyer abhorred Kirk's implication that the age of discussion was over
and that the free use of reason was a dangerous political ideal. "The use
of force against those who propound error is wrong," he thundered, "not
because it is inexpedient but because it is an outrage upon the freedom
of man and, in that, upon the very nature of man."[29]

Between Meyer's appeal to universal truths like "the freedom of the
individual" and Kirk's critique of such "abstractions" in the name of history and concrete circumstances lay a vast gulf. No one was more aware
of it than Kirk himself.[30] But the feud between Kirk and Meyer was
really much more than personal. Other conservative intellectuals were
also disturbed by Kirk's seemingly nostalgic and indiscriminate traditionalism. Kirk, a self-styled "Bohemian Tory" and an author of gothic novels, tended to play the traditionalist, too, living in an old family house in
remote Mecosta, Michigan (pop. 200), and referring to himself as "the
last bonnet laird of the stump country."[31] Kirk's adoration of "the wisdom
of our ancestors" was no doubt useful, Richard Weaver observed on one
occasion, but the question was: which ancestors? "After all, Adam was
our ancestor.... If we have an ancestral legacy of wisdom, we have also an
ancestral legacy of folly...."[32]

In these early years Kirk himself did not hesitate to stoke the fires of
controversy. In *The Conservative Mind* he had said flatly: "True conservatism, conservatism uninfected by Benthamite or Spencerian ideas, rises
at the antipodes from individualism. Individualism is social atomism; con-

servatism is community of spirit."[33] In another book he criticized "individualism" as anti-Christian; one could not logically be a Christian and an individualist at the same time. Kirk distinguished between private property and free enterprise—which he supported—and the ideology of individualism, which he labeled "a denial that life has any meaning except gratification of the ego...." The political result of individualism, he asserted, was anarchy.[34] According to Kirk, Friedrich Hayek and the "Manchesterian" economists, as well as more modern liberals such as Arthur Schlesinger, Jr., were all guilty of superficial and false assumptions about the nature of man. It was wrong to expect that economic doctrines alone would save us; it was wrong to conceive of production and consumption as the proper goals for humanity. Conservatism, while hostile to collectivism, was not the equivalent of laissez-faire, nor could it benignly acquiesce in the current structure of the economy. "As the consolidation of economic power progresses," Kirk warned, "the realm of personal freedom will diminish, whether the masters of the economy are state servants or the servants of private corporations." Perhaps, he even suggested, our economy was "*too* efficient for life on a truly human scale."[35]

If Kirk had reservations about Hayek, the scholarly Austrian economist was even more critical of conservatism. In an essay entitled "Why I Am Not a Conservative," published in 1960, Hayek carefully distinguished his "Old Whig" position from that of the European Right. Conservatism, he asserted, lacked a coherent set of principles and programs with which to combat its foes. It was excessively hostile to innovation and new knowledge, ignorant of free market economics, and altogether too inclined to use the State for its own purposes rather than to limit this threat to liberty. It had often been overly nationalistic and had even been willing to acquiesce in socialism. It was a philosophy of drift, anti-intellectualism, and fear.[36]

With Meyer, Kirk, Weaver, Hayek, and other right-wingers already arguing about fundamentals, a liberal scholar, M. Morton Auerbach, entered the fray in 1959 with *The Conservative Illusion*.[37] Defining conservatism as a philosophy which exalted harmony, tranquillity, the minimization of individual desires, and the maximization of community, Auerbach argued that this philosophy, from Plato to Burke to Kirk, had been impaled by historical and logical "contradictions." America, for example, had never been a conservative country; the twentieth century was "the least congenial period in the history of Western civilization for Conservative ideals. Conservatism seeks 'community,' tradition, harmony, and quiescence. In this century, it has found organization, violence, politi-

cal power, and revolutionary upheaval." [38] Repeatedly Auerbach blud-
geoned conservatives (that is, traditionalists) with "dilemmas." If conservatives sought to "adjust" to "historical development," they became
unconservative. If they chose to fight the tides of history, they were
doomed to futility and alienation. Either way, there was no hope: "For
the twentieth century at least, the divorce between Conservatism and
reality is permanent."[39] In an article in *National Review* in 1962, Auerbach
extended his assault to the classical liberal wing of the new Right. To this
contradiction-minded scholar, it was utterly "fallacious" to combine classical liberalism with the "medieval" new conservatism; the whole movement, in fact, was merely a haphazard "do-it-yourself conservatism."[40]

The conservative reply to Auerbach was unanimous: he did not know
what he was talking about.[41] Responding to his charge that conservatism
was a hodgepodge, M. Stanton Evans, the 28-year-old editor of the *Indianapolis News*, claimed that Auerbach had not distinguished between
fundamental conservative principles and transitory "epiphenomena" peculiar to a given epoch. Russell Kirk agreed; Auerbach's difficulty was
that he adhered to "hollow slogans" and tried to compartmentalize reality without realizing that "great political ideas transcend particular institutions and periods." Edmund Burke, for instance, was an exponent of
Christianity and the Great Tradition of philosophy, not of some abstraction like "medievalism." To defend "aristocracy" was not to be outdated
or medieval either. After all, Adams, Jefferson, and Barry Goldwater
believed in a natural aristocracy; were they therefore "medievalists"? Frank
Meyer contended that Auerbach did not recognize that "the Christian
understanding of the nature and destiny of man, which is the foundation
of Western civilization, is always and everywhere what conservatives strive
to conserve." In short, in one way or another, these conservatives were
proposing an "autonomous" definition of conservatism that was relevant
to the ages and not to a single era.[42]

However vigorously the *National Review* conservatives rebutted
Auerbach, it was increasingly obvious in the late 1950s and early 1960s
that the movement desperately needed to discover unity and clarity.
Conservatives lacked a "recognized intellectual general staff," William
Henry Chamberlin lamented.[43] "The conservative movement in America
has got to put its theoretical house in order," William F. Buckley, Jr.
observed as he noted "the failure of the conservative demonstration."[44] A
European contributor to *National Review*, Erik von Kuehnelt-Leddihn,
felt obliged to conclude in 1962 that the movement still had no "precise
vision"; nor did it have a "concrete program, a blueprint, a coherent 'ideol-

ogy.'" There was too much "contrived vagueness," too much "emphasis on negations."[45] Still another conservative commented that "conservatives today are as hopelessly divided by divergent principles, discordant faiths, and conflicting interests as were the British colonists whose united efforts created the United States."[46] It was indeed a "crucial period" for the emerging conservative counterreformation.[47]

And so, insistently, the question recurred: What *was* conservatism? What held the movement together? Russell Kirk, for one, doubted that anything simple and positive did:

> No simple formula can join inseparably the Northerners and the Southerners, the rural interest and the urban interest, the religious conservatives and the utilitarian oldfangled liberals, the anti-Soviet people and the isolationists—not to mention the anti-fluoridationists, the "philosophical" anarchists, and the protectionists. All that can reasonably be hoped for, so far as the immediate future is concerned, is a series of leagues and coalitions of anti-collectivist elements against the collectivist tendency of the times.[48]

Yet even Kirk hoped that "conservative unity of a higher order" might eventually evolve. In the first years of *National Review* many conservative intellectuals were anxious to help the process along.

Against this background of confusion and disputation there developed in the late 1950s and early 1960s a revival of conservative-oriented political philosophy, much of which was pertinent to the conservatives' efforts to define their common identity. This was particularly the case with the increasing scholarship on Edmund Burke.

Stimulated partly by the release of a collection of Burke's correspondence in 1949, studies and sympathetic invocations of Burke proliferated in the 1950s. Russell Kirk's own *The Conservative Mind* was the most notable of the genre. By 1959, interest in Burke was so great that the quarterly *Burke Newsletter* was established under the auspices of *Modern Age*.[49] But not everyone was enthusiastic about the tendency of some conservatives—notably Kirk—to idolize the British statesman. In *The Ethics of Rhetoric*, for example, Richard Weaver denied that Burke was an adequate spokesman for the right-wing revival. Burke's difficulty, said Weaver, was that he argued from circumstance and expediency, not from definition and high principle. And expediency—the politics of Whiggery—was thoroughly insufficient:

> It is, to make the estimate candid, a politics without vision and

consequently without the capacity to survive.

...[A] party which bases itself upon circumstance cannot
outlast that circumstance very long....

...For the rhetorical appeal on which it will stake its life, a
cause must have some primary source of argument which will
not be embarrassed by abstractions or even by absolutes....
Burke was magnificent at embellishment, but of clear rational principle he had a mortal distrust.[50]

Precisely so, echoed Frank Meyer in his 1955 attack on Kirk. Burke was
simply not a reliable teacher of a "firm political position."[51]

The interpretation of Burke which Weaver and Meyer expressed
had a long and distinguished history. Beginning with the work of Henry
Buckle and John Morley in the nineteenth century, Burke had been widely
portrayed as an empiricist, a utilitarian, a defender of immemorial tradition and "prejudice," and a resolute foe of all "metaphysics" and of the
application of inquisitive reason to politics.[52] Small wonder, then, that
conservatives like Meyer and Weaver—anxious to find a *principled* political philosophy—distrusted a man who allegedly hated potentially explosive "abstractions."

Faced with this challenge to their beloved Burke, some traditionalist conservatives began to develop a new perspective on their hero that
might silence his critics. The most notable example of this impulse was
Peter J. Stanlis's *Edmund Burke and the Natural Law*.[53] Stanlis, then a
professor at the University of Detroit and a good friend of Russell Kirk,
zealously defended Burke, not as the proponent of mindless prescription and "social utility" but as "one of the most eloquent and profound
defenders of Natural Law morality and politics in Western civilization."[54]
Relying heavily on the "ancients-moderns" distinction in Leo Strauss's
Natural Right and History, Stanlis located Burke in the tradition of
Aristotle, Cicero, Aquinas, and Thomas Hooker—the tradition, in other
words, of "natural law" rather than "natural rights" à la Hobbes, Locke,
and Rousseau. Burke, in fact, "regarded the Natural Law as a divinely
ordained imperative ethical norm which, without consulting man, fixed
forever his moral duties in civil society."[55] Burke was a Christian humanist rooted in the best aspects of our culture. He was not a shifty, relativistic defender of the status quo merely because it had existed for generations.

The attractiveness of this view of Burke for many traditionalist conservatives was immense. Here was proof, Russell Kirk triumphantly declared in his foreword to Stanlis's book, that Burke was not a Benthamite

or an opponent of the "true rights of men."[56] Here was the demonstration, one could almost hear the Burkeans saying, that Burke was relevant to postwar America. For them Stanlis had solved the problem of tradition and reason. He had shown Burke to be a defender not merely of peculiar interests but, above all, of a body of *principles*, a tradition of thought that transcended the "epiphenomena" of eighteenth-century England. Burke was not opposed to theory but only to "'bad theory'—theory that is doctrinaire, speculative, abstract, and without adequate reference and relevance to political practice."[57] One could, in other words, be both a traditionalist and a rational man. Edmund Burke was a conservative sage after all.[58]

Stanlis's study signified more than an effort to rescue Burke from contemporary misunderstanding. It reflected as well the continuing conservative search for truth in the premodern past, a development powerfully assisted by the work of Leo Strauss and his disciples. In such works as *Thoughts on Machiavelli* and *What Is Political Philosophy?* Strauss continued to indict the "moderns" and defend the worth of classical political philosophy against positivist and historicist onslaughts. To Strauss the truly evil genius and prophet of modernity was Machiavelli, who had launched a subtle and massive assault on ancient and Christian teachings. To the ancients, the goal of political life was virtue, not freedom, and political philosophy was "guided by the question of the best regime."[59] The audacious and immoral philosophy of Machiavelli, however, "takes its bearings by how men live as distinguished from how they ought to live.... Its symbol is the Beast Man as opposed to the God Man: it understands man in the light of the sub-human rather than of the superhuman."[60] While the ancients emphasized the fixed nature of man, Machiavelli and the moderns asserted the malleability of man and the importance of "institutions" rather than the "formation of character" to control him. [61] While the ancients exalted the life of the seeker of wisdom (the philosopher) and judged regimes in the light of this transcendent good, Machiavelli and his followers lowered their sights and transmogrified philosophy into an instrument "to relieve man's estate or to increase man's power or to guide man toward the rational society...."[62] Conservatives did not always find it easy to apply Strauss's teachings to the present,[63] but they did recognize in his prodigious scholarship an intellectual tour de force. For Strauss was meticulously revealing and critically analyzing the fundamental assumptions of modernity in contrast with the sober, moderate, and still-relevant wisdom of the ancients. And for those who tended to equate modernity with liberalism, Strauss's formidable critiques were welcome indeed.

To many conservatives, then, natural law and other classical teachings were a weapon that could be used against the modern tendency, inaugurated by Machiavelli and Hobbes, to equate right with will and justice with power. It was an assertion of unbending absolutes against the disintegrative ethical relativism of the liberals. It was also a way of affirming a tradition—the Great Tradition—against libertarians who accused traditionalists of being so bemused by history that they did not *stand* for anything.

By the early 1960s the interest in natural law which Stanlis's book exemplified had grown to considerable proportions within the conservative camp. While the scholarly response to Stanlis was decidedly mixed,[64] many conservatives felt that the tide was turning at last. After decades of positivist-relativist dominance, wrote the conservative sociologist Will Herberg in 1962, "the reality of something higher than positive law is again becoming recognized in American ethical and legal thought." In fact, here was a distinction of importance:

> Conservatives, true to the classical tradition of our culture, whether Hebrew or Greek, of course affirm the doctrine of the higher law as the very cornerstone of their moral, social and political philosophy. Liberals, especially in the past century and the earlier part of this, have frequently rejected this doctrine in favor of some form of legal positivism, cultural relativism, and moral pragmatism....[65]

But it was a *conservative* version of natural law that was being propounded. Or, to state the point more accurately, it was natural *law*—an objective moral norm—not subjective natural "rights," that some conservatives now cherished. In many ways, this was a useful conception. To plead the prosaic lessons of history and prudence against the sweeping and alluring liberal doctrine of the "rights of man" was to be at a rhetorical disadvantage, as Richard Weaver had perceptively warned. But to take one's stand for the sweeping, universalistic natural *law* was to enter the debate on more equal rhetorical terms. Moreover, by combining Burke—long the symbol of the appeal to history and expediency—with natural law theory, conservatives were in effect attempting to bridge the gulf between their libertarian and traditionalist wings.

Meanwhile, many traditionalists were examining with enthusiasm a new and grand venture by Eric Voegelin in the philosophy of history. Already known for his influential concept of gnosticism, the German émigré scholar published in 1956 and 1957 the first three volumes of *Order and History*, an attempt to derive the "order of history" from "the history of order."[66] According to Voegelin, "existence is partnership in the community of being," a community or hierarchy which includes an invisible world—that is, transcendent, divine being. Voegelin proposed to examine the history of men's efforts (by "symbolization" in religion, philosophy, and literature) to render intelligible the "order of being" in which they "participated." The history of this symbolization revealed a progression (which he traced in the civilizations of the ancient Near East, Israel, and Greece) from "compact" to "differentiated" experiences and symbols. In fact, twice in the history of mankind there had occurred an extraordinary "leap in being," that "epochal event that breaks the compactness of the early cosmological myth and establishes the order of man in his immediacy under God...."[67] These occasions were Israel's experience of Revelation and Greece's discovery of philosophy. To Voegelin, the "struggle for the truth of order," by which he meant the metaphysical order of being, was "the very substance of history,"[68] and this struggle he proposed to trace. It was a gigantic task—one that could only be undertaken now, in the 1950s. For only now had the scholarly sources and tools become adequate to the task, and only now had "the ideological mortgages on the work of science" vanished. Voegelin listed some of the "forces of the Gnostic age" whose intellectual vitality was waning: "...the varieties of nationalism, of progressivist and positivist, of liberal and socialist, of Marxian and Freudian ideologies, the neo-Kantian methodologies in imitation of the natural sciences, scientistic ideologies such as biologism and psychologism, the Victorian fashion of agnosticism and the more recent fashions of existentialism and theologism...."[69]

Voegelin's massive and learned volumes quickly won recognition among conservative intellectuals. *Modern Age* devoted a special symposium to his work.[70] Frederick Wilhelmsen called it "the most ambitious rival to the work of Spengler and Toynbee," while Gerhart Niemeyer cited Voegelin as one who had "begun to counterattack the intellectual decay of the West."[71] What did conservatives find of value in the often abstruse subject matter and technical vocabulary of this scholar? For one thing, they believed that Voegelin had decisively contributed to a methodological stretching of the scope of political science. As Peter Stanlis commented, Voegelin's work was an "indispensable" antidote to "all modern Gnostic movements which are blind to the religious order in history."[72] Voegelin was an unabashed theist; he spoke of God, the soul, being, and revelation. Moreover, he emphasized the historic conservative concern for order—at the interlocking levels of being, society, and the soul. Above all, he presented a new interpretation of man's collective existence in terms of "attunement" to the order of being, and he spoke of the crises that occurred when men spurned that order and instead pursued "Gnostic" alternatives that scorned "the finite conditions of human life."[73] It was an arresting synthesis that appealed to many religious conservatives struggling to comprehend the disorder of the West.

In a sense, the natural law conservatives and the Voegelinians (usually the same people) were groping for what Frank Meyer later called "an objective moral order based on ontological foundations,"[74] an order above the flux of history. That every society must be grounded in such an order, that every society does and ought to adhere to fundamental truths (an orthodoxy) was, during these years, the persistent theme of the political scientist Willmoore Kendall. In article after article, as well as in *The Conservative Affirmation* (1963), Kendall criticized the liberal notion of an open society. According to the Great Tradition of political philosophy, Kendall argued, "any viable society has an orthodoxy—a set of fundamental beliefs, implicit in its way of life, that it cannot and should not and, in any case, will not submit to the vicissitudes of the market place." The conservative maintained, as did the Great Tradition, that "no society can survive—or should survive—without foundations driven deep in religious belief." America must not become a society so open that anyone had the "unlimited right to think and say what you please, with impunity and without let or hindrance...."[75] Kendall was particularly critical of John Stuart Mill, whom he portrayed as a skeptic and relativist who did not really believe that truth was ultimately attainable at all. In fact, said Kendall, Mill's freedom of speech was "inseparable from...[his] assault on truth," and Mill was "in full rebellion" against religion, philosophy, and traditional society. In the end, Mill's ideal open society would actually become utterly *in*tolerant. Adhering in effect to "a national religion of skepticism," Mill's society would have no unyielding scruples about persecuting *its* dissenters. After all, if everyone's opinions were equal in value, they might be equally valueless, so why worry if unpopular ones were suppressed?

> In order to practice tolerance on behalf of the pursuit of truth, you have first to value and believe in not merely the pursuit of truth *but truth itself, with all its accumulated riches to date. The all-questions-are-open-questions society cannot do that; it cannot, therefore, practice tolerance towards those who disagree with it.*

Even if such a society did not persecute, it would "descend ineluctably into ever-deepening *differences* of opinion, into progressive breakdown of those common premises upon which alone a society can conduct its affairs by discussion, and so into the abandonment of the discussion process and the arbitrament of public questions by violence and civil war." Kendall insisted that he was not seeking a totally closed society. But he wanted to establish above all that the open society concept then being proposed as America's public truth or self-interpretation was historically, logically, and philosophically untenable.[76]

While Kendall and other traditionalists (frequently Roman Catholic, like Kendall himself)[77] were striving to find absolutes on which to rely in a relativistic and secular society, libertarians were also at work on the task of constructing a more coherent philosophy. Their most outstanding effort was Friedrich Hayek's summa, *The Constitution of Liberty*, an erudite case for strictly limited government, a free market, the impersonal rule of law, and social development by spontaneous growth rather than conscious planning and coercion.[78] In making his plea for a free society, Hayek did not, like many conservatives, cite universal and immutable truths. Instead, drawing heavily on the British skeptical empiricist tradition of David Hume, Adam Ferguson, and Adam Smith, Hayek based his case on the ineluctable fact of ignorance: "...no human mind can comprehend all the knowledge which guides the actions of society....[Therefore there is] need for an impersonal mechanism, not dependent on individual human judgments, which will coordinate the individual efforts."[79] The more civilized we are, said Hayek, the *less* we are capable of managing the fantastically complex social organism.[80] Consequently, "the case for individual freedom rests chiefly on the recognition of the inevitable ignorance of all of us concerning a great many of the factors on which the achievement of our ends and welfare depends."[81] Society would be better off if we were *free*. Hayek was no anarchist. On the contrary, he sanctioned a surprising amount of government intervention to provide, for example, a minimum level of protection against suffering and disasters beyond individual control. But he insisted that all such activities be guided by "general abstract rules equally applicable to all."[82] Hayek's enemies were coercion, arbitrariness, discrimination, and the omnivorous administrative discretionary state that tried to *design* progress rather than allow societies to grow under the impersonal rule of law.

Although there was much in Hayek's book that all conservatives could approve (especially his critique of the welfare state), neither it nor any of the other efforts discussed so far commanded universal approbation in the early 1960s. While the increasing sophistication of both libertarian and traditionalist conservative scholars was a mark of maturity, no synthesis of clashing perspectives was discernible. Had a revised Edmund Burke been put forward as a mutually acceptable source of conservative wisdom? Writing in *National Review*, Stephen Tonsor, a young historian at the University of Michigan, emphatically rejected this approach. Burke was not a proper ancestor of the new conservatism. In fact, Tonsor maintained, Burke's heritage was "contradictory." There were *two* Burkes: the conservative-reactionary "who saw liberty as a danger,...who feared moral abstractions,...who considered the state a providential entity...," and the conservative-liberal whose heir was William Gladstone.[83] Was Eric Voegelin's work, then, an agreed-upon rallying point? While many conservatives discussed his books and occasionally quoted his phrases, there was little evidence that he was dazzling the entire movement into discipleship. Furthermore, the naturalistically inclined supporters of Leo Strauss were critical of Voegelin's religious categories and his assumption of the intervention of God in history. Religious faith, implied the Straussians, was an unacceptable point of departure for philosophers—a contention which troubled some theistic conservatives.[84] Nor was the argumentative Kendall a source of unity. His critique of John Stuart Mill and the open, freedom-centered society was hardly likely, for instance, to appease Frank Meyer, whom he even called on one occasion "a great though lovable sinner."[85]

Friedrich Hayek's magisterial *Constitution of Liberty* did not escape criticism, either. To some he appeared to be altogether too oblivious to principles beyond the world of economics. The Austrian conservative Erik von Kuehnelt-Leddihn claimed that Hayek seemed to be arguing that "if freedom were not pragmatically productive, there would be no *reason* for freedom."[86] Frank Meyer was similarly troubled. He did not think Hayek should have defended freedom on utilitarian grounds but on "the nature of men and the very constitution of being." Hayek, as an "Old Whig," suffered, said Meyer, from the weakness of Whiggery: "its fear of acknowledging the absolute transcendent values upon which its strength is founded."[87] As if to complicate matters further, Hayek had concluded his volume with a forceful *rejection* of conservatism![88]

Thus despite the valuable and learned efforts which conservative intellectuals made in the late 1950s and early 1960s to define a satisfactory philosophical posture, they had obviously not succeeded. Not all these books, of course, were expressly intended to serve such a specific purpose. But explicitly or implicitly they all were contributions toward that end. Still, for every thesis propounded, there continued to be many vocal dissents. Even as sober scholarly research went on, the quest for unity was leading to further polemics.

In the early 1960s the already simmering pot boiled over. On one side were the traditionalists: defenders of order, consensus, morality, "right reason," religion, truth, virtue. On the other stood the libertarians, classical liberals, and "Old Whigs," whose "god terms" (to borrow a phrase of Richard Weaver's) were individual liberty, free enterprise, laissez-faire, private property, reason, and yet again individual liberty.

Often, the initiators of the exchanges were aggressive libertarian "individualists," many of them young. Some of the sharpest denunciations of the traditionalists appeared in the *New Individualist Review*, founded in 1961 by graduate students of Friedrich Hayek at the University of Chicago. In one such article James M. O'Connell, a doctoral candidate at the University of Wisconsin, contended that Russell Kirk and the new conservatism were utterly alien to libertarianism. Kirk scorned reason, or what he called "defecated rationality." Yet, O'Connell claimed, tradition was valid only if it conformed to "those principles, discoverable by reason, which regulate human action." Furthermore, Kirk and the new conservatives were overtly hostile to individualism and laissez-faire and did not truly favor freedom. On the contrary, they sought an "aristocratic elite" and "a collectivism of the Right to save us from both the 'inhumanity' of capitalism, with its 'rootless individualism,' and the collectivism of the Left."[89]

Even *National Review* came under fire. According to Ronald Hamowy, a student of Hayek and an associate editor of *New Individualist Review*, Buckley's journal was betraying the libertarian tradition of Garrett, Albert Jay Nock, and Frank Chodorov; it was seeking not to "limit" the State but to "control" it. *National Review* was guilty of an antilibertarian, bellicose foreign policy in the name of anti-Communism. It was willing to squelch civil liberties at home and engage in racist imperialism abroad in violation of the universal natural rights philosophy of the Declaration of Independence. It tended to be arrogant about its Christianity and willing to merge Church and State. It exalted the community over the individual and could muster only "lukewarm" support for a free economy.[90]

Clearly, then, a critical moment in the history of the postwar Right had arrived. At issue was nothing less than the intellectual legitimacy of the coalition that had developed in the mid-1950s, a coalition symbolized and promoted by *National Review*. Did libertarians and traditionalists really have any business associating with one another? What bond united devout

Catholics and secular (or religiously indifferent) economists, people who despised John Stuart Mill and people who praised him, lovers of tradition who criticized militant individualism and others who championed dynamic laissez-faire? Kirk and Meyer, Kendall and Rothbard, Stanlis and Tonsor, Voegelin and Hayek, Wilhelmsen and Chodorov—did such intellectuals have *anything* substantial in common?

In the early 1960s one man more than any other was convinced that they did, that beneath the factional differences lay a genuine consensus of principle and aspiration. This man, of all people, was Frank Meyer—the ever-vigilant Frank Meyer, the very individual who had done so much to illuminate the chasm a few years earlier. Now, in a book and several articles, he attempted energetically to close the fissure that threatened to sunder the conservative movement.[91]

It was not that Meyer was suddenly abandoning his old views: he continued to live as well as preach his individualist philosophy. Residing in a secluded mountain home in Woodstock, New York, he became famous for his crackling, uncompromising creed, often expounded over the telephone long after midnight to conservatives all over the land. So heavily did this intense, cheerfully argumentative, chess-playing, zip code-hating metaphysician of the Right communicate by telephone that Willmoore Kendall once quipped that an "emergency call" from Meyer to his friend Brent Bozell could be defined as "one which interrupts the *regular* call from Frank Meyer to Brent Bozell."[92] In defiance of the compulsory school attendance laws, he was successfully educating his two sons, year after year, at home. When it came to matters of principle, Meyer would not yield an inch.[93]

What were the principles that comprised his attempted synthesis? Absolutely fundamental, he argued, was "the freedom of the person"—"the central and primary end of political society," "the decisive concern of political action and political theory." [94] To Meyer, man was a "rational, volitional, autonomous individual"; freedom was "of the essence of his being"[95]—indispensable, in fact, to his pursuit of virtue. Political order was to be judged according to its contribution to individual freedom. Moreover, the political sphere was sharply limited. The State had but three limited functions: national defense, preservation of domestic order, and the administration of justice between man and man. From this perspective Meyer proceeded to demolish the claims of those—collectivist liberals *and* new conservatives[96]—who disparaged the individual and his reason in the name of the State or "community" or society. There was no such independent entity as society, Meyer contended. Society was a "myth";

the individual was supreme. "Society and the state were made for individual men, not men for them."[97] From Plato and the ancient Athenians to twentieth-century liberals, too many people had hypostatized the State. Even some new conservatives were willing to utilize the State to impose their ideas of virtue upon the citizenry. To Meyer this was utterly wrong. The "achievement of virtue" was not a *political* question at all; it was none of the State's business.[98] Freedom—uncoerced choice—was the absolutely indispensable condition of the pursuit of virtue. "Unless men are free to be vicious they cannot be virtuous. No community can make them virtuous."[99] Freedom was the ultimate *political* end; virtue was the ultimate end of man as man. The new conservatives, unfortunately, could not grasp this distinction: "By their insistence on the use of political power for the inculcation of virtue, by their refusal to take a principled position in defense of a state limited to establishing the conditions of freedom, they disqualify themselves as effective opponents of liberal collectivism."[100] Frank Meyer had devoted fourteen years of his life to the Communist Party. Recoiling from Big Brother, he was not about to let conservatives try to impose *their* version of the good society. People should be left alone to work out their own salvation.

Yet while Meyer continued to level a barrage against certain new conservatives, he was also striving to articulate the common ground which he believed American conservatives actually shared. Time and again he insisted that his conservatism was not mere "nineteenth-century liberalism," which he admitted had been weakened by utilitarianism and excessively antitraditional skepticism and secularism. According to Meyer, the American conservative movement was the victim of a tragic "bifurcation" of the Western tradition in the nineteenth century. On one side were the authoritarian conservatives, rightly concerned for virtue and order but wrongly willing to use government to achieve their ends. They confused the moral and political realms. On the other side were the classical liberals, commendably devoted to the limited state, the autonomous individual, and the free economy. But *they* were increasingly indifferent to the "organic moral order" and unable "to distinguish between the *authoritarianism* with which men and institutions suppress the freedom of men, and the *authority* of God and truth." If Meyer was tenaciously critical of extreme traditionalism, he was fully aware of the traditionalist thesis that liberalism had grown relativistic, unsure of moral principles, parasitic, and ultimately acquiescent to the rise of totalitarian ideologies.

He therefore took his stand for freedom as required not by utility but by "the constitution of being." He too had been reading Voegelin. Meyer was no religious skeptic or scoffer at all tradition. He contended that "the Christian understanding of the nature and destiny of man" was what conservatives were trying to save. He insisted that conservatives must absorb the best of *both* branches of the divided conservative mainstream. This was the true heritage of the West—"reason operating within tradition." While Meyer's position soon became known as "fusionism," he was not happy with the label, for he believed that he was only articulating an instinctive, already existing conservative consensus—the consensus forged so brilliantly by the Founding Fathers in 1787.[101]

To demonstrate that his "fusionist" synthesis was not a fantasy, Meyer edited an entire anthology, *What Is Conservatism?*, published in 1964; both sides contributed to it. Kirk and Kendall defended their brands of traditionalism; M. Stanton Evans (a disciple of Meyer's "fusionism") and Wilhelm Röpke defended libertarianism, while Hayek contributed his famous "Why I Am Not a Conservative." Other conservatives—including Buckley, Stanley Parry, Stephen Tonsor, Garry Wills, John Chamberlain, and Stefan Possony—sought in various ways to transcend or synthesize the theoretical divergence. In an optimistic conclusion, Meyer claimed to discern a true consensus amid the undeniable variations of "emphasis" that pervaded the book. Despite differences, even "eccentric" differences here and there, the conservative intellectuals he assembled agreed, said Meyer, on several fundamentals. First, they all believed in "an objective moral order" of "immutable standards by which human conduct should be judged." Second, whether they emphasized human rights and freedoms or duties and responsibilities, they unanimously valued "the human person" and opposed liberal attempts to use the State "to enforce ideological patterns on human beings." While they disagreed about the extent to which the State should be circumscribed, they all thought that it *should* be circumscribed. They were deeply suspicious of "planning" and attempts to centralize power. They joined in defense of the Constitution "as originally conceived" and shared an aversion to the "messianic" Communist threat to "Western civilization." For Meyer the book abundantly demonstrated the intellectual cohesiveness of the resurgent conservative movement.[102]

The early responses of other right-wing intellectuals to Meyer's efforts, however, suggested otherwise. In the introduction to *The Conservative Affirmation*, for example, Willmoore Kendall suggested that Meyer was a doctrinaire[103]—a charge echoed by Russell Kirk in a blistering review of *In Defense of Freedom* in 1964. Kirk excoriated Meyer for being "filled with detestation of all champions of authority," for striving to turn conservatism into an ideology, for seeking "to supplant Marx by Meyer," for deification of liberty in the abstract, and for arrogant zealotry.[104] Less harsh but also critical was the Duke University professor John Hallowell, another of Meyer's new conservative targets. "For all his avowed concern for the absolute value of human individuals," Hallowell charged, "he is singularly unconcerned about the problems of persons."[105] Even Richard Weaver, to whom Meyer later dedicated *What Is Conservatism?*[106] thought that *In Defense of Freedom* went too far. In his sweeping attacks on those new conservatives who espoused the value of community, Meyer had taken "a long step in the direction of Thoreau's anarchic individualism...."[107] And Felix Morley, reviewing Meyer's anthology, concluded that despite Meyer's "valiant effort," a theoretical consensus had simply not been attained. The conservative edifice remained rickety.[108]

The most extensive scrutiny of Meyer's position came from the very traditionalist Catholic conservative, L. Brent Bozell, brother-in-law of William F. Buckley, Jr. In an incisive essay, Bozell contended that the libertarians and so-called fusionists put altogether too much stress on free choice as a condition of the pursuit of virtue; people *always* have moral freedom to seek salvation, regardless of external circumstances. Hence the libertarian claim that society should constantly maximize freedom in order to encourage virtue was fallacious. In fact, the logic of such a program would result in the destruction not only of State coercion (a presumed enemy of virtue) but of all other institutions that impinge on the freest possible choice. "In short, libertarianism's first command—maximize freedom—applies with equal vigor to all of societies' activities; and the meaning of the command, in effect, is this: *virtue must be made [as] difficult as possible.*" Such was not, Bozell insisted, the *Christian* understanding of politics. For God's purposes included the attempt "to establish temporal conditions conducive to human virtue—that is, to build a Christian *civilization.*" And that included public attempts to "ease the way to virtue." The purpose of politics, in other words, was the promotion not of freedom but of virtue.

What, after all, *was* virtue? If, as Bozell argued, it meant conformity with human nature and "the divine patterns of order," then freedom was simply not necessary to virtue per se. An act could be virtuous even if it were instinctive or coerced. The quest was less important than the achievement. To Bozell freedom, defined as "the urge to be free from God," was *not* the highest value. Ideally, we should strive to limit it, for "true sanctity is achieved only when man loses his freedom—when he is freed of the temptation to displease God."

In building a virtuous Christian commonwealth, how far should the State venture? To Bozell this was a question of prudence; each case must be analyzed separately. It was decidedly not a question to be answered by "ritualistic libertarianism" and Meyer's concept of the trinitarian state.[109] While Bozell professed high regard for the free market, he did not hold it to be the highest good. Relentlessly he hammered his points home: "The chief purpose of politics is to aid the quest for virtue." The State is one of many institutions appropriate to this end. "Political (and economic) freedoms" are means which "the prudent commonwealth will adopt in such measure as they are conducive to the virtue of its citizens." Bozell had no desire to defend the nineteenth century, which had, he asserted, inevitably produced the ghastly twentieth. Nor was he going to join in paeans to the free society. "The story of how the free society has come to take priority over the good society is the story of the decline of the West."[110]

An indirect but even more total challenge to Meyer's fusionist efforts came from another Roman Catholic, Stanley Parry, a priest and professor at Notre Dame and a former student of Willmoore Kendall at Yale. Borrowing heavily from Eric Voegelin (and reminiscent at times of Whittaker Chambers), Parry analyzed the character and options of a society which experiences the most fundamental of disorders: the "civilizational crisis" in which "the very structure of the community's experience of truth in history" is threatened and tradition "falls out of existence." In this ultimate, metapolitical crisis, no political half-measures can save us. Only a new "communal experience of truth," "an authentic revitalization of divine revelation in the soul of every man," can suffice. But if—as the very appearance of Parry's article suggested—this final crisis had arrived, the challenge to Frank Meyer's work was obvious: *even if* a libertarian-traditionalist synthesis could be thrashed out, it would be irrelevant and superficial. Once a civilizational crisis occurs, Parry claimed, it is already too late for man to save himself. And Parry also made it clear that neither "spiritual individualism" nor "economic individualism" was capable of solving the problem of "right social order." [111]

Responding to these challenges, Meyer did not budge from his fusionist position. Freedom and virtue *were* interlocked, and Bozell, despite his disavowals, *was* veering dangerously toward authoritarianism and theocracy: he would give some men the power to impose their imperfect version of God's will on their fellow men. Privately, Meyer believed that the controversy really reflected a split between Catholic and Protestant

Christianity.[112] Publicly, however, he said only that Bozell was abandoning the "humanist element" in the Western heritage by his contrast between the good and the free societies. Against Bozell, Meyer maintained what he called a "balanced" view of mankind and its destiny.[113] As for Father Parry, Meyer simply contended that our civilization had not become irrevocably decayed, that the "civilizational crisis" was not upon us, that conservatism was not irrelevant, that the "prophetic response" transcending evil institutions was not yet imperative.[114]

While Meyer was fending off traditionalist criticism, fusionism was also receiving fire from the more extreme libertarians. In an essay in *Modern Age*, Ronald Hamowy presented once more the complaint already voiced by his teacher Friedrich Hayek. Neo-conservatism was a "polar opposite" of libertarianism. Conservatism was hostile to freedom, anticapitalistic, suspicious of reason, and willing (he cited Bozell) to impose a particular set of values on recalcitrant foes. Hamowy paid little attention to Meyer's "middle way," preferring instead to criticize men like Kirk, Bozell, and Kendall. But he did indicate his dissatisfaction with fusionism: "It is no solution to contend, as does Frank Meyer, that reason must operate *within* tradition when the crucial problem to be answered involves the choice of which tradition to follow."[115]

With this clamor and crossfire disturbing the conservative camp, it is not surprising that John Hallowell, never a member of the *National Review* circle, observed in 1964 that conservatives were "having difficulty agreeing among themselves as to what it is precisely they stand for."[116] It is not surprising that one student of the movement complained of the "cacophony" emanating from it.[117] And yet, rather surprisingly, by the mid-1960s the tumult began to subside. Perhaps, as Meyer remarked, the disputants had run out of fresh things to say.[118] Certainly they had other topics on their mind—the rise of Senator Goldwater, for instance. And as the dust settled, many conservatives began to make a common discovery: that Meyer's fusionism had won. Quietly, with little fanfare, by a process he later called "osmosis," fusionism became for most *National Review* conservatives a fait accompli.[119] Significantly, Meyer's arch-rival (but close friend) L. Brent Bozell, also later agreed that "fusion" did become the de facto consensus.[120] Looking back on the early 1960s, William Rusher, publisher of *National Review* and a self-designated "devout fusionist," called attention to Meyer's "strategic integration" of right-wing thought.[121] Peter Witonski, a young conservative scholar, likewise commented several years later that Meyer was "the first conservative theorist thoroughly to comprehend the uniqueness of American conservatism, and to explain this uniqueness to the conservative rank and file."[122] Naturally, fusionism continued to have its critics, but it was an indication of Meyer's influence that they, not he, remained on the periphery or even left the movement. It was Meyer who would write *The Conservative Mainstream* in 1968—not Hamowy, not Bozell.

If fusionism had indeed triumphed, it is important to recognize precisely what this development meant. The success of Meyer's formulation involved not so much the acceptance of a dogma or system as the ascendancy of a particular way of thinking and acting. Three factors account for its emergence. First, many conservatives adopted fusionism because, one suspects, they *wanted* to. They *wanted* to believe that they had found a base in principle. Perhaps they had tired of factional feuding; more likely they were increasingly cognizant of the need to avoid either quixotic antistatism or morose authoritarianism if their movement was to capture national power and respect. At any rate, after some fierce polemics, Meyer's synthesis was, in effect, accepted. If "fusion" implied practical collaboration with others whose angles of vision did not coincide with one's own, most conservatives were clearly fusionists in this sense by the mid-1960s or even earlier.

Second, fusionism as an attempt at theoretical harmony was immensely assisted by the cement of anti-Communism throughout the years of self-definition. It is extraordinarily noteworthy that anti-Communism, one of the three principal tributaries of the postwar conservative mainstream, was not a significant source of tension in most of these polemics at all.[123] Instead, nearly all conservatives were bound together by consciousness of a common mortal enemy. The threat of an external foe (which included liberalism, too) was an invaluable source of cohesion. Back in 1949 the neo-liberal German economist Wilhelm Röpke had predicted the emergence of a kind of fusion:

> ...the essential thing to understand is that we are now engaged in the final battle between collectivism (totalitarianism) and the forces which fight for the freedom and the dignity of man; in this combat it will become ever more difficult to separate the heritage of Christian social doctrine from all that is essential and lasting in liberalism.[124]

Many conservatives believed that this fusion had occurred. Their sense of combat ("the final struggle") with a common foe helped to keep them together.

Finally, when conservatives turned away from rarefied theoretical disputes about theology or historical genealogy (What think ye of Burke?

or Mill?) and considered the day-to-day conservatism they felt "in their hips" (a phrase of Kendall's), they often found that it was not so difficult to identify what they stood for after all. Few conservatives would have objected to Meyer's list of conservative principles at the end of *What Is Conservatism?* Few would have disagreed with William Henry Chamberlin's brief definition: "Conservatism at all times and in all countries has stood for religion, patriotism, the integrity of the family and respect for private property as the four pillars of a sound and healthy society."[125] Nor would they have had reservations about a more negative but still illuminating description of their views supplied by Meyer:

> American conservatives are united in opposition to the growth of government power—of what is known as the welfare state— and to the centralization of that power in the Federal executive; they are opposed to the characteristic leveling egalitarianism of the time...; they reject what they consider the presently established national policy of appeasement and retreat before Communism, and they stand for firm resistance to its advance and for determined counterattack as the only guarantee of the survival of the American Republic and of our institutions generally.[126]

Definitions like these did not, of course, solve the problems of emphasis which divided many conservatives. But neither were they mere effusions of meaningless rhetoric. Moreover, Meyer and other conservatives never tired of stressing that conservatism was not an ideology, complete with sacred texts or a Fourteen Points. It was part of the wisdom and genius of conservatism that it did not try to encapsulate all its beliefs in a handbook of doctrines. Thus whatever the historical or theoretical incongruity of the conservative alliance, at the level of practical belief it seemed quite natural and sensible to most right-wing intellectuals. What was so strange about simultaneously opposing centralized government, supporting a nonsocialist economy, and adhering to traditional morality? What was so inconsistent about being at once a Christian, an anti-Communist, and a believer in private property and individual responsibility?

Thus fusion (as many conservatives perceived it) was not simply a formalistic contrivance of Meyer; it was the recognition that conservatism was "a house of many mansions"[127] and that ecumenism was the truly logical as well as prudent solution. By the mid-1960s evidence of what William F. Buckley, Jr. called "symbiosis"[128] was increasingly at hand. There was the work of Wilhelm Röpke, a favorite of Russell Kirk and *Modern Age*. Although a firm champion of the free market and a trenchant critic of Keynes and all statism, Röpke did not find his liberalism (old-style) inconsistent with Christianity. At least as early as 1947 he was convinced of the deep and necessary connection between true liberalism and Christianity. Was true liberalism opposed to the totalitarian state?

> It was Christianism [sic] alone which accomplished the revolutionary deed of delivering people as children of God from the stranglehold of the state...the wall which separates us, as far as the concept of freedom is concerned, from antiquity is Christianity, to which we owe the sentence, "Render therefore unto Caesar the things that are Caesar's, and to God the things that are God's." [129]

It was Christianity which had established the dignity of the individual and had created the rationale for the limited state. Fifteen years later, Frank Meyer would say the same thing.[130] Furthermore, in the same article Röpke stressed "how much those of us who are trying to free liberalism from the portentious [sic] follies of the 19th century...owe to Catholic thought."[131] In 1957 the German economist reiterated that "the patrimony of Christian social philosophy...increasingly...merges with all that is essential and enduring in liberalism."[132]

Three years later Röpke's book *A Humane Economy* appeared in the United States;[133] it was the very model of fusionism. Effortlessly Röpke combined an economist's defense of the free market (in terms that libertarians could accept) with a neo-conservative defense of Christian humanism and an assault on "modern mass society." Friedrich Hayek could have written most of the economic analysis; Russell Kirk (whom Röpke often quoted, along with Ortega y Gasset and many other traditionalist saints) could have written the social criticism. Time after time, Röpke reiterated that the two themes were inseparable: "...the market economy is the economic order proper to a definite social structure and to a definite spiritual and moral setting."[134] The market was important, but it was not enough.

> Self-discipline, a sense of justice, honesty, fairness, chivalry, moderation, public spirit, respect for human dignity, firm ethical norms—all of these are things which people must possess before they go to market and compete with each other. These are the indispensable supports which preserve both market and competition from degeneration. Family, church, genuine communities, and tradition are their sources.[135]

Family, church, community, tradition—new conservative terms. Private property, competition, "decentrism," the folly of interventionism—libertarian themes. Röpke felt no contradiction between the two. Perhaps neo-conservatism and neo-liberalism were not so far apart after all; no wonder both libertarians and traditionalists admired him.

Nor was Röpke an aberration. There was William Henry Chamberlin, once an enthusiast for the Russian "experiment," the disillusioned author of *The Confessions of an Individualist* (1940), and author of *The Evolution of a Conservative* in 1959. Recoiling from Communism in the 1930s, Chamberlin had developed a loathing of tyranny and a consequent affinity for classical liberalism's "rejection of state interference with the political, social, and economic freedom of the individual." "Extreme concentration of power" in the Soviet Union had strengthened his individualism. But the Russian adventure had also stimulated his traditionalist side; he had grown to distrust "doctrinaire blueprints" and "change for the sake of change."[136] Gradually, as he studied unhappily the development of liberalism in the twentieth century, he came to identify himself with the conservatism of Burke, Tocqueville, Burckhardt, and John Adams. Yet in doing so, he was not really abandoning his earlier fundamental beliefs; he was reinforcing them. For conservatism was not, as he perceived it, a threat to liberty but a "shield of liberty," a bulwark against "the revolt of the masses, when the equality of men threatens the quality of man."[137] Chamberlin retained his faith in individualism and considered himself a conservative precisely because conservatism was "the best defense of individualism" in the twentieth century.[138] He retained his faith in limited government and private property and linked conservatism with these principles. Checks and balances, decentralization of power, sound money, love of country, opposition to Communism—these were other conservative motifs, according to Chamberlin.[139] Obviously such analysis did not ascend to the metaphysical realms of Meyer or Bozell. Perhaps for that very reason, Chamberlin exemplified with clarity the actual conservative consensus.

In the early and middle 1960s other signs of emerging harmony multiplied. At the first meeting of the Mont Pélerin Society in 1947, for example, not one practicing Roman Catholic had been present.[140] In its early years, Russell Kirk asserted in 1961, many members of the society had been guilty of espousing "Liberal dogmas" and "rationalistic hostility toward Christianity." Now, Kirk proclaimed, this mood had passed. The new trend was symbolized by its incoming president, Wilhelm Röpke ("the most humane of economists"), and by the appearance before it of Otto von Hapsburg—an indication, Kirk said, of how "the totalitarian threat produces a meeting of minds among conservative and Liberal bodies of opinion." [141] Meanwhile, in 1964, a kind of American equivalent of the Mont Pélerin Society was founded. Meeting nationally in 1965 for the first time, the Philadelphia Society at once became a significant forum for divergent elements in the conservative camp. At the first convention 125 right-wing intellectuals—from Meyer to Kirk, Milton Friedman to Brent Bozell—participated in discussion and debate[142] designed to further the society's purpose: "deepening the moral foundations of a free and ordered society and...broadening the understanding of its basic principles and traditions."[143] The very fact that such a society flourished indicated that conservatives believed a working consensus was attainable and a common framework of discourse did exist.

Another sign of healthy cooperation was the growing William Volker Fund Series in the Humane Studies; by 1963, fifteen scholarly volumes had been published under the fund's auspices. Although heavily oriented toward economics (there were three books by Ludwig von Mises), the list reflected traditionalist interests as well. *Scientism and Values* (1960) and *Relativism and the Study of Man* (1961), both edited by Helmut Schoeck and James Wiggins of Emory University, drew upon not just laissez-faire economists but traditionalists like Eliseo Vivas and Richard Weaver as well. Many of the volumes, in fact, severely criticized positivism, scientism, and relativism. The ability of the small and energetic Volker Fund to bring different conservatives together in the symposia from which came many of its books was a sign of the genuine cooperation sustaining the conservative movement. More than that, the steady production of such serious, academically respectable books reflected the developing intellectual maturity of the right.[144]

By 1966, M. Stanton Evans, editor of the *Indianapolis News* and a leading fusionist, was in a mood to celebrate. It was at last "becoming possible to speak of a conservative consensus," he announced. There was even a whole conservative "third force"—including Buckley, Meyer, Tonsor, Weaver, Röpke, Garry Wills, Jeffrey Hart, and William Rickenbacker—that was spearheading the advance.[145] Evans might with justice have singled out William F. Buckley, Jr. for special praise, for more than any other man it was Buckley, as Meyer himself suggested, who personified fusionism.[146] It was Buckley whose *God and Man at Yale* adumbrated within one book both the libertarian theme of antistatism and the traditionalist concern for the decline of Christian values. It was Buckley, the ecumenical editor of *National Review*, who provided a forum for both factions to articulate their positions.

Finally, there were even indications that Meyer and Kirk, antagonists of long standing, were mellowing a little. If Meyer seemed intent on excluding Kirk from the conservative fold in his *In Defense of Freedom* (1962), two years later he included Kirk in his anthology *What Is Conservatism?*, signaling his acceptance of Kirk's traditionalism as an admissible "emphasis" within the much-sought-after consensus. And if his references to "reason operating within tradition" sometimes seemed contrived, they nevertheless demonstrated a compelling impulse to seek points of agreement. As for Kirk, while he did not cease to differ with Meyer, he, too, was not inclined to be sectarian. In 1961 he publicly wished for "a merging of the best elements in the old conservatism and the old liberalism, predicted by Walter Bagehot a century ago."[147] A year later he was even more explicit:

> What we have seen during recent years in this country, and somewhat earlier in Britain, is the gradual fusion [!] of conservatives and old-fangled liberals...into a fairly coherent body of opinion.[148]

Increasingly, also, Kirk's writings were marked by appeals not simply to "the wisdom of our ancestors" but to objective *norms* that transcended the vicissitudes of history.[149]

Had the ordeal of self-definition which marked conservative thought from 1955 to 1965 ended, then, in a genuine harmony? Was the travail really—legitimately—over? At one level the answer was plainly negative. After a decade of strenuous exploration and argument, conservatives had not constructed a unified philosophy satisfactory to all, and they probably never would. The philosophic gap between traditionalism, with its stress on the restraint of man's will and appetites, and libertarianism, with its zeal for individual freedom and (implicitly) *self*-assertion, remained wide. No amount of verbal juggling could produce theoretical unity out of the positions of a Kirk and a Mises, a Meyer and a Bozell, a Kendall and a Hayek. Even Meyer, with his tactful discussion of "emphases," must have realized that philosophical differences within the conservative community were profound.

And yet, in the end, this perspective is inadequate. On one point the conservatives were undeniably right: for all their imposing theoretical vocabulary, they were not trying to build a consistent philosophical system. For all their intense and sometimes rarefied disputes, they were not generally laboring to impose a definitive ideology on their brethren. Conservatism in America in the 1950s and 1960s was not, in its essence, a speculative or theoretical enterprise. It was an intellectual *movement* with definite political implications. It sought not just to understand the world but to preserve, purify, even restore some of it. The crucial question therefore became: were the terms of cooperation sufficiently clear and consistent on the *intermediate* level of intelligent action to justify an alliance of thoughtful men and women in defense of their civilization and its dearest values? For most conservatives the answer to this question was resolutely affirmative. Their ultimate ideals or their intellectual ancestries might differ, but not their intermediate ends. Time and again, on practical matters—from the production of *National Review* and *Modern Age* to the support of specific political leaders and issues—conservatives found themselves able to collaborate with one another. If fusionism as an "ism" at times seemed artificial, fusion on a personal level appeared to be succeeding. If less than a monolithic force, the conservative intellectual movement was more than an ad hoc coalition.

Let the edges be frayed, then. Let the arguments continue—in the knowledge that if the conservative movement had not attained unity, it had achieved an identity. The awkward and unwieldy coalition had become a partnership.

SEVEN

What is Conservatism in America? The Search for a Viable Heritage

As if the search for theoretical harmony were not by itself sufficiently perplexing, conservative intellectuals faced another challenging problem in the late 1950s and early 1960s: the relation of their philosophy to the American environment. In the first decade after 1945—the years of initial protest and ferment—articulate conservatives had been relatively unconcerned with the specifically American features of the heritage they wished to defend. Traditionalists or new conservatives, shocked by totalitarian mass man and mass society, had often looked to Europeans like Burke, Metternich, Ortega y Gasset, and T.S. Eliot for moral and intellectual instruction, a tendency reinforced by the impact of European émigrés on the American conservative renascence. When they did examine the America around them, traditionalists were frequently repelled by its burgeoning "crowd culture." Libertarians, too, felt beleaguered in America and turned to Europeans like Friedrich Hayek, Ludwig von Mises, and Wilhelm Röpke. They, too, were often burdened with the feeling of being a forlorn Nockian Remnant in a nation following a New Deal-Fair Deal Pied Piper into the darkening world of the Total State. Even some of the former Communists who gave the conservative movement its crusading fervor seemed at first little interested in America as America. Instead, they tended to perceive the United States as a world power, the only logical leader of the worldwide struggle against messianic Communism. From such a perspective, America's domestic problems were much less important than the Third World War.

It is not entirely surprising, therefore, that many left-of-center observers soon insisted, and insisted repeatedly, that the postwar Right was "un-American," peculiarly foreign to the American experience. Undoubtedly the most influential example of this line of criticism was Louis Hartz's *The Liberal Tradition in America*, published in 1955. According to Hartz, "Lockean" liberalism was virtually the only tradition in America; conservatism, which he equated with feudalism and hierarchy, had never been truly indigenous. After all, America had lacked a feudal social structure and, consequently, the ideology appropriate to it. In one way or another, a horde of critics elaborated on the same theme. In 1957 Richard Chase argued that a "discontinuity" existed in America between conservative feelings and liberal ideas; our principal literature, while exhibiting conservative sentiments, nevertheless advanced liberal thoughts.[1] In 1962 Elisha Greifer, examining the quest of Henry and Brooks Adams for a "pre-liberal past," concluded that they had not found one. Why? Because it did not exist. There was only one American tradition—the liberal tradition—and conservatism was forever doomed to be an "exotic import."[2]

Five years later, Allen Guttmann reaffirmed the Hartzian critique. Equating philosophical conservatism with the thought of Edmund Burke, Guttmann contended that Burke's views were utterly remote from American life. Burke denied the right to construct new governments, criticized notions of equality, praised the ideal of hierarchy, and evinced reverence for the past. In all these respects, said Guttmann, he was not only antiliberal; he was also worlds apart from America. The American Revolution was not a conservative event. The Declaration of Independence, by the very fact that it claimed a right of revolution, was a liberal document, not a conservative one. Once the Loyalists fled, Guttmann argued, the truly conservative (or Burkean, as he defined it) elements of American society were gone forever. From then on, conservatism (in his special sense) was spent as a political force. As a purely literary phenomenon, however, it had lived on; its central ideas, such as hierarchy, order, and reverence for an aristocratic past, appealed to the imaginations of many of the greatest American writers.[3]

Whenever conservatives suggested a candidate for an American right-wing Hall of Fame, it seemed that a liberal was ready to deny him admission. Was Edmund Burke himself an appropriate patron saint of such a pantheon? No, said Arnold A. Rogow in the *Antioch Review* in 1957; Burke had little in common with the property-conscious, antireformist, "endarkened conservatism" of the Republican Party. In fact, Rogow audaciously claimed, Burke could actually be linked to the liberal tradition of Jefferson, the two Presidents Roosevelt, and Adlai Stevenson. It was this moderate, tolerant, reforming but not radical movement that most genuinely reflected Burkean conservatism.[4] Was John Adams, then, the founder of American conservatism? No, said Allen Guttmann; he was a Lockean who believed in such anti-Burkean notions as the natural rights philosophy and the right of revolution. Moreover, he rejected such Burkean ideas as the defense of monarchy and aristocracy. While Guttmann conceded that Adams had conservative leanings, he was still only a pessimistic liberal, a philosophe in spite of himself.[5] Could the Old South be a source of conservative values? No again, said Guttmann. The antebellum South was capitalist in economics, middle-class (not aristocratic) in family structure, and generally Jeffersonian and liberal, not Burkean, in political philosophy.[6]

Particularly critical of conservative attempts to construct an American genealogy was the historian Arthur Schlesinger, Jr. His principal target was Russell Kirk, who in *The Conservative Mind* had tried to identify just such an ancestry. To Schlesinger, all the new conservatives' "great scurrying about" for roots had produced only "an odd and often contradictory collection of figures":

> John C. Calhoun, the great theorist of slavery and states rights, and John Quincy Adams, the ardent apostle of abolition and nationalism; Francis Lieber, the champion of moral obligation, and Brooks Adams, the advocate of realism; Irving Babbitt, the archbishop of the Genteel Tradition, and George Santayana, its urbane and devastating critic. This miscellany can hardly rise to the dignity of a tradition—certainly not to the dignity of a conservative tradition.

All this, according to Schlesinger, reflected how "astonishingly indifferent" the new conservatives were "to the concrete life of the American people."[7]

The liberal critique of conservatism was a plausible and forceful one—sufficiently so, in fact, to find an echo among many intellectuals on the Right. William Schlamm, a German refugee and "father" of *National Review*, contended in 1955 that Russell Kirk was mistaken in his "desperate attempts" to show that the United States had always been conservative:

> The specifically *American* experience of life...is indisputably a fierce yen for institutionalized "progress" by utopian legislation and industrial gadgetry. Individual Americans, like Calhoun and Adams, may have known better; the American *species* (to the extent that there really is such a thing) is, of course, populist rather than conservative—and for a very

> forceful reason: America happens to be the only society in
> creation built by *conscious* human intent,...and developed,
> by Europeans *tired* of Europe's ancient commitments, and
> determined,...each in his own way, on a "new beginning."

This did not mean, however, that conservatism was irrelevant to the
nation's future. It meant only that conservatism would succeed "not because it owns an historic mortgage on America's social real estate" but
because of "its moral and aesthetic superiority."[8]

Ralph de Toledano was similarly impressed by the seeming self-
contradiction of an "American" conservatism. The fact was that the contemporary Right was mired in "rootlessness and opportunism"; it was
"bound more by frustration than by doctrine." It supported politicians
like Senators Joseph McCarthy and William Knowland despite their ideological aberrations. It embraced a mythical Southern conservatism, when
in reality the South supported the New Deal and was infected with racism as well. Surveying American politics, literature, and religion, Toledano
detected only a "paucity of conservative thought and action." While a
conservative "spirit" was undeniably stirring, he wrote in 1956, the day
was far distant when this impulse would become truly "organic."[9] A few
years later Toledano expatiated on his theme. While conservative "elements and individuals" had graced the country's past, the present era
demanded far more: a radical-conservative reconstruction. "The time was
ripe for an American Disraeli," he wrote, and on the horizon he could
discern only one such leader: Richard Nixon.[10]

Such interpretations of the American past were by no means passing fancies of the 1950s. As late as 1972, Stephen Tonsor, a conservative
historian at the University of Michigan, was struck by the dynamism,
innovation, and hostility to Burkean prescription that permeated American culture. One of the strongest themes of our experience, he observed,
was the urge to escape history. Indeed, "the notion of 'a fresh start' takes
on the proportions of a national purpose."[11]

Underlying the general liberal conception of America as
unconservative were a number of debatable assumptions. If many conservatives in the early postwar years were noticeably oriented toward
Europe, so, too, were their liberal critics. In order to demonstrate how
uncongenial the United States was to conservatism, the critics repeatedly assumed that Burkean and continental conservatism were the only
kinds that existed. But was this truly the case? Why equate conservatism
with Burke? How useful was it to assert that because America lacked a
feudal social structure, it was therefore not "conservative"? Who had

demonstrated that conservatism was solely the ideology of a feudal, hierarchical society? Who had proved that it should be equated only with "medieval" institutions? If America was distinctive, perhaps its conservatism (if any) was also distinctive. To say that the American experience was fundamentally non-Burkean did not establish that it was liberal, only that it was non-Burkean. But had even that claim really been proven? What *did* Burke stand for? How many Burkes were there?[12] Was Burkean conservatism primarily a defense of a particular eighteenth-century status quo, now long dead, or was it the exposition of a body of timeless truths about man and society, as many conservatives increasingly argued?[13] How much should conservative impulses and insights be linked to transient institutions? Might not old wine be placed in new bottles? And just how accurate was the ritualistic assertion that America was essentially— *essentially*—a restless, dynamic country? In many respects, it undeniably was; one thinks of its industrial might, extraordinarily mobile population, and social fluidity (Horatio Alger, rags-to-riches, opportunity for all, free land, "a fresh start"). But were these the only or even the most relevant factors? Had America's material and physical expansiveness been matched by political, moral, or religious experimentation of equal magnitude? Was it not true that in certain mores, attitudes, and even fundamental beliefs, this supposedly liberal people had remained faithful to its Western heritage?

Lurking in the minds of many liberals (and some conservatives), one suspects, was a perception of America made famous long before them by the expatriate Henry James in his study of Nathaniel Hawthorne. America was not Europe, James observed; it lacked so much:

> No State, in the European sense of the word, and indeed
> barely a specific national name. No sovereign, no court, no
> personal loyalty, no aristocracy, no church, no clergy, no army,
> no diplomatic service, no country gentlemen, no palaces, no
> castles, nor manors, nor old country-houses, nor parsonages,
> nor thatched cottages, nor ivied ruins; no cathedrals, nor abbeys, nor little Norman churches; no great Universities, nor
> public schools—no Oxford, nor Eton, nor Harrow; no literature, no novels, no museums, no pictures, no political society,
> no sporting class—no Epsom nor Ascot![14]

James wrote these lines in the 1870s; he might just as well have been scolding Russell Kirk in 1953. But again: was it proper to identify conservative thought with a single kind of society, a peculiar set of institutions that rise and fall and pass away?

America is not Europe: this was the bedrock liberal perception. But what should be done about it? In the mid-1950s, conservatives had as yet no convincing answer. But that it somehow required an answer was, one may fairly conclude, a "given" for many conservatives. This is not to say that conservative intellectuals felt terrorized by Louis Hartz or that they all consciously set out to refute liberal accusations of intellectual illegitimacy. And yet, if the volume of conservatives' output in this area in the 1950s and 1960s indicates anything, it suggests that they felt a need to explain themselves and their tradition, a need to locate a historical basis for a viable American conservatism. The very fact that they did not dismiss the liberal challenge out of hand perhaps conceded something: that the status of conservatism in American life was a *problem*, the solution to which was not self-evident. If it had been, why would they have bothered to make such an effort?

There was more to this quest than the fact that liberals had made an issue out of conservatism's place in American life. First, as the very word "conservatism" suggests, the person who holds its tenets wishes in some sense to conserve something which either exists in the present or has existed in the presumably recoverable past. This does not mean that conservatives are never present-minded or future-oriented; everyone is, to some extent. But for the true conservative the past or "tradition," however interpreted, must have a special claim on his attention. The man of the Left—liberal, radical, or revolutionary—can always repudiate tradition in toto if he wishes. He may deem it irrelevant, outmoded, or even dangerous. This option is never available to the conservative. He need not be indiscriminate, of course; he may select, accepting the good and rejecting the bad. But he cannot toss aside *everything* that has happened before him. He need not go so far as William F. Buckley, Jr., who once claimed "that the truly important in human experience is behind us; that the truly crucial battles have been fought...."[15] But he does believe that *something* has been learned, that what Russell Kirk has called "the wisdom of our ancestors" does exist, and that the wise man should not confront the world and the future with an attitude of total skepticism or blithe insouciance. Thus a significant—and predictable—aspect of the conservative intellectual revival was an intensive reexamination of the American past. If they were *conservatives*, what did they wish to conserve?

Another reason for this search for American roots lay in the peculiar circumstances of the entire conservative movement from the 1940s to the late 1960s. Unlike Edmund Burke, who in the 1790s inveighed against revolutionary France in behalf of a rooted political and social order, American conservatives after World War II occupied a deeply anomalous position: they called themselves conservatives, but their role was that of dissent.[16] Indeed, some right-wing intellectuals—notably Buckley in his first *National Review* editorial[17] and Frank Meyer on many occasions—perceived their position as more counterrevolutionary than conservative (in the narrow sense of preserving the status quo). For conservatism, as Meyer and many others saw it, was responding not to still-unsuccessful assaults on sturdy barricades but to a radical challenge that had already in part succeeded. Conservatives were in the uncomfortable position of opposing a "revolution" already consummated and entrenched. In their desire to stand athwart history, yelling "Stop," conservatives naturally turned to those features of the American past that seemed most opposed to the terrible menaces of the modern age. It was especially urgent that a movement in dissent do so; it needed all the resources, past or present, that it could get.

However anachronistic conservatives might seem to liberal critics, there was at least one consolation. Conservatives had been a minority long enough to appreciate the wisdom of Paul Claudel's remark, "Truth is not concerned with how many it persuades." The first task was to articulate truth-in-tradition, however battered and abandoned the tradition might appear. In the mid-1950s and later, conservative intellectuals evolved a variety of strategies for coping with the assertion that America was a liberal country and that conservatism did not belong here.

One strategy for denying the presumed gap between America and (European) conservatism was to minimize the importance of obvious institutional differences and to assert the existence of a transcendent continuity of *principle* across the Atlantic and across the centuries.

Among the conservatives to whom this approach increasingly appealed was Russell Kirk, the foremost right-wing partisan of Edmund Burke. Kirk had ample reason for adopting this tactic, since many conservatives had accused him of an indiscriminate defense of Western traditions, good and bad. John Hallowell, for instance, wrote that Kirk's discussion of slavery (surely an established institution) in the antebellum South was "evasive."[18] Some conservatives, however, were less interested in criticizing Kirk than in contesting head-on the relevance of his mentor. To Stephen Tonsor, a Midwesterner and a professor of European intellectual history at the University of Michigan, Burke could not be the teacher of contemporary American conservatism. Ours was a "radically" different "environment" from that of the great British statesman. "We are no longer defending an old order from a new society.... No matter then how much we share Burke's prejudices we must all reject his solutions as irrelevant to our age."[19] In another essay, Tonsor chastised Allen Guttmann's *The Conservative Tradition in America* for equating conservatism with Burke. Burke was *not* the fount of modern American conservatism; in fact the "Burkean heritage" conflicted with it:

> American conservatives are "American." They share the common commitment to democratic institutions, the anti-prescriptive bias of American society. Their commitment is to the rational modification of the social order and to the creation of political institutions which serve all rather than a few or a particular group. Though they commonly look to the state for benefits, they mistrust it and possess little of the Burkean reverence for positive government. American conservatives are non-ideological. They have never developed a system which was totally compelling.... It's a wise child that knows its own father, and I suspect that most American conservatives, without benefit of some genealogical study, would not recognize Edmund Burke.[20]

From time to time, other conservatives echoed Tonsor's contentions.[21]

Faced with this challenge from within the conservative community, and aware, too, of liberal attacks, Russell Kirk strove to distinguish what he called the "permanent things" (such as timeless principles of political and moral conduct) from the widely varying, historically conditioned, institutional embodiments of them (such as different forms of government in different nations). Specifically, he attempted to vindicate the insights of Burke in a country which, he recognized, was obviously different from Georgian England. Reviewing the second edition of Clinton Rossiter's *Conservatism in America* in 1962, Kirk vigorously denied Rossiter's claim that the *Federalist Papers* rather than Burke's writings should be the principal source book for modern conservatives. Although Kirk profoundly admired the *Federalist Papers*, he regarded them as primarily a *livre de circonstance*, concerned with problems of "governmental structure" in one nation at one time and therefore of limited value in our revolutionary era. Burke, on the other hand, was neither "provincial" nor outmoded; he still spoke to the crisis which plagued us. Moreover:

> Burke is not *outside* the American tradition; rather, he stands
> in the grander tradition and continuity—the legacy of our
> civilization—of which American life and character are a part
> ....To seek political guidance from Burke is no more exotic or
> alien, for Americans, than to seek humane insights from
> Shakespeare, or to seek religious wisdom from St. Paul.[22]

So Burke *was* relevant—a "genius" whose influence was immense.[23] In
many of his writings in the 1950s and 1960s, Kirk pointed to the perva-
siveness of Burke's influence on American thinkers from John Randolph[24]
to Woodrow Wilson,[25] from the Adamses to Albert Jay Nock, from Calhoun
to Irving Babbitt.[26]

"The grander tradition and continuity"—this phrase of Kirk's suggested another increasingly uttered by conservatives in the 1950s and
1960s: the "Great Tradition." This term was used especially by Leo Strauss
and his disciples to identify the premodern political philosophy of men
like Plato, Aristotle, and Cicero, in contrast to the inferior modern brand
articulated by Machiavelli, Hobbes, and Locke. This concept of a tradition of *truth* that knew limitations neither of time nor of geography was
attractive to conservatives who, like Kirk, were anxious to demonstrate
the wisdom and continuity of the Western experience. Tirelessly Kirk
stressed the eternal verities which commanded conservative allegiance:
"belief in a transcendent order, in an unalterable human nature, and in
a natural law."[27] Here, certainly, were universals that remained true despite the flux of a history and circumstance.

That such a continuity of tradition did exist, that America was linked
with the fundamental truths of Christianity (even Catholic Christianity),
was the argument in 1960 of John Courtney Murray, a distinguished
Jesuit scholar. According to Murray, the United States did have an identifiable "public consensus": "the principles that are structural to the
Western Christian political tradition."[28] Thus, the "American Proposition" *was* reconcilable with ancient and enduring truths. A Catholic (he
might have said conservative) could sincerely applaud much of the American order. What were the constituent parts of this remarkable consensus? First, in the Declaration of Independence and elsewhere, Americans affirmed ("we hold these truths") "the sovereignty of God over nations as well as over individual men."[29] Our nation was "under God."
Second, the "tradition of natural law and natural rights"—"the central
political tradition of the West"—was the solid basis of America's consensus.[30] To Murray, such American beliefs as constitutionalism, limited sovereignty, and the rule of law were not modern innovations at all but

"ancient ideas, deeply implanted in the British tradition in medieval times." Medieval times! Surely this was a twist: asserting America's continuity with those "feudal" Middle Ages. Moreover, Murray intrepidly claimed that by establishing "the consent of the governed," "popular participation in rule," and the distinction between state and society, the "American Proposition" was actually adhering to the Great Tradition. What liberals held to be unconservative, was, on Murray's showing, an organic part of a heritage that went back beyond modern times. He was pleased also by America's assumption that "only a virtuous people can be free."[31] In short, at our deepest level of self-understanding, as "a people organized for action in history," Americans were not cut off from the "patrimony" of our civilization.

Murray's book was acclaimed by several conservative intellectuals. Francis Wilson called him "one of the most creative of the Christian intellectuals of our time."[32] To Willmoore Kendall his book was "a major breakthrough in American political *science*," a book which could tell conservatives just what they ought to be conserving.[33] William F. Buckley, Jr. was sufficiently impressed to include a portion of Murray's work in his anthology of twentieth-century conservative thought.[34]

In a sense, many conservatives during these years were proving by their actions the compatibility of America with the Great Tradition. One of the noticeable features of the conservative intellectual movement after 1945 was the ease with which it established substantial contacts across the Atlantic. If European émigrés contributed significantly to the rebirth of American conservative thought, many right-wing Americans felt at home in Europe. William F. Buckley, Jr. had received part of his education in England and traveled frequently abroad. Russell Kirk earned his doctorate at St. Andrews University in Scotland, eventually bought a home in Pittenweem, Fife, and wandered extensively throughout Europe.[35] James Burnham was coauthor of a book with André Malraux,[36] while Willmoore Kendall, a former Rhodes Scholar, lived at various times in France and Spain. Indeed, Spain exerted a powerful influence on several American conservatives, including Kendall, Francis Wilson,[37] Frederick Wilhelmsen, and L. Brent Bozell, who even educated some of his children there.[38] Through organizations like the Mont Pélerin Society and the European Center for Documentation and Information,[39] through personal acquaintanceships with Otto von Hapsburg (heir to the Austro-Hungarian throne and occasional contributor to *National Review*)[40] and other Europeans, American right-wingers came to display a cosmopolitan outlook. From its inception, *National Review* had correspondents in Europe, and Buckley believed that *National Review*, with its "European" emphasis, made American conservatism more aware of the world, more "urbane."[41]

This evidence could, of course, be interpreted in two ways. If liberal critics had examined the phenomenon, they no doubt would have seen it as a further reflection of inner exile from liberal America, and in a few cases they would have been correct. But the situation was more complex than that. For if Kirk spent part of his year in his ancestral Scotland, or if Buckley repaired annually to Switzerland, or if Kendall lived for a time in Paris and in Spain, the significant fact in these and similar cases was that they *returned*. It was not a simple matter of flight from "progressive" America. It was almost the opposite: conservatives felt a sense of continuity between their homeland and Europe. Conservatism was for many of them a transatlantic philosophy, and the Western heritage an organic tie, binding "American Europe" (a phrase of Kendall's)[42] with the rest of Western civilization.

Yet after all the eternal verities about our common heritage had been expounded, one question still remained: in what form did this heritage survive in the United States? It was reassuring to stress the affinities between the Old World and the New, but America undeniably *was* different: it was not a replica of Europe. Many right-wing intellectuals were understandably anxious to explore the context in which absolute truths existed. What were the *institutional* carriers of the Great Tradition in America? Who were the American heroes whom conservatives should honor?

At the beginning of consolidation in the mid-1950s, two "handbooks" were available to the Right: Russell Kirk's *The Conservative Mind* (1953) and Clinton Rossiter's *Conservatism in America* (1955). Neither was entirely satisfactory to conservatives. Kirk's book, despite its crucial role in the emergence of the New Right, troubled many conservatives because of his heavily Burkean framework. Moreover, while Kirk had offered an American genealogy, Ralph de Toledano wondered whether it was too thin. He was upset by Kirk's remark that "half the history of American conservatism, or nearly that, must be an account of the Adamses." "Four men," Toledano rejoined, "no matter how brilliant, do not make up a tradition."[43] Similarly, the Hungarian émigré Thomas Molnar observed that while *The Conservative Mind* revealed America's "conservative thinkers," they had simply not directed "the course of concrete happenings" and "the shaping of the public philosophy." America had conservative voices, but there was no "conservative tradition *embed-*

ded in the history of the United States...."[44] Cold war strategist Stefan Possony wondered about Kirk's method of selection: his criticism of Hamilton, for instance, but praise for John Randolph, who seemed to Possony "a narrow-minded and quixotic reactionary."[45]

Rossiter's book was far more unacceptable to the Right. For one thing, Rossiter himself declared that he was not even sure he was a conservative; his goal was "to sober and strengthen the American liberal tradition, not to destroy it."[46] For another, in the 1962 edition of his book he severely criticized the postwar conservative movement. Russell Kirk he accused of sounding like "a man born one hundred and fifty years too late and in the wrong country"; most of what Kirk stood for was "gone forever."[47] Rossiter chided such conservatives as Kirk, Richard Weaver, and Anthony Harrigan for their profound, and in his view intemperate, hostility to liberalism. Among his complaints, one—the unforgivable one—stood out. It was Rossiter's use of the liberal theme that conservatism (i.e., Burkeanism) was "irrelevant" to America. Time and again, Rossiter stressed that America was "a progressive country with a Liberal tradition" and "a liberal [political] mind."[48] At most he was willing to accept a kind of conservatism based on the *Federalist Papers* (a "collective Burke") and not too estranged in principle and mood from the dominant liberals. Echoing Arthur Schlesinger, Jr., he called on conservatives to "enlist and serve the interests of American business or abdicate responsibility for the future of the Republic."[49]

No wonder Rossiter's book was anathema to the conservatives. It could not please Kirk, who, aside from the question of Burke's relevance, had indignantly denied in 1954 that his conservatism could or should be identified with businessmen. Conservatism was not a function of classes or laissez-faire economics, he said; "a conservative order is not the creation of the free entrepreneur...." Conservatism was not an ideology of any particular interest group.[50] It could not please the "counterrevolutionary" conservatives who despised the "middle of the road" and who considered liberalism itself to be the enemy. Nor could it satisfy those who denied that the United States was inherently a liberal country.

What *were* the differences between Left and Right, anyway? Were they in part simply ones of "mood and bias," as Rossiter suggested? Did it all boil down to a mere matter of the conservative's wish to "preserve" liberty versus the liberal's wish to "enlarge" it?[51] Not at all, said Gerhart Niemeyer, a conservative political scientist at the University of Notre Dame. Among his arguments against Rossiter was the assertion that conservatism was not (as Rossiter claimed) inherently anxious to restore the

past or to oppose change. Nor was conservatism necessarily hostile to
majority rule or material progress. What divided Left and Right were
profoundly divergent views about the very nature of freedom. This gap
could not be eliminated by dismissing real conservatives as un-American
and neatly homogenizing what remained into a liberal "consensus."[52]
Willmoore Kendall was similarly outraged by this device. It not only assumed that the American mainstream *was* liberal but also excommuni-
cated all who *really* wished to change the direction of the mainstream
rather than play patty-cake with liberals, who were destined, in Rossiter's
scheme, to win no matter what.[53]

So Rossiter would never do; he was a Trojan horse. The task of solving the problem of conservatism in America would have to be undertaken almost from scratch. As Francis Wilson said, "It seems to me fatal
to conservatives to let liberals tell them the kind of conservatism America
ought to have."[54]

In searching for nonliberal elements in the nation's life, many conservatives eagerly looked to the South. There were several reasons why this
discovery was, for the Right, a logical one. The South, as Rossiter pointed
out, had always been the most conservative region of the country.[55] The
Southerner, said Richard Weaver, was "an anomalous American"; only
he had tasted "the cup of defeat" in war and had been taught the meaning of tragedy.[56] In other respects the South was the least "American"—
some might say the least liberal—of sections: in its strong sense of tradition (the Old South, Dixie), its economic "backwardness" and social stability, its religious "piety" (Weaver's phrase) and family loyalties, its suspicion of intellectual presumption and intrusive Yankee "isms," its antipathy toward centralized government and devotion (in theory at least)
to states' rights, its military tradition and attachment to the community
and rural ways. Then, too, only the South was graced (or burdened) with
the lingering memory of the Lost Cause—a poignant source of additional appeal to conservatives, some of whom half-believed at times that
they also had been routed forever from the battlefields of history.

In the 1950s and 1960s signs of conservative affection for the South
multiplied. In 1941 Russell Kirk had received his master's degree from
Duke University; at the time he was avidly interested in Southern history[57] and had written his master's essay on John Randolph of Roanoke.
In 1951 it appeared as a book,[58] which was expanded and reissued in
1964. To Kirk, the eccentric and aristocratic Virginian was "the most

eloquent of American conservative thinkers," the "American Burke."[59] He was a valiant agrarian, states' rightist, strict constructionist, and Old Republican whose opposition to industrialism, social innovation, leveling, and "metaphysical madness" endeared him to Kirk all the more. As editor of *Modern Age*, Kirk devoted an early issue to the South, which he labeled "the Permanence of the American nation."[60] *National Review* also welcomed articles sympathetic to that region. One of its early contributors was the former Southern Agrarian Donald Davidson, whose *The Attack on Leviathan* (1938) Kirk considered "the most important neglected book of this century."[61] In fact, *National Review* was one of the very few journals receptive to the viewpoint of conservative white Southerners in the tempestuous decade after it was founded.

Conservative interest in the South was enormously stimulated by the Supreme Court's 1954 decision in *Brown vs. Board of Education* to outlaw compulsory racial segregation in the schools. While not all right-wing intellectuals initially opposed the decision,[62] the dominant tone at *National Review* was one of criticism of the subsequent governmental drive—at Little Rock and elsewhere—toward integration. Frank Meyer, for instance, declared that the Brown decision "rode roughshod over precedent and reason and constitutional obligation." Moreover, it relied on "positivist sociological assertion" and exemplified "Liberal cant."[63] Richard Weaver was alarmed at the growing use of "racial collectivism" to subvert property rights essential to a truly free society and concluded:

> 1) Integration is not an end in itself. 2) Forcible integration would ignore the truth that equals are not identicals. 3) In a free society, associations for educational, cultural, social, and business purposes have a right to protect their integrity against political fanaticism.[64]

On one occasion *National Review* even bluntly declared:

> The central question that emerges—and it is not a parliamentary question or a question that is answered by merely consulting a catalogue of the rights of American citizens, born Equal—is whether the White community in the South is entitled to take such measures as are necessary to prevail, politically and culturally, in areas where it does not predominate numerically? The sobering answer is *Yes*—the White community is so entitled because, for the time being, it is the advanced race....
>
> *National Review* believes that the South's premises are correct. If the majority wills what is socially atavistic, then to

> thwart the majority may be, though undemocratic, enlight-
> ened....
>   ...Universal suffrage is not the beginning of wisdom or
> the beginning of freedom.[65]

This was too much for William F. Buckley's brother-in-law, L. Brent Bozell, who doubted that "Southern civilization hangs on the thread of Negro disfranchisement" and who accused the journal of condoning Southern white efforts to violate the law and the Constitution.[66] But the magazine's editors did not budge. Instead they called for the South to apply disfranchising laws equally to blacks *and* whites, thereby conforming to the Constitution.[67]

As the racial crisis deepened in the South in 1957, there appeared an able polemic, *The Sovereign States*, written by the outspoken young editor of the *Richmond News-Leader*, James Jackson Kilpatrick.[68] Exploring the history of the Republic from 1776 to 1860 and beyond, Kilpatrick unabashedly revived the old "compact" theory of the Constitution: the nation was a union of States, *sovereign* States, whose powers were confirmed by the Tenth Amendment.[69] Relying heavily on the Virginia and Kentucky Resolutions of 1798 and various state-national conflicts of the young republic, Kilpatrick argued that when a dispute arose between a state and the federal government, the "ultimate umpire" was not the Supreme Court but the people acting in their states. Acting how? By resisting encroachments, by *interposition* of the state's authority between the central government and the state's own citizens. But was this not radical or dangerous? No, thundered Kilpatrick; it was constitutionally logical and historically justified. Nearly half of his book was devoted to examples of states' defiance of federal authority: *Chisholm vs. Georgia*, the protests of 1798 against the Alien and Sedition Acts, the Hartford Convention, the Cherokee removal controversy, nullification in South Carolina, Northern resistance to the Fugitive Slave Act, and many more.

Yet had not this doctrine of state equality (or even supremacy) been invalidated by the Civil War? No, said Kilpatrick. The triumphant North could have established total centralization but did not do so. The Tenth Amendment continued in force. The states remained intact and even benefited from certain Supreme Court rulings. Only after the Court's historic shift to the Left in 1937 had states' rights been dangerously undermined. Now a new and unjustifiable decree—*Brown vs. Board of Education*—was upon us. To Kilpatrick, who believed that "government is least evil when it is closest to the people,"[70] the trend toward "deification of the Federal government, and the steady stultification of the States" was ominous. It was time for "drastic" resistance. The states must use "every device of interposition" to restrain "Federal usurpations."[71]

Fiercely criticized by various liberal reviewers, Kilpatrick quickly achieved eminence on the Right. Soon he was contributing frequently to *National Review*; in time he became one of its more or less "official" spokesmen on constitutional issues and civil rights.[72] Frank Meyer was delighted with *The Sovereign States* and approved its "simple rational and moral truth that the Constitution is a compact between states."[73] In 1959, Felix Morley used Kilpatrick's research to bolster his own *Freedom and Federalism*. Morley, who had grown up in border-city Baltimore and had been editor of the *Washington Post*, president of Haverford College, and coeditor of *Human Events*, argued for a truly federal (that is, decentralized) political system based on strong states. He vigorously opposed the increasing threat of an overweening centralized government responsive only to a Rousseauistic "general will." In these circumstances, Morley welcomed the revival of the theory of interposition as an example of "the tenacity of the federal tradition in American thinking, and a powerful weapon in the armory of those who seek to maintain the Republic." Without this doctrine, the Supreme Court could act without restraint and America's whole system of checks and balances would be imperiled.[74]

While much conservative discussion of the South was obviously related to immediate racial controversies[75]—Morley, too, opposed the Brown judgment[76]—it would be a mistake to reduce conservative affection for the region to a defense of its racial status quo. That the South had more transcendent truths to teach was the persistent theme of the most impressive postwar disciple of the Agrarian movement, Richard Weaver,[77] whose defense of his native region long antedated the integration decision of 1954. Converted from socialism in the late 1930s—in part because of the influence of the Vanderbilt Agrarians—Weaver had presented in his doctoral dissertation a vigorous and sympathetic portrait of a traditional society that even now had not completely succumbed to science, aggressive technology, materialism, commercialism, and other evils of egotistic Northern modernism. In the face of this "revolution of nihilism," the South stood properly but confusedly for so much that was old and true. Alas, while it "needed a Burke or a Hegel [,] it produced lawyers and journalists."[78] Although Weaver did not say so, his career was devoted to filling that gap.

In the years after World War II, this son of North Carolina frequently espoused Southern and explicitly Agrarian values.[79] The South "has been a stumbling block to modernism," he declared.[80] For one thing, he wrote in 1952, the "Southern philosophy" was resistant to corrosive "analysis." The South's distrust of the specialist had helped it remain "humanistic" while other parts of the country followed the false gods of "analysis and science." The South's tradition of rhetoric ("reverence for the word") was an antidote to that "verbal skepticism" which is the beginning of "moral nihilism." In contrast to the Northerner, who was "essentially a child of the Enlightenment," the Southerner piously accepted nature as providential, not as something to be manipulated for selfish ends. Nor was the Southerner motivated by envy and egalitarian urges for somebody else's goods. Finally, while "the typical American" was undeniably the "victorious man," the Southerner was—to repeat a phrase—"an anomalous American"; only he had known defeat and tragedy in his own land. In this respect, as in so many others, the South actually resembled Europe more than the North.[81] Indeed, "the South, with its inherited institutions and its system of values, was a continuation of Western European culture, and...the North was the deviation."[82]

No wonder the liberals hated the South, Weaver wrote on another occasion. More than any other section of the country, the South maintained a "regime," "a system of sustaining forms," "a complex of law, custom, and idiomatic behavior" that acted as a "powerful check against the sense of lostness, the restlessness, and the aimless competition which plague the modern masses and provoke the fantastic social eruptions of our era." Why had the Southern regime survived? Because it had maintained three "strong barriers to anomie": "a structural form of society," "the idea of transcendence," and "its preservation of history." Because, like every regime, it maintained a "principle of exclusion" indispensable to survival. In all these ways the South was an affront to liberalism, which Weaver called "the death-wish of modern civilization":

> In its incapacity for commitment, its nihilistic approach, and its almost pathological fear of settled principle, Liberalism operates to destroy everything and conserve nothing.... A regime can be generous, kindly, humane, even humanitarian, but it cannot be liberal in the sense of perpetually entertaining the question of whether it ought to continue.... [A] regime cannot live exclusively on a diet of self-questioning, to say nothing of self-hate.... Liberalism cannot postulate anything positive, because such affirmations will carry with them exclusions, and the only source Liberalism can recognize for exclusion is intolerance or "narrow-mindedness."
>
> It follows inevitably that the Liberal is exacerbated by the

sight of any independent and healthy growth. Such a growth
can only remind him of his own hollowness. A regime holds
the mirror up to the Liberal.[83]

Weaver was not indifferent, however, to the value of individual freedom. In his essay "The Importance of Cultural Freedom" he not only
raised his familiar theme of the need for consensus and cultural integrity
but also pleaded for considerable artistic freedom and renewal.[84] But
how could individuality and tradition be reconciled? Once again, the
South provided an example: the eccentric John Randolph of Roanoke.
According to Weaver, this Virginian exemplified "'social bond' individualism." Randolph recognized that man was a social animal; he belonged
to the Christian humanist tradition; he struggled for local rights and limited government; he had the rich, earthy historical consciousness of the
rhetorician. In unflattering contrast was Randolph's near-contemporary,
Henry David Thoreau, an abstract "dialectician" who ignored history
and hard fact whenever he desired and preached instead an "anarchic"
perfectionist individualism that was "revolutionary and subversive." It
was Randolph, the Southerner, the conservative, who was our surer
guide.[85]

In inveighing against the foes of the South, past or present, Weaver
moved beyond a critique of secular liberalism, science, and technology
to a dissent even from modern capitalism. Here, too, he was loyal to his
Agrarian roots. "Socialism is by definition anti-conservatism," he argued,
"and capitalism cannot be conservative in the true sense as long as its
reliance is upon industrialism, whose very nature it is to unsettle any
establishment and initiate the endless innovation of technological
'progress.'"[86] Weaver was profoundly concerned by the growth of "mass
plutocracy"—the "greatest danger" America confronted. He distrusted
advertising and lamented the popular views that man was a being of
merely "appetitive function" and that material goods dispensed here and
abroad could save us.[87] Perhaps this sense of duty and self-restraint reflected Weaver's own austere and somewhat incongruous life as a University of Chicago professor. A man who annually returned to his North
Carolina home to plow his land with horses (never a tractor), he lived the
rest of the year in a single room in an undistinguished hotel in Chicago.
A defender of the Christian faith, he attended church but once a year. "A
shy little bulldog of a man," a "little gnome,"[88] this "Puritan in Babylon"
was indeed aloof from the gaudy, frenetic life-style of prosperous
midcentury America.[89] The language of duty and self-discipline—not
"rights," not whims, not mindless indulgence or sneering cynicism—was

the language of Richard Weaver.

At this point, Weaver's contribution to the conservative search for a usable past requires comment. He was not simply a "professional Southerner" or narrow regional apologist.[90] Defending the Agrarian diaspora from the South in the 1940s, he pointed out: "In the battle against antihumanist forces one does not desert by changing his locale for the plain reason that the battle is worldwide.... The sections fade out, and one looks for comrades wherever there are men of good will and understanding."[91] Many of his most trenchant essays were not related to the merits of Southern culture, and conservatives at least would argue that the lessons he taught (on rhetoric, for instance) transcended such vagaries of time and circumstance. Weaver, in fact, had a low opinion of the argument from circumstance,[92] and he warned conservatives, "There cannot be a return to the Middle Ages or the Old South under slogans identified with them. The principles must be studied and used, but in such presentation that mankind will feel the march is forward."[93] Weaver cherished the values and institutions of his region not just because they were Southern but because they were true.

For conservatives anxious to locate an authentic, rooted, American conservatism, however, the "Southern strategy" of Weaver and other regionalists could not totally fulfill their needs. Most of the country, after all, was not Southern. But more importantly, Weaver's historical argument could not be fully satisfactory because it conceded with breathtaking candor precisely what many conservatives wanted most to deny: that the United States was predominantly an aggressive, dynamic, *liberal* country and that the Southerner (conservative) was "anomalous." In his attacks on science, industrialism, and capitalism, Weaver seemed to be underscoring the Hartz-Guttmann-Rossiter-Schlesinger thesis that conservatism *was* un-American! This twist did not seem to trouble Weaver, who knew all about lost causes and who was quite aware that he was resisting what might well be the winning side. It was apparently enough for him to establish that the South survived; at least somewhere in America one could take one's stand against "anti-humanist forces." But could it be enough for other conservatives, too?

It would be wrong to give the impression that conservatives consciously felt this incongruity between Weaver's "regionalism" and their own investigation of the country's past. It is more likely that they did not fully understand him. Most of his "Southern" essays were published in the 1940s and early 1950s in small-circulation academic quarterlies. None of the four works for which conservatives most esteemed him—*Ideas*

Have Consequences (1948), *The Ethics of Rhetoric* (1953), *Visions of Order* (1964), and *Life Without Prejudice and Other Essays* (1965)— waved an Agrarian flag. It was only with the publication of *The Southern Tradition at Bay* in 1968, five years after his death, that the pervasive influence of his Southernness began to be fully appreciated. When conservatives welcomed Weaver to the fold, where he undoubtedly belonged, they did so, one suspects, without fully realizing the uncongenial logic of his historical analysis. For while Weaver was undeniably claiming the South for conservatism, he was simultaneously illuminating a contrast: the Southern exception to the *American* rule. For generations, said Weaver, America's direction had been wrong at some of the deepest levels. This was not the position of those who claimed that America was essentially right (or Right) to begin with.

So the search continued—not in neat time frames or analytic categories, to be sure, but concurrently on a number of fronts. One of these was the field of national political institutions and traditions.

Two books aimed at general audiences in the late 1950s and early 1960s revealed the conservatives' dominant interpretation of the American regime at that time. In 1957 Russell Kirk undertook to elucidate what he called "the American cause."[94] According to Kirk, Americans since 1776 had exhibited "a conservative cast of mind" along with remarkable order and stability. These characteristics he attributed substantially to the "principles" Americans had always affirmed. In the moral realm, they adhered to Greco-Judeo-Christian religious precepts and were undeniably a "Christian nation." To be sure, the United States practiced religious toleration, but this was not indifference. The First Amendment was meant to "shelter religion, not to hamper churches," [95] and throughout our history we had revealed ourselves as a Christian people. "Christian morality," said Kirk, "is the cement of American life."[96] In the political realm, Kirk stressed America's inheritance of British law, political theory, and practice; the classical education and cautious realism of the Founding Fathers; and the "disciplined, traditional, moderate law-respecting freedom" they sought.[97] The United States, Kirk duly noted, was not a centralized "pure" democracy; the Founding Fathers never harbored the "illusion" that most people are "naturally good or wise."[98] Rather, the essence of our political system was "limited, delegated powers," checks and balances, territorial democracy, states' rights, and nonideological parties. In economics, America had devised an extraordinarily successful free-enterprise system "infinitely freer and juster and more orderly than any collectivistic scheme of total regulation."[99] In short, many aspects of the American regime were fundamentally, enduringly, unarguably conservative.

Kirk's basic contentions were pungently reiterated a few years later by Senator Barry Goldwater of Arizona in *The Conscience of a Conservative*,[100] one of the most successful political tracts in American history. Going through more than twenty printings in four years,[101] this hard-hitting polemic (actually written by L. Brent Bozell)[102] galvanized the rumbling popular conservative movement, catapulted Goldwater to national prominence, and helped the Right to capture the Republican Party in the mid-1960s. To what understanding of America's political heritage did this best-seller appeal? "The ancient and tested truths that guided our Republic through its early days," Goldwater declaimed.[103] In a chapter significantly entitled "The Perils of Power," he called the Constitution *"a system of restraints against the natural tendency of government to expand in the direction of absolutism."*[104] It was intended not to set up a democracy but to frustrate "a tyranny of the masses" and "self-seeking demagogues."[105] Ours was a limited federal government, which was forbidden by the Tenth Amendment to infringe on states' rights. Repeatedly Goldwater invoked "strict construction" of the Constitution; nothing in that document, for example, sanctioned federal "intrusion" into agriculture or education. He also sought to demolish the claim that conservatism was "out-of-date":

> The charge is preposterous and we ought boldly to say so. The laws of God, and of nature, have no dateline. The principles on which the Conservative position is based...are derived from the nature of man, and from the truths that God has revealed about His creation. Circumstances do change. So do the problems that are shaped by circumstances. But the principles that govern the solution of the problems do not. To suggest that the Conservative philosophy is out of date is akin to saying that the Golden Rule, or the Ten Commandments or Aristotle's *Politics* are out of date.[106]

The enormous popularity of Goldwater's book and its congruence of interpretation with Kirk's suggest that here at last the Right had discovered its American home. To Felix Morley, American conservatism was simply "Constitutionalism, in a strict rather than pliable interpretation,"[107] and there was no denying that this brand of right-wing thought was indigenous. America *did* have a tradition of limited government; even liberals had to concede that. Liberals might not like this philosophy; they might stress its differences from British conservative thought; they might label it anachronistic. But the antimajoritarian, states' rights, limited government, decentralist philosophy was at least one part of America's past—and that, for conservatives, was what counted. In an era of activist liberal presidents, "creeping socialism," and what Morley called the "Service State," this perspective on our heritage had obvious appeal to the Right. Whatever its merits, it was American.

Yet something was wrong, and conservatives knew it. Back in 1951, reviewing Kirk's *Randolph of Roanoke*, Bernard Iddings Bell spoke plainly:

> Kirk knows as well as Randolph did that, for good or ill, America has repudiated the theory of government which the founding fathers had in mind. The Constitution has been manipulated by loose constructions and judicial interpretations.... The central government has today almost unlimited and anonymous power. It overrides individual rights and local loyalties and peculiarities. It subordinates the states into little more than divisions on a map. By exercise of the taxing power, it dominates all people, all affairs.[108]

While Bell was perhaps gloomier than most, his point was a compelling one. Even if the antimajoritarian conservative cause was grounded in history, it was faltering now. One indication of this mood of pessimism was the appearance of a virtual genre of books portraying political declension. There was Morley's *Freedom and Federalism*, which traced the subversion of the Republic following the Civil War. There was James Burnham's *Congress and the American Tradition*, which documented the decline in power and prestige of Congress since 1933. And there was Gottfried Dietze's *America's Political Dilemma*. Dietze, who had been persecuted by the Nazis while a student in his native Germany, had emigrated to America in 1949 and had eventually become a professor of political science at Johns Hopkins University.[109] As he explored the signs of American decay in the twentieth century, he recognized a principal strand of the process: the trend "from limited to unlimited democracy." This was the subtitle of a book he published in 1968.

Antimajoritarian conservatives also had to cope with the fact that the liberals, too, had a tradition—one which challenged theirs all along the line. The Declaration of Independence, the Bill of Rights, the cult of strong presidents, "broad construction," the "general welfare" clause, the rhetoric of democracy ("one man, one vote")—these, too, were undeniably part of our heritage. So the American Right faced a double challenge: to explain how its tradition had been "derailed"[110] and to deny the superiority of the liberal tradition.

The nature of the conservatives' effort may best be seen by examining a number of "turning points" in America's past that they felt obliged to interpret. The first was the American Revolution itself. To many liberal commentators the United States had been liberal from birth: forged in revolution, America was the natural ally of anticolonialism, even revolutions, abroad. How could a nation conceived in violence and dedicated to universal rights ever be called "conservative"? To this charge conservatives had an easy and (for them) conclusive reply. Relying on the work of such scholars as Daniel Boorstin,[111] they repeatedly contended that the American Revolution was not a cataclysm like the later upheaval in France. It was simply a moderate, limited war for independence and for those *traditional* rights which, said Kirk, the Founders "had inherited from their forefathers."[112] The real radicals had been innovating British imperial officials, not defensive American colonists. To Gottfried Dietze, who believed in the indissoluble linkage of private property, freedom, and order, the American Revolution was notable for its recognition of the value of property rights.[113] It sought to protect the individual from "popular government" (in the form of an unchecked Parliament) and to restore the rule of law. It was, all in all, "evolutionary" rather than wildly innovative.[114] Conservatives also noted approvingly that as early as 1800, Friedrich Gentz, secretary of Metternich, had contrasted the conservative American Revolution with the radical French one. Gentz's essay, translated at the time by John Quincy Adams, was published by the Henry Regnery Company in 1955, with an introduction by Russell Kirk.[115] In short, conservatives tended to stress that the American Revolution was a moderate and prudent affair—hardly a revolution at all.

The Declaration of Independence, with its sweeping, universalistic claims about "inalienable rights" and the equality of men, was more troublesome. Conservatives were acutely conscious of its rhetorical appeal and its current usefulness to liberal reformers. On one occasion, Jeffrey Hart of Dartmouth College in effect conceded the Declaration to the liberals. He then insisted that its doctrine was not the theory of the Constitution, whose Preamble had conspicuously failed to list "rights" or "equality" among the purposes of the new government of 1787. There were, in fact, two theories of government present in the Revolutionary War period, and liberals could claim only one of them.[116] Most conservatives, however, seemed to prefer to stress the compatibility of the Declaration, properly understood, with their views. While none went as far as Boorstin, who emphasized its "technical, legalistic, and conservative character" as a mere "document of imperial legal relations,"[117] the trend of interpretation was clear. According to Kirk, the clause containing the phrase "all men are created equal" meant to the signers simply equality before the law, regardless of one's status. It certainly did not sanction "forcing all men into an artificial and monotonous equality of worldly station, through the power of the state."[118] The Declaration, moreover, was not a product of the Enlightenment but of the circumstances of American life. Liberty under law, not some misty "pursuit of happiness," was the true foundation of our polity.[119] While Kirk acknowledged the existence of "natural rights," he took care to bracket them always with "natural duties."[120] John Courtney Murray insisted that the principles of the Declaration were actually restatements of traditional Western wisdom.[121] Gottfried Dietze pointed out that the Declaration valued the inalienable right to property—surely a laudable feature.[122] In a variety of ways, then, conservatives sought to drain the Declaration of its explosive rhetorical potential.

The next "turning point" which conservatives considered was the Constitution. Here their verdict was enthusiastic: the Constitution "as originally conceived"[123] was, along with the *Federalist*,[124] one of the noblest achievements of Western man. Frank Meyer stated the anti-majoritarian conservative understanding of the document succinctly:

> restriction of government to its proper functions; within government, tension and balance between local and central power; within the Federal Government, tension and balance between the coordinate branches.[125]

In sharp contrast with many (including some of the Founding Fathers) who believed that the Constitution was intended to set up a *stronger* national government than the one under the Articles of Confederation, many conservatives stressed the powers of individuals and states under the federal system. Indeed, at times they seemed to infuse an almost anti-Federalist understanding into the Constitution.[126] In effect, the anti-majoritarian conservatives were often simply—and cheerfully—turning much old Progressive doctrine upside down. Yes, they were saying (as the Progessive scholar J. Allen Smith did fifty years earlier), our system *is* antidemocratic. *And properly so*. Our national government "is not democratic, but representative and republican," Kirk argued.[127] Dietze contended that the primary goal of the Constitution was to safeguard property rights and other "rights of the individual" from "majoritarian despotism."[128] Felix Morley was delighted that "pure" uncurbed democracy was frustrated by the "original Constitution [which] was not merely undemocratic in principle. It also established undemocratic political institutions which have functioned in an undemocratic manner from the outset." Among them were the Senate and the Supreme Court.[129] Morley hastened to point out that democracy was not always an evil; it worked best, however, when "localized."[130] Or as Kirk, borrowing a phrase of Orestes Brownson, stated the case, the United States had been and ought to remain a "territorial democracy."[131]

The conservatives' attitude toward the Bill of Rights was somewhat more ambivalent. It was not that they generally opposed the Bill of Rights. They accepted it, especially—in the cases of Kilpatrick, Morley, and Goldwater, for instance—the philosophy of the Tenth Amendment. As for the rest, John Courtney Murray probably expressed a general conviction when he declared that the Bill of Rights basically incorporated historical "rights of Englishmen," not "eighteenth-century rationalist theory." Like Kirk, he held that the First Amendment clause forbidding the establishment of religion was simply the reasonable "articles of peace" of a pluralistic society.[132] It was not a mandate for liberal secularism. The more states' rights-minded conservatives pointed out that the Bill of Rights was originally intended to be a restraint on the central government only.[133] Nevertheless, the First Amendment in particular—as interpreted by men like Justices Hugo Black and William O. Douglas—caused uneasiness on the Right. At least as much as the Declaration of Independence, it never ceased to be a subject of discussion, if only because "absolutist" liberals went right on making it so.

In general, the pre-Civil War political system met with the approval of the conservatives considered here. But the Civil War itself and the Reconstruction which followed constituted for conservatives one of the two great crises in the decline of the Republic. First, as Morley contended, the adoption of the Fourteenth Amendment had "profoundly and permanently weakened" federalism. It was bad enough that this amendment had been thrust into the Constitution in a "scandalous"[134] fashion (a point made also by Kilpatrick[135]). Even worse was what the amendment signified: "the underlying purpose...was to nullify the original purpose of the Bill of Rights, by vesting its enforcement in the national rather than the State governments." A grave act of consolidation and nationalization had occurred; the states were made "subordinate" to the central authority.[136]

The conservative lament even extended to the greatest folk hero of American politics, Abraham Lincoln. More than one right-winger was troubled by the extraordinary and constitutionally dubious measures which Lincoln took during the war: suspension of habeas corpus, unauthorized expenditure of funds, arrest without due process, the Emancipation Proclamation, and many more. After giving Lincoln a scrupulous hearing, Dietze concluded that while the president was not guilty of "contempt of the Constitution," his administration was a "constitutional tragedy." The Old Republic was *not* preserved unharmed; the seeds of future "arbitrary majority rule," "despotic democracy," and "an omnipotent national executive" were sown.[137] Frank Meyer was far more accusatory. Lincoln was an "ideologue" who had willfully destroyed the traditional "checks and balances" framework "under the spurious slogan of Union." He had operated a "repressive dictatorship" and had sanctioned the horrible military tactics of Grant and Sherman.

> Were it not for the wounds that Lincoln inflicted on the Constitution, it would have been infinitely more difficult for Franklin Roosevelt to carry through his revolution, for the coercive welfare state to come into being and bring about the conditions against which we are fighting today.[138]

Yet even Meyer admitted that Lincoln had only "opened the way to centralized government...."[139] As conservatives saw it, post-Civil War America had displayed remarkable resiliency.[140] Still, in retrospect, ominous developments had occurred. Like Frank Chodorov before him,[141] Felix Morley denounced the Sixteenth Amendment as a "frontal attack on the American system" and as a subversion of state sovereignty. For this and other forms of democratization he particularly blamed William Jennings Bryan. The 1896 campaign "marked the first irreversible turn toward democracy in American political thinking."[142] Dietze pointed to the increasingly popular relativistic theories of "sociological jurisprudence," which served to undermine judicial review, an indispensable antidemocratic bulwark in a property-respecting, limited democracy.[143] On a variety of fronts, in fact, private property—so essential to liberty—was coming under intellectual siege.[144] Much conservative fire was aimed at Justice Oliver Wendell Holmes. While no "Jacobin" or reformer, he was nevertheless, said L. Brent Bozell, a liberal saint and one of the "chief villains" the West ever produced. Why? "The answer is that he emancipated the law from metaphysics.... Holmes was an atheist, skeptic, relativist—and so: a thoroughgoing positivist. He waged unrelentingly his war against the Natural Law—the idea that objective standards of right and wrong exist independently of human preferences...."[145]

The culmination of these trends, conservatives believed, occurred in the years after 1933. Indeed, with rare unanimity the Right believed that the administration of Franklin Roosevelt inaugurated a revolution both in the agenda and structure of American politics. It was the second great crisis in the decline of the Republic. In substance this upheaval sought, as Meyer put it, a form of democratic socialism.[146] In structure the political system was profoundly altered: enormous aggrandizement of the president and federal bureaucracy, the steady weakening of Congress, capitulation of the Supreme Court under pressure in 1937,[147] and, of course, the shackling of the individual and sapping of the states. It is not surprising that some right-wingers, like Meyer, believed that measures of virtually counterrevolutionary proportions were now required. As James Burnham observed, we were living in "the cold civil war of the post-1933 epoch."[148]

What measures? Interposition, perhaps; Morley and Kilpatrick approved of it. Far more practical, however, was the growing conservative tendency to rely on the one branch of government which had proved most immune to radical assault: the Congress. Russell Kirk, for example, coauthored a highly laudatory study of Senator Robert Taft as a sober, prudent defender of America's still valid heritage—the Great Tradition, the "permanent things": a mature party system, liberty under law, restraint on arbitrary power, a free yet humane economy, responsibility among interest groups, a congressional voice in foreign policy.[149]

Yet however much Kirk revered Taft, it must have been obvious to him, as it was to Meyer,[150] that Congress was weakening. This was the well-documented thesis of James Burnham in *Congress and the American Tradition*, one of the most penetrating works of political analysis produced by conservatives since World War II.[151] In a useful analysis of conservative and liberal "syndromes," Burnham conveyed the essential differences between most of the Right and most of the Left in their approach to politics. Conservatives, for example, generally believed in the continuing value of the constitutional tradition, in the diffusion of power, in "representative, mediated government" (as opposed to undiluted "plebiscitary democracy"), in states' rights, decentralization and localization, and (as a presumption) in private enterprise and in Congress rather than the executive.[152] Alas, every one of these values was under the gravest attack. In particular, Congress, once supreme, had declined since 1933 from a "peer of the executive" to a "mere junior partner."[153] Burnham relentlessly amassed the evidence of executive aggrandizement and congressional decay: loss of dominant control over legislation, loss of meaningful power over the bureaucracy, over the vast appropriations, over war making, over treaties. To offset this "constitutional revolution,"[154] Congress was relying heavily on the investigatory power. Yet that, too, was increasingly disparaged, particularly by liberals angered and frightened by Joseph McCarthy.

But did this decline of Congress really matter? To Burnham the stark alternative to a strong Congress was the rampaging ideology of "democratism"—scornful of all "intermediary institutions," unaware of the value of concurrent majorities, impatient of limits and liberties, culminating in the "democratic" dictatorship of a presidential Caesar who "embodies" the people, the "mass men" described by Ortega y Gasset. Even worse: this alternative, Burnham believed in 1959, was now a likelihood. Congress—"the prime intermediary institution" remaining— would probably die, and the "democratist, plebiscitary, bureaucratic, centralist, Caesarean" tendencies which were the "political phase" of the "managerial revolution" would triumph. But, he warned, "if liberty, then Congress; if no Congress, no liberty."[155]

There was one institution to which conservatives conspicuously did not turn for ballast in the 1950s and 1960s: the Supreme Court. There had been a time, back in the 1930s, when the Right had defended the Court and praised judicial review. Gottfried Dietze still did. But ever since the Court first acquiesced in and then increasingly initiated "leftist" policies, antimajoritarian conservatives were deprived of this logical bulwark. Nevertheless, in a curious way, the Supreme Court did come to exert a significant influence on the postwar conservative intellectual movement. It is probably no exaggeration to say that as much as any other liberals, Earl Warren, Hugo Black, William O. Douglas, and their colleagues helped to revitalize American conservatism. By forcing to the surface in the most dramatic cases some of the most profound questions about the nature of American life and the entire political process, by making issues of such supreme gravity public and debatable, the Warren Court helped polarize Left and Right. And polarization is a first step toward self-definition.

Dismay at the Warren Court was integral to American conservatism, whose journals buzzed with angry commentary.[156] "What are the limits, if any, upon the power of the Supreme Court to 'interpret' the Constitution?" James J. Kilpatrick asked. "Where in a government of checks and balances can one find an effective check upon the Court?"[157] Although most leading conservatives at one time or another expressed disgust with the Court, the most systematic and extensive critique emanated from lawyer-author L. Brent Bozell in *The Warren Revolution*. According to Bozell, the United States before 1954 had two "constitutions": the fixed, formal, written Constitution of 1787, and a fluid, informal, unwritten constitution that grew organically by compromise, trial and error, accretion, and consensus. In this process of policy making, the Supreme Court had, via judicial review, "helped discover and develop working consensuses in areas not covered by the fixed constitution."[158] But since 1954 a dramatic change had occurred. No longer content with this traditional role, the Court now asserted an umpire's position in the reshaping of the fluid constitution: "This new kind of constitution-making...*has sought to transfer the solution of some of the most momentous problems of contemporary public policy from the fluid constitution to the fixed constitution—by judicial decree.*" It had transformed itself from being "*an* expounder of the constitution" to being "*the* expounder."[159]

The effects of this rigid innovation were evident in the aftermath of the school integration decision of 1954. Before *Brown vs. Board of Education*, Bozell said, the country had lacked a clear consensus on this issue; no side could attain a constitutional majority. Nevertheless, substantial and permanent racial progress had been made.[160] After the decision, however, "the possibilities of consensual adjustment and accommodation were greatly diminished," as both races were compelled to abide by "the prescriptions of ideology." The "multidimensional" race problem (which included such considerations as justice, preservation of the federal system, and maintenance of order) had been rendered "single-dimensional." The single controlling aim was "satisfying the Negroes' claims." And if the "governed" did not give their "consent"? They now faced the "great anomaly" that "while nine judges can draw up a fixed constitutional provision *without* the authority of a hard constitutional consensus, their decision cannot be reversed *except* on the authority of a hard constitutional consensus."[161]

This hardening of the nation's political arteries was regrettable enough. Also reprehensible to Bozell was the very reasoning of the principal Warren Court rulings. Surely, he argued, the first rule of constitutional interpretation had always been to determine what the framers meant. In the Brown case, the Warren Court—despite some camouflage—deliberately abandoned this firm anchor. The Court's ruling relied on a clause of the Fourteenth Amendment, adopted in 1868, that no state shall "deny to any person within its jurisdiction the equal protection of the laws." Yet the contemporary evidence overwhelmingly demonstrated that the Fourteenth Amendment was *not* intended to outlaw racial segregation in the schools. The very Congress that approved the amendment also established all-black schools in the District of Columbia. Most of the very states that ratified the amendment also permitted or required separate schools, and continued to do so. Indeed, education was then recognized as solely a state and local responsibility.

Ah, but "we cannot turn the clock back to 1868" or 1896, said Chief Justice Warren's opinion. To Bozell this was the supreme outrage. Court decisions before 1954 had not always been proper, but at least the Justices had tried to reconcile tradition with innovation. No more. The Warren Court impudently announced "its emancipation from the anachronisms of an ancient parchment."[162] Apparently Warren believed that the Fourteenth Amendment incorporated a "concept" of "equality" in the equal protection clause and that the Supreme Court was ordained to apply this concept as conditions (or sociologists) dictated.[163] This, Bozell argued, was neither historically justified nor constitutionally wise:

> If the Supreme Court is at liberty to substitute contemporary judgments about the good society for those of the Fourteenth Amendment's framers—and to give those contemporary judgments the force of constitution [sic] law—what is the Court, under the pretense of construing the Constitution, *not* at liberty to do? ...The *Brown* case raises the question of whether the obsolescence of the Constitution should be unilaterally proclaimed by a tribunal charged and sworn to "support and defend the Constitution of the United States."[164]

The pattern established by *Brown vs. Board of Education* was reinforced by other decisions. In the school prayer cases of 1963, for example, the Court had misconstrued the First Amendment, which had clearly prohibited only Congress from establishing a national church or interfering with states' accommodations. After all, many states in 1787 (and for years thereafter) maintained their own religious establishments. Nor could the "no establishment" clause be applied to the states now via the Fourteenth Amendment. Only a few years after the Fourteenth was adopted, *another* amendment had been offered to outlaw state establishment of religion. If the Fourteenth had settled matters, why had this new effort attracted so much support? Why had a new amendment even been thought necessary?

Also alarming were the Court's reapportionment decisions, particularly *Wesberry vs. Sanders* (1964), in which the Court asserted that congressional districts—traditionally the concern of an equal branch of government—must be apportioned according to the "one man, one vote" formula. In a trenchant, history-laden rebuttal, Bozell accused the Court majority of blatant disregard of the indisputable mandate of U.S. tradition. Once again it was evident that the Warren Court sought "to impose the ideology of equality on the American political system, notwithstanding the clear purposes of the architects of the system, and irrespective even of the wishes of the people who now live under it." And once again, the challenge:

> If it is true that a construction of the Constitution by the Supreme Court, no matter how spurious or absurd, no matter how damaging to the organic life of the country, is eo ipso "the law of the land," unchallengeable even by a law made by the people's representatives...then, where, in all candor, are we? If a judicial interpretation of the Constitution is, by definition, *the Constitution*, why then we are in the grips of a judicial despotism.[165]

At this point Bozell swept beyond more conventional right-wing thinking to question not just the decisions of the Warren Court but the idea of judicial supremacy itself.[166] In an audacious and meticulous analysis, Bozell contended that *no* tradition of judicial review of legislative power existed before 1787, that the Founding Fathers did *not* propose anything even remotely resembling judicial supremacy, that virtually no one challenged the "prevailing tradition of legislative supremacy."[167] But if no principle of judicial supremacy was entrenched in 1787,[168] who then was intended to be the "final arbiter"? Nobody! Instead, the Founders deliberately designed a system of tensions and compromise under which *"the business of interpreting and enforcing the Constitution remained a joint enterprise"*—a system which persisted, he believed, right down to 1954.[169] The Constitution established "an intricate consensus machinery,"[170] whose viability required not restraint but energetic fulfillment of functions. If one branch (the Court, at present) gained ascendancy, the system would fail.[171]

Bozell's study exemplifies many features of the conservatives' understanding of the American constitutional system in the 1960s. He reflected their belief that the written Constitution was not an infinitely elastic document or "charter of learning"[172] to be construed in any convenient fashion to attain a transcendent end. If change must come, it should be "organic," not imposed abruptly and apodictically. He reflected the growing conservative apprehension about the imbalance of powers and a growing conservative desire to pull the Court as well as the long-overweening executive back into the constitutional harness. Perhaps above all, he revealed the traumatic and catalyzing effect of the Warren Court on the American Right. The Court drove Bozell and other conservatives back to the *American* fund of political experience, to *American* constitutional sources, and forced them to clarify their self-awareness in *American* terms. Even if they did not always agree, the process itself was useful in their quest for native ground to stand on.

By the mid-1960s, then, conservatives had evolved several strategies for coping with the charge of being "un-American." First, they had articulated a set of principles—such as natural law, Christian revelation, liberty under law, and the limited state—which they held to be "timeless," applicable to any social structure, "feudal" or modern, old or new. Secondly, many of them found in the embattled South a nonliberal bulwark against the rising radical tide. Finally, they successfully located a venerable and obviously indigenous American tradition with which to hammer at post-New Deal liberalism.

What was this tradition to which they repaired? The dominant thrust of the conservative thought discussed in this chapter was deeply and unabashedly antimajoritarian, suspicious of centralization and instant "plebiscitary democracy," and distrustful of innovating "liberals in a hurry" who were impatient with "horse-and-buggy" constitutions. The tradition to which most conservatives appealed was cautious about, even hostile toward, power—above all, concentrated power, whether wielded by popular majorities, by presidents, or by a few men on the Supreme Court. The principal theme of the writings surveyed thus far was resistance, in the name of individual freedom, private property, or the sovereign states, to "the tyranny of the majority" and national consolidation. The general mood was one of pessimism about the declining Old Republic.

Upon reflection, this does not seem surprising. Whatever its validity, this view of America's political development reflected the conservatives' perception of themselves in the 1950s and early 1960s. For theirs was the outlook of a minority, of a movement of protest that was self-consciously challenging many entrenched interests and powerful trends in contemporary American life. Burgeoning government, for instance, controlled by liberals who were kept in power by masses clamoring for more welfare state measures (more Social Security, more farm price supports, more subsidies, higher minimum wage levels): this was what conservatives believed they were confronting. Under these circumstances, it was quite natural for them to be antimajoritarian. After all, they were a minority—or seemed to be. Since the days of Franklin Roosevelt their opponents seemed to command majority support most of the time. Restraint on governmental power (particularly centralized power in Washington) and curbs on the "general will" seemed logical when power was in the hands of their enemies and the "general will" was fickle at best. A view of America's conservative heritage which complemented this view of the present was a very usable past.

Yet the times were changing in the early 1960s; conservatism was beginning a slow and subtle transformation. One sign of it was the fact that from this antimajoritarian mood and orthodoxy a forceful minority of conservatives dissented.

EIGHT

What is Conservatism in America? The Straussians, Willmoore Kendall, and the "Virtuous People"

In 1957 Walter Berns, a professor of government at Cornell University, unleashed a powerful challenge to the liberal interpretation of the First Amendment.[1] Analyzing a number of recent cases involving censorship, free speech, and Communism, Berns excoriated the Supreme Court for confused, tortured, and unjust decisions. The source of the Court's errors was not a particular individual but a pernicious political philosophy called liberalism that had become an American tradition.[2] What was this "liberalism"? It was, said Berns, the philosophy of "natural rights," "individualism," and the idea of the "hostile state" originated by Thomas Hobbes and perpetuated by John Locke. For these men and for all subsequent liberals, political inquiry began with supposedly inalienable, antecedent *rights* of man, against which was poised the state. Liberty *versus* government: this was the liberal conception, of which the Declaration of Independence and the Bill of Rights were American expressions. To be sure, Americans sometimes disagreed about *which* rights to emphasize—property or speech, for example. But always they assumed an opposition between "civilized society" and "government." Moreover, liberalism constantly assumed that freedom was the highest ideal.

The trouble with this "modern" political philosophy was that it was profoundly wrong and unworkable. As the Supreme Court's muddled record in civil liberties cases demonstrated, it was impossible to maintain in practice such an unrealistic doctrine. If we followed Justices Black and Douglas (the leading First Amendment "absolutists") in letting un-checked freedom prevail without ever judging what is *right*, we would ignore the possibility (not farfetched in the twentieth century) that "nox-ious doctrine" might actually prevail over "democratic doctrine." Truth might *lose* in the marketplace. But libertarians did not believe this would happen, Berns observed scornfully. They believed, apparently, in "the operation of the opposite of Gresham's law." *They* believed in "progress"; *they* believed that man was good—unless, perhaps, he was "corrupted" by government. If these assumptions were true, freedom would indeed be "the proper policy for government," and government should be re-stricted drastically. But *were* they true? Was freedom the ultimate politi-cal good? Was government the prime source of threats to liberty? "The gravest threats to freedom may come from the people themselves." This latter fact led Berns to reject the opposing (but also liberal) philosophy of "judicial restraint" espoused by Justice Frankfurter. Logically, it led to the end of judicial review and obeisance before the often dubious "good will and sense of local authorities."[3]

Berns, then, favored an active Supreme Court. But the philosophy it should adopt was profoundly opposed to liberalism. Taking his stand with the "ancients," Berns proclaimed that virtue was the highest good, not freedom. Justice, not "natural rights," was the proper end of govern-ment. To achieve these goals, government and law were indispensable. For "the formation of character is the principal duty of government." "Law *is* concerned with the virtue of citizens...." "Man is by nature not an individual with inalienable rights, but a political being, who can achieve his nature, his end, only in the *polis*, if at all."[4] Berns contended that this understanding of law was recognized by the Constitution. Indeed, the Court's task was to make the Constitution conform to justice, not vice versa.[5] There were, undoubtedly, many practical problems, and Berns insisted that he favored free speech. But freedom was possible and de-sirable only in the community composed primarily of "citizens of good character."[6]

Berns's scholarly polemic was unquestionably a contribution to the postwar reaction against liberalism.[7] Clearly he was not a man of the civil liberties Left, yet his antilibertarian position could not endear him to much of the Right. Frank Meyer disagreed sharply with Berns on sev-eral points; according to Meyer, family, church, and intellectuals—not government—should inculcate virtue.[8] In fact, Berns's book, published by the Henry Regnery Company, articulated a form of conservatism which, in its emphasis on virtue and the good society, resembled the position of

L. Brent Bozell in his exchanges with Meyer in 1962. More than that, it helped to inaugurate within the conservative community a "minority report" on the basis for conservatism in America.

The essentials of this "report" were contained in certain essays which Berns and others contributed to *A Nation of States* in 1963.[9] (The contrast with "mainstream" antimajoritarian conservatism was intensified by the inclusion in this collection of articles by two antimajoritarians, Russell Kirk and James J. Kilpatrick.) In one essay, Professor Martin Diamond of Claremont Men's College reinterpreted the Convention of 1787. Not only was it marked by a conflict between the proponents of "federalism" (that is, a loose league of states) and nationalism, but the ensuing compromise was also a clear victory for the nationalists. The convention had moved in the nationalist direction and had undermined the old notion that liberty was only attainable in small republics. Instead, a new theory had emerged: "a large, powerful republic with a competent national government regulated under a wise Constitution."[10] In another essay, Diamond's colleague Harry Jaffa boldly argued the case for a stronger national government, specifically criticizing the strict-constructionist Kilpatrick along the way.[11] Berns himself argued that the Tenth Amendment, worshipped by states' rightists like Kilpatrick, could only be construed as a "truism," merely "declaratory" of the division of powers in the "original, unamended Constitution." While he conceded that the early Constitution was amenable to diverse interpretations, history had quickly decided in favor of nationalism and of government unhampered by literal construction.[12] With the rather lonely exception of Kirk's and Kilpatrick's pieces, all other essays in this volume favored the "strong government" position.

Sooner or later this brand of conservatism was bound to clash with the prevailing orthodoxy. In a noteworthy exchange between Harry Jaffa and Frank Meyer in 1965, the debate was joined on the issue of Abraham Lincoln. To Jaffa, a political scientist at Claremont and ardent admirer of Lincoln,[13] the formative document, the fount of principle, for the American tradition was the "all men are created equal" clause of the Declaration of Independence. Jaffa was not advocating worldly leveling; he was insisting only that *political* equality was our defining principle: "It was *because* men are by nature equal; *because*, that is, no man is by nature the ruler of another, that government derives its just powers from consent—that is, from the opinion of the governed." In order to obtain such consent, majority rule as a practical matter is required, but the principle of majority rule cannot be divorced from "*the principle of the natural equality of political right of all men.*" This could never be surrendered; it was the basis of our national self-understanding. The Founding Fathers adhered to the principles of the Declaration.[14] So, too, did Abraham Lincoln.

In response to Frank Meyer's strictures on Lincoln, Jaffa made three major points. Siding with the "nationalists" in American history, Jaffa stated that Lincoln had not violated the "original" Constitution. In fact, "the dominant tradition of American statesmanship" was antisecession. Second, fending off charges that Lincoln was a dictator, Jaffa stressed the cautious, undoctrinaire side of the president's policies. Third, chiding Meyer for ignoring antebellum slavery, Jaffa apotheosized Lincoln as "the great prophet of our tradition" who saw

> the inner connection between free, popular, constitutional government, and the mighty proposition, "that all men are created equal." Questions concerning the construction of the Constitution were absolutely subordinate to the principle which gave life and meaning to the whole regime.[15]

Meyer, in rebuttal, noted that Jaffa's "broad constructionism" was not the only possible reading of America's past and reiterated the usual "divided power" themes. Moreover, Meyer bluntly denied Jaffa's claims about the place of equality in America's heritage: "The freedom of the individual person from government, not the equality of individual persons, is the central theme of our constitutional arrangements.... Freedom and equality are opposites...."[16]

The ever-argumentative Frank Meyer was not the only conservative alarmed by Jaffa's apology for Lincoln and equality. Willmoore Kendall feared that Jaffa would "launch" the nation

> upon a political future...made up of an endless series of Abraham Lincolns, each persuaded that he is superior in wisdom and virtue to the Fathers, each prepared to insist that those who oppose this or that new application of the equality standard are denying the possibility of self-government, each ultimately willing to plunge America into Civil War rather than concede his point...and off at the end, of course, the cooperative commonwealth of men who will be so equal that no one will be able to tell them apart.[17]

Francis Wilson accused Jaffa of failing to examine the "historical roots" of the idea of equality in the Declaration of Independence. "Apparently, he does not wish to make any serious inquiry into whether Lincoln's doctrine concerning the Declaration was historically accurate."[18]

So the issue was joined. On one side were those conservatives for whom the nation (particularly as forged by Lincoln) was a locus of value. On the other side were such men as Kirk, Meyer, Weaver, and Kilpatrick, for whom the early and more aristocratic republic before 1865 was something of a golden age. If all this discussion between "nationalists" and states' rightists, broad and strict constructionists, could be reduced to an argument about the distant past, one might be inclined to dismiss the dispute as one of little practical consequence. Certainly both camps were existentially on the Right. Berns, Diamond, and Jaffa all contributed at least once to *National Review*. Jaffa himself was widely believed to be the author of Senator Barry Goldwater's famous "extremism" remark in his acceptance speech at the 1964 Republican convention.[19]

Yet something more than rival interpretations of history was at stake. Here an illuminating clue suggests itself: Berns, Diamond, Jaffa, and certain others who shared their outlook were all disciples of Professor Leo Strauss. Surely this was more than a coincidence. A fundamental tenet of Strauss's thought was the superiority of the "ancients" to the "moderns," of "natural law" to individualistic "natural rights." The implications of this view for an interpretation of American history were immense. If one was not to concede that America was always fully "Lockean," then one had to find non-Lockean elements somewhere. And the tradition of libertarianism, states' rights, and limited government did not always seem a good place to start. For that view was often suffused with a "liberal," modern emphasis on *rights* which Straussians believed to be a massive error. It tended to favor the freewheeling individual over government, and preferred local and state government to the federal level. Frequently it praised the self-sufficient man clutching his bundle of rights and warding off "our enemy, the State." (Thus, an early issue of *National Review* contained praise of Utah Governor J. Bracken Lee for stoutly refusing to pay his income tax because part of it was spent on foreign aid.[20]) Straussian or classical political philosophy, on the other hand, was logically congenial with energetic government designed to improve the polis, inculcate virtue, and help man attain his "natural" end. The nationalistic ideas of Union and of a powerful government determined to implement a "proposition" fitted in very well with Straussianism. For in that conception of politics the libertarian distinction between state and society, between individual and polis (Union), broke down.

Frank Meyer, never one to miss "heresy," saw the conflict clearly. In his book *In Defense of Freedom* he explicitly attacked classical political philosophy for its failure to conceive the State as "a special and limited institution." The ancient Greeks (and by implication their contemporary admirers, including the Straussians) did not "free themselves from the *polis* experienced as an organic being, of which individual men are but cells." Meyer emphasized the superiority of Christianity, with its Incarnation, its stress on the infinite worth of the individual, and its "desanctification" of the State.[21] Nor was Meyer pleased by Straussian interpretations of the American regime; they were too Hamiltonian, even authoritarian, to satisfy a man for whom individual freedom and *limited* government were supreme, and for whom the Tenth Amendment was a good deal more than a "truism."[22]

Straussian doctrine, applied to American history, therefore presented a sharp challenge to antimajoritarian conservatism. For much of the conservatism discussed in the last chapter implicitly or explicitly acquiesced in the natural rights theory of government.[23] Sometimes John Locke was explicitly regarded as a kind of patron saint.[24] Yet here was a group intrepidly claiming that Locke and the moderns were *wrong*. Which side was correct? Could these positions be reconciled? Was America fundamentally Lockean or not? Were most conservatives crypto-liberals after all? What *was* the true meaning of America?

The confusion and problems suggested by the Straussian and antimajoritarian interpretations were visible for all who cared to see.[25] One person who did see—with the penetration, perhaps, of genius—was a remarkable man whom some conservatives came to regard as their greatest interpreter of America's political tradition: Willmoore Kendall.

Few who met Willmoore Kendall ever forgot him. He was born in Konawa, Oklahoma, in 1909, the son of a blind Southern Methodist minister. Kendall's early years were spent in little prairie towns where his father preached—towns like Konawa, Idabel, Mangum. He was a child prodigy who learned to read at the age of two by playing with a typewriter. He graduated from high school at 13, entered Northwestern University the same year, and graduated from the University of Oklahoma at 18. By the time he was 20 he had published a book on baseball and was teaching in a prep school. He was, in the words of a friend, "the boy wonder of Oklahoma."[26]

After completing all nondissertation graduate requirements in Romance languages at the University of Illinois, Kendall became a Rhodes scholar in 1932; his next four years abroad in many respects changed his entire life. It was at Oxford that he enrolled in the Philosophy, Politics, and Economics (P.P.E.) program and discovered his future intellectual passion: political philosophy. One of his tutors was the distinguished philosopher R. G. Collingwood, who, Kendall later remarked, was a major influence. The years in England were ones of excitement, challenge, and intellectual exploration, and in this atmosphere Kendall thrived. He was argumentative, even quarrelsome, and loved to shock people into debate, taking on all comers in disputation far into the night. Kendall's sister provides a glimpse of his arguments with his father, suggesting the pattern at Oxford and wherever he went:

> ...it was not unusual for him and Dad to engage in heated debate of a political issue, ending with one or the other storming out of the room in anger—and then hear them, a few hours later, pick up the same subject, each taking the opposite side of the question under discussion than that held in the previous discussion. It was for them, I think, a very stimulating kind of mental gymnastics—and it made artists of argumentative technique out of both of them.[27]

While Kendall's pugnacious probing at Oxford was generally good-humored, his temperament helps to explain the later troubled personal and academic life of this strangely driven man.

While abroad in the 1930s, Kendall became known as a man of the Left, even (some believed) the Trotskyist Left. While the precise evolution of his beliefs in this period is in some dispute,[28] the testimony of those who knew him at Oxford is solid on one point: he was an enthusiastic admirer of the Spanish Republic. In 1935 he left Oxford for a sojourn as a United Press correspondent in Madrid. There is little doubt that this experience, which ended shortly before the civil war broke out on July 18, 1936, was in political terms one of the decisive moments of his career. Passionately in favor of the leftist Spanish Republic, Kendall became associated with a number of prominent Spanish Trotskyists in Madrid.[29] According to Kendall's first wife, whom he married in 1935, his affinity for the Trotskyists was in large part a reaction against Stalinism. In the turbulent cockpit of Spanish political warfare, Kendall's detestation of Stalin and the Moscow-oriented Communists grew.[30] The dictatorial, totalitarian, antidemocratic aspects of Communism appalled him. He later told a friend that as Spain slid toward civil war he could tolerate the Communists' blowing up the plants of opposition newspapers. But when they deliberately killed opposition *newsboys*—this was too much.[31] Exposure to the Spanish Republic "really shook Willmoore up," one friend recalled, and within a few months, "his thought crystallized into fervent anti-communism."[32] This theme—militant, uncompromising hostility to Communism—became one of the dominant features of his thought. The disintegration of Spain, the awful specter of civil war, started a disillusioned man on the road to the Right. Like so many others of the postwar conservative movement, in Kendall's past was a god—or, more likely in his case, only a demigod—that failed.[33]

But if Kendall's anti-Stalinism was the genesis of a later, broader anti-Communism, it did not make an instant conservative out of him. Returning to the University of Illinois in the fall of 1936, Kendall continued to be a man of the Left. He supported the cause of Republican Spain and was even accused of recruiting students for the Abraham Lincoln Brigade. His first scholarly articles in the late 1930s were of a decidedly left-wing cast; for example, he advocated government ownership of the press[34] and contended that an "economic oligarchy" had always held political power in America.[35] Ever distrustful of elites, Kendall enunciated a radical democratic viewpoint—a position somewhat in vogue in the late 1930s during the debates over majority rule versus the "nine old men" on the Supreme Court. In 1938 he advocated the Ludlow Amendment, under which the United States could not officially go to war (except in case of invasion) until a national referendum was held. "There are those of us," he declared, "who believe that the best judges of a nation's welfare are the people who live in it; and once that belief has been set aside, the door is thrown wide open to the most violent excesses of minority rule."[36]

Meanwhile, Kendall continued his study of political philosophy and obtained his Ph.D. in political science from the University of Illinois in 1940. His dissertation advisor was Francis Wilson, one of the pioneers of the postwar conservative renascence. Kendall's dissertation, published a year later, was true to his temperament: daring, relentlessly argued, and unorthodox.[37] Challenging the conventional notion that John Locke was the champion of inalienable natural rights, Kendall meticulously contended that Locke was actually a "majority rule" democrat. To be sure, Locke talked of natural rights, but in the last analysis he "would entrust to the majority the power of defining individual rights."[38] "...Locke's natural rights are merely the rights vouchsafed by a legislature responsible to the majority...."[39] Society is sovereign, not the individual, whose rights are "a function of, not a limitation on" society.[40] How could Locke have both "rights" and majority dominance? Because, said Kendall, of his "latent premise" that his kind of majority "would never withdraw a right which the individual ought to have."[41]

Kendall's work, which was recognized as a major piece of scholarship on the Locke "problem," inaugurated one of the most unusual academic careers of his time. After government service during and after World War II (including a high position at the Central Intelligence Agency),[42] Kendall joined the Yale University faculty in 1947 and stayed for fourteen tumultuous and bitter years. His letters from this period are full of stories of departmental warfare; never, although he had tenure, did Yale grant him a promotion from associate professor. Finally, in 1961, when Kendall believed it clear that he would never go higher at Yale, he offered to leave—if Yale "bought up" his tenure rights. Yale agreed and paid him a sum in the tens of thousands of dollars. Kendall told a friend that he was "the only man that Yale ever paid to resign from its faculty."[43]

In his early years at Yale,[44] Kendall called himself "an old-fashioned majority-rule democrat"; his principal scholarly enthusiasms were "majority-rule democracy" and the related critique of the "open society."[45] Why was he so unremittingly hostile to the natural rights philosophy? A passage from a critique of one of his favorite targets—John Stuart Mill—provides a clue:

> Start out with Mill's principles, and you end, as Mill himself did, with the anarchistic view that there are no limits whatever upon the degree of "diversity" a society can stomach and still survive (wherefore we must today tolerate, for instance, anti-semitic utterance by our neighbors, because prohibiting it would infringe their "rights" to freedom of speech).[46]

Again and again, in articles and on debate platforms, Kendall denounced the "heresy" that all questions are open questions. He insisted that all societies (including democracies) do have, ought to have, *must* have an orthodoxy, a consensus, a will to survive that they may rightfully defend against those who fundamentally challenge the very core of what they hold dear.[47]

To Kendall these considerations were no airy theoretical fancies. They were truths applicable to the greatest domestic debate of the late 1940s and early 1950s: the status and influence of Communism in American life. Into this fray he moved with characteristic vigor and flamboyance, soon emerging as one of the most capable of the academic defenders of Senator Joseph McCarthy, whom he knew personally. Tirelessly he defended McCarthy's crusade, Whittaker Chambers, and the determination of many Americans to declare Communists beyond the bounds of public protection. He criticized Alger Hiss and J. Robert Oppenheimer[48]—activities not likely to smooth the ruffled feathers of some of his enemies on the Left.

Long after the McCarthy controversy subsided, Kendall labored on—almost quixotically, it seems—in defense of America's deepest meaning as he saw it.[49] There was irony and perhaps pathos in his odyssey: a dissenter pleading the cause of orthodoxy, an individualist who detested notions of absolute rights, a rebel who suffered the displeasure of the local orthodoxy of liberal Yale. Kendall knew, too, the price he was paying for his relentless, irrepressible iconoclasm: hostility at Yale, obstacles to professional advancement, charges that he was a fascist, an authoritarian, a warmonger. Why, one wonders, was he such a persistent, perhaps compulsive, "aginner"? Without attempting to probe Kendall's extraordinary personality (someone has aptly said he was too complicated a man to psychoanalyze), and without wishing in the least to "explain away" his philosophy, we draw attention to two profound and probably formative experiences in his life. First, he said that he learned his deepest lessons about democracy from the closed little towns of his Oklahoma boyhood.[50] Second, the shattering nightmare of Spain, one strongly suspects, taught him the horror of a society without a consensus, a society at war with itself, a society where all people were free to talk—and talked themselves into war. These truths were too dear to him to surrender for the sake of tranquillity in academe.

There was more to his anti-Communism than that. Kendall genuinely believed that Communism was a danger to America and that it simply had to be exposed. Francis Wilson, his dissertation advisor, explained Kendall's convictions:

> Apparently, liberal and kind-hearted Americans believe all men are good and that all issues can be resolved by a little amiable conversation; hence, the communists could hardly be in any case a menace to the security of the United States. But Kendall (and all the conservative critics of communism) have held that this is not so: communists are just not like this. They are engaged in a worldwide conspiracy to bring about the communist revolution everywhere, and the greatest enemy of communistic progress after World War II has been and is the United States.[51]

This unrelenting anti-Communism was undoubtedly a key to his transition from Left to Right. In the 1930s, of course (and later, too), one could be both a man of the Left *and* an anti-Stalinist—a fact which, James Burnham believed, motivated Kendall's "Trotskyism."[52] But to someone like Kendall, the Left in the late 1940s and early 1950s was no longer a likely haven. Certainly not Henry Wallace's Progressivism, which he denounced fiercely. Nor "containment" liberalism, which, to its critics, did not contain.[53] To Kendall, who advocated a "liberation" strategy,[54] the Truman-Acheson foreign policy was hopelessly inadequate.[55]

Kendall's fervent anti-Communism was only one of a number of factors pushing him toward conservatism in the 1940s. As the decade wore on, signs of his estrangement from liberalism multiplied. One early wedge was the great foreign policy debate of 1939-1941. Staunchly anti-interventionist (although still, at that time, a leftist in domestic affairs), Kendall grew increasingly saddened as many of his friends and heroes on the Left began to support war with Germany. Writing to a friend early in 1942, Kendall revealed his disenchantment with the nation's political establishment:

> It is not, in short, my faith in the majority which I've lost. The majority has, in sober truth, arrived at no conclusions in the last couple of years that, on the evidence offered to it, I could fairly have expected it to reject. My concern, and disillusionment, is with the people who could have given them evidence of another kind—with, if you like, the most gigantic and unpardonable *trahison des clercs* of which History offers any record. To think of it makes me sick at heart.[56]

Vehemently anti-Roosevelt, Kendall voted for Willkie in 1940 and hoped for a Republican victory in 1944. He was pleased by the Republicans' gains in the 1946 elections; perhaps, he explained to a friend, he would finally see what he had so long yearned for: "a Congress really asserting its prerogatives vis-à-vis the Executive."[57] None of these positions made Kendall an orthodox conservative; indeed, his correspondence indicates that he was in many respects a man of the Left at least until 1946.[58] But his was a left-wing stance of a decidedly idiosyncratic kind. It is not so surprising, then, that when the great "civil war" over loyalty and Communism erupted in the late 1940s, Kendall moved with apparent ease from Left to Right. So many of his enemies were *already* on the Left.

And one enemy above all: the liberal philosophy of natural rights and civil liberties. In a sense one can say that Kendall in the late 1940s did *not* change fundamentally at all; the Left did. For in the era of Joseph McCarthy, many Americans on the Left asserted with new fervor the value of civil liberties, individual rights, due process of law, checks and balances, and "pluralism." Back in the 1930s, it had been easy to applaud popular sovereignty and sweeping majority rule when the enemy was the Supreme Court, "economic royalists," and Spencerian natural "rights." With the advent of McCarthy and other zealously anti-Communist legislators, however, pure majoritarianism lost much of its appeal. Perhaps the people could be misled, by a *demagogue*; perhaps we need *institutions* and *elites* to limit the untamed general will. To this reorientation in liberal thought, Willmoore Kendall—student of Rousseau,[59] foe of elitism, enemy of John Stuart Mill—was impervious. Others might abandon their undiluted majoritarianism; not Willmoore. Well into the 1950s he strenuously maintained his old position.[60] This unyielding theoretical consistency was one more ingredient in Kendall's deepening antagonism toward liberalism.

So Kendall ended on the Right. At first a supporter of Senator Taft in 1952, he voted for Eisenhower over "Addlepai" Stevenson, "the Ivy League Will Rogers." He even planned at one point (he had so many plans) to write a book to be called "Confession of an American Imperialist Reactionary," which would be "a declaration of war on the intellectuals."[61] Many of his closest student friends at Yale went on to become conservative spokesmen—William F. Buckley, Jr., L. Brent Bozell, Stanley Parry. In 1955, Kendall became a senior editor of *National Review*.

And always he played the role of iconoclast, the man who loved to defend the seemingly impossible cause. In a stunning analysis of Plato's *Apology* and *Crito* in the late 1950s, for example, Kendall attacked head-on the view that Socrates was a faultless hero unjustly persecuted by an ignorant mob. If Athens were so utterly without reason, why did Socrates deliberately elect to stay there and die? If the laws had no legitimate claim over him, why did he not escape? The true point of Plato's drama was the "sheer inevitability of the failure" of Socrates, the tragedy of a conflict of truths. On one side was a man inspired by God, a man with a "divine mission," a "revolutionary agitator" (in the eyes of the Assembly) who candidly and radically questioned the way of life of the polis. On the other was Athens, which did *not* savagely persecute him but first gave him a full hearing *and was not convinced*. How could it have been otherwise? Socrates made it plain that he would not, could not, cease to preach (in effect) the overthrow of the city. He was not harmless; already he had many devoted youthful followers. Therefore, Plato was saying, punishment of Socrates was unavoidable. Athens had offered him all that it possibly could—the Laws, freedom to speak in his own defense, even a chance to flee—and still survive. And Socrates understood this fact. He *refused* to become a modern liberal asserting his absolute "right" to speak regardless of other considerations. He spoke instead in the name of a shattering Truth, of God—*not* in the name of relativistic, "open-minded," free discussion in search of truths that don't exist. We may prefer Socrates, Kendall concluded, but we must "forgive" Athens for its "second-best" choice, which was actually more "realistic" than that of the man who forced it to condemn him.[62]

Meanwhile, another fundamental reorientation of Kendall's life was beginning in the 1950s, a transformation as important as his earlier shift from Left to Right. Writing in 1954 to Henry Regnery, William F. Buckley, Jr. noted a "metamorphosis" in his mentor:

> In 1949, he was rather cynical about the great truths that you had dedicated your life to pressing upon our society. Slowly, but inexorably, he has lost the cynicism he acquired as a precocious scholar at Oxford and as a young and gifted teacher in the turbulent '30's, to the point where he has become, in my experience, one of the few fine and intensely moral figures of our time.[63]

In 1956, Kendall, long a religious skeptic, joined the Roman Catholic Church—impelled in part, he said, by the Church's centuries and centuries of tradition.[64] It is possible that the Church's anti-Communism also had something to do with his conversion.[65]

What were these "great truths" which Kendall increasingly expounded? During the 1950s he became profoundly influenced by two men whose thought, he believed, inaugurated a "revolution in political theory scholarship": Eric Voegelin and Leo Strauss.[66] These two men, he acknowledged freely, dramatically changed his scholarly career. Kendall called Strauss "*the* great teacher of political philosophy, not of our time alone, but of any time since Machiavelli."[67] Under Strauss's influence Kendall modified his view of John Locke[68] and in fact became so affected by the "revolution" that his scholarly standards "changed drastically" and the pace of his own scholarship slowed down. He felt the duty to combat what Strauss called the "illegitimate" (that is, behaviorist, relativist, "value-free") branches of political science.[69] Above all, Kendall absorbed the fundamental Straussian distinction between the Great Tradition and the rebellion against it inaugurated by Machiavelli, Hobbes, and Locke.[70]

In numerous ways, Kendall held, the moderns deviated from the older and better conception of political man. The Great Tradition held that man and society were "coeval"; the "contractarians" saw society as an "artifact" to be altered at will. The Great Tradition emphasized that man is social by nature; the contractarians emphasized instead the self-contained individual, isolated and fearful in a state of nature, who merely made a "contract" or compact to which he gave "consent." The Great Tradition emphasized man's "perfection" or "end"; the contractarians, merely man as he (supposedly) was. The Great Tradition especially emphasized natural law and the duties of men; the "modern" rebellion spoke only of natural "rights" which were not bound by duties or by any moral obligation at all. The only ultimate right, really (said the moderns), was mere self-preservation or self-interest. Indeed, the contract philosophers denied that a higher law existed. That was the question for Kendall: "whether there is or is not a higher law, independent of agreements and contracts, among men."[71]

This new direction in Kendall's thought may seem puzzling on the surface. Natural law, truth, justice, the denigration of "consent"—how was this emphasis compatible with his former absolute majoritarianism? Was not the thrust of his Straussian views at least in spirit antidemocratic? Perhaps. But Kendall's thinking was complex, and one should note the deep continuities between his earlier (leftist) and later (rightist) phases. In both periods, for example, he detested "individual rights" philosophies. In the earlier years he did so in the name of a majority (unhindered by formal Bills of Rights) eager to create and sustain an orthodoxy. Under Strauss's influence he called forth the natural law and duties. Perhaps there is an affinity between absolute majoritarianism and the absolute priority of justice and virtue over freedom and self-interest. At any rate, although he abandoned his absolute majoritarianism in the late 1950s, he did not surrender his belief that the majority should rule. Instead, he now began to speak of *kinds* of majorities, some good, some evil—a transition reflected in his "Two Majorities" article in 1960.[72] What happened, perhaps, was only this: the upholder of the propriety of public orthodoxies had found *the* orthodoxy to defend.

In the final decade or so of his life, Kendall became increasingly absorbed by a new task: the application of his political philosophy to the American tradition. Well before *National Review* was founded, Kendall was, of course, interested in American political institutions[73] and their rescue from both Communists and liberals. But the demonstration that our heritage was reconcilable with the Great Tradition became a dominant theme only in his last years.[74] Animating his writing was the conviction that traditional America was fighting off a "war of aggression," a "Liberal Revolution" which sought to set up, "in Machiavelli's phrase, *new modes and orders*." Conservatism could be empirically defined as the resistance to this revolution.[75] Of what did the liberal threat consist? First, the effort to create a totally "open" society; second, the ceaseless attempt to change the Constitution into a merely plebiscitary system; and third, the attempt to institutionalize a coarse egalitarianism.[76] Kendall contrasted true, conservative criteria for evaluating regimes (justice, the common good) with false, liberal criteria (individual rights, equality). [77] Indeed, there lay the "ultimate issue": natural law versus relativism and self-interest, the Great Tradition versus liberalism. Since liberalism was Lockeanism, conservatism must oppose both.[78]

And so an issue that frequently troubled the postwar conservative movement burst out once more. The "official literature" (to borrow a phrase of Kendall's) taught that the American tradition was inherently liberal. The official literature said that Locke decisively influenced the Founding Fathers, that America was (or ought to be) open, equal, and solicitous of natural rights. Kendall disagreed.

Consider, for example, his interpretation of the Declaration of Independence. If, as liberals often said, the "all men are created equal" clause was a preeminent national commitment in 1776, why was equality not even mentioned in the Preamble to the Constitution only eleven years later? Surely the Founding Fathers did not simply forget to include among the supreme defining purposes of the Constitution the one which everybody supposedly knew underlay all the rest. And why did the *Federalist Papers* and the Bill of Rights also neglect equality? And what did the word "equality" connote, anyway? To Kendall it meant a universal right to justice, to government under law, to treatment as a human being. Equality did not mean liberal egalitarianism—the notion that men should be *made* equal in a material way. That notion emerged only much later, with Abraham Lincoln, whom Kendall found guilty of a tragic "derailment" of our tradition because of his claim that the Declaration of Independence had "constitutional status." Why, it had not even set up a nation, only "a baker's dozen of new sovereignties." The signers actually refused to condemn slavery in the Declaration and gave other indications that the document's phrases had no binding or compelling meaning. Kendall argued that to make the Declaration's equality clause a paradigmatic slogan was to distort grotesquely its limited intent.[79]

Nor did the Constitution or Bill of Rights embody the absolute natural rights theory. Again, the Preamble spoke of insuring justice, tranquillity, and other goals, not absolute individual "rights." Moreover, and astoundingly, the Philadelphia Convention of 1787 had unanimously (and properly) rejected George Mason's proposal to include a bill of rights! How, if the Founders had been such thoroughgoing Lockeans, could they ever have done that? Moreover, there had been no "mandate" or genuine popular demand for a bill of rights, and the one which was adopted was conspicuously not the sort of document Justice Hugo Black later thought it was. It did not proclaim the United States an open society; that question was not even posed in 1790. The First Amendment did not even proclaim a right to free speech. It merely constrained Congress and gave a monopoly of "suppression" to the states! The First Amendment was simply a states' rights amendment.[80]

Moreover, relying on the scholarship of Leonard Levy,[81] Kendall claimed with delight that history vindicated his analysis. Levy showed that the sainted Founding Fathers did not intend (and did not act as if they had intended) to set up a wide-open, "do your own thing" society. The First Amendment was not believed at the time to abolish the common law of seditious libel. Indeed, said Kendall,

> the "people" whose representatives wrote and who themselves ratified the first amendment, with its apparent guarantees of freedom of expression, had no tradition of free speech or a free press, no statesmen who were urging the need for these guarantees, and no political philosophers who had made out a case for them.[82]

Even Jefferson himself had what Levy (but not Kendall) called his "darker side": this verbal libertarian "*did*, while in office, appear to act on the principle that no government should permit qualms about individual rights to get in the way of its policies."[83] Now a critic might berate Jefferson and the Founders for failure to be twentieth-century libertarians. Or he could reprove Jefferson for "ill-considered" grandiloquent pronouncements out of office that could not possibly pass the test of "prudential considerations" in office. Kendall took the latter course.[84]

In fact, he wondered, just where *did* these notions of free speech and open society come from? Clearly, ordinary Americans had no such understanding. In 1955, for instance, two-thirds of them would not even permit Communists and atheists to speak in their town or high school.[85] Now whether this be a sign of intolerance or higher wisdom, it did, Kendall argued, make one wonder whether Americans had ever meaningfully adopted John Stuart Mill's ideas on free speech. It seemed to Kendall—in an extreme, if humorous, statement—that the true American tradition was not "preferred freedoms" but "riding somebody out of town on a rail."[86] And that was the point. America was neither in theory nor in practice an open society. The liberals were *wrong*—wrong on the

Founding Fathers, wrong on the Bill of Rights, wrong on our day-to-day functioning tradition. Whatever the merits of their philosophy, they could not claim the American tradition as a support. That tradition was *ours*— the conservatives'—and liberalism was at best a recent accretion, a foreign body, not organic and not viable.

How could the Left say otherwise? The very fact that American politics is a constant battle about liberal proposals demonstrated, said Kendall, that the tradition itself was conservative.[87] The liberals had not made our country open or equal. From J. Allen Smith to James MacGregor Burns, they had not succeeded in converting the Constitution into an instant-majority-rule document. The French Revolution had not yet occurred in the United States.[88] The liberal rebellion had not captured the barricades.

What barricades? It was not enough for Kendall to deny that the American tradition was exclusively or predominantly liberal. He had to show wherein our tradition was conservative. How did we know that what happened out there in America, away from enclaves of liberals, was not mulishness or ignorance but wisdom?

Something was indeed happening which conventional theory could not explain—this was the thesis of Kendall's pathbreaking article "The Two Majorities." Noting the familiar fact of conflict between a "liberal" president and a "conservative" Congress in recent decades, Kendall sought to understand "an unexplained mystery": the fact that *one and the same electorate maintains in Washington, year after year, a President devoted to high principle and enlightenment, and a Congress that gives short shrift to both....*"[89] Liberals, of course, had an easy explanation for this behavior: the Congress was undemocratic. First, they said, the Constitution itself—by such means as bicameralism, staggered elections, and rural overrepresentation—obstructed the translation of popular sentiment into decisive action. Second, the internal procedures of Congress—like the filibuster and seniority system—further thwarted majority rule. To Kendall, this analysis was superficial and greatly misleading. How could one accuse the Founding Fathers of erecting barriers to a plebiscitary system when such a system was still unheard of? Moreover, the presidential system as we know it was only later "engrafted" onto our system. Citing numerous passages from the *Federalist*, Kendall contended that the Founders *were* majoritarians, but of a special sort.

For what the Founding Fathers wished to achieve *was* majority rule, but a majority decision articulated after "a process of deliberation among virtuous men representing potentially conflicting and in any case different 'values' and interests." This process of deliberation did *not* occur during the ritual of elections, as modern liberals would like. It did not involve deciding at elections between airy principles and visionary programs. It did not involve creation of a binding "mandate" at the polls. Ours was not the British system of government, as that system is usually perceived. Instead, the central process was one of deliberation by Congress itself—a Congress of good men elected by structured local constituencies and *uninstructed* by them, yet always and inevitably aware of them. It was the task of Congress not to implement packaged campaign promises but to weigh and consider, to obtain "feedback" from the local communities—in short, to deliberate. For what purpose? To achieve a "deliberate sense of the community," a *consensus*—not a bare, ragged majority produced after a shrill clash of grandiose principles. It was this undramatic congressional majority that expressed the way the system was originally intended to operate. And rightly so:

> ...insofar as the presidential election encourages the electorate to overestimate its dedication to moral principle, the congressional election encourages them, nay, obliges them, to take a more realistic view of themselves, and to send forth a candidate who will represent, and act in terms of, that more realistic view. By remaining pretty much what the Framers intended them to be, in other words, the congressional elections, in the context of the engrafted presidential election, provide a highly necessary corrective against the bias toward quixotism inherent in our presidential elections.... And it is well they do; the alternative would be national policies based upon a wholly false picture of the sacrifices the electorate are prepared to make for the lofty objectives held up to them by presidential aspirants. And executive-legislative tension is the means by which the corrective works itself out.[90]

Long before it became fashionable, Kendall was a critic of the "imperial presidency."

In siding with Congress and the local constituencies against the president and the centralizing liberals, Kendall, of course, ended in the same camp as most other conservatives. But—and this point is crucial—he came to that position in an "old-fashioned majoritarian" way. Here were no stirring appeals to natural rights, no Goldwaterish blasts at Big Government,[91] no exaltation of abstract individual freedom, no denunciations of universal suffrage or "the tyranny of the majority." Instead, Kendall denied J. Allen Smith's contention (tacitly accepted by many conservatives) that the Constitution was essentially undemocratic.[92] It was not, he insisted, hostile to majority rule per se. Even the Bill of Rights was not really a check on popular sovereignty.

> ...Madison's Bill of Rights, correctly read...leaves the natural rights, in the areas that Justice Black correctly regards as crucial, subject to the general Federalist principles that the deliberate sense of the American community is to be trusted, and that any attempt to put parchment barriers in its way will as a matter of course be ineffective.... If the people wills to do itself hurt—or, we may safely add, good either—who is to say it nay? And the answer, for the American system, would appear to be: in the crucial area, nobody.[93]

But what *kind* of majorities should prevail? Not the plebiscitary ones, which, he stated in one article, "are not good instrumentalities for making public policy" and furthermore tend "to divide us, to make us bad friends with one another."[94]

> We must learn, we conservatives, that the issue is *not* whether the American system is or is not "democratic," but which of two competing definitions of "democracy"—that which equates it with government by the "deliberate sense" of the people, acting through their elected representatives, and that which equates it with direct majority rule and equality—should prevail, and in doing so, learn to expose the falseness of the Liberal's claim that the reforms he proposes can properly be defended in the name of democracy.[95]

In a rousing debate with James MacGregor Burns in 1964, Kendall cheerfully admitted that the American political system as he understood it was not an effective instrument for "translating popular will into action" or "getting government to do things for the people." But that was precisely its design and its virtue:

> Our system was devised by men who feared and disliked *above all things* the operation in politics of sheer, naked will.... It was devised for purposes that had nothing to do with simplistic formulae like "the will of the people".... It was devised to effectuate not the will of the people, but rather, as *The Federalist* puts it, the deliberate sense of the community, the *whole* community, as to what ought to be done, what policies ought to be adopted.[96]

From the majoritarianism of his radical days Kendall had moved to a subtle, "Madisonian," majority-rule posture.

Kendall freely conceded that nothing explicitly written in the Constitution required "deliberate sense" or "consensus" majorities. Indeed, the document itself had—on paper—extraordinary "plebiscitary potential."[97] Consider afresh its words alone. It did not explicitly incorporate any notions of "separation of powers"; on the contrary, the document virtually mandated congressional supremacy. An aroused, sustained majority in Congress could, if it wished, run roughshod over the other two supposedly equal branches. By impeachment and the power of the purse it could control the president. By such tactics as court packing or regulation of appellate jurisdiction it could, if it wished, subdue the Supreme Court. Nothing forbade the emergence of a "mandate" system; Article V, in fact, even allowed the most drastic alterations of the Constitution to be adopted by the country. Clearly Kendall was no ordinary strict constructionist.

And yet this most unconservative constitutional potential had never been actualized. Congress had refrained from using all its powers to dominate the government or to become the vehicle of every passing majority. Our system, said Kendall, had accepted the rise of judicial review, although, as L. Brent Bozell had now "conclusively demonstrated," the Constitution did not, in the eyes of those who wrote it, empower the Court to declare legislative acts unconstitutional. But Kendall held that We the People had, in our wisdom, adopted various political "habits" such as the filibuster, the seniority system, the avoidance of polarized, ideological parties, and the resistance to being "mobilized" for such ends as drastically amending the Constitution. We had absorbed, in short, a particular "constitutional morality."[98] Its purpose—the purpose of these "habits"—was not to thwart majority rule but to create a certain *kind* of majority rule.

And whence had this morality come? Above all, it was articulated in a book which Kendall tirelessly extolled as a "sacred" text: the *Federalist Papers*. It was "Publius" who persuaded Americans to accept a certain interpretation of the Constitution and a certain process by which the country was to be governed. In a luminous passage, Kendall summarized his own distinctive teaching:

> ...what I do take sides on is the thesis of the *Federalist Papers*, namely: That America's mission in the world is to prove to the world that self-government—that is, government by the people through a representative assembly which, by definition, calls the plays—is possible. What I do take sides on is

> our solemn obligation, as Americans, to value the good health
> of the American political system—the system we have de-
> vised in order to prove to the world that self-government is
> possible—above the immediate demands, however just and
> right, of any minority. What I do take sides on is government
> by consensus, which, I repeat, requires of minorities demand-
> ing drastic change that they bide their time until they have
> pleaded their case successfully before the bar of public—not
> merely majority—opinion. What I do take sides on is the Pre-
> amble of the Constitution which gives equal status to justice
> and domestic tranquility, and so pledges us to pursue them
> simultaneously, and not even in the "case" that seems "dear-
> est" to a protesting minority, subordinate domestic tranquil-
> ity to justice.[99]

To Kendall, one of the great strengths of the American system was its
ability to prevent the rise of "pockets of irredentism that produce crises."[100] Perhaps in the back of his mind he was thinking of Spain.

Kendall was shrewd enough to realize that he could not base his
defense of a tradition on a single book that might be dismissed as propaganda.[101] In a posthumously published book he attempted to uncover
the "basic symbols" of America's heritage.[102] Employing the methodology of Eric Voegelin, Kendall argued that any society's self-understanding could be explored by scrutiny of its myths and symbols—in America's
case, its formative public documents from the Mayflower Compact to
the Bill of Rights. According to Kendall, the true tradition—of which
even the Declaration of Independence, properly interpreted,[103] was a
part—was: "the representative assembly *deliberating* under God; the virtuous people, virtuous because deeply religious and thus committed to
the *process* of searching for the transcendent Truth."[104]

And, argued Kendall, this commitment had never been abandoned.
In blunt contrast to nearly every other conservative of his time, many of
whom were deeply skeptical of the masses, Kendall stated, time and
time again, that We the People had not ceased to be "virtuous," to keep
the faith of the Founding Fathers. Oh, the people were inarticulate—he
knew that. Yet they had succeeded in carrying the tradition (the Great
Tradition) "in their hips"—a favorite phrase he attributed to Lincoln
Steffens. Kendall called himself an "Appalachians-to-the-Rockies patriot."
Even in the dark days of 1964 he maintained that "the overwhelming
majority of the American people" were conservative.[105] A frequent un-
dercurrent of his writings was the conviction that in the local communities political wisdom could still be found. He had faith in "neighborli-

ness," which "knocks the edges off the tendency to be doctrinaire."[106] The "Liberal Revolution"—construed especially as an assault on the structure, not the substance, of American politics—had not been consummated. The American people were still bound by a consensus. They had not converted our system to "reliance on the sheer, naked will of the majority."[107] In their hips they knew they were right.

Even the civil rights movement, Kendall said in one of his last essays, had been obliged to conform to the still vital American system. In 1964, a few years before he died, Kendall had predicted that this allegedly revolutionary force would precipitate a "constitutional crisis comparable to and graver than that which precipitated the Civil War...."[108] The American political system, based on government by "consensus" or "the deliberate sense of the community," and biased against "governmentally-induced drastic change,"[109] would clash with a group that demanded such change and that would not take no for an answer. Three years later, even as American cities were wracked by riots, Kendall announced that the civil rights movement had been "killed." His earlier prediction of a constitutional crisis had not come true. Why this unexpected development? First, the movement had lost "steam" because it had been "deserted" by many white liberals. Second, its greatest victories—the congressional legislation of 1964 and 1965—had been won at the price of increasing opposition and of moving the scene of battle from the South to the "more difficult terrain" of the North. Third, by altering its objectives from legal equality to "substantial" equality for blacks, it had increased the obstacles to further success. In other words, the more radical it became, the less the likelihood of victory. Finally—and this was Kendall's favorite explanation—the crisis had been averted because the civil rights forces had been made "a prisoner of the traditional American political system and thus of consensus politics." The movement had been "softened in order to restore equilibrium in the American political system...." How? Precisely by the legislation of 1964 and 1965, which Kendall, virtually alone among conservatives, hailed as "great Conservative victories." Congress had skillfully given the civil rights advocates the appearance of triumph, had domesticated the movement, without giving it in practice what it had conceded in principle.[110] The system still stood.

Still, there was no denying that America faced a massive rebellion. It had been initiated, Kendall said on one occasion, by Abraham Lincoln, whose "legitimate offspring" were today's liberals, "dedicated like Lincoln to egalitarian reforms sanctioned by mandates emanating from national majorities...."[111] To Kendall, Lincoln was the prototype of the modern, liberal, "strong" President. The rebellion was fanned, said Kendall, by a "Liberal Propaganda Machine"[112] and advanced by the Warren Court. The "cancer" that threatened "the very survival of the American political system" was not, however, judicial review as such (which had the sanction of tradition) but the "due process" and "equal protection" clauses of the Fourteenth Amendment, without which the desegregation and school prayer decisions, for instance, would never have been made.[113] On one occasion he even called for the repeal of the amendment or at least a "clarification" of it, or perhaps a congressional removal of the offending clauses from the Court's jurisdiction.[114] On a later occasion he pointed to an ambiguity: "Does the Fourteenth Amendment call for the equal protection of exiting laws? Or does it call for revising existing laws until they confer equal protection?"[115] To Kendall the former meaning was correct—and had been accepted by the Supreme Court for decades.[116]

Kendall was less interested, however, in determining the original intention of the amendment than he was in the meaning of the Court's new interpretation of our entire system. The original Constitution, he noted, had clearly given the monopoly of power in the fields of suffrage, education, religion, and legislative apportionment to the states. The original government, which included the Court, "was to keep its hands off...." This was, as he put it in his distinctive idiom, the "original deal," which the Tenth Amendment "merely hammers down." There was "nothing... sacred" about the deal that "couldn't be revised as time went on." If, he continued, the equal protection clause of the Fourteenth Amendment merely meant "that all are entitled to the impartial application of existing laws," then the "original deal...is still on." But if the other meaning was in force, then the Fourteenth in effect repealed the Tenth! The Supreme Court, by opting for this other meaning, had grossly changed the "deal." It had done so by ignoring the proper process of alteration: constitutional amendment.[117] But, he warned conservatives, do not waste time arguing about the legality of judicial review. Instead, challenge the wisdom of Court decisions. And "get busy and amend the Fourteenth Amendment."[118]

Yet if the menace from the Left was so profound, how could Kendall be sure that We the People would remain "virtuous"? In an essay on Richard Weaver, he gave his answer: a "select minority" (Ortega's phrase) must serve as guardians and teachers of the truths of their culture. To Kendall, Weaver was such an exemplar, and Weaver's *Visions of Order* (1964) was actually the "missing" section of the *Federalist*, the section which would tell us how the virtue requisite to republican self-government would be maintained. [119] Kendall ranked Weaver among the greatest contemporary conservative intellectuals.[120] It was evident from Kendall's writings that Leo Strauss was another such teacher. And it was evident that still another would have to be Kendall himself.

For Kendall was thoroughly dismayed as he surveyed the ranks of those who should serve as teachers of the virtuous people: the contemporary conservative intellectual movement. Time and again, Kendall revealed his exasperation with his fellow intellectuals of the Right. They were, he believed, generally a "poor lot,"[121] full of "false teachers."[122] The movement was disturbingly "rent" by divergent opinions about the very nature of the system it was supposed to be defending. Indeed, it even seemed at times "to be in the *business* of being unprepared intellectually for the next thrust of the Liberal Revolution."[123] There was, for instance, Frank Meyer, "the false sage of Woodstock" (New York),[124] John Chamberlain, and all the other libertarians who perpetuated the liberal "lie" that our tradition was one of "individual rights."[125] There were those— he mentioned Frank Chodorov and Meyer, but nearly all were guilty— who railed against Big Government, even government per se, as inherently evil. The *Federalist* should have taught them otherwise.[126] There were those who ceaselessly lamented that the Right was losing to the Left. The truth was that the Right had not been routed at all.[127] He found Meyer's influential *In Defense of Freedom* "rather frightening."[128] He was "horrified" at the rejoinders of Meyer, Russell Kirk, and M. Stanton Evans to M. Morton Auerbach's critique of contemporary conservatism in *National Review* in 1962.[129] He thought that his revisionist article on the Bill of Rights would "end up getting me expelled from intellectual conservative circles." He noted that *National Review* had once refused to publish an article he wrote on the Declaration of Independence.[130]

Moreover, Kendall was relatively indifferent to laissez-faire economics—perhaps because he had immersed himself in Lord Keynes's thought at Oxford in the 1930s.[131] His conservatism, he proclaimed, had "sworn no vow of absolute fidelity...to free enterprise à la von Mises...."[132] He even attacked the widespread conservative belief that political freedom and free enterprise were inseparable: "Given an appropriate public opinion, I see no reason why a free political system and a socialized economic system couldn't coexist on one and the same piece of real estate."[133] Kendall, like other conservatives, definitely believed in "private initiative" and economic freedom; he was no egalitarian socialist. But unlike

many other conservatives, he did not believe that the primary threat to
"private initiative" came from government at all:

> ...if the future of individual initiative depends on...containing
> the advance of levelling for the sake of levelling, of principled
> egalitarianism, then...we can safely say that private initiative
> is safe for the foreseeable future because, as far as this threat
> is concerned, there exists in America a healthy public opin-
> ion which, when the chips are down, is against levelling.[134]

In fact, some of the most serious dangers came from the private sector:
"the bureaucratization of business enterprise" and "the rise of the
meritocracy."[135] Once again we observe his lifelong distrust of elites,
wherever they existed.

It was not surprising that this self-styled "Appalachians-to-the-
Rockies" conservative was often incensed at the man he labeled "the
benevolent sage of Mecosta," Russell Kirk.[136] Privately he called his own
The Conservative Affirmation a "declaration of war" against Kirk, who
must be shunted aside as an influence on the conservative movement.[137]
For one thing, Kendall disliked Kirk's recurrent appeals to Edmund
Burke. While Kendall found Burke a useful guide on some matters,[138]
he repeatedly emphasized that American conservatism must be grounded
in *American* experience, expressed in American terms; he repudiated
the "Burke 'cultists.'"[139] Burke's thought too often stressed "the tried and
true" as the "essence" of conservatism. But "principled, general opposition to change...was not characteristic of our Founding Fathers, was never
in American conditions, and is not today, a possible political posture...."[140]
In many other ways also, Burkean thought was irrelevant to America's
heritage.[141] Moreover, Kirk was inculcating an "'anti-power' mystique"
that was liberal, not conservative:

> The essence of the American political tradition...lies in the
> exclusion of political power itself from certain *spheres* of hu-
> man activity, thus *not* in the "separation" or "division" of pow-
> ers—in *limited government*...not, I repeat, in any mystique
> about power in the spheres assigned, rightfully, *to* govern-
> ment.... [The] contemporary conservative movement...must
> learn to regard power as *morally neutral*....[142]

Privately Kendall claimed on one occasion that Kirk was really a liberal.[143] On another, he contrasted Kirk's "literary" conservatism with his
own "marketplace conservatism, not very elegant."[144]

Kendall's conservatism, in short, was unique. His was a *political* conservatism, concerned not so much with particular programs as with a process of making decisions. He was quite willing, he said, to let issues be settled "on their merits" in the political arena.[145] He explicitly dissociated himself from the "Tenth Amendmentite anxieties" that James J. Kilpatrick and Russell Kirk expressed in *A Nation of States*. As far as he was concerned, it was part of "the proper business of the American constitutional system to decide when powers reserved to the states and the people shall be moved 'across the line'" to the federal government. Indeed, "the sky's the limit...*provided*...we do not stumble into a constitutional crisis...."[146] Perhaps there was a deeper reason for his divergence from so much conservative thought and his startling unconcern about so many right-wing apprehensions. From the 1930s to the late 1960s, the American Right was often haunted by a fear: what if the majority of the people irrevocably abandons the truths that we hold dear? Deep down inside, Willmoore Kendall, the Middle American boy from Oklahoma, seems never to have felt that fear. Konawa, Idabel, Mangum: the virtuous people, yes.

And it was to the heartland that he returned toward the end of his life. In 1963 he accepted a position at the University of Dallas, a conservative, Roman Catholic institution. There he seemed at last to be happy. He was idolized: Saint Willmoore, they called him. "Kendall for King," proclaimed some student sweatshirts. After two unsuccessful marriages he was happily married at last.[147] Kendall knew, too, that he had come home. In the spring of 1963, just after visiting Dallas and confirming the job offer, he wrote with pride and relief:

> At Dallas, I can be Moses back from the 40 years of his preparation, among *his* people—I found myself sinking into the local accent, which was mine forty years ago, as a weary man sinks into a warm bath.[148]

"[J]'ai survécu," he told Francis Wilson, "and without...any compromise on *any* point."[149] He had escaped the "world of the Buckleys" and felt "surrounded with the warmth and affection of *home*."[150]

Willmoore Kendall died in 1967. Several years earlier, Leo Strauss had told him that he was the best American political theorist of his generation.[151] Nearly everybody—friend and foe alike—agreed that he was one of the most brilliant and remarkable men they had ever met; he was universally regarded as a matchless teacher. His was also a life of restless eccentricity. William F. Buckley, Jr. later called him "the most difficult human being I have ever known...."[152] It was said at *National Review* that he was never on speaking terms with more than one associate at once.[153] Even his closest friends regarded him as "perverse."[154] One referred to Kendall's "raging compulsion to expose error and force recognition of sound principles here and now." [155] In part because of his combativeness, in part because of his marred academic career, Kendall's influence on his profession and the conservative movement was limited in 1967. For these reasons, plus his ardent "egghead McCarthyism,"[156] he never gained while he was alive the full, careful attention he deserved from his professional colleagues.[157] Soon, however, some conservatives and political scientists would begin to feel that he had been ahead of his time.[158]

Some conservatives had their doubts about him. Frank Meyer believed that his effort to reconcile his early left-wing absolute majoritarianism with his later right-wing "Madisonian" majoritarianism was a "mistake."[159] Russell Kirk stressed that Kendall was a "natural aginner" who was too majoritarian, too much influenced by Rousseau's concept of the "general will"—a position "disastrous" to conservatism.[160] Writing to Peter Viereck in 1954, Kirk noted that Kendall was a "devotee" of both Rousseau and Senator McCarthy, and then added: "significantly enough."[161] Similarly, the sociologist Robert Nisbet, who regarded Rousseau as "the real demon of the modern mind,"[162] was cool toward many of Kendall's positions.[163]

These comments by fellow conservatives highlighted one of the distinctive characteristics of Kendall's conservatism: its "populist" overtones. This word, to be sure, is a tricky one, with all sorts of connotations, and Kendall himself eventually repudiated populist (that is, pure, untrammeled, plebiscitary, undeliberative) democracy.[164] His was a special blend of majoritarian and antimajoritarian perspectives. Nevertheless, in the thought of this native son of rural, Democratic Oklahoma, certain themes commonly called "populist" do emerge: a Westerner's distrust of the East and what he once called the "world of the Buckleys"; faith in the inarticulate common man and distrust of "undemocratic" elites—a feature of his thought throughout his life;[165] belief in the virtue still residing out there in the heartland of America. Kendall was in these respects a populist *and* a conservative.[166] The contrast with much aristocratic, even explicitly antipopulist, conservatism in the postwar period was striking.[167]

What had he offered? The most comprehensive and daring reinterpretation of America's political heritage developed by anyone on the Right since World War II. Some have gone further. Professor Jeffrey Hart of Dartmouth College has written: "Willmoore Kendall remains, beyond any possibility of challenge, the most important political theorist to have emerged in the twenty-odd years since the end of World War II."[168] He offered a plausible,[169] "non-Lockean" rejoinder to the "rebels" against the Great Tradition in the United States. An undeniably *American* conservatism—an important legacy to a movement that had often, since 1945, turned to European models in its search for an identity. He once indicated to a friend that he wanted to be, for the contemporary era, an American equivalent of Edmund Burke.[170] At least as much as any other conservative of his time, Willmoore Kendall had a right to make this claim.

It is time to step back and assess the results of the conservative quest for an American identity.

Perhaps the most immediately apparent feature of this search was the very fact that the Right felt the need to undertake it. In part the task was dictated by the structure of avowedly conservative thought, which holds that enduring truths have been found in the past and are embodied in tradition. But it was also dictated by the conservatives' perception that their exact relation to their own country was not self-evident: liberals had told them it was a *problem*. Most of the Right may have felt at home in America, but influential critics considered the movement historically as well as philosophically illegitimate. There was so much, consequently, to explain.

Of course, some conservative intellectuals might conceivably have replied: So what? Suppose that most of us do, in the last analysis, adhere to some form of "natural rights" theory. Suppose that we are Lockean rather than Burkean or "ancient." What then? We are what we are, regardless of semantic stratagems that try to make us all liberals when we know very well that the meaning of liberalism has changed many times in history. We are what we are, and we believe that in our tradition inhere certain truths—label them what you will. At one point Frank Meyer uttered such a sentiment:

> We are told that what is not in the tradition of Burke—or of the medieval synthesis—or of Plato—cannot call itself conservatism: anyone who insists upon freedom in the political and economic sphere together with "legitimate" conservative beliefs, is really half liberal, half conservative, a sad case of intellectual schizophrenia. Such criticism might be answered by simply pointing to actuality, asserting that, whether Euro-

> pean intellectual history blesses us or not, this is the way the
> average contemporary American conservative thinks and
> feels; or by citing the founding documents of the Republic as
> authority—the authority of another, an American, intellec-
> tual history.[171]

In other words, we shall go our own way from the grassroots up. It will
not be the first time that Americans have frustrated the purists. Besides,
conservatism is not a neat ideology anyway.

Although many conservatives may have believed this, they did not
often say it. Instead, they preferred to *argue* that America was not (totally) liberal, however one defined the word. Implicit in their effort was
the belief that America's tradition, properly understood, was indeed con-
gruent with truth as they defined it. But what if this happy belief proved
unfounded? What if one concluded, for example, that Locke in America
was philosophically unsound but historically entrenched? The possibility that truth and tradition were ultimately irreconcilable did not appear
to trouble many conservatives (certainly not Kendall) in the decade or so
after the founding of *National Review*. In time, however, such doubts
would surface in a few places.

What, then, was the dominant theme of this massive conservative
effort? Throughout the second postwar decade there could be no doubt;
despite Kendall, it was antimajoritarianism—the belief that the American political system traditionally stood for and should stand for principles like checks and balances, dispersal of power, limits on power and
majorities. Many conservatives quoted Lord Acton approvingly: "Power
tends to corrupt; absolute power corrupts absolutely." Even if a "liberal"
did say that, it was still wisdom.[172] Frank Meyer and Russell Kirk—to
take two outstanding proponents of this teaching—may have been in
Kendall's eyes "false sages," but they were, in this area at least, at the
center of the conservative intellectual movement.

Nevertheless, the emergence of the Straussian dissent and of the
extraordinary Willmoore Kendall foreshadowed a major transition in the
conservative movement in the late 1960s and early 1970s. For the
antimajoritarian brand of conservatism was in one way peculiarly conditioned: whether true or false, it was the protective doctrine of a minority
consciousness, of a group that in its early days had the beleaguered status of a Remnant. Moreover, in an era of totalitarianism and huge government, the "individual versus authority" formulation acquired additional plausibility. To an ex-Communist like Meyer, who had experienced
tyranny at close range, the individual and his privacy had special worth.

Thus there was logic in the fact that conservatives in their early days launched a revolt against the masses, against "democratic despotism," against majoritarianism, against the State.

Yet by the middle and late 1960s, several factors favored the growth of a more majoritarian conservatism. First, as power was steadily consolidated in the expanding federal government under Presidents Kennedy and Johnson, as the civil rights "revolution" proceeded and the Great Society mushroomed, it was increasingly obvious that concepts like states' rights and interposition were no longer very successful barriers to the liberal onslaught. Second, and more importantly, the appearance of civil rights and other minority movements, each asserting its *rights* and clamoring for power, shocked conservatives into criticism of these seemingly utopian and aggressive Gnostic attacks on the fabric of civilization. No longer did pure, antigovernment, individualistic, libertarian rhetoric seem so universally relevant or persuasive. Not when individuals were expounding the *right* to civil disobedience. Not when people were defying the government by rioting or burning their draft cards. Suddenly a new rhetoric seemed essential. As Francis Wilson put it, "...public order rather than individual rights become [sic] increasingly our contemporary issue."[173]

Finally, the trend toward majoritarianism was enormously stimulated by a series of Supreme Court decisions that aroused not just conservative intellectuals but broad segments of the populace which right-wingers could now, at long last, cultivate. These included policemen and law enforcement officials enraged by Court decisions which protected the "rights" of criminals; millions of Americans who could not understand why the "rights" of atheists should prevent the voluntary reading of the Lord's Prayer and the Bible in public schools; Americans angry about "permissiveness" and Court rulings on pornography; politicians astounded by the Court's reapportionment decisions; and anti-Communists alarmed at the Court's continual blows at congressional investigations and cold war legislation. Just as liberals criticized "nine old men" in the 1930s, so now many conservatives denounced the "ideologues" of the Warren Court who allegedly legislated rather than adjudicated for 200 million Americans. One sign of this mood was L. Brent Bozell's *The Warren Revolution*, which attacked even judicial review itself. But this was only one clue to the evolving conservative posture. It was not the masses but the classes—the elites—which were now seen to be the sources of danger. And the once-distrusted masses (thanks, in part, to the Court) were now accessible to the Right. Antimajoritarian, limited-government, "mainstream" conservatism was a perspective especially congenial to a minority that might never gain power. The perspective of Willmoore Kendall looked forward to the era of the "silent majority."

On one point, conservatives of all persuasions generally agreed: liberal views of conservatism in America were frequently superficial and false. It was an error to equate conservatism with mindless defense of the status quo. It was an error to identify conservatism with medievalism or Burkeanism, if by these terms one meant transient institutional forms. It was an error to perceive the American past as monolithically leftist.

Had conservatives, then, found themselves? If consistency were our only guide, the answer would be no. Some conservatives accepted elements of Lockean liberalism, for example; others did not. There was no single, consistent conservative voice. But there had never been a single voice ("conservatism is not an ideology"); yet, somehow, the movement had continued to thrive. Perhaps, therefore, another criterion should be invoked. For conservatism was not simply an intellectual movement; it was an intellectual movement with political aspirations. For such a phenomenon, an old American measure may be most appropriate: success. From this perspective a different conclusion emerges. As the years went by, the need to articulate a historical rationale for American conservatism seemed to lose some of its urgency. Something *called* conservatism was winning adherents, and in these circumstances it became increasingly difficult to chide it for supposedly not belonging to the main currents of American history.

Many of the liberal critiques, after all, were advanced in the 1950s, when renascent conservatism was still hardly off the ground; plagued by a paucity of intelligent literature, it was unusually dependent on (and influenced by) European intellectuals.[174] Conservatism, said Russell Kirk, "had almost lost the power of language" by the late 1940s.[175] That era was now past.[176] In one respect, time was actually on the conservatives' side. The longer the movement existed and the more scholarly literature it produced, the more legitimate it appeared. The more support it found in the country—Willmoore Kendall's country—the more rooted and organic it became.

NINE

Years of Preparation

In the waning days of the 1956 election campaign, as Dwight Eisenhower was surging toward a landslide victory, William F. Buckley, Jr. pondered the record of the first Republican president in twenty years. It was not a joyful task. Even in 1952, while urging the Republican Party to "acknowledge a domestic enemy, the State," Buckley had not believed that it would ever do so.[1] Now, in 1956, his apprehensions were confirmed. Eisenhower's first term had been marked by "easy and wholehearted acceptance" of "the great statist legacy of the New Deal." The Republican program was at best one of "measured socialism." Buckley realized that for many conservatives the liberal Democratic candidate, Adlai Stevenson, made Eisenhower appealing by contrast. Nevertheless, he warned, the choice in 1956 was only a choice between evils.[2]

In 1958 Buckley again denounced the Eisenhower administration. The president's principal "sin against reality" was his "deficient understanding" of Communism. Neither Eisenhower nor the American people really believed that our adversaries were totally intent on world dominion. Under Eisenhower the West would continue to serve as "a muffler of Communist atrocities"; in the "tranquil world" of Eisenhower, Communism would continue to advance. Faced with the menaces of Communism and domestic statism, Eisenhower adopted "an approach designed not to solve problems, but to refuse, essentially, to recognize that problems exist; and so, to ignore them." The president's "political philosophy," by his own admission, was "incoherent." The Republican Party should "repudiate" him.[3]

Buckley's opposition to the Eisenhower administration was no personal aberration. In the 1950s many conservative intellectuals were appalled by "creeping socialism" at home and by such foreign policy developments as the abortive "spirit of Geneva," the Suez crisis, the failure to rescue Hungary in 1956, and the invitation of Khrushchev to the United States in 1959. Buckley's *National Review* frequently and sharply criticized the Republican incumbent[4]—a cry taken up by several right-wing commentators. The Eisenhower administration, said the traditionalist Anthony Harrigan in 1954, was not conservative. Instead of evincing a religious mode of life and "continuity with the past," it was "the product of the American business community," which was materialistic and even anxious for change. The administration was staffed not by aristocratic conservatives but by "moneymen and hucksters."[5] More typical was Frank Meyer, who was also disenchanted early. Instead of fulfilling his election mandate to fight collectivism, said Meyer, Eisenhower was drifting toward "a somewhat inhibited New Dealism." Instead of recognizing that "either we or they [the Communists] must be destroyed" and that "the overthrow of the Kremlin" must be our goal, Eisenhower was acquiescing in the foreign policy of his predecessors.[6] At the end of the 1950s, Meyer summed up the legacy of the Eisenhower years: "The net balance of 1959, after six years of an administration brought into power by the basic backing of conservative votes, registers an immense slippage in our will to resist Communism and in our position *vis-à-vis* Communism."[7] A few months later, he declared: "Eisenhower...simply floated with the tide."[8]

To Meyer and other conservatives, then, who stressed principle over pragmatism,[9] blandness and moderation could never be enough.[10] Unlike the man in the White House, they wanted to "roll back" both the Iron Curtain and the "Roosevelt revolution": such was the radical imperative for conservatism in a liberal age. "The role of radical is temperamentally alien to the conservative," Meyer acknowledged, "but in the circumstances of Liberal domination under which we live, that role is demanded of him."[11] Not surprisingly, *National Review* declined to endorse a presidential candidate in 1960; Meyer could detect no grounds for preferring Richard Nixon to John Kennedy.[12]

There is probably no better proof of the isolation of the conservative intellectual movement from American politics in the 1950s than its estrangement from the immensely popular President Eisenhower.[13] If postwar conservatism were simply a mood or a set of rarefied ideas, one might be tempted to say that its political posture was irrelevant. Moreover, as Russell Kirk has observed,[14] movements of ideas do not triumph overnight; usually a generation is needed. Yet to most conservatives in the 1950s and 1960s, politics *was* important and time was running out. It was not enough to proclaim their ideals and anathematize the forces of darkness. The defense of Western civilization required that their ideas be implemented, and the war could not be fought solely in academic journals or in *National Review*. Sooner or later the conservative intellectual movement, if it wanted to succeed, would have to shape *political* forces and prevail in the *political* marketplace. It would have to do more than stand athwart history, yelling "Stop."

The need for a practical, popular conservatism was increasingly evident in the late 1950s. Writing shortly after the Republican electoral disaster of 1958, the young historian Stephen Tonsor sounded the alarm:

> If we wait for the American electorate to discover of its own sound reason the virtues of the conservative viewpoint, that discovery will never be made.
>
> I think that the party is in extremes [sic] because it has had no new ideas since the death of Senator Taft. It is suffering from a lack of creative leadership able to hazard the solution of contemporary problems in terms of enduring principle.
>
> We are adrift....
>
> Full employment was the issue which lost the last election.... The Republican Party and conservatism cannot win an election until it has solved the problem of full employment within the framework of a realistic budget.[15]

Tonsor's concerns were shared by Whittaker Chambers. In 1954 he told a friend that while he enjoyed Russell Kirk's *The Conservative Mind*, "if you were a marine in a landing boat, would you wade up the seabeach at Tarawa for *that* conservative position? And neither would I!"[16] Chambers informed Buckley that if the Republican Party did not face reality and develop a program "that means something to masses of people—why, somebody else will. There will be nothing to argue. The voters will simply vote Republicans into singularity."[17] Frequently Chambers argued that the Right must come to grips with technology and the inherent dynamism of capitalism, which he considered "profoundly anti-conservative."[18] "A conservatism that cannot face the facts of the machine and mass production, and its consequences in government and politics," he declared, "is foredoomed to futility and petulance."[19] In 1959 Buckley himself conceded that conservatives had yet to persuade the public about the dangers of the welfare state and the validity of conservative principles.[20]

The agenda for the 1960s was therefore obvious. If conservative intellectuals were ever to break out of their ghetto, they would need to do more than consolidate their forces. Suppose that they did solidify and forge a working coalition. Suppose that they did develop a plausible American line of descent and a historically grounded body of principles. Suppose that these *internal* problems seemed more or less satisfactorily resolved after years of debate and study. What then? What did the movement want to do?

If the decade after 1945 witnessed the birth of the postwar Right, and if the decade or so after 1955 featured a gradual process of self-definition, the early and mid-1960s were to be concurrently years of preparation. The era of Presidents Kennedy and Johnson would see an increasingly sophisticated conservative critique of the Left, elaboration of specific alternatives to liberal programs, and development of a conservative intellectual establishment. The Right, becoming "pragmatized," would make its first significant forays out of the wilderness.

In making their bid for national leadership, conservative intellectuals focused continuously on one principal target: liberalism. In both foreign and domestic policy, the achievements and philosophy of the "liberal establishment"[21] were subjected to relentless criticism.

As conservatives surveyed world crises in the late 1950s and the 1960s, one fundamental fact seemed paramount: the continuous, implacable assault on the West by messianic, revolutionary Communism.[22] Amid all the swirling ephemera of daily events, this transcendent challenge remained constant. We were at war—an "irrepressible conflict," Frank Meyer called it;[23] the "Third World War," James Burnham labeled it in his *National Review* column of that title. In this struggle, there were, according to Meyer and other conservative cold warriors, only two choices: "the destruction of Communism or the destruction of the United States and of Western civilization."[24] In article after article in *Modern Age* and issue after issue of *National Review*, these convictions were either articulated outright or were implicit in the attention paid to the worldwide menace. What Communists were doing in Cuba, Chile, Zanzibar, Laos, or in the American civil rights and peace movements was considered significant. What congressional investigations uncovered about infiltration and subversion was not to be scornfully dismissed or smugly ignored. The Communist enterprise was *real*—as real as deaths in Budapest, barbed wire in Berlin, harangues in Havana, and marines in the mud of Vietnam.

Liberals, of course, might blind themselves to these unpleasant realities—so said conservatives. Liberals might prefer to hope—serenely, pathetically, endlessly, futilely—that maybe now, maybe this time, maybe soon, the Communists would change their spots, cease to be committed revolutionaries, and settle down. Perhaps we could then have peaceful coexistence at last. Meanwhile let us negotiate, "build bridges," engage in cultural exchanges, climb to the summit. Come let us reason together.

Nonsense, said the conservatives. Fatuous delusions. The "Spirit of Geneva" in 1955 did not prevent the Hungarian nightmare of 1956. The "Spirit of Camp David" in 1959 exploded at the Paris summit conference in 1960. The Kennedy-Khrushchev meeting in Vienna in 1961 was followed by the erection of the Berlin Wall and the emplacement of missiles in Cuba. The "Spirit of Glassboro" in 1967 was followed by the invasion of Czechoslovakia in 1968. Would liberals ever recognize that the world was not, every day in every way, getting better and better? The cold war—which was often a hot war—was *not* over. Reacting to "surface phenomena," the Left seemed "oblivious to the hard continuing substance of the Communist battle plan," said Meyer.[25] The revolution is not dead, said James Burnham in 1967, on the fiftieth anniversary of the Bolshevik seizure of power in Russia. Communists had not succumbed to the "law of bourgeoisification"; their revolution had a momentum which could not be halted at will. "Normal international relations" were "impossible" with a regime that had such features as a government monopoly of foreign trade, no domestic political opposition, and a "global ...revolutionary apparatus."[26] Moreover, Robert Strausz-Hupé of the University of Pennsylvania argued, the Kremlin exhibited an "undiminished appetite." "In the cold war, there are no sanctuaries." The Communists had an "enormous" investment in "the arsenal of the cold war," and "good will and reasonable concessions" would never deter them from their objective.

> The Communist system is a conflict system; its ideology is an ideology of conflict and war....
> ...In spite of the twists and turns of the internecine power struggle, the Communist system will endure so long as external pressures do not compound internal strains and bring the system crashing down.[27]

Why would "external pressures" be necessary? Why could not communism gradually mellow and evolve? Pervading conservative writings was the unshakable belief that Communism transcended ordinary laws of diplomatic behavior. In *The Moulding of Communists*, Frank Meyer voiced the conclusions of many other conservatives. The Communist, he asserted, "is different. He thinks differently." He is not "a mirror image of ourselves."[28] Communism is a "secular and messianic quasi-religion"[29] which ceaselessly conditions its converts until they become new men totally dedicated to one mission: "the conquest of the world for Communism."

> Against this vision, the devotion, the determination of Comunist man, there is no recourse in compromise, reasonableness, peaceful co-existence. Only a greater determination can avail, for Communist man poses two stark alternatives for us: victory or defeat.[30]

The Soviet leaders were not "rational," Gerhart Niemeyer of Notre Dame concluded in 1956. Their thought processes and assumptions, sustained by a tenaciously held ideology, were radically different from our own.[31] It was totally unrealistic to expect that Americans could "communicate" with a Communist mind that "shares neither truth nor logic nor morality with the rest of mankind."[32] The Communist view of reality was fundamentally "distorted by their millennial vision and their dialectic reasoning...."[33]

> If Westerners believe that Soviet thoughts are linked to Soviet actions in a way that they can know, understand, and eventually influence rationally, and make this belief a basis of their policy, they are tragically mistaken.[34]

The way to defeat this system was to exploit "Soviet irrationality" and the "deep contradictions of the Soviet system." This could be done by assaulting "Soviet morale at its core: Marxist-Leninist doctrine."[35] Unfortunately, this approach required that Westerners penetrate the alien Communist doctrine sufficiently to expose its fallacies to its apostles.[36] Only a few "specialists" and reformed ex-Communists currently possessed this understanding.[37]

And if the challenge was that grave, if Communism really was "the fundamental break with the unchangeably conservative spirit of western civilization,"[38] some conservatives at least were prepared to contemplate nuclear war as an alternative to their enemy's triumph. While not calling for an immediate "preventive" war in 1959, L. Brent Bozell pointed out that such a course was not inconceivable. He preferred a "new leadership" which, while willing to "drop the Bomb," would first try "an extended war of attrition" which "holds forth reasonable hope of ultimate victory." But if this hope evaporated, we would then have an "obligation" to destroy the enemy "in the middle of the night," knowing that "when the right is pursued, it is God who ordains the cost."[39] Frank Meyer was equally convinced that the rightness of the West's cause was "categorical": "There can be no question of our moral obligation to resist, to counterattack, to destroy, this powerful and proclaimed enemy of man and God."[40] Naturally we should refrain from using nuclear weapons if at all possible in our campaign to destroy the Communist regime. But if the issue of atomic war unavoidably arose, the only question would be: "Given the justice of our cause and the necessity of nuclear force to its victory, what strategy should we adopt?" Should we accept a "deterrence" posture, absorbing a first blow and then destroying the only remaining asset of the enemy: the civilian population? (It would be too late to bomb military targets.) Or should we accept a "counterforce" strategy that would, in these ultimate circumstances, require a first strike on the enemy's military installations only? To Meyer the latter course—aimed not at obliterating civilians but at knocking out nuclear bases—was definitely the morally superior position. But was *any* use of such horrible weapons ever justifiable? To Meyer, the answer was yes:

> ...even granted the most horrendous estimates of the effects of their use, the preservation of human life as a biological phenomenon is an end far lower than the defense of freedom and right and truth. These the victory of Communism would destroy. These it is our duty to defend at all costs.[41]

Did these remarks mean that conservatives were warmongers? William F. Buckley, Jr. did not think so. "All civilized men want peace," he stated. But peace was not identical with pacifism (a "Christian heresy"), and peace was "unthinkable in a community in which plunderers have hold of the city at night." If peace were "the first goal of man," one could simply obtain it by surrendering. The horrors of Hiroshima and Nagasaki, Buckley asserted "cannot compare with the workaday agony of the enslaved world" behind the Iron Curtain. There were, in other words, fates worse than death. Peace is not "thinkable" now because "the West is besieged and the world tyrannized over."

> We must try to win without war: but we must above all try to win, and for the sake of humanity, whose first concern is for the quality of human existence, rather than for life biologically defined.[42]

Better dead than Red, then? Not quite, for these were not the sole alternatives:

...Better the *chance* of being dead, than the certainty of being
Red. And if we die? We die.[43]

Such remarks did not mean that conservatives expected or wanted
Armageddon to occur. On the contrary, they believed that a strong, aggressive cold war posture was America's best hope to avoid a holocaust.
William Schlamm, for instance, argued that the Communists did not want
war—in fact, dearly wished to avert a nuclear war. The enemy, he said,
"*thrives* on peace, *wants* peace, *triumphs* in peace."[44] It exploits the
Western fear of war to advance its own ends. Since war—as the enemy
saw it—was the only obstacle to its success, the "only rational strategy of
the West" was "to keep communism constantly *confronted* with that risk."[45]
Increase the pressure, Schlamm advised. Maintain a "believable" willingness to fight, and the foe will retreat.[46] This was the only way to prevent war. Otherwise Communism would continue to expand until, in a
last act of desperation, a beleaguered America would fight a suicidal
war.[47]

This conservative understanding of foreign affairs as a titanic conflict of ideologies, religions, and civilizations was decisively shaped by
the former Communists and Trotskyists who dominated the *National
Review* circle in its early years. Frank Meyer, James Burnham, Whittaker
Chambers, William Schlamm, William Henry Chamberlin, Willmoore
Kendall, Eugene Lyons, Freda Utley, Max Eastman—all had glimpsed
the Medusa at varying angles. Moreover, many conservative strategists,
including Schlamm, Robert Strausz-Hupé, Stefan Possony, Thomas
Molnar, and Gerhart Niemeyer, were refugees from the totalitarian Europe of the 1930s and 1940s. A number were ardent Roman Catholics;
Bozell and Kendall, for example, were even converts. Such striking biographical information raised many questions. Were these conservatives
trustworthy analysts? If they had been deceived by Communism once in
their lives, could they be depended on now? Or were they perhaps permanently scarred by their experience and inclined to exaggerate the resources of the enemy? Was there not too obvious a yearning for repen-
tance and atonement for past sins? Too much convert's zeal? Were not
these people fanatics who longed for absolutes—first Communism, not
Christianity and Western civilization?

These questions, raised from time to time by liberal observers, had
a ring of plausibility. The Right's conception of Communism was, so to
speak, "historically conditioned." Yet to conservatives the peculiar experience of the ex-Communists and European émigrés was not a handicap
at all. Indeed, it was an advantage. Perhaps these individuals, however

unconventional their past or present lives, had divined the terrible meaning of Communism more profoundly than most others of their time. Perhaps, as Gerhart Niemeyer suggested, they had a peculiarly valuable expertise. After all, they had *seen* the face of evil. And just as artists and writers sometimes lead unorthodox lives but gain a truth at great cost, might not the ex-Communists have special insights to share precisely *because* they lacked the "objectivity" of the uncommitted? "I sometimes feel," wrote William F. Buckley, Jr.,

> that it takes a tainted mind to understand—to really understand—the threat of Communism. To *really* understand Communism is to have touched pitch: one's view of man is forever defiled. To understand Communism means to understand the terrible capacity of man for violence and treachery, an apprehension of which leaves one forever tormented.[48]

André Malraux once wrote to Whittaker Chambers, "You are one of those who did not return from Hell with empty hands."[49] To Chambers and others on the Right, Communism *was* hell. Communists meant what they said. And the Third World War could not be won without countervailing conviction, zeal, and courage.

It was certainly not being prosecuted effectively now, conservatives agreed. The liberal leadership was compiling a melancholy record of retreat, which could not be camouflaged by outrageous assurances that the cold war had ended (why Cuba? why Vietnam?) or by learned references to "polycentrism" in the Communist bloc. M. Stanton Evans, the conservative editor of the *Indianapolis News*, stated the conservative case pungently in 1966:

> The Communists have not in fact been winning the Cold War so much as we have been losing it. We have, on a variety of pretexts, been steadily surrendering the world to the enemy in the Kremlin. We have been losing the fight because, for the most part, the abstractions of Liberalism keep telling us we aren't in it. [50]

William Rickenbacker—son of the war hero Captain "Eddie" Rickenbacker, and contributor to *National Review*—agreed.

> As I see it, recent history can be summed up in a single terrible phrase: *retreat by the West....* The global trend leaps to the eye: the Communist and anti-Western areas have been expanding, the West and pro-Western areas have been shrinking.[51]

It is neither possible nor necessary to examine conservative responses to every foreign policy crisis of the late 1950s and 1960s.[52] A few examples will illustrate why the conservatives did not feel they were being shrill, unreasonable, or doctrinaire. To them the liberal defeats were a matter of *record*. Conservatives did not consider themselves responsible for Cuba, or the Berlin Wall, or our allegedly deteriorating defenses, or the Laotian settlement of 1962, or Vietnam.

Or Hungary. Of all world events since 1955, what Frank Meyer called the "Hungarian slaughter"[53] was undoubtedly the most searing and heartrending for the conservative intellectual movement. For a few precious days in the fall of 1956, the people of Hungary had, conservatives thought, liberated themselves from their masters. Then, as the oppressors returned, the beleaguered freedom fighters pleaded vainly for aid from the West. Silence. Send us arms! Silence. Help us before it is too late!

No answer. No answer.

Conservatives were aghast. Calling for "an immediate suspension of diplomatic relations with the Soviet Union,"[54] *National Review*'s editors took the "Hungary Pledge," calling for a complete cultural boycott of the Soviet Union until all of its forces were withdrawn from Hungary.[55] Conservatives believed that quick intervention by the United States could have exploited the obvious weaknesses of the Kremlin.[56] James Burnham later claimed that Russia's hesitation for a week before sending troops back in was a clear sign that the United States could successfully have issued an ultimatum that would have kept them out.[57] Instead, said *National Review*, not only did American fail the valiant Hungarians; it simultaneously voted in the United Nations to condemn—France, Great Britain, and Israel for failing to withdraw from the Suez area!

> ...*Over the humiliated forms of our two oldest and closest allies, we clasp the hands of the murderers of the Christian heroes of Hungary*, as we run in shameless—and vain—pursuit of the "good will" of Asia and Africa's teeming pagan multitudes.[58]

To Frederick Wilhelmsen (another convert to Roman Catholicism), the American failure to help Hungary had "dishonored" it before the West; this was "the central fact of the mid-century."

> For years our intellectuals have been telling us that Christendom is dead, that the Old Order had run its course. Today we know it was all a lie. It was not the [liberal] dream

of the future and the Full Life that brought those children into the streets of Budapest: it was the call of Honor and the Decency of Death.[59]

A decade later James Burnham reflected that the Hungary-Suez crisis was a "turning point" in the Third World War. Among other bitter lessons, it demonstrated the final collapse of the policy of "liberation," the conferring on the Communist bloc of the status of sanctuary, and the demise of the European foothold in Africa.[60]

If the autumn of 1956 showed the United States (in conservative eyes) paralyzed by fear and liberalism, unable to exploit opportunities that might never come again, American policy toward Africa in the 1960s (said conservatives) showed liberalism at its doctrinaire nadir.[61] Bemused by terms like anticolonialism and self-determination, the United States, in league with an irresponsible United Nations, had foisted freedom on largely primitive and unprepared African tribes and had produced "chaos, communism, and neo-colonialism."[62] Kwame Nkrumah, the so-called "father" of Ghana, turned out to be a ruthless dictator and purveyor of a pseudo-religion. Here and there throughout Africa tribal warfare broke out, and by the late 1960s, all across the continent, crass dictatorships (such as Sékou Touré's in Guinea) proved to be the legacy of the much-heralded end of Western "imperialism." To conservatives it was the West's headlong retreat from Africa, not its former control of the area, which was truly immoral. Do not forget, Frank Meyer bluntly asserted, that the long-despised "white man's burden" did represent "high purpose" as well as "confidence that the truth by which the West lived was the highest truth known to man." The "abdication" of this burden could lead only to upheaval, decay, and Communist penetration.[63] Was *that* moral? Often *National Review* noted approvingly the economic and political stability of the white-dominated states of southern Africa, in contrast to the turmoil in nations to the north.[64] When, the Right wondered, would liberals ever understand that their clichés only made matters worse in Africa, that their projection of an abstract ideology onto the "dark continent" ignored such intractable realities as racial prejudice, tribal strife, cannibalism, and political instability? Could liberals put aside their stereotypes long enough to see that Portuguese control of Angola, for example, was not automatically evil? Contrary to ideology, Portuguese Angola did not practice racial discrimination. The bloody uprising of 1961 was not spontaneous but was carefully prepared by brutal guerrillas aided by Touré and Nkrumah. [65] Jeffrey Hart asked

> when Liberal opinion will assimilate the historical fact that
> parliamentary democracy has produced stable government
> in only a handful of nations...and when having assimilated
> that fact, Liberal opinion will cease expecting it to flourish in
> the Hamnegris [after Hamnegri, an African state in a novel
> by Russell Kirk] of this globe. So resistant is the Liberal imagi-
> nation to so manifest a fact that one is justified in suspecting
> it of a deep hatred of actuality. [66]

For conservatives the fruits of liberal policy in Africa were most bitter in the tragedy of the Congo in the early 1960s. To Frank Meyer the
dissolution of the Congo was "a shameful regression in human history"
for which the West, and especially the United States, must be held responsible.[67] James Burnham charged that instead of protecting Western
interests in the Congo, the Kennedy administration, guided instead by
liberal tenets, favored "supposed neutralist interests." Liberalism dictated that America never act against the Left, only against the Right.[68] In
the Congo the "Right" was represented by Moise Tshombe, a pro-West-
ern, anti-Communist Christian whose province of Katanga was the only
enclave of order in that chaotic land.[69] American conservatives watched
in outrage as the United Nations, financed by the United States, launched
an invasion of Tshombe's province. Ernest van den Haag, a conservative
sociologist who traveled to the Congo late in 1961, discovered what he
considered to be UN record of treachery, looting, murder of civilians,
and blatant interference in the Congo's internal affairs—a record which
the UN desperately tried to conceal and which "set back the Congo twenty
years." Van den Haag was also critical of State Department "experts"
imprisoned by their ideology:

> ...the UN, right or wrong, must be supported by the United
> States; "left" disorder is better than "right" order; left dicta-
> tors are good (progressive); African politicians who are not
> leftists are stooges of colonialism; the UN should not inter-
> vene in the domestic affairs of any country unless it is anti-
> Communist or governed by whites; the way to prevent Com-
> munism from gaining a hold in Africa is to fight African anti-
> Communists and support pro-Communist dictators such as
> Nkrumah, Ben Bella, and Patrice Lumumba (of blessed
> memory).

To van den Haag, the barbarous and dangerous policy of the United
Nations in the Congo necessitated a new American policy toward the
world organization: let it "vegetate" and "atrophy." Meanwhile, what the

Congo needed was decentralization and the return of Belgian officers and administrators. But the UN would not admit that.[70]

Ironically, Moise Tshombe eventually became the leader of the Congo. But in 1967 this conservative hero was kidnapped while in a flight over Spain, taken to Algeria, tortured, and held incommunicado for two years while his enemies in the Congo sought to bring him home to be executed. In 1969 Tshombe died in Algeria, supposedly of a heart attack. William F. Buckley, Jr. sardonically expressed conservative indignation at this injustice: "Can anyone imagine the United Nations interrupting a session on the human rights of mankind in order to plead the human rights of one man, victimized by their beloved Third World?"[71] To Buckley and many other conservatives the United Nations itself was "the true enemy of the native populations of Africa."[72]

Buckley and van den Haag were not the only conservative critics of the United Nations; skepticism about that body was a prominent feature of right-wing commentary in the 1950s and 1960s. To conservatives, liberal praise of the UN as "man's last best hope for peace" and as the embodiment of "world opinion" was preposterous. For one thing, the unwieldy General Assembly, composed increasingly of so-called nonaligned nations, bore little relation to the realities of power in the world. And power, not egalitarian notions (one nation, one vote), was what counted in global politics. James Burnham was most persistently critical of "the motley crew of the U.N. Assembly [which] has come to wield a kind of preventive veto over the Western powers," particularly the United States.[73] Time and again, said Burnham, the United States, instead of following a "Western strategy" oriented toward its NATO allies, allowed itself to be mesmerized by an "Afro-Asian strategy" designed to placate so-called neutral nations.[74]

> Why in the name of minimal common sense does our government allow itself to be denounced, vilified and lied about day after day in the halls of the United Nations by a mob of terrorists, savages, revolutionaries, bankrupts, demagogues, voluptuaries and half-educated opportunists masquerading as representatives of newborn sovereign nations?[75]

The time had come to deflate the pretensions of the world organization, Burnham argued. This the United States could do by proclaiming that it would no longer vote on substantive matters in the UN. Simply that. Without the cooperation of the organization's chief sponsor, the UN's votes would become "automatically meaningless,"[76] and its capacity for harm would be curtailed. "Depoliticize" the UN, he urged.[77]

The United Nations also exemplified what conservatives regarded as one of the most annoying errors of liberalism in foreign policy: its double standard of morality. Sir Arnold Lunn called it "selective indignation";[78] James Burnham labeled it "moral asymmetry."[79] It was so easy for the UN, "world opinion," and American liberals to condemn Portuguese "colonialism" in Angola, said conservatives. But why did no one condemn the utterly bestial uprising of Holden Roberto's Angolan terrorists in 1961? It was so easy to criticize the white government of Rhodesia. Why not also the dismal dictatorship of Nkrumah in Ghana and the racism of the new African nations toward their own minorities? Prime Minister Nehru of India was supposed to be the paragon of Third World virtue. Why was he not chastised more vigorously for his seizure of tiny Goa in 1962, especially when many natives of Goa did not even want to be annexed? Liberals were quick to lavish attention on American misconduct in Vietnam. Why were they so comparatively silent about the systematic torture, assassinations, and other atrocities of the Vietcong? Americans were frequently exhorted to isolate "immoral" regimes in Greece and South Africa, yet were simultaneously urged to "build bridges" to far more monstrous governments in China, Russia, and Eastern Europe. "Right-wing coups by army elements," observed Jeffrey Hart, "are greeted by universal liberal headshaking. Left-wing coups, on the other hand, evoke a capacity for infinite hope."[80] James Burnham commented:

> We can force Britain and France out of the Suez, but we cannot so much as *try* to force the Russian tanks back from Budapest. We can mass our fleet against the Trujillos, but not against the Castros. We can vote in the U.N. against South African apartheid or Portuguese rule in Angola, but we cannot even introduce a motion on the Berlin Wall—much less, give the simple order to push the Wall down.[81]

And what was the result of liberal foreign policy? M. Stanton Evans expressed the conservative position succinctly: "the liquidation of Western hegemony in every quarter of the globe, the transfer of one billion people from the Western world to the armed camp of Communism, and the establishment of a Communist beachhead 90 miles from American shores."[82] William Rickenbacker emphatically concurred. Under Presidents Kennedy and Johnson, America's "retreat" had "accelerated." [83] From Cuba to Laos, from Algeria to Indonesia, from the Berlin Wall to the assassination of Diem in South Vietnam, the American record was ghastly:

> In short, under the Kennedy-Johnson dispensation the
> U.S. has abandoned forward position after forward position
> throughout the world, managed to offend every one of our
> important historic allies, subsidized the rise of socialist re-
> gimes on every continent, given sanctuary if not outright aid
> to the buildup of a Communist military camp in the Carib-
> bean, and demoralized every movement in the world that fa-
> vors being tough with the Communists.[84]

And yet, incredibly (to the conservatives), it was they, the outsiders,
the critics of these disasters, who were accused of "mental aberration."[85]
It was they who were charged with paranoia, extremism, and conspiracy
theories of history. In reply to the common liberal argument that world
events since 1945 were largely inevitable and not controllable by the
United States, Evans stressed the contribution of American foreign policy
to Western defeats. The Bay of Pigs debacle, the overthrow of the anti-
Communist Diem in Vietnam, the U.S. aid which propped up anti-Ameri-
can, Marxist dictators in Ghana and Indonesia for so long—these were
not inevitable developments. They were deliberate policies and decisions. Moreover, if Communism was the wave of the future, why were
pro-Communist leaders deposed in the 1960s in places like British Guiana
and Indonesia? The truth, according to Evans, was that liberals were
"hiding behind the History Theory of Conspiracy": the tendency to as-
cribe liberal failures to the alleged inevitability of history.[86] As the pro-
Western Lebanese statesman Charles Malik wrote in *The Conservative
Papers*:

> If you believe...the outcome of the struggle in China, in
> Korea, in Indochina; the Communist penetration of Asia, Af-
> rica, the Middle East, and Latin America; the absence of any
> effective counteracting force to the Communist Party; the
> relative decline in Western influence and Western economic
> and military strength...*could not have been helped, then you
> are already a Marxist.*[87]

Again and again, conservatives emphasized that the world was not
merely complicated (as liberals insisted) but dangerous. And dangerous
precisely because there really were evil men working tirelessly to bury
the West. Conservative intellectuals were not simplemindedly asserting
that these men were omnipresent and omnipotent. Just the opposite:
Communists could be defeated—*if* the threat were recognized as genuine. For it *was* there, even in unexpected places. The Philby case, for
example, demonstrated that. Harold "Kim" Philby, well-bred, respect-

able, by the early 1950s a senior official in British Intelligence, had fled
to Moscow—a Communist spy who left incredible wreckage behind him.
When Philby published his memoirs in the 1960s, *National Review* proclaimed one of the lessons:

> A whole generation of middle-class youth in the West was
> shattered by the Depression and the rise of Hitler and de-
> luded by the Soviet myth.... In the United States this was the
> generation of Hiss and Chambers.
>   Which brings us back to the McCarthy file.... For the Philby
> scandal finally justifies the essence, if not the detail, of
> McCarthy's approach. The argument centered on the ques-
> tion of whether a sober, respected employee of the state who
> had joined some dim front organization in the early Thirties
> might thereby in the late Forties be a possible security risk.
> For reasons of leftist prejudice or easy-going naïveté,
> McCarthy's opponents said that such affiliations were trivial
> juvenilia. McCarthy insisted that they were relevant (though
> not of course conclusive) character indices. And he has been
> proved right.[88]

Communism was thus not an imaginary conspiracy concocted by fevered
minds. A man could smile and smile and be a villain.

In evaluating liberalism's conduct of foreign policy, conservative intellectuals were driven to meditate on the deeper reasons for the Left's
failures. Liberals, said Meyer, were "innately incapable" of victoriously
resisting Communism.[89] For one thing, the Right suggested, the blandly
rationalistic liberal mind was incapable of grasping the religious,
transnational, and nonrational character of messianic Communism. Too
many liberals emphasized old-fashioned nationalism and geography as
the "real historical counters."[90] Frank Meyer acknowledged that if the
Soviet menace were simply a "Russian" threat, then old-fashioned diplomacy could be employed and peaceful coexistence eventually attained.[91]
But this was not the nature of the enemy; the Soviet Union was instead
"the state form taken by a materialist faith determined to rule the world."[92]
A frequent target of the conservatives was George Kennan, whom many
on the Right regarded as the most eminent liberal strategist. In 1961
Thomas Molnar, a conservative Catholic historian who had survived Nazi
brutality at Dachau, expressed the basic conservative complaint: Kennan
did not understand the recrudescence of "subterranean," "quasi-religious
convictions" in our time. His nineteenth-century *realpolitik* missed the
"ideological component" of power in the twentieth century.[93] As William

Schlamm phrased it, Communism was *not* ordinary; it was "a historical hurricane of unparalleled sweep."[94]

The roots of liberal confusion went even deeper, conservatives believed. Why did liberals fail to recognize that Communism was intrinsically evil? Why did they not understand that it was a "metaphysical faith," that "Communism remains Communism"?[95] Because, said Frank Meyer, liberalism was infected by "a positivism that neither believes in a good for which to fight, nor credits to the enemy the possibility of unstinting devotion to an evil for which he is prepared to fight, come what may."[96] Liberal relativism simply could not distinguish between good and evil.[97] It was virtually a "delusionary psychosis" which preferred "soothing hypotheses derived from flitting changes in the visage of the bear."[98]

Liberal impotence before—even fascination with—this "ultimate challenge to Western civilization"[99] could not be explained, however, simply in terms of liberalism's alleged rationalism and moral relativism. The liberal bond with Communism was more intimate. For what was Communism, said William Schlamm, but

> the final synthesis of all heretical tendencies that have pervaded western civilization for many centuries. Communism is the culminating *hubris* of Promethean man who reaches out for the world and means to remake creation. It is scientism gone political.[100]

Like other conservatives, Schlamm rejected the so-called "stomach" theory of Communism, which asserted that Communism appealed primarily to the economically discontented and the physically miserable. On the contrary, its appeal was mainly to an elite: the intellectuals. Why? Because Communism was "a mutation of the *mind*, a *spiritual* venture, the synthesis of several centuries of all the heretical but *intellectual* unrest in history."[101] Schlamm granted that liberal dislike of "Communism in power" was "sincere." But the underlying magnetic attraction of Communism was continuous. For deep down, the entire Left shared the scientistic faith that man was "about to conquer his fate, to control creation, to manage all life, and God, through applied science!"[102]

In short, conservatives argued, as William F. Buckley, Jr. put it on one occasion, that "the continuing blindness of the liberals" to Communism was not "accidental," not mere "neglect," but a "deep psychological problem" producing paralysis.[103] To L. Brent Bozell this paralysis was a sign of despair. For liberalism was a heresy, a form of gnosticism: the belief in salvation on this earth. "Moderate" gnosticism—that is, liberalism—was dying, and liberals were beginning to perceive

> that the gnostic dream of an earthly paradise can be realized
> (as Khrushchev knows) not by changing society, *but by chang-
> ing man*—by transmutative surgery on the soul. *It follows that
> if gnosticism is ever to triumph, it will triumph in the Com-
> munist form.* Yet Liberals instinctively recoil from that pros-
> pect.... What a pickle—to be possessed by a world view that
> demands the victory of your enemy![104]

Frank Meyer, also relying on the work of Eric Voegelin, similarly stressed that "collectivist Liberalism" and Communism were "forms of the same revolutionary movement."[105] Back in 1954, Whittaker Chambers expressed this fundamental theme of conservative analysis. The "enlightened, ar-ticulate elite" of the West had "rejected the religious roots" of its own civilization for a "new order of beliefs" of which Communism was "one logical expression."

> It is a Western body of belief that now threatens the West
> from Russia. As a body of Western beliefs, secular and ratio-
> nalistic, the intelligentsia of the West share it, and are there-
> fore always committed to a secret emotional complicity with
> Communism of which they dislike, not the Communism, but
> only what, by the chances of history, Russia has specifically
> added to it—slave labor camps, purges, MVD *et al*. And that,
> not because the Western intellectuals find them unjustifiable,
> but because they are afraid of being caught in them. If they
> could have Communism without the brutalities of ruling that
> the Russian experience bred, they have only marginal objec-
> tions. Why should they object? What else is socialism but
> Communism with the claws retracted?[106]

It remained for James Burnham to draw the obvious conclusion in one of the most incisive conservative books of the postwar period.[107] *Sui-cide of the West* was a systematic analysis and indictment of liberal ideol-ogy: its alleged double standard, guilt complex, relativistic theory of truth, and a host of other flaws in its understanding of the world. While Com-munism, for instance, was a threat from the Left, liberalism—"infected" with Communism[108]—was deluded by the false assumption that the true enemy was always on the Right. Indeed, it could "function effectively only against the Right."[109] To Burnham the function of liberalism was starkly clear: the reconciliation of the West to "dissolution." Liberalism was nothing less than "the ideology of Western suicide."[110]

Since Communism was insatiable, and since liberalism (as the British writer Malcolm Muggeridge described it) was "a collective death-wish,"[111] the Right believed that only it could save Western civilization. Yes, conservatives said forthrightly, Western civilization. "We of the Christian West," Bozell declared, "owe our identity to the central fact of history—the entry of God onto the human stage." It is our task to build and defend "a Christian *civilization*."[112] The unique and preeminent value of the truths for which the West stood was a recurrent motif in Meyer's writing as well. According to Charles Malik, no civilization "conceived and developed the human and universal" more than the West.[113] To liberals such judgments no doubt smacked of arrogance and chauvinism; to conservatives the failure to make such judgments showed how diseased liberalism was. They quoted with approval Robert Frost's gibe, "A Liberal is a man too broadminded to take his own side in an argument."[114]

And so conservatives urgently demanded a policy of victory in the cold war. Not containment, Malik urged, but "*an active policy of liberation*."[115] In contrast to liberals like Senator J. William Fulbright, who increasingly stressed the limits of American power and beckoned the nation toward a more "isolationist" posture, Malik and other conservatives contended that the West had not even begun to fight; its resources had never been totally committed to the struggle.[116] Pursue a Western strategy, Burnham exhorted, not a Yalta strategy of attempted collaboration with the Russians or a Third World-UN strategy.[117] Pursue a "Forward Strategy," said Robert Strausz-Hupé and his colleagues.[118] *Why Not Victory?*, Barry Goldwater entitled his second book—one heavily influenced by the conservative cold war expert Gerhart Niemeyer.[119] Occasionally a desperate call for a return to a Fortress America was heard in conservative circles.[120] But such notes were rare in the 1950s and 1960s. The postwar conservative intellectual movement was not predominantly isolationist.[121]

Conservative intellectuals did not confine themselves to militant rhetoric. Although it is not possible to list every foreign policy proposal the Right made, a few examples will suggest the contours of conservative thinking. First, the United States must maintain military supremacy—not parity or "sufficiency." Conservatives distrusted disarmament ideas, the nuclear test ban treaty of 1963, and the military policies of Secretary of Defense Robert McNamara. They supported antiballistic missile development. The United States should not expand its trade with the Communist bloc, aid unfriendly Third World nations, encourage spy-laden "cultural exchanges," or otherwise assist Communism. The United States should support its allies regardless of charges of colonialism, and it should stop courting neutrals. Early in the Vietnam war, some conservatives urged a blockade of Haiphong and other stern measures contrary to the step-by-step escalation strategy of the Johnson administration. Repeatedly conservatives advocated efforts to overthrow the Castro regime in Cuba; at one point James Burnham considered it the first priority.[122] (The trouble with the Bay of Pigs invasion, conservatives believed, was not that it had been tried but that it had failed—a "floundering, half-hearted catastrophe."[123]) The Right believed that successful offensive actions in Vietnam and Cuba alone would reverberate throughout the world. No longer should Communist territory be regarded as a "peace zone" or privileged sanctuary. No longer should American policy be listless, aimless, and uncoordinated. It "must be based," said Strausz-Hupé, Stefan Possony, and William Kintner, "upon the premise that we cannot tolerate the survival of a political system which has both the growing capability and the ruthless will to destroy us. We have no choice but to adopt a Catonic strategy."[124] Conservatives had little faith in the ability of cold war "thaws," destalinization, or the Sino-Soviet split to end the menace or "reduce tensions."[125]

To liberals, of course, such pronouncements seemed wildly simplistic and irresponsible. But whatever the validity of the conservative approach to foreign affairs, an important development occurred during the 1950s and 1960s: the growth of a network of informed conservative foreign policy experts. The Center for Strategic Studies at Georgetown, the Hoover Institution at Stanford, and the American Security Council were among the outposts of scholarly, respectable, conservative cold war analysis. Particularly influential was the Foreign Policy Research Institute of the University of Pennsylvania, founded in 1955 and directed by the Austrian émigré Robert Strausz-Hupé. In 1959 Strausz-Hupé and several colleagues produced a notable analysis of Communist tactics and strategy, *Protracted Conflict*, which markedly affected the Right and impressed many liberals as well.[126] The sequel, *A Forward Strategy for America* (1961), was also well regarded by many conservatives. Eight years later, President Richard Nixon rewarded Strausz-Hupé with the ambassadorship to Ceylon (after Senator Fulbright vetoed an appointment to Morocco).[127]

More and more conservative academics were being heard: men like Stefan Possony, Richard V. Allen, and Milorad Drachkovitch at the Hoover Institution, Warren Nutter at the University of Virginia, David Nelson Rowe at Yale, Frank J. Johnson at the American Security Council, William Kintner and Strausz-Hupé at the University of Pennsylvania, Lev

Dobriansky at Georgetown, Gerhart Niemeyer at Notre Dame, Frank Trager at New York University, Richard Walker at South Carolina, Walter Darnell Jacobs at Maryland, Karl Wittfogel at the University of Washington, and Edward Teller at the University of California. These men and many more were not simply publicists or sloganeers but specialists engaged in scholarly analysis. However controversial their position, they gave to the Right some needed intellectual status and sophistication. If not always taken seriously, conservatives were able by the late 1960s to claim that they *ought* to be taken seriously. Their scholarly output was increasing, and, through *Modern Age*, *National Review*, and journals such as *Orbis* (the quarterly published by the Foreign Policy Research Institute of the University of Pennsylvania), was reaching larger audiences. In a world of Cubas, Vietnams, Czechoslovakias, and massive Russian penetration of the Middle East, the conservative critique of liberal foreign policy gained plausibility. Other Americans, too, doubted that Communists had suddenly become benign.[128]

As the conservatives' assault on America's foreign policy record acquired momentum, so, also, did their critique of the domestic accomplishments of post-New Deal liberalism.

Reasoned suspicion of the State and defense of the free market were not, of course, novel to conservatism in the 1960s. These themes had been developed years before, by men like Nock and Chodorov, Hayek and Mises, Hazlitt and Buckley. Yet by the late 1950s something clearly was missing. For all the learned works of the Austrian economists and their disciples, for all the polemics of publicists, Buckley felt compelled to acknowledge in 1959 that the "conservative demonstration" had failed. Conservatives had been unable to persuade the country that economic freedom (the one most relevant to our everyday lives and choices) was "the most precious temporal freedom." Conservatives had been unable to show the "nexus between individual freedom and property rights."[129]

> Conservatives have not "proved" to the satisfaction either of the public or of the academy that the moderate welfare state has paralyzing economic or political consequences for the affluent society....
> The failure of the conservative demonstration in political affairs rests primarily on our failure to convince that the establishment of the welfare state entails the surrender, bit by bit, of minor freedoms which, added together, can alter the

very shape of our existence.[130]

A new dimension of analysis was therefore needed, one that pushed beyond the repetition of libertarian principles and Hayekian prophecy. In the 1960s conservatism increasingly acquired that dimension. The revolt against the State began to seem less abstract and doctrinaire; it became, in fact, audaciously specific.

One reason for the shift from a paradigmatic to a more pragmatic approach, conservatives argued, was very simple: reality was at last validating their critique. It was no longer quite so necessary to warn about future effects of the welfare state; examples of its present consequences were increasingly at hand. One of the earliest iconoclastic case studies was *The Federal Bulldozer*, an analysis of the urban renewal program by a young Columbia University professor, Martin Anderson.[131] To Anderson urban renewal was objectionable in principle; it was wrong to compel huge numbers of people to abandon their homes and to destroy these homes by eminent domain in order that the land might be put to *private* uses that somebody else deemed preferable. But the core of his analysis was a devastating statistical demonstration that the federal program had not worked. Between 1949 and 1962 it had built about 28,000 homes but destroyed 126,000. Over four times more homes had been eradicated than constructed.[132] Urban renewal had not alleviated the housing problem; it had aggravated it. It had not eliminated slums; it had simply "shifted" them and facilitated their growth. It had killed many small businesses and hurt low-income people for the sake of aesthetic desires of well-to-do elite groups. It had not improved cities' tax bases or stimulated the economy. It had by the early 1960s displaced 1,665,000 people— for no good reason whatsoever.[133]

In contrast to this dreary record, Anderson boldly extolled the private enterprise system. While urban renewal was floundering in the 1950s, "the greatest improvement in housing quality ever shown in the United States" occurred—via free enterprise.[134] It was simply not true that the private sector had been found wanting. "As far as the nonwhite population of the United States is concerned, their housing conditions have been made worse by the federal urban renewal program and have been improved substantially by the free working of the market place."[135] Government intervention itself was the culprit. Free enterprise could do the job. Therefore, Anderson urged, repeal the urban renewal program— totally—now.[136]

Anderson's scholarly tour de force won acclaim among conservatives, who frequently cited urban renewal as a prime illustration of liberal folly. It is easy enough to see why. His book could not be explained away as merely a conservative tirade, published, perhaps, by Regnery or Devin-Adair. While Anderson did openly proclaim his libertarian principles and was capable of righteous indignation, his book was full of hard data that could not be readily dismissed. Furthermore, it was sponsored by the prestigious Joint Center for Urban Studies of MIT and Harvard University; the book had to be taken seriously.

Anderson's study was only the beginning; as the 1960s wore on, an increasingly powerful genre of scholarly conservative muckraking flourished. Unlike the mudraking of an earlier era, its target was not business but government—federal programs created by liberal humanitarian ideology, programs like rent control, public housing,[137] "Medicaid," welfare, farm price supports, and the "war on poverty." Consider, for example, the minimum wage. Who but a person insensitive to suffering could possibly object to a program that set a floor under a person's job earnings? Who could deny the obvious humanitarian benefits of such a scheme? The respected conservative economist Yale Brozen of the University of Chicago did. Armed with tables of statistics, Brozen insisted that the minimum wage "hurt the poor and increased unemployment for unskilled workers." [138] Every single rise in the legal minimum wage since World War II was followed by an *increase* in teenage unemployment. Why? Because artificial increases in the wage rate destroyed low-paying jobs for unskilled people.

> In other words, for many teenagers and particularly for Negro teenagers, the minimum wage has destroyed the beginning jobs where they would normally acquire the skills and discipline to make themselves more productive....
> ...in the interval between the time the minimum is raised and the time productivity catches up, tens of thousands of people are jobless, thousands of businesses fail that are never revived, and teenagers (particularly Negro teenagers) are barred from obtaining the low-wage jobs that have traditionally been their stepping stones to opportunity and advancement.

In addition, these laws stimulated automation, perpetuated segregation, and increased the flight of blacks from the rural South to the already overburdened northern cities.[139] Once again the lesson—to conservatives—was clear: not capitalism, not "racist" white America, but liberalism in government caused economic and social dislocation.

Consider the federal regulatory agencies: the ICC, FTC, FPC, CAB, and dozens of others. Were they truly useful or even necessary institutions any longer? After surveying the evidence, Yale Brozen concluded, "The fact is that most of these regulatory agencies have ended up setting price floors to protect industry, not price ceilings to protect consumers—and regulated industry has tended to become more inefficient as a result."[140] If anything, these powerful bureaucracies had, conservatives insisted, clogged and distorted the economy. But what about the monopoly power of big business? Milton Friedman, a colleague of Brozen's at the University of Chicago, declared that the impact of monopoly on the U.S. economy had been greatly exaggerated. Aside from a few "technical" or natural monopolies and some temporary, unstable private arrangements, "the most important source of monopoly power" was government itself, dispensing such favors as tariffs, tax breaks, and exemption of union monopolies from antitrust laws.[141] Relentlessly, conservative intellectuals, citing the record, drove their point home:

> ...it is the government itself that causes much of the hardship and poverty that concerns us, partly by its many interventions in the free market and partly by the taxes required to support these programs.[142]

The conservative critique of the welfare state extended even to what the Right learned to its sorrow in 1964 was virtually a sacred cow in American politics: Social Security. Conservatives had long been troubled by this program but had often tended to stress philosophical rather than empirical objections to it. William F. Buckley, Jr., for instance, stated in 1959 that its "compulsory character" was "the most serious argument" against it.[143] Milton Friedman also based part of his case on these moral grounds.[144] But as time went on, this objection was supplemented by others directed at the mechanics of the program itself. In 1962 Friedman summarized some of its practical defects:

> It has deprived all of us of control over a sizable fraction of our income, requiring us to devote it to a particular purpose, purchase of a retirement annuity, in a particular way, by buying it from a government concern. It has inhibited competition in the sale of annuities and the development of retirement arrangements. It has given birth to a large bureaucracy that shows tendencies of growing by what it feeds on.... And all this, to avoid the danger that a few people might become charges on the public.[145]

Nor was this all. Another conservative student of Social Security, economist Colin Campbell of Dartmouth College, cited statistics revealing numerous defects in the system. The tax rate, for example, was dreadfully regressive, especially for the poor. There was only a "very loose relationship" between the costs of a person's Social Security plan and the benefits he could expect to receive. In particular, young workers just entering the system could not hope to get back later what they would put in for most of their lives.[146] By the late 1960s and early 1970s, as Congress voted election-year benefit increases with seemingly mechanical regularity, and as Social Security taxes soared in consequence, conservative intellectuals became ever more convinced that the program was, in Meyer's word, "fraudulent" in practice as well as objectionable in principle.[147] The whole program seemed to be totally out of control. Social Security taxes had increased seven times since 1950, M. Stanton Evans noted in 1972. By 1974 Social Security taxes would reach $1,320 on an income of $12,000, with obligations still far in excess of assets. Evans cited studies showing that workers could obtain much better annuities from private sources, and at much less cost.[148] In 1972, Milton Friedman publicly trod where Barry Goldwater had never ventured. *Abolish* Social Security, he urged—in the liberal-oriented *Washington Monthly*.[149] The idea no longer seemed so shocking.

As liberal programs came under intellectual siege from the Right, as conservative scholars challenged not simply the morality of government action but what Buckley called the very "competence of the state" to remedy social ills,[150] conservatives turned often to the most disruptive domestic issue of the 1960s: the relation between black and white America. Many prominent right-wing intellectuals had been critics of the civil rights movement from the beginning. *National Review* persistently and forcefully challenged the integrationists' tactics and ultimate goals, despite the initially adverse climate of opinion. The conservative leadership strenuously abjured any notions of innate black inferiority. No ranting, vulgar racism besmirched *National Review* or *Modern Age*. Barry Goldwater even declared in *The Conscience of a Conservative* that integrated schools were, in his judgment, "wise and just."[151] Conservatives pointed out that Goldwater had helped to integrate the Arizona Air National Guard and the Phoenix Sky Harbor Airport.[152] Frank Meyer insisted that every person has "innate value" and every citizen the right to "equal treatment before the law." Moreover, Meyer knew (as did other conservatives) that "the Negro people have suffered profound wrongs." But, he added (and here he no doubt voiced a conservative consensus), black grievances could not be remedied "by destroying the foundations of a free constitutional society." Legalized coercion in favor of desegregation was as much a "monstrosity" as legalized coercion in favor of segregation. Governmental regulation of individual relationships always brought "disaster to a free society."[153]

Conservative hostility to governmental coercion and belief in the unconstitutionality of civil rights legislation was deeply and sincerely felt. In the 1960s, however, these objections in principle were supplemented by a more pragmatic argument: integration, even if constitutional, did not *work*. Probably the most scholarly conservative critic of integration in the schools was the New York University sociologist Ernest van den Haag. According to van den Haag, the "factual" basis of *Brown vs. Board of Education* was utterly worthless. The Supreme Court had relied on "modern authority" (studies cited by Kenneth Clark, a black psychologist) to prove that racially separate schools were "inherently unequal" since black children suffered psychic damage because of segregation. To van den Haag, however, Clark's studies proved no such thing at all.[154] His scholarship was flatly and suspiciously distorted and wrong;[155] there was "no evidence...that separation *per se* is injurious to Negroes, or that any damage is suffered therefrom."[156] The obvious present educational deficiencies of black children could not, said van den Haag, be solved by placing black children in white schools; such "mixed education" would "impair" the learning of both groups. For the moment, black children did not "on the average" respond as well as white children to "the stimulation given by average white schools." Therefore black children should be educated "separately," while black schools must strive to overcome the "culturally deprived home environment" of many black youngsters. Improved education for all was dependent on separation according to ability. "And this," van den Haag said candidly, "means very largely according to race."[157]

While this sociologist was undermining the claim that integrated schools were a solution to racial problems, other conservatives relied heavily on *Beyond the Melting Pot*, in which two political liberals, Nathan Glazer and Daniel Patrick Moynihan, demonstrated that ethnic groups had never been totally "integrated" into a homogeneous pattern in New York City. Conservatives used this study to attack the integrationist ethos in toto. Integration, claimed Jeffrey Hart, was based on what we now know was the "myth" of homogeneity. The attempt to effect "total Negro integration" was an effort to set up "a novel and abstract pattern" to which no other ethnic group had conformed.[158] For that matter, *National Review* editorialized in 1967, "there is no country with genuine racial integration," and even blacks did not want it so much any more. Look at the "black power" movement. Divested of its revolutionary dimension, it suggested an impulse toward "black responsibility." Why not experiment with black administration of black schools, for example, if that was what a majority of black parents really wanted? Why be shackled by clichés about integration?[159]

Clichés, empty and dangerous clichés: this was the verdict which conservatives emphatically pronounced on the Report of the National Advisory Commission on Civil Disorders (the Kerner Commission) in March 1968. In their response to the commission's examination of the racial crisis, conservatives presented their case with more fervor than ever before. The report, they agreed, was a disaster—and a compelling indication of the intellectual bankruptcy and irresponsibility of liberalism. In 1966, as the wave of urban riots in America gained momentum, Frank Meyer claimed that the black protest movement was shifting from "civil rights" to a revolutionary agitation for "confiscatory socialism."[160] Now, in the bleak early days of 1968, Martin Luther King was actually publicly planning, in his own words, a "massive dislocation" of the nation's capital "until America responds."[161] In the face of "incipient revolution," which confronted "the survival of a free society" with the threat of "endemic disorder," what did the Kerner Commission recommend for the short term? Nothing. Instead, it "put the blame everywhere but where it belongs": on the rioters, abetted by the liberals "who, with their abstract ideology, prepared the way for the riots by their contempt for social order and their utopian, egalitarian enticements and incitements." Ignoring the elementary fact that a free society cannot exist if it cannot quell violent threats from within, the commission repeated on a "grandiose" scale the central error of the liberal approach: the creation among blacks of the "false hope" that "by an act of government, without strenuous effort, without the time always needed for beneficent social change, instant Utopia could be created." *That* was the fundamental cause of the riots.[162]

Moreover, M. Stanton Evans stressed, the commission's specific proposals were also defective. The report was "impervious" to the failures of "welfarism"; it could suggest only—more welfarism. It worried about teenage unemployment in the ghettos but advocated a rise in the minimum wage that would magnify the problem. It wanted more public housing, more urban renewal—despite evidence that these programs were failing. If standard liberal nostrums were valid, why, Evans wondered, had the worst riot of 1967 occurred in liberal Detroit, which had received huge amounts of federal money and energetically carried out the war on poverty? "There is little to suggest," Evans concluded, "that poverty caused the Detroit riots or that welfarism could have prevented them."[163]

A more extensive dissection of the Kerner Commission Report was performed by Ernest van den Haag. The conservative sociologist emphasized what the report did not: that "in all material respects, the fate of Negroes has improved faster than ever before...." In fact, "there has been more improvement in the last twenty years than in the previous two hundred." Yet while measurable progress was occurring, severe problems remained which the commission, by blaming riots on "those rioted against," only tended to exacerbate. Even worse, confronted by a mounting desire among some blacks to fight whites, the commission recommended appeasement, buying off the rioters, on the theory that "we must be at fault if they are dissatisfied." As if riots were a "rational phenomenon." As if the yearning for violence, now "independent of material effects," could be eliminated by rewarding it. No wonder many blacks were outraged by the "pitiful" groveling of white liberals. To alter the conditions that produced the desire to riot, he continued, would take a long time. Moreover, government might not always be the agency to alter them. In the meantime, in the short run, government must *govern*: it must increase the costs of rioting by swift and rigorous enforcement of the law.[164]

Equally critical of the Kerner Report was Jeffrey Hart. Like other conservatives, he was angered by the commission's blaming the riots on "white racism" and not at all on the rioters themselves. Like Meyer, he was disturbed by "an erosion of concern for law and for public order." This decline was encouraged by the spread of "civil disobedience" and the "frivolous attitudes" of liberals like Adlai Stevenson, who suggested early in the 1960s that a jail sentence in the cause of civil rights was an honorable and perhaps even politically profitable thing. Such "remarkably casual" talk, Hart warned, would have to cease. Furthermore, it was not true that white racism was the basic cause of black distress. At the professional level, for instance, blacks were advancing rapidly. All across the board, legal walls of discrimination were crumbling. While it took other ethnic groups three generations or more to move from manual labor to significant white-collar status, there were signs that the new urban Northern black minority would make this transition even more quickly. Adopting what he called a "toughly realistic" approach, Hart emphasized the deeper and more intractable dimensions of the blacks' plight. In part that problem was not one of "white racism" at all but the natural "lag" that occurs when a formerly rural group strives to adjust to an urban environment. Moreover, blacks suffered many additional handicaps: they seemed unable to develop coherent institutions (including businesses) and "group solidarity," like the Puerto Ricans, Chinese, and other minorities. They were impeded by "the chronic instability of the Negro family." (Once again, the influence of Moynihan was apparent.) These problems, Hart argued, would not be quickly solved—certainly not by mere disbursement of money, nor by more street protests.[165]

What, then, should be done about the racial problems? At the most immediate level, conservative intellectuals resolutely demanded the restoration of order and the quelling of violence. This was an eminently proper tactic for a decent and free society. "Repression," said William F. Buckley, Jr., after analyzing Martin Luther King's plan to paralyze Washington, D.C., "is an unpleasant instrument, but it is absolutely necessary for civilizations that believe in order and human rights. I wish to God Hitler and Lenin had been repressed."[166] But conservatives did not stop here; they went on to specify solutions of their own. Eliminate minimum wage laws and arrange welfare payments so as not to reduce the incentive to work, counseled van den Haag.[167] Eliminate rent control and attack racially restrictive labor union practices, urged Hart. In addition, Hart vigorously called for more black-owned businesses, more blacks on urban police forces, and the development, via education (perhaps at the pre-school level), of a stable Negro middle class. Perhaps black self-consciousness was not such a bad thing.[168] Hart was not the only conservative to urge blacks to organize and rely more upon themselves. Buckley suggested that whites "acquiesce even in impulses to separatism"; perhaps, he added, black unions should be organized.[169] In 1965, while a candidate for mayor of New York City, Buckley stated succinctly one of the fundamental conservative tenets: "The *principal* problems that are faced by Negroes today...are *not* solved by government. They are solved by the leadership of their own people."[170]

Finally, conservatives pleaded: eschew the rhetoric of endless promises. Stop the stimulation of hopes that cannot be instantly fulfilled. Do not overlook the unpublicized but extraordinary achievements of the free enterprise system. Again and again, they stressed that, in Hart's words, "we cannot expect spectacular results in the short run."[171] The path to improvement, *National Review* declared in 1967, was primarily economic—a route that necessitated "hard work and self-discipline."[172] Frank Meyer referred to the "great insight" of Booker T. Washington that "respect and access to jobs must be earned by the Negroes themselves." [173] Large numbers of "solid Negro families," he said, were doing just that.[174] Jeffrey Hart uttered what seemed to conservatives an obvious if unpleasant truth: "Some problems are complicated and recalcitrant enough to admit of no immediate solution; such problems cannot be solved but only endured...."[175] But improvement, conservatives also insisted, *was* quietly and steadily occurring, even if the Kerner Report seemed to minimize it. It might not be easy to dramatize, but it could not be denied.

Whatever the merit of these conservative proposals and approaches, they had one definite rhetorical vulnerability. It was easy to dismiss an appeal for patience, prudence, and self-help as moralistic indifference to suffering. How often conservatives had been told that they were selfish and lacked compassion. Fully aware of this criticism, conservatives sought to account for liberalism's claims to superior sensitivity. In *Suicide of the West*, James Burnham developed the most systematic analysis. The liberal, he observed, is "relentlessly driven" by an irrational feeling of guilt which he seeks to discharge by attempting to "cure every social evil":

> ...he must *do something* about the social problem even when there is no objective reason to believe that what he does can solve the problem—when, in fact, it may well aggravate the problem instead of solving it....
>
> ...The real and motivating problem, for the liberals, is not to cure the poverty or injustice or what not in the objective world but to appease the guilt in their own breasts; and what that requires is *some* program, some solution, some activity, whether or not it is the correct program, solution and activity....the liberal...[is] morally disarmed before those whom the liberal regards as less well off than himself.[176]

Conservatives believed that this analysis was vindicated by the racial upheaval of the late 1960s. The Kerner Commission, "morally disarmed" by evident social injustices, could only engage in what van den Haag called "pathetic handwringing."[177] It could only condemn "white racism."

The cleavage between Left and Right was profound indeed. For conservatives were rejecting not just a program here and there but—in domestic affairs, at least—an entire style of politics: the politics of righteous indignation, moralistic crusades, New Frontiers, Great Societies, Wars on Poverty, the recurrent urge to advertise one's feelings of sympathy for the poor. Was the only way to improve society the way which required that one endlessly verbalize one's good intentions? Were good intentions enough? Did the absence of political zeal mean the absence of compassion? Did reliance on the market imply indifference to the poor?

Yet there was power in the liberal critique, and one unorthodox conservative, Richard Cornuelle, knew it. As a young man in the 1940s, Cornuelle had been converted from a vague belief in socialized medicine by Friedrich Hayek's *The Road to Serfdom*. As an active proponent of limited government and free enterprise, he became an editorial assistant to the redoubtable libertarian journalist Garet Garrett and later an executive of the Volker Fund. Annoyed by Cornuelle's "tidy ideology," Garrett told the young enthusiast to visit the coalfields of Kentucky. The suffering he saw there shook him greatly and led him to discover "a lack of humanity in my conservative position."[178] The dilemma was painful: humanity and freedom seemed irreconcilable. After years of intense searching, Cornuelle found a way to resolve the problem. On one side, he argued in 1965, were the conservatives, properly devoted to limited government, yet unable to present a specific and convincing program. On the other side were the liberals, ever ready with massive federal programs which now, in the 1960s, were failing. The alternative was a long-neglected but still viable American tradition: the "independent sector" of voluntary action motivated by neither profit nor power but by "the desire to serve others."[179] This sphere, brilliantly analyzed by Alexis de Tocqueville (who called it "associations"), *was* capable of competing with government and of tapping Americans' enormous desire to do good. Churches and foundations, for example, were doing much and could do more. Government was simply not the sole alternative to apathy and neglect. Cornuelle cited example after example of what the "independent sector" could do. It was a private organization, not government, which virtually eliminated polio. Alcoholics Anonymous, a private concern, was accomplishing substantial good in that area. Cornuelle's own United Student Aid Funds, Inc. was demonstrating that loans for college students need not be a federal responsibility. In Southern cities "independent leadership" was a force for racial harmony. Given recognition and zestful reorganization, this sphere could do again what it had done before the Great Depression: "build a humane society and a free society together."[180]

Cornuelle's brisk little book won quick acclaim in conservative circles and from such unexpected sources as Saul Alinsky and (at that moment) Irving Kristol. William F. Buckley, Jr. also praised Cornuelle's "refreshing thesis."[181] Frank Meyer stressed that Cornuelle's ideas could not thrive in a statist environment and were compatible with conservative principles. He was pleased that Cornuelle, through his Foundation for Voluntary Welfare and his book, was compensating concretely for a conservative defense of the free society which was, Meyer conceded, "largely general and dry."[182]

Perhaps Meyer sensed what Buckley had felt in 1959 in *Up from Liberalism*: that it was neither politically nor intellectually satisfying for conservatives simply to reiterate truisms about the free market, even if they were true. The conservative case for the free society needed a fresh practical restatement in the 1960s. Fortunately for the movement, it was forthcoming—from the irrepressibly brilliant economist Milton Friedman and the rising Chicago School of economics.

Born in 1912 of immigrant parents from Ruthenia, Friedman graduated in the early 1930s from Rutgers, where he was influenced by an exciting teacher, Arthur Burns, later an advisor to President Eisenhower and chairman of the Federal Reserve Board. In 1932 Friedman began graduate work in economics at the University of Chicago and at once became immersed in its electric atmosphere, dominated by some of the greatest twentieth-century free-market economists: Frank Knight, Jacob Viner, and Henry Simons. Another future conservative economist, George Stigler, was a fellow graduate student. After work at the U.S. Treasury during much of World War II, Friedman returned to Chicago and became part of a circle including Simons, Knight, and Friedman's brother-in-law Aaron Director—a group which turned this empirically and theoretically directed economist toward questions of government policy. Shortly after the war, Friedman had a new colleague, Friedrich Hayek, whose *Road to Serfdom* the young economist regarded as "an extraordinarily insightful and prescient book." In 1947 Friedman attended the founding session of the Mont Pélerin Society, through which his circle of friends abroad widened significantly.

During the 1950s, as the conservative intellectual renascence slowly made its way, Friedman participated in a number of conferences which, in retrospect, he considered "extremely significant" both for him and for the struggling movement. Sponsored primarily by the small but highly useful Volker Fund, these sessions, held at Wabash College, Claremont, and a few other institutions, brought together such libertarian scholars as Hayek, David McCord Wright, John Jewkes of England, and Bruno Leoni of Italy for lectures and discussion. These meetings, Friedman later recalled, enabled their participants to explore and refine their views, a much-needed task in those years.[183]

In 1962 Friedman published one result of these conferences: a compact, hard-hitting book called *Capitalism and Freedom*. It was one of the most significant works of conservative[184] scholarship of the 1960s. In the first two chapters of the book, he articulated lucidly the philosophy of nineteenth-century liberalism. Freedom was the ultimate social ideal; governmental power, while necessary, must be limited and decentralized. Interventionism was baneful and dangerous. Economic freedom—that is, capitalism—was an indispensable condition for political liberty. In a centralized socialist state, by contrast, individual endeavor and political dissent would become very difficult: where could dissenters find funds to oppose, for example, state socialism itself? Since all jobs in a fully socialized state would be controlled by the government, who would risk—would the state allow?—significant intellectual and political challenges to the "system"? Capitalism and freedom, Friedman asserted, were inseparable. The government should serve as an umpire, an enforcer of rules, not as a participant in the game itself.

These and other ideas of Friedman's were not, of course, new to conservatives in 1962; Hayek and Simons, for example, had enunciated similar themes years before.[185] What was truly striking was the task Friedman went on to perform in *Capitalism and Freedom*: a daring and iconoclastic assault on conventional twentieth-century liberal wisdom and an incisive indictment of liberal failures. Why, he asked, should the federal government retain a monopoly of the post office? Why did it forbid by law any competition?

> If the delivery of mail is a technical monopoly, no one will be able to succeed in competition with the government. If it is not, there is no reason why the government should be engaged in it. The only way to find out is to leave other people free to enter.[186]

Why should the government control the price of gold? Why not adopt flexible, floating exchange rates? [187] In the field of education, state insistence on minimum amounts of schooling and even state financial support of this schooling were justified. But did the state *have* to administer ("nationalize") the schools themselves?

> Governments could require a minimum level of schooling financed by giving parents vouchers redeemable for a specified maximum sum per child per year if spent on "approved" educational services.... The educational services could be rendered by private enterprises operated for profit, or by nonprofit institutions....

> In terms of effects, denationalizing schooling would widen
> the range of choices available to parents.... Parents could ex-
> press their views about schools directly by withdrawing their
> children from one school and sending them to another....
>   ...The injection of competition would do much to promote
> a healthy variety of schools. It would do much, also, to intro-
> duce flexibility into school systems.[188]

There was the tax system, another example of pernicious governmental
activism: "An income tax intended to reduce inequality and promote the
diffusion of wealth has in practice fostered reinvestment of corporate
earnings, thereby favoring the growth of large corporations, inhibiting
the operation of the capital market, and discouraging the establishment
of new enterprises."[189]

From farm price supports to social security, from the minimum wage
to urban renewal, liberal solutions, said Friedman, had not achieved their
aims. If in the 1920s and 1930s most intellectuals had understandably
believed capitalism to be "defective" and governmental controls the panacea, the times were finally changing. For now at last there was a record
of intervention; experience belied the statist dream.[190]

Friedman was also anxious to refute various criticisms of the free
market. Capitalism was not "racist," for instance; the emergence of capitalism was marked by a *reduction* of discrimination and the dramatic
opening of new opportunities for minorities.[191] The "great achievement"
of capitalism, in fact, was the increase of opportunities and the creation
of less inequality than in any other economic system.[192] By far his most
important contention, however, was his reply to the standard liberal argument that the free market had proved itself a failure in the Great Depression. If capitalism was so laudable, why the disaster of the 1930s?
Relying on research later published as part of his monumental *Monetary
History of the United States, 1867-1960*, Friedman refuted this persistent taunt. The free enterprise system did *not* produce the Great Depression; "government mismanagement" did:

> A governmentally established agency—the Federal Reserve
> System—had been assigned responsibility for monetary policy.
> In 1930 and 1931, it exercised this responsibility so ineptly as
> to convert what otherwise would have been a moderate con-
> traction into a major catastrophe....
>   ...[The] evidence persuades me that...the severity of each of
> the major contractions—1920-21, 1929-33, and 1937-38—is
> directly attributable to acts of commission and omission by

the Reserve authorities and would not have occurred under
earlier monetary and banking arrangements....

The Great Depression in the United States, far from being a
sign of the inherent instability of the private enterprise system, is a testament to how much harm can be done by mistakes on the part of a few men when they wield vast power
over the monetary system of a country.[193]

Friedman's liberating revisionism rapidly became part of the conservative scholarly arsenal.

The publication of *Capitalism and Freedom* and Friedman's emergence as a preeminent economist among conservatives constituted a major
landmark in the evolution of the postwar Right.[194] Here was a man of
increasing prestige within his profession, a man whom even opponents
respected as one of the very best American economists, who was articulating conservative viewpoints with a felicitous combination of learning
and wit. In 1967 he was elected president of the American Economic
Association; by the end of the 1960s he was probably the most highly
regarded and influential conservative scholar in the country, and one of
the few with an international reputation.[195]

In several ways Friedman and the Chicago School represented an
advance, for conservatives, over Hayek, Mises, Hazlitt, Rothbard, and
the Austrian School.[196] Aside from certain differences of viewpoint concerning the gold standard and monetary questions,[197] the Chicago economists tended to be more pragmatic than the "Austrians," more oriented
toward the use of mathematics than, for example, Mises, who was notably suspicious of "quantitative economics."[198] In an increasingly math-
ematics-oriented profession, this was an advantage, which explains in
part the Chicago School's greater academic status. While Mises labored
at a gigantic philosophy of human action which opposed interventionism
on principle, men like Friedman, George Stigler, and Yale Brozen were
particularly interested in the way government programs actually mal-
functioned in practice. In his study of the Federal Reserve Board and his
contributions to monetary theory, Friedman broke new ground in a way
that "Austrians" did not. While the two schools were united in their devotion to the free market, it was the Chicago circle that was "in the vanguard of contemporary economic thought."[199] The Chicago School's empirical and skeptical tendencies fitted in well with the general
"pragmatization" of conservative thought in the 1960s.

There was another reason for Friedman's impact on the Right: his
ability to generate a dazzling array of programs based on his libertarian

principles. As much as any intellectual of the 1960s, Friedman was responsible for the growing acceptability of the volunteer army concept. In 1968 the editor of the influential *Why the Draft?* wrote: "If the ideas in this book can be traced to a single individual, that person is Professor Milton Friedman...." Friedman was also credited by some conservatives with persuading President Nixon's Commission on an All-Volunteer Armed Force to endorse the concept in 1970.[200] On another front, as many of the nation's schools became racked by racial violence, and as secularism in the schools seemed triumphant, many conservatives turned with increasing interest to Friedman's voucher plan for education.[201] His tax reform program won the support of Buckley.[202] His "negative income tax" concept was as provocative a plan to alleviate poverty as any other offered in the 1960s.[203]

Friedman's ideas did not, of course, invariably sweep conservatives off their feet. Not all right-wingers, for example, favored a volunteer army.[204] The negative income tax was vehemently denounced by Henry Hazlitt, who voiced the skepticism of many in labeling Friedman's idea a politically naive guaranteed annual income scheme that was "not only economically but morally indefensible."[205] But the point remains that the writings of Friedman and his disciples bristled with *specific, arguable* alternatives to liberal programs. For an antiestablishment force that had to fight off charges of negativism and fetishistic devotion to outmoded ideas, this development was a most welcome boon. In 1968 Buckley sensed the changing climate:

> There is in the air a sense of great excitement among American conservatives who have reason to believe that their time is coming. In the past few years any number of ideas developed in the garrets of conservative scriveners and roundly dismissed as radical and irrelevant have suddenly begun to appear in the classiest political shopwindows.[206]

If there was any single individual he might have thanked, it was Milton Friedman.[207]

Yet not Friedman alone. Rather, an increasing number of conservative academics like George Stigler, Yale Brozen, Colin Campbell, Ernest van den Haag, Gordon Tullock, Warren Nutter, James Buchanan, James Wiggins, and many more.[208] Nor could one ignore the continuing contributions of individuals like Hayek, Mises, Hazlitt, Rothbard, and John Chamberlain.[209] Conservative scholarship was proliferating; networks of influence in economics departments and elsewhere were being established; a presence was being felt. These individuals were contributing to one of the significant intellectual currents of the 1960s: disillusionment with government and the remarkable revival of "neoclassical" economics.[210]

By the early 1960s, paralleling the deepening intellectual challenge to the Left, signs of conservative resurgence were multiplying. Conservatives felt it; in 1961 M. Stanton Evans discerned a conservative "revolt on the campus" against liberal conformity and collectivism.[211] Liberals felt it, too; one result was a flood of popular articles on conservatism, Senator Goldwater, the "radical Right," and the John Birch Society. Why did this seemingly sudden upsurge occur? Explanations varied. Some argued that the "Ike Age" was over and that both Left and Right were stirring:[212] Young Americans for Freedom (YAF) was formed at Buckley's home in 1960, while the Students for a Democratic Society was organized in 1962. Many hostile observers saw the revival as merely the quest of frustrated, insecure, resentful extremists for easy answers, simple solutions, a purer, older, and largely mythical America.

Conservatives naturally had different ideas. After all, Evans pointed out, the movement was stirring well before Eisenhower's departure. In part, he noted, campus conservatism represented not "a revolt of generation against generation" but the emergence of "an 'inner-directed underground'—a generation of parents who, in an age of other-direction, have held fast to traditional values, and bootlegged them to their children."[213] Loyal to their parents' beliefs, defiant of the prevailing liberal climate, these young people were sustained by the growth of conservative thought in the 1950s. "The key to the conservative uprising has thus been the development of an intellectual community to provide alternatives to the Liberal orthodoxy, and of an agency to unite that community with the prospective rebels."[214] This agency was Frank Chodorov's quiet but very significant Intercollegiate Society of Individualists (ISI). Since its founding in 1953, ISI had in eight years increased its mailing list from 600 to more than 13,000 and had distributed conservative literature to about 40,000 students. ISI, Evans properly observed, was an indispensable link between right-wing scholars and college students.[215] It had established a "loose confederation" of youthful conservatives[216] who would become, through YAF and other channels, important intellectual and political exponents of the cause. The seeds sown by isolated scholars in the 1940s and 1950s and nurtured by such journals as *National Review* and *Modern Age* were at last beginning to bear fruit.

The climax of conservatism's burst into prominence in the early 1960s was Senator Barry Goldwater's 1964 presidential campaign. We are concerned here not with the strictly political aspects of the Goldwater candidacy but with its relation to the burgeoning conservative intellectual movement. The first important point is that the two *were* related to a degree that politics and intellectuals had not been for a long time. Every campaign organization, to be sure, has its "idea men," speechwriters, and cast of supporting academics. Still, the Goldwater experience was not an ordinary phenomenon. From an early date, prominent conservative intellectuals significantly assisted the Arizona senator.[217] *National Review* enthusiastically promoted his candidacy. Russell Kirk helped to prepare a few of his speeches and was an early supporter.[218] Harry Jaffa wrote at least part of his acceptance speech; Milton Friedman served as his economic adviser.[219] William Rusher was heavily involved from the start.[220] Kirk, Meyer, Buckley, Bozell, even Ayn Rand:[221] right-wingers of nearly every variety endorsed Goldwater.[222] The Arizona senator's campaign represented the first thrust of the postwar New Right into presidential politics. Indeed, it is likely that without the patient spadework of the intellectual Right, the conservative *political* movement of the 1960s would have remained disorganized and defeated. Without *The Conscience of a Conservative* (actually written by L. Brent Bozell), which sold 3,500,000 copies by 1964,[223] Goldwater would probably not have attained national stature. Ideas did have consequences, as Richard Weaver had long before observed.

The conservative intellectual movement had certainly come a long way from the ghetto-like isolation of the early postwar years. What a contrast with the era of Senator Taft! Back in 1953 a reporter had asked the Ohio senator whether he had read Russell Kirk's book *The Conservative Mind*. No, he indicated, and added with a chuckle, "You remind me of Thurber's *Let Your Mind Alone*." On the same occasion Taft remarked, "There are some questions that I haven't thought very much about. But I'm a politician, not a philosopher."[224] Eleven years later, conservatives at last had a colorful political champion who doubled as a philosopher and gathered intellectuals to his side.

The crusade of 1964 ended, of course, in overwhelming electoral defeat. Nevertheless, for conservative intellectuals it was an intensely educational experience. One lesson drawn by many of them was that the campaign revealed the immense power and blatant bias of the news media and the utter unscrupulousness of their presumably responsible liberal foes. It was, said Buckley, a "vile campaign,"[225] and conservatives were deeply stung and embittered by it. "Goldwater Republicanism is the closest thing in American politics to an equivalent of Russian Stalinism," said Senator Fulbright. "We see dangerous signs of Hitlerism in the Goldwater campaign," said Martin Luther King. "All we needed to hear [at the Republican convention] was 'Heil Hitler,'" commented Governor Brown of California. "[The Republicans] had *Mein Kampf* as their political bible," charged the mayor of San Francisco. "Goldwater is mentally unbalanced— he needs a psychiatrist," said Walter Reuther. These and other statements by responsible liberals[226] had a searing and lasting impact on the intellectual Right.[227] In 1965, for instance, M. Stanton Evans devoted a chapter of *The Liberal Establishment* to what he regarded as willful distortion of Goldwater's views and performance by the principal national news media in 1963 and 1964.[228] "The mass-communication network, solidly in Liberal hands, is even more formidable an opponent than conservatives had thought," Frank Meyer mused shortly after the election.[229] It became a settled conviction. The events of 1964 reinforced conservative awareness of the strength of the opposition and of their own status as an antiestablishment movement.

They did not, however, concede defeat. To be sure, Frank Meyer admitted, there was much to be done. Conservatives needed to "translate" their principles into issues more effectively. They needed to find a way to refute liberal charges that the Right wanted instant and "radical tearing down of established institutions." But on one point, he and other conservatives were uncompromising: America had *not* repudiated the conservative philosophy. This position had *not* proved intellectually bankrupt.[230] As Ronald Reagan, writing in *National Review*, put it, conservatism was not routed; only a "false image" of it was.[231] Despite all sorts of handicaps, conservatism had made "remarkable progress" in 1964, James Burnham asserted. An "idea in a few hundred heads" a decade ago now had millions of conscious adherents.[232] "Rivulets," Gerhart Niemeyer asserted, had been united into a "great stream": "conservatism in America is now an articulate, inclusive movement of the people."[233]

Niemeyer was surely correct. As an intellectual and political movement, conservatism did not peak with Goldwater and did not die thereafter. What seems most noteworthy in retrospect was not the magnitude of the movement's defeat at the polls in 1964 but the rapidity of its recovery. The extraordinary resiliency of the Right was apparent in the increasing ties between intellectuals and politicians. In New York, the Conservative Party (an explicitly *conservative* party, no less), founded in 1961, was steadily growing, and writers like Frank Meyer were intimately involved in its activities.[234] In 1965 William F. Buckley, Jr. ran for mayor of New York City, gaining unprecedented exposure for his philosophy (and 13 percent of the vote) in the very citadel of liberalism.[235] Such a venture would have been impossible a decade earlier. Increasingly, too, politicians were emerging as foci of conservative enthusiasm—in particular, after 1966, Ronald Reagan. Many of these political figures were also willing to cooperate with their academic brethren. The barriers between conservative thought and political activity were breaking down. It was becoming more and more difficult to separate the two.

Another sign of the growing political sophistication of the intellectual Right after 1964 was its increasingly firm dissociation from the prime symbol of right-wing extremism, the John Birch Society. Ever since the national press had discovered the society in 1961, many conservatives had been embarrassed by the sweeping and irresponsible statements of its leader, Robert Welch. William F. Buckley, Jr. believed that Welch's well-publicized activities were being exploited by a liberal press in order to "anathematize the entire American right wing."[236] For several years the *National Review* circle concentrated its fire on Welch but refused to condemn the society as a whole. In 1961 Buckley stressed his "grave differences" with Welch and condemned his allegation that President Eisenhower was a Communist. On the other hand, he hoped that the society itself, most of whose members had never even heard of Welch's wild charges, would prosper—*if* it could distinguish "subjective motives" from "objective consequences" of a person's behavior.[237] In early 1962, shortly after a meeting in Miami of several conservative leaders,[238] various conservatives again tried to bury the Birch issue. In *Commonweal*, Russell Kirk lambasted a number of extremists, particularly Welch, who was harming "responsible conservatism" far more than Communism. While many decent people belonged to the society, it was controlled by "the lunatic fringe"—namely, Welch.[239] Almost simultaneously, *National Review* denounced Welch (but not the entire society) for "damaging the cause of anti-Communism," endangering conservative action, and continuing to detect no difference between "an active pro-Communist" and "an ineffectually anti-Communist Liberal."[240]

By 1965, however, the distinction between Welch and his followers no longer seemed tenable, and the editors of *National Review*, in a special feature section, condemned the entire society.[241] Welch's allegedly paranoid views (which the editors cited in detail) could not be dismissed as merely his own; they dominated the society, whose members gave every evidence of supporting him. These views, the editors believed, were false and increasingly harmful to informed anti-Communism. The society could not, therefore (said Meyer), be considered merely "misguided." Its "psychosis of conspiracy" (such as the new assertion that America was "60-80 percent" Communist-dominated) was dangerous to the defense of America's national interests.[242]

While the respectable Right was repudiating Birchism, there was increasing evidence of intellectual maturity and recognition as well. The divisive philosophical quarrels of the early 1960s were yielding (at least temporarily) to a kind of cease-fire sanctified by fusionism. Slowly, here and there, conservatives appeared to be "making it." *National Review*'s circulation, which had been about 30,000 in 1960, jumped to 60,000 by 1963, over 90,000 in 1964, and, after a postelection slump, around 95,000 in 1965 and more than 100,000 in the late 1960s.[243] Buckley's syndicated column, founded in 1962 with thirty-eight charter newspapers,[244] continued to increase its outlets until it became by the early 1970s one of the two or three most widely syndicated columns in the country (with more than 300 subscribers). in 1966 Buckley successfully inaugurated *Firing Line*, a popular television debate series. Later that same year, Milton Friedman became a regular columnist in *Newsweek*.[245] Meanwhile ISI coordinated scores of lectures on campuses by conservative intellectuals and assisted dozens of conservative clubs. Its *Intercollegiate Review*, founded in 1965, quickly became a principal conservative journal, with a press run of 45,000 by 1967.[246] In April 1964 the Conservative Book Club was formed; obtaining 25,000 members within eight months, it reached 30,000 in 1965.[247] Books by nearly every major conservative figure were featured by the club and published by its associate, Arlington House, which was also founded in 1964 and which soon became the leading conservative publisher.[248]

Surveying these and other developments, a conservative youth-oriented magazine, *Rally*, observed in 1967:

> ...the last three years have witnessed the evolution of an ideological infrastructure that now unites what was, before 1964, a loose congeries of publications and interest groups. The communications, activist, and academic sectors have coalesced into a conservative commonwealth, with sophisticated internal communication and division of labor.

The feeling was in the air: the phase of consolidation, the years of preparation, were ending. Conservatives were less and less intellectual pariahs. In 1964, Nelson Rockefeller and the "liberal establishment" told conservatives that they did not belong to the "mainstream" of American life. Four hectic years later, these same conservatives helped capture the presidency of the United States.

Yet even as power seemed within reach, the ground appeared to be quaking. The agonies of Vietnam and the ghettos, mounting disorder on the campuses, and numbing fear of crime in the cities were a few of the immediate factors which led many conservative intellectuals to feel—more intensely, perhaps, than ever before—that a truly profound crisis was at hand in the late 1960s.[250] Beyond what they regarded as liberalism's practical failures at home and abroad, they perceived a deeper threat: *disorder* and the decay of the spiritual and moral foundations of civilization. Alarmed at what they saw as moral breakdown fostered by nihilistic relativism[251] and by the literally subversive doctrine of civil disobedience,[252] conservatives asked: what did the malaise signify?

James Burnham, analyzing the riots, supplied their answer in one phrase: "a collapse of the morale of the governing elite." [253] It was the disintegrating elite, the liberal establishment—above all, the radicalized intellectuals—who were creating the crisis of authority and values in the West. According to Will Herberg, the respected conservative sociologist of religion, America was witnessing the "defection" of an uprooted intelligentsia whose "self-extrusion" from ordered society was leading it to war against its own tradition. Once upon a time, he said, dissent had signified disagreement within a basic consensus. No more. Now it was total, "without fixed content," "the mask and the instrument" of rage and revolution against a society which refused the floating intellectuals the power they sought.[254]

Perhaps, though, these clouds had a silver lining, Stephen Tonsor suggested in 1968. For the American people as a whole were not "degenerate"; our society as a whole was not "diseased." What was occurring was something else: "the last hours of the great liberal ascendancy." The dominant liberal elite—decadent, "yearning for apocalypse," sentimentally infatuated with the revolutionary life-styles of a Che Guevara or a Malcolm X, lacking the will to survive—was dying. It was, said Tonsor, "the end of an era."[255] In the traumatic days of the late 1960s and early 1970s, conservatives sought to fill the vacuum.

TEN

Things Fall Apart

James Burnham's contention in 1964 that liberalism was the ideology of Western suicide must have seemed a bit fanciful, even to conservatives, in that year of Lyndon Johnson, the Great Society, "consensus," and the massive rejection of Barry Goldwater. The tide seemed so inexorably moving to the Left. Within five years, however, the liberal mood and perhaps the liberal tide had ebbed. Conservatives were increasingly convinced that their hour was approaching and that liberalism as a coherent intellectual and political force was fragmenting and expiring. Yet out of its ashes was emerging a challenge even more ominous. In the summer of 1968, Jeffrey Hart prophesied, "Spreading political violence of a revolutionary character now seems inevitable in America."[1]

Ironically (to conservatives), its source was not that much-publicized phenomenon of the early 1960s, the "Radical Right." It was not the John Birch Society, the Christian Anti-Communist Crusade, or any other fringe elements that had been sedulously investigated by the popular press in the era of President Kennedy. The real revolutionary danger, conservatives argued, emanated squarely from the Left. It came from groups and individuals like the Students for a Democratic Society, the Black Panthers, the *New York Review of Books*, and Herbert Marcuse—leftists all. As usual (said conservatives), liberals could not recognize the enemy when it appeared. How could they? They shared so much of its point of view. James Burnham summed it up in *Suicide of the West*: for liberals there was never an unappeasable enemy to their Left. Their preferred opponent *had* to be on the Right.[2]

What were the roots of bankrupt liberalism and the radical mystique? Above all, their institutional locus was alleged to be the two most liberal-dominated institutions of the 1960s: the universities and the mass media. If conservatism was to succeed as an intellectual or political movement, it would have to cope with the demise of liberalism, the radicalization of the Left, and the immense powers which still resided in the left-oriented intellectual and cultural centers of the nation. Conservatives contended that it was not the vast "producing majority" of Americans (as Frank Meyer called them)[3] who were generating the developing revolutionary upsurge. This fact was to be of the greatest significance in shaping the character and prospects of the conservative intellectual movement in the late 1960s and 1970s.

By the end of the 1960s the condition of American higher education was a principal issue in national politics and the subject of a torrent of conservative analysis. Reports from the campus were at times an almost continuous feature of *National Review*, while *Modern Age* and *Intercollegiate Review* frequently contained articles on "student unrest," the "counterculture," and related phenomena. At one time or another, virtually every major conservative intellectual analyzed the crisis; several contributed in 1969 to an entire book of conservative interpretations of academic disorder.[4] Pervading these writings was a sense of the utter seriousness of the mounting upheavals. Conservatives rejected explanations which found the roots of protest in legitimate outrage about the Vietnam war, racism, or other presumed ills of American society. They denied that the new generation was the best educated in American history. They condemned what they regarded as automatic liberal horror at the use of police on campus. As William F. Buckley, Jr. stated, "...policemen are, in certain circumstances, precisely the agents of civilization and humanity. Their availability is something that the forces of reason and enlightenment should celebrate, rather than deplore."[5]

Beyond the question of tactics and immediate causation lay the deeper problem: why? What was responsible for the ugly ferment on the campuses? And why so particularly on the campuses? Why had the universities, by the end of the 1960s, replaced the ghettos as the scene for spectacular rebellions and violence? Conservatives offered a variety of hypotheses. To Russell Kirk, author of *National Review*'s regular "From the Academy" column and a devotee of the stern educational theories of Albert Jay Nock and Bernard Iddings Bell, the student protests were a vindication of nearly twenty years of scathing criticism of academe. Back in 1953, Kirk had resigned from the faculty of Michigan State College (now Michigan State University) rather than submit to what he considered a deliberate lowering of standards in order to increase enrollments.[6]

Ever since, he had relentlessly criticized the mindless, aggrandizing boosterism of "Behemoth University."[7] The root of the trouble, said Kirk, was boredom. Huge and ever-increasing numbers of ill-prepared, rootless students, often imbued with "America's Pelagian heresy" that education would save us all,[8] had enrolled at typically impersonal, mass campuses "preoccupied with vocationalism and sociability." Drifting about aimlessly in a sea of mediocrity, intellectual irrelevance, and ethical purposelessness, these permissively reared, undisciplined students understandably became bored, resentful, and rebellious. No wonder trouble developed. Kirk recommended that the size of universities be reduced, that only "real students" be admitted, and that the curriculum be revised. (Down with "antiquarianism," survey courses, hotel administration for undergraduates, and most courses in education and sociology.) In effect, Kirk pleaded for a return to a rigorous liberal arts curriculum—for those who could benefit from it. Other kinds of schools should accommodate young people with different interests. Remove boredom, restore the "moral imagination" and "ethical ends" to learning, and we would go far to eliminating the malaise in academe.[9]

Perhaps this was so, commented Will Herberg in 1969. But Herberg wondered whether Kirk was merely projecting "his own personal experience" onto the current crisis. Was not the problem far more profound? "What we are witnessing today...is the final outcome of the social and moral disintegration of the stable, organized, integrated society we think of as characterizing the high Middle Ages in the West, where everyone normally had a place in society, and found no difficulty in defining his identity in terms of his belonging." It was not the proletariat (sustained by "conservative, antidisintegrative" labor unions) which was failing to cope with alienation and social upheaval. It was the intellectual—that is, "the free floating journalist, the *littérateur*, or the junior academician"— who was responding to pressure by attempting to subvert and destroy "the existing social order." This peculiar "vulnerability" of the intellectuals, noticeable first in Europe and then in Latin America, was finally reaching America: the United States was becoming "Europeanized" at last.[10] It was not "youth" that was causing the upheaval, said Gerhart Niemeyer of Notre Dame a year later, but "a radical ideology," "notions," and "slogans" which comprised a "cult" that was "more characteristic of uprooted Western intelligentsia, Julien Benda's *clercs* than of youth."[11]

This developing conservative theme was powerfully expounded by Jeffrey Hart in the fifteenth anniversary issue of *National Review* in 1970. Hart's point of departure was "the habitually antagonistic, and some-

times even treasonous, relationship" of intellectuals "to their surrounding society." "This settled antagonism, this spirit of inner defection, exists in its most concentrated form in the academy (the only American
institution, let us note, that is entirely run by liberals, and, not coinci-
dentally, the institution furthest along toward disintegration)." According to Hart, this "adversary" posture of truly "fundamental antagonism"
was a comparatively novel development in Western culture. Only in the
early nineteenth century had artists and intellectuals begun to adopt such
a stance—one increasingly common to Left and Right alike, from
Mallarmé to Marx, Matthew Arnold to Baudelaire, *Partisan Review* to
T.S. Eliot. Who was their enemy? The philistines, the bourgeoisie, "respectable" society. Until World War II, Hart continued, the "adversary
writers" were little known to the society about them. Now, however, the
situation had utterly changed. Now we had "a *mass* intelligentsia" and a
"mass adversary culture."

> During the past 25 years there has occurred a sort of cultural
> explosion: paperbacks, Eliot reading his poems to fifty thou-
> sand students in a Midwestern football stadium, LP records,
> Mailer and Genet "covering" the Democratic Convention,
> Mailer and Genet and de Sade appearing in mass circulation
> journals, the op-art and pop-art and porno phenomena.
>
> All of these things, along with affluence, the GI Bill and
> the assumption, implicit in democratic theory and increas-
> ingly the premise of government action, that absolutely ev-
> eryone must go to college, has now given rise to a vast stu-
> dent proletariat. Twenty-five years ago, about ten per cent of
> the college-age population attended college; today the per-
> centage approaches 50 and it will continue to climb. Much of
> this proletariat absorbs the attitudes of the adversary culture....

More and more students were thus becoming exposed to a phenomenon
that was now, said Hart, "fixed, habitual, and coarse."[12]

What Hart called the adversary culture Gerhart Niemeyer (following Theodore Roszak) labeled the "counter-culture" in an article published in *National Review* in mid-1970.[13] The New Left, he contended,
was a movement which sought "the destruction of the entire social order
and the reversal of all values in Western countries." It was heavily dependent on the "counterculture" (or "anti-culture"), which had made a "cult"
of "negation." Niemeyer stressed the utter completeness of the revolt,
the "limitless discontent" of the enragés.[14] And he noted the intensifying
moral and intellectual malaise in society's leadership elite—the courts,

for example, and the administrators of universities. Steeped in positivism, they seemed unable to distinguish between right and wrong, between freedom and license, between "rational dialogue and the clash of irrationalities." Unless this decline of rationality was halted, could an order-restoring Fortinbras be far behind?

What was the ideological source of the revolutionary threat? Indeed, whence came the distinctive nihilism itself? Conservative analysts dismissed what they generally regarded as superficial differences between Old and New Left. Instead, they hammered away at an old theme: the fundamental continuity of the Left. While individual liberals might courageously condemn the destructive behavior of radical youth, conservatives insisted that liberalism was inescapably responsible for its progeny. Did not many sociological studies demonstrate that radical students were usually the children of liberal or radical parents? In fact, wrote M. Stanton Evans in 1966, "the New Left is not...a rebellion at all."

> The root premises of the New Left...include a vague commitment to collectivism, permissiveness in morals, militant egalitarianism, hostility to patriotic sentiment, and strident pacifism. These are also, as it happens, the root premises of the Liberal orthodoxy. On all doctrinal matters, the New Left is merely American Liberalism writ large....[15]

Reviewing Sidney Hook's *Academic Freedom and Academic Anarchy* in 1970, Russell Kirk praised Hook's personal example but questioned his social-democratic premises. Was not ritualistic liberalism, which Hook skillfully dissected, merely Hook's own "'realistic liberalism' carried to absurdity"? Did not *both* Hook and the youthful Left espouse "Marxist dogma" and "Dewey's democratism"?[16] To Frank Meyer the fundamental thrust of the turmoil was equally clear. The "student revolt" was "simply a radical speed-up of the glacier-like erosion" of the standards of Western civilization, an erosion caused by liberalism.[17] Radicalism was "the logical conclusion" of the inherent egalitarianism and relativism of the liberals. What was the hippie counterculture, with its call to "do your own thing," but "an extreme extension" of liberalism's relativist assault on the verities of the West?[18]

One alarming and saddening aspect of the crisis, for conservatives, was that at times it seemed so inevitable. For years they had inveighed against pernicious doctrines espoused by entrenched elites in the universities. Now, they charged, the chickens were coming home to roost. In the early 1960s, well before the decay had become outwardly visible, Richard Weaver trenchantly exposed the intellectual heresy that was allegedly sapping the foundations of our culture. For fifty years American education had been controlled by "revolutionaries" whose "grand pundit" was John Dewey.[19] For fifty years America had been the victim of an unprecedented and

> systematic attempt to undermine a society's traditions and beliefs through the educational establishment which is usually employed to maintain them.... The result has been an educational system not only intrinsically bad but increasingly at war with the aims of the community which authorizes it....[20]

In what ways did these so-called progressives challenge the "Judeo-Christian-classical heritage of the West"?[21] Weaver listed their subversive tenets:

> 1. There is no such thing as a body of knowledge which reflects the structure of reality.... Knowledge is viewed as an instrumentality which is true or false according to the way it is applied to concrete situations or the way it serves the needs of the individual.... there is no final knowledge about anything....
> 2. This being so, the object of education is not to teach knowledge, but to "teach students.".…
> 4. The teacher must not think of himself as being in authority, because authority is evil....
> 6. The mind is not to be exalted over the senses....
> 8. The general aim is to train the student so that he will adjust himself not simply to the existing society, as is sometimes inferred from their words, but to society conceived as social democracy.[22]

Weaver argued that the twentieth-century progressives were remarkably similar to ancient Gnostics. Both, for example, saw man as naturally divine. Both saw law and traditions as repressive and the material world as evil and remediable.[23] And that was the true goal of the educationists: to remedy the alleged imperfections of their environment and to produce (whether they knew it or not) a "secular communist state."[24] For this purpose recruits were needed, and these recruits were to be students. The "real aim" of these "gnostics of education" was "conditioning the young for political purposes."[25] A few years later many conservatives would wonder whether the "Gnostics" had succeeded.

Most conservatives seemed willing to accept men like Sidney Hook as at least temporary allies in the fight against extremism. Nevertheless, such tactical necessities, they felt, must not obscure the truth: that liberalism as a philosophy "remains," in Meyer's words, "an enemy—the more so, having given birth to a radical progeny...."[26] Back in 1949, at the very beginning of the postwar conservative revival, Peter Viereck wrote: "What worries the conservative is not so much the liberal as his grandson. The liberal himself is a benign and beamish soul, as well behaved as you could wish, for he is still living on the moral capital accumulated by past conservatives."[27] But comes the relativist second generation and then the nihilistic third....

The result was that the 1960s, said the conservative sociologist Robert Nisbet, were "the single most critical, crisis-ridden decade in the history of American higher education."[28] To Jeffrey Hart, the nation's colleges and universities, which had once served as our "dispersed capital," now were being converted into a "dispersed Sierra Maestre."[29] Without conservative ballast, unchecked liberalism was rampant. It was liberals, observed one conservative political scientist, who had developed the huge egalitarian "multiversity" and who had urged students to become politically committed.[30] Could it be, Stephen Tonsor suggested, that student radicals were learning the ways of closed-mindedness from their professors?[31] Surely, he insisted, one of the stultifying features of academe was the absence of philosophical and political diversity.

> The ideological and cultural uniformity of higher education in America is a disgrace. Why is it that our colleges and universities have conformed themselves over the past two decades to the orthodoxy of secular liberalism? Why has the atmosphere been so increasingly hostile to open debate? [32]

On another occasion, Tonsor was even more emphatic. Many intellectuals, he asserted, simply did not want the university to be an "open forum." Most state universities slighted religion in their curriculum and, until lately, had tended to discriminate against Roman Catholics. Nor was this all:

> How does it happen that in the history department to which I belong, out of over fifty faculty members, only one is an identifiable Republican?... I believe...that a process of selection and exclusion has been at work for nearly sixty years which has now produced a marvelous homogeneity of viewpoint.[33]

Conservative intellectuals realized that no simple conspiracy was at work and that many institutional pressures tended to generate political imbalance.[34] Tonsor believed that the tenure system encouraged "the homogenization of thought within the academy" and the perpetuation of "the liberal establishment."[35] But the idea that gross and undesirable imbalance did exist was a certitude on the Right. Many believed that conservative professors were often discriminated against by what Erik von Kuehnelt-Leddihn called the "Holy Liberal Inquisition."[36] They cited studies by the sociologist Seymour Martin Lipset indicating that most academics were left-leaning and that most students moved leftward while in college.[37] William F. Buckley, Jr. discerned the danger of "ideological indoctrination" in the fact that in 1968 more faculty members at Princeton University voted for comedian Dick Gregory for president than for Richard Nixon.[38] James Burnham contrasted liberals' treatment of revolutionaries with their treatment of conservatives:

> Nearly all liberals believe communists should be allowed to speak on college campuses, and most liberals believe communists should be permitted to teach in college.... There is no comparable liberal solicitude for fascists or even for those belonging to what liberals like to refer to as "the Radical Right."[39]

In 1971 *National Review* published the results of a poll of undergraduates at twelve American campuses in 1969-1970. The results were deeply disheartening to conservatives. For example:

> Three-fifths [of the respondents] call themselves political liberals, fully 17% are self-proclaimed radicals.... almost half favor the socialization of all basic industries; seven out of ten want their country unilaterally to suspend atomic weapons development. 40% say American society is "sick"; just over half believe that organized religion is harmful or worse. Given the alternatives of war or surrender in a confrontation with the Soviet Union, 54% would have the United States surrender.

Conservative opinion on the campus was in sharp decline.[40]

Yet it is unlikely that these findings really surprised conservative intellectuals, who undoubtedly already knew that, numerically at least, they maintained only a small foothold in academe. They recognized that their movement was maturing in defiance of academic orthodoxy. Ironically, conservatism's very weakness among intellectuals proved in a way to be an advantage. For when the demoralization of the universities occurred, it was widely perceived as a *liberal* failure. No one could blame conservatives for mismanaging the campuses. The popular symbols of capitulation to student radicals were "liberal" college presidents like Clark

Kerr of California, James Perkins of Cornell, and Kingman Brewster of Yale. Suddenly conservatives—the outsiders, the gadflies—found themselves on the popular side of a national issue and visibly closer than ever before to the mainstream of American life.

What was happening on the campus? More than at any other time, probably, in the nation's history, American faith in the wisdom of higher education was tottering. Many parents feared for their sons and daughters in college: what would become of them? Drugs, radicalism, loss of religious faith, changes in sexual mores, estrangement from home, the "conflict of generations"—it was a bitter and unhappy time. What was *happening* on the campuses? Where culture, civility, and learning were supposed to prevail, many Americans now saw barbarism. And many drew the same conclusions about cause-and-effect as did conservative intellectuals. From time to time, William F. Buckley, Jr. was quoted as saying that he would rather be governed by the first 2,000 names in the Boston telephone directory than by the entire Harvard faculty.[41] In the passionate, polarized atmosphere of the late 1960s and early 1970s, many Americans would undoubtedly have agreed.

The crisis in higher education accelerated the emergence of conservatism as a potent intellectual and political force in the 1970s. Indeed, postwar conservatism may be seen in part as a critique of (liberal) intellectuals and of the universities which rose to such enormous size, affluence, and prestige after 1945.[42] Yet it would be facile and inaccurate to describe postwar conservatism as one more outbreak of the anti-intellectualism which some historians believe is embedded in the American mind. For one thing, the complaints we have been examining came from people who were themselves intellectuals, often professors, certainly not uncultured "populists" of the stereotype fashionable in the 1950s. More importantly, while conservatives were severely critical of liberal intellectuals, they did not denigrate intellect as such. In fact, it was precisely because they appreciated the power of the mind that they chastised those who, in their view, misused their talents and their solemn responsibilities. Not ideas, not scholarship, but intellectual irresponsibility and arrogance were the objects of conservative fire. The belief that "ideas, theories, and doctrines...guide human action"[43] was a deep-seated one among all segments of the Right. Such was their tribute to intellect that they held *intellectuals* to the strictest accounting. And their position increasingly coincided with the national mood in the first Nixon administration.

Academe was not alone. Another popular target of the Right was the powerful national news media, particularly the television networks and the Eastern metropolitan, liberal press. Like the hostility to liberal-dominated higher education, antagonism toward the media was not a new feature of conservative commentary. It had surfaced dramatically at the Republican convention in 1964 when former President Eisenhower denounced "sensation-seeking columnists and commentators." It figured in conservative explanations of Senator Goldwater's defeat that year. In 1966 M. Stanton Evans asked why the media "relentlessly publicized" the New Left and ignored the numerically larger Right. (While SDS had perhaps 2,000 members at that point, Young Americans for Freedom had 28,000.) The answer, he suggested, was that the media were liberal, caught up in the assumption that the future had to be liberal and that youthful revolt could only emanate from the Left.[44]

The theme of media bias became increasingly urgent as the conservative intellectual revival gained political momentum. The Right was jubilant when Vice-President Spiro Agnew criticized the television networks in 1969. In *The Conscience of a Majority*, Barry Goldwater devoted two lengthy chapters to a detailed examination of unfair coverage by the media.[45] In columns and even entire books, right-wing spokesmen sought to document instances of "liberal" distortion of the news and of conservatism itself.[46] Particularly welcome to the conservatives was the appearance in 1971 of Edith Efron's *The News Twisters*, a controversial statistical analysis of national television news coverage of the presidential candidates in the autumn of 1968.[47] The results of her study were unmistakable. While Hubert Humphrey and George Wallace received roughly equal or (on balance) somewhat negative coverage by the three networks, Richard Nixon received *ten times* as much unfavorable as favorable coverage. Network news was simply overwhelmingly anti-Nixon. Moreover, according to Efron, the "related issues" of the campaign were presented in a lopsidedly liberal manner. The antiwar viewpoint on Vietnam, for example, was virtually the only opinion presented. While the white middle class was portrayed as racist, authoritarian, and banal, "the kids" were merely labeled "hecklers" and "demonstrators," and the militant Left was seen as "harmless, friendly, idealistic, young, 'restless,' and trustworthy."

To conservatives, Efron's best-selling book—filled with graphs and tabulations—was a devastating and unimpeachable vindication of their decade-old critique.[48] The conservative complaint found an echo in a review by Irving Kristol, editor of *The Public Interest*. Examining Efron's book in *Fortune*, Kristol declared that "ideological bias in television newscasting" was not a "malicious invention" of Vice-President Agnew;

such left-of-center observers as Theodore H. White, Howard K. Smith, and Daniel Patrick Moynihan had all raised the issue before. There *was* self-righteous, liberal bias in the media—"extreme bias"—and it was "an exceedingly serious problem." Efron's book "takes good aim and scores many direct hits."[49]

And so the contours of the national crisis became increasingly obvious to the Right. America itself was not "sick"; liberalism was. Conservatives believed that their war was not with America but with what they considered its ruling elite. It was the liberal universities, along with the fashionable media and some of the foundations and churches, which were the sources of the profound malaise afflicting the nation. The "verbalizers," James Burnham called them. The radicalized liberal establishment. Was there not a syndrome here, conservatives asked? Radical chic, Leonard Bernstein's party for the Black Panthers, the *New York Review of Books*, the lionization of Eldridge Cleaver, Angela Davis, the Woodstock Nation, Charles Reich, *Hair*, Charles Manson, the Chicago Seven, "the kids," drugs, "do your own thing," *Easy Rider*, civil disobedience, pornography, "permissiveness." Conservatives believed that these phenomena were philosophically related.[50]

In the summer of 1972, Robert Nisbet analyzed what he considered a grave challenge: the contemporary "revolt against authority" which "has already reached a higher point than in any other period in the West since perhaps the final years of the Roman Empire."[51] The revolt took many forms: against language, against form in culture, against the very ideas of objectivity and rationality. "I think it would be difficult to find a single decade in the history of Western culture when so much barbarism—so much calculated onslaught against culture and convention in any form, and so much sheer degradation of both culture and the individual—passed into print, into music, into art, and on to the American stage as the decade of the 1960s." The "adversary culture," he continued, became in the 1960s "an all-out nihilism against culture." Linked to the developing threat was "the collapse of academic authority" that had occurred when "the mission of the university was so profoundly changed from that of education to that of serving, saving, healing, reforming, even revolutionizing, the social order." The very intellectuals who were deliberately undermining "traditional authority" were simultaneously seeking power—power attained by crusades and deposited in "a single charismatic person."

> The revolt against authority, the consecration of disorder, waste, and anarchy in traditional society, these are in-

deed icons of all Left intellectuals at the present time.... What
we may now expect, in rising volume and intensity, is the cor-
relative theme...: the appeal for power, which will be called
freedom—for elites, which will be called equality—and for
collectivism, which will be called humanitarianism.[52]

What Nisbet articulated in a respected intellectual journal was increasingly common currency at all levels of the Right, from the bitter
remarks of the rank-and-file about "limousine liberals" and "Porsche
populists" to the speeches of Vice-President Agnew. In 1969 Agnew defined the problem in stinging terms: "A spirit of national masochism pre-
vails, encouraged by an effete corps of impudent snobs who characterize
themselves as intellectuals."[53] It was a mark of the polarization of the
time that what the Left perceived as an outrageous smear and a cynical
political tactic, the Right applauded as the simple truth.

If the challenge from the Left was truly that fundamental, the Right
must make an equally fundamental response. This was the new, more
visceral perception of the late 1960s. In 1971 William F. Buckley, Jr.
reflected that by the end of the decade conservatives had been compelled to defend more basic values. The very survival and virtue of the
United States were now at stake. Because of the alleged disparagement
of American values by the intelligentsia, the Right had been pushed
deeper than opposition to New Deal programs, down to the "bedrock
conservatism" of the majority of the country. Conservatives were now
defending a new "establishment" consisting of those who "were not prepared to give up on America."[54] In 1969 Buckley wrote:

> I see it as the historical role of the new conservatives not
> to abandon their traditional concerns, but to accept the ne-
> cessity of gut affirmations respecting America's way of doing
> things, some of which were traditionally espoused by the lib-
> erals and the progressives, whose contemporary uncertainty
> about them...imposes special burdens on the conservatives.[55]

In the face of left-wing defections, it was the conservatives who must
now defend democracy and due process and work to facilitate upward
mobility. It was a peculiar position for the Right to occupy, Buckley knew.
After all, "the abuse of due process [by government] was rampant, but
how valuable due process becomes, up against Marcusean furies."[56] It
was now up to conservatives—often the critics of twentieth-century
America—to stand *for* it. "At all costs. Against any enemy, foreign or
domestic."[57]

Yet how does one restore order—in the State and in the soul—without succumbing to tyranny? How does one inculcate respect for authority and love of the "permanent things"? One can teach and preach the recovery of "norms," as Russell Kirk did with learning and skill in 1969.[58] But was persuasion enough? Was there time? Could the conservative movement do it?

At least a few were driven to somber reflection.

In the fifteenth anniversary issue of *National Review* in 1970, there appeared a searching article by James Burnham. Much of his analysis was, no doubt, familiar enough to conservatives. Liberalism was "moribund," devoid of self-confidence and creative energy, unable to cope with the "Augean wave" of immorality and the New Left. Liberalism's "secular relativism and permissiveness" were an inadequate "metaphysical foothold." Relying on the insights of Christopher Dawson and T.S. Eliot, Burnham argued that liberalism was parasitically dependent on preliberal authority. "That authority is now dissolving," and liberalism could not stop it.

From here on, however, Burnham ventured into new territory. Could it be that the United States government was itself on the verge of collapse, that the regime itself (in the Aristotelian sense) to which *both* conservatism and liberalism subscribed was "moribund"?

> Can the American type of government under the pluralistic compete—bargain—compromise rules survive the decay of liberalism? How can authority be reasserted in the moral and political mash compounded during the permissive epoch? Can a post-liberal government be authoritative without being authoritarian?... Can an effective post-liberal government be constructed within the framework of the Constitution?

Burnham offered no glib answers, and the tone of his remarks was not optimistic.[59]

Burnham was not the first conservative to ponder the bleak implications of apparent liberal collapse. Late in 1969, Donald Atwell Zoll, then a professor at the University of Saskatchewan, bluntly asked what conservatives should do in the face of the "death wish" of liberalism and its inability to control the revolutionary Left.

> The problem for conservatism, thus, is either to go down with liberalism, clinging to the common values and abiding by the traditional rules of the game or to elect to fight, uninhibited

by the liberal *thanatos* or by liberal proprieties as to method. It is not an easy choice to make.

On the one hand, conservatism was naturally reluctant to employ extreme measures; on the other hand, it was devoted to "the conservation of cultural values." If—as seemed quite possible to Zoll in 1969—the "moderate, pluralistic" American system fell into danger of a successful revolution in the next few years, conservatism's duty in that ultimate crisis would be clear. In order to head off the neo-fascist "primitive Right," it would have to "acknowledge the primacy of social conservation," shed the "anti-authoritarian inhibitions" of liberalism, and use "techniques generally ignored by contemporary Western conservatives.... [A] Bismarck is much to be preferred to a Robespierre."[60]

Zoll's unsettling essay touched off a strenuous debate with Frank Meyer which lasted several months. To Meyer, the chief architect of fusionism, Zoll's analysis was false and dangerous. In his apparent attachment to order for its own sake, and in his rejection of an order designed to achieve individual liberty and civility, Zoll, said Meyer, was actually rejecting the American tradition itself: "the tradition of the Constitution and the Founding Fathers." The alternatives were not anarchy or an "iron state." If American conservatives were to be *conservatives*, they must defend the historic libertarian regime bequeathed to them.[61]

Zoll struck back with equal vigor. Yes, he said, he *was* rejecting Meyer's vaunted "American tradition."

> I, like most conservatives, would be more than willing to reject a very considerable part of the "American tradition," dominated as it is by influences scarcely harmonious with the conservative cast of mind.

Annoyed by Meyer's "stentorian platitudes," Zoll accused Meyer of being a classical liberal who, like all liberals, saw order as but one of many competing values, when actually order was "a pre-theoretical condition upon which all civilized political alternatives rest." Civility and freedom were based upon order, not vice versa. Zoll claimed that he wanted not an "iron state" but a "high Toryism" which would support ontological order and curb the repressive radical Right.[62]

Meyer was still not mollified. For one thing, Zoll had a "contempt for freedom" and did not recognize that the "freedom of the person" was the "condition toward which our order is directed." Western civilization, informed by the Incarnation, held "the person" to be "the ordering principle, the fount and end of social being." American conservatism was "both Tory and Whig."[63] Moreover, Zoll, postulating only the most stark alternatives for the near future, and showing antagonism toward American "liberty under law," ignored the resources currently at hand. Meyer insisted that "no radical extra-Constitutional steps" were required to save the country. The laws and constitutional sanctions were there, *"if they are enforced....* Given the will to defend the Republic, they can be invoked...." Meyer then enumerated a long list of suggestions.[64]

Not everyone was satisfied by this answer to Zoll's specter of Jacobin hordes fighting primitive rightists. Thomas Molnar, a traditionalist Catholic professor at Brooklyn College, criticized Meyer's "incantations": "All Meyer does is to state that such restoration [of law and authority] is possible *if* the Constitution and the laws are enforced. But the whole debate hinges on the question why are they not enforced?" [65] The intensity and duration of the dispute, and the profundity of the questions raised, suggested that this was more than a routine exchange of polemics. Indeed, the Meyer-Zoll debate revealed that, in the dark days of the late 1960s and early 1970s, deep fissures were reappearing in the conservative movement. The whole fusionist synthesis, constructed (or, as Meyer claimed, articulated) in the early 1960s, seemed for a time to be cracking under pressures of unprecedented intensity.

At the center of one estranged camp was L. Brent Bozell and the magazine he edited, *Triumph.* Bozell's journal, established in 1966, was the product of a long feud between liberal and conservative Catholics that was traceable to the publication of William F. Buckley, Jr.'s *God and Man at Yale* in 1951. At that time and ever since, Buckley, as a devotee of free enterprise, had been repeatedly accused by fellow Catholics of "grave variance" with the allegedly anticapitalist social teachings of the Church, particularly the encyclicals *Rerum Novarum* (1891) and *Quadragesimo Anno* (1931).[66] Repeatedly, too, Buckley and other conservatives denied that Christianity and the free market were incompatible.[67] The debate reached new proportions in 1961 when Pope John XXIII promulgated *Mater et Magistra,* an encyclical which appeared to many conservatives to ignore the Communist menace and economic progress of free nations and to lend support to the welfare state. In the July 29, 1961 issue of *National Review,* a brief unsigned editorial criticized the encyclical as "a venture in triviality coming at this particular time in history."[68] In the next issue *National Review* published a soon-to-be-famous quip: *"Mater, sí; Magistra, no."*[69]

Immediately the storm broke. Liberal Catholics, led by *America* and *Commonweal,* accused Buckley and his journal of slanderous, insulting behavior toward the Church. *America* even refused to accept any further advertisements from *National Review*. The dispute about conservatism, the Church, clericalism, and related issues raged for nearly a year; eventually a book was written about it.[70] Out of this dispute came *Triumph*, designed to be the desperately needed conservative Catholic answer to what Bozell considered to be liberal domination of Church periodicals.[71]

It was not long, however, before Bozell—deeply concerned about the need to construct a Christian civilization and impressed by the Christian social order of Spain[72]—pushed far beyond the boundaries of Meyer's conservative consensus, from which, even in 1962, he had dissented. In an essay in *Triumph* early in 1968 he proclaimed that he would never write his promised sequel to *The Warren Revolution*. First, as the failure of Congress to declare war constitutionally in Vietnam and a host of other developments demonstrated, the American Constitution was no longer "an operative charter of government"; it was merely "an occasionally convenient supplement to *Bartlett's Quotations*." Checks and balances, the "constitutional morality," were disintegrating. Nobody—not even the conservatives—really seemed to care. Why? This led to Bozell's second point: the American commonwealth—from the very start—was corrupt and "bound to fail." For it deliberately left God out of the political order and relied instead on a self-interested autonomous republic, based not on God (as Christianity taught) but solely on the people. God was not even mentioned or recognized as sovereign in the Constitution. The Founding Fathers had "built a house in which secular liberalism could live...."[73]

And now, *Triumph* editorialized a few months later, "the liberal Republic is coming down." It chided Frank Meyer for advocating "repriming the wellsprings of the country's origins" in order to recover "national virtue and health." What Meyer could not see was that America always had been and still was liberal. The Founding Fathers "quite legitimately" considered themselves "liberal."

> Now the central tenet of liberalism, yesterday and today, is that man is on his own. His personal life is neither dependent on nor answerable to any external Authority; nor, in its own sphere, is the public order he constructs. It follows, as the necessary antidote to disillusionment and despair, that human life and human society are perfectible by the agency of man....
>
> This...synopsis of liberalism...is also a synopsis of the

American creed. It comes down to a revolt against God.

...To call [like Meyer] for moral authority without explicitly identifying that authority with God is as senseless and as mischievous as to call for the brotherhood of man without acknowledging the Fatherhood of God. Moral authority implies, in the absence of the Author, the authority of man; and that is the beginning and the end of all our troubles.[74]

In the spring of 1969, while most conservatives were still sympathetic to the new Republican administration, Bozell told his former brethren that their movement—antistatist, nationalist, anti-Communist, constitutionalist—was dead, repudiated in every salient feature by Richard Nixon. To be sure, "secular liberalism" was also dead, but no one believed that conservatives had defeated it. In fact, the conservatives were the victims of two grand illusions. First, they still believed that American conservatism and liberalism were essentially different, when in fact they were "branches of the same tree." Despite the unsuccessful attempts to fuse traditionalism and libertarianism, despite the struggle of Russell Kirk and other traditionalists to influence the conservative movement, it remained at heart "nineteenth-century liberal." It was bemused by the idea of secular self-fulfillment, preoccupied with economics and material things, and indifferent to the "public life." This was the second conservative illusion: "that politics—the ordering of the public life—can proceed without reference to God." The public life, Bozell insisted, was supposed "to help open men to Christ," to "provide inducements to virtue and occasions of grace." At present, it was an "enormous obstacle to virtue" and "a fierce agent of Satan."[75] Bozell acknowledged that Christianity was not itself a civilization. But "Christian politics" should nevertheless accept God's sovereignty, "help a man be a Christian," and strive to create a new Christendom.[76] To Bozell, contemporary conservatism was no longer relevant; it was part of the problem. The rise of legalized abortion was yet another revelation of America's moral decadence. In 1970 Bozell and some of his followers, known as the Sons of Thunder, were arrested while demonstrating against abortion at the George Washington University clinic in Washington, D.C.[77] To Bozell, to his close friend Frederick Wilhelmsen, and to the editors of Triumph, America seemed increasingly hostile and doomed.

It was only logical that Triumph would turn its fire on a man who symbolized a fusion it considered untenable: Willmoore Kendall. Kendall had been both a Catholic and a devout believer in the goodness of the American people and their system. In a posthumously published book,

Kendall and George Carey of Georgetown argued that the "basic symbols of the American tradition" included the virtuous people under God searching for "transcendent Truth."[78] In an article in 1970, Michael Lawrence, an editor of *Triumph*, accepted Kendall's portrayal of the American tradition. But was this tradition "satisfactory" to a Christian? Lawrence answered forcefully that it was not. For on Kendall's own showing, a central part of the American "myth" was the "uniquely American" creation of a "wedge" between the political and religious realms, between government and society. This separation, said Lawrence, was "a knife in the heart of the Christian tradition." Reflecting the thinking of Bozell, he declared:

> The purpose of politics, then, is to assist man in his efforts to be virtuous. This is to be accomplished, concretely, in large part by the infusion of Christianity into the world's political and social institutions so that these institutions become intrinsically and organically Christian....
>
> ...In this light the American "wedge" can be seen as an explicit and official abandonment of that ideal....
>
> ...[T]he wedge...is also an open declaration that government—that most crucial of human institutions, the one explicitly invested with the agency of God's authority—is *not* to be infused with Christianity, not to be made a vehicle of divine grace. There could be no more direct a repudiation of the supreme symbol of the Christian political tradition.

What, then, was to be done? We must start over. We must "make a new compact" with ourselves and with God to spread the "grace of God" in this "New World."[79]

While mainstream conservatism was coming under attack from a few militant Catholic traditionalists, it confronted as well a revolt on another front: the radical libertarian anarchists. These defectors were led principally by the Misesian economist Murray Rothbard and by Karl Hess, Barry Goldwater's principal speechwriter in 1964 and an avowed "left-wing anarchist" four years later.[80] Long a critic of the anti-Communist conservatives at *National Review*,[81] Rothbard published in 1968 his "confessions" in the New Left journal *Ramparts*. In the 1940s and early 1950s, he asserted, the American Right had been libertarian and isolationist, fervently opposed to conscription, militarism, President Truman's "imperialist aggression" in Korea, and statism at home. Its heroes had been men like Jefferson, Paine, Thoreau, Herbert Spencer, Lysander Spooner, Benjamin R. Tucker, H.L. Mencken, Albert Jay Nock, and Frank

Chodorov. But then a terrible change had occurred. With the rise of McCarthyism and *National Review*, the Old Right succumbed to "the blight of anti-Communism." A fiery band of ex-Communists, Catholic zealots (such as Bozell and Kendall), and devotees of "foul European conservatism" seized the leadership of the Right. Rothbard accused the *National Review* circle of wishing to destroy the Soviet Union in a nuclear war and of abandoning its vestiges of libertarianism as it attained political respectability. "Something *has* gone wrong," he argued: "the right wing has been captured by elitists and devotees of the European conservative ideals of order and militarism, by witch hunters and global crusaders, by statists who wish to coerce 'morality' and suppress 'sedition.'"[82]

By the early 1970s, radical libertarianism was receiving more than casual attention, and Rothbard was writing hopefully of "a burgeoning split" on the Right.[83] In the *New York Times*,[84] in Rothbard's *Libertarian Forum*, and in books like Jerome Tuccille's manifesto *Radical Libertarianism*,[85] the anarcho-capitalists were at least being heard. A tumultuous clash at the Young Americans for Freedom (YAF) convention in 1969 precipitated a secession by the militant libertarians and the establishment of the Society for Individual Liberty (SIL) shortly thereafter.[86] Soon an aggressive new company, Libertarian Enterprises, was selling a huge array of libertarian literature.[87] By 1972 the movement had attained enough of a following to organize a Libertarian Party with a presidential candidate: John Hospers, chairman of the philosophy department at the University of Southern California.[88]

For all the outpouring of tracts and treatises, the rebellion's message was simple and direct: pure laissez-faire, "radical decentralization" (Tuccille's phrase), voluntarism, anarchy.

> The libertarian doctrine begins, not with the conservative community or state but with the individual. Every individual as an independent acting entity possesses the absolute right of "self-ownership": that is, to own his or her person without molestation by others.... The libertarian holds that the state is permanent aggression and disorder....[89]

In their unyielding hostility to government coercion, the paradigmatic libertarians sometimes offered truly startling proposals. Tuccille, for example, argued that government should not be allowed to monopolize defense: let individuals, groups, even nations contract in the free market with private companies that would compete to provide defense for their customers.[90] Some argued that the highways should be privately owned and that the police function should be handled by private enterprise.

Other ideas were more conventional: abolish the draft, antiabortion laws, drug laws. Underlying these suggestions, of course, was a natural rights philosophy so pure that it would have astounded even Willmoore Kendall, the scourge of all who spoke of natural rights.

This purity was probably one source of the movement's appeal to the young. For radical libertarianism (or anarchism, or radical capitalism—the names seemed interchangeable) drew most of its support not from established right-wing intellectuals but from college students. On the campuses the phenomenon often had cultic dimensions—for example, the eager following acquired by Ayn Rand and by the science fiction novelist Robert Heinlein,[91] and the proliferation of buttons, sweatshirts, and posters, some having the words "laissez-faire" superimposed on a red clenched fist. The animus of the anarcho-capitalists was apparent in their slogans (they had many slogans): Anarchy forever! Sock it to the State! MYOB (Mind Your Own Business)! Leave us alone! I am an enemy of the State! Taxation is theft! Caution: military service may be hazardous to your health. Clearly Rothbard and his followers were appealing to the antiestablishment impulses so widely shared by young Americans in the late 1960s. Indeed, radical libertarianism was not so much a reaction to the ferment of those years as a product of it. "This is the beauty of anarcho-libertarianism," said Tuccille: "utter and complete toleration for any and all styles of life so long as they are voluntary and nonaggressive in nature."[92]

Above all, the phenomenon was a consequence of the Vietnam war and the decline of cold war anti-Communism. It was the conflict in Asia which catapulted Karl Hess out of the conservative movement.

> Conservatives like me had spent our lives arguing against Federal power—with one exception. We trusted Washington with enormous powers to fight global Communism. We were wrong—as Taft foresaw when he opposed NATO.... Vietnam should remind all conservatives that whenever you put your faith in big government for *any* reason, sooner or later you wind up as an apologist for mass murder.[93]

Even before Vietnam, Murray Rothbard, influenced by the revisionist historian D. F. Fleming, had concluded that "the United States was solely at fault in the Cold War, and that Russia was the aggrieved party."[94] As Rothbard's friend Leonard Liggio, a revisionist historian at City College, explained:

> Buckley supports the big state because he's concerned mainly

with anti-communism. He sees the Christian West besieged
by communism and colored infidels. We saw the need for
détente.[95]

Not surprisingly, opposition to the draft (and the war) was a principal
feature of the radical libertarian platform; the issue of resistance to the
draft helped to split YAF in 1969.[96]

The emergence of this challenge to the conservative establishment
underscored the importance of anti-Communism as the cement of the
postwar conservative intellectual movement. When this unifying force
lost some of its appeal, one of the constituent elements of the grand
coalition began—at least on the fringes—to slip out of orbit. Barry
Goldwater minus anti-Communism became the anarchist Karl Hess.[97]
More than one SDS member in the late 1960s had supported Goldwater
in 1964. To state the point another way: anti-Communism had never
convinced Rothbard. But only when an arduous new war occurred, at a
time when a new generation of young people had emerged for whom the
cold war was less and less an immediate reality—only then could radical
libertarianism arise.

To these flank assaults from the ultratraditionalists and
ultralibertarians the conservative center responded with vigor. Most leading right-wing intellectuals rejected L. Brent Bozell's neo-Hartzian argument that American had always been secular-liberal. William F. Buckley,
Jr. pointed out that the Constitution, so condemned by Bozell, contained
a Bill of Rights which John Courtney Murray had shown to be "an essentially Christian idea," "the product of Christian history."[98] Nor did most
conservatives seem willing to give up hope for the country. Jeffrey Hart
pointed to hopeful developments in the early Nixon administration, while
National Review's editorial board declared:

> We have got, in America, what we have got. It is not what we
> would have, but neither is it as bad as what we might have. To
> dismiss even contemporary America as one vast plot against
> the survival of our eternal souls is Manichean and boring.[99]

Many conservatives were especially alarmed by the theocratic and
"angelistic" implications of Bozell's arguments.[100] Neil McCaffrey, the
Catholic president of the Conservative Book Club, warned Bozell, "His
Kingdom is not of this world."[101] Gerhart Niemeyer cautioned, "The salvation of society...is not in our power."[102] When Bozell and a band of
followers, wearing the red berets of Spanish Carlists and shouting "Viva
Christo Rey!", protested against abortion in 1970, *National Review* criti-

cized their "exotic" and violent confrontation with the police.[103] In *Cruising Speed* William F. Buckley, Jr. admitted that he had become "estranged" from his brother-in-law; *Triumph* had "elided now into an organ of militant anti-Americanism...."[104]

Nor were leading conservatives any less critical of the anarchist challenge. They denied that anti-Communism was an outmoded, immoral, statist sellout. As James Burnham and others argued week after week, the world was not a serene place; Communism was not benign and was not dead. Were it not for America's "statist" containment of "aggressive powers" in the last few decades, Buckley said pointedly, Rothbard would be living in a "zoo."[105] The trouble with the Rothbards and the Hesses, said Frank Meyer (that ever-alert scenter of heresy), was that they were "ideologues" and "libertines":

> The libertine impulse that masquerades as libertarianism ...disregards all moral responsibility, ranges itself against the minimum needs of social order, and raises the freedom of the individual...to the status of an absolute end.

But it was *not* an "absolute end"; it was, to Meyer, the highest *political* end. What, after all, were people, once freed from governmental coercion, supposed to *do* with their freedom? "The libertine answers that they should do what they want." That reply, said Meyer, "ignores the hard facts of history...civilization is a fragile growth, constantly menaced by the dark forces that suck man back towards his brutal beginnings."[106] Similarly, Buckley warned that "the absolutization of freedom" was "the oldest and most tempting heresy," and laughed at some of Rothbard's "amiable lunacies":[107]

> My all-time favorite is Mr. Rothbard's proposal that the lighthouses that throw out their welcome to storm-tossed ships should be privately owned, the lighthouse keeper zooming out to collect a dollar from any ship which can be proved to have treated itself to a bearing drawn from the private stock of the owner's electricity.[108]

More "nauseating" to Buckley was Karl Hess's statement "that the Soviet Union is slightly to be preferred to the United States, because the Soviet Union executed Beria, and we still have J. Edgar Hoover."[109] Buckley and other conservatives shared much of the economic analysis of the radical libertarians; both sides respected such scholars as Hayek, Hazlitt, and Mises.[110] Many conservatives agreed with Rothbard's opposition to the military draft. But the overlap was limited. The conservative accepted the State along with a *"presumption"* against its expansion, said Buckley.[111] But a doctrinaire application of the capitalist paradigm to every sphere—no.

What was the significance of these polemics and well-publicized defections from the conservative mainstream? Intellectually, of course, they revealed that the fusionist synthesis—so central to the conservative revival—was still, after years of trial, under stress. They highlighted the diverse tendencies which comprised the movement and demonstrated how easy it was—intellectually—to stray from the fold. And yet, for all the sound and fury and discussion of a "burgeoning split," one durable fact stood out: the conservative center was not disintegrating in practical terms. The dissenters remained dissenters; the extremes remained the extremes—not the center. Aside from Frederick Wilhelmsen and some lesser-known figures, few conservative intellectuals appeared to be moving in the militant direction of Bozell. While many Catholic conservatives, such as Jeffrey Hart and Russell Kirk, contributed on occasion to *Triumph*, they obviously did not share its total ethos.[112] Nor did the Rothbard-Hospers group appear to be attracting or creating leaders of the national influence and stature of a Buckley, Meyer, or Milton Friedman.[113] At the YAF convention of 1969, the radical libertarians had, after all, been a distinct minority. While the broad antistatist impulse was very strong on the Right, the radical libertarian form of this impulse was not.

Times, of course, could change; the possibilities were there. Years before, Whittaker Chambers had concluded that the cause of the West was hopeless. If in the 1970s a spectacular national disaster occurred or the pace of moral disintegration accelerated, if America seemed to succumb to the revolutionary Left, the perspective of Bozell might well find new adherents. If the revolt against the state gained new momentum, if the vaunted "greening" of America and the "do your own thing" life-style spread, if American pluralism evolved into polarized sectarianism, then the anarchist tendency might flourish more than ever. But these were as yet only possibilities, not history. At the beginning of the 1970s, most conservative intellectuals seemed content to pursue what appeared to be the commonsense middle course, veering away from paradigmatic purity. Such an approach was not, perhaps, philosophically tidy; it would not please those whom they branded ideologues. But then, conservatism was not supposed to be an ideology, anyway.

And when all the theoretical arguments about principle were thoroughly aired, conservatives were not tempted by their critics for two additional reasons: a momentous rightward shift of many influential liberals, and the emergence at last of conservatism as a credible competitor for national leadership.

ELEVEN

Can the Vital Center Hold?

In 1966 Jeffrey Hart, a young conservative scholar and Dartmouth College professor, published *The American Dissent*, a survey of the ideas of the *National Review* circle. Toward the close of the book he ventured a prediction about the future of American liberalism:

> ...under the pressure of the world revolution, as contradictions and evasions are exposed to an ever greater extent, liberalism most certainly will undergo fragmentation. Many liberals will move to the Left, jettisoning their remaining Western cultural attachments. Others, just as inevitably, will move to the Right, becoming more conservative.[1]

Far more than he probably ever anticipated, Hart proved to be a prophet. For during the next decade, conservatives watched with interest as increasing numbers of prominent liberal scholars began to utter conservative thoughts.

One of the earliest signs of the new posture was an address by the liberal sociologist Daniel Patrick Moynihan before the national board of Americans for Democratic Action (ADA) in September 1967. In that dismal autumn, as war raged in Asia and riotous demonstrations erupted at home, Moynihan implored his fellow liberals—who were, after all, in power in the United States—to learn some unusual lessons:

> 1. Liberals must see more clearly that their essential interest is in the stability of the social order; and given the present threats to that stability, they must seek out and make much more effective alliances with political conservatives who share their interest....

2. Liberals must divest themselves of the notion that the nation—and especially the cities of the nation—can be run from agencies in Washington.

Finally, Moynihan warned liberals to stop trying to excuse everything, "however outrageous," done by blacks. A wave of terrorism was now inevitable; nothing could be done to appease black or white militants. Among Moynihan's proposals for the crisis, one was especially striking: "informed conservatives" were needed to preserve order. Moynihan called forthrightly for "the politics of stability."[2]

The Harvard sociologist was not in the vanguard for long. Increasingly in these troubled years, many liberals rediscovered the virtues of order, tradition, and firm standards. In 1971, for instance, in an article significantly entitled "The Limits of Social Policy," Moynihan's colleague Nathan Glazer remarked that "the breakdown of traditional modes of behavior is the chief cause of our social problems" and that "some important part of the solution to our social problems lies in...traditional restraints."[3] In the same year, Irving Kristol, a self-styled "conservative liberal,"[4] wrote for the *New York Times Magazine* an article entitled "Pornography, Obscenity, and the Case for Censorship," in which he explicitly acknowledged the influence of the conservative Straussian scholar Walter Berns.[5]

Above all, this new awareness of conservative values must be attributed to the fiery, polarizing effects of the student revolt in the universities in the late 1960s and early 1970s. As campus after campus exploded in wild confrontations and riots, the need for order, restraint, and standards of excellence seemed ever more apparent to at least a segment of the academic community. The universities were under radical *attack*. As Hart had predicted, professors were forced to choose; some suddenly found themselves in a "conservative" situation. This is not to say, of course, that the defense of elementary order, academic freedom, professional standards, an open university, and sheer human civility were in any sense the exclusive concern of conservatives. Nevertheless, the very act of protecting these values—the *need* to do so—had a profoundly "conservatizing" effect on many liberal intellectuals. This time the enemy was on the Left.

In no one was this process more readily discernible than in Nathan Glazer, a veteran of uprisings at Berkeley and Harvard. "How," he asked, "does a radical, a mild radical, it is true, but still one who felt closer to radical than to liberal writers and politicians in the late 1950s, end up a conservative, a mild conservative, but still closer to those who call themselves conservative than to those who call themselves liberal in early 1970?"[6] One principal answer, he explained in a series of brilliant essays, was the developing student revolt of the 1960s. Elsewhere, too, the trend was evident—for example, in the University Center for Rational Alternatives, founded in 1969 by Sidney Hook, Oscar Handlin, Lewis Feuer, and a number of other professors anxious to fend off the extremists. While liberal sponsorship of UCRA was clear, especially interesting was the participation of several conservative scholars, including Milton Friedman, Will Herberg, Leo Strauss, and Ernest van den Haag.[7] Here was something new: a *coalition* of conservatives and moderate liberals against the common radical foe. Frank Meyer called Hook's efforts "exemplary."[8]

Meanwhile certain trends in foreign affairs were simultaneously exerting a rightward influence on some liberals. As the Vietnam war divided the Left and undermined cold war liberal internationalism,[9] at least a few anti-Communist liberals—alienated from their brethren—unexpectedly found sympathetic listeners on the Right. In 1969 Eugene V. Rostow, once a Johnson administration official, criticized some "end-the-war" proposals in *National Review*;[10] a year later a commentary on the war by his brother Walt was published in *Human Events*.[11] Toward the end of his life the urbane, acerbic Dean Acheson—once the *bête noire* of many conservatives—was receiving favorable book reviews and approving commentary from *National Review*.[12] Of particular interest was John Roche—a political scientist at Brandeis, former chairman of the ADA, and adviser to President Johnson. Roche insisted that his basic world outlook had not changed. He was a John F. Kennedy liberal internationalist in 1961, and he remained one ten years later. Yet (or was it therefore?) in the years after 1968, Roche emerged in his newspaper column as a caustic opponent of student activism and a frequent supporter of President Nixon's foreign policies. On one occasion *National Review* reprinted a critique by Roche of the opponents of Vice-President Agnew.[13] From time to time, also, conservatives found themselves collaborating loosely with cold war liberals on such matters as support for antiballistic missile development, funding for the Voice of America, and opposition to drastic reduction of the American military presence in Europe.

In part, this tendency toward convergence reflected a subtle change in the conservative foreign policy of the early 1970s. While still vigilant about Communism and distressed by its military buildup and expansionist tendencies (as conservatives saw them), the Right no longer talked very often or very loudly about victory, as many of its spokesmen had in the 1950s and early 1960s. There was little serious discussion of "liberation" or "rollback" any more.[14] Perhaps in this quiet way the defeat of Goldwater, the Vietnam war, and the foreign policy initiatives of President Nixon made their imprint on the conservative movement. But as this tacit shift occurred, conservative foreign policy more and more came to resemble the old liberal policy of containment! One conservative duly noted that "Mr. Acheson's internationalism (Mr. Truman's internationalism for that matter) is in many ways closer to today's conservative position than to the left-wing isolationism of Eugene McCarthy and his supporters."[15] And so, on foreign policy as on the campus issue, many conservatives found themselves defending what Arthur Schlesinger, Jr. had once called the "vital center." Meanwhile many liberals—outraged by the Vietnam war, influenced by "New Left" cold war revisionist historiography, and anxious to reorder national priorities—appeared (at least to their critics) to be evolving toward neo-isolationism. In these circumstances, an alliance of conservative and liberal *internationalists* was possible, in the face of the anti-internationalist enemy to the Left.

The contours of this alliance developed rapidly in 1972 with the presidential campaign of Senator George McGovern. Faced with a man who admired Henry Wallace, such long-time cold war liberals as Irving Kristol and Oscar Handlin found themselves supporting President Nixon for reelection.[16] George Meany, one of the staunchest "cold warriors" in the labor movement, vehemently criticized McGovern's views on foreign affairs, while John Roche accused McGovern of "repudiation of the liberal tradition of the past quarter of a century": the South Dakota senator was "a throwback to the liberal isolationists of the 1930's." "I, at least," said Roche, "am proud of the liberal foreign policy formulated by Harry Truman and Dean Acheson."[17]

Even more harsh was the old social-democratic warhorse, Sidney Hook, who denounced McGovern in the Socialist Party newspaper *New America* in the fall of 1972. His "open letter" described McGovern's foreign policy views as "appeasement" based on the "illusions" of Henry Wallace in 1948:

> If it be true that the Kremlin now seeks a *détente*, it is in virtue of the measures America took to contain Communist aggression—measures you have condemned.... I doubt whether you are really aware of what a Communist system is.... You condemn the unintentional bombing of civilians by the U.S., but have not condemned the deliberate and system-

atic terror practiced by the other side [in Vietnam]....
Is there any wonder then that to many liberals and democrats your foreign policy smells of "the spirit of Munich"...?

Hook was also "appalled" at McGovern's "ill-informed and illiberal attitudes toward the universities...." McGovern, he charged, had "encouraged, perhaps unwittingly, non-violent disruption of classes and labora-
tories." Consequently, for the first time in his life, Hook decided to vote
Republican for president. Richard Nixon was the "lesser evil."[18]

The student issue and foreign policy were not the only sources of
what might be called right-wing liberalism. Of all the factors operating in
the late 1960s to produce it, perhaps the most encouraging one for conservatives was the increasing evidence of liberal disillusionment with
government and with conventional liberal approaches to social reform.
Throughout the decade the conservative "revolt against the state" had
acquired new point and plausibility as it examined, pragmatically, the
record of liberal programs. Now many liberals themselves were joining
in. In 1967 Richard Goodwin, an adviser to Presidents Kennedy and
Johnson, lamented the enormous growth of federal power in recent decades and urgently called for decentralization to curb the alarming spread
of individual powerlessness and frustration.[19] In his speech to the ADA
that same year, Moynihan criticized not only the belief that the country
could be governed from Washington but also the conventional wisdom
that held "the national government and national politics" to be "the primary sources of liberal social innovation."[20] On another occasion—an
essay for the *Republican Papers* (Moynihan's appearance there was itself
noteworthy)—the Harvard social scientist commented: "Somehow liberals have been unable to acquire from life what conservatives seem to be
endowed with at birth, namely, a healthy skepticism of the powers of
government agencies to do good."[21]

This was only the beginning. By the end of the decade, expressions
of disenchantment with what Michael Oakeshott called "rationalism in
politics" seemed almost commonplace. In 1970 Peter Schrag wrote in
dismay:

> It is ten years later, and the great dream has come to an end.
> We thought we had solutions to everything—poverty, racism,
> injustice, ignorance; it was supposed to be only a matter of
> time, of money, of proper programs, of massive assaults.... it
> is now clear that the confidence is gone, that many of the
> things we *knew* no longer seem sure or even probable.[22]

In terms often reminiscent of Friedrich Hayek's *The Constitution of Liberty*, liberal social scientists and other observers confessed humility and lack of expertise. "We are facing a problem we do not fully understand and certainly do not know how to solve," Moynihan observed.[23] In *Maximum Feasible Misunderstanding*, he analyzed the numbing failure of the community action program of the War on Poverty; radical activists, liberal reformers, and bureaucrats did not come off particularly well. In essence,

> A program was launched that was not understood, and *not explained, and this brought about social losses that need not have occurred....* The government did not know what it was doing. It had a theory. Or, rather, a set of theories. Nothing more.[24]

Moynihan chided his fellow liberals, who "underestimate difficulties, overpromise results, and avoid any evidence of incompatibility and conflict...."[25] He did not advocate "immobilism" or even caution but "great care."[26] A few years later, Harry Schwartz in the *New York Times* publicized a "law" discovered by Jay W. Forrester of MIT: "...in complicated situations efforts to improve things often tend to make them worse, sometimes much worse, on occasion calamitous."[27] Social reform was not easy to achieve.

Similarly, the well-known management consultant Peter Drucker argued in 1969 that the actual record of government since the 1930s was "dismal."[28] In welfare, agriculture, the urban crisis, and other areas, its policies were failures:

> During the past three decades, federal payments to the big cities have increased almost a hundredfold for all kinds of programs. But results from the incredible dollar flood into the cities are singularly unimpressive. What is impressive is the administrative incompetence. We now have ten times as many government agencies concerned with city problems as we had in 1939.[29]

Government today was big but not strong; in recent times it had been able to do only two things well: "wage war" and "inflate the currency."[30] Government simply was not a "doer," Drucker insisted. His analysis of "the sickness of government" won the enthusiastic attention of William F. Buckley, Jr.[31]

By 1972 scholarly disillusionment extended to one of the great liberal commitments of the day: school busing to achieve racial balance.

Ever since the celebrated Coleman Report in 1966, liberal faith in the school environment as a means of improving performance of children from disadvantaged backgrounds had been faltering.[32] Now Nathan Glazer, in a long article in *Commentary*, asked, "Is Busing Necessary?" No, he concluded, and the journal's editor, Norman Podhoretz, agreed with him.[33] A major new study of the problem by David Armor of Harvard, appearing in the Summer 1972 issue of *The Public Interest*, seemed to confirm this growing skepticism: case studies showed that nearly every goal of the proponents of busing had not been achieved. Massive compulsory busing, Armor concluded, could not presently be justified.[34]

As if to sum up the trend, in May 1972 the Brookings Institution released a study of national priorities; the next day Jack Rosenthal interpreted the verdict in the *New York Times*:

> The glory days of the Great Society...are over.... [A group of Brookings Institution economists] concludes[s] that the multiplication of dollars and programs brought not solutions...but a multiplication of dilemmas. And now the dilemmas threaten to become paralyzing.
> In the end, they argue, the critical lack has not been money. How could it be when the Federal social spending has soared from \$30-billion to \$110-billion in ten years...?
> The underlying shortage...has been knowledge.[35]

A few months later Alan Otten of the *Wall Street Journal* reported a "dearth of creative new ideas coming from the entire liberal intellectual community." So many liberal "solutions" had "clearly failed" or were encountering "increasing criticism." "For the past several decades, the traditional liberal medicine for social ills has been large doses of federal funds.... Now, in the face of increasing evidence, most liberals realize their past panaceas were too simplistic." The War on Poverty, public housing, aid to education, manpower training—the list of disaster areas was growing.[36]

At the center of this wave of scholarly disillusionment was a journal with a small circulation but a significant readership among the opinion molders and governing classes of America. Founded in 1965 as a venture in "revisionist liberalism," *The Public Interest*, edited by Irving Kristol and sociologist Daniel Bell, soon developed themes and promulgated findings that did not sustain routine liberal assumptions.[37] On pornography, for instance: when the journal published in 1971 an article by Walter Berns on "the case for censorship," Kristol observed that this was "a topic we would not have dealt with two or three years ago."[38] Or reapportionment, a source of much optimism among reformers in the early 1960s: surveying the evidence, *The Public Interest* concluded that "most of the great expectations hanging upon reapportionment are going to be dashed."[39] Or the difficulty of reform and the dangers of bureaucratization—two of the most persistent themes of the journal's articles. (The "discovery" of bureaucracy was surely one of the key elements in the liberal disillusionment.[40]) Or the turmoil in the universities and the "twilight of authority."[41] On occasion, *The Public Interest* could be stinging in its criticism of liberal leaders. In 1969 Kristol and Paul Weaver, a Harvard political scientist, castigated the allegedly smug UESSE (Upper East Side and Suburban Elite) of New York City. These "cosmopolitan parochials," including an apocalypse-oriented mass media, were incredibly ignorant of the true nature of the city which they arrogantly presumed to guide.[42]

Another increasingly noteworthy forum for disillusioned liberals was *Commentary*, edited by Norman Podhoretz. Reacting to the catastrophic 1967 New York City teacher's strike (which pitted blacks against Jews), the demands on some campuses for racial quotas (which offended many Jews), and alleged New Left anti-Semitism and hostility to Israel, many American Jews began to move to the right at the end of the 1960s. One manifestation of this trend was the evolving position of Podhoretz, whose journal was seen by many observers as a rival to the radical *New York Review of Books*.[43] By 1971 and 1972 virtually every issue of *Commentary* crackled with at least one right-wing liberal analysis of social issues—articles with significant tiles like "The Limits of Social Policy," "Is Busing Necessary?", "Liberty and the Liberals," "Growth and Its Enemies," and "Liberalism vs. Liberal Education." Articles criticizing the allegedly radical bias of the American Civil Liberties Union and the efforts of the Department of Health, Education, and Welfare to compel universities to hire equal numbers of women or lose federal aid. Articles attacking the "population controllers" and the proponents of "apocalyptic thinking."[44]

By 1972 the increasing conservatism of American Jews, including some Jewish intellectuals, was a topic of interest to pundits, pollsters, and politicians. Reflecting on this trend, Irving Kristol argued that Jews had not, all by themselves, moved to the Right. Rather, the Left had moved further left—"probably the crucial political development of the past fifteen years." Unlike the Old Left, which had been "humanistic," the New Left preached "utter contempt for liberal values." Precisely because Jews remained committed to these liberal values, they were now of necessity becoming "conservative." Kristol concluded with an intriguing speculation: Jews might give American conservatism "an intellectual vigor and cultural buoyancy it has sadly lacked until now."[45]

The rise of chastened liberalism (especially among social scientists) was paralleled by mounting interest in conservative approaches to reform. In 1966, for example, the Harvard sociologist Christopher Jencks, openly citing Milton Friedman, endorsed the voucher plan concept for the schools; Friedman quickly hailed his new ally.[46] In 1969 Alan Altshuler, a political scientist at M.I.T., declared:

> Men of the left have been appropriating principles of the right (or what used to be such) on a wholesale basis in recent years. That is to say, men devoted to egalitarian ends have come increasingly to appreciate the "conservative" critique of government—at least of government by direct control, as opposed to government by the structuring of market incentives and cash transfers—as an instrument of social policy.

The "classic" example of this trend, said Altshuler, was the popularity of Friedman's negative income tax proposal.[47] There were others. In 1970 the press publicized a memorandum in which Daniel Moynihan, then an adviser to President Nixon, urged a period of "benign neglect" of the race problem;[48] many well-known liberals were aghast.[49] Their anger only increased when, almost simultaneously, there appeared a book that seemed to encapsulate the new social science: Edward Banfield's *The Unheavenly City*.

If ever there was an iconoclastic book, this was it. One observer labeled it "a political scientist's version of Milton Friedman's *Capitalism and Freedom*."[50] Indeed, Banfield—yet another Harvard social scientist—was a conservative, a close friend of Friedman (who read the manuscript before publication), and a former adviser to President Nixon.[51] Banfield systematically challenged a host of prevailing assumptions. It was not true, for instance, that all urban problems were becoming worse, or that a disastrous crisis was impending:

> The plain fact is that the overwhelming majority of city dwellers live more comfortably and conveniently than ever before ....There is still much poverty and much racial discrimination. But there is less of both than ever before.[52]

(Of course, he added, constant *talk* about crisis, coupled with soaring expectations, might produce a crisis of a different sort.) It was not true (to take another example) that racial prejudice was the principal obstacle to black advancement: "...the situation of most Negroes would not be fundamentally different even if there were no racial prejudice at all...."[53] Central to Banfield's analysis was the contention that there existed a pathological, disoriented, present-minded "lower class" which was simply not amenable to ordinary reforms and was not about to disappear. Again and again, Banfield stressed that urban problems were not going to go away, that government especially could not expect to improve matters. (It had often made them worse.) "The import of what has been said in this book is that...there are very few problems that can be solved...."[54]

This did not mean that he counseled despair and indifference. Toward the end he offered twelve proposals of his own. Among them: "Avoid rhetoric tending to raise expectations to unreasonable and unrealizable levels...." Repeal the minimum wage laws and legislation which protects monopolistic powers of labor unions. Lower the school-leaving age to fourteen. Abandon the "elastic" concept of "relative deprivation" as a measure of poverty. Give birth-control advice to the "incompetent poor." Pay "problem families" to send their children to nurseries where they can be introduced into "normal culture." "Confine and treat drug addicts" and punish rioters severely.[55] Banfield candidly acknowledged that his ideas stood little chance of acceptance. Government was more likely to *increase* expectations, to exaggerate the importance of "white racism," and to increase the minimum wage, while powerful "veto groups" (civil rights activists, labor unions, teachers, social workers) would oppose his suggestions.[56] Above all, Banfield believed that he would fail because he was challenging a deep-seated, powerful, and dangerous American ethos: the ethos of upper-middle-class, guilt-ridden, activist liberal reform— the politics of righteous indignation. Among the causes, no doubt, for the outrage that greeted Banfield's book were passages like this one:

> The frightening fact is that large numbers of persons are being rapidly assimilated to the upper classes and are coming to have incomes—time as well as money—that permit them to indulge their taste for "service" and doing good in political action.... Doing good is becoming—has already become—a growth industry, like the other forms of mass entertainment, while righteous indignation and uncompromising allegiance to principle are becoming *the* motives of political commitment.[57]

No conservative could complain that Banfield's book was ignored. Widely, vehemently, sometimes viciously criticized,[58] *The Unheavenly*

City rapidly achieved a *succès de scandale*; by 1972 it had sold over 100,000 copies. [59] One conservative reviewer noted that the book was circulated in the White House before the publication date.[60] Not surprisingly, conservatives greeted the book with delight. It was "a genuine classic and work of genius," Jeffrey Hart declared;[61] Robert Nisbet was equally laudatory.[62] Left and Right seemed to agree that Banfield had prepared a formidable indictment of current orthodoxy.[63] Of special interest in the present context was Irving Kristol's evaluation of *The Unheavenly City* as "easily the most enlightening book that has been written about the 'urban crisis' in the U.S."[64] But perhaps Kristol's welcome of the conservative scholar's book should not surprise us. For Banfield in 1970 was *already* part of a widening circle that included Kristol, Glazer, Moynihan, James Q. Wilson, and other contributors to *The Public Interest*.[65] Once more the ideological lines were blurring, as dissenting professors converged in scholarly opposition to the "enemy" on the Left.

At this point a caveat may be in order. The phenomenon of right-wing liberalism should not be equated with orthodox *National Review* conservatism. Some of the people discussed here continued to regard themselves as liberals,[66] and Moynihan's ideas on welfare (reflected in President Nixon's Family Assistance Plan) were definitely not popular with many conservatives. Nevertheless, as the phenomenon intensified, there were more and more indications that a momentous intellectual realignment was taking place in the early 1970s. In 1972 James Burnham suggested that while disillusioned liberalism was still in a "transitional state," it was "bound to develop further into a more integral outlook"—although not necessarily into conventional conservatism, much of which was itself obsolescent.[67] If Burnham was correct, it would not be the first time in the history of the conservative intellectual movement that refugees from the Left had rejuvenated the Right; one thinks of the remarkable number of former Communists who shaped the post-1945 conservative revival. This latest tendency, of course, was in part a reaction against radicalism rather than a revolt from within liberalism. But the thrust—Left to Right—was the same.

Signs of a new infusion increased within the conservative camp. There was the odyssey of the new "mild conservative," Nathan Glazer. In 1955 he had contributed to Daniel Bell's critical collection of essays *The New American Right*. In the summer of 1972, for the first time, his work appeared within the covers of *National Review*.[68] What 'had happened? Principally, of course, the student revolt and other events of the 1960s.[69]

But also, to some extent, the personal example of men like Kristol, Banfield, and a Communist-turned-conservative, Will Herberg.[70] If men like these had conservative ideas or leanings, surely one must take conservatism seriously. To a certain degree, Glazer's friendship with Frank Meyer affected him, too. Meyer, who introduced Glazer to William F. Buckley, Jr., had "played a role" in Glazer's avoidance of "psychologizing" since his piece for Daniel Bell's anthology in 1955. Back in the days of Senator McCarthy, Glazer had thought Buckley's defense of the senator "absolutely outrageous" and had considered *McCarthy and His Enemies* a "terrible" book. By 1972, however, both (Old) Left and Right were mellowing. Glazer now regarded Buckley's columns as "consistently sensible" and "intelligent."[71]

Glazer was not an anomaly. Surely it was no coincidence that in 1972 alone, Glazer, Sidney Hook, Lewis Feuer, and Seymour Martin Lipset appeared in *National Review*.[72] What did these men have in common? None had been previously known as a conservative. All were Jewish. Three (Glazer, Feuer, and Lipset) had been at Berkeley (birthplace of the student revolution) early in the 1960s. All had written extensively on student unrest.[73] Perhaps most interesting was the fact that all had at one time been "radical" in the social-democratic sense. Just as ex-Stalinists and ex-Trotskyists were prominent in early postwar conservatism, so (Glazer observed) were old-time *anti*-Communist Socialists conspicuous in the new antiradical upsurge.[74]

Another product of (and contributor to) the new alignment was *The Alternative*. Founded in 1967 by conservative students at Indiana University, this sprightly monthly magazine, edited by R. Emmett Tyrell, Jr., had acquired by 1975 a national circulation of about 25,000 and the status of one of the two most important "under-30" conservative periodicals in the country. (*Intercollegiate Review* was the other.) Aimed at and largely produced by undergraduate and graduate students, *The Alternative* was unabashedly (and wittily) conservative. It was also open to right-wing liberals, as articles by and about Senator Henry Jackson indicated.[75]

In the autumn of 1971, *The Alternative* sponsored a collegiate "Education for Democracy" conference in Cambridge, Massachusetts. The list of speakers clearly showed the converging lines of force: Martin Diamond, a former student of Leo Strauss and analyst of *The Federalist Papers*; Norman Podhoretz, editor of *Commentary*; Garret Scalera of the Hudson Institute; Alexander Bickel, professor of law at Yale Law School;[76] Paul Weaver, a political scientist at Harvard; and the conservative sociologist Robert Nisbet. It was more than symbolically significant that one of the principal coordinators of this conference (as well as a senior editor of *The Alternative*) was Irving Kristol's son, then an undergraduate at Harvard.

Indeed, it began to appear that the principal figure in the developing realignment might well be Irving Kristol himself. The June 1972 issue of *The Alternative*, for instance, contained four articles about him, including tributes by Nathan Glazer and William F. Buckley, Jr. [77] Buckley declared that Kristol was "writing more sense in the public interest these days than anybody I can think of."[78] In a perceptive analysis, Robert Bartley, associate editor of the *Wall Street Journal*, contended that Kristol and his journal were forging an "alliance of empirical social scientists and classical political philosophers" into a neo-conservative movement including such men as Herman Kahn and Leo Strauss. This neo-conservatism, said Bartley, avoided the sometimes doctrinaire laissez-faire purism and "apocalyptic" anti-Communism of the older Right. It also addressed with penetration the most profound questions America faced in the 1970s:

> Intellectually, the neo-conservative themes *are* the central themes of our time. The collapse of values. The place of tradition in a time of change. The need not only for outward material progress but for the inner satisfaction of living in what seems to be a proper society. The place of an intellectual elite in a nation where, *The Public Interest* is careful to tell us, only eleven percent of adults have completed four years of college.

Perhaps, Bartley ventured, the most remarkable event in the intellectual history of the 1960s would turn out to be "the evolution of a new and newly relevant conservatism."[79]

In 1972 Kristol published a collection of essays which promised to be one of the most significant conservative books of the 1970s.[80] In the preface to *On the Democratic Idea in America*, Kristol acknowledged his deep debt to Lionel Trilling and Leo Strauss;[81] the influence of classical political philosophy was apparent in every chapter. The subject of his book was simply stated:

> the tendency of democratic republics to depart from...their original, animating principles, and as a consequence to precipitate grave crises in the moral and political order.
>
> In the United States, these original principles firmly linked popular government to a fair measure of self-government (i.e., self-discipline) on the part of the individual citi-

zen. The departure from these principles has taken the form of a "liberation" of personal and collective selves—a freeing of self-interests, personal aspirations, private fantasies—in the realms of economics, politics, education, and culture. It is assumed, on the basis of various benign theories about human nature and human history, that the actions of self-serving men will coalesce into a common good, and that the emancipation of the individual from social restraints will result in a more perfect community. I do think that, within limits, the notion of the "hidden hand" has its uses in the marketplace.... I believe the results are disastrous when it is extended to the polity as a whole, which can go bankrupt only once, and whose destiny is finally determined by the capacity of its citizenry to govern its passions and thereby rightly understand its enduring common interests.[82]

Again and again, in a manner similar to the traditionalist new conservatives, Kristol condemned the relativism, the nihilism, the "do your own thing" ethos rising in the land: "Self-government, the basic principle of this republic, is inexorably being eroded in favor of self-seeking, self-indulgence, and just plain aggressive selfishness."[83]

Fearlessly challenging libertarian assumptions, Kristol urged, among other things, a discreet censorship of pornography. Democracy depends on values and on the character of those who try to govern themselves. It depends on what the Founding Fathers labeled "republican virtue," which we should strive to preserve: "if you care for the quality of life in our American democracy, then you have to be for censorship."[84] In a way reminiscent of Willmoore Kendall,[85] Kristol contrasted America's "transcendentalist populism," its streak of flatulent utopianism, with the prudent, tempered democratic *philosophy* of the Founding Fathers. Frequently he scourged America's intellectuals—a growing "mass movement" with inordinate and alarming pretensions.[86] Always he beckoned to a public philosophy, a *good* society, a civilization that could resolutely answer "the ultimate subversive question: 'Why not?'"[87]

And if in the early 1970s Irving Kristol was becoming a leader of a newly invigorated conservative movement, it was symbolically appropriate. For Kristol, too, like so many others,[88] had once been a man of the far Left. A graduate of City College in 1940, Kristol had been a youthful Trotskyist. Gradually during the late 1930s and early 1940s, he had withdrawn from the far Left; he once remarked that he had been moving steadily to the Right since 1942.[89] During he 1940s and 1950s he had become a cold war liberal, serving as an editor of *Commentary, Encoun-*

ter, and the *Reporter*.[90] In 1952 he rocked *Commentary* with a searing attack on the fellow-traveling, anti-anti-Communist Left.[91] Like so many other liberals who eventually moved to the Right, Kristol in the 1950s was critical of then-emerging conservatism,[92] but the polarization of the 1960s altered his perspective. Just as Jeffrey Hart had prophesied, the barriers between moderates of Left and Right were crumbling.

In 1970 Frank Meyer argued that if liberalism was now "moribund," "not a small part of the cause has been the growing strength of conservatism...."[93] This was no doubt an overstatement. For while conservatism was in fact gaining strength, it was not the body of conservative thought as such but the larger pressures of reality which were independently propelling many liberals to the Right.[94] Still, it is important to recognize that as polarization increased within the liberal camp, the conservative alternative was already there. If it was acquiring new allies and even recruits from the Left, the Right was also, on its own, finally entering the mainstream of American thought and politics.

The year 1970, a year of disasters on the campuses and fears of national disintegration, was also a year of symbolic success for the conservative intellectual movement. It saw the stunning election of William F. Buckley's brother James to the United States Senate from the very citadel of liberalism, New York. It saw Young Americans for Freedom celebrate its tenth anniversary; an organization of fewer than 100 members in 1960 (it had first met in William F. Buckley's living room), YAF now had more than 50,000, making it "the largest non-party political action organization in the country."[95] In 1970 also, *National Review*, with more than 100,000 subscribers, celebrated its fifteenth birthday. While the anniversary issue of *National Review* that year was preoccupied with the uncertain national destiny, one of the essays did find much to celebrate. Surveying the variety and volume of contemporary conservative thought, Peter Witonski, a young conservative historian, discerned "the growing intellectual maturity of the conservative movement, as well as NR's influence on that movement. Conservative writers and writings are no longer just something to hope for; they are here for us to read."[96]

Witonski was undoubtedly correct. By the early 1970s the production of explicitly conservative literature had become a torrent. Libertarianism, traditionalism, and anti-Communism—the fundamental constituent elements of postwar conservative thought—continued to find expression in scholarly books. Particularly noteworthy was the increasing number of conservative analyses of turmoil in the Christian churches.[97] A few conservative books, including Edward Banfield's *The Unheavenly City* and works by William F. Buckley, Jr., became best-sellers. There was renewed interest in Albert Jay Nock.[98] Both in books and in periodicals, conservatives continued to explore their varied tradition;[99] in 1970 and 1971 alone, three anthologies of conservative thought were published.[100]

Also heartening to conservatives was their success in disseminating their ideas. *National Review*, *Modern Age*, the *Intercollegiate Review*, and *The Alternative* continued to churn out a vast respectable literature.[101] Another sign of health was the Washington-based *Human Events*. Starting with a readership of 127 at its founding in 1944, it had attained a circulation exceeding 100,000 twenty years later.[102] Under the editorship of Thomas Winter, *Human Events* grew rapidly in prestige in the late 1960s and became in the Nixon years perhaps the most influential conservative journal in the Washington political community.[103] Week by week it covered politics and served as a medium for the growing number of syndicated conservative columnists. In fact, the movement was especially blessed with columnists, including not only the preeminent William F. Buckley, Jr. but also John Chamberlain, Jeffrey Hart, James J. Kilpatrick, Russell Kirk, Kevin Phillips, George F. Will, and numerous others. The Conservative Book Club continued to distribute its offerings at a robust rate to its 30,000 members, while the Hoover Institution in California and the American Enterprise Institute (a respected, conservative-leaning "think tank" in Washington, D.C.) published studies by conservative scholars.[104] The American Conservative Union, founded in the aftermath of the Goldwater debacle, had become by the early 1970s an effective Washington lobby, with 60,000 members supporting its expanding activities.[105]

Even the television networks—the objects of so much conservative wrath—seemed to be opening their doors a bit to conservative spokesmen. Three articulate right-wing journalists—M. Stanton Evans, Jeffrey St. John, and James J. Kilpatrick—became commentators on the CBS radio *Spectrum* series. The National Educational Television network debate series, *The Advocates*, featured Left-Right confrontations on contemporary issues, with William Rusher of *National Review* and J. Daniel Mahoney (chairman of the Conservative Party of New York) as frequent defenders of the conservative side. And there was that urbane evangelist, the versatile personification of conservatism, William F. Buckley, Jr.; it is difficult to imagine what (or where) the movement would have been without this gifted popularizer. In 1969 his *Firing Line* won an Emmy for "outstanding program achievement in television."[106] A year later Will Herberg exulted:

> ...today the tables are turned.... In bringing about this reversal, no one in this country has been more effective than William F. Buckley, Jr....[107]

Clearly the upheavals of the 1960s were benefiting both libertarians and traditionalists. The wave of skepticism about government was generating renewed interest in the Chicago School[108] and was helping to sustain the substantial influence of Milton Friedman.[109] Peter Drucker labeled Friedman's suggestion that the economy be regulated by an automatic, fixed, annual expansion of the money supply "the most radical proposal in economics since Adam Smith...."[110] The ability of libertarians to devise specific proposals for public policy also contributed to their continuing impact.[111] In 1972 the Mont Pélerin Society celebrated its twenty-fifth anniversary; John Chamberlain claimed that it "could look back to some very considerable victories."[112] One of the most pleasant (and, for conservatives, most unexpected) came in 1974, when Friedrich Hayek was named a co-recipient of the Nobel Prize for economics. To jubilant libertarians it was a symbolic recognition of their increasing respectability and influence.

Yet as Russell Kirk, Robert Nisbet, Leo Strauss, Irving Kristol, and many others taught, the crisis penetrated to far deeper levels of human behavior than the economic. In the late 1960s the "revolt against the state" merged with a broader phenomenon, a revolt against custom and authority: in the Roman Catholic Church, in academe, in racial and sexual mores—in every sphere, it seemed, of American society. Suddenly ideas like tradition, order, authority, restraint, duty, morality, and community seemed to many Americans to address the truly basic perplexities of the time. Irving Kristol believed that beneath the pervasive rhetoric of "liberation" and "equality" lay "an acute yearning for order and stability."[113] In addition, the proliferation of what conservatives deemed "Gnostic" movements drove many right-wing intellectuals to defend more than ever the Voegelinian "constitution of being" against its utopian foes.[114] The massiveness of radical negations (extending to assaults on family structure, private property, and the very ideals of objectivity and rationality) produced traditionalist replies at equally fundamental levels. As the example of Kristol alone demonstrated, the writings of Leo Strauss continued to exert a compelling influence on some conservatives. William F. Buckley, Jr. regarded Strauss as "unquestionably one of the most influential teachers of his age."[115]

Paralleling these intellectual trends were auspicious developments in politics. In 1969, for the first time since their postwar revival began, conservatives had access to the presidency. Richard Nixon, a self-styled "Disraeli conservative,"[116] was a friend of such conservatives as Russell Kirk and an admirer of Kirk's *A Program for Conservatives*.[117] A number of right-wing scholars found niches, at least for a time, in the Nixon administration: Arthur Burns at the Federal Reserve Board, Warren Nutter at the Defense Department, Richard V. Allen of the Hoover Institution on the staff of Henry Kissinger, and Martin Anderson (author of *The Federal Bulldozer*) on the White House staff, to name some of the most prominent. William F. Buckley, Jr. received an appointment to an advisory commission to the United States Information Agency. Some of Spiro Agnew's young speechwriters were conservatives, including John Coyne, who left *National Review* in 1971 to work for the vice-president for a time. Agnew became, for several years, a conservative hero.

This unprecedented leverage on power did not, however, prevent rising conservative disenchantment with President Nixon, which rapidly deepened in 1971 and 1972. In domestic affairs, many (but not all) conservative intellectuals were disturbed by Nixon's apparent leftward drift and opportunism, signified by huge budget deficits, wage and price controls, expanding bureaucracy, and the Family Assistance Plan.[118] Even more alarming were his China policy, his cultivation of what one writer called "the illusion of *détente*,"[119] and—more than anything else—"his failure to call public attention to the deteriorated American military position," which conservatives viewed as gravely and steadily weakening. Accordingly, on July 26, 1971, Buckley, Burnham, Meyer, and several other prominent conservatives "suspended their support" of the administration.[120] The American Conservative Union and many leading right-wing publicists and scholars endorsed the protest candidacy of Representative John Ashbrook for president early in 1972.[121] While virtually all eventually supported Nixon for reelection, M. Stanton Evans expressed a rather widespread sentiment that summer when he declared that the Nixon years "have not been especially happy ones" for the Right.[122]

Despite these political setbacks (which were partially offset by conservative victories, especially the Supreme Court appointments), American conservatives in the Nixon years believed that they had achieved an intellectual and political breakthrough. With new confidence they rejoiced that they had "made it." "Conservatism has become of age," Stephen Tonsor announced in 1969:

> Out of power, rejected even by the party to which every natu-
> ral and unreflecting conservative belonged, without major fi-
> nancial support and denied access to the public by the mo-
> nopoly the establishment maintained in the academy, the
> churches and the news media, Conservatism made itself heard
> because it has the arguments and it has the men.[123]

The veteran journalist John Chamberlain agreed: "The great story of our age is that of the conservative counter-culture's success in making a new climate for itself."[124]

Reflecting this perceived change in status was an intriguing change in conservative rhetoric. In the 1940s and 1950s conservatism had often appeared to be, in Clinton Rossiter's phrase, a "thankless persuasion," and the rhetoric of the Right reflected its seemingly forlorn minority status. Some conservatives sought solace in Nock's concept of the Remnant and spoke of the need to "stand athwart history yelling 'Stop.'" *National Review* even questioned the wisdom of universal suffrage in the South;[125] in 1961 William F. Buckley, Jr. labeled universal suffrage "a mockery of true democracy."[126] The spirit of Mencken, of an aristocratic revolt against the masses, noticeably affected the early issues of *National Review*.[127] In the early 1960s, with the advent of Barry Goldwater, conservatism's minority consciousness started to fade. Still, its rhetoric remained that of an embattled losing side. "Twenty-seven million Americans can't be wrong," proclaimed bumper stickers after Goldwater's defeat. Defiant language, yes, but not the language of victory.

In the late 1960s and early 1970s, however, this older rhetoric, while not dead, was supplanted by an optimistic new theme: conservatives were no longer pariahs but the voice of the "silent majority" of the American people.[128] Early in 1970, Arlington House announced itself in advertisements as the publisher "for the silent majority."[129] In 1970 Barry Goldwater published *The Conscience of a Majority*. "I am the voice of the new politics," Senator-elect James Buckley said exultantly on election night in 1970.[130]

As most conservatives became more fervently convinced that America as a whole was still healthy and that only an elite was decadent, there emerged what Kevin Phillips aptly labeled "populist conservatism."[131] "Middle America is the last heir of Western civilization," Frank Meyer thundered in 1971.[132] Thus it was no coincidence that there was renewed interest in that Oklahoma celebrant of the virtuous people, Willmoore Kendall, many of whose writings were gathered into one volume in 1971. It was no coincidence that James Burnham criticized "verbalists" and admired the heartland.[133] Conservatives had no illusions that as an intellectual movement they had swept all before them. Nor did talk of "populism" mean that they embraced the principal "populist" in the land, George Wallace.[134] But they were more confident than ever before that "the people" could now be reached.[135]

Yet nagging internal tensions remained. On the fringes, Bozell, Rothbard, and their respective camps were active, revealing the fissures that had never disappeared. Ayn Rand maintained a devoted following, and in 1967 *National Review* again felt the need to censure her.[136] In 1971 Peter Viereck, long self-exiled from most of the Right, zestfully denounced "rightist touts" and authoritarians who, in his view, were not conservative at all.[137] Closer to the actual center of the movement, perennial controversies lingered on. There was the persistent claim that America was really a liberal country.[138] There was the recurrent problem of determining the limits of the capitalist model; on one occasion William F. Buckley, Jr. even chastised Milton Friedman and his son for tending to make laissez-faire a "dogmatic theology."[139] There was the still-felt need, in some quarters, to demonstrate that Christian morality and the free market were really compatible.[140] From time to time, the old question of defining the American conservative tradition (and the place of Lincoln in it) aroused renewed controversy.[141] Conservatives also continued to disagree about the extent to which continental conservatism was relevant to the New World.[142] Libertarians and traditionalists clashed on such issues as pornography, censorship, and the legalization of certain drugs;[143] should marijuana, for example, be decriminalized?[144] Old disputes never died; they faded and then reappeared.

How important were these differences? Was conservatism merely an ill-assorted temporary coalition, or was there substantial common ground? In 1971 Donald Atwell Zoll bluntly attacked Frank Meyer's fusionism: "...he confuses expedient eclecticism with compatible integration." The divisions on the Right, said Zoll, were too deep to justify "ecumenism."[145] Similarly, Robert Nisbet doubted that conservatives (so much more individualistic than the "homogeneous" liberals) could create a lasting movement out of the current unstable coalition.[146] Publisher Devin Garrity believed that the movement was dividing into "traditionalism" and "anarchism."[147]

On the other hand, many influential right-wing intellectuals deeply believed that a consensus *was* there—and that Frank Meyer had proved it. "No single man's efforts to make it [the "instinctive consensus"] survive have counted more than Frank Meyer's," said Buckley in 1969.[148]

Peter Witonski claimed that "a conservative consensus does exist.... We are all libertarians; we are all traditionalists."[149] M. Stanton Evans, a devout fusionist, insisted that a "continuum" did exist among conservatives, despite obvious disagreements and dissimilar preoccupations.[150] Whatever the philosophical validity of these men's position, the historically noteworthy fact was that so many conservatives clearly thought that common ground existed. Fusionism in fact *was* the conservative consensus, Buckley observed.[151]

Obviously many wanted to believe this was so. One senses such a desire in the outpouring of tributes to Frank Meyer which *National Review* printed in 1972. A few hours before he died on April 1, 1972, Frank Meyer—an ardent, argumentative libertarian, as well as one of the formative personal influences on the conservative revival—became a member of the Roman Catholic Church.[152] For many conservatives, one suspects, his conversion was the great symbolic reconciliation, the ultimate fusion.

How, then, shall we resolve the question? First, on a purely philosophical or "ideological" level, American conservatism did not speak with a single voice. It had never done so and probably never would. There was a continuing gap between the traditionalist ethos of self-restraint, of limits on will, and the libertarian ethos of self-assertion, self-cultivation, and resistance to the State.[153] There was at least a rhetorical gap between a journal devoted to the "public interest" and a libertarianism that was suspicious of the very idea of "public interest" and "social responsibility" of business.[154] "It is very hard," Irving Kristol observed, "to be for tradition...and at the same time to celebrate the unqualified virtues of individualism."[155] Much of the new conservatism of the 1950s and beyond sought to articulate a "public philosophy." At the heart of much of libertarianism was a "private philosophy" and the wish to be let alone.

This desire was evident in the conservatism of the greatest popular symbol of postwar conservatism, William F. Buckley, Jr. As a Roman Catholic, as a disciple of Nock, Kendall, Chambers, and Kirk,[156] Buckley embodied not only the libertarian brand of conservatism but also its traditionalist and anti-Communist varieties. Nevertheless, it was the libertarian ethos which decisively influenced Buckley's famous "style." For despite his public reputation as a celebrity and sword bearer for the Right, despite the wit and elegance that helped to make him a public figure, deep down, one suspects, Buckley did not really seek or cherish the "firing line." Rather, this was a role which the unwelcome tides of history had compelled him to accept. His public appearances were often marked by a certain aristocratic reserve, which some thought was hauteur—an aloofness, even at times a sense of resignation, which some mistook for arrogance or conceit. In 1970 Buckley told conservatives that they must teach "the need for superordinating the private vision over the public vision."[157] A few years before he had spoken with heartfelt conviction about the conservative's plight in the modern age:

> Politics, it has been said, is the preoccupation of the quarter-educated, and I do most solidly endorse that observation, and therefore curse this century above all things for its having given all sentient beings very little alternative than to occupy themselves with politics.

He deplored "this century's most distinctive aggression, which is against privacy, publicly understood." He resented the absence of alternatives to taking the heat in Harry Truman's famous kitchen.[158]

Conservatism was obviously no monolith. Yet to dwell exclusively on its various internal differences is to miss much—perhaps the essence—of the matter. The truly remarkable fact was that most conservatives managed with ease to remain united and cooperative. Rent by disagreements as the movement (like any movement) was, said Thomas Molnar, conservatism was still effective in action.[159] On practical day-to-day issues there was a surprising amount of convergence on the Right (except for its farthest fringes). Thus, Russell Kirk—a traditionalist through and through—was a proponent of the voucher plan and volunteer army.[160] Both libertarians and traditionalists opposed urban renewal, though not always for the same reasons.[161] Some of the most perceptive comments on this subject came from John Chamberlain, the pro-capitalist libertarian author. Chamberlain found no practical quarrel between religious and nonreligious conservatives; both shared a common morality. Nor was it difficult to find areas of agreement with someone like Russell Kirk, whose "traditions" and prescriptions harmonized nicely with Chamberlain's "principles." Many of the "fights" disappeared, he noted, when conservatives moved from "first principles" to "first practices."[162] In 1970 another libertarian luminary, Henry Hazlitt, whose early idols had included John Stuart Mill and Herbert Spencer, found himself writing, in an article entitled "In Defense of Conformity," observations that traditionalists could applaud. Hazlitt had always considered himself a libertarian, but now he adhered also to a conservatism which taught: "Let us change our moral codes, our laws, our political institutions, when we find this to be necessary, but let us do so cautiously, gradually, piecemeal...." Hazlitt denounced the destructive cult of "dissent" and proclaimed the necessity for "prevailing conformity" in order to achieve "mutual cooperation" and "genuine progress." Without "basic conformity" in such areas as manners, morals, and speech, "civilized society could hardly survive."[163] And always, as an example of conservatism's unity as well as its diversity, there was William F. Buckley, Jr., a diplomat who did much, especially in the early years, to hold the movement together.[164]

Perhaps, on closer inspection, the divergent emphases of the movement were more intimately related than some realized. Both libertarians and traditionalists evinced, for instance, a strong distrust of "intellectuals"—a point on which everyone from Hayek to Kristol could agree. Hayek and Kirk both preached the gospel of humility and opposition to presumptuous rationalism. All shared a revulsion against "gnosticism" and utopian "social engineering,"[165] and a sense of the complexity of the social order.[166] None worshipped the State, although their formulations and policies differed. Libertarians reacted against the State as a threat to individual liberty and economic progress. Traditionalists, *sharing much of this critique*, also reacted against the total State as an expression of the collapse of moral and spiritual authority. "Society," said Burke (and traditionalists echoed him), "cannot exist, unless a controlling power upon will and appetite be placed somewhere; and the less of it there is within, the more there must be without."[167] Anti-Communists reacted against the State in its most despotic and ominous contemporary forms, the Soviet Union and China.

One could go on, but the point is clear. There was a fascinating heterogeneity in conservative thought, yet most right-wing intellectuals readily agreed on certain fundamental "prejudices" which they articulated and refined in many different ways: a presumption (of varying intensity) in favor of private property and a free enterprise economy; opposition to Communism, socialism, and utopian schemes of all kinds; support of strong national defense; belief in Christianity or Judaism (or at least the utility of such belief); acceptance of traditional morality and the need for an inelastic moral code; hostility to positivism and relativism; a "gut affirmation" of the goodness of America and the West. These were but a few constituent elements of the working conservative consensus.

And so, with the greatest opportunity of their lives before them, conservatives faced the future. The past had often been bitter, and conservatives had long been conditioned to accept defeat. Writing in his diary in December 1970, William F. Buckley, Jr. described himself as "a conservative grown up in the knowledge that victories are not for us."[168] Perhaps he remembered the haunting words Whittaker Chambers once wrote to him:

> Those who remain in the world, if they will not surrender on its terms, must maneuver within its terms. That is what conservatives must decide: how much to give in order to survive at all; how much to give in order not to give up the basic principles. And, of course, that results in a dance along a precipice. Many will drop over, and, always, the cliff dancers will hear the screaming curses of those who fall, or be numbed by the sullen silence of those, nobler souls perhaps, who will not join the dance.[169]

Maturity and opportunity did not insure success. In the fall of 1971, William Rusher observed that while the "product" of conservatism was substantial, its "impact" was still small.[170] Frank Meyer acknowledged that the conservative movement had not yet had a profound influence on American life and had not taken control of the country. Its major contribution remained the critique of liberalism.[171] Thomas Molnar agreed. Conservatives had succeeded in presenting an alternative to the country and had brought "new colors" to the American scene, but they had not yet triumphed.[172] Progress had been made, of course. Twenty years before, said Robert Nisbet, academe had regarded many conservatives as "bizarre." Now many of the new conservative positions of the 1950s were accepted, even commonplace.[173] Still, conservatives knew—and painful was their knowledge—that among intellectuals they remained a minority.

As the first term of President Nixon came to a close, there were signs that the conservative intellectual movement was in "drift"[174] and that a crucial period of soul-searching was in the offing. Shortly after the 1972 elections, political analyst Kevin Phillips addressed his fellow conservatives, many of whom were alarmed by the president's policies. Conservatives, he argued, had won the elections of 1968, 1970, and 1972, but these had turned out to be negative and inconclusive victories, mere repudiations of the Left. If the Right was to achieve the decisive breakthrough that was possible, it must recognize that "the fulcrum of ideological gain is not adherence to classic conservatism, but rather hostility toward the emerging liberal elite of amorality-activists and social-change merchants...." The Right must stop harping on such "wrong issues" as wage-price controls or the president's visits to Moscow and Peking. Above all, it must become "activist" and "positive."[175]

Was this prescription valid? Each element in the conservative movement had much thinking to do. Consider the libertarians. Could they imaginatively hold off the burgeoning bureaucratic State and what William F. Buckley, Jr. once called the "passion to centralize"?[176] Helped by "the happy accident of massive federal failures,"[177] could they convincingly prove to millions their assertion of the superiority of the free enterprise system? Could the Banfield—Kristol—*Public Interest* social scientists convert their skepticism about government efforts to "do good" (as Banfield put it) into a workable alternative approach?

Consider the traditionalists. In an increasingly nomadic,[178] pluralistic, and hedonistic country, could the neo-conservative themes, however relevant, be made the basis of effective action? (Here the libertarians had an advantage: their principles, oriented so much to economics, were easily convertible into policy proposals.) What role, if any, should government play in preserving the nation's spiritual health? Could the conservative *case* for authority, morals, tradition, and truth be translated into popular *acceptance* of authority, morals, tradition, and truth? Or had the decline of the West gone too far? Could the "Gnostic" intellectuals be contained? Could "the wisdom of conservatism" be articulated not only to Chambers's marine on the beach of Tarawa but to the generation that had grown up with the war in Vietnam?

Particularly problematic was the future of anti-Communism. What would happen to the movement if its greatest unifying force disintegrated? Most conservatives no doubt still believed that Communism was evil and a menace to the West.[179] Yet, as President Nixon's trip to China, the SALT agreements, anti-Vietnam war sentiment, and expanding East-West trade demonstrated, the tide of *détente* and public opinion seemed to be running against the traditional conservative posture. How would the Right respond to this uncongenial situation? Suppose, for instance, that the clouds of fate lowered over a weary America in the late 1970s. Could conservatives rally the nation in time? Suppose that the conservatives were wrong about the Communist threat and that a "multipolar" world had replaced the stark simplicities of yesteryear. Could a movement that was so much a product of the cold war survive the end of the cold war (if it had ended)? Could conservatism fall back to a hard-headed, neo-Metternichian, balance-of-power strategy, as James Burnham seemed to be counseling?[180] Was America, was democracy itself, stable and patient enough for this kind of foreign policy to succeed?

Conservatives were living in a revolutionary age, and the pleasant new sensation of victories at the polls could not dispel their disquieting perception of this fact. If "the revolution" ever succeeds in conquering the United States and the Roman Catholic Church, Thomas Molnar predicted, "then the West is finished."[181] The very fact that conservatives could think in such terms showed how deep the chasm seemed to be.

How tempting it was and would continue to be to succumb to the nihilist's siren call: "Why not?" All values are relative—*why not?* God is dead and everything is permitted—*why not?* America and the West are no better than Communist Russia and China—*why not?* When terrorists at home and abroad demand capitulation—*why not?* Because, answered American conservatives, we *stand* for certain things—the "permanent things"—which transcend us and which we must defend lest our civilization collapse. Willmoore Kendall said it forcefully:

> Survival, in itself, is *not* the highest value; on the *contrary*: under the ethos of Western civilization as revealed to us by that civilization's central teaching, survival is a relatively *low* value; above it, for example, ranks truth; above it also, for example, ranks beauty; above it, far above it, rank justice, and along with justice true religion; above it finally...ranks *freedom*, and along with freedom those processes of rational deliberation and discussion...that we know to be the characteristic features of truly civil society.[182]

In 1965 William F. Buckley, Jr., in a moment of sober reflection, declared:

> It is undoubtedly necessary, every now and then, to bare one's teeth; and we do so, preferably, in the course of smiling. But the smiles have a way of freezing, as the sadness rolls in. The joys of warmaking [for conservative causes] presuppose the eventual stillness of victory: and that, so far as I can see, is beyond our reach. Perhaps it was meant to be so.[183]

Perhaps. But one must *resist*—this was a conservative lesson, too. For the drama was not over. Conservatism—and America—were still in "the middle of the journey." By the early 1970s conservatives had finally won an opportunity. But an opportunity to do what? In his last letter to Buckley, Whittaker Chambers wrote that "each age finds its own language for an eternal meaning."[184] Here was the challenge: to defend enduring truths in a language appealing to America in the 1970s. In the words of T.S. Eliot, if this was not a lost cause, it was never a gained cause, either.

In an endeavor so ambitious, conservatives would often need to recall the words of Robert Frost:

> *Ah, when to the heart of man*
> *Was it ever less than a treason*
> *To go with the drift of things...?* *

*From "Reluctance," from *The Poetry of Robert Frost*, edited by Edward Connery Lathem. Copyright 1934, © 1969 by Holt, Rinehart and Winston, Inc. Copyright © 1962 by Robert Frost. Reprinted by permission of Holt, Rinehart and Winston, Publishers.

EPILOGUE

Conservatism Ascendant: The Age of Reagan and Beyond

Twenty years have now passed since the preceding pages were first published. Time never stands still, and neither, in this period, did the conservative intellectual movement in the United States. By the mid-1970s, conservatives had established a hard-won presence in the American public square and an opportunity to shape their nation's destiny. Still, it was *only* an opportunity, and no conservative with knowledge of past travails could be sure that history would finally listen to those who had stood athwart it yelling "Stop!" Nevertheless, this time history—in the form of the American electorate—did respond. In 1980 what had once seemed unattainable came to pass. With the election of Ronald Reagan to the presidency, the intellectual forces described in this book achieved a decisive breakthrough in their quest for political and cultural influence.

The nineteenth-century Italian nationalist Giuseppe Mazzini once remarked: "Ideas rule the world and its events. A revolution is the passage of an idea from theory to practice. Whatever men say, material interests never have caused, and never will cause a revolution." In 1981 the United States entered an era of what some soon called the "Reagan Revolution." Such a description, of course, was hyperbole. But in one sense—Mazzini's sense—the use of the word "revolution" was precisely correct. In the decade of the Eighties, America witnessed the passage of an idea from theory to practice. That idea, that philosophy, was called conservatism.

As readers of this book have already discovered, conservatism at the dawn of the Reagan years was no monolith. It was, in fact, a compound of diverse and not always consistent impulses, each sharing a deep antipathy to twentieth-century liberalism. To the libertarians, modern liberalism was the ideology of the ever-aggrandizing bureaucratic, welfare state. If unchecked, it would become a totalitarian state, destroying individual liberty and private property—the wellsprings of a prosperous society. To the traditionalists, liberalism was a disintegrative philosophy which, like an acid, was eating away at the ethical and institutional foundations of Western civilization, creating a vast spiritual void into which totalitarian false gods would enter. To the Cold War anti-Communists, modern liberalism—rationalistic, relativistic, secular, anti-traditional, quasi-socialist—was by its very nature incapable of vigorously resisting an enemy on its left. Liberalism to them was part of the Left and could not effectively repulse a foe with which it shared so many underlying assumptions. As James Burnham had put it, liberalism was essentially a means for reconciling the West to its own destruction. Liberalism was the ideology of Western suicide.

Joining the conservative coalition in the Seventies and Eighties was a fourth component, identified earlier in this book as "right-wing liberalism" but now known as "neoconservatism." Irving Kristol's definition conveyed its essence: "A neoconservative," he said, "is a liberal who has been mugged by reality." According to another definition, a neoconservative was a person who uttered two cheers for capitalism instead of three: a reflection of the fact that many neoconservatives in their younger days had been staunch New Deal Democrats or socialists. In any case, one of the salient developments of the 1980s was to be the continuing journey of various liberals and social democrats into conservative ranks. By the end of the Reagan decade such neoconservative writers as Kristol, Norman Podhoretz, Midge Decter, and Jeane Kirkpatrick were prominent figures in the American Right's intelligentsia.

In part the neoconservative phenomenon could be interpreted as a recognition that good intentions alone do not guarantee good governmental policy, and that the actual consequences of liberal social activism in the 1960s and 1970s had been devastating. Neoconservatism was also a reaction of moderate liberals to the polarizing upheavals of the 1960s (particularly on the campuses) and to the shattering rise of the New Left, with its tendency to blame America first for world tensions and its hostility to an American military presence abroad. Many neoconservatives, in fact, had been anti-Communist, "vital center" liberals of the Harry Truman-Hubert Humphrey wing of the Democratic Party who found themselves bereft of a political home after the capture of their party by the followers of Senator George McGovern in 1972.

The rightward migration of disillusioned liberals was not the only development which profoundly altered the intellectual configuration of American conservatism in the 1980s. Another—and one destined to have enormous political consequences—was the rapid emergence of the so-called New Right, or, as it usually came to be labeled, the Religious Right. Initially the New Right was not primarily a movement of intellectuals at all. It was, rather, a grassroots movement of protest by aroused citizens, many of them Protestant fundamentalists, evangelicals, and pentacostals, with some Roman Catholics and Orthodox Jews as well. While New Right leaders like Jerry Falwell and Pat Robertson generally shared the foreign policy and economic perspectives of other conservatives, their guiding preoccupations lay elsewhere, in what became known as the "social issues": abortion, school prayer, pornography, drug use, crime, sexual deviancy, the vulgarization of mass entertainment, and more. Convinced that American society was in a state of vertiginous moral decline, and that secular humanism—in other words, modern liberalism—was the fundamental cause of this decay, the New Right exhorted its hitherto politically quiescent followers to enter the public arena in defense of traditional moral values.

In a very real sense the Religious Right of the 1980s and 1990s was closest in its concerns to the traditionalist conservatism depicted earlier in this book. But whereas the traditionalists of the 1940s and 1950s had largely been academics in revolt *against* secularized, mass society, the New Right was a revolt *by* the "masses" against the secular virus and its aggressive carriers in the nation's elites. And whereas the conservative intellectual movement since 1945 had heretofore concentrated mostly on national issues and politics, the New Right was essentially the product of traumas experienced by "ordinary" people in their everyday lives. Its anguish was that of parents who discovered that their children were being offered condoms at school, were being taught that homosexual behavior was just another lifestyle, and were being instructed that biblical standards of right and wrong were "relative," "sexist," and "homophobic." Above all, the religious conservatives derived their fervor from an unremitting struggle against what most of them considered the supreme abomination of their time: legalized abortion, a practice that from 1973 to the mid-1990s took the lives of more than 30,000,000 unborn American children.

In time the New Right acquired intellectually influential voices outside its religious precincts—notably the neoconservative William Bennett, whose compilation, *The Book of Virtues*, became a best seller in 1993. Many other conservative writers shared and articulated the Religious Right's disquietude. The phenomenon gained further momentum from its organic ties to a growing, evangelical Protestant subculture: a "parallel universe"(as one observer called it)[1] of Christian colleges, schools, periodicals, television and radio stations, publishing houses, philanthropies, and bookstores. Spearheaded at the political level by the Moral Majority (1979-1989) and Christian Coalition (created in 1989), the Religious Right brought to American conservatism a moral intensity and populist dimension not seen since the Goldwater campaign of 1964.

By the end of President Reagan's second term, the American Right encompassed five distinct impulses: libertarianism, traditionalism, anti-Communism, neoconservatism, and the Religious Right. And just as William F. Buckley, Jr. had done for conservatives a half-generation before, so Ronald Reagan in the Eighties did the same: he performed an emblematic and ecumenical function. Much of Reagan's success as a spokesman for conservatism derived from his embodiment of all these impulses simultaneously.

And as these disparate elements merged into a political and intellectual force, they experienced a stirring passage from the world of ideation to the world of political activism. It is not possible to discuss in detail here the myriad books, issues, personalities, and controversies that marked this great transition. But from the perspective of the mid-1990s, certain aspects of it deserve note.

Perhaps the most immediately striking feature of conservative intellectual activity in the 1980s was that there was so much of it. The publication of conservative books, essays, articles, and syndicated columns—already substantial in the 1970s—attained in the Reagan era the proportions of an avalanche. Gone were the days when Lionel Trilling could assert that liberalism was the "sole intellectual tradition" in the United States. Now it was possible for serious students of American culture and politics to devote every waking hour to the writings of conservative intellectuals alone.

Gone, too, was the time when *National Review*, *Modern Age*, *Human Events*, and *The Freeman* comprised the virtual totality of intelligent conservative journalism in the United States. By the late 1980s, and increasingly thereafter, it seemed that every strand of the conservative movement had its own publication—its own literary branch, as it were, on the family tree. For libertarians there were such periodicals as *Reason* and *The Cato Journal*; for militant traditionalists, *Chronicles*; for militant Southern traditionalists, the *Southern Partisan*; for neoconservatives, *Commentary*, *The Public Interest*, *The National Interest*, and *New Criterion*. For conservatives interested in social and religious issues, there were such periodicals as *Crisis* (formerly *Catholicism in Cri-*

sis), *The Family in America* (formerly *Persuasion at Work*), the *Human Life Review*, and *First Things*. Conservative historians had *Continuity: A Journal of History*; conservative political scientists had the annual *Political Science Reviewer*; for Straussian political philosophers there was for a time the *Claremont Review of Books*. For conservative (and liberal) scholars appalled by the plague of "political correctness" and erosion of standards in colleges and universities, the journal *Academic Questions*, published by the National Association of Scholars, provided a forum. In Michigan, Hillsdale College—honored among conservatives for its principled resistance to federal intrusion into higher education—published a monthly called *Imprimis*, whose circulation rose into the hundreds of thousands.

During the 1980s, too, literally dozens of conservative student newspapers sprang up on the nation's campuses, often with financial and technical assistance from right-minded foundations. A number of these publications, particularly the *Dartmouth Review*, took hold and became, in a sense, farm teams for the conservative big leagues: bridges between older activists and the rising "third generation."

Not all the flourishing conservative media confined themselves to well-defined market niches. In the mid-1980s the *American Spectator* (formerly *The Alternative*), edited by R. Emmett Tyrrell, Jr., moved its offices from Bloomington, Indiana to the vicinity of Washington, D.C. With its Menckenesque blend of humor and iconoclasm, Tyrrell's monthly had long attracted students and younger conservatives, as well as many neoconservatives-in-the-making. By the late Eighties it was ready to transcend its origins.

In the early Nineties the tempestuous battle over the nomination of Clarence Thomas to the Supreme Court provided the opportunity. Thanks to some extraordinary reporting on this controversy, and to well-timed advertising on Rush Limbaugh's conservative radio talk show, the *American Spectator's* subscription list rose from around 40,000 to more than 200,000 in a matter of months. The jaunty magazine that had been founded in an Indiana farm house in 1967 had become the most widely read conservative opinion journal in the nation.

This cascade of conservative literature was intimately linked to a second accelerating trend: the development of a burgeoning network of conservative media, foundations, research centers, and intellectual advocacy groups, from the shores of the Potomac to the farthest corners of the country. A few of these, like the Hoover Institution and American Enterprise Institute, were already well-established by the early 1970s. When Ronald Reagan took power, they became senior fellows (so to speak) in the emerging conservative public policy establishment. But most were much younger than that, and by the late Eighties they were almost too numerous to count. There were the Heritage Foundation, the Cato Institute, the Ethics and Public Policy Center, the Manhattan Institute for Public Policy Research, National Journalism Center, Claremont Institute for the Study of Statesmanship and Political Philosophy, Committee for the Free World, Center for Strategic and International Studies, Shavano Institute at Hillsdale College, Rockford Institute in Illinois, and scores of others.

Once again, it seemed, the principle of market specialization was at work. In the legal profession, for instance, a growing array of public interest law firms such as the Pacific Legal Foundation and Washington Legal Foundation challenged overweening government in the courts. Among law students and legal scholars, the Federalist Society and the Center for Judicial Studies articulated conservative approaches to jurisprudence and constitutional interpretation. In the field of environmental and natural resource policy—an increasingly contentious arena of dispute in the Reagan era—the Political Economy Research Center, based in Bozeman, Montana, championed a paradigm shift known as free market environmentalism. For Religious Right activists and others interested in social issues, James Dobson's Focus on the Family organization and Gary Bauer's Family Research Council provided an arsenal of ammunition.

Not all these clusters of intellectual energy set up offices in the nation's capital. One of the noteworthy trends of the 1980s was the proliferation of free-market-oriented think tanks in the states. Focusing on such close-to-home subjects as school choice and local regulatory policies, the state-level think tanks carried conservative thinking into new territory. By the mid-1990s they had established beachheads in nearly three-quarters of the states.

And so it went. Perhaps one statistic more than any other illumined the extraordinary transformation in the reach and orientation of American conservatism after the mid-1970s. In 1996 the Heritage Foundation published its first *Directory of Public Policy Organizations* on the American Right. The volume listed a staggering 288 such entities.

Of these, one above all bore a distinctive relationship to the increasingly specialized conservative intellectual community. Established in 1973, the Heritage Foundation became in the 1980s the nerve center of the "Reagan Revolution." Far more than a conventional think tank, the foundation deliberately assumed the role of facilitator, liaison, and clearinghouse for the entire conservative public policy network. The foundation established a

Resource Bank, which eventually comprised more than 2000 right-of-center academics and activists around the world. It produced an annual *Guide to Public Policy Experts*. It published a monthly compilation of announcements and publication abstracts called *The Insider*: an invaluable guide to conservative activity at home and abroad. It hosted lectures by conservative scholars, seminars on the history of conservatism for "third generation" activists, and innumerable forums for public policy specialists from near and far. In its journal *Policy Review*, it regularly gave conservatives of many stripes the opportunity to present their agendas and debate their intramural differences. It was not surprising, then, that for self-conscious, "movement" conservatives, the Heritage Foundation was not just a skillful disseminator of ideas "inside the Beltway." It was the institutional equivalent of Ronald Reagan: an ecumenical presence.

By the 1980s it was apparent that, whatever the future vicissitudes of politics, conservatism was no passing spasm of protest. It was too well organized for that. As the movement reached institutional maturity, a change in the texture and focus of conservative literature became perceptible. Largely gone, now, was the restless quest for self-definition and philosophic coherence that had animated so much discourse on the Right in the first two decades after World War II. Instead, conservative writing was becoming ever more programmatic. If there was a characteristic mode of conservative expression from the late Seventies onward, it was not the rarefied tome of political philosophy or cultural criticism; it was the policy study.

Fueling this transition was a deepening collaboration between conservative intellectuals and like-minded politicians. Such a symbiosis, of course, had long been common on the other side of the ideological spectrum. From the New Deal of Franklin Roosevelt to the New Frontier of John Kennedy to the Great Society of Lyndon Johnson, prominent academicians had supplied "idea power" to the American Left. With mounting intensity in the 1980s, the "intellectualization" of our politics extended to the American Right as well.

There was no more dramatic example of this trend than the appearance in the 1970s of a body of conservative thought called "supply-side economics," initially identified with Professor Arthur Laffer of the University of Southern California. In a remarkably short time Laffer's work was enthusiastically publicized by several influential conservative writers until, in the form of tax reduction legislation sponsored by Representative Jack Kemp and Senator William Roth, it became the official tax policy of the Republican Party. Ronald Reagan heartily endorsed the proposal and signed a modified form of it into law early in his presidency. No more could it be charged that conservative politicians were stodgy reactionaries lacking in fresh ideas. To the contrary, many of them—especially younger ones in the House of Representatives—*craved* ideas and found in supply-side economics a way of taking the intellectual offensive. In supply-side economics, theory and practice merged.

In the 1990s the Republicans' receptivity to conservative ideas reached another crescendo in the 1994 election manifesto known as the Contract with America. How far indeed the Grand Old Party had come in a single generation. When Republicans captured control of the House of Representatives in 1994 for the first time since the 1950s, they elected as Speaker no conventional, unimaginative politician but a former college professor thoroughly at home in the world of conservative ideas: Newt Gingrich. It was more than a little significant that Gingrich held a Ph.D. in history—the first Speaker of the House ever to do so—and that his deputy, the new House majority leader, Richard Armey, was a former college professor himself, with a doctorate in economics. It was also symbolically fitting that Gingrich was closely associated with a think tank: the Progress and Freedom Foundation.

All this did not mean that conservative intellectuals had become exclusively present-minded. In journals like *Modern Age* and the *Intercollegiate Review*, scholars on the Right continued soberly to address philosophical and cultural questions that underlay the ephemera of current contentions. Similarly, the Intercollegiate Studies Institute and the Liberty Fund continued to disseminate an impressive collection of serious books on traditionalist and libertarian themes. And in 1988 Transaction Publishers began to publish the Library of Conservative Thought, a set of conservative classics selected and edited by Russell Kirk. By the time of Kirk's death in 1994, the series had grown to thirty volumes. Each of these projects gave depth and historical perspective to a movement increasingly embroiled in day-to-day political disputation.

The decade of the Eighties also saw the publication of important right-of-center books, including George Gilder's *Wealth and Poverty*; Michael Novak's *The Spirit of Democratic Capitalism*; Charles Murray's *Losing Ground: American Social Policy, 1950-1980*; Richard John Neuhaus's *The Naked Public Square: Religion and Democracy in America*; and Thomas Sowell's *A Conflict of Visions*. Conservatives also acclaimed their British confrere Paul Johnson's massive *Modern Times*, an audacious reinterpretation of twentieth-century history emphasizing the staggering evil wrought by "the rise of moral relativism, the decline of moral responsibility, the repudiation of Judeo-Christian values," intellectual hubris, and the unconstrained, ideologically driven State.[2] To those who believed that "an enlarged state could increase the sum total of human happiness," the ex-Socialist Johnson taught otherwise:

> The experiment had been tried in innumerable ways; and it had failed in nearly all of them. The state had proved itself an insatiable spender, an unrivalled waster. It had also proved itself the greatest killer of all time.[3]

By the 1990s, Johnson declared in the second edition of his book, "state action had been responsible for the violent or unnatural deaths of some 125 million people during the century.... Its inhuman malevolence had more than kept pace with its growing size and expanding means."[4]

Still, it was not so much for scholarly treatises that the American Right was known in the Eighties as for *applied* conservatism, forged in the fires of heated political controversy. Not everyone on the Right was happy with the result. As the Reagan Revolution passed into history, some of its intellectual architects—especially libertarians—wondered what it had really accomplished: after eight years of free-market rhetoric and critiques of the welfare state, in 1989 gargantuan government was still in place, and bigger than ever. For their part, in the mid-1980s a number of academically oriented traditionalists lamented that conservatism (in their judgment) was being reduced to political scheming, deprived of ethical vision, and deflected from its larger mission of cultural renewal.

By far the most serious source of discontent on the Right was the role played within its ranks by the erstwhile liberals known as the neoconservatives. To an increasingly angry group of traditionalists who took the label "paleoconservatives," the "neocons" were "interlopers" and "impostors" who despite their recent rightward journey remained essentially secular, Wilsonian, and welfare statist in their philosophy.[5] In other words, not conservative at all. Where, for instance, conservatives had resisted Communism in the name of Western civilization, the neoconservatives of the 1980s did so (said their rightwing critics) in the name of a neo-Wilsonian ideology of "global democratic capitalism." As if (said disgusted "paleos") "capitalism" and "global democracy" were the sum and substance of the conservative cause. Two of the most outspoken paleoconservative writers, Paul Gottfried and Thomas Fleming, charged that neoconservatives had captured much of the conservatives' financial base in the 1980s and had "weakened and defunded" more genuinely conservative alternatives to the status quo.[6]

The conflict between the two factions surfaced in 1981, when President Reagan selected the neoconservative academic William Bennett (over the Southern traditionalist, Professor M.E. Bradford) to chair the National Endowment for the Humanities, after a bitter lobbying battle that left many scars.The feud erupted again in 1986 when Bradford and his allies subjected the neoconservatives to a fierce critique at the annual meeting of the Philadelphia Society and in the *Intercollegiate Review*.[7] But it was in 1989 and 1990, and on into the presidential campaign of 1992, that the lingering animosities flared into a firestorm that threatened the unity of the conservative grand alliance. If the paleoconservatives considered the "neos" to be ossified liberals eager to marginalize anyone on their right, the disproportionately Jewish neoconservatives had grievances of their own. In the utterances of the paleoconservative columnists Joseph Sobran and Patrick Buchanan about Israel, and in the feisty pages of the "paleo" journal *Chronicles*, perturbed neoconservatives detected ominous signs of something not seen on the mainstream Right in a generation: a neoisolationist nativism tinged with antisemitism.[8]

Personalities aside, pugnacious paleoconservatism had clearly introduced a discordant element into conservative circles. Fiercely and defiantly "nationalist" (rather than "internationalist"), skeptical of "global democracy" and entanglements overseas, fearful of the impact of Third World immigration on America's Europe-oriented culture, and openly critical of the doctrine of free trade, Buchananite paleoconservatism increasingly resembled much of the American Right *before* 1945: before, that is, the onset of the Cold War. When Buchanan himself campaigned for the presidency in 1992 under the pre-World War II, anti-interventionist banner of "America First," the symbolism seemed deliberate and complete.

As the neo/paleo furor intensified, a number of observers on the Left and the Right opined that the conservative coalition was either dead or in hopeless disarray. Certainly some paleoconservative strategists believed this and were acting on their separatist convictions. As if in counterpoint to the ecumenically inclined Philadelphia Society, a group of paleoconservatives formed their own organization, the John Randolph Club, and even reached out to the "paleolibertarian" economist Murray Rothbard, a man long outside the mainstream of the *National Review*-dominated Right. Once again the symbolism was apt. In their reaction against the neoconservative "interlopers," zealous paleos had no desire merely to return to the status quo ante 1980 or even to the fusionism exemplified by *National Review* in its early days. For paleoconservatives, *their* intellectual forbears were the *Old* Right: the Right that had existed before the ascendancy of the Buckleyites.

It did not escape notice that the conservatives' uncivil strife coincided with the collapse of Communism in Europe and the stunning end of the Cold War. Inevitably the question arose: could a movement so identified with anti-Communism survive the disappearance of the adversary in the Kremlin? Or would centrifugal tendencies (such as the paleoconservatives' defection) now prevail in the conservative community, as they were doing in the former Soviet empire?

In certain respects these questions were quickly answered. Contrary to the fears (and hopes) of some observers, the conservative intellectual movement did not disintegrate in the early 1990s. Reports of its demise proved to be exaggerated. Conservatism since 1945, after all, had always encompassed more than geopolitical anti-Communism. The downfall of the Soviet Union did not render obsolete the deeper, civilizational concerns of Hayek, Weaver, Voegelin, Strauss, or Kirk. Moreover, in the "great debate" of 1989-1992, most of the conservative establishment either opposed, or expressed reservations about, the Buchananite tendency. While certain paleoconservative themes—notably anxiety about unrestricted immigration to America's shores—resonated in parts of the conservative camp, the "Old Right" did not dominate conservative discourse. Significantly, the circulation of *Chronicles* remained small compared to that of *National Review* and the *American Spectator*.

Nevertheless, it was undeniable that anti-Communism had been a crucial unifying agent in the post-1945 conservative coalition and that the fall of Communism in Europe had attenuated the fusionist imperative for American conservatives. As the post-Cold War era settled in, many conservatives appeared to be searching for a new "vital center." As they did so, many questions remained. Had the conservative coalition grown too successful and too variegated to *have* a vital center any longer? Without the clarity supplied by an external enemy, without the life-and-death seriousness imparted by the Cold War, would a movement of such diverse origins lose its "movement consciousness" and with it the capacity to govern America? Or would other assaults from the Left—multiculturalism, the metastasis of the welfare state, the politics of victimhood and identity, the "culture wars"—provide the Right another adhesive force? No one, with assurance, could say.

And so, in the mid-1990s, American conservatives entered an awkward period best described as the best and the worst of times. Certainly it was among the best of times, considered from the perspective of forty years before. The world was a far less lonely place for conservatives than it had been in 1953 when a young don from Michigan named Russell Kirk brought forth a book he originally intended to call *The Conservatives' Rout*. By 1996 intellectual conservatism had built an elaborate infrastructure that was nonexistent a generation earlier; the expression of conservative sentiments had been professionalized. Moreover, between the organized conservative elite and the vast electorate once known as the "silent majority" there now flourished a phalanx of mediators led by the remarkable Rush Limbaugh, whose 1992 book *The Way Things Ought to Be* quickly sold more than 2,000,000 copies, making it the fastest selling hardcover book of all time.

Other signs of maturity and success abounded. In 1995 Russell Kirk's memoir, *The Sword of Imagination*, appeared, as did Irving Kristol's *Neoconservatism: The Autobiography of an Idea*. Increasingly, eminent men of the Right like James Burnham, Friedrich Hayek, Leo Strauss, Eric Voegelin, and Richard Weaver were becoming the subjects of scholarly attention. In fact, conservatism itself—both in its intellectual and grassroots manifestations—was rapidly becoming a field of historical study: a recognition of its durability and importance.

And yet, for many on the Right, there loomed a profoundly disturbing paradox: while the conservative mind in America was more articulate than ever before, and while conservative politicians in Washington were more numerous than they had been in decades, conservative influence on American culture appeared to be diminishing. If ideas have consequences (as conservatives insisted), then it was painfully clear that conservative ideas were not the only ideas in circulation in the post-Cold War age. For an entire generation, significant sectors of America had moved not to the right but to the left, even as the conservative resurgence gained momentum. Particularly in the area of "lifestyles"—of drug use, sexual mores, acceptance of pornography, and tastes in mass entertainment—popular attitudes and behavior had veered noticeably toward permissiveness. Some called it "liberation"; some called it "expressivist" individualism. Whatever the label, the vectors of social change did not point unequivocally in a conservative direction.

If anyone doubted this point, he need only have consulted *The Index of Leading Cultural Indicators* that William Bennett prepared in 1993. In it he demonstrated empirically what many conservative social critics had long contended: that from the turbulent Sixties to the narcissistic Nineties, the United States had "experienced substantial social regression."[9] Whatever the causes of this declension, the conservative critique of it had been unable to reverse the slide.

By the beginning of 1996 there was a growing consensus among conservatives that "sixty years of liberalism" had left America's "social fabric" "in tatters" and that negative remedies, such as "dismantling Big Government," would not alone suffice to restore it. Conservatives, wrote Adam Meyerson in *Policy Review*, must now effect nothing less than a "restoration of civil society" from the bottom up: a task that could take a generation. "Entirely new institutions," he argued, would have to be established, and others rebuilt, outside the usual sphere of public policy, if the cataclysms of "family collapse," rampant crime, and failing public education were to be overcome.[10] Other conservatives were even more sweeping in their prescriptions for societal renewal. In the fiftieth-anniversary issue of *Commentary* in November 1995, a striking number of conservative intellectuals declared approvingly that America was on the verge of, or even in the midst of, a religious revival akin to the eighteenth-century Great Awakening.[11] In no other way, it seemed to many on the Right, could the needed regeneration of America come about: so vast and decadent now was the wasteland created by liberal relativism and "infectious nihilism."[12]

Whatever the future might bring, conservatives in the post-Cold War era were realizing anew the truth of Ortega y Gasset's remark more than half a century before: "The simple process of preserving our present civilization is supremely complex, and demands incalculably subtle powers." If at times it might seem that the struggle naught availeth, conservatives could take courage from their own history since 1945: however entrenched and fearsome the evils of the hour, they are not insuperable. The future does not always belong to the present.

APPENDIX

Interviews and Correspondence

I. Interviews

Edward Banfield: December 8, 1970.
L. Brent Bozell: April 26, 1972.
Cleanth Brooks: December 1, 1973.
William F. Buckley, Jr.: November 26, 1971.
James Burnham: February 4, 1972.
John Chamberlain: April 6, 1972.
Herbert Cornuelle: November 17, 1972.
W. M. Curtiss: November 18, 1971.
Milton Friedman (reply by tape): March 1972.
Devin Garrity: August 5, 1972.
Nathan Glazer: December 4, 1972.
Jeffrey Hart: September 10, 1971.
Henry Hazlitt: August 30, 1973.
Charles Hyneman: March 8, 1974.
Katherine Kendall: October 21, 1973.
Russell Kirk: April 21, 1971.
Evron Kirkpatrick: October 24, 1973.
Irving Kristol: November 9, 1973.
Frank S. Meyer: September 4, 1971.
Thomas Molnar: November 4, 1972.
Robert Nisbet: November 29, 1971.
Edmund Opitz: November 17-18, 1971.
Paul Poirot: November 16, 1971.
Austin Ranney: December 30, 1971.
Leonard Read: November 17, 1971.
Murray Rothbard: March 23, 1972.
William Rusher: October 30, 1971.
Peter Viereck: informal interviews and
    conversations on several occasions, 1971-1975.
Henry Wells: November 9, 1973.

II. Correspondence

The following individuals, in letters to the author, shared recollections and anecdotes, verified facts, or otherwise provided valuable information: Carl Albert, John Alvis, Juan and Maria Andrade, Polly Weaver Beaton, Daniel Boorstin, Lyle H. Boren, L. Brent Bozell, M. E. Bradford, R.F. Bretherton, Cleanth Brooks, William F. Buckley, Jr., James Burnham, George Carey, Charles H. Commons, Glenn D. Commons, Thomas Cook, George Core, Morris Cox, Louis Dehmlow, Martin Diamond, John Fischer, Barry Goldwater, E. A. Grant, Edward Harrison, Henry Hazlitt, Will Herberg, Hubert Humphrey, Charles Hyneman, Bertrand de Jouvenel, Katherine Kendall, Nellie D. Kendall, Russell Kirk, Arthur Larson, Savoie Lottinville, Yvona K. Mason, Neil McCaffrey, R.B. McCallum, Frank S. Meyer, Thomas Molnar, Robert Nisbet, Edmund Opitz, Austin Ranney, Murray Rothbard, David N. Rowe, Mulford Q. Sibley, Allen Tate, Stephen Tonsor, Ernest van den Haag, Paul Varnell, Eliseo Vivas, Henry Wells, Francis Wilson, Thomas Winter.

NOTES

CHAPTER ONE

1. This phrase has been attributed to Harry Hopkins.
2. Harold Macmillan, *Tides of Fortune* (New York, 1969), p. 36; *New York Times*, August 2, 1945, pp. 1, 9.
3. Mortimer Smith, "Individualism Talks Back," *Christian Century* 62 (February 14, 1945): 202.
4. *Ibid.*, p. 203.
5. Friedrich A. Hayek, *The Road to Serfdom* (Chicago, 1944). In 1956 this book was reprinted with a new foreword; we shall cite this later edition (Chicago, 1956). This important foreword is reprinted as chap. 15 of Friedrich A. Hayek, *Studies in Philosophy, Politics and Economics* (Chicago, 1967). For biographical information on Hayek, see Mary Sennholz, ed., *On Freedom and Free Enterprise* (Princeton, 1956), pp. 3-4.
6. Hayek, *Road to Serfdom*, p. 70.
7. *Ibid.*, pp. 35, 42.
8. *Ibid.*, p. 92.
9. *Ibid.*, p. 31.
10. *Ibid.*, pp. 3-4.
11. *Ibid.*, p. 17.
12. "In no system that could be rationally defended would the state just do nothing" (*ibid.*, p. 39).
13. For example, see *ibid.*, pp. 17, 36. On the latter page he called the laissez-faire attitude "dogmatic."
14. *Ibid.*, p. 72.
15. *Ibid.*, pp. 36-37, 120-121. They might not always be wise policy, however.
16. *Ibid.*, p. 42. For a concise statement of Hayek's distinction, see his radio debate with Professor Charles Merriam and Professor Maynard Kreuger, April 22, 1945, entitled "The Road to Serfdom," *University of Chicago Round Table*, no. 370.
17. See, for example, George Orwell's review in the *Observer*, April 9, 1944, reprinted in *As I Please, 1943-1945* (New York, 1968), pp. 117-119. A surprisingly favorable review came from Lord Keynes in a letter to Hayek, June 28, 1944: "In my opinion it is a grand book. We all have the greatest reason to be grateful to you for saying so well what needs so much to be said. You will not expect me to accept quite all the economic dicta in it. But morally and philosophically I find myself in agreement with virtually the whole of it;

and not only in agreement with it, but in a deeply moved agreement" (quoted in *The Life of John Maynard Keynes*, by R.F. Harrod [New York, 1951], p. 436).

18. Barbara Wootton, M.P., *Freedom Under Planning* (London, 1945), and Herman Finer, *The Road to Reaction* (Boston, 1945).

19. *New York Times*, June 6, 1945, p. 4. Harold Macmillan later recalled that Churchill read *The Road to Serfdom* before he gave his famous 1945 election radio address denouncing socialism as a threat to British liberties (Macmillan, *Tides of Fortune*, p. 32). For Hayek's retrospective analysis of the success of his book in Great Britain, see his 1956 foreword, pp. iv-v.

20. Hayek, *Road to Serfdom*, p. v. For a discussion of the peculiar response of at least one publisher to the book, see William Miller, *The Book Industry* (New York, 1949), p. 12, and W.T. Couch, "The Sainted Book Burners," *The Freeman* 5 (April 1955): 423.

21. C. Hartley Grattan, "Hayek's Hayride: Or, Have You Read a Good Book Lately?" *Harper's* 191 (July 1945): 48.

22. Hayek, *Road to Serfdom*, p. v.

23. Grattan, "Hayek's Hayride," p. 48.

24. Lawrence K. Frank, "The Rising Stock of Dr. Hayek," *Saturday Review* 28 (May 12, 1945): 5.

25. Henry Hazlitt, "An Economist's View of 'Planning,'" *New York Times Book Review*, September 24, 1944, p. 1. Hazlitt believes that this front-page review in one of the nation's principal newspapers made Hayek's book a best-seller (interview by telephone, August 30, 1973).

26. John Davenport, review of Hayek's book in *Fortune* 30 (November 1944): 218-221.

27. Smith, "Individualism Talks Back," p. 203.

28. "Poor Mr. Hayek," *New Republic* 112 (April 23, 1945): 543; "In Justice to Mr. Hayek," *New Republic* 112 (May 21, 1945): 695.

29. Stuart Chase, "Back to Grandfather," *Nation* 160 (May 19, 1945): 565.

30. Charles Merriam, in *American Political Science Review* 40 (February 1946): 135.

31. Aaron Director and Eric Roll, in *American Economic Review* 35 (March 1945): 173-180. In introducing these reviews, the editor mentioned the "ideological character" of Hayek's book.

32. Hayek's reaction, given in the *Chicago Sun*, is quoted in Grattan, "Hayek's Hayride," p. 50.

33. Hayek, *Road to Serfdom*, pp. v-vi.

34. "In Justice to Mr. Hayek," p. 695.

35. Grattan, "Hayek's Hayride," p. 45.

36. Paul Hutchison, "Is a Planned Economy Slavery?" *Christian Century* 62 (January 3, 1945): 18.

37. Hayek, *Road to Serfdom*, pp. vi-vii.

38. Chase, "Back to Grandfather," p. 565.

39. For biographical information on Mises, see Sennholz, ed., *On Freedom*, pp. ix-xii. For a discussion of his intellectual ancestry, see his own *The Historical Setting of the Austrian School of Economics* (New Rochelle, N.Y., 1969).

40. Henry C. Simons, in *Annals of the American Academy of Political and Social Science* 236 (November 1944): 192.

41. See Sennholz, ed., *On Freedom*, pp. x-xi.

42. Friedrich A. Hayek, "A Rebirth of Liberalism," *The Freeman* 2 (July 28, 1952): 730.

43. Ludwig von Mises, *Omnipotent Government* (New Haven, 1944), *Bureaucracy* (New Haven, 1944). Both were published by Yale University Press.

44. University of Chicago Professor Henry C. Simons, for instance, called Mises "the greatest living teacher of economics" and "the toughest old liberal or Manchesterite of

his time." But alas, he added, "he is also perhaps the worst enemy of his own libertarian cause" (in *Annals*, 192).

45. Antonin Basch, in *American Economic Review* 34 (December 1944): 903.

46. Mises, *Omnipotent Government*, p. 55.

47. *Ibid.*, p. 48.

48. *Ibid.*, pp. 58, 284.

49. Simons, in *Annals*, p. 192.

50. John Cort, "More Books of the Week," *Commonweal* 41 (November 3, 1944): 78. This is a review of *Bureaucracy*. The purity of Mises's opposition to any governmental power beyond the minimum necessary for the preservation of domestic peace and the market is suggested by an anecdote that Leonard Read tells about him. In 1940, shortly after arriving in the United States, Mises was a guest of Read, then general manager of the Los Angeles Chamber of Commerce. One evening at a party, someone asked Professor Mises: Suppose he was the dictator of the United States and could impose any change he deemed advisable. What would he do? Instantly Mises replied, "I would abdicate!" Interview with Leonard Read, president of the Foundation for Economic Education, Irvington-on-Hudson, N.Y., November 17, 1971.

51. Mises, *Omnipotent Government*, p. 6.

52. See *ibid.*, passim, and Ludwig von Mises, *Planned Chaos* (Irvington-on-Hudson, N.Y., 1947).

53. Mises, *Bureaucracy*, p. iii.

54. *Ibid.*, p. 125.

55. Henry Hazlitt, *New York Times Book Review*, October 1, 1944, p. 5.

56. Russell Kirk to W. C. McCann, November 3, 1944, Russell Kirk Papers, Clarke Historical Library at Central Michigan University, Mount Pleasant, Mich.

57. Sennholz, ed., *On Freedom*, p. xi. Paul Poirot, managing editor of *The Freeman*, and the journalist Henry Hazlitt recall that it was necessary to pay New York University to hire Mises. Because of the university's reluctance to appoint the Austrian economist, a number of his American friends, including Hazlitt, Leonard Read, and Lawrence Fertig (an NYU trustee), had to channel funds to the university to support him. Interview with Paul Poirot, Irvington-on-Hudson, N.Y., November 16, 1971; interview with Henry Hazlitt (by telephone), August 30, 1973.

58. Ludwig von Mises, *Human Action* (New Haven, 1949). Leonard Read states that Yale University Press never would have published the book had Read not paid the press $7,500 for 750 copies, which he distributed to colleges and universities in the United States (interview, November 17, 1971).

59. Alfred Sherrard, "The Free Man's Straitjacket," *New Republic* 122 (January 9, 1950): 18-19.

60. Seymour E. Harris, "Capitalist Manifesto," *Saturday Review* 32 (September 24, 1949): 31.

61. John Kenneth Galbraith, "In Defense of Laissez-Faire," *New York Times Book Review*, October 30, 1949, p. 45.

62. Henry Hazlitt, "The Case for Capitalism," *Newsweek* 34 (September 19, 1949): 70.

63. William Henry Chamberlin to Mrs. Chamberlin, July 5-6, 1949, William Henry Chamberlin Papers, Providence College, Providence, R.I.

64. Frank S. Meyer, "Richard M. Weaver: An Appreciation," *Modern Age* 14 (Summer-Fall 1970): 243.

65. Henry Regnery, "A Conservative Publisher in a Liberal World," *The Alternative* 5 (October 1971): 15.

66. Robert M. Crunden, *The Mind and Art of Albert Jay Nock* (Chicago, 1964), p. 179.

67. Nock distinguished between government, which performed the limited and negative

function of preserving the peace, and the State, which was always predatory and exploitative.

68. Albert Jay Nock, *Our Enemy, the State* (New York, 1935).

69. It is significant that Nock's essay "Isaiah's Job" was reprinted by William F. Buckley, Jr. in his anthology *American Conservative Thought in the Twentieth Century* (Indianapolis, 1970), pp. 509-522. Two recent biographies of Nock are Robert M. Crunden's, cited above, and Michael Wreszin's *The Superfluous Anarchist: Albert Jay Nock* (Providence, 1972).

70. Interview with Robert Nisbet, Northampton, Mass., November 29, 1971.

71. Russell Kirk mentioned Nock in his letters to W.C. McCann on May 14, 1945, July 19, 1945, and September 4, 1945, Kirk Papers. In this last letter, Kirk said of the recently deceased Nock, "There are few of his stamp left."

72. Interview with the Reverend Edmund Opitz, Foundation for Economic Education, Irvington-on-Hudson, N.Y., November 17, 1971.

73. Edmund Opitz, "Catalyst of Liberty," *National Review* 17 (January 12, 1965): 26. Opitz eventually helped to found the Nockian Society.

74. John Chamberlain, "People on Our Side: 1. Frank Chodorov," *The Freeman* 2 (May 5, 1952): 504; reprinted as the introduction to Frank Chodorov, *One Is a Crowd: Reflections of an Individualist* (New York, 1952), pp. vii-xii. Chamberlain, a radical in the early 1930s, had also been moved by William Graham Sumner's *Folkways*. See Malcolm Cowley and Bernard Smith, eds., *Books that Changed Our Minds* (New York, 1938), pp. 75-87. For a recent study of Chamberlain, see Frank Annunziata, "The Political Thought of John Chamberlain: Continuity and Conversion," *South Atlantic Quarterly* 74 (Winter 1975): 52-71.

75. Interview with William F. Buckley, Jr., Stamford, Conn., November 26, 1971.

76. An excellent and moving essay on Chodorov is William F. Buckley's eulogy in Buckley, *The Jeweler's Eye: A Book of Irresistible Political Reflections* (New York, 1968), pp. 343-349. See also Frank Chodorov, *Out of Step: The Autobiography of an Individualist* (New York, 1962), especially chaps. 7, 14. For other appreciations of Chodorov (who died in 1966), see the eulogies by Oscar B. Johannsen *et al.* in *Fragments* 5 (January-March 1967): 1-16.

77. Chodorov, *Out of Step*, p. 79.

78. *Ibid.*, pp. 79-82.

79. *Ibid.*, p. 80. See also Edmund A. Opitz, "Witness to the Truth," *Fragments* 4 (October-December 1966): 2.

80. Chodorov, *Out of Step*, p. 80.

81. Chodorov, promotional letter to readers of *analysis* (n.d.); copy in possession of Opitz, Foundation for Economic Education, Irvington-on-Hudson, N.Y.

82. Chodorov, promotional letter to readers of *analysis* (n.d., but about April 1945); copy in possession of Opitz. It is indicative of Chodorov's political views that in 1912 he voted for Theodore Roosevelt for president; he never again voted in a presidential election (Chodorov, *Out of Step*, p. 36).

83. In one of his early promotional letters Chodorov said that Nock had agreed to become a contributing editor of *analysis*. Death, of course, intervened.

84. Chodorov, "What This Country Needs Is Guts," *analysis* 2 (February 1946): 3.

85. *analysis* 3 (February 1947): 4.

86. *analysis* 2 (October 1946): 4.

87. Chodorov, *Out of Step*, p. 80.

88. Opitz recalls being told that Chodorov had no money for his enterprises and lived on one meal a day (interview, November 17, 1971).

89. In his interview with the author on November 26, 1971, Buckley cited Chodorov

along with Nock as a principal libertarian influence on him in the 1940s.

90. Opitz, "Witness to the Truth," p. 2.

91. James J. Martin, "Frank Chodorov: Journalist," *Fragments* 4 (October-December 1966): 7.

92. Chodorov, "Taxation Is Robbery," *Out of Step*, pp. 216-239.

93. Murray Rothbard to the author, December 14, 1971.

94. Henry Hazlitt, *Economics in One Lesson* (New York, 1946), p. ix.

95. Frank Knight, *Freedom and Reform: Essays in Economic and Social Philosophy* (Chicago, 1947).

96. Aaron Director, prefatory note to Henry C. Simons, *Economic Policy for a Free Society* (Chicago, 1948), p. v. While not fully agreeing with Simons's views, Hayek recognized his book as an outstanding and important work; see Hayek, "The Intellectuals and Socialism," *University of Chicago Law Review* 16 (Spring 1949): 417-433. This essay is reprinted in Hayek, *Studies in Philosophy, Politics and Economics*, pp. 178-194.

97. For two assessments of Simons, see John Davenport, "The Testament of Henry Simons," *Fortune* 34 (September 1946): 116-119, and Charles Oscar Hardy, "Liberalism in the Modern State: The Philosophy of Henry Simons," *Journal of Political Economy* 56 (August 1948): 305-314. For both Knight and Simons, see William Breit and Roger L. Ransom, *The Academic Scribblers* (New York, 1971), chaps. 12, 13. A recent essay on Simons is George J. Stigler, "Henry Calvert Simons," *Journal of Law and Economics* 17 (April 1974): 1-5.

98. Friedrich A. Hayek, *Individualism and Economic Order* (Chicago, 1948).

99. *Ibid.*, p. 6.

100. *Ibid.*, p. 32.

101. *Ibid.*, p. 11.

102. According to Milton Friedman (interview by tape, March 1972), three University of Chicago professors—John U. Nef, Aaron Director, and Henry Simons—persuaded the small, conservative Volker Fund to pay a portion of Hayek's salary at the university for a long time. Otherwise, presumably, the Austrian economist would never have joined its faculty. Hayek became a member of the prestigious Committee on Social Thought; Friedman recalls hearing that the department of economics was reluctant to hire him.

103. Felix Morley, *The Power in the People* (New York, 1949); John T. Flynn, *The Road Ahead* (New York, 1949).

104. Regnery, "Conservative Publisher," p. 14.

105. The president of Devin-Adair Company was Devin A. Garrity, who had met Frank Chodorov at the Henry George School in the 1930s and had been impressed by him ever since. Devin-Adair published all four of Chodorov's books. See Devin A. Garrity, "Frank Chodorov: Prophet," *Fragments* 4 (October-December 1966): 5. Caxton Printers was founded in 1907 by James Herrick Gipson, brother of the famous historian Lawrence Henry Gipson. For a brief reminiscence of this individualistic publisher, see Lawrence Henry Gipson, "James Herrick Gipson, RIP," *National Review* 17 (June 15, 1965): 508.

106. John Chamberlain, "A Reviewer's Notebook," *The Freeman* 2 (July 14, 1952): 702-703.

107. Interview with Read, November 17, 1971.

108. *Ibid.*

109. *Ibid.*; Chamberlain, "A Reviewer's Notebook," p. 703. Read's libertarianism was not merely theoretical; he vigorously protested the removal of Japanese-American citizens from their homes on the west coast during the war.

110. Interview with Read, November 17, 1971.

111. These were Donaldson Brown, vice-chairman, General Motors Corporation; Pro-

fessor Fred Rogers Fairchild, Yale University; David M. Goodrich, chairman, B.F. Goodrich Company; Henry Hazlitt, *New York Times*; Claude Robinson, president, Opinion Research Corporation; Professor Leo Wolman, Columbia University (*ibid.*).

112. Interview with Paul Poirot, November 16, 1971; interview with W.M. Curtiss, Irvington-on-Hudson, N.Y., November 18, 1971.

113. Interview with Read, November 17, 1971.

114. Interview with Poirot, November 16, 1971.

115. On October 1, 1947, the foundation was nearly bankrupt, with a $120,000 mortgage, $70,000 in unpaid bills, and no money in the bank. Two small conservative foundations—the Relm Foundation and the Volker Fund—put up the money for the mortgage. Within less than three years, Read, an excellent fund raiser, had paid off this debt and established FEE's solvency (interview, November 17, 1971). The role of the Volker Fund and Relm Foundation in financing intellectual conservative causes was unobtrusive but frequently crucial.

116. *Ibid.*

117. Interview with Curtiss, November 18, 1971. Read was not an anarchist. See his *Government—An Ideal Concept* (Irvington-on-Hudson, N.Y., 1954), a book dedicated to W.C. Mullendore.

118. John Chamberlain, "A Reviewer's Notebook," *The Freeman* 5 (October 1954): 144.

119. Chamberlain, "A Reviewer's Notebook," *The Freeman* 2 (July 14, 1952): 702. In the late 1950s the list reached 50,000, where it has hovered ever since (interview with Poirot, November 16, 1971).

120. Interview with Read, November 17, 1971. Probably more than anyone else, Read is responsible for the great interest in Frédéric Bastiat on the American Right. Incidentally, in the preface to *Economics in One Lesson*, Henry Hazlitt stated that his greatest debt therein was to an essay by Bastiat.

121. *Essays on Liberty* (Irvington-on-Hudson, N.Y., 1952).

122. Leonard Read, *Outlook for Liberty* (Irvington-on-Hudson, N.Y., 1951), quoted in *A Free Man's Library* by Henry Hazlitt (New York, 1956), p. 137. For further comments on Read, see William F. Buckley, Jr., *The Governor Listeth: A Book of Inspired Political Revelations* (New York, 1970), pp. 408-411.

123. Hayek, *Studies*, p. 199n.

124. Quoted in *Le colloque Walter Lippmann* (Paris, 1939), p. 13. This is a transcript of the proceedings of the five-day conference.

125. Information about this meeting can be found in Hayek's opening remarks, reprinted in *Studies*, pp. 148-159. The participants from America were Karl Brandt, John Davenport, Aaron Director, Milton Friedman, Harry Gideonse, Frank Graham, F.A. Harper, Henry Hazlitt, Frank H. Knight, Fritz Machlup, L.B. Miller, Ludwig von Mises, Felix Morley, Leonard Read, George Stigler, and V.O. Watts. It was virtually a directory of intellectuals of the American libertarian Right. It is quite noteworthy that the Volker Fund "made possible the participation" of these individuals (Hayek, *Studies*, p. 159). Among the European conferees were Hayek, Bertrand de Jouvenel, John Jewkes, Michael Polanyi, Karl Popper, Lionel Robbins, and Wilhelm Röpke; for the complete list, see Hayek, *Studies*, p. 148n.

126. From the "Statement of Aims" of the Mont Pélerin Society, adopted April 8, 1947; copy in possession of the author.

127. *Ibid.*

128. Hayek had thought of naming the society after Lord Acton or Alexis de Tocqueville, but instead a neutral name was preferred (Hayek, *Studies*, p. 158).

129. Quoted by John Davenport in "The Radical Economics of Milton Friedman," *Fortune* 75 (June 1, 1967): 147.

130. Interview with Friedman, March 1972.

131. Among the Americans who could not attend the first Mont Pélerin Society meeting but who later agreed to join were William Henry Chamberlin, Max Eastman, Hans Kohn, Walter Lippmann, and Henry Wriston. Europeans included Luigi Einaudi, Salvador de Madariaga, Jacques Rueff, and G.M. Young (Hayek, *Studies*, p. 152n).

132. For example, papers presented at the society comprised the core of Friedrich Hayek, ed., *Capitalism and the Historians* (Chicago, 1954).

133. Hayek, "Rebirth of Liberalism," p. 731.

134. "The Faith of the Freeman," *The Freeman* 1 (October 2, 1950): 5.

135. At the end of its first year *The Freeman* listed among its owners Chamberlain, Hazlitt, La Follette, Mises, Read, and Roscoe Pound (*The Freeman* 2 [October 22, 1951]: 34).

136. *Ibid.*

137. This was the subtitle which the magazine adopted with its issue of April 7, 1952.

138. These men sent greetings to *The Freeman* on its second anniversary. See "Birthday Greetings," *The Freeman* 3 (October 20, 1952): 43-45.

139. Interview with Read, November 17, 1971. The title was retained but was transferred to the former *Notes on Liberty*, FEE's monthly collection of short articles and homilies similar in format to the *Reader's Digest*.

140. Under the direction of William Bradford Huie, who succeeded Lawrence Spivack as editor late in 1950, the *American Mercury* moved further to the Right.

141. Quoted in Eckard V. Toy, "Spiritual Mobilization: The Failure of an Ultra-conservative Ideal in the 1950's," *Pacific Northwest Quarterly* 61 (April 1970): 78.

142. "Dear Mr. Bennett: Dear Mr. Opitz:" *Faith and Freedom* 4 (April 1953): 3-6, and 4 (May 1953): 10-15.

143. Interview with Opitz, November 17, 1971. Since 1955, Opitz has been on the staff of the Foundation for Economic Education.

144. Since the days of H.L. Mencken, for instance, the *American Mercury* had considerable prestige. *Faith and Freedom* was sent to a literate, professional clientele (the ministry), and Spiritual Mobilization attracted some distinguished sponsors in the 1940s and 1950s. See Toy, "Spiritual Mobilization," pp. 77-86.

145. Both were published by Devin-Adair, which Garrity headed.

146. Interview with Buckley, November 26, 1971. In *One Is a Crowd*, Chodorov argued for the abolition of the government postal monopoly—one mark of his intransigence.

147. Devin A. Garrity recalls Chodorov's delight in saying that no one was further right than he (interview, South Hadley, Mass., August 5, 1972). The importance of Chodorov's influence and the quiet way in which it spread are both evident in an anecdote told by M. Stanton Evans, later a leading conservative writer and activist. While an undergraduate at Yale in the 1950s, Evans discovered *One Is a Crowd*. It was the first libertarian book he had ever read, and it "opened up more intellectual perspectives to me than did the whole Yale curriculum." Evans came to believe that Chodorov "probably had more to do with the conscious shaping of my political philosophy than any other person" ("Frank Chodorov: Editor," *Fragments* 4 [October-December 1966]: 5).

148. Frank Chodorov, "A Fifty-Year Project to Combat Socialism on the Campus," *analysis* 6 (October 1950): 1-3. Buckley recalls that Chodorov always thought in terms of the distant future. In fact, Chodorov was very pleased to attract an audience of only thirty or forty people, which he considered "almost massive" (interview with Buckley, November 26, 1971).

149. William F. Buckley, Jr., *God and Man at Yale: The Superstitions of "Academic Freedom"* (Chicago, 1951), p. 113. This book was published by the Henry Regnery Company.

150. *Ibid.*, p. 46.

151. *Ibid.*, p. v.

152. Buckley did not remain president for long. In an amusing letter to him that Buckley delights in, Chodorov wrote: "Am removing you as president. Making myself pres. Easier to raise money if a Jew is president. You can be V-P. Love. Frank" (quoted in Buckley, *Jeweler's Eye*, pp. 347-348).

153. See F. R. Buckley, "Revolt of the Classes," *The Freeman* 5 (September 1955): 653-656.

154. Frank Chodorov, "The Sophomores Are Coming," *Human Events* 13 (September 26, 1956). ISI started with 600 members.

155. For an excellent survey of its work as of 1961, see M. Stanton Evans, *Revolt on the Campus* (Chicago, 1961), pp. 57-73.

156. Frank Chodorov, "The Seven Thousand Unequals," *Human Events* 14 (September 14, 1957).

157. F.R. Buckley, "Revolt of the Classes," p. 655.

158. *Ibid.*, p. 654; Chodorov, "Sophomores Are Coming."

159. The founding of ISI is one more reason why William F. Buckley, Jr. has concluded that Chodorov "deeply influenced the postwar conservative movement." See William F. Buckley, Jr., "Nay-Sayer to the Power-Hungry," *National Review* 13 (December 4, 1962): 446-447.

160. Not all, however. The journalist Garet Garrett, author of *The Revolution Was* and other anti-New Deal tracts, apparently became so despondent and angry about the nation's affairs that he actually retired to live in a cave in Tuckahoe, N.J. He died in 1954. See Garet Garrett, *The People's Pottage* (Boston, 1965), p. 140.

161. Hayek, "Rebirth of Liberalism," pp. 729-731.

162. Erik von Kuehnelt-Leddihn, "Resurgence of Liberalism," *The Freeman* 3 (February 9, 1953): 337-339.

163. Hayek, ed., *Capitalism and the Historians*, p. 10. This book was not simply a scholarly enterprise; it was quite consciously a declaration of war against the work of J.L. Hammond and Barbara Hammond and the ideological uses to which their "pessimistic" interpretation of the Industrial Revolution had been put. For a recent discussion of this controversy, see Brian Inglis, "The Poor Who Were with Us," *Encounter* 37 (September 1971): 44-55.

164. Frank Chodorov, "Things *Are* Looking Up," *The Freeman* 5 (October 1954): 117.

165. Keith Hutchinson, "A Study in Whitewash," *The Nation* 178 (June 12, 1954): 508.

166. Eric Lampard, in *American Historical Review* 60 (October 1954): 65.

167. Arthur Schlesinger, Jr., in *Annals of the American Academy of Political and Social Science* 293 (May 1954): 177-78.

168. Simons, *Economic Policy for a Free Society*, p. 51.

169. Milton Friedman recalls that this issue repeatedly divided meetings of the Mont Pélerin Society (interview, March 1972).

170. Erik von Kuehnelt-Leddihn, "Letter from the Continent," *National Review* 1 (April 4, 1956): 19.

171. *Ibid.* See also Carl Friedrich, "The Political Thought of Neo-Liberalism," *American Political Science Review* 49 (June 1955): 509-525.

172. See Robert Taft, *A Foreign Policy for Americans* (Garden City, N.Y., 1951), p. 117.

173. For an example of this more positive assessment of America, see the symposium "Our Country and Its Culture," *Partisan Review* 19 (1952): 282-326, 419-450, 562-597. Another clue to the new mood was the changing trend in historiography; attacks on "robber barons" were giving way to more sympathetic treatments of "free enterprise" and its heroes.

174. Hayek, *Road to Serfdom*, p. xiii.

175. Max Eastman, *Reflections on the Failure of Socialism* (New York, 1955).

176. See Karl Brandt, "A Life for Freedom and Human Dignity—Wilhelm Röpke (1899-1966)," *Modern Age* 10 (Summer 1966): 246-250. For an autobiographical essay, see Wilhelm Röpke, "The Economic Necessity of Freedom," *Modern Age* 3 (Summer 1959): 227-236. In 1953 the West German government awarded Röpke the Grand Cross of Merit for his contribution to the German economic recovery. One example of conservative esteem for Röpke is Karl Brandt's statement: "The remarkable prosperity of the German economy during the fifties and sixties would have been impossible without the 'Working Party for the Socially Responsible Market Economy,' of which Wilhelm Röpke was a founding member" (p. 249).

177. Quoted in *Modern Age* 10 (Spring 1966): 221. A more extensive laudatory statement by Erhard is quoted in Brandt, "Life for Freedom," p. 249.

178. For example, see Wilhelm Röpke, "The Malady of Progressivism," *The Freeman* 1 (July 30, 1951): 687-691, and "Economic 'Miracle' in Germany," *The Freeman* 3 (August 24, 1953): 843-846.

179. H. Stuart Hughes, "Capitalism and History," *Commentary* 17 (April 1954): 407.

180. Interview with Friedman, March 1972.

CHAPTER TWO

1. This is the title of a book William F. Buckley, Jr. started to write several years ago but put aside, at least temporarily (interview with Buckley, Stamford, Conn., November 26, 1971).

2. Richard M. Weaver, "Up from Liberalism," *Modern Age* 3 (Winter 1958-1959): 29-30. This is an autobiographical essay, and the next several paragraphs of the chapter are based on this source. Also useful is an unpublished memorial essay by Kendall Beaton, "Richard M. Weaver: A Clear Voice in an Addled World"; copy in possession of the author. Beaton was Weaver's brother-in-law. I am grateful to George Core for providing a copy of this essay.

3. *Ibid.*, p. 30.

4. *Ibid.*, p. 22.

5. *Ibid.*

6. *Ibid.*, p. 23.

7. *Ibid.*

8. *Ibid.*, p. 24.

9. *Ibid.*

10. *Ibid.*, pp. 25-28. The title of the dissertation was "The Confederate South, 1865-1910: A Study in the Survival of a Mind and Culture." It was published in 1968, five years after Weaver's death, as *The Southern Tradition at Bay: A History of Postbellum Thought*, ed. George Core and M.E. Bradford (New Rochelle, N.Y., 1968). This book is substantially the same as the dissertation except for an introduction and epilogue written shortly afterward by Weaver. Page references will be to the published version, which also contains an enlightening foreword by a leading Agrarian, Donald Davidson. Weaver's introduction (p. 33) discusses Ortega's concept of the "spoiled child" psychology; p. 44 contains a quotation from Ortega's *The Revolt of the Masses*, first published in 1930.

11. Weaver, *Southern Tradition*, p. 29.

12. *Ibid.*, pp. 30-31.

13. *Ibid.*, p. 59.

14. *Ibid.*, p. 388.

15. *Ibid.*, p. 391.

16. For a perceptive analysis of Weaver's intellectual roots, see M.E. Bradford, "The Agrarianism of Richard Weaver: Beginnings and Completions," *Modern Age* 14 (Summer-Fall, 1970): 249-256.

17. Ortega y Gasset, *The Revolt of the Masses* (New York, 1932), p. 73; quoted in Weaver, *Southern Tradition*, p. 44.

18. Polly Weaver Beaton to the author, February 3, 1972. Mrs. Beaton is a sister of Richard Weaver.

19. Frank S. Meyer, "Richard M. Weaver: An Appreciation," *Modern Age* 14 (Summer-Fall 1970): 243.

20. Richard M. Weaver, *Ideas Have Consequences* (Chicago, 1948), p. 1.

21. *Ibid.*, pp. 2-3.

22. *Ibid.*, p. 3.

23. *Ibid.*, p. 4.

24. *Ibid.*, pp. 4-17. The foregoing is a partial summary of the introduction.

25. *Ibid.*, p. 23.

26. *Ibid.*, p. 24.

27. *Ibid.*, p. 35.

28. *Ibid.*, p. 113.

29. *Ibid.*, p. 103.

30. *Ibid.*, pp. 130-131.

31. *Ibid.*, p. 131.

32. *Ibid.*, p. 133.

33. *Ibid.*, p. 147. See chap. 7 of his book for the full argument.

34. *Ibid.*, p. 148.

35. *Ibid.*, p. 158.

36. *Ibid.*, p. 165.

37. *Ibid.*, p. 166.

38. *Ibid.*, p. 169.

39. *Ibid.*, chap. 7.

40. Weaver to Donald Davidson, February 28, 1948, Donald Davidson Papers, Joint University Libraries, Nashville, Tenn.

41. Their comments can be found on the book jacket and on the back cover of the paperback edition published in 1959 by the University of Chicago Press.

42. Eliseo Vivas, "Historian and Moralist," *Kenyon Review* 10 (Spring 1948): 346.

43. Willmoore Kendall, in *Journal of Politics* 11 (February 1949): 261.

44. Charles Frankel, "Property, Language, and Piety," *Nation* 166 (May 29, 1948): 609-610.

45. Howard Mumford Jones, "Listing Mankind's 'Wrong Turnings,'" *New York Times Book Review*, February 22, 1948, pp. 4, 25. Jones claimed that Weaver's book made irresponsible and unfounded generalizations, lacked charity and humor, and ignored four-fifths of the human race. Jones deplored "the irresponsibility of intellectuals—who condemn without comprehension, in the name of an austere intellectualism, the total life of our time."

A few weeks later Weaver replied to Jones's criticisms. He insisted that he *had* been responsible: he had made his premises quite clear—principles that many other "thinkers in the Platonic-Christian tradition" had also advocated. As for the charge that he was "concerned with only a small portion of mankind," Weaver declared: "Actually the book was written out of concern for the millions over the earth, in bread lines, in bombed homes, in prison camps, whose sufferings, material and spiritual, are traceable to the kind of pragmatism which Jones so egregiously flaunts" (Weaver, letter to the editor, *New York Times Book Review*, March 21, 1948, p. 29).

46. W.E. Garrison, "Unraveling Mr. Weaver," *Christian Century* 65 (May 5, 1948): 416.

47. George R. Geiger, "We Note...the Consequences of Some Ideas," *Antioch Review* 8 (Spring 1948): 251.

48. Weaver to Davidson, February 28, 1948, Davidson Papers.

49. Several years later Weaver admitted that his book "met a response far beyond anything anticipated..." (foreword to the first paperback edition [Chicago: Phoenix Books, 1959], p. v).

50. Beaton, "Richard M. Weaver," p. 3. Weaver's sister was not aware of her brother's work until she discovered it in a New York City bookstore (Polly Weaver Beaton to the author, February 3, 1972).

51. Weaver later wrote in his 1959 foreword: "The book was written in the period immediately following the second World War, and it was in a way a reaction to that war—to its immense destructiveness, to the strain it placed upon ethical principles, and to the tensions it left in place of the peace and order that were professedly sought" (*Ideas Have Consequences*, p. v).

52. Herbert J. Muller, "The Revival of the Absolute," *Antioch Review* 9 (March 1949): 99-110.

53. See Felix Oppenheim, "Relativism, Absolutism, and Democracy," *American Political Science Review* 44 (December 1950): 950-959. This article contends that there are no necessary correlations among the philosophical and political views examined. A philosophical "absolutist" need not be a supporter of political absolutism, for example.

54. See John Hallowell, *The Moral Foundation of Democracy* (Chicago, 1954).

55. August Heckscher, *A Pattern of Politics* (New York, 1947).

56. *Ibid.*, p. 223.

57. *Ibid.*, pp. 229-230.

58. Gordon Keith Chalmers, *The Republic and the Person* (Chicago, 1952).

59. *Ibid.*, p. 22.

60. Quoted in *ibid.*

61. *Ibid.*, p. 24.

62. John Hallowell, "Politics and Ethics," *American Political Science Review* 38 (August 1944): 639-655. This essay, along with an opposing article by William F. Whyte, provoked a noticeable controversy among political scientists. See Gabriel Almond, Lewis Dexter, William F. Whyte, and John Hallowell, "Politics and Ethics—A Symposium," *American Political Science Review* 40 (April 1946): 283-312.

63. Hallowell, "Politics and Ethics," p. 641.

64. *Ibid.*, p. 643.

65. *Ibid.*, p. 650.

66. *Ibid.*, pp. 651-652, 653.

67. John Hallowell, "Modern Liberalism: An Invitation to Suicide," *South Atlantic Quarterly* 46 (October 1947): 459. See also John Hallowell, *The Decline of Liberalism as an Ideology* (Berkeley, 1943). This book was originally Hallowell's doctoral dissertation at Princeton. One of his mentors was Gerhart Niemeyer, a German émigré who became a leading conservative intellectual after World War II.

68. Hallowell, "Modern Liberalism," p. 460.

69. *Ibid.*, p. 462.

70. Bernard Iddings Bell, *Crisis in Education* (New York, 1949), p. 25.

71. Bernard Iddings Bell, *Crowd Culture* (New York, 1952). The book was reprinted in 1956 by Henry Regnery Company with a valuable introduction by Russell Kirk. Page references are to the 1956 edition.

72. *Ibid.*, p. 1.

73. *Ibid.*, p. 83.

74. *Ibid.*, p. 91.

75. Anthony Harrigan, "The New Depravity in American Literature," *Contemporary Review* 183 (February 1953): 106, 108. Harrigan was much impressed by William Watts Ball and eventually edited his writings. See Anthony Harrigan, ed., *The Editor and the Republic: Papers and Addresses of William Watts Ball* (Chapel Hill, N.C., 1954).

76. Anthony Harrigan, "The New Yorker," *Catholic World* 174 (March 1952): 444, 447.

77. Anthony Harrigan, "The Modern Temper," *Dalhousie Review* 33 (Summer 1953): 134. See also Harrigan, "Our Liberal Elders," *South Atlantic Quarterly* 50 (October 1951): 514-518, and "Thoughts on the Managerial Class," *Prairie Schooner* 27 (Summer 1953): 145-150.

78. Bell, *Crisis in Education*, p. 229.

79. *Ibid.*, p. 145.

80. *Ibid.*, p. 124.

81. See Mortimer Smith, *And Madly Teach* (Chicago, 1949) and *The Diminished Mind* (Chicago, 1954); Arthur Bestor, *Educational Wastelands* (Urbana, Ill., 1953) and *The Restoration of Learning* (New York, 1955); Gordon Keith Chalmers, *The Republic and the Person* (Chicago, 1952).

82. In a semiautobiographical essay published many years later, Vivas declared that by the end of the 1930s he had "begun to perceive" that "what I had been engaged in up to then was the more or less conscious effort to destroy my culture." Vivas had been shocked by the advent of the war and particularly the fall of France: "What the catastrophe revealed was the inner crumbling of a people—the French—because they had been corrupted by the liberal ethos." Vivas himself felt some responsibility for France's collapse: "Not directly, of course. But because what had brought France down was a movement in which I, as teacher and writer, had eagerly cooperated. I stood convicted before my conscience: as a liberal I was responsible for the destruction of my culture" ("Apologia Pro Fide Mea," *Intercollegiate Review* 2 [October 1965]: 131).

83. Eliseo Vivas, *The Moral Life and the Ethical Life* (Chicago, 1950), p. ix.

84. *Ibid.*, p. viii. For another account of Vivas's intellectual development, see A. Campbell Garnett, "A Search Rewarded," *Christian Century* 68 (February 7, 1951): 175.

85. Vivas, *Moral Life*, pp. 127-128.

86. Bell, *Crisis in Education*, p. 166.

87. Vivas, *Moral Life*, p. 133. Elsewhere in his book (p. 175), Vivas stated that "naturalistic moral philosophy" was "infected with radical theoretical errors which lead to frightful practical consequences."

88. *Ibid.*, p. x.

89. See entry for Voegelin in *Who's Who in America*, 37th ed., 1972-1973 (Chicago, 1972), p. 3271. Voegelin taught successively at Harvard, Bennington College, the University of Alabama, and LSU. In a letter to Francis Wilson on May 31, 1957, Francis Wilson Papers, University of Illinois, Urbana, Ill., Voegelin alluded to Elliott's aid in getting him out of Austria in 1938.

90. Eric Voegelin, *The New Science of Politics* (Chicago, 1952), p. 126.

91. *Ibid.*

92. *Ibid.*, pp. 121, 129, 107, 124, 129, 152. See in general chap. 4.

93. *Ibid.*, p. 110.

94. *Ibid.*, pp. 117, 119, 111. These symbols included "the conception of history as a sequence of three ages," "the leader," "the prophet of the new age," and "the brotherhood of autonomous persons" (pp. 111-112).

95. *Ibid.*, p. 134.

96. *Ibid.*, p. 167.

97. *Ibid.*, p. 172.

98. *Ibid.*, p. 132. For a review of Voegelin's book by a new conservative, see John Hallowell, in *Louisiana Law Review* 13 (March 1953): 525-530.

99. See entry for Leo Strauss in *Who's Who in America*, 37th ed., 1972-1973 (Chicago, 1972), p. 3077. See also Joseph Cropsey, ed., *Ancients and Moderns* (New York, 1964), pp. v-vi.

100. Leo Strauss, *The Political Philosophy of Hobbes* (Chicago, 1952), p. viii. This book, published in 1936 in England, was appropriately published in the United States in 1952, at the height of the early new conservative revival.

101. *Ibid.*, p. 2. See also p. 3.

102. *Ibid.*, pp. 159-160.

103. Leo Strauss, *Natural Right and History* (Chicago, 1953), p. 5.

104. *Ibid.*, p. 6. For Strauss's views on positivism and historicism, see chaps. 1-2. See also Leo Strauss, "Political Philosophy and History," *Journal of History of Ideas* 10 (January 1949): 30-50; reprinted in Strauss, *What is Political Philosophy? and Other Studies* (Glencoe, Ill., 1959).

105. Robert Nisbet, *The Quest for Community* (New York, 1953); reprinted as *Community and Power* (New York, 1962).

106. *Ibid.*, p. 98.

107. *Ibid.*, p. 126.

108. *Ibid.*, p. 147.

109. *Ibid.*, p. 154.

110. In fact, he used the word "vacuum" on p. 203.

111. *Ibid.*, p. 222.

112. John Hallowell, *Main Currents in Modern Political Thought* (New York, 1950), p. 84. See also Hallowell, "Modern Liberalism," pp. 453-466.

113. Hallowell, *Main Currents*, p. 91.

114. Hallowell, "Modern Liberalism." p. 455.

115. James Burnham, *Suicide of the West* (New York, 1964), p. 297.

116. J.L. Talmon, *The Rise of Totalitarian Democracy* (Boston, 1952), p. 250. See in general the introduction and conclusion.

117. Lord Percy of Newcastle, *The Heresy of Democracy* (Chicago, 1955), p. 16.

118. Albert Salomon, *The Tyranny of Progress: Reflections on the History of French Sociology* (New York, 1955), p. 97.

119. *Ibid.* Another scholar who emphasized the pernicious influence of Hegel, Saint-Simon, and Comte was Friedrich Hayek, *The Counter-Revolution of Science* (Glencoe, Ill., 1952). The "scientism" of these and other nineteenth-century intellectuals, said Hayek, had begotten the totalitarianism of the twentieth century. Scientism—the fallacious application of the methods of the natural sciences to the moral and social sciences—underlay modern attempts to engineer and consciously control society. "Scientistic hubris" and the engineering mentality were responsible, for example, for the current vogue of "economic planning." The "scientistic approach" to society was inherently collectivistic.

120. Not all the intellectuals discussed thus far necessarily considered themselves conservatives during this period. Nevertheless, their contributions were recognized, and applauded, by many who did call themselves conservatives.

121. Peter Viereck, *Shame and Glory of the Intellectuals* (Boston, 1953), p. 84.

122. *Ibid.*, p. 87.

123. *Ibid.*, pp. 78-91. See also Peter Viereck, *Metapolitics: From the Romantics to Hitler* (New York, 1941).

124. All this emphasis on ideas did not go unchallenged. In a review of Salomon's *Tyranny of Progress*, the revisionist historian Harry Elmer Barnes criticized the growing

tendency to interpret "contemporary totalitarianism as an ideological rather than an operational product." To Barnes "the exaggerated concentration on the social significance of totalitarianism and the even more fantastic search for its origins in past social thought" were signs of contemporary intellectual "degradation." It was "utterly absurd" to see Saint-Simon and Comte as "in any direct and effective sense, forerunners of contemporary totalitarianism." "Modern total war," he insisted, was the result of "the rise of mass communications and emotional engineering (systematic propaganda)." To understand totalitarianism, Barnes asserted, one should read such works as James Burnham's *The Managerial Revolution*, John T. Flynn's *As We Go Marching*, and George Orwell's *1984* rather than Salomon's book. See Harry Elmer Barnes, in *Annals of the American Academy of Political and Social Science* 302 (November 1955): 178-179.

CHAPTER THREE

1. William Barrett, "Art, Aristocracy, and Reason," *Partisan Review* 16 (June 1949): 664.

2. Robert Gorham Davis, "The New Criticism and the Democratic Tradition," *American Scholar* 19 (Winter 1949-1950): 10.

3. Clinton Rossiter, "Wanted: An American Conservatism," *Fortune* 41 (March 1950): 95.

4. Lionel Trilling, *The Liberal Imagination* (New York, 1950), p. ix.

5. Most of the specific examples in the paragraph are drawn from William L. Miller, "The 'Religious Revival' and American Politics," *Confluence* 4 (April 1955): 44-56. See also Sarah Wingate Taylor, "The Retreat from Materialism," *Catholic World* 167 (July 1948): 298-305, and Will Herberg, "The Religious Stirring on the Campus," *Commentary* 13 (March 1952): 242-248.

6. For President Eisenhower's prayer at his inauguration, see *New York Times*, January 21, 1953, p. 19. For his speech on faith for the American Legion, see *New York Times*, February 8, 1954, p. 1. The President's religious activities were frequently reported by the *Times* during these years.

7. "The New Boy," *Time* 51 (March 15, 1948): 56, 58.

8. See Arthur M. Schlesinger, Jr., "Reinhold Niebuhr's Role in American Political Thought and Life," in *Reinhold Niebuhr: His Religious, Social, and Political Thought*, ed. Charles Kegley and Robert Bretall (New York, 1956), vol. 2, pp. 125-150.

9. Ernest van den Haag, "An Open Letter to Sidney Hook," *Partisan Review* 17 (July-August 1950): 607-608.

10. Quoted in James Rorty, "Faith and Force," *The Freeman* 1 (January 8, 1951): 253.

11. William F. Buckley, Jr., *God and Man at Yale: The Superstitions of "Academic Freedom"* (Chicago, 1951), p. xii.

12. John Hallowell, *Main Currents in Modern Political Thought* (New York, 1950), p. 655.

13. *Ibid.*, p. 651. It is of interest that the presidential address at the 1948 American Historical Association convention was a defense of Christianity's approach to history, by Kenneth Scott Latourette. See Latourette, "The Christian Understanding of History," *American Historical Review* 54 (January 1949): 259-276.

14. Hallowell, "Modern Liberalism: An Invitation to Suicide," *South Atlantic Quarterly* 46 (October 1947): 462.

15. Richard M. Weaver, "Up from Liberalism," *Modern Age* 3 (Winter 1958-1959): 29.

16. *Ibid.*

17. Eliseo Vivas, *The Moral Life and the Ethical Life* (Chicago, 1950), p. 133.

18. Bernard Iddings Bell, *Crowd Culture* (New York, 1952), p. 71.

19. Gertrude Himmelfarb, "The Prophets of the New Conservatism," *Commentary* 9 (January 1950): 78.

20. Weaver, "Up from Liberalism," p. 29.

21. Hallowell, *Main Currents*, p. 652.

22. Frederick Wilhelmsen, "The Conservative Vision," *Commonweal* 62 (June 24, 1955): 295-299. For another expression of Wilhelmsen's apotheosis of the Middle Ages, criticism of such phenomena as the Industrial Revolution, and desire for a Christian culture, see Wilhelmsen, "The Conservative Catholic," *Commonweal* 57 (February 20, 1953): 491-493. In 1953, Wilhelmsen was 30 years old. With a B.A. from the University of San Francisco and an M.A. from Notre Dame, he eventually earned a Ph.D. at the University of Madrid.

23. Frederick Wilhelmsen to the editor, *Commonweal* 57 (April 2, 1953): 651. This letter was in reply to "'Liberal' vs. 'Conservative'" (editorial), *Commonweal* 57 (February 20, 1953): 488.

24. "Journalism and Joachim's Children," *Time* 61 (March 9, 1953): 57-61.

25. "Religion and the Intellectuals: Editorial Statement," *Partisan Review* 17 (February 1950): 103.

26. H. Stuart Hughes, "Our Social Salvation," *Saturday Review* 34 (March 3, 1951): 14.

27. See Leo Strauss, *Natural Right and History* (Chicago, 1953); "On Classical Political Philosophy," in *What Is Political Philosophy? and Other Studies* (Glencoe, Ill., 1959), chap. 3.

28. See Gertrude Himmelfarb, "Political Thinking: Ancients vs. Moderns," *Commentary* 12 (July 1951): 76-83.

29. Interview with William F. Buckley, Jr., Stamford, Conn., November 26, 1971.

30. John Hallowell, *The Moral Foundation of Democracy* (Chicago, 1954), pp. 24-25.

31. *Ibid.*, p. 83.

32. *Ibid.*, p. 128.

33. An excellent anthology of the controversy is Thomas L. Thorson, ed., *Plato: Totalitarian or Democrat?* (Englewood Cliffs, N.J., 1963). See also John Wild, *Plato's Modern Enemies and the Natural Law* (Chicago, 1953) and John Hallowell, "Plato and His Critics," *Journal of Politics* 27 (May 1965): 273-289.

34. Richard M. Weaver, *The Ethics of Rhetoric* (Chicago, 1953). Weaver's interest in the role of rhetoric in preserving values was lifelong, and his professional impact significant. See Richard L. Johannesen et al., eds., *Language is Sermonic: Richard M. Weaver on the Nature of Rhetoric* (Baton Rouge, La., 1970).

35. Walter Lippmann, *Essays in the Public Philosophy* (Boston, 1955), pp. 69, 79, 123. The interest in natural law was broadly based: "The revival of natural law ideas...which attained increasing momentum in the last decade, has brought in its train a renewed interest in ethics and the normative side of human conduct" (Edgar Bodenheimer, "A Decade of Jurisprudence in the United States of America: 1946-1956," *Natural Law Forum* 3 [1958]: 45).

36. Robert Nisbet, *Tradition and Revolt* (New York, 1968), p. 4.

37. Interview with Robert Nisbet, Northampton, Mass., November 29, 1971.

38. Alexis de Tocqueville, *Democracy in America*, ed. Phillips Bradley (New York, 1945).

39. William J. Schlaerth, S.J., ed., *A Symposium on Alexis de Tocqueville's Democracy in America* (New York, 1945). This was the first symposium of Fordham's newly founded Burke Society.

40. John Lukacs, *Historical Consciousness* (New York, 1968), p. 321.

41. This paragraph is based on "Erik Ritter von Kuehnelt-Leddihn: Curriculum Vitae and lecture topics" (1972); copy in possession of the author. Kuehnelt-Leddihn published *The Menace of the Herd* (Milwaukee, 1943) under the pseudonym Francis Stuart Campbell.

42. Erik von Kuehnelt-Leddihn, *Liberty or Equality: The Challenge of Our Time* (Caldwell, Idaho, 1952).

43. *Ibid.*, p. 3.

44. *Ibid.*, p. 9.

45. *Ibid.*, p. 21. Kuehnelt-Leddihn was, of course, using the word "liberal" in its "classical" rather than its twentieth-century (social-democratic) sense.

46. *Ibid.*, p. 247.

47. *Ibid.*, p. 268.

48. Kuehnelt-Leddihn was also an acerbic critic of liberalism. In a vehement review of Morris Cohen's *The Faith of a Liberal* in 1946, Kuehnelt-Leddihn claimed that neither Cohen nor his "heroes," Dewey and Justice Holmes, had any "'answer' for the satanism" of our time. Cohen's "scientific," agnostic near-relativism, said Kuehnelt-Leddihn, could not cope with the horrors of Nazism and Communism. After all, "there is no scientific reason why one should not make lampshades out of reactionaries. None whatsoever." Kuehnelt-Leddihn urged instead the "Christian Revolution" as the only antidote to nihilism. See Erik von Kuehnelt-Leddihn, "Thoughts on 'The Faith of a Liberal,'" *Catholic World* 163 (July 1946): 310-318.

49. Peter Viereck, *Conservatism Revisited: The Revolt against Revolt* (New York, 1949).

50. See Niel M. Johnson, *George Sylvester Viereck* (Urbana, Ill., 1972).

51. Conversation with Peter Viereck, South Hadley, Mass., September 20, 1972.

52. Peter Viereck, "But—I'm a Conservative!" *Atlantic Monthly* 165 (April 1940): 539.

53. *Conservatism Revisited* was dedicated to his brother's memory.

54. Viereck, *Conservatism Revisited*, pp. 31, 9, 10-11 (for the quotations). See in general chap. 1.

55. *Ibid.*, pp. 6, 28, 30.

56. See, for example, Henry Kissinger, *A World Restored* (Boston, 1957), another sympathetic study of Metternich.

57. See Irwin Ross, "No Quarrel With Liberalism," *New Leader* 32 (October 15, 1949): 8, and Dwight Macdonald, "Back to Metternich," *New Republic* 121 (November 14, 1949): 34-35. Macdonald claimed to detect "a good deal of sheepish liberalism beneath his [Viereck's] conservative wolfskin" (p. 35).

58. Peter Viereck, *Conservatism Revisited*, rev. ed. (New York, 1962), p. 16.

59. Interview with Nisbet, November 29, 1971.

60. See "The Occasion and Need of a Burke Newsletter," *Modern Age* 3 (Summer 1959): 321-324, for a survey of the Burke revival among scholars. This was the first issue of the *Burke Newsletter*.

61. Ross J.S. Hoffman to Russell Kirk, September 20, 1960, Russell Kirk Papers, Clarke Historical Library at Central Michigan University, Mount Pleasant, Mich.

62. Schlaerth, ed., *Tocqueville's Democracy in America*, p. 5.

63. Ross J.S. Hoffman and Paul Levack, eds., *Burke's Politics* (New York, 1949), pp. xxxiv-xxxv.

64. Crane Brinton, "Burke and Our Present Discontents," *Thought* 24 (June 1949): 199.

65. Russell Kirk, *Randolph of Roanoke: A Study in Conservative Thought* (Chicago, 1951), pp. 18-19.

66. The following account relies on two sources: Russell Kirk, *Confessions of a Bohemian Tory* (New York, 1963), pp. 3-30 (an illuminating autobiographical essay), and Kirk's rich and extensive correspondence files in the Kirk Papers.

67. Kirk, *Confessions*, p. 6.

68. *Ibid.*, p. 16.

69. *Ibid.*, p. 18.

70. Kirk to W.C. McCann, February 5, 1941, Kirk Papers. Kirk's substantial wartime correspondence with McCann contains many interesting and valuable details about his political and intellectual interests.

71. Kirk to McCann, March 3, 1941, Kirk Papers.

72. Kirk to McCann, January 26, 1941, Kirk Papers.

73. Kirk to McCann, January 25, 1941, Kirk Papers.

74. Russell Kirk, "Jefferson and the Faithless," *South Atlantic Quarterly* 40 (July 1941): 226-227.

75. Kirk to McCann, January 18, 1942, Kirk Papers.

76. Kirk to McCann, n.d. (probably April 1941), Kirk Papers.

77. *Ibid.*; Kirk to McCann, October 31, 1941, Kirk Papers.

78. See, for example, Kirk to McCann, February 2, 1942, Kirk Papers.

79. Kirk to McCann, March 13, 1942, Kirk Papers.

80. Kirk to McCann, March 4, 1942, Kirk Papers.

81. Kirk to McCann, September 10, 1941, Kirk Papers.

82. Kirk to McCann, October 31, 1941, Kirk Papers.

83. Kirk, *Confessions*, pp. 19-20.

84. Kirk to McCann, April 2, 1941, Kirk Papers.

85. Kirk to McCann, September 10, 1944, Kirk Papers.

86. Kirk to McCann, November 19, 1943, Kirk Papers.

87. Kirk to McCann, December 12, 1943, Kirk Papers.

88. See, for example, Kirk to McCann, July 19, 1945, Kirk Papers.

89. Kirk to McCann, June 1, 1944, Kirk Papers.

90. Russell Kirk, "Conscription *Ad Infinitum*," *South Atlantic Quarterly* 45 (July 1946): 315, 319.

91. Russell Kirk, "A Conscript on Education," *South Atlantic Quarterly* 44 (January 1945): 87, 88.

92. *Ibid.*, p. 88.

93. *Ibid.*, p. 98.

94. Bernard Iddings Bell to Russell Kirk, April 26, 1945, Kirk Papers.

95. Kirk, *Confessions*, p. 23.

96. *Ibid.*, p. 27.

97. *Ibid.*, p. 26.

98. Kirk to McCann, June 28, 1943, Kirk Papers.

99. *Review of Politics* 13 (October 1951): 398.

100. Russell Kirk, *The Conservative Mind: From Burke to Santayana* (Chicago, 1953), pp. 7-8.

101. *Ibid.*, pp. 6, 5, 399, 428.

102. *Ibid.*, p. 9. See also pp. 24-25.

103. *Ibid.*, p. 325. In 1944, Kirk had referred to himself as "thoroughly un-machined." (He did not drive a car at the time.) The only machine he had mastered, he said, was a typewriter (Kirk to McCann, September 22, 1944, Kirk Papers).

104. Henry Regnery, "A Conservative Publisher in a Liberal World," *The Alternative* 5 (October 1971): 15. Within a year the book had gone into a fourth printing. See Russell Kirk, "The American Conservative Character," *Georgia Review* 9 (Fall 1954): 249.

105. Robert Nisbet to Kirk, May 27, 1953 and September 10, 1953, Kirk Papers.

106. T.S. Eliot to Kirk, August 6, 1953, Kirk Papers.

107. Kirk to Eliot, October 21, 1953, Kirk Papers. For other new conservative or tradi-

tionalist reactions (all generally favorable), see Peter Viereck, "Conservatism vs. Smugness," *Saturday Review* 36 (October 3, 1953): 38-39; August Heckscher, "Toward a True, Creative Conservatism," *New York Herald Tribune Book Review*, August 2, 1953, p. 4; John Hallowell, in *Journal of Politics* 16 (February 1954): 150-152. An interesting criticism of Kirk by a prominent British conservative in the tradition of Hume rather than Burke is Michael Oakeshott, "Conservative Political Thought," *Spectator* 193 (October 15, 1954): 472, 474. A lavish review from the libertarian end of the conservative spectrum is Edmund Opitz, in *Faith and Freedom* 5 (March 1954): 22.

108. Regnery, "Conservative Publisher," p. 16. On another occasion Regnery stated that the appearance of *The Conservative Mind* was "a landmark in the intellectual history of the postwar period" ("Some Men of Integrity," *Imprimis* 2 [July 1973]: 5).

109. See Gordon Keith Chalmers, "Goodwill Is Not Enough," *New York Times Book Review*, May 17, 1953, pp. 7, 28.

110. The foregoing account is based on three sources: an interview with Russell Kirk, Cambridge, Mass., April 21, 1971; a lecture by Kirk at Harvard University on the same day; and a letter from Kirk to the author, January 7, 1974. For *Time*'s review, see [Max Ways], "Generation to Generation," *Time* 62 (July 6, 1953): 88, 90-92.

111. Kirk, Harvard lecture, April 21, 1971.

112. Interview with Jeffrey Hart, Hanover, N.H., September 10, 1971.

113. Regnery, "Conservative Publisher," p. 16.

114. See, for example, Richard Weaver, "The Older Religiousness in the South," *Sewanee Review* 51 (April 1943): 237-249; "Southern Chivalry and Total War," *Sewanee Review* 53 (April 1945): 267-278; "Lee the Philosopher," *Georgia Review* 2 (Fall 1948): 297-303; "Agrarianism in Exile," *Sewanee Review* 58 (Autumn 1950): 586-606.

115. Francis Wilson, *The Case for Conservatism* (Seattle, 1951), p. 72. Wilson had been investigating and developing conservative political theory for many years. See, for example, his "A Theory of Conservatism," *American Political Science Review* 35 (February 1941): 29-43, and "The Ethics of Political Conservatism," *Ethics* 53 (October 1942): 35-45.

116. Daniel Boorstin, *The Genius of American Politics* (Chicago, 1953).

117. Robert Nisbet later recalled that before he read Viereck's and Kirk's books, he had always thought of conservatism as a European intellectual tradition, unrelated to the big business, anti-New Deal "conservatism" prevalent in the United States. Viereck and Kirk changed his perspective (interview with Nisbet, November 29, 1971).

118. See, for instance: Daniel Aaron, "Conservatism, Old and New," *American Quarterly* 6 (Summer 1954): 99-110; Noel Annan, "Revulsion to the Right," *Political Quarterly* 26 (July-September 1955): 211-219; Stuart Gerry Brown, "Democracy, the New Conservatism, and the Liberal Tradition in America," *Ethics* 66 (October 1955): 1-9; Phillip C. Chapman, "The New Conservatism: Cultural Criticism v. Political Philosophy," *Political Science Quarterly* 75 (March 1960): 17-34; Francis W. Coker, "Some Present-Day Critics of Liberalism," *American Political Science Review* 47 (March 1953): 1-27; Bernard Crick, "The Strange Quest for an American Conservatism," *Review of Politics* 17 (July 1955): 359-376; Ludwig Freund, "The New American Conservatism and European Conservatism," *Ethics* 66 (October 1955): 10-17; Franklyn S. Haiman, "A New Look at the New Conservatism," *Bulletin of the American Association of University Professors* 41 (Autumn 1955): 444-453; Chadwick Hall, "America's Conservative Revolution," *Antioch Review* 15 (June 1955): 204-216; Ralph L. Ketcham, "The Revival of Tradition and Conservatism in America," *Bulletin of the American Association of University Professors* 41 (Autumn 1955): 425-443; Gordon K. Lewis, "The Metaphysics of Conservatism," *Western Political Quarterly* 6 (December 1953): 728-741; H. Malcolm MacDonald, "The Revival of Conservative Thought," *Journal of Politics* 19 (February

1957): 66-80; Eric McKittrick, "'Conservatism' Today," *American Scholar* 27 (Winter 1957-1958): 49-61; C. Wright Mills, "The Conservative Mood," *Dissent* 1 (Winter 1954): 22-31; Ralph Gilbert Ross, "The Campaign Against Liberalism, Cont.," *Partisan Review* 20 (September-October 1953): 568-575; E. V. Walter, "Conservatism Recrudescent: A Critique," *Partisan Review* 21 (September-October 1954): 512-523; Harvey Wheeler, "Russell Kirk and the New Conservatism," *Shenandoah* 7 (Spring 1956): 20-34; Esmond Wright, "Radicals of the Right," *Political Quarterly* 27 (October-December 1956): 366-377.

119. Viereck, "But—I'm a Conservative!" p. 543.

120. See, for example, Viereck, *Shame and Glory of the Intellectuals* (Boston, 1953), pp. 251-255.

121. Viereck, *Conservatism Revisited*, rev. ed. (1962), p. 123.

122. Kirk, "American Conservative Character," p. 249.

123. Haiman, "New Look at the New Conservatism," p. 444. In an interview with the author on November 26, 1971, William F. Buckley, Jr. stated that the phrase "new conservative" was "a way in which liberals designated people they thought respectable." It was a means by which the "enemy" separated "approved" conservatives (Viereck, Rossiter) from those who eventually clustered around *National Review*.

124. H. Malcolm Macdonald, "Revival of Conservative Thought," p. 67.

125. Born in Budapest in 1923, educated at Cambridge University and the University of Budapest, Lukacs joined the history department of Chestnut Hill College in 1947 and remained there. A specialist in diplomatic history and the history of modern Europe, he contributed frequently to *Commonweal* and other periodicals in the 1950s. He was one of the original editorial advisers of Russell Kirk's avowedly conservative journal, *Modern Age*, founded in 1957. Although not the activist that Kirk and Viereck were, Lukacs must be counted as part of the traditionalist conservative renascence after World War II. (See footnote 138 below.) For basic biographical information, see the entry for Lukacs in *Directory of American Scholars*, 5th ed. (New York, 1969), vol. 1, p. 316.

126. Interview with Thomas Molnar, Chestnut Hill, Mass., November 4, 1972; Molnar to the author, December 11, 1974. For his account of his experiences at Dachau, see Thomas Molnar, "Last Days at Dachau," *Commonweal* 65 (November 16, 1956): 169-172. For basic biographical data, see Russell Kirk, foreword to *The Future of Education* by Thomas Molnar (New York, 1961), p. 10, and entry for Molnar in *Who's Who*, 37th ed., 1972-1973 (Chicago, 1972), p. 2218.

127. Russell Kirk, *Enemies of the Permanent Things* (New Rochelle, N.Y., 1969), p. 254.

128. Kirk had been brought up in a family where no one went to church or was deeply interested in religion. As a youth he had become an atheist (Kirk, *Confessions*, pp. 14-15). In 1942 he told a friend he was not a Christian but "the Gibbon of Michigan" (Kirk to McCann, June 1, 1942, Kirk Papers). By 1953, Kirk was obviously sympathetic to Anglican and Catholic Christianity (as seen in Burke and Newman, for example) in *The Conservative Mind*. Although Kirk still proclaimed his "heterodoxy" in *Academic Freedom* (Chicago, 1955), he was nevertheless convinced that "the fountain of learning, and of liberty, is religion" (pp. 30-31). In 1964, Kirk became a Roman Catholic; see George Scott Moncrieff to Kirk, May 4, 1964, Kirk Papers.

129. Peter Viereck to Francis Wilson, February 23, 1951, Francis Wilson Papers, University of Illinois, Urbana. Viereck added, however, that he did not expect to go further. He could not accept the supremacy of the bishop of Rome over other bishops. In 1975 Viereck amplified: "Catholicism remains the global force most immune—morally, spiritually—to Stalinism as well as to the neo-Stalinizers of, say, Portugal. And even in the belt of semi-fascist countries stretching from Brazil to Spain (in contrast to earlier clerical authoritarianism), Catholic idealists today are increasingly an effective political as

well as moral pressure in defense of the rights of the poor.... I feel a downright emotional admiration both for the Michael Novak kind of Catholic and for the Reinhold Niebuhr kind of Protestant." Viereck to the author, August 8, 1975.

130. Viereck, *Shame and Glory*, p. 45. "But for the 1970s" (according to Viereck's later, revised aphorism) "it is anti-semitism that's the anti-semitism of the liberals"—an allusion to "the new respectability of Arab terrorists among the international progressives." Viereck to the author, August 8, 1975. See Viereck's updating essay in *New York Times Book Review*, October 31, 1971, pp. 56-57.

131. Sidney Hook, *Heresy, Yes; Conspiracy, No* (New York, 1953), p. 220.

132. Frank Chodorov, arch antistatist, actually praised Viereck's *Conservatism Revisited*. See his review in *analysis* 6 (August 1950): 4; reprinted as "Not Merely Gossip: A Supplement to *Human Events*," *Human Events* 7 (August 2, 1950).

133. See Viereck, *Shame and Glory*, pp. 248, 251-255.

134. Kirk, "American Conservative Character," p. 254 (see also pp. 249-260); Russell Kirk, *A Program for Conservatives* (Chicago, 1954), p. 23.

135. Kirk, *A Program for Conservatives*, p. 147.

136. Russell Kirk, "The Age of Discussion," *Commonweal* 63 (November 11, 1955):

138. Kirk also called Chodorov's *Freeman* "baneful." Kirk to Peter Viereck, July 20, 1954; copy in possession of the author.

137. Robert Nisbet, *The Quest for Community* (New York, 1953), p. 278.

138. Frederick Wilhelmsen also denied the applicability of the word "conservative" to nineteenth-century laissez-faire: "...in a very real sense Catholic Rightists have fought that order from the raising of the banner of Charles I at Nottingham to the tragedy of Versailles" ("Conservative Catholic," p. 491). Similarly, Erik von Kuehnelt-Leddihn contended that "true liberalism" was "hardly compatible with an unlimited capitalism of the Manchester school" (*Liberty or Equality*, p. 5). John Lukacs, a European émigré, attacked the "muddled and dreadful liberal terminology" of calling the Republican Party conservative. For Lukacs, conservatism meant Adams, Calhoun, and Tocqueville, not "ad-men and used-car dealers in the mid-West" (Lukacs to the editor, *Commonweal* 61 [November 12, 1954]: 168-169).

139. Viereck to Wilson, February 23, 1951, Wilson Papers.

140. Weaver, "Lee the Philosopher," p. 301.

141. Louis Filler to the editor, *Modern Age* 2 (Winter 1957-1958): 102.

142. Raymond English, "Conservatism: The Forbidden Faith," *American Scholar* 21 (Autumn 1952): 393-412. For a further assessment of American conservatism by Professor English, a British subject and political scientist, see his letter to the editor, *The Listener* 55 (March 29, 1956): 319.

143. Clinton Rossiter, *Conservatism in America: The Thankless Persuasion*, 2nd ed., rev. (New York, 1962).

144. Cushing Strout, "Liberalism, Conservatism, and the Babel of Tongues," *Partisan Review* 25 (Winter 1958): 102.

145. Clinton Rossiter, "The Giants of American Conservatism," *American Heritage* 6 (October 1955): 56.

CHAPTER FOUR

1. This title is taken from a documentary on Communist Russia which appeared on television some years ago.

2. Jeffrey Hart, "The Pattern of Our War," *National Review* 18 (January 11, 1966): 31.

3. Allen Guttmann, *The Wound in the Heart: America and the Spanish Civil War* (New York, 1962).

4. See Murray Rothbard, "The Transformation of the American Right," *Continuum* 2 (Summer 1964): 220-231.

5. The leading works of right-wing revisionism after World War II were Charles A. Beard, *President Roosevelt and the Coming of the War, 1941* (New Haven, 1948); Harry Elmer Barnes, ed., *Perpetual War for Perpetual Peace* (Caldwell, Idaho, 1953); William Henry Chamberlin, *America's Second Crusade* (Chicago, 1950); George Morgenstern, *Pearl Harbor: The Story of the Secret War* (New York, 1947); Charles C. Tansill, *Back Door to War: The Roosevelt Foreign Policy* (Chicago, 1952). *Human Events*, founded in 1944 by Felix Morley, Frank Hanighen, and Henry Regnery (the latter active in America First), was another source of right-wing criticism of Roosevelt's foreign policies. For a survey of the significance of revisionism, see Selig Adler, *The Isolationist Impulse: Its Twentieth-Century Reaction* (New York, 1957), pp. 384-388. See also Henry Regnery, "A Conservative Publisher in a Liberal World," *The Alternative* 5 (October 1971): 14-16.

6. Barnes, ed., *Perpetual War*, p. 658.

7. Chamberlin, *America's Second Crusade*, p. 353.

8. Russell Kirk to W.C. McCann, February 13, 1944, Russell Kirk Papers, Clarke Historical Library at Central Michigan University, Mount Pleasant, Mich.

9. Chamberlin, *America's Second Crusade*, p. 353.

10. Eugene Lyons, *The Red Decade: The Stalinist Penetration of America* (Indianapolis, 1941). For a brief sketch of Lyons, see Daniel Aaron, *Writers on the Left* (New York, 1961), p. 248.

11. Aaron, *Writers on the Left*, p. 248.

12. Lyons, *Red Decade*, p. 14.

13. *Ibid.*, p. 17.

14. For Lyons's discussion of the pact, see *ibid.*, chap. 28. For a summary of the Open Letter, see *New York Times*, August 14, 1939, p. 15. The Open Letter, dated August 10, was printed in full in *Nation* 149 (August 23, 1939): 228. See also "In Reply to a Committee," *New Republic* 100 (August 23, 1939): 65.

15. See Frank A. Warren III, *Liberals and Communism: The 'Red Decade' Revisited* (Bloomington, Ind., 1966).

16. Eugene Lyons, *Moscow Carousel* (New York, 1935) and *Assignment in Utopia* (New York, 1937).

17. Freda Utley, *The Dream We Lost* (New York, 1940); Max Eastman, *Artists in Uniform* (New York, 1934) and *Stalin's Russia and the Crisis in Socialism* (New York, 1940); William Henry Chamberlin, *Collectivism: A False Utopia* (New York, 1937) and *The Confessions of an Individualist* (New York, 1940).

18. Chamberlin, *Confessions*, p. 159.

19. Walter Krivitsky, *In Stalin's Secret Service* (New York, 1941); Benjamin Gitlow, *I Confess* (New York, 1940); Jan Valtin, *Out of the Night* (New York, 1941).

20. Interview with James Burnham, Kent, Conn., February 4, 1972.

21. Eugene Lyons, "Appeasement in Yalta," *American Mercury* 60 (April 1945): 461-468.

22. Athan Theoharis, *The Yalta Myths: An Issue in U.S. Politics, 1945-1955* (Columbia, Mo., 1970), p. 1. See also chap. 2.

23. See Arthur Bliss Lane, *I Saw Poland Betrayed* (Indianapolis, 1948).

24. James Burnham, *The Coming Defeat of Communism* (New York, 1950), p. 56.

25. See Joseph Keeley, *The China Lobby Man: The Story of Alfred Kohlberg* (New

Rochelle, N.Y., 1969), pp. 194-206.

26. Freda Utley, *The China Story* (Chicago, 1951); John T. Flynn, *While You Slept: Our Tragedy in Asia and Who Made It* (New York, 1951). It is noteworthy that both books were issued by right-wing publishers—Regnery and Devin-Adair, respectively. The heads of both firms had been "isolationists" in the 1930s.

27. See, for example, Theoharis, *Yalta Myths*; Robert Griffith, *The Politics of Fear: Joseph R. McCarthy and the Senate* (Lexington, Ky., 1970); and Ronald J. Caridi, *The Korean War and American Politics* (Philadelphia, 1968). For a brief conservative critique of the foreign policy of the Truman administration, see William F. Buckley, Jr., "Dean Acheson's Record," *The Freeman* 2 (March 10, 1952): 378-380.

28. See Robert Strausz-Hupé and Stefan T. Possony, *International Relations* (New York, 1950); Stefan T. Possony, *A Century of Conflict: Communist Techniques of World Revolution* (Chicago, 1953); Gerhart Niemeyer, *An Inquiry into Soviet Mentality* (New York, 1956).

29. Niemeyer, a political scientist, was born in Germany in 1907 and came to the United States in 1937. During the next thirteen years he taught at Princeton and Oglethorpe universities. From 1950 to 1953 he was a planning adviser in the State Department; from 1953 to 1955, a research analyst for the Council on Foreign Relations. In 1955 he joined the faculty of Notre Dame University.

Possony, a native of Vienna, earned his doctorate at the age of 20 (in 1933) and came to America in 1940. A specialist in military strategy, he was already known for *Tomorrow's War* (London, 1938). During World War II he worked first at the Institute for Advanced Study and then for the U.S. Navy. In 1946 he began fifteen years of work for the air force as well as fifteen years as a professor in the Graduate School of Georgetown University. In 1961 he became director of the International Political Studies Program of the Hoover Institution.

Like Possony, Strausz-Hupé was born in Vienna. In 1923 (at the age of 20) he emigrated to the United States and eventually became a political scientist specializing in foreign affairs. Early in the 1940s he published *The Russian-German Riddle* (Philadelphia, 1940), *Axis-America* (New York, 1941), and *Geopolitics* (New York, 1942), followed by several other works later in the 1940s and in the 1950s. In 1953 he lectured at the Air War College. Like Niemeyer and Possony, Strausz-Hupé had close connections with the U.S. government.

For biographical data on Niemeyer, Possony, and Strausz-Hupé, see *Who's Who*, 37th ed., 1972-1973 (Chicago, 1972), pp. 2336, 2529, and 3077, respectively. See also Robert Strausz-Hupé, *In My Time* (New York, 1965), and Morton A. Kaplan, "Robert Strausz-Hupé: Scholar, Gentleman, Man of Letters," *Orbis* 14 (Spring 1970): 58-70.

30. Bogdan Raditsa, "Beyond Containment to Liberation," *Commentary* 12 (September 1951): 226, 227, 231.

31. William Henry Chamberlin, *Beyond Containment* (Chicago, 1953), p. 376.

32. Peter Viereck, *Shame and Glory of the Intellectuals* (Boston, 1953), pp. 164, 163, 162, 185.

33. This paragraph is based on two sources: an interview with Burnham, February 4, 1972, and James Burnham, *The Managerial Revolution* (Bloomington, Ind.: Midlands ed., 1960), pp. v-vi.

34. James Burnham, *The Machiavellians: Defenders of Freedom* (1943; Chicago: Gateway ed., 1963), p. viii. Burnham wrote these remarks as part of a special preface to the 1963 edition.

35. James Burnham, *The Struggle for the World* (New York, 1947); interview with Burnham, February 4, 1972.

36. Burnham, *Struggle*, p. 55.

37. *Ibid.*, pp. 127, 181.

38. *Ibid.*, p. 160.

39. *Ibid.*, p. 177.

40. *Ibid.*, pp. 182, 184.

41. *Ibid.*, p. 190. See chaps. 14-16 for the full discussion of Burnham's proposals.

42. *Ibid.*, pp. 222-223.

43. *Ibid.*, p. 230.

44. *Ibid.*, pp. 240, 247.

45. Burnham, *Coming Defeat of Communism*, p. 9n.

46. *Ibid.*, p. 137.

47. *Ibid.*, p. 131.

48. See *ibid.*, pp. 145-148. Burnham indicated that the decision of whether to initiate "an immediate total attack" on the Soviet Union was only "a problem of expediency." At the moment circumstances did not dictate an all-out war, but circumstances might change. Burnham believed that his plan for "offensive political warfare" was the only way to avoid a full-scale war.

49. *Ibid.*, p. 143.

50. James Burnham, *Containment or Liberation? An Inquiry into the Aims of United States Foreign Policy* (New York, 1953), p. 43.

51. *Ibid.*, p. 41.

52. *Ibid.*, p. 43.

53. *Ibid.*, pp. 251-252.

54. *Ibid.*, p. 98.

55. *Ibid.*, p. 112.

56. See *ibid.*, part 3.

57. *Ibid.*, p. 204.

58. *Ibid.*, pp. 205-206.

59. *Ibid.*, pp. 206, 207, 209.

60. See "Blueprint for Empire," *Christian Century* 64 (May 21, 1947): 646-648; "Blueprint for Destruction," *Christian Century* 64 (May 28, 1947): 678-679; "The Truman-Burnham Parallel," *Christian Century* 64 (June 4, 1947): 702-703.

61. Burnham, *Containment or Liberation?*, p. 255. According to one historian, *The Coming Defeat of Communism* "struck profoundly sympathetic chords" among influential officials in the State Department, Defense Department, and CIA early in 1950 (Townsend Hoopes, *The Devil and John Foster Dulles* [Boston, 1973], p. 118).

62. Burnham, *Coming Defeat of Communism*, p. 217.

63. *New York Times*, July 23, 1951, p. 1.

64. Harvey Breit, "Talk with James Burnham," *New York Times Book Review*, February 26, 1950, p. 16.

65. In *The Game of Nations* (London, 1969), p. 259, a British author, Miles Copeland, stated that Burnham was a "consultant" to the CIA after World War II. Similarly, in *Undercover: Memoirs of an American Secret Agent* (New York, 1974), p. 69, E. Howard Hunt, a former CIA agent, identified Burnham as a "consultant" to the CIA's Office of Policy Coordination, c. 1950. In an interview with the author on February 4, 1972, Burnham declined to discuss directly his work with the government in those years.

66. For a hostile study of the American Committee for Cultural Freedom, see Christopher Lasch, "The Cultural Cold War: A Short History of the Congress for Cultural Freedom," in *Toward a New Past: Dissenting Essays in American History*, ed. Barton J. Bernstein (New York, 1967), pp. 332-359.

67. Excerpts from *The Struggle for the World* appeared also in *Commonweal* 48 (March 14, 1947): 534-538. A portion of *The Coming Defeat of Communism* was published in

Partisan Review 17 (January 1950): 47-63. Clearly Burnham's ideas were widely disseminated by journals of differing political views, one mark of an important thinker.

68. Frank S. Meyer, "Books in Review," *American Mercury* 76 (May 1953): 73; Eugene Lyons, "Let's Take the Initiative," *The Freeman* 3 (April 6, 1953): 497-499.

69. Raymond Moley, "The End of a Blind Trail," *Newsweek* 41 (March 9, 1953): 92.

70. See, for example, Louis Budenz, *This Is My Story* (New York, 1947); Elizabeth Bentley, *Out of Bondage* (New York, 1951); Bella Dodd, *School of Darkness* (New York, 1954); Hede Massing, *This Deception* (New York, 1951).

71. Richard Crossman, ed., *The God that Failed* (New York, 1950); Julien Steinberg, ed., *Verdict of Three Decades: From the Literature of Individual Revolt Against Soviet Communism, 1917-1950* (New York, 1950).

72. Nathaniel Weyl is another. A member of a Communist cell (the Ware Group) in the 1930s, Weyl eventually broke, testified about his past, and became a contributor to *The Freeman*.

73. The information in this paragraph is drawn from Meyer's testimony before the Senate Internal Security Subcommittee on February 26, 1957. See U.S., Congress, Senate, Committee on the Judiciary, *Hearings Before the Subcommittee to Investigate the Internal Security Act and Other Security Laws*, 85th Cong., 1st sess., 1957, pp. 3577-3609.

74. Interview with Meyer (by telephone), September 4, 1971.

75. In 1949, Meyer testified in *Dennis et al.* vs. *U.S.*, the trial of the principal U.S. Communist Party leaders. Meyer, *Hearings*, p. 3601.

76. Frank S. Meyer, "Richard M. Weaver: An Appreciation," *Modern Age* 14 (Summer-Fall 1970): 243.

77. William A. Rusher, *Special Counsel* (New Rochelle, N.Y., 1968), pp. 164-165.

78. In his interview with the author on September 4, 1971, Meyer stated that he worked briefly for the *American Mercury* as a book reviewer. Meyer's early contributions to *The Freeman* also were book reviews.

79. One popular account of the case is Alistair Cooke, *A Generation on Trial* (New York, 1950), but see Rebecca West's critical review in *University of Chicago Law Review* 18 (Spring 1951): 662-677. A critical review by an American conservative is John Chamberlain, "An Era on Trial," *The Freeman* 1 (October 2, 1950): 25-26.

80. Arthur M. Schlesinger, Jr. to the editor, *American Mercury* 75 (December 1952): 64. Another prominent liberal intellectual who accepted Chambers's account was Lionel Trilling; see his recent essay "Whittaker Chambers and the Middle of the Journey," *New York Review of Books* 22 (April 17, 1975): 18-24. See also Leslie Fiedler, "Hiss, Chambers and the Age of Innocence," *Commentary* 12 (August 1951): 109-119.

81. Arthur Schlesinger, Jr., "Whittaker Chambers and His *Witness*," *Saturday Review* 35 (May 24, 1952): 9; reprinted in Arthur Schlesinger, Jr., *The Politics of Hope* (Boston, 1962), pp. 183-195.

82. Burnham, *Containment or Liberation?*, p. 207.

83. Whittaker Chambers, *Witness* (New York, 1952), p. 793.

84. Ralph de Toledano, *Lament for a Generation* (New York, 1960), pp. 29, 40. The details of Toledano's background given in these paragraphs are drawn from this source, his autobiography.

85. *Ibid.*, pp. 61, 64.

86. *Ibid.*, pp. 146-147.

87. Ralph de Toledano, "The Liberal Disintegration—a Conservative View," *The Freeman* 1 (November 13, 1950): 109, 110.

88. Toledano, *Lament*, p. 172.

89. *Ibid.*, pp. 126-127.

90. *Ibid.*, p. 127.

91. Ralph de Toledano and Victor Lasky, *Seeds of Treason: The True Story of the Hiss-Chambers Tragedy* (New York, 1950). Chambers later stated that *Seeds of Treason* "enormously" contributed to the nation's understanding of the case (Chambers, *Witness*, p. 794). When Chambers died in 1961, Toledano published a eulogy: "Let Only a Few Speak for Him," *National Review* 11 (July 29, 1961): 49-51. See also, in the same issue, Duncan Norton-Taylor, "Wisdom Is the Most Terrible Ordeal" (pp. 48-49).

92. Sidney Hook, "The Faiths of Whittaker Chambers," *New York Times Book Review*, May 25, 1952, p. 1. Arthur Schlesinger, Jr. called *Witness* "one of the really significant American autobiographies" (Schlesinger, "Chambers and His *Witness*," p. 8).

93. John Chamberlain, "Whittaker Chambers: Witness," *The Freeman* 2 (June 2, 1952): 580.

94. Interview with William F. Buckley, Jr., Stamford, Conn., November 26, 1971.

95. Chambers, *Witness*, p. 769.

96. Chambers to Buckley, April 6, 1954, quoted in *Odyssey of a Friend: Whittaker Chambers' Letters to William F. Buckley, Jr., 1954-1961*, ed. William F. Buckley, Jr. (New York, 1970), pp. 60-62.

97. Chambers, *Witness*, p. 9.

98. *Ibid.*, p. 16.

99. *Ibid.*, p. 17.

100. *Ibid.*, p. 699.

101. Eric Voegelin, *The New Science of Politics* (Chicago, 1952), p. 175.

102. For criticisms from the Left of Chambers's philosophy, see Schlesinger, "Chambers and His *Witness*," pp. 8-10, 39-41; Sidney Hook, "Faiths of Whittaker Chambers," pp. 1, 34-35; and Philip Rahv, "The Sense and Nonsense of Whittaker Chambers," *Partisan Review* 19 (July-August 1952): 472-482.

103. Chambers, *Witness*, p. 472.

104. *Ibid.*, pp. 473, 741-742.

105. Interview with Buckley, November 26, 1971. In their book reviews Schlesinger and Rahv also noted the "un-American" intensity and quality of Chambers's mind. Rahv was reminded of Dostoevsky.

106. Interview with William A. Rusher, Cambridge, Mass., October 30, 1971; Rusher, *Special Counsel*, p. 17.

107. Chamberlain, "Witness," pp. 579-581.

108. Viereck, *Shame and Glory*, pp. 119, 125.

109. *Ibid.*, pp. 172, 168.

110. *Ibid.*, pp. 170n, 175.

111. *Ibid.*, pp. 306-307.

112. *Shame and Glory of the Intellectuals* was essentially a compilation of previously published articles.

113. Forrest Davis, "The Treason of 'Liberalism,'" *The Freeman* 1 (February 12, 1951): 305.

114. *Ibid.*, p. 307.

115. Interview with Burnham, February 4, 1972.

116. Quoted in William F. Buckley, Jr. and L. Brent Bozell, *McCarthy and His Enemies: The Record and Its Meaning* (Chicago, 1954), p. 153. For Lattimore's side of the story, see Owen Lattimore, *Ordeal by Slander* (Boston, 1950). For a critique of Lattimore's book by a cold war liberal who later became a neo-conservative, see Irving Kristol, "Ordeal by Mendacity," *Twentieth Century* 152 (October 1952): 315-323.

117. Quoted in James Burnham, *The Web of Subversion: Underground Networks in the U.S. Government* (New York, 1954), p. 219.

118. Interview with Jeffrey Hart, Hanover, N.H., September 10, 1971.

119. Interview with Burnham, February 4, 1972. *Reader's Digest* published excerpts from the book.

120. Burnham, *Web of Subversion*, pp. 219, 221. Burnham's allusion to Guatemala was to the leftist regime of Jacobo Arbenz, the "Red Colonel," who was overthrown in 1954. For different views of Burnham's evidence, see Robert Gorham Davis, "A Machiavellian Views Subversion," *New Leader* 37 (May 10, 1954): 16-18, and Irving Kristol, "The Web of Realism," *Commentary* 17 (June 1954): 609-610.

121. This is the title of chap. 6 of Toledano's *Lament for a Generation*.

122. Suzanne La Follette, "The Strategy of Defeat," *The Freeman* 1 (September 10, 1951): 793-795.

123. Dwight Macdonald, "Scrambled Eggheads on the Right," *Commentary* 21 (April 1956): 368.

124. John Chamberlain, "A Reviewer's Notebook," *The Freeman* 2 (August 11, 1952): 777.

125. *Ibid.*, p. 776.

126. Buckley and Bozell, *McCarthy*, p. 245.

127. *Ibid.*, p. 340.

128. *Ibid.*, p. 335.

129. *New York Times*, March 31, 1954, p. 16. According to Buckley, McCarthy considered the book too critical; see *Odyssey of a Friend*, ed. Buckley, p. 47.

130. *New York Times*, March 31, 1954, p. 16.

131. See, for example, John P. Roche, "Explaining Away McCarthy," *New Leader* 37 (May 24, 1954): 24-25; Francis W. Coker, in *Journal of Politics* 17 (February 1955): 113-122. While Coker in his exceptionally long review (perhaps an indication of the book's importance) judged the book inadequate, he conceded that it did prove laxity in the State Department and misconduct by the Tydings Committee.

132. Frank Chodorov, in *Faith and Freedom* 5 (June 1954): 32-33.

133. Max Eastman, "Facts and Logic re McCarthy," *The Freeman* 4 (April 19, 1954): 534.

134. William F. Buckley, Jr., "For the Record," *National Review* 16 (March 10, 1964): 188; *New York Times*, March 14, 1954, p. 46, and March 15, 1954, p. 16. McCarthy eventually filmed his own televised reply to Murrow; see *New York Times*, April 7, 1954, p. 18.

135. Richard Rovere, *Senator Joe McCarthy* (New York, 1959), pp. 225, 241, 241n.

136. *New York Times*, April 6, 1953, p. 7.

137. This was presumably a reference to McCarthy's encounter with General Zwicker in the Army-McCarthy hearings of 1954.

138. *New York Times*, November 16, 1954, p. 28.

139. *New York Times*, July 29, 1954, p. 9.

140. Viereck, *Shame and Glory*, p. 58.

141. Viereck's remarks are taken from his essay, "The Revolt Against the Elite," in *The New American Right*, ed. Daniel Bell (New York, 1955), pp. 91-116.

142. Peter Viereck, *The Unadjusted Man* (Boston, 1956), p. 165.

143. *Ibid.*, p. 178.

144. *Ibid.*, p. 166.

145. For basic data, see entry for Herberg in *Who's Who*, 37th ed., 1972-1973 (Chicago, 1972), p. 1411. Herberg confirmed his Communist background in a letter to the author, January 19, 1973.

146. For Herberg's intellectual development in the 1950s, see Will Herberg, "Historicism as Touchstone," *Christian Century* 77 (March 16, 1960): 311-313.

147. Will Herberg, "Government by Rabble-Rousing," *New Leader* 37 (January 18, 1954):

15, 16.

148. Interview with Robert Nisbet, Northampton, Mass., November 29, 1971.

149. Chambers to Buckley, quoted in *Odyssey of a Friend*, ed. Buckley, pp. 52, 102, 57, 177.

150. See Toledano, *Lament for a Generation*, pp. 205-213.

151. Russell Kirk, "Conformity and Legislative Committees," *Confluence* 3 (September 1954): 343.

152. Kirk to Viereck, October 3, 1952; copy in possession of the author.

153. "I know his [Taft's] deficiencies; but I think him our chief hope in this sorry time. I was immensely grieved at his defeat in Chicago, and I am now in an Olympian calm down here in my slum-alley, careless who wins the election" (*ibid.*).

154. Kirk to Viereck, August 5, 1954; copy in possession of the author.

155. See, for example, his remarks on Owen Lattimore in *Academic Freedom* (Chicago, 1955), p. 135.

156. *Ibid.*

157. *Ibid.*, pp. 76, 135; Russell Kirk, *A Program for Conservatives* (Chicago, 1954), p. 281.

158. See Will Herberg, "McCarthy and Hitler: A Delusive Parallel," *New Republic* 131 (August 23, 1954): 13-15; Ernest van den Haag, "McCarthyism and the Professors," *Commentary* 27 (February 1959): 179-182. Herberg's article concludes: "It is about time someone challenged the McCarthy myth. Joe McCarthy is not the superman of the anti-McCarthyite imagination; he is not the Hitler of American Fascism; he is not a sinister fanatic plotting a totalitarian revolution. He is just a political swashbuckler from Wisconsin who—almost accidentally—struck it rich and is determined to exploit his strike to the utmost.... The first step in ending McCarthyism is to understand just who and what Joe McCarthy really is" (p. 15).

159. Kirk, "Conformity and Legislative Committees," p. 345.

160. *Ibid.*, p. 351.

161. The Senate Munitions Investigating Committee, chaired by Senator Gerald P. Nye, attempted to prove in its hearings (1934-1936) that bankers and munitions makers, anxious for a profit, had engineered American entry into World War I. An energetic counsel to the committee, incidentally, was Alger Hiss.

162. Kirk, "Conformity and Legislative Committees," p. 347.

163. Interview with Russell Kirk, Cambridge, Mass., April 21, 1971.

164. Peter Viereck, *Conservatism Revisited*, rev. ed. (New York, 1962), pp. 145-146. The quotation is from book 2: "The New Conservatism—What Went Wrong?"

165. Interview with Rusher, October 30, 1971. For Rusher's account of his work with the Senate Internal Security Subcommittee, see his *Special Counsel*.

166. Interview with Burnham, February 4, 1972.

167. James Burnham, "A Letter of Resignation," *Partisan Review* 20 (November-December 1953): 716-717.

168. Rusher, *Special Counsel*, pp. 246-247.

169. William F. Buckley, Jr., "Senator McCarthy's Model?" *The Freeman* 1 (May 21, 1951): 531.

170. See, for example, Aubrey Herbert [Murray Rothbard], "Along Pennsylvania Avenue," *Faith and Freedom* 6 (February 1955): 14-15. Rothbard traced the liberals' strident hostility to McCarthy to their fear that conservatives had finally found a man who could reach the masses and threaten liberals in power.

171. James Burnham, "The Third World War: Re-Legitimization," *National Review* 3 (June 1, 1957): 518.

172. Buckley and Bozell, *McCarthy*, pp. 323-324. For their full discussion, see chap. 14.

173. *Ibid.*, p. 326.

174. *Ibid.*, pp. 311, 316, 319, 329, 334, 329.

175. *Ibid.*, pp. 332, 329, 328.

176. Kendall claimed that much of its writing and analysis was, directly or indirectly, his (Kendall to Austin Ranney, April 13, 1954; copy in possession of the author). Certainly some of the book's prose—even the diction—sounds like Kendall's. In 1954, Buckley wrote of Kendall, "I attribute whatever political and philosophical insights I have to his tutelage and his friendship. As you know, he helped me a great deal with my books" (Buckley to Henry Regnery, September 25, 1954, Buckley Papers, Yale University Library, New Haven, Conn.).

177. Kendall's career will be examined in detail in Chapter Eight.

178. Willmoore Kendall, *John Locke and the Doctrine of Majority Rule* (Urbana, Ill., 1941).

179. Kendall to the editor, *Yale Daily News*, April 28, 1950; Kendall to Ranney, April 13, 1954; *Yale Daily News*, April 18, 1950.

180. See Willmoore Kendall, *The Conservative Affirmation* (Chicago, 1963), chap. 3.

181. Viereck, *Shame and Glory*, p. 191.

182. Ernest van den Haag, "Controlling Subversive Groups," *Annals of the American Academy of Political and Social Science* 300 (July 1955): 62-71.

183. Publisher Devin A. Garrity recalled that the dispute was "utterly intense"; some people would not speak to one another because of it. Garrity remembered vividly the "intolerance" and "arrogance" of liberals during this period (interview, South Hadley, Mass., August 5, 1972).

184. One adverse effect of McCarthyism for conservatives was the straining and even disruption of their cold war alliances with the anti-Communist Left. James Burnham's resignation from *Partisan Review* was one sign of the split; friction within the American Committee for Cultural Freedom another. See also an exchange of letters in 1955 between William F. Buckley, Jr. and Daniel Bell, Buckley Papers.

185. Toledano, *Lament for a Generation*, p. 206.

186. The conservative Chicago businessman Sterling Morton, for example, wrote to Buckley: "I read your book on McCarthy with a great deal of interest but am disgusted that he yielded to the very great temptation to attack the President. Not that he didn't have just cause to do it, but it was just a foolish, even worse, stupid, thing for him to do. Of course, the pseudo-liberals will say that McCarthy's eclipse is due to the so-called censure action, but those one-sided proceedings enhanced his stature in the eyes of many people. Then he made his silly attack on the President and alienated a very large number of his followers" (Morton to Buckley, December 30, 1954, Sterling Morton Papers, Chicago Historical Society).

187. Interview with Buckley, November 26, 1971. Garrity, however, believed that McCarthy strengthened the conservative movement (interview with Garrity, August 5, 1972).

188. Burnham, *Struggle for the World*, p. 7. Peter Viereck also considered this a "blunder"; see Viereck, *Shame and Glory*, p. 159. Unlike many postwar conservatives, Viereck had been an interventionist before Pearl Harbor. While a graduate student at Harvard, he had participated actively in the campus chapter of the Committee to Defend America by Aiding the Allies (conversation with Viereck, December 3, 1974).

189. See Kirk to McCann, April 16, 1944 and June 1, 1944, Kirk Papers.

190. Burnham, *Struggle for the World*, p. 8; Kirk to McCann, January 10, 1945, Kirk Papers.

191. Harry Elmer Barnes, in *Annals of the American Academy of Political and Social Science* 252 (July 1947): 106.

192. Felix Morley, in *Human Events* 4 (July 30, 1947).

193. Leonard Read, *Conscience on the Battlefield* (Irvington-on-Hudson, N.Y., 1951), pp. 19, 23, 18, 24.

194. Interview with Leonard Read, Irvington-on-Hudson, N.Y., November 17, 1971. Significantly, Read stated in the interview that his Foundation for Economic Education was criticized more for this pamphlet than for anything else it has ever done.

195. Felix Morley, "The Early Days of *Human Events*," *Human Events* 34 (April 27, 1974): 26, 28, 31.

196. William Henry Chamberlin to Mrs. Chamberlin, July 17, 1949, William Henry Chamberlin Papers, Providence College, Providence, R.I.

197. Buckley to the author, February 22, 1972. Buckley attended an America First rally at the age of 15.

198. William F. Buckley, Jr., "The Party and the Deep Blue Sea," *Commonweal* 55 (January 24, 1952): 391-393.

199. See (in order of their appearance): Aubrey Herbert [Murray Rothbard], "The Real Aggressor," *Faith and Freedom* 5 (April 1954): 22-27; William Henry Chamberlin, "Appeasement on the Right," *New Leader* 37 (May 17, 1954): 21; William Henry Chamberlin, "Crisis of American Foreign Policy," *Faith and Freedom* 6 (September 1954): 12-15; Frank Chodorov, "The Return of 1940?" *The Freeman* 5 (September 1954): 81-82; William S. Schlamm, "But It Is Not 1940," *The Freeman* 5 (November 1954): 169-171; Frank Chodorov, "A War to Communize America," *The Freeman* 5 (November 1954): 171-174; William Schlamm vs. Aubrey Herbert [Rothbard], "Fight for Formosa or Not?" *Faith and Freedom* 6 (May 1955): 6-9; William Schlamm vs. Aubrey Herbert [Rothbard], "Fight for Formosa or Not? II," *Faith and Freedom* 6 (June 1955): 18-21. In a letter to the author on December 14, 1971, Rothbard confirmed that he used "Aubrey Herbert" as a pseudonym; he was thinking of the late-nineteenth-century British libertarian and disciple of Herbert Spencer, Auberon Herbert.

200. William F. Buckley, Jr., "A Dilemma of Conservatives," *The Freeman* 5 (August 1954): 51-52.

201. Buckley to the editor, *The Freeman* 5 (January 1955): 244.

202. Buckley and Rothbard, interviews with the author, November 26, 1971, and March 23, 1972, respectively.

203. Interview with Rothbard, March 23, 1972.

204. Chamberlin, "Crisis of American Foreign Policy," p. 15.

205. Max Eastman, *Reflections on the Failure of Socialism* (New York, 1955).

206. Frank Chodorov, "McCarthy's Mistake," *Human Events* 9 (November 12, 1952).

207. Interview with Rothbard, March 23, 1972.

208. Burnham never became a Mises-style libertarian (interview with Burnham, February 4, 1972). In the 1940s and later, he was vehemently critical of what he regarded as the "abysmal ignorance" displayed by American businessmen toward Communism. He opposed large-scale trade with the Communist bloc and believed that "the best soldiers in the fight against Communism" were ex-Communists. See Burnham, *Coming Defeat of Communism*, chap. 17.

209. Perhaps it should be noted that conservative leaders, while often critical of *intellectuals*, did not disparage intelligence or scholarship as such. They did believe that intellectuals as a group had much to atone for. See Frank Meyer, "The Unrepentant Left," *The Freeman* 4 (June 14, 1954): 677-678, and William F. Buckley, Jr., "The Colossal Flunk," *American Mercury* 54 (March 1952): 29-37.

210. Chambers, *Witness*, pp. 793-794; Burnham, *Coming Defeat of Communism*, p. 277; Willmoore Kendall, "Bipartisanship and Majority-Rule Democracy," *American Perspective* 4 (Spring 1950): 146-156; William Schlamm, introduction to *McCarthy and*

His Enemies by Buckley and Bozell, p. xv.

211. See Allen J. Matusow, ed., *Great Lives Observed: Joseph R. McCarthy* (Englewood Cliffs, N.J., 1970), pp. 131-132.

212. These are the words of William F. Buckley, Jr., Murray Rothbard, and William Rusher, respectively (interviews with the author).

213. Burnham, *Struggle for the World*, p. 223; Peter Viereck, "Thirty Days to Save the Peace," *New York Herald Tribune*, July 21, 1950, p. 14.

214. One example is Kendall to Ranney, January 29, 1952; copy in possession of the author.

215. Chambers to Buckley, August 5, 1954, quoted in *Odyssey of a Friend*, ed. Buckley, pp. 67-68.

CHAPTER FIVE

1. Interview (by telephone) with Frank S. Meyer, September 4, 1971.

2. See Eric Goldman, *Rendezvous with Destiny* (New York, 1961), chap. 17.

3. Bernard Sternsher, "Liberalism in the Fifties: The Travail of Redefinition," *Antioch Review* 22 (Fall 1960): 315-331.

4. John Fischer, "The Lost Liberals," *Harper's* 194 (May 1947): 386.

5. Arthur Schlesinger, Jr., "Abstraction and Actuality," *Nation* 164 (April 26, 1947): 489.

6. See Richard Chase, "The Progressive Hawthorne," *Partisan Review* 16 (January 1949): 96-100; exchange of letters among Newton Arvin, Robert Gorham Davis, Daniel Aaron, and Richard Chase, *Partisan Review* 16 (February 1949): 221-223; William Barrett, "What Is the 'Liberal' Mind?" *Partisan Review* 16 (March 1949): 331, 333-336; Richard Chase, Lionel Trilling, and William Barrett, "The Liberal Mind: Two Communications and a Reply," *Partisan Review* 16 (June 1949): 649-665.

7. Joseph C. Harsch, "Are Liberals Obsolete?" *Reporter* 7 (September 30, 1952): 13-16.

8. Eric Goldman, "The American Liberal: After the Fair Deal, What?" *Reporter* 8 (June 23, 1953): 25-28.

9. A useful discussion of Niebuhr and his influence on liberals is [Whittaker Chambers], "Faith for a Lenten Age," *Time* 51 (March 8, 1948): 70-72, 74-76, 79. In *Witness* (New York, 1952), p. 505, Chambers identified this essay as one that he wrote while at *Time*.

10. Arthur Schlesinger, Jr., *The Vital Center* (Boston, 1949).

11. Interview with Robert Nisbet, Northampton, Mass., November 19, 1971. For a discussion of the origins of the ADA, see Clifton Brock, *Americans for Democratic Action* (Washington, D.C., 1962).

12. One particularly famous article was Irving Kristol, "'Civil Liberties,' 1952—A Study in Confusion," *Commentary* 13 (March 1952): 228-236.

13. Schlesinger, "Abstraction and Actuality," p. 489.

14. Arthur Schlesinger, Jr., "The Need for an Intelligent Opposition," *New York Times Magazine* (April 2, 1950): 13, 56-58.

15. Arthur Schlesinger, Jr., "Calhoun Restored," *Nation* 170 (April 1, 1950): 302.

16. John Fischer, "Unwritten Rules of American Politics," *Harper's* 197 (November 1948): 27-36.

17. Chester Bowles, "The Challenge to the Conservatives," *New York Times Magazine* (October 10, 1948): 42.

18. Lionel Trilling, *The Liberal Imagination* (New York, 1950), p. ix.

19. See Arthur Schlesinger, Jr. and Russell Kirk, "Conservative vs. Liberal," *New York Times Magazine* (March 4, 1956): 11, 58, 60, 62 (Schlesinger), and 11, 63-64 (Kirk).

20. Samuel P. Huntington, "Conservatism as an Ideology," *American Political Science Review* 51 (June 1957): 445.

21. *Ibid.*, 472, 473. Huntington's argument was challenged from the Right in Murray Rothbard, "Huntington on Conservatism: A Comment," *American Political Science Review* 51 (September 1957): 784-787. For Huntington's rebuttal, see *American Political Science Review* 51 (December 1957): 1063-1064.

22. *Nation* 171 (October 21, 1950): 355.

23. Arthur Schlesinger, Jr., in *Annals of the American Academy of Political and Social Science* 293 (May 1954): 178.

24. Arthur Schlesinger, Jr., "World War III," *Nation* 164 (April 5, 1947): 398-399, and "Middle-Aged Man With a Horn," *New Republic* 128 (March 16, 1953): 16-17.

25. Stephen J. Tonsor to the editor, *Reporter* 13 (August 11, 1955): 8.

26. James Burnham, in *Annals of the American Academy of Political and Social Science* 298 (March 1955): 216.

27. Willmoore Kendall, "The Liberal Line: By Ulysses out of McCloskey," *National Review* 2 (November 3, 1956): 17.

28. Gerhart Niemeyer, in *Journal of Public Law* 4 (Fall 1955): 441.

29. Frank S. Meyer, "Collectivism Rebaptized," *The Freeman* 5 (July 1955): 562.

30. John Roche, "I'm Sick of Conservatism: It's Irrelevant to Today's America," *New Leader* 38 (August 22, 1955): 6-7.

31. Stuart Gerry Brown, "Democracy, the New Conservatism, and the Liberal Tradition in America," *Ethics* 66 (October 1955): 8. For other contemporary examples of this interpretation of American history, see Louis Hartz, *The Liberal Tradition in America* (New York, 1955); Bernard Crick, "The Strange Quest for an American Conservatism," *Review of Politics* 17 (July 1955): 359-376; Arthur Schlesinger, Jr., "The New Conservatism in America: A Liberal Comment," *Confluence* 2 (December 1953): 61-71; Peregrine Worsthorne, "The Misreading of American History," *New Republic* 134 (February 13, 1956): 16-18; Arnold Rogow, "Edmund Burke and the American Liberal Tradition," *Antioch Review* 17 (June 1957): 255-265.

32. Arthur Schlesinger, Jr., "The New Conservatism: Politics of Nostalgia," *Reporter* 12 (June 16, 1955): 9-12.

33. T.W. Adorno et al., *The Authoritarian Personality* (New York, 1950).

34. Daniel Bell, ed., *The New American Right* (New York, 1955).

35. Herbert McClosky, "Conservatism and Personality," *American Political Science Review* 52 (March 1958): 27-45. The quotations are from pp. 38, 40.

36. William F. Buckley, Jr., *Up from Liberalism* (New York, 1959), pp. 59, 62. See in general pp. 59-62.

37. Frank S. Meyer, "The Scholarly Journals," *National Review* 1 (February 8, 1956): 23-24.

38. Both men cited Richard Christie and Marie Jahoda, eds., *Studies in the Scope and Method of "The Authoritarian Personality"* (Glencoe, Ill., 1954), a study that mounted a very serious challenge to the Adorno book.

39. Russell Kirk, in *Annals of the American Academy of Political and Social Science* 305 (May 1956): 185. For another conservative critique of Bell's book, see W.T. Couch, in *Shenandoah* 7 (Spring 1956): 55-61.

40. For Kendall's criticisms, see *American Political Science Review* 52 (June 1958): 506-510. For a critique of McClosky's research by Morton J. Frisch and a reply to both critics by McClosky, see *American Political Science Review* 52 (December 1958): 1108-1112.

41. Russell Kirk, "The Dissolution of Liberalism," *Commonweal* 61 (January 7, 1955): 374-378.

42. William F. Buckley, Jr. to C.L. Anderson, November 23, 1954, William F. Buckley, Jr. Papers, Yale University Library, New Haven, Conn.

43. Arthur Krock, "The Superior Articulation of the Left," *New York Times*, July 14, 1949, p. 26; Krock, "The Superior Articulation of the Left, II," *New York Times*, July 19, 1949, p. 28.

44. William F. Buckley, Jr., *God and Man at Yale: The Superstitions of "Academic Freedom"* (Chicago, 1951), p. xii. Interestingly, Frank Chodorov examined Buckley's manuscript before he submitted it for publication. (Letter from William F. Buckley, Jr. to David P. Berenberg, February 22, 1952, Buckley Papers.) A few years later Buckley acknowledged his indebtedness to Chodorov: "It is quite unlikely that I should have pursued a career as a writer but for the encouragement he gave me just after I graduated from Yale." (Letter from Buckley to E. Victor Milione, June 6, 1960, Buckley Papers.)

45. Buckley to chairman of *Yale Daily News*, November 26, 1951, Buckley Papers.

46. McGeorge Bundy, "The Attack on Yale," *Atlantic Monthly* 188 (November 1951): 51. See also William F. Buckley, Jr., "The Changes at Yale," *Atlantic Monthly* 188 (December 1951): 78, 80, 82, and McGeorge Bundy, "McGeorge Bundy Replies," *ibid.*, pp. 82, 84.

47. Max Eastman, "Buckley versus Yale," *American Mercury* 73 (December 1951): 22-26; Felix Wittmer, "Collectivism at Yale," *The Freeman* 2 (October 22, 1951): 58-60.

48. E. Merrill Root, *Collectivism on the Campus: The Battle for the Mind in American Colleges* (New York, 1955).

49. Felix Wittmer, *Conquest of the American Mind: Comments on Collectivism in Education* (Boston, 1956).

50. Nancy Jane Fellers, "God and Woman at Vassar," *The Freeman* 3 (November 3, 1952): 83-86. The article caused a storm of interest. See also "Vassar Answers Nancy Fellers," *The Freeman* 3 (December 1, 1952): 160-163, and Patricia Buckley Bozell, "Liberal Education at Vassar," *The Freeman* 3 (January 12, 1953): 269-272. Mrs. Bozell is William F. Buckley, Jr.'s sister.

51. Interview with Murray Rothbard, Cambridge, Mass., March 23, 1972.

52. John Chamberlain, "The Literary Market: 1952-53," *Human Events* 10 (August 19, 1953): 4.

53. Kevin Corrigan to Buckley, April 25, 1953, Buckley Papers.

54. Henry Regnery, "To all Yale Men," n.d., Buckley Papers. This was a promotional letter for *God and Man at Yale*.

55. Regnery to Al Hill, March 23, 1953, Buckley Papers.

56. Russell Kirk, "The Age of Discussion," *Commonweal* 63 (November 11, 1955): 137, 138.

57. Interview with Russell Kirk, Cambridge, Mass., April 21, 1971.

58. Kirk to the author, September 29, 1971. The journal, which appeared in 1950 and 1951, was published quarterly by the Henry Regnery Company. Its board of editors consisted of Daniel Boorstin, David Grene, Robert Hutchins (chairman), John U. Nef, Robert Redfield, Henry Regnery, and Otto G. von Simson.

59. See Kirk to Ross Hoffman, April 5, 1951; Peter Stanlis to Kirk, June 5, 1954; Boorstin to Kirk, June 10, 1955. These letters are in the Russell Kirk Papers, Clarke Historical Library at Central Michigan University, Mount Pleasant, Mich.

60. The quotations in these two paragraphs are drawn from Russell Kirk, "The Principles of a Monthly Journal," a six-page undated typescript. Kirk sent a copy of this prospectus to Peter Viereck on May 14, 1954; copy in possession of the author.

61. *Ibid.*, pp. 2-3.

62. Kirk to the author, September 29, 1971. In this letter Kirk noted that for a time it appeared that the Committee on Social Thought at the University of Chicago would

sponsor his journal, but this did not finally happen. For Kirk's explanation of the likely reasons for the collapse of this proposal, see Kirk to Buckley, September 10, 1957, Buckley Papers.

63. Buckley told Kirk that he was "a little perplexed" at Kirk's failure to include some *National Review* editors, especially John Chamberlain and James Burnham, on this list of "advisers" to *Modern Age* (Buckley to Kirk, September 10, 1957, Kirk Papers).

64. For the full list, see *Modern Age* 1 (Summer 1957), inside front cover.

65. Interview with Kirk, April 21, 1971.

66. Kirk to the author, September 29, 1971. Kirk departed after a dispute with the associate editor, David Collier.

67. The information given in this paragraph is based on two sources: William S. Schlamm to the author, April 15, 1972; interview with John Chamberlain, Cheshire, Conn., April 6, 1972.

68. Interview with Chamberlain, April 6, 1972. According to Chamberlain, funds were not available, and Luce had become interested in founding *Sports Illustrated*. See also W.A. Swanberg, *Luce and His Empire* (New York, 1972), pp. 215-216, and Robert T. Elson, *The World of Time, Inc.* (New York, 1973), pp. 206-207, for brief accounts of Schlamm and his magazine.

69. Schlamm to the author, April 15, 1972. In this letter Schlamm said he left his position with Luce "partly for personal reasons, partly because I disapproved of Harry Luce's political 'pragmatism.'..."

70. Schlamm's letter is the basis for this account, which is confirmed in all essentials by the author's interview with Chamberlain. In 1955, Buckley called Schlamm and James Burnham "my two closest partners in this enterprise"—that is, the founding of *National Review* (Buckley to Frank Cullen Brophy, May 3, 1955, Buckley Papers).

71. This paragraph is based on five sources: "Battle for *The Freeman*," *Time* 61 (January 26, 1953): 74-75; interview with Chamberlain, April 6, 1972; Schlamm to the author, April 15, 1972; interview with Henry Hazlitt (by telephone), August 30, 1973; "*The Freeman*," Post-Presidential Subject File, Herbert Hoover Papers, Herbert Hoover Presidential Library, West Branch, Iowa. The last source contains many detailed memos and letters to Hoover from both factions. Hoover had been actively involved in the founding and promotion of *The Freeman*.

72. Leonard Read, "From the New Publisher," *The Freeman* 5 (June 1954): 5.

73. Interview with William F. Buckley, Jr., Stamford, Conn., November 26, 1971.

74. Buckley to Margaret Ailshie, October 1, 1955, Buckley Papers.

75. Buckley to Ruth Alexander, January 23, 1956, Buckley Papers.

76. Buckley to John W. Beck, December 2, 1954, Buckley Papers.

77. "Ortega y Gasset," *National Review* 1 (November 26, 1955): 7.

78. "The Magazine's Credenda," *National Review* 1 (November 19, 1955): 6.

79. Joseph R. McCarthy, "Acheson Looks at Acheson," *National Review* 1 (December 28, 1955): 26-28.

80. See L. Brent Bozell, "'This Was a Man,'" *National Review* 3 (May 18, 1957): 468; Frank S. Meyer, "The Meaning of McCarthyism," *National Review* 5 (June 14, 1958): 565-566; "*Esquire's* World and Joe McCarthy's," *National Review* 6 (August 2, 1958): 102; L. Brent Bozell, "'Smear and Unsupported Charges,'" *National Review* 7 (July 4, 1959): 183-184.

81. "Credenda," p. 6.

82. William F. Buckley, Jr., "Publisher's Statement," *National Review* 1 (November 19, 1955): 5.

83. "The Editors of *National Review* Believe:" *National Review* 1 (November 19, 1955): 8.

84. William A. Rusher, "Report from the Publisher," *National Review* 4 (July 27, 1957): 101.

85. Frank S. Meyer, "The Meaning of McCarthyism," *National Review* 5 (June 14, 1958): 566.

86. Buckley, "Publisher's Statement," p. 5.

87. Interview with Peter Viereck, South Hadley, Mass., September 21, 1971; Allen Tate to the author, November 1971.

88. T.S. Eliot to Kirk, January 13, 1956 and February 3, 1958, Kirk Papers. See also Eliot to Buckley, December 5, 1956 and November 22, 1957, Buckley Papers.

89. Kirk to Eliot, December 22, 1955, Kirk Papers.

90. See Meyer, "Collectivism Rebaptized," pp. 559-562; Jeffrey Hart, *The American Dissent* (New York, 1966), p. 199n. The Kirk-Meyer feud will be discussed further in the next chapter.

91. See Kirk, "Age of Discussion," p. 138. In his interview with the author, Kirk declared that he felt closer to the socialist Norman Thomas than to the anarcho-capitalist Murray Rothbard.

It is also conceivable that Kirk felt aloof from the ex-radicals at *National Review*. Back in 1953 he had privately criticized Max Eastman's efforts (as Kirk saw them) to establish a "new party line" at *The Freeman*. "Very few of the ex-communists," Kirk observed, "manage to cut themselves free of their former tactics" (Kirk to Viereck, June 4, 1953; copy in possession of the author).

92. See Kirk to Buckley, September 1, October 5, and November 29, 1955, and April 2, 1956, Buckley Papers. In his letter of September 1, Kirk stated that Chodorov and Meyer had sent a copy of the issue of *The Freeman* containing Meyer's criticism of Kirk to all the editorial advisers of Kirk's *Conservative Review* (the eventual *Modern Age*). According to Kirk, many of his advisers were jubilant at this sign of distance between Kirk and his libertarian rivals. Under these circumstances, Kirk felt he could not become an editor of a magazine in which Meyer's and Chodorov's work appeared.

93. Kirk to Buckley, November 29, 1955, Buckley Papers. In this letter Kirk said that *National Review* too much resembled the pre-1953 *Freeman*, and he urged *National Review* to shun the allegedly doctrinaire style and clientele of its predecessor.

94. Interview with Kirk, April 21, 1971. Kirk noted in this interview that *National Review* had been affected by certain "radical" and "unsound" influences at its inception but had outgrown these in the first year or two. For Buckley's comments on the masthead question and Kirk's differences with Frank Meyer, see Buckley to Kirk, n.d. (summer 1955?), December 6, 1955, February 13, 1956, and April 6, 1956, Kirk Papers. See also Buckley to Kirk, September 14, 1955, Buckley Papers. Buckley was very anxious to keep Kirk's name on the masthead and urged him not to feel responsible for the magazine's editorials. He also insisted that Meyer and Chodorov were not out to "get" Kirk.

95. There were also occasional reservations of a more technical nature. The conservative journalist William Henry Chamberlin, for instance, thought that the first four issues of *National Review* "made a pretty amateurish impression" (diary of William Henry Chamberlin, December 18, 1955, William Henry Chamberlin Papers, Providence College, Providence, R.I.).

96. Clinton Rossiter to the editor, *National Review* 2 (June 20, 1956): 22.

97. The magazine's average circulation per issue was 18,000 in its first year, 19,419 in its second, 19,080 in its third, and 25, 835 in its fourth. By early 1960 it passed 30,000. See William F. Buckley, Jr., annual publisher's statement in *National Review* 2 (October 20, 1956): 23; William Rusher, annual publisher's statement in *National Review* 4 (October 19, 1957): 358; Rusher, annual statement in *National Review* 6 (October 11, 1958): 255; Rusher, annual statement in *National Review* 7 (October 24, 1959): 438; Rusher in

"Notes and Asides," *National Review* 8 (January 16, 1960): 34.

98. See the fund-raising letter from Buckley to Sterling Morton, July 5, 1958, Sterling Morton Papers, Chicago Historical Society, and William F. Buckley, Jr., "Can a Little Magazine Break Even?" *National Review* 7 (October 10, 1959): 393-394, 407.

99. Buckley to Morton, July 5, 1958, Morton Papers.

100. William F. Buckley, Jr., *Rumbles Left and Right* (New York, 1963), p. 66. The complete text of Buckley's address is included in this book.

101. John Fischer, "The Editor's Easy Chair," *Harper's* 212 (March 1956): 16, 18, 20, 22; Murray Kempton, "Buckley's National Bore," *The Progressive* 20 (July 1956): 13-16; Dwight Macdonald, "Scrambled Eggheads on the Right," *Commentary* 21 (April 1956): 367-373.

102. See especially William F. Buckley, Jr., "A Report from the Publisher: Reflections on the Failure of 'National Review' to Live Up to Liberal Expectations," *National Review* 2 (August 1, 1956): 7-12; Murray Rothbard to the editor, *Commentary* 21 (June 1956): 584-585; John Chamberlain, introduction to *The National Review Reader*, ed. John Chamberlain (New York, 1957), pp. ix-xiv.

103. Willmoore Kendall, "The Liberal Line," *National Review* 1 (March 14, 1956): 14.

104. Interview with William Rusher, Cambridge, Mass., October 30, 1971.

105. *Modern Age* was a quarterly, *The Freeman* and *American Mercury* monthlies. In 1956, *The Freeman* became essentially a digest of brief essays, usually on libertarian economics; it offered no commentary on day-by-day political developments. In the late 1950s the *American Mercury* became anti-Semitic, in the opinion of William F. Buckley, Jr., Frank Meyer (interview, September 4, 1971), and other conservatives. It therefore ceased to be a significant forum for leading right-wing intellectuals. On April 1, 1959, Buckley issued a memorandum to writers for *National Review* stating that his magazine would not include on its masthead names which also appeared on the masthead of the *American Mercury*. Although *National Review* would not decline to publish articles written by people who also wrote for the *Mercury*, each editor of *National Review* agreed not to contribute to the *Mercury* until it acquired new management. This memorandum is in the Buckley Papers; see also Buckley to C.D. Batchelor, January 1, 1957, and Buckley to Ethel Morse, June 15, 1959, Buckley Papers.

CHAPTER SIX

1. William F. Buckley, Jr., to Russell Kirk, April 6, 1956, Russell Kirk Papers, Clarke Historical Library at Central Michigan University, Mount Pleasant, Mich.

2. For the best account of this early period in *National Review*'s history, see William F. Buckley, Jr., "Notes Towards an Empirical Definition of Conservatism," in *What Is Conservatism?* ed. Frank S. Meyer (New York, 1964), pp. 211-226; reprinted in William F. Buckley, Jr., *The Jeweler's Eye: A Book of Irresistible Political Reflections* (New York, 1968), pp. 15-31.

3. Peter Viereck, *The Unadjusted Man: A New Hero for Americans* (Boston, 1956), p. 252.

4. See *ibid.*, part 4. For a sympathetic study of Viereck by a political scientist who was himself a Viereck-style new conservative, see Thomas I. Cook, "Viereck Revisited: In Search of Continuity and Values," *Tri-quarterly* (Spring 1965): 173-178. See also Cook to the editor, *Hopkins Review* 5 (Fall 1951): 88-90, and his "Conservatism Purified," *New Leader* 39 (November 5, 1956): 18-20.

5. Frank S. Meyer, "Counterfeit at a Popular Price," *National Review* 2 (August 11,

1956): 18. For another critique of Viereck from the Right, see Max Eastman, "Equivocal Conservatism," *The Freeman* 3 (March 9, 1953): 423-424. Eastman deplored Viereck's "equivocation on the essential issue": "the dependence of all our freedoms on the free market economy."

6. Interview with William F. Buckley, Jr., Stamford, Conn., November 26, 1971.

7. Ayn Rand, *Atlas Shrugged* (New York, 1957).

8. "Playboy Interview: Ayn Rand," *Playboy* 11 (March 1964): 36.

9. *Ibid.*, pp. 39-40.

10. *Ibid.*, p. 39.

11. *Ibid.*, p. 35. For an able discussion of Ayn Rand's life and philosophy, see Nathaniel and Barbara Branden, *Who Is Ayn Rand?* (New York, 1962).

12. "Playboy Interview: Ayn Rand," p. 35.

13. Whittaker Chambers, "Big Sister Is Watching You," *National Review* 4 (December 28, 1957): 594-596.

14. E. Merrill Root, "What About Ayn Rand?" *National Review* 8 (January 30, 1960): 76-77. See also letters to the editor, *National Review* 8 (February 13, 1960): 116-117.

15. See John Chamberlain, "A Reviewer's Notebook," *The Freeman* 7 (December 1957): 53-56, and Chamberlain to the editor, *National Review* 5 (February 1, 1958): 118.

16. Murray Rothbard to the editor, *National Review* 5 (January 25, 1958): 95. Rothbard subsequently abandoned his objectivist beliefs (interview with Rothbard, Cambridge, Mass., March 23, 1972).

17. Russell Kirk to the editor, *National Review* 5 (February 1, 1958): 118.

18. See Russell Kirk, *Confessions of a Bohemian Tory* (New York, 1963), pp. 181-182.

19. Frank S. Meyer, "Why Freedom," *National Review* 13 (September 25, 1962): 223-225.

20. Garry Wills, "But Is Ayn Rand Conservative?" *National Review* 8 (February 27, 1960): 139.

21. Richard Weaver was another conservative unimpressed by Ayn Rand. In 1960 he told a friend: "I do not find Ayn Rand particularly upsetting (though I haven't read her long novel). What is evident is that she is very much of an amateur as a philosopher. Her stuff is an undigested compound of truths, half truths, and untruths.... I cannot believe that she will be an influence for very long. Most probably college students are aroused over the novelty of a novelist out preaching large ideas. When her ideas have to stand on their own legs, I predict that they won't because of her general superficiality and lack of sophistication in the better sense.... I think a campaign against her would be too much like swatting hard at a gnat" (Weaver to Louis Dehmlow, August 18, 1960; copy in possession of the author).

The Reverend Edmund Opitz of the Foundation for Economic Education was also critical of Rand and appreciative of the Chambers review. See Opitz to Buckley, January 17, 1958, Buckley Papers, Yale University Library, New Haven, Conn.

22. Buckley, "Notes," pp. 214-216.

23. "Playboy Interview: Ayn Rand," pp. 42-43.

24. For Eastman's attitudes, see his *Reflections on the Failure of Socialism* (New York, 1956) and his "Am I Conservative?" *National Review* 16 (January 28, 1964): 57-58. On p. 84 of his book Eastman wrote: "Whittaker Chambers is very profoundly wrong when he says in his book, *Witness*, that the issue between Soviet Communism and the free world is between religion and irreligion, or between belief in man and belief in God." William S. Schlamm later commented in a review of Eastman's autobiography, *Love and Revolution*: "There were Communists who one day discovered that Communism was a false religion; and so they left it. Then there were Communists who one day discovered a true religion; and they therefore left Communism. And there also were Communists

who discovered that Communism *was* a religion; whereupon they left the party in horror." According to Schlamm, Eastman had become disillusioned with Communism for the latter reason. Schlamm labeled him a "happy pagan" who "gaily looks forward to the Promised Land of Science" ("Eastman's Loves and Revolutions," *National Review* 17 [January 26, 1965]: 65-66).

25. Eastman to Buckley, November 28, 1958, Buckley Papers; quoted in Buckley, "Notes," p. 222. See also Eastman to Buckley, January 28, 1958, Buckley Papers. Eastman was especially disturbed by *National Review's* support of Father Hugh Halton, a zealous Roman Catholic priest who had aroused the animosity of many professors at Princeton University (where he was a chaplain) and had been dismissed. For Buckley's comments on Eastman, see Buckley, "Notes," pp. 222-224, and Buckley to Kirk, December 16, 1958, Kirk Papers.

26. Buckley, "Notes," p. 222. A few months before he resigned from the masthead of *National Review*, Eastman published in that journal a defense of John Dewey—one of the bêtes noires of traditionalist conservatives. His essay was followed by a vigorous rejoinder from Russell Kirk. See Max Eastman, "The Reaction Against John Dewey," *National Review* 6 (June 21, 1958): 9-11; Russell Kirk, "John Dewey Pragmatically Tested," *ibid.*, pp. 11-12, 23. This exchange illuminates some of the differences between Eastman and other intellectuals on the Right.

27. Frank S. Meyer, "Collectivism Rebaptized," *The Freeman* 5 (July 1955): 559-562. John Chamberlain was similarly disturbed by the new conservatives' disparagement of "individualism"; see his "A Reviewer's Notebook," *The Freeman* 5 (August 1955): 617.

28. Russell Kirk, "Mill's 'On Liberty' Reconsidered," *National Review* 1 (January 25, 1956): 23-24.

29. Frank S. Meyer, "In Defense of John Stuart Mill," *National Review* 1 (March 28, 1956): 24. For another interesting conservative analysis of Mill, see Stephen J. Tonsor, "To Educate the Present," *National Review* 13 (November 20, 1962): 396-398.

30. See Chapter Five for further details on the Kirk-Meyer clash.

31. Kirk to T.S. Eliot, December 22, 1955, Kirk Papers. For samples of Kirk's fiction, see his bestselling novel, *Old House of Fear* (New York, 1961), and his ghost stories full of "social significance" (conservative-style), *The Surly Sullen Bell* (New York, 1962).

32. Richard Weaver, "Which Ancestors?" *National Review* 2 (July 25, 1956): 21. This is a review of Kirk's *Beyond the Dreams of Avarice* (Chicago, 1956). Political scientist Walter Berns, a student of Leo Strauss, made a similar point about Kirk's *A Program for Conservatives*: "For the criteria for the judgment of good and evil provided by political philosophy, Mr. Kirk, like Burke before him, would substitute the criteria provided by ancestors..." (in *Journal of Politics* 17 [November 1955]: 686).

33. Russell Kirk, *The Conservative Mind: From Burke to Santayana* (Chicago, 1953), p. 211.

34. Russell Kirk, *Academic Freedom* (Chicago, 1955), pp. 121, 124, 123.

35. Russell Kirk, "Ideology and Political Economy," *America* 96 (January 5, 1957): 388-391.

36. Friedrich Hayek, "Postscript: Why I Am Not a Conservative," in *The Constitution of Liberty* (Chicago, 1960), pp. 395-411. Hayek was not the only free market economist who disliked the label "conservative"; see David McCord Wright, "When You Call Me a Conservative, Smile," *Fortune* 43 (May 1951): 76-77, 190-192.

37. M. Morton Auerbach, *The Conservative Illusion* (New York, 1959).

38. *Ibid.*, p. 85.

39. *Ibid.*, p. 238.

40. M. Morton Auerbach, "Do-It-Yourself Conservatism?" *National Review* 12 (January 30, 1962): 57-58.

41. For conservative critiques of Auerbach's book see M. Stanton Evans, "Exorcising Conservatism," *National Review* 8 (January 30, 1960): 81-82; Richard Weaver, "Illusions of Illusion," *Modern Age* 4 (Summer 1960): 316-320; Willmoore Kendall, *The Conservative Affirmation* (Chicago, 1963), pp. 139-142.

42. M. Stanton Evans, "Techniques and Circumstances," *National Review* 12 (January 30, 1962): 58; Russell Kirk, "Conservatism Is Not an Ideology," *ibid.*, 59, 74; Frank S. Meyer, "The Separation of Powers," *ibid.*, 59. For a discussion of "aristocratic," "autonomous," and "situational" definitions of conservatism, see Samuel P. Huntington, "Conservatism as an Ideology," *American Political Science Review* 51 (June 1957): 454-473.

43. William Henry Chamberlin, *The Evolution of a Conservative* (Chicago, 1959), pp. 248-249.

44. William F. Buckley, Jr., *Up from Liberalism* (New York, 1959), pp. 161, 159.

45. Erik von Kuehnelt-Leddihn, "American Conservatives: An Appraisal," *National Review* 12 (March 13, 1962): 167.

46. Revilo P. Oliver, "Conservatism and Reality," *Modern Age* 5 (Fall 1961): 398.

47. Stanley Parry, "Conservatism and the Social Bond," *Modern Age* 4 (Summer 1960): 306. Parry also referred to the current "struggle for theoretical coherence."

48. Russell Kirk, "The Seventh Congress of Freedom," *National Review* 5 (May 3, 1958): 418.

49. See "The Occasion and Need of a Burke Newsletter," *Modern Age* 3 (Summer 1959): 321-324. The newsletter eventually became an independent periodical, *Studies in Burke and His Time*. For a perceptive conservative interpretation of Burke which reveals much about his appeal to the postwar American Right, see Jeffrey Hart, "Burke and Radical Freedom," *Review of Politics* 29 (April 1967): 221-238.

50. Richard Weaver, *The Ethics of Rhetoric* (Chicago, 1953), pp. 76, 77, 83.

51. Meyer, "Collectivism Rebaptized," p. 561.

52. See Peter J. Stanlis, *Edmund Burke and the Natural Law* (Ann Arbor, Mich., 1958), p. ix.

53. See also Francis P. Canavan, "Edmund Burke's Conception of the Role of Reason in Politics," *Journal of Politics* 21 (February 1959): 60-79, and his *The Political Reason of Edmund Burke* (Durham, N.C., 1960).

54. Stanlis, *Edmund Burke*, p. xi.

55. *Ibid.*, p. 73.

56. *Ibid.*, p. viii.

57. Ronald F. Howell, in *Journal of Politics* 22 (November 1960): 730.

58. As Stanlis put it, "Burke is a restorative of the Christian-humanist wisdom of Europe, based on the Natural Law.... Throughout Western history the Natural Law has played a vital role in the dramatic struggle to preserve and extend the traditions of civil and religious liberty, and men who wish to gain fresh insights into its applied principles will have their faith in liberty renewed by turning to the political writings of Edmund Burke" (*Edmund Burke*, pp. 249-250). For a sustained attempt to relate Burke to the present day, see Peter J. Stanlis, ed., *The Relevance of Edmund Burke* (New York, 1964). For an interesting case of one scholar's evolving attitudes toward Burke, see Gertrude Himmelfarb's two strikingly different essays about him in her *Victorian Minds* (New York, 1968), pp. 3-31.

59. Leo Strauss, *What Is Political Philosophy? and Other Studies* (Glencoe, Ill., 1959), p. 34.

60. Leo Strauss, *Thoughts on Machiavelli* (Glencoe, Ill., 1958), pp. 296-297.

61. Strauss, *Political Philosophy*, p. 43.

62. Strauss, *Machiavelli*, p. 296.

63. See Frederick Wilhelmsen, "Classical Political Theory and the Western Mind," *Commonweal* 73 (November 4, 1960): 152, 154.

64. Some reviewers thought his book rather polemical and unbalanced. For critical comments on Stanlis's thesis, see Stephen R. Graubard, in *New England Quarterly* 31 (September 1958): 411-416; Donald C. Bryant, "Edmund Burke: A Generation of Scholarship and Discovery," *Journal of British Studies* 2 (November 1962): 91-114; and Paul E. Sigmund, Jr., in *Natural Law Forum* 4 (1959): 166-174. This last article was also severely critical of Leo Strauss. For more favorable assessments, see Warren Fleischauer, in *Fordham Law Review* 27 (1958): 303-306, and Will Herberg, "Natural Law and History in Burke's Thought," *Modern Age* 3 (Summer 1959): 325-328. A critical review that nevertheless accepts Stanlis's basic thesis is Thomas H.D. Mahoney, in *William and Mary Quarterly,* 3rd series, 15 (October 1958): 552-554.

65. Will Herberg, "Conservatives, Liberals, and the Natural Law, I," *National Review* 12 (June 5, 1962): 422; Herberg, "Conservatives..., II," *National Review* 12 (June 19, 1962): 458.

66. Eric Voegelin, *Order and History* (Baton Rouge, La.), vol. 1: *Israel and Revelation* (1956); vol. 2: *The World of the Polis* (1957); vol. 3: *Plato and Aristotle* (1957).

67. Voegelin, *World of the Polis*, p. 1. This paragraph is based on Voegelin's explanation of his enterprise in the preface and introduction to vol. 1 and the introduction to vol. 2.

68. *Ibid.*, p. 2.

69. Voegelin, *Israel and Revelation*, p. xii.

70. "The Achievement of Eric Voegelin," *Modern Age* 3 (Spring 1959): 182-196. Frederick Wilhelmsen and Peter Stanlis contributed to this symposium. See also Ellis Sandoz, "Voegelin's Idea of Historical Form," *Cross Currents* 12 (Winter 1962): 41-63; Dante Germino, "Eric Voegelin's Contribution to Contemporary Political Theory," *Review of Politics* 26 (July 1964): 378-402.

71. Frederick Wilhelmsen, "Israel and Revelation," *Modern Age* 3 (Spring 1959): 188; Gerhart Niemeyer, "Eric Voegelin's Achievement," *Modern Age* 9 (Spring 1965): 138.

72. Peter Stanlis, "The World of the Polis," *Modern Age* 3 (Spring 1959): 190.

73. Frank S. Meyer, "Where There is Vision...," *National Review* 6 (August 16, 1958): 137.

74. Frank S. Meyer, "Conservatism," in *Left, Right, and Center*, ed. Robert A. Goldwin (Chicago, 1965), p. 5.

75. Willmoore Kendall, "Three on the Line," *National Review* 4 (August 31, 1957): 181. See also Willmoore Kendall, "Do We Want an 'Open Society'?" *National Review* 6 (January 31, 1959): 491-493.

76. Willmoore Kendall, *The Conservative Affirmation* (Chicago, 1963), pp. 108, 110, 114, 115, 116, 111. These quotations are from chap. 6: "Conservatism and the 'Open Society.'" Kendall privately referred to this essay as "unabashedly egghead McCarthyism" (Kendall to Francis Wilson, August 4, 1960, Francis Wilson Papers, University of Illinois, Urbana). Kendall's theme was also stressed in an article by his friend Frederick Wilhelmsen: "In order to be, a society must defend itself against whatever and whoever might threaten its existence. The inability to defend oneself against the enemy has always been the sign of approaching death.... Orthodoxy is nothing other than a law of being.... [M]en can live and act together only if they are bound together by code and custom, myth and legend, sculpture and song—all bespeaking some common confrontation of the Absolute. Where such an underlying orthodoxy is lacking we find ourselves in the midst of an aggregate of ghettos, not a society.... The proposition that America is bound to a discussion potentially infinite in duration is the proposition that America is destined to fall" ("'My Doxy Is Orthodoxy,'" *National Review* 12 [May 22, 1962]: 365-366). The Voegelinian overtones ("in order to be," "law of being," "confrontation of the

Absolute") of this passage are evident.

77. Stanlis and Wilhelmsen, for example, were also Catholic, Niemeyer an Episcopalian, Voegelin a "pre-Reformation Christian," and Kirk a Catholic (as of 1964).

78. For a significant sympathetic review of Hayek's book by a free market conservative, see John Davenport, "'An Unrepentant Old Whig,'" *Fortune* 61 (March 1960): 134-135, 192, 194, 197-198. For a critical response, see Sidney Hook, "Of Tradition and Change," *New York Times Book Review*, February 21, 1960, p. 28.

79. Hayek, *Constitution of Liberty*, p. 4.

80. *Ibid.*, p. 26.

81. *Ibid.*, p. 29.

82. *Ibid.*, p. 284.

83. Stephen J. Tonsor, "Disputed Heritage of Burke," *National Review* 10 (June 17, 1961): 390-391.

84. See Dante Germino, "The Crisis in Community: Challenge to Political Theory," in *Nomos II: Community* (New York, 1959), ed. Carl J. Friedrich, p. 98n. Willmoore Kendall was also aware of the split between reason and revelation among conservative philosophers (Kendall to Alfred Balitzer, August 26, 1965; copy in possession of the author).

One Christian neo-conservative who criticized Strauss's exclusive reliance on "the perspective of classical paganism" was John Hallowell. While Hallowell admired "the wisdom of the Greeks," it was "insufficient"; St. Paul, he asserted, "had a more profound understanding of man's predicament and need than did Aristotle" (in *American Political Science Review* 48 [June 1954]: 538-541). Gerhart Niemeyer also noted Strauss's significant "omission of Christian political philosophy from his periodization" and his unwillingness to recognize that Christian revelation and "the wholly novel idea of transcendence flowing from Christ made an essential difference in political thought" (Niemeyer, "What Is Political Knowledge?" *Review of Politics* 23 [January 1961]: 101-107.

The scholarly methods and assumptions of the Straussians—particularly Strauss's theory of "secret writing," of what Russell Kirk called the tendency "to detect arcane doctrine concealed beneath the rhetoric" of great political philosophers—also aroused skepticism among some conservatives. See Kirk, "Bolingbroke, Burke, and the Statesman," *Kenyon Review* 28 (June 1966): 429.

85. Kendall, *Conservative Affirmation*, p. xi.

86. Quoted in Buckley, "Notes," p. 224.

87. Frank S. Meyer, "Champion of Freedom," *National Review* 8 (May 7, 1960): 304-305.

88. Hayek, *Constitution of Liberty*, pp. 395-411.

89. James M. O'Connell, "The New Conservatism," *New Individualist Review* 2 (Spring 1962): 17-21.

90. See Ronald Hamowy vs. William F. Buckley, Jr., "'National Review': Criticism and Reply," *New Individualist Review* 1 (November 1961): 3-11. See also Ralph Raico vs. Robert Croll, "Individualist, Libertarian or Conservative—Which Are We?" *The Individualist* 4 (May 1960): 1, 2, 4. Interestingly, Raico was also a graduate student under Hayek at the University of Chicago. *The Individualist* was a publication of Frank Chodorov's Intercollegiate Society of Individualists (ISI).

In the early 1960s, ISI was brushed by the ongoing effort of the Right to define itself. On September 1, 1960, William F. Buckley, Jr. formally proposed that the organization change its name. Buckley explained that in the early years after World War II it was not yet obvious what the movement would be called. Leonard Read wanted to label it "libertarian"; Frank Chodorov favored "individualist." At that time Buckley, too, was searching for the proper word ("conservative" did not seem precise enough), although he had reservations about the "solipsistic overtones" of "individualism." But by 1960, Buckley argued, the movement had, for better or worse, acquired the label "conservative," and the now-odd name Intercollegiate Society of *Individualists* was increasingly an obstacle to the organization's acceptance on campuses and in fund raising (Buckley to E. Victor Milione, September 1, 1960, Buckley Papers).

The responses of conservatives to this suggestion varied; see Frank S. Meyer to Milione, October 22, 1960; Frank Chodorov to William H. Brady, Jr., January 14, 1961; and Buckley to Brady, February 7, 1961, Buckley Papers. While Chodorov was willing to acquiesce in a change of names, he still liked "individualist" (because it stood for the philosophy of freedom, self-reliance, and limited government) and disdained "conservative." Buckley's idea was not immediately accepted, and ISI retained "Individualist" in its title until 1966 (the year of Chodorov's death), when it became the Intercollegiate Studies Institute.

91. Frank S. Meyer, *In Defense of Freedom: A Conservative Credo* (Chicago, 1962). Meyer's theoretical articles appeared in *Modern Age* and *National Review*; the principal ones are conveniently reprinted in Frank S. Meyer, *The Conservative Mainstream* (New Rochelle, N.Y., 1969), chap. 1: "What is Conservatism?" See also his "Conservatism," in *Left, Right, and Center*, ed. Goldwin, pp. 1-17.

92. Quoted in Priscilla L. Buckley, "Notes on a Fifth Birthday," *National Review* 9 (November 19, 1960): 308.

93. Meyer's death from lung cancer on April 1, 1972, elicited a large number of informative tributes to him by former colleagues and friends. See "Frank S. Meyer, R.I.P.," *National Review* 24 (April 28, 1972): 466-473, 475; John Chamberlain, "The Pervasive Influence of Frank Meyer," *Human Events* 32 (April 15, 1972): 13; Jameson G. Campaigne, Jr., "Frank Meyer, R.I.P.," *The Alternative* 5 (June-September 1972): 14-15; Murray Rothbard, "Frank S. Meyer, R.I.P.," *Libertarian Forum* 4 (May 1972): 8.

94. Meyer, *In Defense of Freedom*, pp. 1, 10.

95. *Ibid.*, pp. 22-23.

96. By new conservatives he meant primarily Russell Kirk, Peter Viereck, Clinton Rossiter, Robert Nisbet, and John Hallowell. Meyer excluded Eric Voegelin, Leo Strauss, Willmoore Kendall, Richard Weaver, and Frederick Wilhelmsen, who, he said, were both more thoroughly anticollectivist than the first group and not inclined to worship tradition against reason. The latter group, he noted approvingly, esteemed the use of reason to work out the principles of conservatism (*ibid.*, pp. 38-40).

97. *Ibid.*, p. 27. On p. 28, Meyer referred to "the myth of society."

98. *Ibid.*, p. 136.

99. *Ibid.*, p. 166.

100. *Ibid.*, p. 137.

101. These paragraphs are based primarily on Frank S. Meyer, "Freedom, Tradition, Conservatism," *Modern Age* 4 (Fall 1960): 355-363, reprinted in slightly revised form in *What Is Conservatism?*, ed. Meyer, pp. 7-20. For his objection to the word "fusion," see Meyer, "Why Freedom," p. 223. "Fusionism" was a term coined by one of Meyer's critics, L. Brent Bozell.

102. Meyer, ed., *What Is Conservatism?*, pp. 229-232.

103. Kendall, *Conservative Affirmation*, p. xi.

104. Russell Kirk, "An Ideologue of Liberty," *Sewanee Review* 72 (April-June 1964): 349-350.

105. John Hallowell, in *American Political Science Review* 58 (September 1964): 688.

106. The book was dedicated to Richard M. Weaver, "pioneer and protagonist of the American conservative consensus." Meyer regarded Weaver as an exemplar of that consensus. See Frank S. Meyer, "Richard M. Weaver: An Appreciation," *Modern Age* 14 (Summer-Fall 1970): 243-248.

107. Richard M. Weaver, "Anatomy of Freedom," *National Review* 13 (December 4, 1962): 444. Weaver in turn was accused of misreading Meyer. See Stephen J. Tonsor to the editor, *National Review* 13 (December 31, 1962): 521-522.

108. Felix Morley, "American Conservatism Today," *National Review* 16 (March 24, 1964): 235-236.

109. This was a reference to Meyer's claim that the State had only three proper functions: national defense, domestic order, and the administration of justice.

110. This account is drawn from L. Brent Bozell, "Freedom or Virtue?" *National Review* 13 (September 11, 1962): 181-187, 206.

111. Stanley Parry, "The Restoration of Tradition," *Modern Age* 5 (Spring 1961): 125-138. See also Stanley Parry, "Reason and the Restoration of Tradition," in *What Is Conservatism?*, ed. Meyer, pp. 107-129, and "Dilemma of Conservatism," *National Review* 5 (February 22, 1958): 185-186.

112. Interview with William Rusher, Cambridge, Mass., October 30, 1971. At the time Meyer was a nondenominational Christian. On April 1, 1972, a few hours before he died, he became a Roman Catholic. For more on Meyer's religious views, see *In Defense of Freedom*, p. 165n, and "Frank S. Meyer, R.I.P.," *National Review* 24 (April 28, 1972): 466-473, 475.

113. Meyer, "Why Freedom," pp. 223-225.

114. Frank S. Meyer, "Conservatism and Crisis: A Reply to Fr. Parry," *Modern Age* 7 (Winter 1962-1963): 45-50.

115. Ronald Hamowy, "Liberalism and Neo-Conservatism: Is a Synthesis Possible?" *Modern Age* 8 (Fall 1964): 351. For other comments on fusionism, see Murray Rothbard, "Conservatism and Freedom: A Libertarian Comment," *Modern Age* 5 (Spring 1961): 217-220; Ralph Raico, "The Fusionists on Liberalism and Tradition," *New Individualist Review* 3 (Autumn 1964): 29-36; M. Stanton Evans, "Raico on Liberalism and Religion," *New Individualist Review* 4 (Winter 1966): 19-25 (a fusionist's reply to Raico); Ralph Raico, "Reply to Mr. Evans," *ibid.*, pp. 25-31.

116. Hallowell, in *American Political Science Review*, p. 687.

117. Allen Guttmann, *The Conservative Tradition in America* (New York, 1967), p. 163.

118. Interview (by telephone) with Frank S. Meyer, September 4, 1971.

119. This was Meyer's view, expressed to the author in the interview previously cited. One influential individual who admired Meyer's work was William F. Buckley, Jr. Before *In Defense of Freedom* was published, Buckley told a friend that "it goes further than anything I have seen to develop a conservative metaphysic.... I think he provides a more satisfactory philosophical answer to the question why should we have freedom, than has anyone else" (Buckley to Henry Regnery, April 25, 1960, Buckley Papers).

120. Interview (by telephone) with L. Brent Bozell, April 26, 1972. Bozell did not, however, abandon his own position.

121. Interview with Rusher, October 30, 1971.

122. Peter P. Witonski, "The Political Philosopher," *National Review* 24 (April 28, 1972): 468.

123. *National Review*'s cold war policies were a target of *New Individualist Review* libertarians, however.

124. Wilhelm Röpke, "Liberalism and Christianity," *Commonweal* 46 (July 18, 1947): 332.

125. William Henry Chamberlin, "Conservatism in Evolution," *Modern Age* 7 (Summer 1963): 254.

126. Meyer, ed., *What Is Conservatism?*, pp. 3-4.

127. Raymond English, in *Burke Newsletter* 5 (Winter 1963-1964): 296.

128. Buckley, "Notes," p. 226.

129. Röpke, "Liberalism and Christianity," pp. 328-329.

130. Meyer, *In Defense of Freedom*, pp. 87-89.

131. Röpke, "Liberalism and Christianity," p. 329.

132. Wilhelm Röpke, "Liberalism and Christianity," *Modern Age* 1 (Fall 1957): 134. Significantly, Röpke sought to demonstrate in this article that the Papal encyclical *Quadragesimo Anno* (1931), usually interpreted as advocating corporatism, was in fact reconcilable with Röpke's brand of free market neo-liberalism.

133. Wilhelm Röpke, *A Humane Economy: The Social Framework of the Free Market* (Chicago, 1960).

134. *Ibid.*, p. 93.

135. *Ibid.*, p. 125.

136. Chamberlin, *Evolution of a Conservative*, p. 15. See in general chaps. 1, 4.

137. *Ibid.*, p. 55.

138. *Ibid.*, p. 274.

139. See *ibid.*, chap. 15: "An American Conservative Manifesto."

140. Röpke, "Liberalism and Christianity" (1957), p. 128.

141. Russell Kirk, "The Mt. Pélerin Society," *National Review* 11 (October 21, 1961): 271. Kirk's article was rebutted by three "Chicago School" economists—Aaron Director, Milton Friedman, and George Stigler—in a letter to the editor, *National Review* 11 (December 2, 1961): 390. They insisted that the society had always been tolerant and that liberal dogmas and anti-Christian views had not pervaded the first conference or subsequent meetings. The "shift" Kirk claimed to discern was merely an indication of that tolerance.
    Kirk, however, held to his convictions. Although he welcomed current tendencies, he told Buckley that tension between the Christians and extreme nineteenth-century liberals within the society continued. (Kirk to Buckley, December 20, 1961, Buckley Papers.) Regardless of the validity of Kirk's estimate, it is significant that he perceived the situation in this way in 1961 and approved of what he thought was a new mood of conciliation.

142. Guy Davenport, "The Need to Maintain a Civilization," *National Review* 17 (April 6, 1965): 283-284. See also Erik von Kuehnelt-Leddihn, "The Philadelphia Society," *National Review* 17 (November 2, 1965): 986.

143. From "The Philadelphia Society: Statement of Purpose"; copy in possession of the author.

144. Among the leading books in this series were Ludwig von Mises, *The Free and Prosperous Commonwealth* (Princeton, 1962); Felix Morley, ed., *The Necessary Conditions for a Free Society* (Princeton, 1963); Helmut Schoeck and James Wiggins, eds., *Scientism and Values* (Princeton, 1960), *Relativism and the Study of Man* (New York, 1961), and *The New Argument in Economics* (Princeton, 1963). For the full list as of 1963, see Morley, ed., *Free Society*, p. ii.

145. M. Stanton Evans, "The Maturing of Conservatism," *Rally* 1 (July 1966): 11-13.

146. Frank S. Meyer, "The Growth of Conservative Thought," *National Review* 17 (November 30, 1965): 1097.
    As early as 1958, Buckley optimistically pointed out to a friend "the growing compatibility of political decentralization cum economic freedom cum moral absolutism, a fusion which has not, to be sure, swept the nation, but which appears, e.g., in the columns of *National Review*, to be making for a coherent basis for American neo-conservatism" (Buckley to Ralph de Toledano, June 4, 1958, Buckley Papers).

147. Kirk, "Mt. Pélerin Society," p. 270.

148. Kirk, "Conservatism Is Not an Ideology," p. 59.

149. This characteristic is especially evident in Russell Kirk, *Enemies of the Permanent*

Things: Observations of Abnormity in Politics and Literature (New Rochelle, N.Y., 1969).

CHAPTER SEVEN

1. Richard Chase, "Neo-Conservatism and American Literature," *Commentary* 23 (March 1957): 254-261.
2. Elisha Greifer, "The Conservative Pose in America: The Adamses' Search for a Pre-Liberal Past," *Western Political Quarterly* 15 (March 1962): 5-16.
3. Allan Guttmann, *The Conservative Tradition in America* (New York, 1967). See especially the introduction and chap. 1.
4. Arnold A. Rogow, "Edmund Burke and the American Liberal Tradition," *Antioch Review* 17 (June 1957): 255-265.
5. See Guttmann, *Conservative Tradition*, chap. 1.
6. *Ibid.*
7. Arthur Schlesinger, Jr., "The New Conservatism in America: A Liberal Comment," *Confluence* 2 (December 1953): 65. See also Arthur Schlesinger, Jr., "The New Conservatism: Politics of Nostalgia," *Reporter* 12 (June 16, 1955): 9-12.
8. William S. Schlamm, "Civilized Conversation," *The Freeman* 5 (December 1954): 233. This was a review of Kirk's *A Program for Conservatives* (Chicago, 1954).
9. Ralph de Toledano, "Notes for a Controversy," *National Review* 2 (September 22, 1956): 15-16. For a rebuttal to Toledano by a fellow conservative, see Gerhart Niemeyer, "Too Early and Too Much," *National Review* 2 (October 13, 1956): 19, 23.
10. Ralph de Toledano, *Lament for a Generation* (New York, 1960), pp. 183, 220, 224. See in general chaps. 9-11.
11. Stephen J. Tonsor, "A Fresh Start: American History and Political Order," *Modern Age* 16 (Winter 1972): 3.
12. See Stephen J. Tonsor, "Disputed Heritage of Burke," *National Review* 10 (June 17, 1961): 390-391.
13. See Peter Stanlis, *Edmund Burke and the Natural Law* (Ann Arbor, Mich., 1958) for an exposition of the latter view.
14. Henry James, *Hawthorne* (New York, 1880), pp. 42-43.
15. William F. Buckley, Jr., "Conservatism," *Saturday Review* 40 (June 8, 1957): 37.
16. For a vigorous treatment of this point, see Peter L. Berger, "Two Paradoxes," *National Review* 24 (May 12, 1972): 507-511.
17. William F. Buckley, Jr., "Publisher's Statement," *National Review* 1 (November 19, 1955): 5. In this article Buckley used the term "radical conservatives" to identify the people for whom *National Review* would presumably speak.
18. John Hallowell, in *Journal of Politics* 16 (February 1954): 150-152.
19. Stephen J. Tonsor, in *Burke Newsletter* 8 (Winter 1966-1967): 684.
20. Stephen J. Tonsor, in *Studies in Burke and His Time* 10 (Winter 1968-1969): 1192-1193.
21. Notably Willmoore Kendall, whom we shall discuss in the next chapter.
22. Russell Kirk, in *Burke Newsletter* 4 (Winter 1962-1963): 190-193.
23. Russell Kirk, *Edmund Burke: A Genius Reconsidered* (New Rochelle, N.Y., 1967), p. 209.
24. Russell Kirk, *John Randolph of Roanoke*, rev. ed. (Chicago, 1964).
25. Russell Kirk, "Wilson: Abstraction, Principle, and the Antagonist World," *Confluence* 5 (Autumn 1956): 204-215.
26. See, for example, Russell Kirk, "Burke and the Principle of Order," *Sewanee Review*

60 (Spring 1952): 187-201. The impact of Burke on American thought was, of course, a major theme of his *The Conservative Mind* (Chicago, 1953), as well as a recurrent motif of his columns in *National Review*.

27. Russell Kirk, *Beyond the Dreams of Avarice* (Chicago, 1956), p. 25.

28. John Courtney Murray, *We Hold These Truths: Catholic Reflections on the American Proposition* (New York, 1960), pp. 10, 43.

29. *Ibid.*, p. 28. The next sentence reads: "This is the principle that radically distinguishes the conservative Christian tradition of America from the Jacobin laicist tradition of Continental Europe."

30. *Ibid.*, p. 30.

31. *Ibid.*, pp. 33-36.

32. Francis Wilson, in *Catholic Historical Review* 47 (April 1961): 42.

33. Willmoore Kendall, "Natural Law and 'Natural Right,'" *Modern Age* 6 (Winter 1961-1962): 93-96.

34. William F. Buckley, Jr., ed., *American Conservative Thought in the Twentieth Century* (Indianapolis, 1970), pp. 4, 37-51. In a review, Buckley acclaimed the book as a "noble statement" and went on to declare the natural law philosophy (argued by Murray) to be "the neglected, tatterdemalion lode from which, if we set out to do it, we can mine a public philosophy which will bring the West out alive" ("Nihil Obstat," *National Review* 10 [January 28, 1961]: 56-57).

35. See Russell Kirk, *Confessions of a Bohemian Tory* (New York, 1963), especially part 2.

36. André Malraux and James Burnham, *The Case for De Gaulle: A Dialogue* (New York, 1948).

37. See Francis Wilson, "The New Conservatives in Spain," *Modern Age* 5 (Spring 1961): 149-160; Francis Wilson, "Ramiro de Maeztu: Critic of the Revolution," *Modern Age* 8 (Spring 1964): 174-185.

38. Interview (by telephone) with L. Brent Bozell, April 26, 1972.

39. See Rafael Calvo-Serer, "They Spoke for Christian Europe," *National Review* 4 (July 27, 1957): 109, 112. This article is an account of the organization's sixth annual Congress, held in Spain's Escorial and chaired by the Archduke Otto von Hapsburg. The topic of the conference was the "misunderstanding" between America and Europe. Calvo-Serer, a distinguished Spanish intellectual, was impressed by "the profoundly European consciousness and sense of responsibility of the American participants," including Burnham, Kendall, and Wilhelmsen.

40. See William F. Buckley, Jr., *Cruising Speed: A Documentary* (New York, 1971), pp. 163-165, for a discussion of his friendship with Otto von Hapsburg. See also Russell Kirk's sympathetic portrait of him in his *Confessions of a Bohemian Tory*, pp. 145-147.

41. Interview with William F. Buckley, Jr., Stamford, Conn., November 26, 1971.

42. Quoted in Calvo-Serer, "They Spoke for Christian Europe," p. 109.

43. Toledano, "Notes for a Controversy," p. 16.

44. Thomas Molnar, "French Conservative Thought Today," *Modern Age* 3 (Summer 1959): 283.

45. Stefan Possony, "Conservatism Reappraised," *New Leader* 37 (January 25, 1954): 22.

46. Clinton Rossiter to the editor, *Reporter* 13 (August 11, 1955): 7.

47. Clinton Rossiter, *Conservatism in America*, 2nd ed., rev. (New York, 1962), pp. 222, 221.

48. *Ibid.*, pp. 262, 69.

49. *Ibid.*, p. 252.

50. Russell Kirk, "The American Conservative Character," *Sewanee Review* 8 (Fall 1954):

255 and passim.

51. Gerhart Niemeyer, in *Journal of Public Law* 4 (Fall 1955): 441-447.

53. Willmoore Kendall, "Who's Coming and Who's Going?" *National Review* 13 (August 28, 1962): 151-152.

54. Francis Wilson, in *Journal of Politics* 18 (May 1956): 359. A few years later Wilson attempted to define the new conservatism and to refute the numerous criticisms of it by liberal observers. See Wilson, "The Anatomy of Conservatives," *Ethics* 70 (July 1960): 265-281. For a libertarian critique of Rossiter see John Chamberlain, "A Reviewer's Notebook," *The Freeman* 5 (May 1955): 484-485. Chamberlain feared that Rossiter, with all his talk about "the primacy of the community," was insensitive to the value of "individual variation" and the dangers of coercion (the great menace) in the name of the community.

55. Rossiter, *Conservatism in America* (1962), p. 227.

56. Richard Weaver, "Aspects of the Southern Philosophy," *Hopkins Review* 5 (Summer 1952): 15, 17.

57. See Kirk's letters at the time to W.C. McCann, Russell Kirk Papers, Clarke Historical Library at Central Michigan University, Mount Pleasant, Mich.

58. Russell Kirk, *Randolph of Roanoke: A Study in Conservative Thought* (Chicago, 1951).

59. *Ibid.*, pp. 1, 18.

60. Russell Kirk, "Norms, Conventions, and the South," *Modern Age* 2 (Fall 1958): 344.

61. Donald Davidson, "The New South and the Conservative Tradition," *National Review* 9 (September 10, 1960): 141-146; Kirk, *Confessions of a Bohemian Tory*, p. 154.

62. See "'All Men Are Created Equal,'" *The Freeman* 4 (June 14, 1954): 655-656, for a statement of support by the libertarian Right.

63. Frank S. Meyer, "In the Great Tradition," *National Review* 3 (June 1, 1957): 527-528.

64. Richard M. Weaver, "Integration is Communization," *National Review* 4 (July 13, 1957): 67-68.

65. "Why the South Must Prevail," *National Review* 4 (August 24, 1957): 149.

66. L. Brent Bozell, "The Open Question," *National Review* 4 (September 7, 1957): 209.

67. "A Clarification," *National Review* 4 (September 7, 1957): 199.

68. James J. Kilpatrick, *The Sovereign States: Notes of a Citizen of Virginia* (Chicago, 1957).

69. The Tenth Amendment reads: "The powers not delegated to the United States by the Constitution, nor prohibited by it to the States, are reserved to the States respectively, or to the people."

70. Kilpatrick, *Sovereign States*, p. ix.

71. *Ibid.*, pp. 304, 305.

72. In the middle and late 1950s, Kilpatrick was also influential in Virginia politics and was the principal journalistic and constitutional theorist of "massive resistance." See Benjamin Muse, *Virginia's Massive Resistance* (Bloomington, Ind., 1961), pp. 20-21, and J. Harvie Wilkinson, III, *Harry Byrd and the Changing Face of Virginia Politics, 1945-1966* (Charlottesville, Va., 1968), pp. 127-129.

73. Meyer, "Great Tradition," p. 527. For hostile reviews, see Robert J. Harris, in *Journal of Politics* 20 (February 1958): 229-232; Charles Black, Jr., "Constitutional Issues Today," *Yale Review* 47 (September 1957): 117-125.

74. Felix Morley, *Freedom and Federalism* (Chicago, 1959), pp. 187-188.

75. Kilpatrick, for example, contended that the Supreme Court had "commanded" the South "to breach the immutable law by which the South's character has been preserved."

He believed that school integration in the South would produce "a relationship forbidden by the mores of the people" and would "risk, twenty or thirty years hence, a widespread racial amalgamation and debasement of the society as a whole" (*Sovereign States*, pp. 280-281). See also William D. Workman, *The Case for the South* (New York, 1960), and James J. Kilpatrick, *The Southern Case for School Segregation* (New York, 1962). The former was reviewed in Richard Whalen, "As the South Sees It," *National Review* 8 (February 13, 1960): 109-110, the latter in L. Brent Bozell, "To Mend the Tragic Flaw," *National Review* 14 (March 12, 1963): 199-200. Both reviews, while showing understanding of the Southern position, were also critical of it.

In later years, Kilpatrick altered his views on the social consequences of *Brown vs. Board of Education*. On the twentieth anniversary of the Brown decision, he declared in his syndicated column that the black children in the desegregation cases of 1954 had made "a lasting contribution...toward a better life for their people." Despite "the tensions, the hardships, and the new abuses that have been created in uprooting the old way, it has to be said that this way is better. It is not perfect, but it is better." Kilpatrick continued to believe, however, that "as a matter of jurisprudence" the Brown decision was wrong. One of its adverse effects was the rise of doctrinaire and unjustified judicial decisions, including "bizarre" and "disgraceful" rulings to achieve racial balance in the schools ("From Warren to Weinstein," *Springfield* [Mass.] *Sunday Republican*, May 12, 1974, p. 39).

76. Morley, *Freedom and Federalism*, pp. 183-187.

77. An excellent study of this dimension of Weaver's thought is M.E. Bradford, "The Agrarianism of Richard Weaver: Beginnings and Completions," *Modern Age* 14 (Summer-Fall 1970): 249-256.

78. Richard M. Weaver, *The Southern Tradition at Bay: A History of Postbellum Thought*, ed. George Core and M.E. Bradford (New Rochelle, N.Y., 1968), p. 389.

79. Weaver often examined and praised his Agrarian mentors. See, for example, his "Agrarianism in Exile," *Sewanee Review* 58 (Autumn 1950): 586-606; "The Tennessee Agrarians," *Shenandoah* 3 (Summer 1952): 3-10; "The Southern Phoenix," *Georgia Review* 17 (Spring 1963): 6-17. This last essay is a discussion of the 1930 Agrarian manifesto, *I'll Take My Stand*. A virtually complete bibliography of Weaver's writings is included in *Southern Tradition*.

80. Weaver, "Southern Phoenix," p. 9.

81. See Weaver, "Aspects," pp. 5-21.

82. Weaver, "Tennessee Agrarians," p. 4.

83. All quotations in this paragraph are from Richard M. Weaver, "The Regime of the South," *National Review* 6 (March 14, 1959): 587-589. See also Weaver's "Roots of the Liberal Complacency," *National Review* 3 (June 8, 1957): 541-543.

84. Richard M. Weaver, "The Importance of Cultural Freedom," *Modern Age* 6 (Winter 1961-1962): 21-33.

85. Richard M. Weaver, "Two Types of American Individualism," *Modern Age* 7 (Spring 1963): 119-134. A related essay is Richard M. Weaver, "Two Orators [Webster and Hayne]," *Modern Age* 14 (Summer-Fall 1970): 226-242. These two articles were intended to comprise part of a book Weaver was writing when he died in 1963. It was to have consisted of contrasts between Southern and New England cultures, as seen in Randolph vs. Thoreau, William Byrd vs. Cotton Mather, and others. Weaver's distrust of uncontrolled "dialectic" and his belief in the need for balancing "rhetoric" are recurrent themes of his work. See Weaver, *The Ethics of Rhetoric* (Chicago, 1953), especially chaps. 1-2; Weaver, *Visions of Order* (Baton Rouge, 1964), especially chap. 4; and Richard Johannesen et al., eds., *Language is Sermonic: Richard M. Weaver on the Nature of Rhetoric* (Baton Rouge, 1970).

86. Weaver, "Southern Phoenix," p. 8. The alleged antagonism between conservatism and capitalism (and technology) was also much emphasized by Whittaker Chambers. See William F. Buckley, Jr., ed., *Odyssey of a Friend: Whittaker Chambers' Letters to William F. Buckley, Jr., 1954-1961* (New York, 1969), pp. 79-84, 227-231, 246-247.

87. See Richard M. Weaver, "Mass Plutocracy," *National Review* 9 (November 15, 1960): 273-275, 290.

88. These are descriptions of Weaver offered by Russell Kirk and Bernard Iddings Bell, respectively. See Kirk's foreword to *Visions of Order: The Cultural Crisis of Our Time*, by Richard M. Weaver (Baton Rouge, 1964), pp. vii-viii.

89. This biographical information is drawn from two tributes to Weaver: Kirk, *Confessions of a Bohemian Tory*, pp. 193-196; Eugene Davidson, "Richard Malcolm Weaver—Conservative," *Modern Age* 7 (Summer 1963): 226-230. The phrase "Puritan in Babylon" was first applied by William Allen White to Calvin Coolidge.

90. As M.E. Bradford points out, he had a "nationalist" side. See Richard M. Weaver, "The American as a Regenerate Being," *Southern Review* 4 (Summer 1968): 633-646. This piece was edited by George Core of the University of Georgia. In an interview with the author (Cambridge, Mass., April 21, 1971), Russell Kirk placed Weaver in the Southern Whig tradition.

91. Weaver, "Agrarianism in Exile," pp. 601-602.

92. See his critique of Burke in Richard M. Weaver, *The Ethics of Rhetoric* (Chicago, 1953), chap. 3.

93. Weaver, *Southern Tradition*, pp. 394-395.

94. Russell Kirk, *The American Cause* (Chicago, 1957). In 1966 a special edition of this book was published with an introduction by John Dos Passos.

95. *Ibid.*, p. 40. Kirk quoted with approval (p. 41) Justice William O. Douglas's statement in a 1951 Supreme Court decision: "We are a religious people whose institutions presuppose a Supreme Being."

96. *Ibid.*, p. 36.

97. *Ibid.*, p. 67.

98. *Ibid.*, p. 73.

99. *Ibid.*, p. 111.

100. Barry Goldwater, *The Conscience of a Conservative* (Shepherdsville, Ky., 1960).

101. Twenty-two by August 1964.

102. F. Clifton White, *Suite 3505: The Story of the Draft Goldwater Movement* (New Rochelle, N.Y., 1967), p. 21. Bozell's authorship had been more or less "common knowledge" for some time; see Richard Rovere, "The Conservative Mindlessness," *Commentary* 39 (March 1965): 38. Senator Goldwater himself called Bozell the "guiding hand" of the book; his comment was placed on the dustjacket of Bozell's own *The Warren Revolution: Reflections on the Consensus Society* (New Rochelle, N.Y., 1966).

103. Goldwater, *Conscience*, p. 5.

104. *Ibid.*, p. 18.

105. *Ibid.*

106. *Ibid.*, p. 5.

107. Felix Morley, "American Conservatism Today," *National Review* 16 (March 24, 1964): 236.

108. Bernard Iddings Bell, in *Commonweal* 54 (September 21, 1951): 579.

109. Gottfried Dietze, *In Defense of Property* (Baltimore, 1963), p. 2.

110. A phrase of Willmoore Kendall's.

111. Daniel Boorstin, *The Genius of American Politics* (Chicago, 1953). It is noteworthy that certain historians' emphasis in the 1950s on the conservative features of the American Revolution coincided with the emergence of the conservative intellectual move-

ment and the widespread feeling that America's role in the world was inherently conservative.

112. Kirk, *American Cause*, p. 53.

113. Dietze, *In Defense of Property*, p. 59.

114. Dietze, *America's Political Dilemma: From Limited to Unlimited Democracy* (Baltimore, 1968), pp. 7-9.

115. Russell Kirk, ed., *The French and American Revolutions Compared* (Chicago, 1955).

116. See Jeffrey Hart, "Conservatism: Literary and Political," *Kenyon Review* 30 (1968): 697-702.

117. Boorstin, *Genius of American Politics*, pp. 82, 84. This was in contrast, he stressed, to the French "Declaration of the Rights of Man and Citizen" of 1789.

118. Kirk, *American Cause*, pp. 62-63.

119. See Russell Kirk, "Conservatism: The Shield of Liberty," *Catholic World* 189 (August 1959): 381-386.

120. Kirk, *American Cause*, pp. 30-33.

121. See Murray, *We Hold These Truths*, foreword and chap. 1.

122. Dietze, *In Defense of Property*, pp. 59-60. Dietze said also: "The most significant principle of the Declaration is not equality, but freedom" (p. 60).

123. Frank S. Meyer, "Conservatism and Republican Candidates," *National Review* 19 (December 12, 1967): 1385.

124. See Gottfried Dietze, *The Federalist: A Classic on Federalism and Free Government* (Baltimore, 1960).

125. Meyer, "Conservatism and Republican Candidates," p. 1385.

126. Clyde Wilson, a young conservative historian, even argued that the anti-Federalists were the true conservatives of 1787, while the Federalists could be seen as "innovators" and "tinkerers" who constructed an abstract system which failed to reckon with the possibility that nonconservative forces would seize control of the presidency and judiciary. Wilson's view of the Federalists is atypical. See Clyde Wilson, "The Jeffersonian Conservative Tradition," *Modern Age* 14 (Winter 1969-1970): 36-48.

127. Russell Kirk, "The Prospects for Territorial Democracy in America," in *A Nation of States: Essays on the American Federal System*, ed. Robert A. Goldwin (Chicago, 1963), p. 45.

128. Dietze, *America's Political Dilemma*, pp. 14-15.

129. Morley, *Freedom and Federalism*, p. 14.

130. *Ibid.*, p. 53.

131. See Kirk, "Territorial Democracy," pp. 42-64. Kirk admired the writings of Orestes Brownson, the nineteenth-century radical-turned-conservative whose *The American Republic* (1865) Kirk regarded as a masterpiece. In 1955, Kirk edited Brownson's *Selected Essays*, published by the Henry Regnery Company. A number of years later he counted Brownson "among the ten or twelve most important men of ideas in the American national experience" ("The Enduring Orestes Brownson," *University Bookman* 13 [Spring 1973]: 51).

132. Murray, *We Hold these Truths*, pp. 38-39 and chap. 2.

133. See Morley, *Freedom and Federalism*, p. 66.

134. *Ibid.*, pp. 59, 68. See in general chap. 6.

135. Kilpatrick, *Sovereign States*, pp. 258-261. Kilpatrick lambasted the "palpably unconstitutional" ratification procedure. See also "A Clarification," *National Review* 4 (September 7, 1957): 199.

136. Morley, *Freedom and Federalism*, pp. 67, 92. Morley believed that "in the enlargement of centralized power and in the encouragement of democratic theory, the Civil War had profound effects upon our form of government" (p. 80). See also Dietze,

America's Political Dilemma, pp. 108-116.

137. *Ibid.*, chap. 2.

138. Frank S. Meyer, "Lincoln Without Rhetoric," *National Review* 17 (August 24, 1965): 725. For a severe critique of Lincoln's allegedly Gnostic and "millennial" rhetoric by a latter-day Agrarian conservative, see M.E. Bradford, "Lincoln's New Frontier: A Rhetoric for Continuing Revolution," *Triumph* 6 (May 1971): 11-13, 21, and 6 (June 1971): 15-17.

139. Meyer, "Lincoln Without Rhetoric," p. 725.

140. See Morley, *Freedom and Federalism*, chap. 7; Kilpatrick, *Sovereign States*, chaps. 15-16.

141. See, for example, Frank Chodorov, "Dewey Out-Centralizes Hamilton," *Human Events* 4 (November 26, 1947): 1-4, and *The Income Tax: Root of All Evil* (New York, 1954). In the article Chodorov asserted: "The unique American experiment of a union of independent states was not finished by civil war, but rather by the Sixteenth Amendment. The 'War Between the States' settled the question of the right of secession, leaving the autonomy of the states in other matters where it was. Federal income taxation, however, destroyed the integrity of the states by abolishing their 'commonwealth' status."

142. Morley, *Freedom and Federalism*, pp. 79, 83. See in general chap. 7.

143. See Dietze, *In Defense of Property*, especially chap. 4, and *America's Political Dilemma*, pp. 152-160. On p. 159 of the former book, Dietze acclaimed judicial review, "exercised for the sake of freedom from democratic action," as "an outstanding feature of American government." Dietze became atypical on this point as the "Warren Court" became a conservative target.

144. Dietze, *In Defense of Property*, chap. 4.

145. L. Brent Bozell, "Legal Libertine," *National Review* 11 (November 18, 1961): 340-341.

146. Frank S. Meyer, "Conservatism," in *Left, Right, and Center*, ed. Robert A. Goldwin (Chicago, 1965), p. 4.

147. A theme developed particularly by Dietze in his two books.

148. James Burnham, *Congress and the American Tradition* (Chicago, 1959), p. 331.

149. Russell Kirk and James McClellan, *The Political Principles of Robert A. Taft* (New York, 1967).

150. See Frank S. Meyer, "The Revolt Against Congress," *National Review* 1 (May 30, 1956): 9-10; "The Attack on the Congress," *National Review* 16 (February 11, 1964): 109-110; "The Court Challenges the Congress," *National Review* 16 (March 24, 1964): 233.

151. Fifteen years later, in the wake of the Watergate affair, Irving Kristol—by then a neo-conservative—acclaimed Burnham's book as "a critical analysis of the emerging 'imperial presidency' that is still the most perceptive and thoughtful of the lot" (Kristol, "The Inexorable Rise of the Executive," *Wall Street Journal*, September 20, 1974, p. 12).

152. Burnham, *Congress*, pp. 121-123.

153. *Ibid.*, p. 128.

154. *Ibid.*, p. 259.

155. *Ibid.*, p. 344. The preceding summary is based on part 3 of his book.

156. Both *Modern Age* and *National Review* featured many critiques of Warren Court decisions.

157. James J. Kilpatrick, "Conservatism and the South," in *The Lasting South*, ed. Louis D. Rubin and James J. Kilpatrick (Chicago, 1957), p. 204.

158. Bozell, *Warren Revolution*, p. 29.

159. *Ibid.*, pp. 25, 30.

160. A point asserted also in Kilpatrick, *Sovereign States*, pp. 285-286. Kilpatrick contended that the Brown decision had actually increased Southern white intransigence and set back racial progress.

161. Bozell, *Warren Revolution*, pp. 33-34.

162. *Ibid.*, p. 54.

163. *Ibid.*, p. 56.

164. *Ibid.*, p. 57.

165. *Ibid.*, pp. 110-112.

166. Contrast Dietze, who held judicial review (i.e., supremacy) to be a crucial and established component of a properly functioning federal system.

167. With one exception: under Article VI *state* judges were exempted from their former subordination to their state legislatures. This was done, said Bozell, "for the purpose of enforcing the Union's supremacy over its component states" (*Warren Revolution*, p. 331).

168. Bozell promised to explore post-1787 developments in a second volume, but he did not do so, for reasons to be examined in Chapter Ten.

169. Bozell, *Warren Revolution*, p. 340.

170. *Ibid.*, p. 336.

171. For assessments of Bozell's book by conservatives, see Charles E. Rice, in *Fordham Law Review* 35 (May 1967): 760-765; Martin Diamond, "Challenge to the Court," *National Review* 19 (June 13, 1967): 642-644.

172. This is a description of the Constitution used by Robert Hutchins in a public debate with Bozell about the 1954 school decision. See *Dialogues in Americanism* (Chicago, 1964), pp. 65-100, for the text of the debate.

CHAPTER EIGHT

1. Walter Berns, *Freedom, Virtue and the First Amendment* (Chicago, 1957).

2. *Ibid.*, p. 46.

3. This paragraph is based on *ibid.*, chap. 8.

4. *Ibid.*, pp. 253, 226, 247.

5. *Ibid.*, p. 162.

6. *Ibid.*, p. 256.

7. See David Spitz, "Freedom, Virtue, and the New Scholasticism," *Commentary* 28 (October 1959): 313-321.

8. See Frank S. Meyer, "Freedom, Virtue, and Government," *National Review* 4 (October 12, 1957): 329; "A Specter Is Haunting Yale," *National Review* 5 (February 15, 1958): 160.

9. Robert A. Goldwin, ed., *A Nation of States: Essays on the American Federal System* (Chicago, 1963).

10. Martin Diamond, "What the Framers Meant by Federalism," *ibid.*, p. 37.

11. Harry Jaffa, "The Case for a Stronger National Government," *ibid.*, pp. 106-125.

12. Walter Berns, "The Meaning of the Tenth Amendment," *ibid.*, pp. 126-148.

13. Jaffa was the author of *Crisis of the House Divided* (Garden City, N.Y., 1959), a penetrating study of the Lincoln-Douglas debates.

14. Harry Jaffa, *Equality and Liberty* (New York, 1965), pp. 82-84. It should be noted that Jaffa appeared to find in the Declaration of Independence not the full Lockean inalienable rights theory (which Berns saw in it) but only one eternal truth: that all men

are created politically equal. This was the only clause of the Declaration to which Jaffa regularly referred.

15. See Harry Jaffa, "Lincoln and the Cause of Freedom," *National Review* 17 (September 21, 1965): 827-828, 842. Elsewhere Jaffa admitted that "no American statesman ever violated the ordinary maxims of civil liberties more than did Lincoln...." But, he went on: "...civil liberties are, as their name implies, liberties of men in civil society. As such, they are to be correlated with the duties of men in civil society, and they are subject to that interpretation which is consistent with the duty of men to preserve the polity that incorporates their rights.... For Lincoln, the preservation of the Union...meant above all the preservation of a body whose soul remained *dedicated* to the principles of the Declaration of Independence" (*Equality and Liberty*, pp. 170, 172-173).

16. See Frank S. Meyer, "Again on Lincoln," *National Review* 18 (January 25, 1966): 71, 85.

17. Willmoore Kendall, "Source of American Caesarism," *National Review* 7 (November 7, 1959): 462.

18. Francis Wilson, "Politics and Literature," *Modern Age* 10 (Fall 1966): 424.

19. William F. Buckley, Jr., ed., *American Conservative Thought in the Twentieth Century* (Indianapolis, 1970), p. 214. The controversial remark was: "Extremism in the defense of liberty is no vice; moderation in the pursuit of justice is no virtue." Presumably Jaffa believed the latter clause to be an unexceptionable restatement of Aristotle's teaching, and the former clause a mere rendition into principle of what Lincoln correctly did in practice.

20. Sam M. Jones, "From Washington Straight," *National Review* 1 (May 30, 1956): 2, 11.

21. Frank S. Meyer, *In Defense of Freedom* (Chicago, 1962), pp. 83, 86, 87-89.

22. Meyer to William F. Buckley, Jr., February 8, 1964, William F. Buckley, Jr., Papers, Yale University Library, New Haven, Conn. In this letter he specifically criticized the contributions of Berns, Diamond, and Jaffa to *A Nation of States*.

23. While this was the definite rhetorical tendency, one should generalize cautiously. John Courtney Murray emphasized natural rights *and* natural law and was severely critical of Locke; see his *We Hold These Truths* (New York, 1960), p. 286ff. Lockean rights were not the only rights. Russell Kirk often linked rights to duties and liked to quote Burke to the effect that restraints are among the true rights of man. (One is reminded of a phrase in the ceremony awarding degrees to graduates of Harvard Law School: "the wise restraints that make men free.") On the other hand, Frank Meyer denied that the exercise of rights was contingent on the performance of duties or the practice of virtue; see his *In Defense of Freedom* and Meyer to the editor, *National Review* 6 (September 13, 1958): 190.

24. Often because of his presumed rationale for the right to private property; see Gottfried Dietze, *In Defense of Property* (Baltimore, 1962), pp. 26-28, and John Chamberlain, *The Enterprising Americans* (New York, 1963), p. xvi. Meyer's influential conception of the limited state (for defense, internal order, and administration of justice) was strongly reminiscent of Locke's belief that government was instituted to protect the life, liberty, and property of individuals.

25. A personal anecdote may be illuminating. In 1971 the author attended a seminar on conservative thought at Harvard University. In one session two conservatives—one a person who talked of Aristotle and the polis, the other a very thorough libertarian—disagreed about governmental regulation of drugs. The question arose: "Are we our brother's keeper?" Yes, said the Aristotelian. No, said the libertarian. It was another illustration of the distance between the "ancients" and the "moderns"—and between differing schools of conservative political philosophy.

26. This biographical portrait is based on a large variety of published and unpublished sources. Rather than burden the text with a citation for every single biographical datum, the author lists here the material used. For published information on Kendall's life, see George W. Carey, "Willmoore Kendall, 1909-1967," *Western Political Quarterly* 20 (September 1967): 799; Neal B. Freeman, "Recollections of an Impossible Man," *Rally* 2 (September 1967): 22, 28; Jeffrey Hart, "Willmoore Kendall: American," in *Willmoore Kendall Contra Mundum*, ed. Nellie D. Kendall (New Rochelle, N.Y., 1971), pp. 9-26; Charles S. Hyneman, "In Memoriam," *P.S.: Newsletter of the American Political Science Association* 1 (Winter 1968): 55-56; and "Kendall, Willmoore," *Encyclopedia of Biography* (n.d., copy supplied by Nellie D. Kendall). The author has been permitted to read "Willmoore Kendall: American Conservative," an unpublished tribute by Professor Leo Paul S. de Alvarez, a former colleague at the University of Dallas, The following individuals have supplied information about Kendall by correspondence and, in many cases, by interview as well: Carl Albert (a friend of Kendall at Oxford and later); John Alvis (a political scientist and former student); Juan and Maria Andrade (two old friends from Spain); Alfred Balitzer (a political scientist and a former student); Lyle H. Boren (a friend from childhood on); L. Brent Bozell; R.F. Bretherton (Kendall's tutor in economics at Oxford); Cleanth Brooks (a friend of Kendall's at LSU and Yale); William F. Buckley, Jr.; James Burnham; George W. Carey (a close collaborator in later years); John Chamberlain; Charles H. Commons (a cousin); Glenn D. Commons (a cousin); Martin Diamond (a political scientist and friend); John Fischer (a friend from Oxford days on); E.A. Grant (a British friend at Oxford and later); Edward Harrison (a friend from Oklahoma); Hubert Humphrey; Charles Hyneman (a political scientist and friend); Bertrand de Jouvenel (a French political theorist and friend); Katherine Kendall (his first wife); Nellie D. Kendall (his third wife); Russell Kirk; Evron Kirkpatrick (a political scientist and friend); Arthur Larson (a former roommate at Oxford); Yvona K. Mason (Kendall's sister); R.B. McCallum (Kendall's tutor in politics at Oxford); Frank S. Meyer; Robert Nisbet; Edmund Opitz; Austin Ranney (coauthor of a book with Kendall); Mulford Q. Sibley (a political scientist and friend); Henry Wells (a political scientist and friend); Francis Wilson (Kendall's dissertation adviser). A large number of Kendall's letters are in the Francis Wilson Papers, University of Illinois, Urbana, and in the Buckley Papers at Yale. In addition, Professors Balitzer, Hyneman, Ranney, and Wells have very kindly allowed the author to examine letters from Kendall in their possession. The responsibility for fact and interpretation, of course, is the author's alone.

The remark about Kendall as "the boy wonder of Oklahoma" is from Arthur Larson to the author, December 29, 1971.

27. Yvona K. Mason to the author, April 20, 1972.

28. Kendall's sister and Lyle H. Boren have stated their belief (in letters to the author) that Kendall was never a full-fledged "Trotskyite." (Mrs. Mason did say, however, that after returning from Spain he did for a time "argue in favor of certain aspects of that philosophy.") On the other hand, several who knew him at Oxford have recalled that he was left-wing and even (more or less) a "Trotskyite." Kendall himself, in a letter to Henry Wells on April 20, 1942, referred to his "notorious Trotskyite sympathies from 1935 down to 1938" (copy in possession of the author). In a letter to the author on January 7, 1973, James Burnham recalled that although Kendall was never a Trotskyist member in the late 1930s, he was "on the fringe" of a loose group of "fellow travelers of the Trotskyite faction." This "satellite group," said Burnham, included Sidney Hook, Suzanne La Follette, Mary McCarthy, and Dwight Macdonald. "Most of these intellectuals swerved toward Trotsky primarily because of Trotskyism's anti-Stalinism (which for many of them, as for me, was in reality potential anti-Communism) and, related to this, the issue of the Moscow Trials. Most of them, including Kendall, supported the

committee that arranged the countertrial in Mexico." Probably Mulford Q. Sibley has most accurately summed up the matter: "If he was not actually a Trotskyite, he was at times close to their position" (Sibley to the author, January 6, 1972).

29. One of his closest friends was Juan Andrade, a leader of the semi-Trotskyist Partido Obrero de Unificacion Marxista (POUM).

30. Interview (by telephone) with Katherine Kendall, October 21, 1973.

31. Interview with Charles Hyneman, Washington, D.C., March 8, 1974.

32. Lyle H. Boren to the author, May 17, 1972. James Burnham recalls: "I do remember his strong interest in the Spanish Civil War. I believe it was his knowledge of the Communist operations there, combined with the Moscow Trials, that pulled him away from the degree of liberalism he had gone along with, and directed him toward hard anti-Communism and, over the years, to his special sort of conservatism" (Burnham to the author, January 7, 1973).

33. Austin Ranney of the University of Wisconsin recalls that Kendall told him that his experience in Spain was a great formative influence on him: it made an anti-Communist out of him (interview by telephone, December 30, 1971).

34. See Willmoore Kendall, "Should the Government Control the Press?" *The Quill* 27 (May 1939): 10-12.

35. See Kendall, "On the Preservation of Democracy in America," *Southern Review* 5 (Summer 1939): 53-68.

36. Kendall, "A Letter to a Congressman," *The American Oxonian* 25 (April 1938): 93.

37. Kendall, *John Locke and the Doctrine of Majority-Rule* (1941; reprint ed., Urbana, Ill., 1965).

38. *Ibid.*, p. 54.

39. *Ibid.*, p. 58.

40. *Ibid.*, p. 101.

41. *Ibid.*, p. 135.

42. He was chief of the Latin American division of the CIA's Office of Reports and Estimates. The author is grateful to Nellie D. Kendall for supplying a curriculum vitae for Kendall.

43. John Fischer to the author, January 20, 1972. Kendall appears to have been paid $42,500, the equivalent of five years' salary.

44. Actually, he was on leave much of the time. From 1950 to 1954, for example, he was a major in the air force in the area of psychological warfare. His work (which included analysis of the effectiveness of propaganda and preparation of manuals) took him frequently to the Far East.

The merits of Kendall's controversy with Yale are impossible to weigh here and are, at any rate, largely irrelevant to the issues at hand. The case did attract considerable comment within the profession. At one point late in the 1950s, Kendall, in desperation, had a substantial number of academic friends write to Yale attesting to his scholarly reputation. Apparently Yale contended that his record of publication was inadequate. In addition, there was probably some animus against his immersion in "nonprofessional" work as a senior editor of *National Review*. Personal factors were also undoubtedly important.

45. See Kendall, letter to the editor, *Yale Daily News*, April 28, 1950.

46. Kendall, in *Journal of Politics* 8 (August 1946): 427. For Kendall's most extended critique of Mill, see *The Conservative Affirmation* (Chicago, 1963), chap. 6.

47. This was a persistent theme in his writings, early and late. See, for example, Kendall, *Conservative Affirmation*, esp. chaps. 3, 4, 6. See also Frederick Wilhelmsen and Willmoore Kendall, "Cicero and the Politics of the Public Orthodoxy," *Intercollegiate Review* 5 (Winter 1968-1969): 84-100.

48. See William F. Buckley, Jr., ed., *Odyssey of a Friend: Whittaker Chambers' Letters*

to William F. Buckley, Jr., 1954-1961 (New York, 1970), pp. 53-54; Buckley, "The Ivory Tower: Professor Kendall Speaks at Harvard on Oppenheimer," *National Review* 3 (May 4, 1957): 430.

49. In a letter to the author on November 25, 1972, Kendall's sister pointed out that he persisted in defending what people called McCarthyism after others had stopped. Francis Wilson has said: "...it is probable that toward the end of his life he may have been among the very few who were willing to stand before a university audience and affirm the danger of communism and the necessity of exposing communists" ("The Political Science of Willmoore Kendall," *Modern Age* 16 [Winter 1972]: 45).

50. According to Kendall's colleague, Leo Paul S. de Alvarez of the University of Dallas, Kendall often said this. See de Alvarez, "Difficult, Singular, and Legendary," *National Review* 23 (August 24, 1971): 935-936.

51. Wilson, "Political Science of Willmoore Kendall," p. 44.

52. Interview with James Burnham, Kent, Conn., February 4, 1972. Burnham also believed that Kendall's political shift paralleled Burnham's own from anti-Stalinist Left to anti-Communist Right.

53. In a noted speech before the European Center for Documentation and Information in 1957, Kendall asserted: "American Europe can become free, can resume the living of the good life as Europe has always conceived it, only by liberating itself and the rest of Europe from every form of subjection to Communism. And this it can do only by destroying the military power of the Soviet Union" (quoted in Rafael Calvo-Serer, "They Spoke for Christian Europe," *National Review* 4 [July 27, 1957]: 109).

54. Charles Hyneman, an old friend of Kendall's, recalled in an interview (March 8, 1974) that Kendall advocated preventive war during the early cold war years. For Kendall's position on war, pacifism, and Christianity, see Kendall and Mulford Q. Sibley, *War & the Use of Force: Moral or Immoral, Christian or Unchristian?* (Denver, 1959). This is the transcript of a lively debate held at Stanford University in 1959.

55. For an important example of Kendall's critique of liberal foreign policies and assumptions about Communism in this period, see his introduction to *A Communist Party in Action*, by A. Rossi (New Haven, 1949), pp. v-xxiv. Kendall translated this book from the original French version.

56. Kendall to Henry Wells, April 20, 1942; copy in possession of the author.

57. Kendall to Wells, November 6, 1946; copy in possession of the author.

58. Quite in contrast to many conservatives in the mid-1940s, for example, Kendall disliked Friedrich Hayek's influential critique of socialism, *The Road to Serfdom*. Instead, he praised Herman Finer's rebuttal, *The Road to Reaction* (Boston, 1945).

59. After Kendall completed his dissertation on John Locke, he planned to write an equally revisionist study of Rousseau. But although he studied the French philosopher intensively throughout his life, and although he translated two of Rousseau's books, Kendall never completed his projected work. For Kendall's analysis of Rousseau, see his introductions in his own translations of *The Social Contract* (Chicago, 1954) and *The Government of Poland* (Indianapolis, 1972).

60. See, for example, his "Prolegomena to Any Future Work on Majority Rule," *Journal of Politics* 12 (November 1950): 694-713.

61. Kendall to Wells, October 24, 1952; copy in possession of the author.

62. Willmoore Kendall, "The People Versus Socrates Revisited," *Modern Age* 3 (Winter 1958-1959): 98-111.

63. Buckley to Henry Regnery, September 25, 1954, Buckley Papers.

64. The author is indebted here to Professor de Alvarez's unpublished memorial essay, listed above. One of Kendall's students, Father Stanley Parry, appears to have been a significant influence on his religious conversion.

65. Lyle Boren suspects that this was the case (Boren to the author, May 17, 1972).

66. Kendall, in *American Political Science Review* 59 (June 1965): 473.

67. Kendall, "Who Killed Political Philosophy?" *National Review* 8 (March 12, 1960): 175. Kendall also called the Straussian interpretation of modern political philosophy "the decisive development in modern political philosophy since Machiavelli himself" (in *Philosophical Review* 75 [April 1966]: 251-252).

68. See Kendall, "John Locke Revisited," *Intercollegiate Review* 2 (January-February 1966): 217-234.

69. Kendall to Francis Wilson (received March 4, 1960), Wilson Papers. Kendall attributed his low productivity at this point to the fact that Strauss and Voegelin had "changed drastically" Kendall's "standards." In this letter Kendall described Strauss's *Thoughts on Machiavelli* (Seattle, 1958) as very unsettling, "the most upsetting work of our time."

70. See especially Kendall, *Conservative Affirmation*, pp. 83-99.

71. *Ibid.*, p. 99. This paragraph is also based on Willmoore Kendall, "Social Contract," *International Encyclopedia of the Social Sciences* (New York, 1968), vol. 14, pp. 376-381.

72. Willmoore Kendall, "The Two Majorities," *Midwest Journal of Political Science* 4 (November 1960): 317-345.

73. See Austin Ranney and Willmoore Kendall, *Democracy and the American Party System* (New York, 1956), a combination explanation/defense of the system, using absolute majority-rule criteria. The book was begun several years before Kendall joined *National Review*.

74. This new orientation meant that Kendall had to change his mind on many things. For example, in his radical days he had highly regarded J. Allen·Smith's *The Spirit of American Government* (1907). By the late 1950s and 1960s Kendall perceived Smith's book as the origin of the twentieth century "'Liberal attack' on the inherited political system of the United States." See Willmoore Kendall and George W. Carey, eds., *Liberalism versus Conservatism: The Continuing Debate in American Government* (Princeton, 1966), p. xvi. See also Kendall, *Contra Mundum*, pp. 285-286. Kendall's correspondence indicates that he occasionally dreamed in his later years of writing a full-scale rejoinder to Smith's book.

75. See Kendall, *Conservative Affirmation*, pp. 8, 10. See in general pp. 1-20.

76. See Willmoore Kendall, "Three on the Line," *National Review* 4 (August 31, 1957): 179-181, 191.

77. Willmoore Kendall, "The Cure that Kills," *National Review* 11 (November 18, 1961): 346.

78. Kendall, *Conservative Affirmation*, p. 99.

79. Kendall talked about these matters often. See especially Kendall, *Conservative Affirmation*, pp. 17-18, 249-252; Kendall and George W. Carey, *The Basic Symbols of the American Political Tradition* (Baton Rouge, 1970), chaps. 5-6; Kendall, *Contra Mundum*, pp. 350-352.

80. Willmoore Kendall, "The Bill of Rights and American Freedom," in *What Is Conservatism?* ed. Frank S. Meyer (New York, 1964), pp. 41-64.

81. Leonard Levy, *Legacy of Suppression* (Cambridge, Mass., 1960) and *Jefferson and Civil Liberties: The Darker Side* (Cambridge, Mass., 1963).

82. Kendall, in *Stanford Law Review* 16 (May 1964): 759.

83. *Ibid.*, p. 764.

84. *Ibid.*, p. 765.

85. See Samuel Stouffer, *Civil Liberties, Communism, and Conformity* (Garden City, N.Y., 1955). Kendall called this "a very favorite book of mine" (*Conservative Affirmation*, p. 81).

86. *Ibid.*, p. 82. Kendall was not opposed to free speech. In fact, he said (*Conservative Affirmation*, p. 77) that he sided "temperamentally" with the "let-'em-speak" people rather than the "shut-'em-up" people. But he refused to make a universally true, always applicable, absolute doctrine out of his preference.

87. Kendall, "Three on the Line," p. 180.

88. This was a major point of Willmoore Kendall and George W. Carey, "Towards a Definition of 'Conservatism,'" *Journal of Politics* 26 (May 1964): 406-422.

89. Kendall, "Two Majorities," p. 328.

90. *Ibid.*, p. 344.

91. In a debate with James MacGregor Burns in 1964, Kendall explicitly denied that he was the kind of conservative who believed, "The more government, the less freedom" (*Dialogues in Americanism* [Chicago, 1964], p. 112).

92. This was a change from the late 1930s, when Kendall—still on the Left—believed that an "economic oligarchy" had always controlled political power in America and that the Constitution, "as it now operates, is as little congenial to majority-rule as it could possibly have become without abandoning the make-believe of democratic leanings" (Kendall, "On the Preservation of Democracy for America," *Southern Review* 5 [Summer 1939]: 54, 58.

93. Kendall, "The Bill of Rights," pp. 63-64.

94. Kendall, "Three on the Line," p. 181.

95. Kendall, *Contra Mundum*, p. 417.

96. Kendall, in *Dialogues in Americanism*, p. 136. For Burns's view of his differences with Kendall, see also "The Conservative Negation," *New Leader* 46 (September 30, 1963): 16-17.

97. Kendall, "Three on the Line," p. 181.

98. This paragraph is based primarily on Kendall, "Three on the Line," and Kendall's essay "How to Read 'The Federalist,'" reprinted in Kendall, *Contra Mundum*, pp. 403-417. Kendall's conception of a "constitutional morality" is similar to Bozell's idea of the "unwritten Constitution." Kendall's reference to Bozell's "conclusive" research is in *Contra Mundum*, p. 413.

99. Willmoore Kendall, "What Killed the Civil Rights Movement?" *Phalanx* 1 (Summer 1967): 43.

100. Willmoore Kendall and George W. Carey, "The 'Intensity' Problem and Democratic Theory," *American Political Science Review* 62 (March 1968): 22. One outstanding element in the American political system was the political parties, which Kendall vigorously endorsed; see Kendall and Ranney, *Democracy and the American Party System.* For example: "Fostering consensus, then, is the phase of popular consultation on which our parties make their best showing..." (p. 517). Kendall was a great believer in government by consensus and was very impressed by the "civil-war potential" in American society (*ibid.*, pp. 464-467). Political parties helped to counteract this danger.

101. Charges that he attempted to refute in his essay on the *Federalist*. See Kendall, *Contra Mundum*, pp. 403-417.

102. Kendall and Carey, *Basic Symbols*, cited above. Although Kendall wrote four of the chapters, Carey edited that portion and added several chapters of his own. However, since Carey was a close friend and collaborator, and since Carey's own chapters utilize Kendall's lecture notes, it is safe to follow the reviewers and call this book a part of Kendall's oeuvre.

103. While Kendall often appeared to attack the Declaration of Independence, his targets were slightly different: the liberal (also Lincolnian, he thought) *interpretation* of the document, and the effort to make the document (or one clause of it) the single absolute American principle before which all else was to be sacrificed. He could on

occasion acclaim the Declaration on conservative grounds. Following John Courtney Murray, whom he called "the true sage of Woodstock" (Maryland), he appeared, in an unfinished essay, to approve the Declaration's emphasis on absolute truths ("we hold these truths") in opposition to the relativism of the liberals. See Kendall, *Contra Mundum*, pp. 74-89, especially pp. 88-89.

104. Kendall and Carey, *Basic Symbols*, p. 154.

105. Kendall, *Contra Mundum*, p. 360. The author has been told that Kendall voted for Lyndon Johnson in 1964. He was definitely not enthusiastic about Senator Goldwater, whom he considered "very bad news for the cause" (Kendall to Buckley, July 17, 1963, Buckley Papers). See also Kendall to Buckley (received July 23, 1963, Buckley Papers). For a published critique, see Kendall, "Quo Vadis, Barry?" *National Review* 10 (February 25, 1961): 107-108, 127.

106. Kendall, "American Conservatism and the 'Prayer' Decisions," *Modern Age* 8 (Summer 1964): 258.

107. Kendall, in *Dialogues in Americanism*, p. 141.

108. Kendall, "The Civil Rights Movement and the Coming Constitutional Crisis," *Intercollegiate Review* 1 (February-March 1965): 54.

109. *Ibid.*, pp. 60, 57, 61. Kendall did not believe, however, that America was opposed to all change. In fact, he later said, our political system has a bias "in favor of leaving drastic changes (they do happen in America, often more swiftly than they could happen anywhere else) to free spontaneous action by individuals out in American society" ("What Killed the Civil Rights Movement?", p. 41).

110. Kendall, "What Killed the Civil Rights Movement?", pp. 37-43.

111. Kendall, "Source of American Caesarism," p. 462.

112. A phrase he used frequently in his column for *National Review*. Kendall did not use this term in any literal, conspiratorial sense. Rather, he meant to convey by it what later conservatives meant by the "liberal establishment."

113. Kendall, "'Prayer' Decisions," p. 254.

114. *Ibid.*

115. Kendall, *Contra Mundum*, p. 354.

116. See *ibid.*, pp. 354-355.

117. *Ibid.*, pp. 354-357.

118. Kendall, "'Prayer' Decisions," pp. 255, 259. Kendall's ability to translate sometimes controversial conservative positions into a fresh and arresting idiom is evident in his discussion of the religion clause of the First Amendment. The notion that this clause established a "wall of separation" between church and state was "an Old Wives' Tale." "In point of fact, the wall of separation in America has always been as full of holes as a kitchen sieve.... The American answer to the problem of having it both ways here, the *traditional* American answer, which to our misfortune we have all too rarely tried to put into words, has been this: Maintain a wall; celebrate it in myth and song; celebrate it, indeed, as a wall that cannot and must not be breached. But let that wall be *porous*..." (*ibid.*, pp. 256-257).

119. See Willmoore Kendall, "How to Read Richard Weaver: Philosopher of 'We the (Virtuous) People,'" *Intercollegiate Review* 2 (September 1965): 77-86.

120. *Ibid.*, p. 83. Kendall had enthusiastically approved Weaver's *Ideas Have Consequences* when it appeared in 1948. In a review of this book Kendall unabashedly nominated Weaver for "the captaincy of the anti-Liberal team" (*Journal of Politics* 11 [February 1949]: 259-261).

121. Kendall, in *American Political Science Review* 57 (June 1965): 473.

122. Kendall, "How to Read Richard Weaver," p. 81.

123. Kendall, "'Prayer' Decisions," p. 250.

124. This was Kendall's epithet for Meyer and the projected title of a chapter on Meyer

in Kendall's never-finished *Sages of Conservatism*. Interview (by telephone) with Frank Meyer, September 4, 1971.

125. Kendall, "How to Read Richard Weaver," p. 81.

126. *Ibid.* and Kendall, *Conservative Affirmation*, p. xi.

127. Kendall, "How to Read Richard Weaver," pp. 81-82.

128. Kendall to Wilson (received August 17, 1962), Wilson Papers.

129. Kendall to Wilson, February 3, 1962, Wilson Papers. Auerbach's critique of conservatism, and various rebuttals, appeared in *National Review* 12 (January 30, 1962): 57-59, 74.

130. Kendall to Wilson (received December 4, 1962), Wilson Papers. In 1957, Kendall had submitted an essay to *National Review* critical of the political philosophy of the Declaration of Independence and even the Constitution. His piece was rejected, partly on the grounds that it was too technical and not readable enough for the magazine's readers and partly because Buckley did not find Kendall's essay either persuasive or up to Kendall's standard. See William F. Buckley, Jr., memorandum to the editors of *National Review*, November 19, 1957, and his memo to L. Brent Bozell (with a copy of a memo to Kendall), February 5, 1958, Buckley Papers.

Kendall may have believed that *National Review* would not dare to publish so iconoclastic an article. The rejection probably reinforced his oft-expressed contention that *National Review* was merely "the Right-wing organ of the Establishment" (Kendall to Buckley, January 16, 1964, Buckley Papers).

131. The author learned this fact in correspondence with two of Kendall's tutors, R.F. Bretherton and R.B. McCallum.

132. Kendall, *Conservative Affirmation*, p. xi.

133. Kendall, *Contra Mundum*, p. 601.

134. *Ibid.*, p. 600.

135. *Ibid.*, p. 605. See in general pp. 594-608 (a speech Kendall delivered in 1966).

136. See Kendall, *Contra Mundum*, pp. 29-57, for an analysis of Kirk's conservatism.

137. Kendall to Wilson (received April 11, 1963), Wilson Papers.

138. See Kendall and Carey, "Towards a Definition of 'Conservatism,'" pp. 406-422.

139. Kendall, "How to Read Richard Weaver," p. 83. See also Kendall's introduction to *Conservative Affirmation*.

140. Kendall, *Contra Mundum*, p. 37. See in general pp. 29-57.

141. *Ibid.*, pp. 46-47.

142. *Ibid.*, pp. 53-54.

143. Kendall to Wilson (received March 7, 1963), Wilson Papers.

144. Kendall to Wilson (n.d.; probably March 1963), Wilson Papers.

145. Kendall, in *Dialogues in Americanism*, p. 112.

146. Kendall, "Constitutional Crisis," pp. 53-54. It should be noted that Kendall was discussing what *could* be done under our political system, not what *ought* to be done. On many, probably most, policy issues of the day, Kendall agreed with his fellow conservatives.

147. Even in private life Kendall was unusual. Thrice married, he may have been the only person in the history of the Roman Catholic Church to have two marriages annulled simultaneously.

148. Kendall to Wilson (n.d., but Spring 1963), Wilson Papers.

149. Kendall to Wilson, May 1963, Wilson Papers.

150. Kendall to Wilson (received January 13, 1964), Wilson Papers.

151. Leo Strauss to Kendall, May 14, 1961, Wilson Papers.

152. William F. Buckley, Jr., *Cruising Speed—A Documentary* (New York, 1971), p. 73.

153. In 1963, Kendall resigned as a senior editor of *National Review*, from which he was

increasingly estranged. See Kendall to Buckley, September 22, 1963, Buckley Papers.

154. Both Frank Meyer and George W. Carey used this word to describe (but certainly not dismiss) Kendall. Interview with Frank Meyer (by telephone), September 4, 1971; George Carey, "How to Read Willmoore Kendall," *Intercollegiate Review* 8 (Winter-Spring 1972): 63.

155. Charles S. Hyneman, "In Memoriam," *P.S.: Newsletter of the American Political Science Association* 1 (Winter 1968): 56.

156. Kendall used the term "unabashedly egghead McCarthyism" to describe his article "The Open Society and Its Enemies" (Kendall to Wilson, August 4, 1960, Wilson Papers).

157. Kendall once wrote: "...the single most depressing fact about contemporary America is that the finest men and women one knows...those who embody most fully the so-called 'values of the West,' finally seek their destinies outside the nation's leading educational and governmental and opinion-forming institutions, avoid their cocktail parties, and pass up their literature" ("To High Heaven," *National Review* 2 [December 22, 1956]: 20). He may well have been thinking of himself.

158. In his memorial essay on Kendall, Hyneman stated that "few of his generation in American political science can match his claim for attention over the decades immediately ahead" (p. 56).

159. Interview with Meyer, September 4, 1971.

160. Interview with Russell Kirk, Cambridge, Mass., April 21, 1971.

161. Kirk to Peter Viereck, August 5, 1954; copy in the possession of the author.

162. Robert Nisbet to Kirk, September 10, 1953, Russell Kirk Papers, Clarke Historical Library at Central Michigan University, Mount Pleasant, Mich.

163. Nisbet to Kirk, January 3, 1963, Kirk Papers. On the other hand, Nisbet did acknowledge that Kendall was a "formidable" and "towering" figure for those who knew his work (interview with Nisbet, Northampton, Mass., November 29, 1971).

164. See his late essay with George W. Carey, "'Intensity' Problem and Democratic Theory," especially part 4.

165. See his early essay "The Majority Principle and the Scientific Elite," *Southern Review* 4 (Winter 1939): 463-474.

166. These remarks are not, of course, meant to imply that Kendall was in any way unsophisticated.

167. Compare, for example, Peter Viereck's attacks on "populist" McCarthyism in *The Unadjusted Man: A New Hero For Americans* (Boston, 1956).

168. Jeffrey Hart, "Willmoore Kendall: American," in *Contra Mundum*, p. 9. John P. East, a political scientist at East Carolina University, has more recently concurred with Hart's appraisal. East declares that Kendall must be placed on any "list of the most important political scientists of the post-World War II era. Moreover, as regards the American political tradition, it is easily argued that Kendall is the most original, innovative, and challenging interpreter of any period" ("The Political Thought of Willmoore Kendall," *Political Science Reviewer* 3 [1973]: 201).

169. An analysis of the merits of Kendall's thought would require a separate and different study. As Garry Wills said, "One has to answer Kendall in books—the mark of an important thinker" (in *Commonweal* 93 [December 18, 1970]: 306). Our own concern here, of course, is not the validity but the evolution and impact of Kendall's thought.

170. Thus, one should not conclude that Kendall "disliked" Burke. He sought rather to "translate" him—where applicable—into an American vocabulary. Nor should one conclude that because Kendall was such a fervent American he was any less at home in Europe. He spent many years abroad and was, for example, very interested in Spain. Frederick Wilhelmsen (a close friend) stated that Kendall once said to him upon seeing

Spain's Escorial, "This is my favorite church in all Christendom" (Wilhelmsen to the editor, *National Review* 24 [June 23, 1972]: 672-673).

171. Frank S. Meyer, *In Defense of Freedom: A Conservative Credo* (Chicago, 1962), p. 6.

172. Some conservatives openly admired Acton. See Stephen J. Tonsor, "The Conservative Search for Identity," in *What Is Conservatism?* ed. Frank S. Meyer (New York, 1964), pp. 133-151.

173. Francis Wilson, "Politics and Literature," *Modern Age* 10 (Fall 1966): 424.

174. On this point see Clyde Wilson, "The Jeffersonian Conservative Tradition," *Modern Age* 14 (Winter 1969-1970): 36.

175. Russell Kirk, *Beyond the Dreams of Avarice* (Chicago, 1956), p. 19.

176. This is not to imply that as American conservatism became more articulate, it shunned or repudiated Europe. On the contrary, it welcomed contributions from the Old World. One of the most notable of these was the conservative British philosopher Michael Oakeshott, whose *Rationalism in Politics and Other Essays* (New York, 1962) evoked admiration from the intellectual American Right. See Francis Wilson, "Oakeshott and Conservatism," *University Bookman* 4 (Autumn 1963): 19-23; Harry Jaffa, "A Celebration of Tradition," *National Review* 15 (October 22, 1963): 360-362; Buckley, *Cruising Speed*, p. 250. In 1970, Buckley included an essay by Oakeshott in his anthology *American Conservative Thought in the Twentieth Century* (Indianapolis, 1970). For a recent appraisal of the British philosopher, see Gertrude Himmelfarb, "The Conservative Imagination: Michael Oakeshott," *American Scholar* 44 (Summer 1975): 405-420.

CHAPTER NINE

1. William F. Buckley, Jr., "The Party and the Deep Blue Sea," *Commonweal* 55 (January 25, 1952): 391-393.

2. William F. Buckley, Jr., "Reflections on Election Eve," *National Review* 2 (November 3, 1956): 6-7.

3. William F. Buckley, Jr., "The Tranquil World of Dwight D. Eisenhower," *National Review* 5 (January 18, 1958): 57-59.

4. For a sample of the journal's early criticisms of Eisenhower and the "age of progressive moderation," see John Chamberlain, ed., *The National Review Reader* (New York, 1957), pp. 185-213.

5. Anthony Harrigan, "Is Our Administration Conservative?" *Catholic World* 179 (April 1954): 24-28. In a similar vein, see Harrigan's essay "The Realities of the American Situation," *Catholic World* 184 (March 1957): 458-464.

6. Frank S. Meyer, "Where Is Eisenhower Going?" *American Mercury* 78 (March 1954): 123-126.

7. Frank S. Meyer, "Slippage and the Theory of the Lesser Evil," *National Review* 6 (February 28, 1959): 556.

8. Frank S. Meyer, "The Politics of 'The Impossible,' II: 1960 Dilemma," *National Review* 7 (December 19, 1959): 555.

9. Not all conservatives agreed with Meyer. In a letter to the editor, *National Review* 4 (December 21, 1957): 573, Ralph de Toledano, later a biographer of Richard Nixon, stressed that politics was, after all, a matter of acquiring power. "Moral: Democrats win elections because they keep their eye on the ball. Republicans, like Trotskyite splinter groups, get their kicks from ideological purity." For Meyer's rebuttal, see his "On What Ball?" *National Review* 5 (January 4, 1958): 17.

10. Richard Weaver was another conservative who rejected Eisenhower-style "modera-

tion." "Properly speaking," Weaver observed, "middle-of-the-road-ism is not a political philosophy at all. It is rather the absence of a philosophy or an attempt to evade having a philosophy" ("The Middle of the Road: Where It Leads," *Human Events* 12 [March 24, 1956]). See also Weaver, "The Middle Way: A Political Meditation," *National Review* 3 (January 19, 1957): 63-64. In this essay he declared: "It seems clear that 'the middle of the road' is one of the guises worn by relativism. And relativism is the means by which Liberalism is descending into mindlessness."

11. Frank S. Meyer, "The Politics of 'The Impossible,'" *National Review* 7 (November 7, 1959): 459. Said Meyer on another occasion: "Conservatives are by definition defenders of [Western] civilization; and in a revolutionary age this means that they are, and must be, counterrevolutionaries" ("On What Ball?" p. 17).

12. "*National Review* and the 1960 Elections," *National Review* 9 (October 22, 1960): 233-234; Frank S. Meyer, "Only Four More Years to 1964," *National Review* 9 (December 3, 1960): 344.

Behind *National Review*'s editorial silence on the 1960 election was a dispute among editors about whether or not to endorse Richard Nixon. Meyer, of course, was adamantly against it; see his memorandum to William F. Buckley, Jr., May 10, 1960, William F. Buckley, Jr. Papers, Yale University Library, New Haven, Conn. *National Review*'s publisher, William Rusher, also opposed a public endorsement of Nixon; see his memoranda to Buckley of September 14 and October 10, 1960, Buckley Papers. On the other side (despite his lack of personal enthusiasm for Nixon) was James Burnham; see Burnham to Buckley, October 9, 1960, Buckley Papers.

13. William S. Schlamm, for instance, an important figure at *National Review* in its early years, detested Eisenhower. For an amusing anecdote about Schlamm, see "Confidential: Among Ourselves," *National Review* 2 (December 1, 1956): 15. When Schlamm went on vacation, the magazine's staff prankishly decorated his entire office with photographs of President Eisenhower. It also prepared a mock issue of *National Review* in which Schlamm urged that both parties nominate Dwight and Milton Eisenhower for president and vice-president. See also William S. Schlamm, *Germany and the East-West Crisis* (New York, 1959), pp. 199-202, for a severe critique of Eisenhower. Schlamm was particularly angered by Eisenhower's remark "War is unthinkable," which Schlamm called "logically without meaning, morally untenable, and politically suicidal."

14. Lecture by Russell Kirk at Harvard University, Cambridge, Mass., April 21, 1971.

15. Stephen Tonsor to the editor, *National Review* 6 (December 20, 1958): 412.

16. Whittaker Chambers, *Cold Friday* (New York, 1964), p. 221.

17. Chambers to Buckley, November [23?], 1958, quoted in *Odyssey of a Friend: Whittaker Chambers' Letters to William F. Buckley, Jr., 1954-1961*, ed. William F. Buckley, Jr. (New York, 1970), p. 216.

18. Chambers to Buckley, May 7, 1959, quoted in *ibid.*, p. 247.

19. Chambers to Buckley, September 1954, quoted in *ibid.*, p. 79.

20. See William F. Buckley, Jr., *Up from Liberalism* (New York, 1959), part 2.

21. A frequently used term in conservative circles. See especially M. Stanton Evans, *The Liberal Establishment* (New York, 1965).

22. To Whittaker Chambers, the Russian Revolution was "the central fact of the first half of the twentieth century," and Communism the "central issue" of the entire century (*Cold Friday*, p. 109).

23. Frank S. Meyer, "'New Ideas' or Old Truth," *National Review* 3 (February 2, 1957): 108.

24. *Ibid.*

25. Frank S. Meyer, "Saved by the U-2," *National Review* 8 (June 4, 1960): 365.

26. James Burnham, "Is the Revolution Dead?" *National Review* 19 (October 31, 1967):

1162, 1164, 1220.

27. See Robert Strausz-Hupé, "The Kremlin's Undiminished Appetite," *National Review* 20 (February 27, 1968): 180-182, 205.

28. Frank S. Meyer, *The Moulding of Communists: The Training of the Communist Cadre* (New York, 1961), p. 4.

29. *Ibid.*, p. 5.

30. *Ibid.*, p. 171.

31. Gerhart Niemeyer, with the assistance of John S. Reshetar, Jr., *An Inquiry into Soviet Mentality* (New York, 1956). This book was published under the auspices of the Foreign Policy Research Institute of the University of Pennsylvania, founded by Robert Strausz-Hupé. At the beginning of the book, Niemeyer explicitly thanked Strausz-Hupé and Stefan Possony for their assistance.

32. *Ibid.*, p. 70.

33. *Ibid.*, p. 69.

34. *Ibid.*, pp. 72-73.

35. *Ibid.*, p. 74.

36. *Ibid.*

37. *Ibid.*, p. 72.

38. Schlamm, *Germany and the East-West Crisis*, p. 172.

39. L. Brent Bozell, "They Gave the Orders, II," *National Review* 7 (October 24, 1959): 419.

40. Frank S. Meyer, "Just War in the Nuclear Age," *National Review* 14 (February 12, 1963): 105-106.

41. *Ibid.*, p. 112.

42. William F. Buckley, Jr., "Peace and Pacifism," *National Review* 7 (October 24, 1959): 427.

43. William F. Buckley, Jr., "On Dead-Red," *National Review* 13 (December 4, 1962): 424.

44. Schlamm, *Germany and the East-West Crisis*, pp. 184, 169.

45. *Ibid.*, p. 183.

46. *Ibid.*, pp. 170, 184.

47. *Ibid.*, p. 170.

48. Buckley, "Tranquil World," pp. 57-58.

49. Quoted in *Odyssey of a Friend*, ed. Buckley, p. 78.

50. M. Stanton Evans, *The Politics of Surrender* (New York, 1966), p. 21.

51. William F. Rickenbacker, *The Fourth House: Collected Essays* (New York, 1971), p. 37. Rickenbacker was describing the period from 1945 to 1965.

52. See *ibid.*, pp. 36-59, for a representative synopsis of conservative attitudes toward many foreign policy developments in the postwar era.

53. Meyer, "'New Ideas' or Old Truth," p. 107.

54. "The Week" [unsigned editorial], *National Review* 2 (November 3, 1956): 3.

55. "The Hungary Pledge," *National Review* 2 (December 8, 1956): 5.

56. See, for example, Frank S. Meyer, "An American Tragedy," *National Review* 2 (December 8, 1956): 12.

57. James Burnham, "Prisonhouse of Nations," *National Review* 20 (September 10, 1968): 897.

58. "Abstractions Kill the West," *National Review* 2 (December 6, 1956): 6.

59. Frederick D. Wilhelmsen, "The Bankruptcy of American Optimism," *National Review* 3 (May 11, 1957): 449, 451. A few years later Wilhelmsen wrote an essay on "the heresy of co-existence" with Communism; see "Towards a Theology of Survival," *National Review* 17 (January 12, 1965): 17-19.

60. James Burnham, *The War We Are In: The Last Decade and the Next* (New Rochelle, N.Y., 1967), pp. 15-19.

61. Conservative critiques of developments in Africa were extensive. *National Review* editorialized frequently on the subject. See also Frank S. Meyer, ed., *The African Nettle: Dilemmas of an Emerging Continent* (New York, 1965), and Thomas Molnar, *Africa: A Political Travelogue* (New York, 1965).

62. Burnham, *War We Are In*, p. 19.

63. Frank S. Meyer, "Abdication of Responsibility," *National Review* 10 (April 8, 1961): 218.

64. See, for example, James J. Kilpatrick, René Albert Wormser, and Walter Darnell Jacobs, "Rhodesia: A Case History," *National Review* 19 (May 16, 1967): 512-526.

65. See Burnham, *War We Are In*, pp. 225-226.

66. Jeffrey Hart, "African Gothic," *National Review* 18 (July 26, 1966): 733.

67. Meyer, "Abdication of Responsibility," p. 218.

68. James Burnham, "Tangle in Katanga," *National Review* 11 (December 30, 1961): 446.

69. See Buckley's eulogy of Tshombe in William F. Buckley, Jr., *The Governor Listeth: A Book of Inspired Political Revelations* (New York, 1970), pp. 403-405, for an example of conservative esteem for him.

70. See Ernest van den Haag, "The Lesson of the Congo," *National Review* 16 (September 8, 1964): 771-773, 785. See also Ernest van den Haag, "The UN War in Katanga," *National Review* 12 (March 27, 1962): 197-202, and "The UN's Idiot Policy in the Congo," *National Review* 17 (January 26, 1965): 61-62. The UN's record in the Congo, including documented charges of atrocities, is analyzed by M. Stanton Evans in *The Politics of Surrender*, chap. 27. Another prominent, conservatively inclined critic of the UN's Congo policy was Arthur Krock of the *New York Times*.

71. Buckley, *Governor Listeth*, p. 404.

72. William F. Buckley, Jr., "Must We Hate Portugal?" *National Review* 13 (December 18, 1962): 468.

73. James Burnham, "Arithmetic of the United Nations," *National Review* 8 (February 13, 1960): 99. See also Burnham's essay in *The African Nettle*, ed. Meyer, pp. 243-253.

74. James Burnham, "Root Fallacy," *National Review* 12 (January 16, 1962): 24; "No Friends Allowed," *National Review* 12 (January 30, 1962): 60, 73.

75. James Burnham, "Why Do We Take It?" *National Review* 17 (January 12, 1965): 20.

76. James Burnham, "What to Do About the UN," *National Review* 12 (April 24, 1962): 284. See also Burnham, "Emancipation Proclamation," *National Review* 13 (November 6, 1962): 348.

77. Burnham, "Arithmetic of the United Nations," p. 99.

78. Sir Arnold Lunn, "Selective Indignation," *National Review* 19 (October 3, 1967): 1081-1082.

79. James Burnham, *Suicide of the West* (New Rochelle, N.Y., 1964), p. 205.

80. Jeffrey Hart, *The American Dissent: A Decade of Modern Conservatism* (Garden City, N.Y., 1966), p. 102.

81. Burnham, "Tangle in Katanga," p. 446.

82. Evans, *Politics of Surrender*, p. 531.

83. Rickenbacker, *Fourth House*, p. 49.

84. *Ibid.*, p. 58.

85. Evans, *Politics of Surrender*, p. 531.

86. See *ibid.*, pp. 521-525.

87. Charles Malik, "The Challenge to Western Civilization," in *The Conservative Papers*, ed. Melvin Laird (Garden City, N.Y., 1964), p. 4.

88. "The Lesson of Philby," *National Review* 19 (October 31, 1967): 1155. Not surprisingly, conservatives continued to support congressional investigations of Communist subversion at home and abroad. See, for example, William F. Buckley, Jr. et al., *The Committee and Its Critics: A Calm Review of the House Committee on Un-American Activities* (Chicago, 1962).

89. Frank S. Meyer, "What Is Under the Bed?" *National Review* 12 (April 10, 1962): 244.

90. James Burnham, "Is Communism Folding Up?" *National Review* 17 (July 27, 1965): 631. Burnham labeled this "the Kennan-de Gaulle-Morgenthau-Lippmann approach."

91. Frank S. Meyer, "Nature of the Enemy," *National Review* 3 (March 23, 1957): 283.

92. Frank S. Meyer, "Dilemmas of Foreign Policy," *National Review* 5 (March 29, 1958): 303.

93. Thomas Molnar, "All-Too-Hasty Wisdom," *National Review* 11 (July 15, 1961): 20-21.

94. Schlamm, *Germany and the East-West Crisis*, p. 172.

95. Frank S. Meyer, "Communism Remains Communism," *National Review* 2 (October 13, 1956): 11, 12.

96. *Ibid.*, p. 12.

97. Frank S. Meyer, "The Relativist 'Re-evaluates' Evil," *National Review* 3 (May 4, 1957): 429.

98. Frank S. Meyer, "An American Tragedy," *National Review* 2 (December 8, 1956): 12.

99. Schlamm, *Germany and the East-West Crisis*, p. 174.

100. *Ibid.*, p. 172.

101. *Ibid.*, p. 173.

102. *Ibid.*, pp. 174-175.

103. William F. Buckley, Jr., *The Jeweler's Eye: A Book of Irresistible Political Reflections* (New York, 1968), pp. 48-49.

104. L. Brent Bozell, "To Magnify the West," *National Review* 12 (April 24, 1962): 286.

105. Frank S. Meyer, "What Time Is It?" *National Review* 6 (September 13, 1958): 180.

106. Chambers, *Cold Friday*, pp. 225-226.

107. James Burnham, *Suicide of the West: An Essay on the Meaning and Destiny of Liberalism* (New York, 1964). R.H.S. Crossman, a prominent Labour M.P. in Great Britain, considered this book a "powerful" work of "corrosive clarity." Crossman warned the Left not to underestimate Burnham's book and acknowledged that Burnham often scored against liberalism, particularly its "moral asymmetry." See R.H.S. Crossman, "Radicals on the Right," *Partisan Review* 31 (Fall 1964): 555-565.

108. "What communism does is to carry the liberal principles to their logical and practical extreme: the secularism; the rejection of tradition and custom; the stress on science; the confidence in the possibility of molding human beings; the determination to reform *all* established institutions; the goal of wiping out all social distinctions; the internationalism; the belief in the welfare state carried to its ultimate form in the totalitarian state" (Burnham, *Suicide of the West*, p. 289).

109. *Ibid.*

110. *Ibid.*, pp. 305, 297.

111. See Malcolm Muggeridge, "The Great Liberal Death-Wish," *National Review* 18 (June 14, 1966): 573-574.

112. Bozell, "To Magnify the West," p. 287.

113. Malik, "Challenge to Western Civilization," p. 14.

114. Quoted in Guy Davenport, "First National Poetry Festival: A Report," *National Review* 14 (January 15, 1963): 26.

115. Malik, "Challenge to Western Civilization," pp. 5-6.

116. *Ibid.*, p. 16.

117. See Burnham, *War We Are In*, especially chap. 3, for an analysis of these alternatives.

118. Robert Strausz-Hupé, William R. Kintner, and Stefan T. Possony, *A Forward Strategy for America* (New York, 1961).

119. Barry Goldwater, *Why Not Victory?* (New York, 1962), p. 19. Goldwater said that Niemeyer's "views on the Communist War have proved an invaluable help in my research." Goldwater's bibliography lists some of the books then influencing conservative opinion on foreign policy.

120. Frank Meyer's columns sometimes contemplated this possibility as a grim alternative to the more aggressive policy he preferred.

121. See James Burnham, "The New Isolationism," *National Review* 17 (January 26, 1965): 60.

122. James Burnham, "The Choking Point," *National Review* 12 (March 27, 1962): 203.

123. Burnham, *War We Are In*, p. 17.

124. Strausz-Hupé, Kintner, and Possony, *Forward Strategy*, pp. 405-406.

125. In 1960 *National Review* published a special supplement of eight scholarly articles on China and Russia; it concluded that no Sino-Soviet split would occur. In 1966 Jeffrey Hart, in *The American Dissent*, pp. 157-158, acknowledged that these conservatives had made a mistake. Nevertheless, Hart, reflecting the predominant conservative view, questioned how "significant" this split would be to the West. After all, he said, Russia and China did remain our sworn ideological foes, divided at most over how best to bury us.

126. Robert Strausz-Hupé et al., *Protracted Conflict* (New York, 1959). The dust jacket included highly laudatory comments by such politically diverse people as Dean Acheson, C.L. Sulzberger, Senator Stuart Symington, Henry Hazlitt, Henry Kissinger, and Adm. Arleigh Burke. M. Stanton Evans declared that the book was "the most important discussion of foreign policy that I have seen since James Burnham's *Struggle for the World*" ("Moscow Formula for Victory," *National Review* 7 [August 1, 1959]: 248-249). James Burnham eventually changed the title of his column to "The Protracted Conflict" and called that work an "excellent book" ("Hungary, Tibet and the Caribbean," *National Review* 7 [July 18, 1959]: 203). For another sign of conservative esteem for this scholar, see Russell Kirk, "The Sagacity of Dr. Strausz-Hupé," *National Review* 19 (November 14, 1967): 1276.

127. *New York Times*, December 23, 1969, p. 11.

128. For a discussion of growing *liberal* disillusionment with the United Nations, see Hart, *American Dissent*, pp. 158-161.

129. Buckley, *Up from Liberalism*, pp. 179-183.

130. *Ibid.*, pp. 181, 184.

131. Martin Anderson, *The Federal Bulldozer: A Critical Analysis of Urban Renewal, 1949-1962* (Cambridge, Mass., 1964).

132. *Ibid.*, p. 67.

133. See *ibid.*, pp. 219-233 for a summary of these and other conclusions.

134. *Ibid.*, pp. 219-220.

135. *Ibid.*, p. 213.

136. *Ibid.*, p. 230.

137. In 1962 a young lawyer wrote an article in *The Freeman* describing the successful campaign of the citizens of Winsted, Conn. to defeat a proposed federal housing project in their town. Three times the people decisively rejected the idea in referenda. The lawyer delineated the ways in which the public housing program undermined freedom, private property, and the solution of housing problems. "Giant government," he warned,

"has outgrown the capacity of the institutions designed to restrain its encroachments and abuses." He pointed to Winsted as an inspiring example of resistance to the "service state." The lawyer was Ralph Nader. See Nader, "How Winstedites Kept Their Integrity," *The Freeman* 12 (October 1962): 49-53.

138. Yale Brozen, "The Untruth of the Obvious," in *Republican Papers*, ed. Melvin Laird (New York, 1968), p. 145. See in general pp. 144-153.

139. *Ibid.*, pp. 149-150, 152-153.

140. *Ibid.*, p. 157.

141. See Milton Friedman, *Capitalism and Freedom* (Chicago, 1962), p. 129. See in general chap. 8: "Monopoly and the Social Responsibility of Business and Labor."

142. Brozen, "Untruth of the Obvious," p. 159.

143. Buckley, *Up from Liberalism*, p. 177.

144. See Friedman, *Capitalism and Freedom*, pp. 185-189.

145. *Ibid.*, p. 189.

146. See Colin D. Campbell, "Social Security: The Past Thirty Years," in *Republican Papers*, ed. Laird, pp. 325-337.

147. Frank S. Meyer, "Is Social Security a Sacred Cow?" *National Review* 17 (June 1, 1965): 463.

148. M. Stanton Evans, "At Home," *National Review Bulletin* 24 (July 28, 1972): B118.

149. Milton Friedman, "The Poor Man's Welfare Payment to the Middle Class," *Washington Monthly* 4 (May 1972): 11-12, 15-16. Friedman's proposal was supported in the same issue (p. 14) by Nicholas von Hoffman, a well-known liberal columnist increasingly influenced by libertarian economics—particularly as expressed by Murray Rothbard.

150. Buckley, *Jeweler's Eye*, p. 34.

151. Barry Goldwater, *The Conscience of a Conservative* (Shepherdsville, Ky., 1960), p. 37.

152. Rob Wood and Dean Smith, *Barry Goldwater* (New York, 1961), p. 79.

153. Frank S. Meyer, "The Negro Revolution," *National Review* 14 (June 18, 1963): 496.

154. See William F. Buckley, Jr., "Footnote to *Brown v. Board of Education*," *National Review* 10 (March 11, 1961): 137.

155. See Ernest van den Haag, "Social Science Testimony in the Desegregation Cases—A Reply to Professor Kenneth Clark," *Villanova Law Review* 6 (Fall 1960): 69-79.

156. Ernest van den Haag, "Negroes and Whites: Claims, Rights, and Prospects," *Modern Age* 9 (Fall 1965): 358.

157. Ernest van den Haag, "Intelligence or Prejudice?" *National Review* 16 (December 1, 1964): 1061.

158. Jeffrey Hart, "The Negro in the City," *National Review* 20 (June 18, 1968): 604.

159. "What Price Integration?" *National Review* 19 (August 22, 1967): 887-888.

160. Frank S. Meyer, "The Negro Revolution—A New Phase," *National Review* 18 (October 4, 1966): 998.

161. Frank S. Meyer, "Showdown with Insurrection," *National Review* 20 (January 16, 1968): 36.

162. Frank S. Meyer, "Liberalism Run Riot," *National Review* 20 (March 26, 1968): 283.

163. M. Stanton Evans, "At Home," *National Review Bulletin* 20 (April 16, 1968): B62. Evans's analysis was corroborated on one point by Moynihan: "Detroit had everything the Great Society could wish for a municipality: a splendid mayor and a fine governor. A high-paying and, thanks to the fiscal policies of the national government, a booming industry, civilized by and associated with the hands-down leading liberal trade union of the world.

"Moreover, it was a city whose Negro residents had every reason to be proud of the position they held in the economy and government of the area" ("Where Liberals Went Wrong," in *Republican Papers*, ed. Laird, p. 132).

164. Ernest van den Haag, "How Not to Prevent Civil Disorders," *National Review* 20 (March 26, 1968): 284-287.

165. Hart, "Negro in the City," pp. 603-606, 623.

166. Buckley, *Jeweler's Eye*, p. 137.

167. Van den Haag, "Civil Disorders," pp. 286-287.

168. Hart, "Negro in the City," pp. 606, 623. Van den Haag also strongly criticized union discrimination.

169. Buckley, *Governor Listeth*, p. 101.

170. William F. Buckley, Jr., *The Unmaking of a Mayor* (New York, 1966), p. 147.

171. Hart, "Negro in the City," p. 623.

172. "What Price Integration?" p. 188.

173. Meyer, "Liberalism Run Riot," p. 283; Meyer, "Showdown with Insurrection," p. 36.

174. Meyer, "Liberalism Run Riot," p. 283.

175. Hart, "Negro in the City," p. 606.

176. Burnham, *Suicide of the West*, pp. 195, 196-197.

177. Van den Haag, *"Civil Disorders,"* p. 287.

178. Richard C. Cornuelle, *Reclaiming the American Dream* (New York, 1965), p. xiii. The biographical information in this paragraph is drawn from "A Personal Summary," pp. xi-xv. See also the biographical sketch of Cornuelle at the end of the book.

179. *Ibid.*, p. 55.

180. *Ibid.*, p. 26.

181. The back cover of the paperback edition contains plaudits from Alinsky, Kristol, and Buckley.

182. Frank S. Meyer, "Richard Cornuelle and the Third Sector," *National Review* 17 (February 9, 1965): 103.

183. The quotations and biographical information presented in these two paragraphs are drawn from taped responses by Friedman to questions submitted by the author, February 26, 1972. See also John Davenport, "The Radical Economics of Milton Friedman," *Fortune* 75 (June 1, 1967): 131-132, 147-148, 150, 154. In the preface to *Capitalism and Freedom* (Chicago, 1962), Friedman stated that the Volker Fund conferences were "among the most stimulating intellectual experiences of my life."

184. In his taped reply to the author, Friedman stressed that he never called himself a conservative, for the reasons given by Hayek in his essay "Why I am Not a Conservative." Friedman even protested at times that he was not a conservative. His dislike of the label did not, of course, lessen his impact on the Right or his association with it. Friedman clearly belonged within the "conservative" tent.

185. See especially Friedrich Hayek, *The Constitution of Liberty* (Chicago, 1960), and Henry C. Simons, *Economic Policy for a Free Society* (Chicago, 1948).

186. Friedman, *Capitalism and Freedom*, p. 29.

187. See *ibid.*, chap. 4.

188. *Ibid.*, pp. 89, 91, 93.

189. *Ibid.*, p. 198.

190. *Ibid.*, pp. 196-198.

191. *Ibid.*, pp. 108-109.

192. *Ibid.*, p. 169.

193. *Ibid.*, pp. 38, 45, 50. In 1963 Friedman and Anna Schwartz published *A Monetary History of the United States, 1867-1960* (Princeton, 1963). Chap. 7 contained their scath-

ing critique of the Federal Reserve Board's conduct from 1929 to 1933. In 1965, chap. 7 was published in paperback as *The Great Contraction, 1929-1933* (Princeton, 1965). On p. ix of the preface, Friedman and Schwartz summarized their conclusions: "The drastic decline in the quantity of money during those years and the occurrence of a banking panic of unprecedented severity were not the inevitable consequence of other economic changes.... Throughout the contraction the System had ample powers to cut short the tragic process of monetary deflation and banking collapse." As late as mid-1931 the System could have acted successfully to alleviate the contraction and even to terminate it "at a much earlier date."

194. Friedman's professional reputation rested, of course, on other books as well, including *Essays in Positive Economics* (Chicago, 1953), *A Theory of the Consumption Function* (Princeton, 1957), and the *Monetary History* cited above.

195. See Serge-Christophe Kolm, "De l'utilité du liberalisme," *Le Monde*, December 7, 1971, p. 18, a discussion of Friedman's *Capitalism and Freedom* (recently translated into French).

196. For a revealing clash between a leading "Austrian" and a leading "Chicago" economist, see: Frank H. Knight, "Absolute Economics as Absolute Ethics," *Ethics* 76 (April 1966): 163-177; Henry Hazlitt, "A Reply to Frank Knight," *Ethics* 77 (October 1966): 57-61; Frank H. Knight, "A Word of Explanation," *Ethics* 78 (October 1967): 83-85. This exchange was generated by Knight's critical review of Hazlitt's *The Foundations of Morality* (New York, 1964). In general, Knight favored more extensive governmental involvement in the economy than Hazlitt did, in order "to prevent intolerable divergences from free market conditions and ...to prevent intolerable consequences that would prevail if society were organized solely through exchange by individuals in the nearest possible approach to the perfectly competitive markets of 'pure' economic theory." Hazlitt, for his part, was alarmed that the "drift" of Knight's thinking "seems to be a defense of the enormous growth in government power in this country in the last thirty years."

It seems clear that the Austrian School was more antigovernment than the Chicago School. For a severe critique of Friedman by an economist profoundly influenced by Mises, see Murray N. Rothbard, "Milton Friedman Unraveled," *The Individualist* 3 (February 1971): 3-7. Rothbard denounced Friedman as "the Establishment's Court Libertarian" who "has functioned not as an opponent of statism and advocate of the free market, but as a technician advising the State how to be more efficient in going about its evil work." Among Friedman's many misdeeds, said Rothbard, one of the "most disastrous" was his role at the Treasury Department in World War II in establishing the withholding system for the income tax, a keystone of "the present Leviathan State in America." Another error was Friedman's advocacy of complete governmental control of the money supply, an "inherently inflationary" proposal.

197. Friedman's willingness to abandon the gold standard and adopt floating exchange rates was controversial among right-wing economists. In his taped reply to the author's questionnaire, Friedman stated that this issue was the most continually debated one at the annual meetings of the Mont Pélerin Society since 1947. Friedman's proposal that the U.S. money supply be increased at a fixed, regular rate (thereby removing the discretionary powers of the Federal Reserve Board) also attracted criticism both from "Austrians" and Keynesians. Both sets of critics agreed that Friedman overemphasized the importance of monetary policy. See Milton Friedman and Walter Heller, *Monetary vs. Fiscal Policy: A Dialogue* (New York, 1969), and Rothbard, "Milton Friedman Unraveled," pp. 5-6. For a useful survey of conservative economists, see Peter P. Witonski, "Rough and Tumble among Conservative Economists," *National Review* 24 (February 4, 1972): 91-95, 114.

198. See Ludwig von Mises, "The Plight of Business Forecasting," *National Review* 1

(April 4, 1956): 17-18. In this article he declared, "There is not, and there cannot be such a thing as quantitative economics."

199. Witonski, "Rough and Tumble," p. 93. For a survey of differences between the Austrian and Chicago schools, see Israel M. Kirzner, "Divergent Approaches in Libertarian Economic Thought," *Intercollegiate Review* 3 (January-February 1967): 101-108. For an interesting exchange between Henry Hazlitt and Ernest van den Haag on the question "Must Conservatives Repudiate Keynes?" see *National Review* 8 (June 4, 1960): 361-364. Hazlitt said yes; van den Haag, no. Hazlitt was editor of *The Critics of Keynesian Economics* (Princeton, 1959) and author of *The Failure of the New Economics* (Princeton, 1959).

200. James C. Miller, ed., *Why the Draft?: The Case for a Volunteer Army* (Baltimore, 1968), p. 5; "The Week," *National Review* 22 (March 10, 1970): 236.

201. See, for example, William F. Buckley, Jr., "Notes for the Platform Committees: III. Civil Disobedience, Education, Housing, Labor," *National Review* 20 (June 4, 1968): 571. Friedman was not, of course, the only conservative proponent of this idea. It was advanced at least as early as 1958 by the Australian economist Colin Clark; see Clark, "The Horrible Proposals of Mr. Galbraith," *National Review* 6 (October 11, 1958): 239. But it seems safe to say that Friedman's vigorous advocacy of the voucher plan in *Capitalism and Freedom* was at least as important as any other influence in bringing the matter to national attention.

202. William F. Buckley, Jr., "Notes for the Platform Committees: II. Fiscal Policies & Poverty," *National Review* 20 (June 4, 1968): 570. The plan called for elimination of all personal deductions, increase of exemptions to $1,200, and a flat (nonprogressive) tax of about 20 percent.

203. See Milton Friedman, "The Case for the Negative Income Tax," in *Republican Papers*, ed. Laird, pp. 202-220, and Friedman, "The Case for the Negative Income Tax," *National Review* 19 (March 7, 1967): 239-241. Friedman first propounded the idea in *Capitalism and Freedom*, pp. 190-195.

204. William Rusher, publisher of *National Review*, opposed it (interview, Cambridge, Mass., October 30, 1971). In 1967, James Burnham criticized the youthful Left-Right antidraft coalition as a danger, under the circumstances, to America's national interests ("The Anti-draft Movement," *National Review* 19 [June 13, 1967]: 629).

205. Henry Hazlitt, "The Coming Crisis in Welfare," *National Review* 19 (April 18, 1967): 416. *National Review* itself criticized Friedman's proposal; see "The Week," *National Review* 18 (August 23, 1966): 814. Murray Rothbard called Friedman's plan "catastrophic." "The libertarian approach to the welfare problem," Rothbard said, "...is to abolish all coercive, public welfare, and to substitute for it private charity based on the principle of encouraging self-help; bolstered also by inculcating the virtues of self-reliance and independence throughout society. But the Friedman plan, on the contrary, moves in precisely the *opposite* direction; for it establishes welfare payments as an automatic *right*, an automatic, coercive claim upon the producers" ("Milton Friedman Unraveled," p. 5).

206. Buckley, *Governor Listeth*, p. 127. This was part of a column written by Buckley on January 13, 1968.

207. Two economists summarized Friedman's attack on the "new economics" as follows: "First, he painstakingly reconstructed and tested the quantity theory of money. Second, he re-emphasized the power of monetary policy. Third, he questioned the Lerner view of the flexibility and potency of fiscal policy and the Lerner-Samuelson belief in the trade-offs between inflation and employment. Fourth, he argued that the orthodox interpretation of the Great Depression was incorrect and constructed his own formula for preventing such catastrophes in the future. Fifth, he challenged the logic of the Veblen

and Chamberlin methodologies and, lastly, restated the classical liberal philosophy in terms pertinent to his own time" (William Breit and Roger L. Ransom, *The Academic Scribblers: American Economists in Collision* [New York, 1971], p. 227).

For a lucid and lively exposition of Friedman's views, see "Playboy Interview: Milton Friedman," *Playboy* 20 (February 1973): 51-54, 56, 58-60, 62, 64, 66, 68, 74.

208. The Volker Fund Series, mentioned in Chapter Six, was another sign of the academic revival of laissez-faire; it included contributions by such men as Mises, Hazlitt, and Rothbard. For a history of government-promoted monopolies and their consequences, see William Wooldridge, *Uncle Sam, the Monopoly Man* (New Rochelle, N.Y., 1970).

209. See, for example, Murray Rothbard's massive *Man, Economy, and State*, 2 vols. (Princeton, 1962). Henry Hazlitt acclaimed it as "the most important general treatise on economic principles since Ludwig von Mises' *Human Action* in 1949" ("The Economics of Freedom," *National Review* 13 [September 25, 1962]: 232). See also Hazlitt's review essay, "The Development of Economic Thought," *National Review* 17 (November 30, 1965): 1102, 1104, which lists the principal libertarian contributions in economics between 1955 and 1965.

210. For a survey of Knight, Simons, and Friedman, see Breit and Ransom, *Academic Scribblers*, part 4: "The New Neoclassicism."

211. M. Stanton Evans, *Revolt on the Campus* (Chicago, 1961). See also Patrick Riley, "Conservatism on the Campus," *American Mercury* 84 (April 1957): 39-42.

212. See Eugene V. Schneider, "The Radical Right," *Nation* 193 (September 30, 1961): 199-203; "Conservatism on the Campus," *Newsweek* 57 (April 10, 1961): 35.

213. Evans, *Revolt on the Campus*, pp. 54-55.

214. *Ibid.*, p. 58.

215. *Ibid.*, pp. 65-66.

216. *Ibid.*, p. 71.

217. William Baroody, president of the conservative American Enterprise Institute, was a key adviser. Other important intellectuals who assisted in the campaign included Gerhart Niemeyer; W. Glenn Campbell, director of the Hoover Institution; Richard Ware of the Relm Foundation; David Nelson Rowe; Stanley Parry; Karl Brandt; Stefan Possony; Warren Nutter; and Yale Brozen. See Karl Hess, *In a Cause That Will Triumph* (Garden City, N.Y., 1967), pp. 28, 34-37.

218. The Russell Kirk Papers in the Clarke Historical Library at Central Michigan University, Mount Pleasant, Mich., contain interesting correspondence between Kirk and Goldwater. In a letter to Kirk on July 12, 1963, Goldwater thanked him for his substantial role in a speech Goldwater delivered at Notre Dame University. Not long after his nomination, Goldwater, in a letter to Kirk dated August 22, 1964, noted Kirk's involvement in the Goldwater movement at the very start. In a letter to the author on April 29, 1972, Kirk stated that Senator Goldwater was the only conservative politician for whom he worked in this capacity. He mentioned that he "had a hand in" not only the Notre Dame speech but also a lecture delivered by Goldwater at Yale University in 1962. In response to a letter from William F. Buckley, Jr. on July 19, 1963 (in Kirk Papers), Kirk wrote "The Mind of Barry Goldwater," *National Review* 15 (August 27, 1963): 149-151.

219. Davenport, "Radical Economics of Milton Friedman," pp. 148-150.

220. Rusher's activities are examined at various points in F. Clifton White, *Suite 3505: The Story of the Draft Goldwater Movement* (New Rochelle, N.Y., 1967).

221. Rand's statement of support can be found in *Look* 28 (November 3, 1964): 53.

222. A list of some academic supporters of Goldwater was printed in the *Chicago Tribune*, September 29, 1964, sec. 1, p. 6.

223. White, *Suite 3505*, p. 21n.

224. Duncan Norton-Taylor, "Robert Taft's Congress," *Fortune* 48 (August 1953): 145.

225. William F. Buckley, Jr., "The Vile Campaign," *National Review* 16 (October 6, 1964): 853-856, 858. This is a discussion of what Buckley regarded as smears of conservatives and Goldwater by such sources as George Meany, the *Saturday Evening Post*, and the Anti-Defamation League.

226. These and similar quotations were compiled in Kenneth Paul Shorey, "Letter to an American," *Modern Age* 10 (Spring 1966): 131-145.

227. Probably the most famous controversy involved Ralph Ginzburg, publisher of *Fact*. In this magazine, in hundreds of thousands of leaflets, and in advertisements printed in the *New York Times* and elsewhere, Ginzburg publicized a personal "survey" of psychiatrists under such headlines as "Is Barry Goldwater Psychologically Fit to Be President of the United States?" The psychiatrists (none of whom had ever examined Goldwater) said no. See Shorey, "Letter," p. 145. In 1970 Goldwater won a $75,000 libel judgment against Ginzburg (*New York Times*, January 27, 1970, p. 32).

228. See Evans, *Liberal Establishment*, pp. 33-50. See also Lionel Lokos, *Hysteria, 1964: The Fear Campaign Against Barry Goldwater* (New Rochelle, N.Y., 1967).

229. Frank S. Meyer, "What Next For Conservatism?" *National Review* 16 (December 1, 1964): 1057.

230. *Ibid.*

231. Ronald Reagan, comment in *National Review* 16 (December 1, 1964): 1055. His remarks were part of a symposium, "The Republican Party and the Conservative Movement," pp. 1053-1056, 1078. Contributors included George Bush, John Davis Lodge, Russell Kirk, Gerhart Niemeyer, and Reagan.

232. James Burnham, "Must Conservatives Be Republicans?" *National Review* 16 (December 1, 1964): 1052.

233. Gerhart Niemeyer, comment in "Republican Party," p. 1056.

234. See Daniel Mahoney, *Actions Speak Louder* (New Rochelle, N.Y., 1968), a history of the Conservative Party by one of its founders.

235. See Buckley, *Unmaking of a Mayor*, for an account of his campaign.

236. William F. Buckley, Jr., "The Uproar," *National Review* 10 (April 23, 1961): 243. Russell Kirk believed that the furor was a tempest in a teapot. See Russell Kirk, "Conservatives and Fantastics," *Commonweal* 106 (February 17, 1962): 644.

237. See Buckley, "Uproar," pp. 241-243.

238. In December 1961, Goldwater, Kirk, Buckley, William Baroody, and Dr. Jay Gordon Hall met in Miami. One of the main subjects of the discussion was the John Birch Society and the need for a clear dissociation of Goldwater from Welch; among the results of the meeting were the articles in *Commonweal* (cited in 236) and *National Review* (cited in 240). This information was supplied in Kirk to the author, April 20, 1972.

239. Kirk, "Conservatives and Fantastics," p. 644. See also Kirk to Francis X. Gannon of the John Birch Society, January 20 and 29, 1962, in William F. Buckley, Jr. Papers, Yale University Library, New Haven, Conn.

240. See "The Question of Robert Welch," *National Review* 12 (February 13, 1962): 83-88. See also Buckley to William S. Schlamm, January 2, 24, and February 1, 1962, Buckley Papers.

241. "The John Birch Society and the Conservative Movement," *National Review* 17 (October 19, 1965): 914-920, 925-929.

242. Meyer, *ibid.*, p. 920.

243. See Hart, *American Dissent*, p. 31n, for approximate circulation figures through 1964. See also Priscilla L. Buckley, "Notes on a Tenth Anniversary," *National Review* 17 (November 30, 1965): 1115.

244. "A Chance to Holler," *Time* 79 (April 6, 1962): 49.

245. See *Newsweek* 68 (September 12, 1966): 15 for the announcement. Six years later,

Friedman published a collection of his *Newsweek* essays; see his *An Economist's Protest: Columns in Political Economy* (Glen Ridge, N.J., 1972).

246. M. Stanton Evans, *The Future of Conservatism* (New York, 1968), p. 107.

247. Neil McCaffrey to the author, August 3, 1971. Mr. McCaffrey was founder-president of the Conservative Book Club. The Club continued to sustain a membership hovering around 30,000 through 1975.

248. See Anne Edwards, "The Story of the Conservative Book Club," *Human Events* 27 (May 20, 1967): 8-9, and "An Interview with Neil McCaffrey," *ibid.*

249. "The Call to Battle," *Rally* 2 (June 1967): 80.

250. The sense of uncertainty and transition was reflected in a memorandum by Frank Meyer, May 23, 1966, Buckley Papers. Meyer observed that powerful changes were occurring in American politics and society which urgently required conservative analysis. The establishment, he noted, was dividing—a fissure not confined to foreign policy issues.

251. See, for example, M. Stanton Evans, "At Home," *National Review Bulletin* 18 (June 21, 1966): B6.

252. This philosophy was often attacked by conservatives. See, for example, Will Herberg, "A Religious 'Right' to Violate the Law?" *National Review* 16 (July 14, 1964): 579-580, which argued that Martin Luther King's doctrine of civil disobedience was un-Christian and heretical. See also Harry Jaffa, "The Limits of Dissent," *National Review* 20 (September 10, 1968): 911-912.

253. James Burnham, "The Right to Riot," *National Review* 20 (October 8, 1968): 1000.

254. Will Herberg, "Alienation, 'Dissent,' and the Intellectual," *National Review* 20 (July 30, 1968): 738-739. By "intellectual" Herberg meant not the professional scholar but "the free-floating journalist, the *littérateur*, or junior academician, who feels it is his high prerogative, self-conferred, to destroy the existing order..." (p. 739).

255. Stephen J. Tonsor, "On Living at the End of an Era," *National Review* 20 (July 30, 1968): 756-758.

CHAPTER TEN

1. Jeffrey Hart, "The Coming Revolution in America," *National Review* 20 (July 2, 1968): 646.

2. See James Burnham, *Suicide of the West* (New Rochelle, N.Y., 1964), chap. 11.

3. Frank S. Meyer, "Reaping the Whirlwind," *National Review* 22 (January 27, 1970): 89.

4. Frederick Wilhelmsen, ed., *Seeds of Anarchy: A Study of Campus Revolution* (Dallas, 1969). Contributors included Ronald Reagan, Russell Kirk, Jeffrey Hart, John C. Meyer (son of Frank Meyer), Thomas Molnar, M. Stanton Evans, Erik von Kuehnelt-Leddihn, Jane Bret, and Michael Lawrence (an editor of *Triumph*).

5. William F. Buckley, Jr., "Harvard and the Police," *National Review* 21 (May 6, 1969): 455.

6. See Russell Kirk, "Rebellion Against Boredom," in *Seeds of Anarchy*, ed. Wilhelmsen, pp. 26-37, for a discussion of his differences with Michigan State University and an explanation of his educational philosophy.

7. See Russell Kirk, *The Intemperate Professor and Other Cultural Splenetics* (Baton Rouge, 1965), pp. 1-70, for a convenient collection of his essays on higher education.

8. Kirk attributed this phrase to Ernest van den Haag. Kirk, "Rebellion Against Boredom," p. 27.

9. This paragraph is based on *ibid.*, pp. 26-37. See also Kirk's columns in *National Review*, passim. For a succinct comment on campus turmoil see Kirk, "The Scranton Report," *National Review* 22 (November 17, 1970): 1212.

10. Will Herberg, "The Student Left: Cause and Consequence," *National Review* 21 (July 29, 1969): 754-756.

11. Gerhart Niemeyer, "The Homesickness of the New Left," *National Review* 22 (July 28, 1970): 783.

12. Jeffrey Hart, "Secession of the Intellectuals," *National Review* 22 (December 1, 1970): 1278-1282.

13. Niemeyer, "Homesickness of the New Left," pp. 779-783, 800. *National Review*, in introducing this article, remarked that it "may be the most cogent analysis of the philosophical underpinning of New Leftist ideology yet to appear in print." See "In This Issue," *National Review* 22 (July 28, 1970): 763.

14. Another conservative who emphasized the bedrock nihilism of the New Left was William Rusher, publisher of *National Review* and a frequent speaker on campuses. See Rusher, "Memo on the New Left," *National Review* 21 (August 12, 1969): 803-804, 817.

15. M. Stanton Evans, "Orthodox Rebels," *National Review* 18 (July 12, 1966): 687.

16. Russell Kirk, "Academic Freedom 1970," *National Review* 22 (January 27, 1970): 91-92.

17. Frank S. Meyer, in *National Review* 22 (April 7, 1970): 348.

18. Meyer, "Reaping the Whirlwind," p. 89.

19. Richard M. Weaver, *Visions of Order: The Cultural Crisis of Our Time* (Baton Rouge, 1964), pp. 114, 116.

20. *Ibid.*, p. 114.

21. *Ibid.*, p. 115.

22. *Ibid.*, pp. 115-116.

23. *Ibid.*, pp. 119-125.

24. *Ibid.*, p. 133.

25. *Ibid.*, p. 132.

26. Meyer, "Reaping the Whirlwind," p. 89.

27. Peter Viereck, *Conservatism Revisited: The Revolt against Revolt* (New York, 1949), p. 129.

28. Robert Nisbet, "Dismal Decade for the Academy," *National Review* 22 (December 29, 1970): 1409.

29. Hart, "Revolution in America," p. 647.

30. John P. East, "Why So Few Conservatives on Campus?" *Wall Street Journal*, July 2, 1970, p. 6.

31. Stephen J. Tonsor, "Alienation and Relevance," *National Review* 21 (July 1, 1969): 638.

32. *Ibid.*, p. 661.

33. Stephen J. Tonsor, "Faculty Responsibility for the Mess in Higher Education," *Intercollegiate Review* 6 (Spring 1970): 86.

34. See East, "Conservatives on Campus," p. 6, for an analysis of some of them.

35. Tonsor, "Faculty Responsibility," p. 89.

36. Quoted in Kirk, *Intemperate Professor*, p. 13. Kirk cited the case of Dr. W. Glenn Campbell, director of the Hoover Institution at Stanford University. "No sooner had he arrived than the local liberal inquisitors asked if he had any sympathy with the political and economic views of Mr. Herbert Hoover, founder of the institution. When they discovered him so heretical as to express substantial agreement with Mr. Hoover, they persuaded the Stanford faculty senate to pass a resolution—by a narrow majority—denouncing the appointment of Dr. Campbell" (*ibid.*).

37. See East, "Conservatives on Campus," p. 6.

38. William F. Buckley, Jr., "The Brownsville Affair: II," *National Review* 21 (January 14, 1969): 41.

39. Burnham, *Suicide of the West*, p. 214.

40. "Opinion on the Campus," *National Review* 23 (June 15, 1971): 635, 637. For a conservative graduate student's graphic account of life at Berkeley in the 1960s, see John R. Coyne, Jr., *The Kumquat Statement* (New York, 1970).

41. William F. Buckley, Jr., *Rumbles Left and Right: A Book About Troublesome People and Ideas* (New York, 1963), p. 134.

42. See Robert Nisbet, *The Degradation of the Academic Dogma* (New York, 1971). For a history and critique of the intellectual as a social type, see Thomas Molnar, *The Decline of the Intellectual* (Cleveland, 1961).

Some conservative scholars so disliked the term "intellectual" that they preferred not to be identified as one. To them the word usually suggested rootlessness, superficiality, officiousness, and presumption. See Will Herberg's strictures on "intellectuals," cited in this chapter and the last. See also Russell Kirk, *Beyond the Dreams of Avarice* (Chicago, 1956), pp. 5-15.

43. Ludwig von Mises, *Planned Chaos* (Irvington-on-Hudson, N.Y., 1947), p. 62.

44. Evans, "Orthodox Rebels," pp. 687-688.

45. See Barry Goldwater, *The Conscience of a Majority* (New York, 1970), chaps. 7-8.

46. See, for example, Joseph Keeley, *The Left-Leaning Antenna* (New Rochelle, N.Y., 1971) and John Coyne, *The Impudent Snobs: Agnew vs. The Intellectual Establishment* (New Rochelle, N.Y., 1972). Significantly, *National Review* began to offer *Frankly Speaking*, a collection of Vice-President Agnew's 1969 speeches, as part of some of its subscription drives in the early 1970s.

47. Edith Efron, *The News Twisters* (Los Angeles, 1971). Efron was a staff writer for *TV Guide*.

48. See John Chamberlain, "Edith Efron's Murderous Adding Machine," *National Review* 23 (November 5, 1971): 1225-1226, 1253, for an enthusiastic review of Efron's book by a conservative.

49. Irving Kristol, "Does TV News Tell It Like It Is?" *Fortune* 84 (November 1971): 183, 186. For another review, which accepted much of Efron's data showing bias but which offered a different explanation of it, see Paul Weaver, "Is Television News Biased?" *The Public Interest*, no. 26 (Winter 1972): 57-74. A sharply critical review of Efron's book is Nelson W. Polsby, "Truth and/or Fairness in the News," *Harper's* 244 (March 1972): 88-89, 91.

50. *Triumph*, for example, a very conservative Catholic magazine, interpreted the hippie movement as "the last expression of modern WASP culture, which rests on the base hope that man is fundamentally good and needs no discipline.... They [hippies] are a standing and visible reproach to the moral imbecility of liberalism beginning with Locke and Mill, and working down through John Dewey to Robert Kennedy" ("Hippie, Son of WASP," *Triumph* 3 [February 1968]: 37).

51. Robert Nisbet, "The Nemesis of Authority," *Encounter* 39 (August 1972): 11.

52. *Ibid.*, pp. 16, 17, 19, 20.

53. Quoted in Coyne, *Impudent Snobs*, p. 248.

54. Interview with William F. Buckley, Jr., Stamford, Conn., November 26, 1971.

55. William F. Buckley, Jr., *The Governor Listeth: A Book of Inspired Political Revelations* (New York, 1970), p. 137.

56. *Ibid.*, p. 138.

57. *Ibid.*, p. 139.

58. Russell Kirk, *Enemies of the Permanent Things* (New Rochelle, N.Y., 1969).

59. James Burnham, "Notes on Authority, Morality, Power," *National Review* 22 (December 1, 1970): 1283-1289.

60. Donald Atwell Zoll, "Shall We Let America Die?" *National Review* 21 (December 16, 1969): 1261-1263. Zoll, a political scientist, was author of *The Twentieth Century Mind* (Baton Rouge, 1967).

61. Frank S. Meyer, "What Kind of Order?" *National Review* 21 (December 30, 1969): 1327.

62. Donald Atwell Zoll, "Order and Repression," *National Review* 22 (March 10, 1970): 259-260.

63. Frank S. Meyer, "In Re Professor Zoll: I—Order and Freedom," *National Review* 22 (March 24, 1970): 311.

64. Frank S. Meyer, "In Re Professor Zoll: II—Defense of the Republic," *National Review* 22 (April 7, 1970): 362, 373.

65. Thomas Molnar to the editor, *National Review* 22 (May 19, 1970): 529.

66. An early and representative Catholic critique was Christopher Fullman, "God and Man and Mr. Buckley," *Catholic World* 175 (May 1952): 104-108. Father Fullman accused Buckley of driving a "wedge of cleavage between God and man" (p. 108). "In Chapter I he is all for Christ and in the rest of the book he seems to be all for Adam Smith" (p. 105). The phrase "grave variance" is found in Kevin Corrigan, "God and Man at 'National Review,'" *Catholic World* 192 (January 1961): 206-212. In a review of Buckley's *Up from Liberalism* (1959), Irving Kristol asserted that Buckley adhered to "two incompatible ideals: he is a devout Catholic and an exponent of *laissez-faire* capitalism after the fashion of Herbert Spencer" ("On the Burning Deck," *Reporter* 21 [November 26, 1959]: 47).

67. See, for example, William F. Buckley, Jr., "Father Fullman's Assault," *Catholic World* 175 (August 1952): 328-333, and "A Very Personal Answer to My Critics," *Catholic World* 192 (March 1961): 360-365. Buckley flatly denied that he was a utilitarian or Spencerian individualist. In condemning idolatrous "nineteenth-century liberalism" and individualism, the popes, he said, had criticized "a perversion of free market economics" of the kind linked with Herbert Spencer then and Ayn Rand now. Buckley claimed that he knew the Church's social teachings very well and pointed out that papal encyclicals had also denounced socialism and explicitly defended private property. Buckley denied that he was a doctrinaire antistatist; government had necessary functions to perform. But *only* certain functions. Calling himself a "subsidiarist," Buckley allied himself with the papal doctrine of subsidiarity, according to which large units of government should do only those tasks that smaller units clearly cannot. Was this not a legitimate ground for opposing "the passion to federalize"? Many Catholics—including the free enterprise economist Colin Clark—supported *National Review*'s stand, he noted. He told Father Fullman that "the great American adjustment—economic freedom—has presented highly convincing credentials as a basically humanitarian, dignified, and realistic system of economic behavior" (p. 330). As for Irving Kristol's charge, Jeffrey Hart found it "hopelessly confused": "Once we admit that one can be a Christian and also live in society, then the question arises of how we can best organize life in society. The argument, obviously, is not between Christianity and the free market, but between two economic doctrines; and it turns on the question of which produces the greater well-being and which is the more equitable" (*The American Dissent: A Decade of Modern Conservatism* [Garden City, N.Y., 1966], pp. 232-233). For Hart and most conservatives, of course, the "presumption" (Hart's word) was "in favor of the free market," while the Left had a presumption "toward central control and planning from 'above'" (*ibid.*, p. 227).

68. "The Week," *National Review* 11 (July 29, 1961): 38.

69. "For the Record," *National Review* 11 (August 12, 1961): 77. The quip appeared to

imply that conservative Catholics would accept their Church as a mother (*mater*) but not—at least in this instance—as a teacher (*magistra*).

70. See Garry Wills, *Politics and Catholic Freedom* (Chicago, 1964). Part 1 is an excellent review of the dispute. Developments in the Roman Catholic Church (particularly *Aggiornamento* and the liberal-conservative cleavage) were a frequent subject of commentary in *National Review* throughout the 1960s. For instance, the May 4, 1965 issue of *National Review* contained several articles under the heading: "What in the name of God is going on in the Catholic Church?" The magazine also commented from time to time on the state of Protestantism. See, for example, Harold O.J. Brown, "The Protestant Deformation," *National Review* 17 (June 1, 1965): 464-466.

In 1961 *National Review* appointed Will Herberg, the Jewish philosopher and sociologist, its religion editor. During the 1960s he produced many thoughtful essays on conservatism and religion, including "Conservatives and Religion: A Dilemma," *National Review* 11 (October 7, 1961): 230, 232; "Reinhold Niebuhr, Burkean Conservative," *National Review* 11 (December 2, 1961): 378, 394; "Conservatism, Liberalism, and Religion," *National Review* 17 (November 30, 1965): 1087-1088. Herberg's article on Niebuhr provoked a dissent from Jeffrey Hart, who argued that Niebuhr and Burke differed profoundly on many issues. See Hart to the editor, *National Review* 12 (January 16, 1962): 34-36.

71. Two sources contain much illuminating information on the activities of Bozell and other conservative Catholics in the 1960s: Bozell's correspondence with Russell Kirk, in the Russell Kirk Papers, Clarke Historical Library at Central Michigan University, Mount Pleasant, Mich., and the file marked "Catholic Conservatives, 1965-1966" in the Francis Wilson Papers, University of Illinois, Urbana.

72. In an interview (by telephone) with the author on April 26, 1972, Bozell emphasized the impact upon him of the Christian social order of Spain. Willmoore Kendall had a great "analytical" influence on him, Frederick Wilhelmsen a greater "substantive" influence. Bozell stated that his intellectual odyssey was not affected by the defeat of Barry Goldwater in 1964.

73. L. Brent Bozell, "The Death of the Constitution," *Triumph* 3 (February 1968): 10-14.

74. "The Autumn of the Country," *Triumph* 3 (June 1968): 7, 9.

75. L. Brent Bozell, "Letter to Yourselves," *Triumph* 4 (March 1969): 11-14.

76. L. Brent Bozell, "Politics of the Poor," *Triumph* 4 (April 1969): 11-13.

77. See "Abortion," *National Review* 22 (June 30, 1970): 658-659. See also the July 1970 and the October 1970 issues of *Triumph* for lengthy discussions of this incident.

78. Willmoore Kendall and George W. Carey, *The Basic Symbols of the American Political Tradition* (Baton Rouge, 1970), p. 154.

79. Michael Lawrence, "What's Wrong with the American Myth?" *Triumph* 5 (December 1970): 16-19.

80. Hess's fascinating intellectual journey is chronicled in James Boyd, "From Far Right to Far Left—and Farther—With Karl Hess," *New York Times Magazine* (December 6, 1970): 48-49, 152, 154, 156, 159, 161, 164, 166, 168.

81. See Chapter Four for an analysis of Rothbard's foreign policy posture in the 1950s.

82. Murray Rothbard, "Confessions of a Right-Wing Liberal," *Ramparts* 6 (June 15, 1968): 47-52.

83. Murray Rothbard, "The New Libertarian Creed," *New York Times*, February 9, 1971, p. 37. See also Murray Rothbard, *For a New Liberty* (New York, 1973), chap. 1.

84. See Rothbard, "New Libertarian Creed," p. 37. See also Stan Lehr and Louis Rossetto, Jr., "The New Right Credo—Libertarianism," *New York Times Magazine* (January 10, 1971): 24-25, 86-88, 93-94; Jerome Tuccille, "A Split in the Right Wing," *New York*

Times, January 28, 1971, p. 35.

85. Jerome Tuccille, *Radical Libertarianism: A Right Wing Alternative* (Indianapolis, 1970).

86. For a dramatic, radical libertarian view of the crucial 1969 YAF convention, see *ibid.*, afterword. For an assessment which emphasized the numerical weakness of the dissidents, see David Keene, "Libertarian into Anarchist," *National Review* 22 (October 6, 1970): 1065-1066. Keene was national chairman of YAF. For a Catholic traditionalist perspective on the problems of YAF, see Brad Evans, "The Young Conservatives: Coming Unglued?" *Triumph* 5 (November 1970): 11-15.

87. By 1972, Libertarian Enterprises offered more than 200 books by Ludwig von Mises, Henry Hazlitt, Frédéric Bastiat, Murray Rothbard, Milton Friedman, Ayn Rand, Harry Elmer Barnes, and many others. Another important source was the flourishing Institute for Humane Studies, founded by F.A. Harper (formerly of the Foundation for Economic Education) in 1959 in California. According to Lehr and Rossetto, Mises was the movement's "chief economist" ("New Right Credo," p. 94).

88. "Politics '72: Libertarian Party," *Human Events* 32 (August 5, 1972): 14. Hospers was the author of *Libertarianism* (Los Angeles, 1970). He and his running mate received a few thousand votes—and one electoral vote, when a Virginia elector defected from President Nixon. In 1975 this elector, Roger Lea MacBride, became the Libertarian Party's 1976 nominee for president (*New York Times*, August 31, 1975, p. 20).

89. Rothbard, "New Libertarian Creed," p. 37.

90. See Tuccille, *Radical Libertarianism*, chap. 5: "Toward a Rational Foreign Policy: Defending the Nonstate."

91. Lehr and Rossetto (at the time, seniors at Columbia College) cited Ayn Rand as the "key philosopher" of libertarianism ("New Right Credo," p. 94). In *Radical Libertarianism*, p. 4, Tuccille stated that the "seeds" of the later "eruption" of the phenomenon were planted with Ayn Rand's *Atlas Shrugged* (1957). Some libertarians eventually became disenchanted with Rand. See Tuccille, *Radical Libertarianism*, p. 6, and his sequel, *It Usually Begins with Ayn Rand* (New York, 1971).

Robert Heinlein's novel, *The Moon is a Harsh Mistress*, was popular among many campus libertarians. The acronym TANSTAAFL (There Ain't No Such Thing as a Free Lunch), which appeared in the novel, was a popular slogan in the breakaway movement.

An active young anarcho-capitalist was David Friedman, son of the economist. Appearing in December 1971 at Harvard University to deliver a speech (which the author attended), Friedman wore around his neck a large medallion, on which was engraved a dollar sign and the acronym TANSTAAFL. In 1973 Friedman published *The Machinery of Freedom: A Guide to a Radical Capitalism* (New York, 1973).

92. Tuccille, *Radical Libertarianism*, p. 51.

93. Quoted in Boyd, "Karl Hess," p. 49.

94. Rothbard, "Confessions," p. 51.

95. Quoted in James Dickenson, "'Abolish Government,'" *National Observer*, March 1, 1971, p. 18.

96. According to Tuccille's afterword to *Radical Libertarianism*, the climactic polarizing moment came when a radical libertarian defiantly burned a draft card, thereby precipitating a riot.

97. Hess claimed that Goldwater "would have made a great anarchist" and noted, "As soon as I educated myself to the fact that Communism wasn't just plain Stalinism, which I was hung up on, the rest was easy" (quoted in Dickenson, "'Abolish Government,'" p. 18).

98. William F. Buckley, Jr., to the editor, *Triumph* 3 (April 1968): 3. The latter quoted phrase is Murray's.

99. Hart's and *National Review*'s reactions were printed in "Letters from Yourselves," *Triumph* 4 (June 1969): 17, 40. Other contributors were John Chamberlain, John Davenport, Will Herberg, and Gerhart Niemeyer.

100. The word "angelistic" was *National Review*'s (*ibid.*, p. 40).

101. Neil McCaffrey to the editor, *Triumph* 3 (April 1968): 6.

102. In "Letters from Yourselves," p. 40.

103. See "Abortion," pp. 658-659.

104. William F. Buckley, Jr., *Cruising Speed—A Documentary* (New York, 1971), p. 236. Buckley devoted several pages of this book to the Bozell movement, particularly its summer institute in Spain. Buckley quoted at length a letter from a disillusioned participant in the institute who had discovered its intense hostility to John Courtney Murray, Willmoore Kendall, and the idea that America's "patrimony [was] properly Christian and constitutional" (p. 238).

105. William F. Buckley, Jr., "The Conservative Reply," *New York Times*, February 16, 1971, p. 33.

106. Frank S. Meyer, "Libertarianism or Libertinism?" *National Review* 21 (September 9, 1969): 910.

107. William F. Buckley, Jr., "The Right-Radicals," *National Review* 23 (February 9, 1971): 162.

108. Buckley, "Conservative Reply," p. 33.

109. Buckley, "Right-Radicals," p. 162.

110. Buckley did consider Rothbard a "talented" economist (*ibid.*). In 1972, M. Stanton Evans suggested that Vice-President Agnew could profit from discussions with Milton Friedman "or, [for] that matter, with Murray Rothbard" ("The Political Odyssey of Spiro T. Agnew," *National Review* 24 [August 18, 1972]: 900). It is noteworthy that many of the economics books distributed by Libertarian Enterprises were perfectly acceptable to more conventional conservatives.

111. Buckley, "Conservative Reply," p. 33.

112. Hart, for example, was a leading disciple of Willmoore Kendall. Significantly (and again not surprisingly), *Triumph* took great interest in Spain. Wilhelmsen was a Carlist (interview with Russell Kirk, Cambridge, Mass., April 21, 1971), and the Society for the Christian Commonwealth's annual summer institute was held at the magnificent Escorial palace in Madrid. An advertisement in 1970 for this institute described the Escorial as the "symbol of the *res publica Christiana*" (*Triumph* 5 [April 1970]: 31).

113. It is worth mentioning, however, that in his taped response to the author's questionnaire in March 1972, Professor Friedman said that his colleague George Stigler's studies of the actual effect of government policies had driven Friedman in a libertarian, even anarchistic, direction and had made him more pessimistic than ever about effecting social change by government. It is also interesting that some radical libertarians believed that they did have a national political leader who shared their bold decentralist views: Senator Mark Hatfield of Oregon.

CHAPTER ELEVEN

1. Jeffrey Hart, *The American Dissent: A Decade of Modern Conservatism* (Garden City, N.Y., 1966), p. 106.

2. See Daniel P. Moynihan, "The Politics of Stability," *New Leader* 50 (October 9, 1967): 6-10. This is the text of his speech to the ADA, adapted for publication. The quotations here are from this published version of Moynihan's address.

3. Nathan Glazer, "The Limits of Social Policy," *Commentary* 52 (September 1971): 54.

4. This was the phrase Kristol used in an interview in the *New York Times*, November 12, 1970, pp. 41, 48.

5. Irving Kristol, "Pornography, Obscenity, and the Case for Censorship," *New York Times Magazine* (March 28, 1971): 24-25, 112-114, 116. Kristol was indebted to a recent essay by Berns in *The Public Interest*.

6. Nathan Glazer, *Remembering the Answers: Essays on the American Student Revolt* (New York, 1970), p. 3.

7. These men were listed on UCRA stationery as charter sponsors of the organization; copy, dated May 5, 1969, in possession of the author.

8. Frank S. Meyer, "The Revolution Eats Its Parents," *National Review* 21 (June 3, 1969): 541.

9. See William F. Buckley, Jr., *The Jeweler's Eye: A Book of Irresistible Political Reflections* (New York, 1968), pp. 50-52, for a conservative reaction to the decline of what Buckley called "left anti-Communism."

10. Eugene V. Rostow, "Three Questions for President Brewster and Mayor Lee," *National Review* 21 (November 4, 1969): 1113-1114, 1127, 1129.

11. Walt W. Rostow, "Why We Can't Cut and Run," *Human Events* 30 (July 18, 1970): 8, 13-14.

12. In 1956 one of Acheson's books had been reviewed in *National Review* by Senator Joseph McCarthy. In contrast, see Jared C. Lobdell, "The Old Acheson and the New," *National Review* 21 (December 30, 1969): 1330-1331. See also David Brudnoy, "Whatsoever Things Are True," *National Review* 23 (November 19, 1971): 1310-1311. A comment which mixed praise and criticism was "Dean Acheson, RIP," *National Review* 23 (November 5, 1971): 1219-1220.

13. John Roche, "A Diagnosis of the Anti-Spiro Jitters by a Former Chairman of ADA," *National Review* 22 (August 25, 1970): 878.

14. In an essay in 1969, William F. Buckley, Jr. noted the decline of "evangelistic" anti-Communism in America and the consequent conservative problem: "...conservatives, who continue to be, loosely speaking, the most orthodox anti-Communists in America, look for new forms through which to express themselves. The Soviet Union does not let too much time go by without giving them cause, though every time it becomes a little tougher on account of the general attrition of anti-Communism and the great symbolic rupture of 1959 [Khrushchev's visit to the United States]." William F. Buckley, Jr., *The Governor Listeth: A Book of Inspired Political Revelations* (New York, 1970), p. 135.

15. Lobdell, "Old Acheson and the New," p. 1331.

16. For a list of scholars for Nixon in 1972, see *New York Times*, October 15, 1972, sec. 4, p. 7.

17. John Roche, "Go Home McGovern!" *New America* 10 (October 25, 1972): 3.

18. Sidney Hook, "An Open Letter to George McGovern," *New America* 10 (September 30, 1972): 4-5, 7.

19. Richard N. Goodwin, "The Shape of American Politics," *Commentary* 43 (June 1967): 25-40.

20. Moynihan, "Politics of Stability," p. 8.

21. Daniel P. Moynihan, "Where Liberals Went Wrong," in *Republican Papers,* ed. Melvin Laird (New York, 1968), p. 138.

22. Peter Schrag, "End of the Impossible Dream," *Saturday Review* 53 (September 19, 1970): 68.

23. Moynihan, "Where Liberals Went Wrong," p. 142.

24. Daniel P. Moynihan, *Maximum Feasible Misunderstanding* (1969; paperback ed., New York, 1970), pp. xiii-xiv, 170. Page references are to the paperback edition, which contains an expanded preface.

25. *Ibid.*, p. liv.

26. *Ibid.*, p. 192.

27. Harry Schwartz, "Forrester's Law," *New York Times*, June 14, 1971, p. 37.

28. Peter F. Drucker, *The Age of Discontinuity* (New York, 1969), p. 217.

29. *Ibid.*, p. 219.

30. *Ibid.*, p. 217.

31. William F. Buckley, Jr., "Nixon's 'Workable' Proposals," *National Review* 21 (May 6, 1969): 454.

32. See Daniel Patrick Moynihan and Frederick Mosteller, eds., *On Equality of Educational Opportunity* (New York, 1972).

33. Nathan Glazer, "Is Busing Necessary?" *Commentary* 53 (March 1972): 39-52; Norman Podhoretz, "School Integration and Liberal Opinion," *ibid.*, p. 7.

34. David Armor, "The Evidence on Busing," *The Public Interest*, no. 28 (Summer 1972): 90-126.

35. Jack Rosenthal, "An Epitaph for the Great Society," *New York Times*, May 25, 1972, p. 32.

36. Alan L. Otten, "Politics and People: Intellectual Aridity," *Wall Street Journal*, December 7, 1972, p. 28.

37. According to Kristol, a formative influence on him and Bell was Bell's membership on President Johnson's Commission on Automation. This experience intensified their awareness of the need for rigorous analysis and criticism of dubious clichés of public policy—such as Great Society slogans—then popular in many quarters. In addition, the founders of *The Public Interest* were anxious to learn more about what was actually happening in the world and to locate and publicize significant but often little-known social science scholarship. Interview with Irving Kristol, New York City, November 9, 1973.

38. Walter Berns, "Pornography and Democracy: The Case for Censorship," *The Public Interest*, no. 22 (Winter 1971): 3-24; Irving Kristol, "Editorial Note," *ibid.*, p. 3.

39. "Current Reading: 'One Man, One Vote—So What?'" *The Public Interest*, no. 7 (Spring 1967): 124.

40. On this point, see Moynihan, *Maximum Feasible Misunderstanding* (1970 ed.), pp. xviii-xxvii. See also James Q. Wilson, "The Bureaucracy Problem," *The Public Interest*, no. 6 (Winter 1967): 3-9, and Alan Altshuler, "The Potential of 'Trickle Down,'" *The Public Interest*, no. 15 (Spring 1969): 46.

41. See, for example, Robert Nisbet, "The Twilight of Authority," *The Public Interest*, no. 15 (Spring 1969): 3-9.

42. See Irving Kristol and Paul Weaver, "Who Knows New York?" *The Public Interest*, no. 16 (Summer 1969): 41-59.

43. For an interesting account of Podhoretz's career and that of his rival Jason Epstein (editor of the *New York Review of Books*), see Merle Miller, "Why Norman and Jason Aren't Talking," *New York Times Magazine* (March 26, 1972), pp. 34-35, 104-111.

44. The articles mentioned (in order of publication) are these: Nathan Glazer, "The Limits of Social Policy," *Commentary* 52 (September 1971): 51-58; Samuel McCracken, "Apocalyptic Thinking," *Commentary* 52 (October 1971): 61-70; Joseph W. Bishop, "Politics and ACLU," *Commentary* 52 (December 1971): 50-58; Norman Podhoretz, "Liberty and the Liberals," *Commentary* 52 (December 1971): 4, 6; Paul Seabury, "HEW and the Universities," *Commentary* 53 (February 1972): 38-44; Nathan Glazer, "Is Busing Necessary?" *Commentary* 53 (March 1972): 39-52; Samuel McCracken, "The Population Controllers," *Commentary* 53 (May 1972): 45-53; Rudolf Klein, "Growth and Its Enemies," *Commentary* 53 (June 1972): 37-44; James Q. Wilson, "Liberalism vs. Liberal Education," *Commentary* 53 (June 1972): 50-54.

45. Irving Kristol, "Why Jews Turn Conservative," *Wall Street Journal*, September 14, 1972, p. 18.

46. Christopher Jencks, "Is the Public School Obsolete?" *The Public Interest*, no. 2 (Winter 1966): 18-27; Milton Friedman, "A Free Market in Education," *The Public Interest*, no. 3 (Spring 1966): 107.

47. Altshuler, "'Trickle Down,'" p. 46.

48. Moynihan's memorandum was printed in the *New York Times*, March 1, 1970, p. 69. The controversial passage read: "The time may have come when the issue of race could benefit from a period of 'benign neglect.' The subject has been too much talked about. The forum has been too much taken over to hysterics, paranoids, and boodlers on all sides. We may need a period in which Negro progress continues and racial rhetoric fades."

49. See the reply of civil rights leaders in the *New York Times*, March 6, 1970, p. 27. For a favorable reaction to the celebrated memorandum, see "Mr. Moynihan's Apostasy," *Wall Street Journal*, March 13, 1970, p. 8.

50. T.R. Marmor, "Banfield's 'Heresy,'" *Commentary* 54 (July 1972): 86.

51. Banfield once contributed a review of *Capitalism and Freedom* to *National Review*. See Edward Banfield, "Freedom and the Market," *National Review* 13 (November 20, 1962): 401-403. (He was not, however, close to the *National Review* circle.) In 1968 he headed President-elect Nixon's Task Force on Urban Affairs. See *New York Times*, January 15, 1969, pp. 1, 35, for some of the group's recommendations.

52. Banfield, *The Unheavenly City: The Nature and Future of Our Urban Crisis* (Boston, 1970), pp. 3-4.

53. *Ibid.*, p. 85.

54. *Ibid.*, p. 261.

55. *Ibid.*, pp. 245-246.

56. *Ibid.*, pp. 246-248.

57. *Ibid.*, pp. 253-254.

58. See Marmor, "Banfield's 'Heresy,'" pp. 86-88, for a discussion of the heated controversy.

59. *Ibid.*, p. 86.

60. J. Bernard Burnham, "'Thinking May Make It So,'" *National Review* 22 (April 21, 1970): 420.

61. Jeffrey Hart, "The City and the Alchemist," *National Review* 22 (May 19, 1970): 520.

62. Robert Nisbet, "The Urban Crisis Revisited," *Intercollegiate Review* 7 (Fall 1970): 3-10.

63. "If Banfield is right, at least, the noblest efforts of the past thirty years have been wrong, what progress has occurred has been accidental, and only a 180-degree shift in sensibility can begin to save us" (Richard Todd, "A Theory of the Lower Class: Edward Banfield: The Maverick of Urbanology," *Atlantic* 226 [September 1970]: 52).

64. Irving Kristol, "The Cities: A Tale of Two Classes," *Fortune* 81 (June 1970): 197.

65. See "Intellectuals for the City," *The Public Interest*, no. 7 (Spring 1967): 127-128, for a review of Martin Meyerson and Edward Banfield, *Boston: The Job Ahead*.

66. Nathan Glazer supported Senator McGovern for President in 1972. See Nathan Glazer, "McGovern and the Jews: A Debate," *Commentary* 54 (September 1972): 43-47.

67. James Burnham, "Selective, Yes. Humanism, Maybe," *National Review* 24 (May 12, 1972): 516.

68. Nathan Glazer, "Seeking the Tap Root," *National Review* 24 (August 18, 1972): 903-904.

69. Interview with Nathan Glazer, Cambridge, Mass., December 4, 1972. One disillu-

sioning influence, Glazer recalled, was the War on Poverty. Another influence was Jane Jacobs's blistering critique of urban renewal, *The Death and Life of Great American Cities* (New York, 1961). Significantly, William F. Buckley, Jr. included an excerpt from this book in his anthology *American Conservative Thought in the Twentieth Century* (Indianapolis, 1970). He called Jacobs a "tenacious challenger of the urban abstractionist" (p. 220).

70. Herberg joined the Young Communist League in the 1920s and rose to influential positions in the Party. Expelled along with Jay Lovestone for resisting the Stalinization of the Party, Herberg became an active "Right-Opposition" Communist for a time in the early 1930s. In 1934 he became educational director of the International Ladies Garment Workers Union and gradually continued his drift to the Right. By the 1950s he regarded himself as a "Burkean Conservative." He retained his friendships with labor union activists, however (Herberg to the author, January 19, 1973).

71. Interview with Glazer, December 4, 1972.

72. See Sidney Hook, introduction to Ernest van den Haag, "Civil Disobedience," *National Review* 24 (January 21, 1972): 29; Nathan Glazer, "Seeking the Tap Root," *National Review* 24 (August 18, 1972): 903-904; Lewis Feuer, "Democrats versus Democracy," *National Review* 24 (October 27, 1972): 1178-1180; Seymour Martin Lipset, "No Easy Answers," *National Review* 24 (December 22, 1972): 1411, 1413.

73. See Glazer, *Remembering the Answers*; Sidney Hook, *Academic Freedom and Academic Anarchy* (New York, 1970); Lewis Feuer, *Conflict of Generations* (New York, 1969); Seymour M. Lipset, ed., *The Berkeley Student Revolt* (Garden City, N.Y., 1965) and later books.

74. Interview with Glazer, December 4, 1972.

75. As of the summer of 1972, *The Alternative*'s advisory board included Edward Banfield, Jameson G. Campaigne, Jr., George Carey, Philip Crane, Martin Diamond, M. Stanton Evans, Nathan Glazer, Robert Nisbet, Henry Regnery, William Rusher, C.H. Simonds, Ernest van den Haag, and Paul H. Weaver (letterhead in possession of the author).

76. Alexander Bickel's book *The Supreme Court and the Idea of Progress* (New York, 1970), which criticized many leading decisions of the Earl Warren era, was another manifestation of right-wing liberalism. It received a sympathetic reception in Walter Berns, "What Was Wrong with the Warren Court," *National Review* 22 (April 21, 1970): 414-415.

77. These four essays were: Robert Bartley, "Irving Kristol and the Public Interest Crowd," *The Alternative* 5 (June-September 1972): 5-6; Nathan Glazer, "Kristol and the New York Intellectual Establishment," *ibid.*, pp. 6-7; William F. Buckley, Jr., "Re Irving Kristol," *ibid.*, pp. 7-8; R. Emmett Tyrell, Jr., "On the Democratic Idea in America," *ibid.*, pp. 8-9.

78. Buckley, "Re Irving Kristol," p. 7.

79. Bartley, "Public Interest Crowd," pp. 5-6. This article was adapted from Bartley, "Irving Kristol and Friends," *Wall Street Journal*, May 3, 1972, p. 20.

80. Irving Kristol, *On the Democratic Idea in America* (New York, 1972). The jacket of this book contained highly laudatory comments from Seymour Martin Lipset and Robert Nisbet. Nisbet predicted that it would become a "modern classic." See also M. Stanton Evans, "The Middle of the Journey," *National Review* 24 (July 21, 1972): 800-801, for a generally favorable review.

81. In his interview with the author on November 9, 1973, Kristol cited Trilling's essay "'Elements That Are Wanted,'" *Partisan Review* 7 (September-October 1940): 367-379, as one which had a profound influence on him.

82. Kristol, *Democratic Idea*, pp. vii-viii.

83. *Ibid.*, p. 27.

84. *Ibid.*, p. 43.

85. It is probably not coincidental that in his preface Kristol mentioned his close friend Martin Diamond, a Straussian political scientist who was a good friend and admirer of Willmoore Kendall and who shared many of Kendall's views on the nature of the American political system.

86. Kristol suggested that "under the strain of modern life" many segments of the populace, especially the "educated classes," were "entering what can only be called, in the strictly clinical sense, a phase of infantile regression" (*Democratic Idea*, p. 104).

87. *Ibid.*, p. 20.

88. Kristol's friend Martin Diamond had also been a man of the Left in his youth. At one point he had worked for Norman Thomas and the Socialist Party. For more on Diamond, see "To Profess with a Passion," *Time* 87 (May 6, 1966): 84-85.

89. Quoted in *New York Times*, November 12, 1970, p. 41. In his interview with the author, Kristol cited two writers above all who influenced him in the early 1940s: John Dewey and Reinhold Niebuhr.

90. For biographical information about Kristol, see his "Memoirs of a 'Cold Warrior,'" *New York Times Magazine* (February 11, 1968): 25, 90, 92, 94-97.

91. Irving Kristol, "'Civil Liberties,' 1952—A Study in Confusion," *Commentary* 13 (March 1952): 228-236.

92. See Irving Kristol, "On the Burning Deck," *Reporter* 21 (November 26, 1959): 46-48, and "Old Truths and the New Conservatism," *Yale Review* 47 (March 1958): 365-373.

93. Frank S. Meyer, "Authoritative or Authoritarian?" *National Review* 22 (December 29, 1970): 1407.

94. Both Jeffrey Hart and Russell Kirk made this point in their interviews with the author.

95. "YAF 10," *New Guard* 10 (September 1970): 7. This issue of *New Guard* was devoted to reflections on the organization's anniversary.

96. Peter P. Witonski, "The Conservative Consensus," *National Review* 22 (December 1, 1970): 1307.

97. See, for example, Harold O.J. Brown, *The Protest of a Troubled Protestant* (New Rochelle, N.Y., 1969), and *Christianity and the Class Struggle* (New Rochelle, N.Y., 1970); Arnold Lunn and Garth Lean, *Christian Counterattack* (New Rochelle, N.Y., 1970).

98. See Michael Wreszin, *The Superfluous Anarchist* (Providence, R.I., 1971), and Edmund Opitz, "Speaking to Our Condition," *National Review* 24 (June 23, 1972): 701-702.

99. A few important examples among many: Jeffrey Hart, "David Hume and Skeptical Conservatism," *National Review* 20 (February 13, 1968): 129-132; Byron C. Lambert, "Paul Elmer More and the Redemption of History," *Modern Age* 13 (Summer 1969): 277-288; George Carey, "The 'New' American Political Tradition," *Modern Age* 15 (Fall 1971): 358-369; Murray Rothbard, "Ludwig von Mises and the Paradigm for Our Age," *ibid.*, 370-379; Donald Atwell Zoll, "The Social Thought of Russell Kirk," *Political Science Reviewer* 2 (Fall 1972): 112-136; John P. East, "The Conservatism of Frank Straus Meyer," *Modern Age* 18 (Summer 1974): 226-245.

100. William F. Buckley, Jr., ed., *American Conservative Thought in the Twentieth Century* (Indianapolis, 1970); Robert Schuettinger, ed., *The Conservative Tradition in European Thought* (New York, 1970); Peter P. Witonski, ed., *The Wisdom of Conservatism*, 4 vols. (New Rochelle, N.Y., 1971). In 1973 appeared yet another: David Brudnoy, ed., *The Conservative Alternative* (Minneapolis, 1973).

101. The *Political Science Reviewer*, an annual volume established in 1971, promised to

become another outlet for conservative scholarship. Its co-editor was George Carey, a professor at Georgetown University and a former collaborator of Willmoore Kendall's. Its first issue included articles about Friedrich Hayek and Eric Voegelin; contributors included Carey and Gerhart Niemeyer.

Another increasingly influential source of thoughtful conservatism was the *Wall Street Journal*. Paul Weaver, associate editor of *The Public Interest*, declared that the *Journal's* editorial page "comes as close to the ideal of rational political discourse as any daily publication in America" ("The Public Discourse," *The Alternative* 6 [November 1972]: 18). Significantly, in autumn 1972, Irving Kristol began to contribute monthly articles to the *Wall Street Journal*.

Yet another addition to conservative media was the monthly journal (in newsletter format) *Imprimis*, established as the organ of the Center for Conservative Alternatives (CCA) at Hillsdale College in 1972. By 1975 it had attained a circulation of 18,000. The CCA was founded by Hillsdale's young conservative president, George C. Roche III, and quickly became a major outlet of conservative intellectual activity. Hillsdale College itself, since its establishment in 1844, had never accepted any government aid.

102. *New York Times*, January 11, 1964, p. 23. This article is an obituary for Frank Hanighen (1900-1964), a founder of *Human Events*.

103. See "The Right Way," *Newsweek* 78 (September 6, 1971): 75.

104. The president of the American Enterprise Institute (AEI) was William Baroody, a close adviser to Senator Barry Goldwater before and during the campaign of 1964. For an excellent account of the increasingly important and extensive activities of the Hoover Institution and AEI in the early 1970s, see Daniel J. Balz, "Washington Pressures/AEI, Hoover Institution voices grow in policy debates during Nixon years," *National Journal Reports* 5 (December 22, 1973): 1893-1901.

105. The ACU's monthly publication, *Battle Line*, was another reflection of the increasing interrelationship of conservative thought and political action.

106. *National Review* 21 (July 1, 1969): 649.

107. Will Herberg, "Words that Slay, Wisdom that Mends," *National Review* 22 (July 14, 1970): 739.

108. See Leonard Silk, "Frank Knight and the 'Chicago School,'" *New York Times*, May 21, 1972, sec. 3, p. 3.

109. See Milton Viorst, "*friedmanism*, n. Doctrine of most audacious U.S. economist; esp. theory 'only money matters,'" *New York Times Magazine* (January 25, 1970): 22-23, 80, 82-84.

110. Drucker, *Age of Discontinuity*, p. 167.

111. On this point, see the discerning comments of Jeffrey Hart, "The Relevance of Burke," *National Review* 19 (September 19, 1967): 1023.

112. John Chamberlain, "The View Twenty-Five Years Later," *National Review* 24 (October 13, 1972): 1127. One of those who delivered a paper at this anniversary meeting was Irving Kristol.

113. Kristol, *Democratic Idea*, p. 105.

114. Eric Voegelin's influence on some conservatives continued to be profound. See, for example, Kirk, *Enemies of the Permanent Things*, pp. 253-281; Gerhart Niemeyer, *Between Nothingness and Paradise* (Baton Rouge, La., 1971). See also Dante Germino, *Beyond Ideology: The Revival of Political Theory* (New York, 1967), which includes a highly laudatory chapter on Voegelin as well as a generally sympathetic discussion of Leo Strauss and other critics of positivism and behaviorism in the social sciences. For Voegelin's own continuing contributions, see especially *Science, Politics and Gnosticism* (Chicago, 1968) and *The Ecumenic Age* (Baton Rouge, La., 1974), vol. 4 of his *Order and History*. For a penetrating essay on conservatism which draws upon some of Voegelin's

insights, see Stephen J. Tonsor, "Gnostics, Romantics, and Conservatives," *Social Research* 35 (Winter 1968): 616-634.

115. Buckley, ed., *American Conservative Thought*, p. 398. One reviewer called Strauss "America's most important political philosopher" (Frederick K. Sanders, "Our Secular Circe," *Sewanee Review* 78 [Winter 1970]: 193). One of the most sophisticated books in a Straussian vein was Harry M. Clor, *Obscenity and Public Morality* (Chicago, 1969), which challenged libertarian views on this issue and called for a moderate censorship along the lines advocated by Walter Berns and Kristol. Not surprisingly, one of Clor's advisers was the Straussian political scientist Joseph Cropsey of the University of Chicago.

When Leo Strauss died in 1973, *National Review* published four very interesting tributes by his former students. See Walter Berns, Herbert J. Storing, Harry Jaffa, and Werner J. Dannhauser, "The Achievement of Leo Strauss," *National Review* 25 (December 7, 1973): 1347-1349; 1352-1357. Also of unusual value is Allan Bloom, "Leo Strauss: September 20, 1899-October 18, 1973," *Political Theory* 2 (November 1974): 372-392.

116. This was President Nixon's description of himself in an interview published in the *New York Times*, November 10, 1972, p. 20.

117. See the Nixon-Kirk correspondence in the Russell Kirk Papers, Clarke Historical Library at Central Michigan University, Mount Pleasant, Mich. Kirk actively supported Nixon for the Republican nomination in 1968. For Nixon's appreciation of *A Program for Conservatives*, see Nixon to Kirk, June 22, 1966, Kirk Papers. In April 1972, Kirk met with the president; Nixon had reread *A Program for Conservatives* and had passed out copies to some members of his staff (Kirk to the author, April 20, 1972).

118. Some conservatives, notably Frank Meyer, were not at all happy about "Disraeli conservatism." Meyer had long been a critic of Nixon and had supported Governor Ronald Reagan of California for president in 1968. See Frank S. Meyer, "Why I Am for Reagan," *New Republic* 158 (May 11, 1968): 17-18. Said Meyer on one occasion: "Neither Disraeli nor Nixon ever stood firmly upon principle" ("Reform Without Principle," *Modern Age* 5 [Spring 1961]: 196).

119. See "John Ashbrook's 'Manifesto,'" *Battle Line* 6 (January 1972): 1.

120. See "A Declaration," *National Review* 23 (August 10, 1971): 842. The American Conservation Union concurred a month later; see "ACU Suspends Support," *Battle Line* 5 (October 1971): 4.

121. See "We're for Ashbrook," *Battle Line* 6 (January 1972): 2.

122. M. Stanton Evans, "The Political Odyssey of Spiro T. Agnew," *National Review* 24 (August 18, 1972): 894.

123. Stephen J. Tonsor, "The Drift to Starboard," *Modern Age* 13 (Summer 1969): 330.

124. John Chamberlain, "Dean of Conservative Columnists," *National Review* 22 (July 14, 1970): 742.

125. "Why the South Must Prevail," *National Review* 4 (August 24, 1957): 148-149.

126. William F. Buckley, Jr., "An Interview with William F. Buckley, Jr.," *Mademoiselle* 53 (June 1961): 121.

127. See William S. Schlamm, "To Mencken—In His Spirit," *National Review* 1 (February 15, 1956): 25, and John Abbot Clark, "Bring on the Menckens!" *National Review* 1 (February 29, 1956): 22-23.

128. Goldwater had adumbrated this theme in the early 1960s with his appeals to the "forgotten American," but it had not caught on; see Goldwater, *The Conscience of a Majority* (New York, 1970), chap. 1. In the 1960s, conservatives often addressed themselves to and tried to win the support of "forgotten Americans." Only in the late 1960s and early 1970s did they really seem to *feel* that they represented the "silent majority."

129. See its advertisement in *National Review* 22 (February 10, 1970): 107.

130. *New York Times*, November 4, 1970, p. 1.

131. See Kevin Phillips, *The Emerging Republican Majority* (New Rochelle, N.Y., 1969), chap. 1, for an influential discussion of antiestablishment conservatism and political realignments.

132. Frank S. Meyer, "The Course of Garry Wills," *National Review* 22 (July 28, 1970): 791.

133. "...I am not alone in finding, or feeling, when I get out of cities like New York into the vast hinterland—as I frequently and rather thoroughly do—that things are not so bad after all, that it's a great country as we always said, and Americans a marvelous people" (James Burnham, "Notes on Authority, Morality, Power," *National Review* 22 [December 1, 1970]: 1288).

134. *National Review* frequently criticized Governor Wallace. See, for example, Frank S. Meyer, "The Populism of George Wallace," *National Review* 19 (May 16, 1967): 527; John Ashbrook, "And Anyway Is Wallace a Conservative?" *National Review* 20 (October 22, 1968): 1048-1049; Barry Goldwater, "Don't Waste a Vote on Wallace," *ibid.*, pp. 1060-1061, 1079; "George Wallace: Moment of Truth," *National Review* 22 (April 7, 1970): 344-345. See also William F. Buckley, Jr. to John A. Thiers, October 31, 1968, William F. Buckley, Jr. Papers, Yale University Library, New Haven, Conn.

135. M. Stanton Evans repeatedly cited polls showing a continuous popular trend to the right on various issues. See Evans, "Odyssey of Spiro T. Agnew," p. 894.

Not all conservatives, however, apotheosized the "silent majority." For one thing, Thomas Molnar observed, it was silent; what did we know about it? Was it not misled at times by demagogues? Did it always vote correctly? As a European, Molnar said, he could not believe that the people were "the fount of wisdom" (interview with Molnar, Chestnut Hill, Mass., November 4, 1972). Molnar believed that the silent majority would "shrink," and compared faith in the "silent majority" to faith in the Noble Savage (lecture at Boston College, November 4, 1972).

136. M. Stanton Evans, "The Gospel According to Ayn Rand," *National Review* 19 (October 3, 1967): 1059-1063. Evans praised Rand's anti-Communism and "excellent grasp" of free market economics but criticized her assault on the moral matrix within which capitalism needs to operate—namely, "the Christian culture which has given birth to all our freedoms."

137. Peter Viereck, review of Peter P. Witonski, ed., *The Wisdom of Conservatism* in *New York Times Book Review*, October 31, 1971, pp. 56-57.

138. See Peter Berger, "Two Paradoxes," *National Review* 24 (May 12, 1972): 507-511. See, in reply, Jeffrey Hart, "Peter Berger's 'Paradox,'" *ibid.*, pp. 511-513.

139. This dispute involved carrying the libertarian imperative to what Buckley considered the extremes of legalizing hard drugs. Buckley invited the Friedmans to inspect the "real world" of Harlem, where narcotics were a "contagious disease." He asked: "How does libertarian theory, pursued *à outrance*, handle moral problems, other than by denying their existence?" He warned against "fantasizing" and thereby "discrediting" the "wholesome major contentions of libertarian theory" (*Governor Listeth*, pp. 129-134).

140. See Edmund Opitz, *Religion and Capitalism: Allies, Not Enemies* (New Rochelle, N.Y., 1970), and M. Stanton Evans, "The Religious Roots of Liberty," *National Review* 22 (July 28, 1970): 796-797.

141. See Clyde Wilson to the editor, *National Review* 22 (November 3, 1970): 1139; Harry Jaffa, "The Open Question: Weathermen and Fort Sumter," *National Review* 22 (December 29, 1970): 1403, 1419; Clyde Wilson to the editor, *National Review* 23 (February 9, 1971): 116, 118.

142. Stephen J. Tonsor, "Athena's Bat," *National Review* 22 (February 10, 1970): 160-

161; Thomas Molnar to the editor, *National Review* 22 (March 10, 1970): 230.

143. See David Brudnoy, "Comstock's Nemesis," *National Review* 23 (September 14, 1971): 1064-1066.

144. Late in 1972, *National Review* published a debate on the marijuana laws; it was a fascinating tour of the many compartments of the contemporary American conservative mind. See Richard C. Cowan, "American Conservatives Should Revise Their Position on Marijuana," *National Review* 24 (December 8, 1972): 1344-1346; James Burnham, "What's the Rush?" *ibid.*, pp. 1346-1348; Jeffrey Hart, "Marijuana and the Countercul- ture," *ibid.*, p. 1348; William F. Buckley, Jr., "The Spirit of the Law," *ibid.*, pp. 1348, 1366.

145. Donald Atwell Zoll, "Philosophical Foundations of the American Political Right," *Modern Age* 15 (Spring 1971): 126, 128.

146. Interview with Robert Nisbet, Northampton, Mass., November 29, 1971.

147. Interview with Devin Garrity, South Hadley, Mass., August 5, 1972.

148. William F. Buckley, Jr., "The Old Man in the Back of the Room," *National Review* 21 (March 21, 1969): 288. Stephen Tonsor reached a similar conclusion: "That the im- plicit sectarianism of Conservatism has been contained and restrained is due in no small part to Frank Meyer's catholic leadership." Tonsor, "Drift to Starboard," p. 330.

149. Witonski, "Conservative Consensus," pp. 1305-1306.

150. M. Stanton Evans, "Varieties of Conservative Experience," *Modern Age* 15 (Spring 1971): 137.

151. Interview with William F. Buckley, Jr., Stamford, Conn., November 26, 1971.

152. "Frank S. Meyer, RIP," *National Review* 24 (April 28, 1972): 466-473, 475. For a sympathetic assessment of Meyer's thought by a young conservative whom he deeply influenced, see David Brudnoy, "The Living Legacy of Frank S. Meyer," *The Alterna- tive* 6 (April 1973): 16-20.

153. This gap has been stressed by many critics of conservatism. See, for example, Jean Worrall Ward, "Value Contradictions in Contemporary American Conservatism" (un- published doctoral dissertation, University of Minnesota, 1967).

154. See Milton Friedman, "Social Responsibility: A Subversive Doctrine," *National Review* 17 (August 24, 1965): 721-723. See also Friedman's *Capitalism and Freedom* (Chicago, 1962), pp. 1-2, wherein Friedman vigorously attacked the "paternalistic" and "organismic" statement by John F. Kennedy: "Ask not what your country can do for you—ask what you can do for your country."

155. "A Conversation with Irving Kristol," *The Alternative* 2 (May-June 1967): 10. Kristol was critical of Friedrich Hayek; see his *Democratic Idea*, chap. 6.

156. Buckley's deep indebtedness to Nock, Kendall, and Chambers has already been indicated. For his high esteem of Kirk, see his letters to Kirk, especially one dated September 17, 1968, Kirk Papers.

157. William F. Buckley, Jr., "In the Beginning...," *National Review* 22 (December 1, 1970): 1265.

158. William F. Buckley, Jr., "Remarks at the Anniversary Dinner," *National Review* 17 (November 30, 1965): 1128.

159. Interview with Molnar, November 4, 1972.

160. See Russell Kirk, "Free Choice: A Voucher Plan," *National Review* 21 (June 17, 1969): 599, and Kirk, "Rebellion and Boredom," in *Seeds of Anarchy: A Study of Cam- pus Revolution*, ed. Frederick Wilhelmsen (Dallas, 1969), p. 36. In the latter essay, Kirk said that students either ought to be conscripted in the same way as others "or else no one ought to be conscripted, a volunteer army developing instead."

161. Traditionalist reasons included the adverse effect of urban renewal on the organic community. Libertarian arguments emphasized the interference with individual free-

dom and the failure of urban renewal to improve the housing supply.

162. Interview with John Chamberlain, Cheshire, Conn., April 6, 1972.

163. Henry Hazlitt, "In Defense of Conformity," *Intercollegiate Review* 7 (Fall 1970): 25-29.

164. According to Jeffrey Hart, *National Review* was plagued in its first decade by vehement clashes among such men as Meyer, Kendall, Bozell, and Schlamm. After all, Hart said, a number of *National Review*'s early senior editors were "thorny" "underground men." This initial phase eventually passed, and harmony developed. Interview with Jeffrey Hart, Hanover, N.H., September 10, 1971.

165. One of the most systematic and perceptive conservative analyses of utopian thinking was Thomas Molnar, *Utopia, the Perennial Heresy* (New York, 1967). To Molnar the utopian dream of the perfect society—"the city of God on earth"—was a "delirious ideal" which led to the "heresy" of "self-divinization" and "the denial of God" (p. vii).

166. Irving Kristol expressed this conservative position well: "I have observed over the years that the unanticipated consequences of social action are always more important, and usually less agreeable, than the intended consequences" (*Democratic Idea*, p. ix). In 1972, Kristol wrote an essay decrying the rise of "radical egalitarianism" as a "gnostic" eruption on the part of a growing intelligentsia that had lost its sense of meaning and purpose; see "About Equality," *Commentary* 54 (November 1972): 41-47.

167. Edmund Burke, *A Letter to a Member of the National Assembly*, in *The Works of the Right Honorable Edmund Burke*, rev. ed. (Boston, 1866), vol. 4, p. 52.

168. William F. Buckley, Jr., *Cruising Speed—A Documentary* (New York, 1971), p. 158.

169. Whittaker Chambers to Buckley, September 1954, quoted in *Odyssey of a Friend: Whittaker Chambers' Letters to William F. Buckley, Jr., 1954-1961*, ed. William F. Buckley, Jr. (New York, 1970), p. 83.

170. Interview with William Rusher, Cambridge, Mass., October 30, 1971.

171. Interview (by telephone) with Frank S. Meyer, September 4, 1971.

172. Interview with Molnar, November 4, 1972.

173. Interview with Nisbet, November 29, 1971.

174. R. Emmett Tyrrell, Jr. to the editor, *National Review* 24 (December 8, 1972): 1330. See also the postelection editorial "What Next?" *National Review* 24 (November 24, 1972): 1287.

175. Kevin Phillips, "The Future of American Politics," *National Review* 24 (December 22, 1972): 1398.

176. Buckley, "Interview" (1961), p. 120.

177. Interview with Buckley, November 26, 1971.

178. See Vance Packard, *A Nation of Strangers* (New York, 1972).

179. For example, see George F. Will, "The Intentions of the Enemy," *National Review* 23 (April 6, 1971): 374-375. Will emphasized the Soviet leaders' continued adherence to Communist "orthodoxy" and predicted that pending any "mutation" in their system (and none had yet occurred) the "future will be like the past—dangerous."

180. See James Burnham, "Why Not Some Yankee Trading?" *National Review* 24 (September 15, 1972): 998. Burnham recognized that East-West contacts, especially trade, were going to increase. But at least, he said, let the United States extract some concessions in return for its aid to the Soviet bloc. At least try to "open up" Communist societies.

181. Interview with Molnar, November 4, 1972. See also Thomas Molnar, *The Counter-Revolution* (New York, 1969), p. 202.

182. Willmoore Kendall, *Willmoore Kendall Contra Mundum*, ed. Nellie D. Kendall (New York, 1971), p. 631.

183. Buckley, "Remarks at the Anniversary Dinner," p. 1128.

184. Chambers to Buckley, April 9, 1961, quoted in *Odyssey of a Friend*, ed. Buckley, p. 293.

EPILOGUE

1. Doug Bandow, "Christianity's Parallel Universe," *American Enterprise* 6 (November/December 1995): 58-61.

2. Paul Johnson, *Modern Times: The World from the Twenties to the Eighties* (New York, 1983), revised and reissued as *Modern Times: The World from the Twenties to the Nineties* (New York, 1991). The words quoted in my Epilogue appear on page 784 of the revised edition.

3. Johnson, *Modern Times* (revised edition), p. 783.

4. *Ibid.*

5. The words "impostor" and "interlopers" were used by the paleoconservative professors Clyde Wilson and M.E. Bradford, respectively, in *Intercollegiate Review* 21 (Spring 1986): 7, 15.

6. Paul Gottfried and Thomas Fleming, *The Conservative Movement* (Boston, 1988), pp. 73, 108. See also Paul Gottfried, *The Conservative Movement* (revised edition: Boston, 1993), especially chaps. 6 and 7.

7. "The State of Conservatism: A Symposium," *Intercollegiate Review* 21 (Spring, 1986): 3-28.

8. Concise summaries of the neo/paleo controversy may be found in Sara Diamond, *Roads to Dominion: Right-Wing Movements and Political Power in the United States* (New York and London, 1995), pp. 279-289, and John Ehrman, *The Rise of Neoconservatism: Intellectuals and Foreign Affairs, 1945-1994* (New Haven, 1995), pp. 185-186. The story is told in much greater detail, from a paleoconservative perspective, in Paul Gottfried's *Conservative Movement* (cited in note 6). For a neoconservative account of some aspects of the dispute, see Norman Podhoretz, "Buchanan and the Conservative Crackup," *Commentary* 93 (May 1992): 30-34. During the uproar William F. Buckley, Jr., wrote an entire book about issues of anti-Semitism raised by the feud: William F. Buckley, Jr., *In Search of Anti-Semitism* (New York, 1992).

9. William J. Bennett, *The Index of Leading Cultural Indicators* (Washington, D.C., 1993). Bennett's compilation was published jointly by the Heritage Foundation and Empower America.

10. Adam Meyerson, "Letter to Our Readers," *Policy Review: The Journal of American Citizenship*, no. 75 (January/February 1996): 5-6.

11. "The National Prospect: A Symposium," *Commentary* 100 (November 1995): passim; A.J. Bacevich, "*Commentary* Gets Religion," *Weekly Standard* 1 (December 4, 1995): 34-35.

12. The phrase is Midge Decter's in her contribution to the *Commentary* symposium cited in note 11.

BIBLIOGRAPHICAL ESSAY

FOR THE ORIGINAL EDITION

Anyone investigating recent American conservatism will soon become aware of a paradox of abundance and scarcity. Because the subject is so contemporary and because so many postwar conservative leaders are still alive, published materials by and about them are plentiful and continue to proliferate. Significant collections of private papers and unpublished sources, however, are few. Nevertheless, they include three of exceptional worth and importance: the William F. Buckley, Jr. Papers, Yale University Library, New Haven, Conn.; the Russell Kirk Papers, Clarke Historical Library at Central Michigan University, Mount Pleasant, Mich.; and the Francis Wilson Papers, University of Illinois, Urbana.

The Buckley Papers are voluminous, well organized, and invaluable. At the time of my initial research, only a portion of them was generally available to scholars; this part was useful for correspondence and clippings relating to *God and Man at Yale* and also contained such items as videotapes of many of Buckley's *Firing Line* television shows. More recently, the Buckley Papers have been enhanced by the accession of a massive and extremely interesting set of papers focusing on *National Review* and covering, in varying depths, the years 1954-1973. This diverse acquisition includes (among other items) copies of Buckley's syndicated column "On the Right," a clipping file for several years of *National Review*, tapes of many *Firing Line* shows, and—most important of all—more than eighty boxes of Buckley's correspondence between 1954 and 1973. These files include illuminating—and, in many cases, extensive—correspondence with nearly every major conservative figure of the past two decades. Also of unusual interest are in-house memoranda written by members of the staff of *National Review* from the 1950s through 1969.

These behind-the-scenes communications reveal much about the intellectual and publishing history of *National Review*, the varying perspectives and activities of the magazine's contributors, and the sometimes stormy development of the conservative movement.

As this book goes to press, the manuscripts for 1954-1973 in the Buckley Papers are not yet generally open to researchers. Before preparing the final draft of my manuscript, however, I obtained the permission of William F. Buckley, Jr. to examine these papers in entirety and without restriction. This enabled me to clarify, amplify, and confirm many points in the book.

The Kirk Papers are also rich and extensive and contain informative correspondence with a wide variety of prominent conservatives, including Bernard Iddings Bell, L. Brent Bozell, William F. Buckley, Jr., T. S. Eliot, Barry Goldwater, and Robert Nisbet. Also valuable is a substantial file of letters written by Kirk before and during World War II; these reveal in detail the evolving attitudes and intellectual interests of one of the preeminent postwar conservatives.

The Wilson Papers likewise contain a rewarding assortment of letters from such men as Bozell, Buckley, Stanley Parry, Peter Viereck, and (most notably and extensively) Willmoore Kendall. Also helpful is a file of correspondence on activities of Roman Catholic conservatives leading to the establishment of *Triumph*.

Several other archival sources are of significant, although lesser, value. The William Henry Chamberlin Papers at Providence College, Providence, R.I., contain a few interesting letters, scrapbooks of his articles in the *Wall Street Journal*, and a diary of occasional usefulness. The Donald Davidson Papers, Joint University Libraries, Nashville, Tenn., include about a dozen letters from Richard Weaver. As of early 1975, the Special Collections Department of the Joint University Libraries was assembling documents for eventual inclusion in a collection to be called the Richard M. Weaver Papers. The task of acquiring and processing materials is not yet complete, however. Some correspondence, mostly minor, of Buckley, Kendall, and Kirk with Herbert Hoover can be found in the ex-president's papers at the Herbert Hoover Presidential Library, West Branch, Iowa. The Post-Presidential Subject File of the Hoover Papers also includes material pertaining to *Human Events* and an extensive file concerning the internal difficulties of *The Freeman* in 1952 and 1953. The Sterling Morton Papers at the Chicago Historical Society contain several significant letters from Buckley discussing the financial problems of *National Review* in its early years. A few relatively unimportant letters from Buckley are in the Charles Parsons Papers, Yale University Library.

Because of the nature of the subject, it was possible to obtain additional primary source material in two important ways. First, a large number of conservative intellectuals and other persons (including friends and relatives of prominent conservatives) responded generously and often repeatedly to my letters of inquiry. Their correspondence enabled me to supplement the public record with valuable reminiscences and fresh viewpoints on old events, issues, and personalities. In addition, the following individuals kindly permitted me to examine primary sources (including letters and clippings) in their personal possession: Alfred Balitzer, Polly Weaver Beaton, Louis Dehmlow, Charles Hyneman, Nellie D. Kendall, Yvona K. Mason, Edmund Opitz, Austin Ranney, Peter Viereck, and Henry Wells.

Second, the very fact that so many postwar conservative intellectuals are still alive and active proved to be an advantage, for I was able to interview a significant number of them, sometimes at great length. In most cases these interviews were conducted in person, in a few cases necessarily by telephone. As with correspondence, interviews yielded abundant autobiographical information, anecdotes, and other recollections which simply could not be found in published sources. The names of interviewees and principal correspondents are listed in the Appendix.

In contrast to the relatively small number of collections of unpublished sources is the ever-increasing volume of published primary materials, in itself a sign of the resurgence of the intellectual American Right since 1945. As a group, conservative scholars and publicists were astonishingly prolific. Most of their major writings (other than books) were conveniently clustered in a few periodicals, the best known and most valuable of which was *National Review*, founded in 1955 and edited by William F. Buckley, Jr. It is safe to say that no significant facet of the conservative renascence after this date escaped *NR*'s notice. Nearly every prominent conservative intellectual wrote at least one article for it; many were regular contributors. Here, too, many of the crucial intramural debates on conservative thought and strategy were conducted. If any single publication mirrored and even dominated the development of the Right after the mid-1950s, *National Review* was it.

Also valuable were several other publications which, while less famous than *National Review*, should not be neglected. *The Freeman*, revived in 1950, was an essential source of pungent right-wing commentary, particularly of a libertarian and nationalist-anti-Communist sort, for 1950-1954. In later years, under the sponsorship of the Foundation for

Economic Education, *The Freeman* became a kind of *Reader's Digest* of the "freedom philosophy," with short monthly articles by libertarians like John Chamberlain, Edmund Opitz, and Leonard Read. Most of these dealt with free market principles and refrained from involvement in immediate controversies, presumably in accordance with Read's emphasis on education rather than political activism. Also useful for the pre-*National Review* period were *Faith and Freedom* and the *American Mercury*. The former, established in 1950 as the organ of Spiritual Mobilization, featured articles of a generally libertarian nature, as well as some revealing right-wing debates on the cold war in the early 1950s. The latter was for several years a forum for such anti-Communist (and often ex-radical) journalists as Eugene Lyons, William Henry Chamberlin, Max Eastman, and Ralph de Toledano. *Human Events*, founded in 1944, eventually became one of the most successful and politically influential journals of the Right. A week-by-week source of conservative political commentary, it became—especially in later years—an outlet for the expanding number of conservative columnists. Frank Chodorov's *analysis*, also founded in 1944, was for a few years a virtually one-man effort by an arch-individualist.

Indispensable for the traditionalist side of conservative thought is *Modern Age*, founded by Russell Kirk in 1957. It and the *Intercollegiate Review* (published since 1965 by the Intercollegiate Studies Institute) remain the most important conservative academic quarterlies; they continue to be important sources of serious and mature conservative thought. The *Burke Newsletter*, originally published as a part of *Modern Age* and eventually as *Studies in Burke and His Time*, illuminated this strand of conservative scholarship. The *University Bookman*, a quarterly established in 1960 by Russell Kirk, was dedicated to the reformation of higher education along traditionalist lines. *The Political Science Reviewer*, an annual volume founded in 1971 and edited primarily by conservatives, regularly featured valuable scholarly articles by and about conservative intellectuals. *Imprimis*, the monthly publication of the Center for Constructive Alternatives at Hillsdale College, was established in 1972 and became another flourishing medium for reflective conservative writing. For the estranged Catholic ultratraditionalism of L. Brent Bozell and his circle, *Triumph*, founded in 1966, was the principal forum.

A few publications of conservative youth proved to be worth examining. The *New Individualist Review*, established in 1961 by graduate students of Friedrich Hayek at the University of Chicago, was, before its demise in the late 1960s, an excellent source of articles in the Hayek-

Friedman mold. The *New Guard*, founded in 1961 as the organ of Young Americans for Freedom, served mostly as an indication of the developing strength of the "under-30" segment of the movement; especially interesting was its tenth anniversary issue (September 1970). *Rally* (1966-1967) was a sprightly but short-lived monthly produced by young conservatives, while *The Alternative*, founded in 1967, rapidly became an important journal which both reflected and encouraged the growing fusion of conservatives and right-wing liberals.

To sustain these periodicals, conservatives obviously wrote an enormous number of articles. They also published a substantial number of books. At this point, it would be redundant to mention particular books and essays; most of the important ones have already been discussed in the text or cited in the footnotes. In my judgment, these items are the essential sources for a study of intellectual conservatism in the United States since 1945. Of course, anyone wishing to study the more ephemeral writings (such as day-to-day political commentary) of conservative intellectuals should ferret out lesser articles not mentioned in this book; conservative periodicals are the best place to begin. Another good source is the syndicated columns of such men as Buckley, Kirk, John Chamberlain, Jeffrey Hart, Ralph de Toledano, James J. Kilpatrick, and Kevin Phillips; the best single source for a weekly selection of their output is *Human Events*. The conservative journalist William Henry Chamberlin frequently contributed book reviews and other essays to the *Wall Street Journal* in the 1950s and 1960s; he also wrote often for the *New Leader*. Milton Friedman has had a regular column in *Newsweek*, beginning in 1966. Two frequent outlets for Irving Kristol's writings were *Fortune*, for which he wrote book reviews, and the *Wall Street Journal*, to which he has contributed a monthly column since autumn 1972. In the early 1970s the "Op Ed" page of the *New York Times* rather frequently printed prices by right-wing spokesmen.

Fortunately for those who wish to explore the burgeoning literature produced by the American Right, many leading conservatives have gathered their principal essays into books. In this department William F. Buckley, Jr. has been especially assiduous, periodically collecting his writings into best-selling books with intriguing titles. See his *Rumbles Left and Right: A Book About Troublesome People and Ideas* (New York, 1963); *The Jeweler's Eye: A Book of Irresistible Political Reflections* (New York, 1968); *The Governor Listeth: A Book of Inspired Political Revelations* (New York, 1970); *Inveighing We Will Go* (New York, 1972); and *Execution Eve—And Other Contemporary Ballads* (New York, 1975).

Many of James Burnham's columns on foreign policy from 1955 to the mid-1960s are reprinted in *The War We Are In: The Last Decade and the Next* (New Rochelle, N.Y., 1967), while Milton Friedman's articles in *Newsweek* from 1966 to 1972 have been assembled in *An Economist's Protest: Columns in Political Economy* (Glen Ridge, N.J., 1972). Some of the best essays of Friedrich Hayek have also been collected; see *Individualism and Economic Order* (Chicago, 1948) and *Studies in Philosophy, Politics, and Economics* (Chicago, 1967). Two indispensable collections of Willmoore Kendall's writings are *The Conservative Affirmation* (Chicago, 1963) and *Willmoore Kendall Contra Mundum*, ed. Nellie D. Kendall (New Rochelle, N.Y., 1971). Among Russell Kirk's book are three stimulating sets of essays: *Beyond the Dreams of Avarice: Essays of a Social Critic* (Chicago, 1956); *Confessions of a Bohemian Tory: Episodes and Reflections of a Vagrant Career* (New York, 1963); and *The Intemperate Professor and Other Cultural Splenetics* (Baton Rouge, 1965). Frank S. Meyer's *The Conservative Mainstream* (New Rochelle, N.Y., 1968) is an invaluable and carefully organized compilation of the main writings of this influential conservative spokesman during the 1950s and 1960s. For an introduction to Leo Strauss and his school, several sets of essays are useful: Leo Strauss, *What Is Political Philosophy? and Other Studies* (Glencoe, Ill., 1959) and *Liberalism Ancient and Modern* (New York, 1968); Leo Strauss and Joseph Cropsey, eds., *History of Political Philosophy* (Chicago, 1963); Herbert Storing, ed., *Essays On the Scientific Study of Politics* (New York, 1962); and Joseph Cropsey, ed., *Ancients and Moderns: Essays on the Tradition of Political Philosophy in Honor of Leo Strauss* (New York, 1964). For Eric Voegelin, see *Science, Politics, and Gnosticism* (Chicago, 1968), a small but important collection of essays on a subject of increasing interest to the intellectual Right. After Richard Weaver's death in 1963, eight of his previously published articles, including the autobiographical "Up from Liberalism," were brought together in *Life without Prejudice and Other Essays* (Chicago, 1965).

Also convenient for the student of postwar conservatism are several published bibliographies which have facilitated my research and which need not be duplicated here. Most useful was Clinton Rossiter's, appended to his *Conservatism in America: The Thankless Persuasion*, 2nd ed., rev. (New York, 1962). Also well worth consulting is the bibliographical essay in Ronald Lora, *Conservative Minds in America* (Chicago, 1971). William F. Buckley, Jr., ed., *American Conservative Thought in the Twentieth Century* (Indianapolis, 1970), includes an essay on sources that reflects Buckley's conservative position. It is thus a helpful primary source as well as an introduction to modern American conservative writings. Robert Schuettinger, ed., *The Conservative Tradition in European Thought* (New York, 1970), contains a good bibliographical essay on conservatism on the other side of the Atlantic. A nearly complete bibliography of Richard Weaver's work (along with a list of many articles about him) can be found at the back of his posthumously published *The Southern Tradition at Bay: A History of Postbellum Thought*, ed. George Core and M.E. Bradford (New Rochelle, N.Y., 1968). For Leo Strauss's published writings up to 1964, see the already cited Festschrift, *Ancients and Moderns*. Also very helpful is David L. Schaefer, Jr., "The Legacy of Leo Strauss: A Bibliographical Introduction," *Intercollegiate Review* 9 (Summer 1974): 139-148. A complete bibliography of Friedrich Hayek's publications is contained in Erich Streissler, ed., *Roads to Freedom: Essays in Honor of Friedrich A. von Hayek* (London, 1969).

The status of secondary sources is different. No full-length history of post-war conservative intellectuals exists; the closest approximation to one is Jeffrey Hart, *The American Dissent: A Decade of Modern Conservatism* (Garden City, N.Y., 1966), a sympathetic survey of the views of the *National Review* circle during the magazine's first ten years. (Portions of Hart's book were printed in the tenth anniversary issue of *National Review*.) Hart's book is not a full-fledged history but an attempt to demonstrate the intellectual seriousness and respectability of contemporary conservative thought.

Some books do treat conservatism in historical terms. Clinton Rossiter's *Conservatism in America*, 2nd ed., rev. (New York, 1962) is still the most comprehensive treatment of the subject. His chapters on conservatism since 1945 are generally critical, emphasizing the severe intellectual problems faced by the Right in a dynamic and (presumably) liberal country. In fact, this section of the book is almost as much prescription as description; not surprisingly, conservatives have accepted neither. For their principal replies to Rossiter, see John Chamberlain, "A Reviewer's Notebook," *The Freeman* 5 (May 1955): 484-485; Russell Kirk, in *Burke Newsletter* 4 (Winter 1962-1963): 190-193; Gerhart Niemeyer, in *Journal of Public Law* 4 (Fall 1955): 441-447; and Francis Wilson, in *Journal of Politics* 18 (May 1956): 358-360. See also Willmoore Kendall, *The Conservative Affirmation* and *Willmoore Kendall Contra Mundum*, each of which contains incisive critiques of Rossiter. Ronald Lora's *Conservative Minds in America* (Chicago, 1971), a general survey of the Right since John Adams, has predominantly critical chapters on

Russell Kirk and Peter Viereck and on William F. Buckley, Jr. and *National Review*. Because his book appeared about a decade after Rossiter's, Lora's volume is a more up-to-date brief introduction to the postwar conservative movement; however, his chapters on recent conservatism are of limited scope. Thus Richard Weaver is discussed in a single paragraph, while Friedrich Hayek, Willmoore Kendall, and Leo Strauss receive only a few passing references, and Milton Friedman, Eric Voegelin, and Robert Nisbet are not mentioned at all.

In general, secondary works on recent American conservatism tend to be critical and to fall into three categories. The most popular genre asserts the incompatibility of much of conservatism with America's supposedly dominant liberal tradition. Both Rossiter and Lora advance this argument, as do numerous other writers, most of whose articles have already been mentioned in the text and footnotes. The most influential example of this school of thought is Louis Hartz, *The Liberal Tradition in America* (New York, 1955); see also Allen Guttmann, *The Conservative Tradition in America* (New York, 1967). When Guttmann's book appeared, it received very critical reviews by several conservative scholars. See Jeffrey Hart, "Conservatism: Literary and Political," *Kenyon Review* 30 (1968): 697-702; Stephen J. Tonsor, in *Studies in Burke and His Time* 10 (Winter 1968-1969): 1188-1193; and Peter P. Witonski, "Literary Historian Awash," *National Review* 19 (October 31, 1967): 1214-1216. In his bibliographical essay at the beginning of *American Conservative Thought in the Twentieth Century*, William F. Buckley, Jr., accused Guttmann of relying solely on liberal sources, hence coming inevitably to liberal conclusions. While this liberal assault on postwar conservatism has made a definite impact on the Right and has helped to illuminate tensions in the conservative movement, it can easily become a way simply to dismiss conservatism or score a semantic victory over it, without coming to terms with the reality of the multi-faceted conservative revival.

A second kind of critique emphasizes purported psychological and sociological inadequacies of conservatives and, in general, the "irrational" roots of their behavior. The most famous example of this genre is Daniel Bell, ed., *The New American Right* (New York, 1955), expanded into *The Radical Right* (New York, 1963). These collections of essays contain many stimulating observations that have some validity. Thus, an element of "populist" Western resentment against Eastern liberal elites *was* present in some conservatism during the 1950s—a strain that grew stronger in the late 1960s and early 1970s. Conservatives *were* often embittered toward liberals. Many right-wingers *did* perceive themselves as outsiders, as rebels against a "respectable" liberal consensus. An especially vivid illustration is William S. Schlamm, "Across McCarthy's Grave," *National Review* 3 (May 18, 1957): 469-470.

The two collections, however, also have certain defects. The rather indiscriminate lumping of serious right-wing intellectuals with John Birchers into the "Radical Right," the stress on alleged "status anxieties" of conservatives, and a general tendency to see conservatism as eccentric if not dangerous—all weaken the value of these books for the historian who seeks in them an adequate understanding of intellectual conservatism. These books are marked by relatively little discussion of conservative thought. Indeed, one is apt to come away feeling that there was no such thing—only deep and illegitimate resentments. These books were very much a product of the McCarthy controversy, during which some liberals, fearful of an eruption of the masses led by rightist demagogues, discovered the value of (a pro-New Deal) consensus and of nondemocratic (but presumably liberal and enlightened) elites. In this respect, the books are rewarding to the historian. But whatever their applicability to mass movements may be, the use of social-psychological categories like "status anxiety" to explain the activities of highly sophisticated, self-conscious, often idiosyncratic *intellectuals* is a hazardous undertaking at best.

The books edited by Bell also exemplify the third principal kind of critique: often polemical portraits of the Radical Right. At the beginning of my research, I read a considerable number of such articles, which appeared in such periodicals as *Time*, *Newsweek*, *Look*, and the *New Republic* in the early 1960s. Few of these, however, proved to be of value. For one thing, my subject was intellectuals, not the sometimes colorful extremist groups so much discussed by the media. For another, this genre was usually more concerned with establishing a *menace* from the Right than with dispassionate historical inquiry. The easiest way to locate such materials is to consult the heading "Conservatism" in the *Reader's Guide to Periodical Literature*.

Upon closer examination, these three main types of critical secondary sources appear to have shared two important assumptions: that the postwar Right was in some sense illegitimate, and that the true American consensus was fundamentally liberal. These kinds of criticism can all be understood as responses to *emerging* conservatism, to *youthful* conservatism, the nature of which alarmed some liberals. But as the conservative movement has matured, these criticisms—based, again, on the almost automatic assumption of liberal supremacy and consensus in America—have fallen into decline. It has apparently become less plausible to dismiss conservatism as simply outside of the American mainstream, or as the ideology of an insecure "*lumpen*-bourgeoisie" (Dwight Macdonald's term in 1956), of as mere crude and irascible extremism. The reasons for this change are, of course, part of the subject of this book. It is interesting to see fashions in historiography reflecting intellectual and political trends.

As postwar conservatism has become established as an articulate intellectual and political force, several of its spokesmen have increasingly received recognition and scholarly attention. This is especially true of Friedrich Hayek, Leo Strauss, Eric Voegelin, and other pillars of the revival of political philosophy in the United States since 1945. A lucid survey of this phenomenon is Dante Germino, *Beyond Ideology: The Revival of Political Theory* (New York, 1967). Significant essays on Hayek, Strauss, Voegelin, and Michael Oakeshott are contained in a recent anthology: Anthony de Crespigny and Kenneth Minogue, eds., *Contemporary Political Philosophers* (New York, 1975). The death of Leo Strauss in 1973 occasioned a number of important reflections on his distinguished career and work. See Allan Bloom, "Leo Strauss: September 20, 1899-October 18, 1973," *Political Theory* 2 (November 1974): 372-392, and Walter Berns, Herbert J. Storing, Harry V. Jaffa, and Werner J. Dannhauser, "The Achievement of Leo Strauss," *National Review* 25 (December 7, 1973): 1347-1349, 1352-1357. When he died, Strauss was associated with St. John's College, Annapolis, Maryland; its publication, *The College*, devoted its January 1974 issue to remarks on Strauss by his former colleagues and students. See also Milton Himmelfarb, "On Leo Strauss," *Commentary* 58 (August 1974): 61-66, and Emma Brossard, "Leo Strauss: Philosopher and Teacher, Par Excellance [sic]," *Academic Reviewer* (Fall-Winter 1974): 1-5. The latter essay contains a list of eulogies and other articles about Leo Strauss that have appeared since his death.

The death of Ludwig von Mises in 1973, the publication that same year of the first volume of a new trilogy by Friedrich Hayek, and the awarding of the Nobel Prize in economics to Hayek in 1974 have stimulated new interest in and respect for the Austrian School of economics. See Henry Hazlitt, F. A. Hayek, Lawrence Fertig, and Israel Kirzner, "Tribute to von Mises," *National Review* 25 (November 9, 1973): 1244-1246, 1260; Ralph Raico, "Ludwig von Mises," *The Alternative* 8 (February 1975): 21-23; James Grant, "Hayek: The Road to Stockholm," *The*

Alternative 8 (May 1975): 10-12; Ralph Raico, "A Libertarian Maestro," ibid., 21-23.

One other special secondary source deserves mention. In the course of assessing the intellectual impact of postwar conservatism, I examined many reviews of conservative books in order to ascertain scholarly and nonconservative reactions. On several occasions this strategy was fruitful, as in the case of Friedrich Hayek's *The Road to Serfdom*, and I have noted many of these reviews in the book. But even more rewarding than left-of-center responses to right-of-center books were reviews by conservatives of one another's books. These often provided revealing insights into an exceedingly diverse movement for which self-definition was a recurrent passion and need.

As with the primary sources, it would be superfluous to record again titles which have already been discussed in footnotes and text. For additional secondary references, see the bibliographies compiled by Buckley, Lora, Rossiter, and Schuettinger. An annotated bibliography of the principal sources consulted for a preliminary version of this book is contained in the author's doctoral dissertation, "A Dance Along the Precipice: The Conservative Intellectual Movement in America, 1945-1972" (Harvard University, 1973).

BIBLIOGRAPHICAL POSTSCRIPT

As readers of the Epilogue are already aware, the literature of conservatism has grown prodigiously since this book was first published: so much so that it would require an elaborate bibliographical essay to encompass it. Fortunately, no such effort is really necessary here. Thanks to a rapidly developing literature *about* conservatism—much of it generated by conservative writers themselves—the intellectual movement chronicled in this book is more accessible to study than ever before.

As conservatism since 1945 has come of age, it has created a genre of writing largely absent when my book initially appeared: autobiographies and memoirs by leading participants. Especially noteworthy are: John Chamberlain, *A Life with the Printed Word* (Chicago, 1982); Russell Kirk, *The Sword of Imagination* (Grand Rapids, 1995); Irving Kristol, *Neoconservatism: The Autobiography of an Idea* (New York, 1995); Felix Morley, *For the Record* (South Bend, 1979); Norman Podhoretz, *Breaking Ranks: A Political Memoir* (New York, 1979); and Henry Regnery, *Memoirs of a Dissident Publisher* (New York and London, 1979). The shattering impact of the Sixties is vividly documented in John H. Bunzel, ed., *Political Passages: Journeys of Change Through Two Decades, 1968-1988* (New York, 1988), a collection of autobiographical essays by twelve ex-leftists who moved in varying degrees to the right. Part memoir, part history, is William A. Rusher's *The Rise of the Right* (New York, 1984; rev. ed., 1993), a story well told by a conservative "insider" and longtime publisher of *National Review*.

The conservative intellectual movement has also begun to inspire biographies and biographically focused monographs. Notable in this category are Shadia Drury, *The Political Ideas of Leo Strauss* (New York,

1988); Samuel T. Francis, *Power and History: The Political Thought of James Burnham* (Lanham, Md., 1984); John B. Judis, *William F. Buckley, Jr.: Patron Saint of the Conservatives* (New York, 1988); Kevin J. Smant, *How Great the Triumph: James Burnham, Anticommunism, and the Conservative Movement* (Lanham, Md., 1992); and Fred Douglas Young, *Richard M. Weaver, 1910-1963: A Life of the Mind* (Columbia, Mo., 1995). Although Russell Kirk has not yet been the subject of a biography, biographical details abound in the Festschrift completed shortly before he died in 1994: James E. Person, ed., *The Unbought Grace of Life: Essays in Honor of Russell Kirk* (Peru, Illinois, 1994). Kirk's place in American conservatism is also evaluated from many perspectives in the Fall 1994 *Intercollegiate Review*, a "tribute issue" containing contributions from twenty scholars. A lively Festschrift for the "godfather" of neoconservatism is Christopher DeMuth and William Kristol, eds., *The Neoconservative Imagination: Essays in Honor of Irving Kristol* (Washington, D.C., 1995). Not to be overlooked, either, are two recent scholarly biographies of the man who carried the conservatives' standard in the pivotal 1964 presidential election: Lee Edwards, *Goldwater: The Man Who Made a Revolution* (Washington, D.C., 1995) and Robert Alan Goldberg, *Barry Goldwater* (New Haven, 1995).

Another sign of conservative maturity has been the appearance of anthologies of conservative thought, including Russell Kirk, ed., *The Portable Conservative Reader* (New York, 1982) and William F. Buckley, Jr. and Charles R. Kesler, eds., *Keeping the Tablets: Modern American Conservative Thought* (New York, 1988). Also worth noting are Terry Teachout, ed., *Ghosts on the Roof: Selected Journalism of Whittaker Chambers, 1931-1959* (Washington, D.C., 1989) and Joseph Scotchie, ed., *The Vision of Richard Weaver* (New Brunswick, N.J., 1995).

A number of broader studies of conservative thought have also appeared in the last decade. Outstanding among these are: Patrick Allitt, *Catholic Intellectuals and Conservative Politics in America, 1950-1985* (Ithaca and London, 1993); John P. East, *The American Conservative Movement: The Philosophical Founders* (Chicago, 1986); John Ehrman, *The Rise of Neoconservatism: Intellectuals and Foreign Affairs, 1945-1994* (New Haven and London, 1995); Bruce Frohnen, *Virtue and the Promise of Conservatism* (Lawrence, Kansas, 1993); Paul Gottfried, *The Search for Historical Meaning: Hegel and the Postwar American Right* (Dekalb, Illinois, 1986); Paul Gottfried and Thomas Fleming, *The Conservative Movement* (Boston, 1988); Paul Gottfried, *The Conservative Movement* (rev. ed.: New York, 1993); and J. David Hoeveler, *Watch on the Right: Conservative Intellectuals in the Reagan Era* (Madison, 1991). The anti-Communist dimension of American conservatism receives attention in Richard Gid Powers, *Not Without Honor: The History of American Anticommunism* (New York, 1995), an important new work. Less scholarly in character, but brimming with wit and provocative observation, are studies of conservatism's recent tribulations by two of the movement's foremost journalists: R. Emmett Tyrrell, Jr., *The Conservative Crack-Up* (New York, 1992) and David Frum, *Dead Right* (New York, 1994). For an articulate paleoconservative perspective on much the same subject, see Samuel Francis, *Beautiful Losers: Essays on the Failure of American Conservatism* (Columbia, Mo., 1993).

Finally, the conservative intellectual movement since 1945 is now old enough to be the subject of two useful bibliographies: Gregory Wolfe, *Right Minds: A Sourcebook of American Conservative Thought* (Chicago, 1987), an excellent, annotated guide; and Russell Jenkins, John R. Virtes, and Frederick W. Campano, comps., *The* National Review *Politically Incorrect Reference Guide: Your Handbook for the Right Information Sources* (New York, 1993). A comprehensive, ongoing, de facto bibliography of conservative publications in the domain of public policy is provided monthly by *The Insider*, produced by the Heritage Foundation in Washington, D.C.

At this point I am acutely conscious of the many worthy books and articles that I have *not* mentioned in this brief addendum. (A few, of course, have already been noted in the Epilogue.) But again, a piling of title upon title here would be supererogatory. In the books and reference tools already cited, the interested reader will find abundant points of entry into a subject of increasing complexity and sophistication. Of one thing such a researcher can be sure: there will be no dearth of reading matter to assimilate.

INDEX